TUTORIAL:

COMPUTER GRAPHICS: IMAGE SYNTHESIS

Kenneth I. Joy, Charles W. Grant, Nelson L. Max, and Lansing Hatfield

Computer Society Order Number 854
Library of Congress Number 88-61363
IEEE Catalog Number EH0281-6
ISBN 0-8186-8854-4

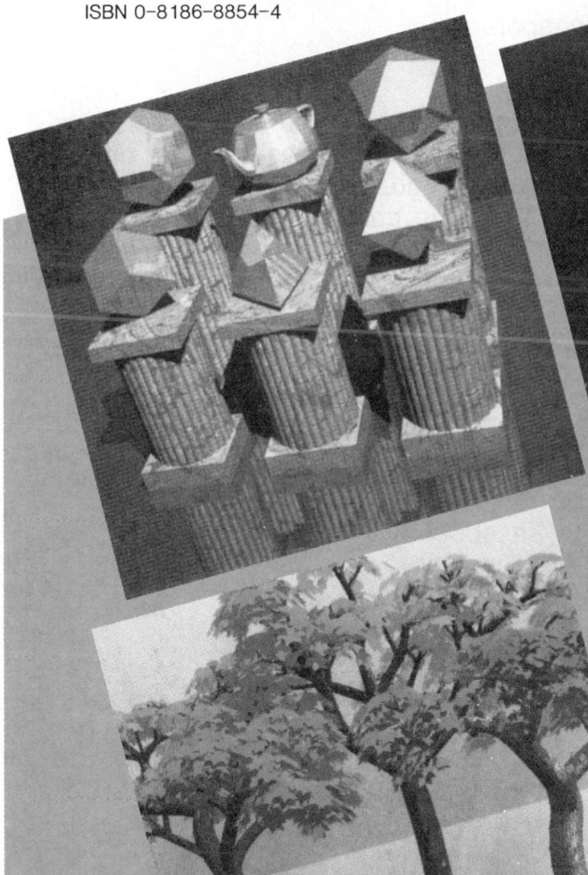

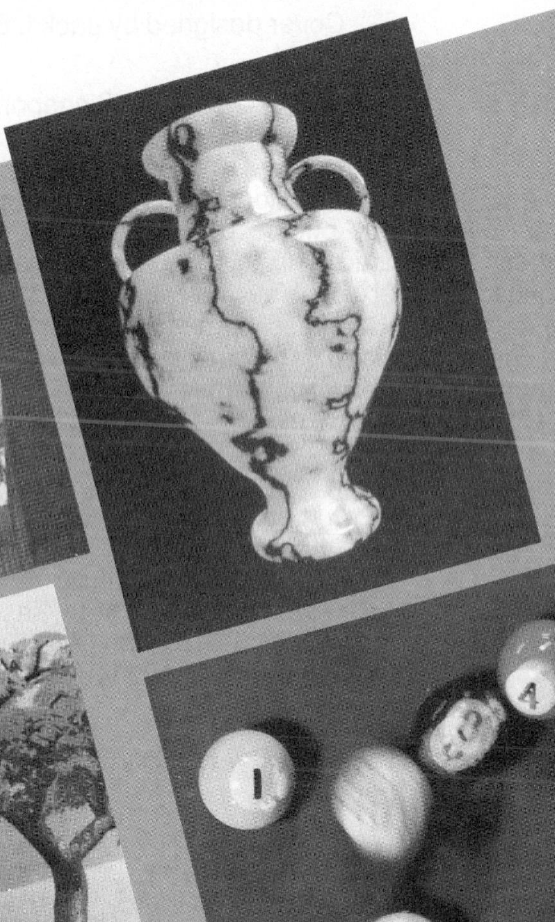

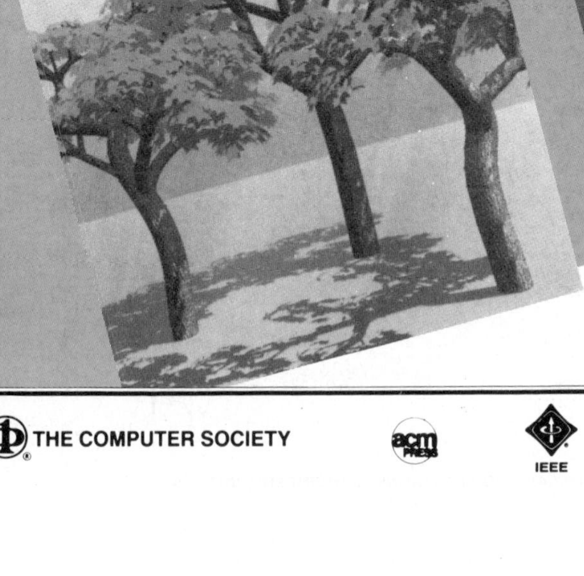

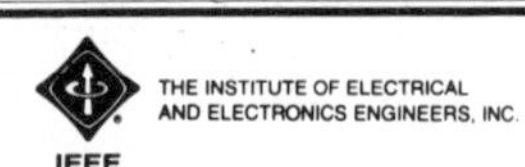

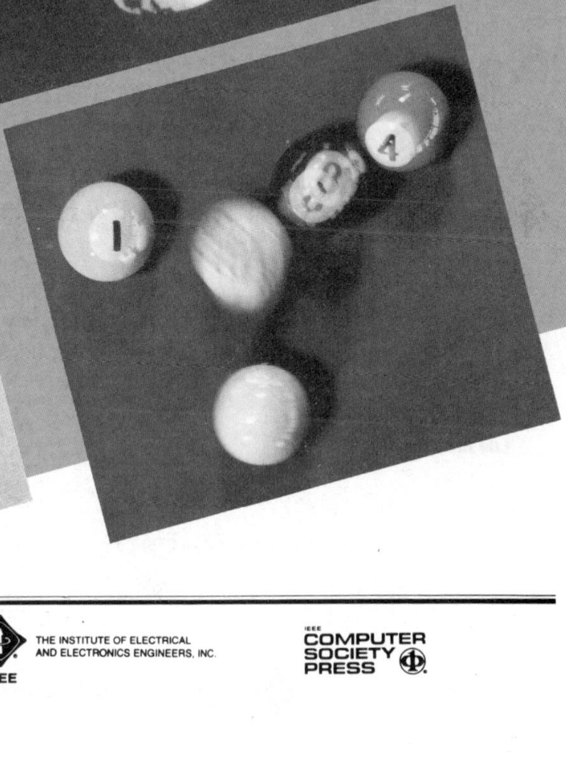

Published by

IEEE Computer Society Press
10662 Los Vaqueros Circle
P.O. Box 3014
Los Alamitos, CA 90720-1264

Cover designed by Jack I. Ballestero

Printed in Singapore

IEEE Computer Society Press Order Number 854
Library of Congress Number 88-61363
IEEE Catalog Number EH0281-6
ISBN 0-8186-8854-8 (Casebound)
ISBN 0-8186-4854-6 (Microfiche)
SAN 264-620X

Additional copies can be ordered from

IEEE Computer Society Press
Customer Service Center
10662 Los Vaqueros Circle
P.O. Box 3014
Los Alamitos, CA 90720-1264

IEEE Computer Society
13, avenue de l'aquilon
B-1200 Brussels
BELGIUM

IEEE Computer Society
Ooshima Building
2-19-1 Minami-Aoyama,
Minato-Ku
Tokyo 107, JAPAN

IEEE Service Center
445 Hoes Lane
P.O. Box 1331
Piscataway, NJ 08855-1331

THE INSTITUTE OF ELECTRICAL AND ELECTRONICS ENGINEERS, INC.

Preface

The goal of this tutorial is to provide the information necessary to advance from an introductory level in computer graphics to the understanding and use of state-of-the-art research results in image synthesis. The papers reprinted in this tutorial were selected for their relevance to this area. Some contain important background material, while others report on very recent research.

The two main subject areas of image synthesis that are addressed in this collection are (1) visible-surface algorithms and (2) algorithms for shading, texturing, and antialiasing. Conceptually, these are different problems but practically there is much overlap. Various decisions made in the design of the algorithms for one area will usually impact the other areas. Many of the papers reprinted here make significant contributions to more than one area.

This material should be accessible to professionals who have a basic knowledge of three-dimensional computer graphics—including basic plotting techniques, mathematical foundations of graphics, raster-scan techniques, transformational geometry, and clipping. Thus it will be accessible material for those interested readers who have had a one semester course in computer graphics, those who have attended a tutorial or seminar in introductory computer graphics, or those who are familiar with most of one of the major introductory textbooks. Both the computer professional who wishes a more advanced background in image-synthesis techniques, and the advanced student who has the background material for the understanding of the state-of-the-art topics, will find this tutorial useful.

A temptation when compiling a volume of this type is to include every paper that makes a significant contribution to the field. Unfortunately, practical limitations make this impossible, and decisions (often difficult) have to be made as to the papers that will eventually make up the collection. We made two decisions that affect the character of this book. First, we made the decision to make this an "up-to-date" collection, and thus many of the "classical" papers from the early- and mid-1970s have been omitted. These papers are adequately reviewed in virtually all of the current computer-graphics textbooks, or in the earlier computer-graphics tutorials published by the Computer Society of the IEEE. Reviews of these works appear in the introductory sections to each chapter.

Second, we made the decision to limit the collection to only the area of image synthesis. This meant leaving out many excellent papers whose primary results are in computer-graphics modeling. These results are central to the description of complex scenes, and can affect the rendering methods that might be used for such a scene. To compensate for this, we placed a high priority on the inclusion of image-synthesis papers that give descriptions of modeling techniques. We also do not discuss hardware, either computing or display. There have been many advances in this area, but fundamental image-synthesis algorithms have tended to be independent of particular hardware.

We have also invested considerable time on the annotated bibliography. A complete collection must make the reader aware of not only the fundamental papers of the field but also the papers that constitute further reading in the field. Thus, the reader will not find the bibliography to be comprehensive, but will find the major works, both background and research, and where they can be located.

Whereas textbooks form a basis from which introductory knowledge of a field can be obtained, developing a working knowledge of the original research results is indispensable for gaining a basis from which to do research. This tutorial is our attempt to present these original research results in one volume. These are the papers that we learned from, and we hope that you can use them in the same way.

Kenneth I. Joy
Charles W. Grant
Nelson L. Max
Lansing Hatfield

Table of Contents

Chapter 1: Image Synthesis

Introduction

Image synthesis is the subfield of computer graphics that attempts to produce realistic pictures. One goal of image synthesis is to create synthetic images indistinguishable from photographs of real objects. These images are primarily useful in applications where it is desirable to visualize an object without having to physically construct the object. Image synthesis has developed applications in fields including advertising, architecture, art, computer-aided design, defense, education, entertainment, manufacturing, medicine, scientific visualization, and simulation.

Image synthesis is to some degree a simulation of the optical processes at work in the real world. The actual physics of light propagation and interaction with matter is vastly too complicated and detailed to simulate over macroscopic distances, therefore simplified models have been developed. The emphasis in image synthesis has been placed on getting something that "looks good enough" rather than exact models of physical reality. There is a tradeoff present in all image-synthesis applications between realism and computation. Increased realism can be obtained by using more complex models and algorithms, but this will cause increased computational expense in terms of time and memory requirements.

The papers included in this tutorial cover most of the significant developments in image synthesis. These include methods that advance the level of realism possible, as well as methods that represent good tradeoffs between realism and computation. For example, recent research in image synthesis has uncovered techniques for modeling the effects of mirror reflections, fuzzy reflections, glossy reflections, transparency, refraction, indirect lighting with color bleeding, caustics, directional-light sources, smooth shadows with umbras and penumbras, motion blur, depth of field, realistic surface textures, fog, and haze.

Based on a simulation of light propagation in the real world, image synthesis can be divided into the following three subproblems:

- *image formation*—the determination of the components of the image that are dependent on the position of the viewpoint in the scene. This includes analyzing the distribution of light leaving the visible objects and producing an image from a particular viewpoint (direct image formation), and analyzing the distribution of light from objects not directly visible from the viewpoint, producing viewpoint dependent effects (indirect image formation).

  Direct image formation has been historically referred to as "the hidden-surface problem,"[1] or "the visible-surface problem," but it is only one of the many "visibility-determination steps" that must take place in the complete image-synthesis process. The indirect-image-formation step includes the calculation of reflections from mirrored surfaces, and refractions through transparent objects. This involves additional visibility-determination steps with different viewpoints.

- *illumination*—the determination of the components of the image that are dependent on the light propagation throughout the scene and independent of the position of the viewpoint. This includes the processes of distributing the incident light from the light sources directly to the surfaces of the objects (direct illumination) and of calculating the incident light on each object, which is not due to direct propagation from the light source to the object (indirect illumination).

  Direct illumination is often referred to as the "shadow" problem, which involves visibility determination from the viewpoints of the light sources. Indirect illumination can include reflections (both diffuse and specular) from other objects and light passing through transparent or translucent objects. Visibility determination, with viewpoints distributed over the surfaces of each object, is required here.

[1]Surfaces are by far the most commonly used modeling primitives in image synthesis, so the name "hidden-surface problem" has endured, but there are other primitives. Points, lines, volumes, and slices of higher-dimensional objects have all been used. More generally, we speak of "visibility determination."

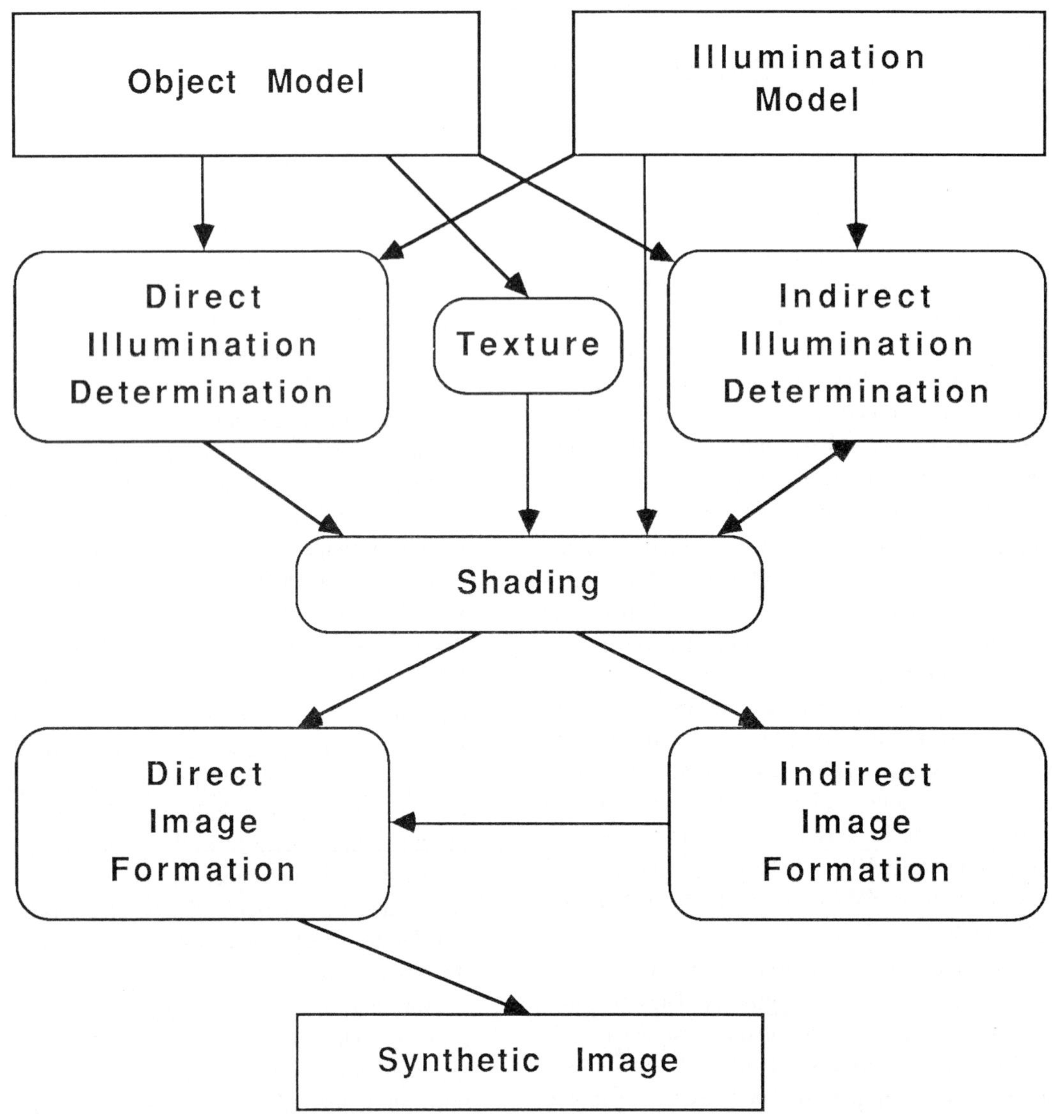

Figure 1.1: Subproblems of Image Synthesis

- *shading*—the process of determining the distribution of light leaving a surface, given the incident light and the optical properties of the surface. In its most general form, this is described by a bidirectional distribution function[2] $R(\theta_{in},\phi_{in},\theta_{out},\phi_{out},x,y,z)$. This function describes what fraction of the light that strikes the point (x,y,z) on the object from angle (θ_{in},ϕ_{in}), leaves the object at angle $(\theta_{out},\phi_{out})$. Calculating the (x,y,z) dependence of this function is usually referred to as texturing.

[2]Both the bidirectional-reflection-distribution function and the bidirectional-transmission-distribution function can be combined into a single bidirectional-distribution function.

These subproblems of image synthesis are shown in Figure 1.1. There are several things to note in this figure. Most steps involve visibility determination, which is the dominate cost in most image-synthesis systems.

Incorporating all of these subproblems into a single image-synthesis system is an elaborate undertaking. At this writing, no system does a satisfactory job on all subproblems. Simulating just a few optical effects can be very expensive.

Visibility Determination

Visibility determination is a fundamental and recurring subproblem in image synthesis, which occurs in several forms. The simple visibility problem with a single fixed viewpoint at a single moment in time is one most often studied. This is the problem for both simple direct-image formation with direct illumination from point-light sources. The algorithms to solve this simple visibility problem form the basis for extensions to solve higher-order visibility problems (such as those calculating motion blur, depth of field, or indirect-illumination effects). The visible-surface problem for this simple case of the direct image formation problem can be stated as:

Given.
a set of surfaces in three dimensions,
a viewpoint,
an oriented image plane,
and a field of view
For each point on the image plane within the field of view *do*
Determine which point on which surface lies closest
to the viewpoint along a line from the viewpoint through
the point in the image plane

This is a very abstract description of the problem. In a complete rendering system, the algorithm for solving this subproblem will not be as isolated as the problem description shown here but will be interconnected with the other subproblems in various ways. However, studying all of the basic algorithms to solve this subproblem in isolation is very instructive in understanding the techniques available to use on the larger problem.

There are two basic classes of algorithms to solve this problem: *continuous algorithms* and *point-sampling algorithms*. Each class attacks the above problem quite differently. Continuous algorithms operate by performing visibility determination over continuous areas covering the entire image plane. Every visible piece of each surface will be detected regardless of location or size. Continuous filtering and shading algorithms may be used to process the output. Point-sampling algorithms form an approximate solution to the visible-surface problem. These algorithms determine visibility only at a finite number of sample points and make assumptions about the visibility of objects between sample points.

Any continuous algorithm can be transformed into a point-sampling algorithm simply by point sampling the continuous output. Although there may be a more efficient transformation, this brute-force technique will always work. Unfortunately, it is not necessarily possible to generalize a point-sampling algorithm into a continuous one.

In practice, the theoretical advantages of the continuous algorithms are far outweighed by their tremendous complexity and the limited primitives and effects they can support. Usually only polygons are supported with no indirect-lighting effects. Point-sampling algorithms for solving this visibility and shading problems allow many advanced effects and complex models to be used (e.g., multiple reflections and refractions from curved surfaces), which are very difficult, if not impossible, for any continuous algorithm.

Visible-surface algorithms can be classified in several ways. The two broadest classes are continuous algorithms and point-sampled algorithms. A further subdivision of this classification can be made by looking at the general algorithmic structures in more detail. Based on these structures, seven fundamental types of visible-surface algorithms have been identified.

- point-sampling algorithms
  - Z-buffer algorithms
  - ray-tracing algorithms
  - painter's algorithms
  - scan-line algorithms
- continuous algorithms
  - area/volume subdivision algorithms
  - scan-plane algorithms
- other algorithms
  - wavefront propagation algorithms

Here we consider only the simplest and most idealized form of each algorithm. These simplified algorithms demonstrate the known basic strategies for solving the visibility problems, without the obscuring efficiency details and combinations of techniques present in real algorithms.

The first six basic algorithms all operate using a very simple model of light propagation. Light is assumed to travel in a homogeneous media, in straight rays, and only interacts with objects at their surfaces according to the rules of geometric optics. Diffraction, phase, polarization, and any relation between the sizes of the objects and the wavelength of the light are ignored. There is no time dependence on any aspect of the light rays, and an infinite number of rays are assumed to fill the scene (no quantization effects). On the other hand, the wavefront propagation algorithm treats light as a complex-valued wave phenomenon, which propagates in spherical wave fronts from every point in the scene. Some experiments have been reported that use the wave model of light (see [Mora81]), but the results have been discouraging due to limitations on primitive sizes and spacing, massive amounts of data and calculations, serious diffraction problems, and coherent light speckle. At this time, it seems unreasonable to expect that realistic image synthesis by this method will ever compete with geometric-optics methods, and thus only algorithms using the geometric-optics model of light are considered in this volume.

Point-Sampling Algorithms

Four point-sampling algorithms are used in the bulk of today's image synthesis work. In their seminal analysis, Sutherland, et al. [Suth74], identified sorting order as a major distinction between types of point-sampling algorithms[3] and identified algorithms using most of the possible sorting orders. The sorting order classification is expanded in the following analysis. The four point-sampling algorithms are listed below with a description of the sorting and comparisons used in each.

Z-Buffer Algorithm

for all objects {
  for all covered pixels (x,y) {
    compare z }}

Ray-Tracing Algorithm

for all pixels (x,y) {
  for all objects {
    compare z }}

Painter's Algorithm

sort objects by z, for all objects {
  for all covered pixels (x,y) {
    paint }}

Scan-Line Algorithm

sort objects by y, for all y {
  sort objects by x, for all x {
    compare z }}

The Z-buffer and ray-tracing algorithms differ by the nesting order of their main loops. Whereas the Z-buffer algorithm handles one object at a time and operates on all pixels that this object covers, the ray-tracing algorithm handles one pixel at time and compares every object's depth at this pixel. Thus, the Z-buffer and ray-tracing algorithms are duals with respect to loop-nesting order.

The Z-buffer and painter's algorithms differ in when the depth comparisons are made. Whereas the Z-buffer algorithms make depth comparisons throughout the calculations in the inner loop, the painter's algorithm makes all of its depth comparisons in a preliminary sorting phase (assuming a valid sorted order exists and can be found). Thus the Z-buffer and painter's algorithms are duals with respect to the time of depth determination.

The scan-line algorithm differs from the Z-buffer algorithm in that the scan-line algorithm first divides the two-dimensional image into a sequence of one-dimensional "scan lines" and then applies a simplified one-dimensional visible-surface algorithm to each scan line. Only those primitives, that intersect the scan line, are included in the visible-surface problem for that scan line. This sorting and division by scan line occurs before any operations of the visible-surface algorithm that is applied to each scan line. This is an attempt to reduce the complexity of the subproblems. Applying scan-line subdivision and then using the Z-buffer, ray-trac-

[3]No continuous algorithms had been published as of 1974.

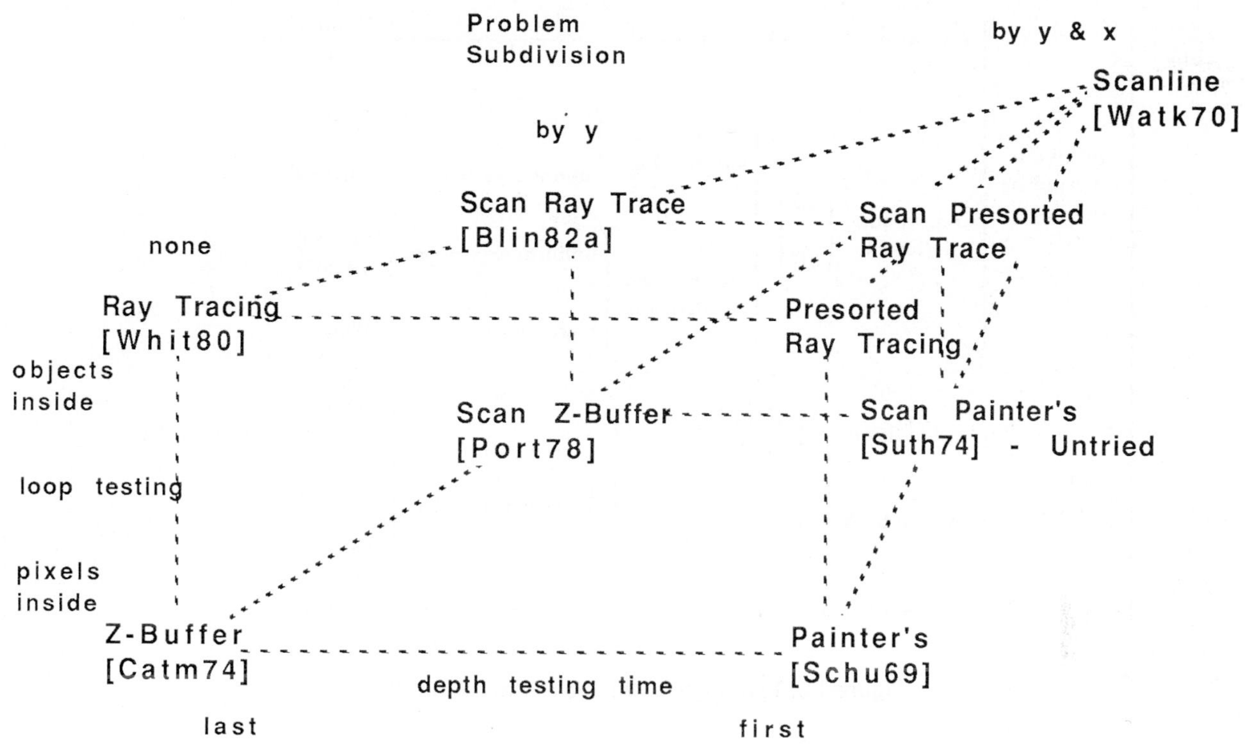

Figure 1.2: Sorting Order Classification for Point Sampling

painter's algorithms on each scan line yields scan line versions of these algorithms. The application of two levels (y then x) of this divide-and-conquer principle is possible, yielding division of the one-dimensional scan lines into zero-dimensional single pixel subproblems. The single pixel version of the Z-buffer and ray-tracing algorithms are identical, since the x and y loops have degenerated to a single iteration and only the object loop remains. The single pixel version of the painter's algorithm (sort all the objects by depth then select the closest one) becomes identical to the other two after a trivial optimization. Thus, with respect to problem subdivision, the Z-buffer, ray-tracing, and painter's algorithms are all duals to the y-x division scanline algorithm.

Since three of the point-sampling algorithms have been shown to be simple transformations of the Z-buffer algorithm, it is natural to construct a "three-dimensional space" of point-sampling algorithms on this basis. This is shown in Figure 1.2 (from [Gran87]). Various algorithms are plotted in this space based on the simple structural ideas that they utilize. Each of the algorithms embodies enhancements, which are ignored in this classification, to make it more efficient. It can be seen that many combinations of the simple algorithmic transformations for point-sampling algorithms have been implemented or described.

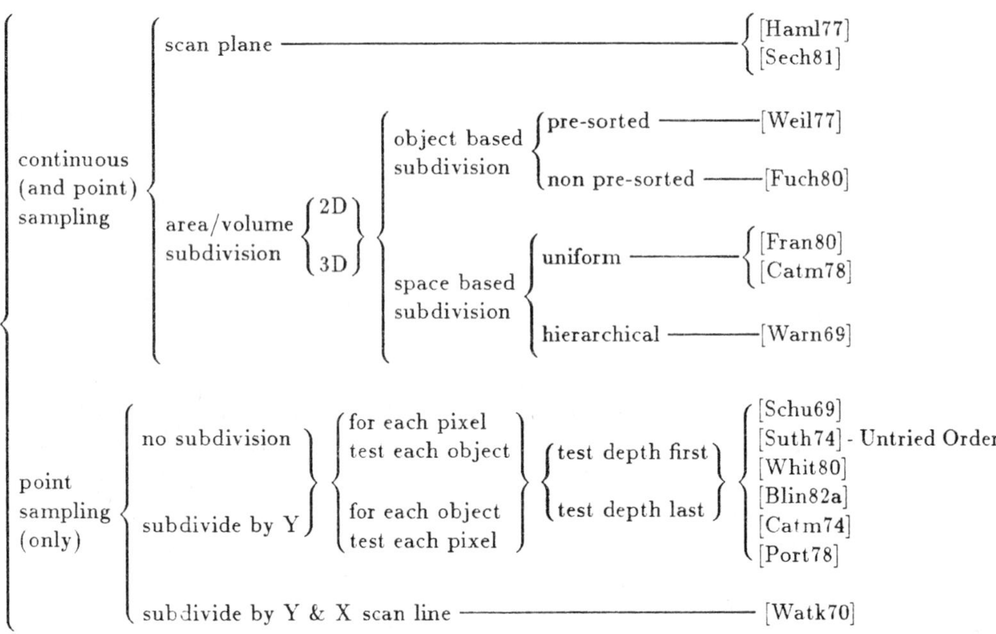

Figure 1.3: Taxonomy of Visible Surface Algorithms

Continuous Algorithms

Continuous visibility algorithms return descriptions of the continuous visible areas from a particular viewpoint. This is a "polygons-in, polygons-out" operation. There are two subclasses of continuous algorithms: the scan-plane algorithms [Haml77,Sech81,Sequ85], which move a plane through the environment to collect data that allow the generation of an exact polygonal reconstruction of the visible objects in the scene; and subdivision algorithms, which partition the environment, seeking a reduced problem that can be solved by simpler methods. Scan-plane algorithms in computer graphics are similar to scan-plane algorithms from computational geometry (see [Prep85]). Subdivision algorithms can be further classified by the way the subdivision is done. This can be two dimensional or three dimensional, at fixed points in space or at object vertices, edges or faces, uniformly or hierarchically, and with or without presorting. A more complete taxonomy of algorithms has been given by Grant [Gran87] and is shown in Figure 1.3.

Some algorithms that were originally developed as point-sampling algorithms are classified here as continuous algorithms because they use continuous techniques and then point sample for output. For example, Warnock's [Warn69] algorithm is easily extended to produce continuous output since all intermediate calculations are continuous.

Combinations of Algorithms

Most algorithms, in practice, combine techniques from several of the basic algorithms. Some scan-line algorithms perform the vertical subdivision on each scan line separately and then use a continuous algorithm on the resulting lower-dimensional subproblems. This allows for continuous anti-aliasing in the horizontal direction but not in the vertical direction.

The subdivision algorithms have proven useful as preprocessing steps for point-sampling algorithms. The subdivision reduces the size of the problems that the rest of the algorithm must solve. This has recently been used as a technique for speeding up ray tracing. Fujimoto [Fuji86], with a three-dimensional space-based uniform subdivision, Kaplan [Kapl85] and Glassner [Glas84], with a three-dimensional space-based hierarchical subdivision, Rubin [Rubi80] and Kay and Kajiya [Kay86], with a three-dimensional object-based hierarchical subdivision, and Dippé [Dipp84], with a three-dimensional space-based semi-regular subdivision, have all utilized this method. Cleary et al. [Clea86] compare two-dimensional and three-dimensional space-based regular subdivision techniques for ray tracing on a multiprocessor. Fuchs [Fuch80] uses a three-dimensional object-based subdivision as a preprocessing step for the painter's algorithm. Franklin [Fran80] has shown that proper subdivision can reduce the complexity of visible-surface determination to be linear in the number of objects.

In 1974 memory was very expensive and processors were slow. This caused Sutherland et al. [Suth74] to conclude that the ray-tracing and Z-buffer algorithms were hopelessly inefficient brute-force techniques (which they were). However with today's cheap memory, faster CPUs, and parallel processing, the Z-buffer algorithm has clearly emerged as the most widely used visible-surface algorithm. Nearly every piece of graphics hardware that supports a built-in visible-surface algorithm uses the Z-buffer algorithm. Some hardware, particularly those that are designed to solve the visible-surface problem in real time at video rates, use scan-line algorithms, but this is a small number compared to those that utilize the Z-buffer algorithm. Relatively inexpensive parallel processing machines using the Z-buffer algorithm are also commercially available.

In research environments, the most popular algorithm has been ray tracing, because of the great flexibility of the algorithm. Early ray-tracing algorithms suffered from great slowness and severe aliasing, but many recent advances have made ray tracing competitive with the other algorithms. Ray tracing is no longer the brute-force technique it once was.

Direct Illumination

The direct-illumination-determination problem, or shadowing, is very similar to the direct-image-formation problem. Parts of objects are illuminated if they are visible to the light source. With most shadow algorithms, multiple light sources can be treated with independent applications of the same algorithm to each light source. Using many light sources will quickly cause the illumination-processing time to dominate the image-formation processing time.

A continuous algorithm of the "polygons-in polygons-out" type can be used as a preprocess to calculate "shadow polygons," which are then combined with the original polygons as a texture and rendered with any type of direct-image formation algorithm. Atherton et al. [Athe78] do this by using the same polygon-subdivision algorithm for both passes.

Other types of preprocessing are possible. Williams [Will78] creates a "depth map," which is a Z-buffer image computed from the viewpoint of the light source. Only the z component (distance to the light source) is calculated and stored. Then, while rendering the scene, the distance to the light source from the visible object is calculated at each pixel. This distance is compared to the corresponding location in the depth map. If the depth map holds a smaller value, then an object exists intervening between that pixel of the visible object and the light source. Therefore, that pixel of the visible object is in shadow. Reeves et al. [Reev87] improve on this algorithm by adding stochastic supersampling and storing floating-point values in the depth buffer. Max [Max86a] presents a horizon-map algorithm, which is closely related to the Z-buffer shadow algorithm, for shadowing bumped-map textures.

Crow [Crow77a] suggests adding polygons that bound "shadow volumes" to the input of a scan-line algorithm. This increases the number of polygons that the scan-line algorithm must process, but with a little additional processing it is easy to determine if a visible span is inside any shadow volume. This technique is further refined by Nishita and Nakamae [Nish83], Bergeron [Berg86], and Max [Max86b].

Other combinations of algorithms calculate the direct illumination at each pixel independently, without preprocessing. The shadow-mask sweep algorithm of Grant [Gran86] uses the painter's algorithm for both image formation and direct illumination. The algorithms of Berlin [Berl85] and Garcia [Garc86] use polygon subdivision for indirect illumination and the painter's algorithm for direct-image formation. Shadow volume testing is done in parallel at each pixel by Fuchs et al. [Fuch85] in a system that uses the Z-buffer algorithm for direct-image formation. Ray tracing for direct illumination with a scan-line direct-image-formation algorithm was implemented by Bouknight [Bouk70b].

Shadow testing by ray tracing fits well with direct-image formation by ray tracing [Whit80]. Haines and Greenberg [Hain86] propose a method of accelerating the testing of shadow rays by using a two-dimensional subdivision of the scene from the viewpoint of the light sources. The more general three-dimensional subdivision techniques of Glassner [Glas84], Kaplan [Kapl85], and Fujimoto et al. [Fuji86] accelerate the testing of shadow rays as well as all other rays.

Indirect-image-formation effects (reflection, transparency, and refraction) are elegantly handled by ray tracing [Whit80]. The general problems of reflections from curved surfaces, refraction, and glossy reflections have only really been handled well with the ray-tracing algorithm. The distributed ray-tracing system of Cook et al. [Cook84a] probably has implemented the greatest number of effects. The synthetic image, *1984* (see [Cook84a]), created with this system is probably the most realistic synthetic image published at this time. The limited case of planar mirror reflections has been handled with the painter's algorithm by Garcia [Garc86] and Berlin [Berl85]; a three-dimensional space-subdivision algorithm, beam tracing, by Heckbert and Hanrahan [Heck84]; and by Wallace et al. [Wall87] with the Z-buffer algorithm. Planar refractions are more difficult and were approximated by Heckbert and Hanrahan [Heck84].

In Chapters 2-6 of this tutorial, we shall examine the various types of visible-surface algorithms in detail. These chapters cover Z-buffer algorithms, painter's algorithms, ray-tracing algorithms, scan-line algorithms, and continuous algorithms, respectively. Most of the papers in these chapters concentrate on the direct-image-formation application of these algorithms (a few discuss shadows), but they are all suitable for solving some of the other visibility problems in image synthesis.

Shading

Shading is the process of determining the light intensity leaving an object, given the incoming light distribution and the properties of the object. Indirect illumination involves the repeated application of local shading as light travels between objects. The best approximations to the calculations of indirect illumination are through the techniques of radiosity, first reported by Goral et al. [Gora84] and Nishita and Nakamae [Nish83]. Many works have expanded on this important area of research. The subjects of indirect illumination and shading are presented in Chapter 7.

Aliasing

The output of the image-synthesis process is a raster image—a discrete representation of a continuous image. The process of converting a continuous signal into a discrete signal is called *sampling*. The spacing of the samples limits the amount of detail that can be represented in the discrete signal. Any attempt to represent finer detail (higher spatial frequencies) will result in the introduction of an unwanted coarse signal (lower spatial frequency). This unwanted signal is called an *alias* and this process is known as *aliasing*. The process of preventing aliasing is called *antialiasing*. To perform antialiasing, the continuous signal must be filtered before sampling to eliminate all detail which is too small. The familiar stairstep edge or "jaggies" is an example of spatial aliasing caused by sampling without filtering. Temporal aliasing can occur when creating a sequence of images for animation. Temporal antialiasing of images has become known as *motion blur* since the effect of the filtering is to blur the moving objects. Proper antialiasing is absolutely essential to creating realistic images. Antialiasing is required in all visibility-determination stages in the image-synthesis process, not just the final image-formation stage. This topic is covered in Chapter 8.

Texturing

Texture is the surface detail of a displayed object, which is generated by varying the optical properties of the objects. There are two main problems associated with texturing: the inverse mapping problem and the antialiasing problem. The mapping problem is to find out what point in the image corresponds to a point on the object. This is a simple projection. The inverse mapping problem involves determining what region of the texture corresponds to a given pixel in the image. The texture antialiasing problem involves representing the properties of this region of texture with a single sample without introducing aliasing. Texturing is the subject of Chapter 9.

Modeling

Our environments consist of objects, and modeling is used to define the objects we wish to visualize. This process includes the definition of the shape, location, and orientation of each object, the optical properties of each object, and the location, color, and intensity distribution of each light source. Objects are usually modeled by describing their surfaces. Various forms of surfaces can be used: polygons, spheres, cylinders, parametric patches, and implicit equations, for example. Each is usually only an approximation to the desired shape of the actual object. Again there is a tradeoff between the additional realism of using a more accurate model and the additional expense that it involves. Because of space restrictions and the volume of literature in this area, we were forced to exclude a chapter in this important field. However, we have included many works which go into some detail describing modeling and how it is accomplished.

Chapter 2: Z-Buffer Algorithms

Introduction

Of all algorithms for image synthesis, the Z-buffer (or depth-buffer) algorithm is perhaps the simplest. For each pixel on the display, we keep a record of the depth of the primitive in the scene that is closest to the viewer, plus a record of the intensity that should be displayed to show the object. When a new polygon is to be processed, a *z*-value and intensity value are calculated for each pixel that lies within the boundary of the polygon. If the *z*-value at a pixel indicates that the polygon is closer to the viewer than the *z*-value in the Z-buffer, the *z*-value and the intensity values recorded in the buffers are replaced by the polygon's values. After processing all polygons, the resulting intensity buffer can be displayed (see Figure 2.1 for an outline of the algorithm).

The development of this algorithm is usually attributed to Catmull [Catm74], who was using subdivision methods on bicubic patches to reduce the patches to "pixel size," which could then be drawn, giving a representation of the surface. The Z-buffer strategy was necessary to accurately show scenes containing multiple surfaces, or surfaces containing one or more silhouette edges.

The basic problem with the Z-buffer algorithm is aliasing, created by the point-sampling nature of the algorithm. In essence, the Z-buffer methodology is equivalent to the initial level of ray tracing, and thus the same sampling problems exist. Unfortunately, having each Z-buffer location correspond to one pixel limits the application of the solutions used in the ray-tracing scheme.

Carpenter [Carp84] (included in this chapter) proposes an enhancement to the Z-buffer, an A-buffer, containing a 32-bit mask that can be used to contain coverage information. Comparison of polygons that intersect the same pixel can be implemented through Boolean operations and thus are quite efficient. The technique is implemented in software, and the Z-buffer is kept only scan line by scan line. This technique effectively increases the resolution of the Z-buffer algorithm several times.

The REYES rendering system, described by Cook et al. [Cook87] (included in this chapter), utilizes a "stochastic" Z-buffer, which uses many samples per pixel, each sample jittered within the pixel (see [Cook86]). This makes the typical scan-conversion process much more difficult, because the samples are not in a fixed position. However, by using a weighted average of the intensities at the subpixels, a high-quality antialiased image can be produced. This algorithm follows Catmull's example closely because all objects in the scene are subdivided until they are less than one-half of a pixel in area. These small objects can then be considered polygonal and can be given a flat shade before processing. The Z-buffer then accomplishes the hidden-surface calculation.

Williams [Will78] (included in this chapter) has shown how to use the Z-buffer algorithm to produce shadows. A view of the scene is first constructed from the point of view of the light source in which only the *z*-values are retained. A Z-buffer image of the scene is then constructed from the ordinary image-space viewpoint. A three-dimensional linear transformation is determined that maps (x,y,z) points in the image space into (x,y,z) points in the light-source space. As each point is generated in image space, it is transformed into the light-source space and tested for visibility against the Z-buffer produced by the light-source view. If this point is farther from the light source than the Z-buffer value, it is determined to be in shadow, and its intensity is modified accordingly. This algorithm still exhibits aliasing artifacts, especially if the light source is "nearly perpendicular" to the viewing plane. Reeves et al. [Reev87] have developed a method (which is based upon the REYES system [Cook87]) by which these artifacts can be reduced.

Duff [Duff85] (included in this chapter) has developed an extension of the image composition algorithm of Porter and Duff [Port84] (included in Chapter 3: Painter's Algorithms), which includes *z*-depth information in a picture file. For each pixel, the method stores the usual RGB-intensity information, an α-coverage factor (from [Port84]), and a *z*-depth value. Two images can then be composed (pixel-by-pixel), by using the depth information from the *z*-values. This allows three-dimensional composition of scenes instead of the usual 2½-dimensional method. Elementary antialiasing can also be accomplished, based upon the α and z-depth values. The algorithm utilizes a run-length encoder to reduce the size of the image files.

The simplicity of the Z-buffer algorithm makes it most appropriate for hardware implementation. Several authors have developed systems based upon the Z-buffer paradigm. These include Parke [Park80], who discusses a multiprocessor implementation of the Z-buffer algorithm, and Fuchs and his colleagues [Fuch81,Fuch85], who have developed a unique massively parallel display with Z-buffer capability.

```
Z-Buffer Algorithm
    Given
        List of polygons {P1, P2, ..., Pn }
        An array z-buffer[x,y] initialized to +∞
        An array Intensity[x,y]
    begin
        for each polygon P in the polygon list do {
            for each pixel (x,y) that intersects P do {
                calculate z-depth of P at (x,y)
                if z-depth < z-buffer[x,y] then {
                    Intensity[x,y] = intensity of P at (x,y)
                    z-buffer[x,y] = z-depth
                    }
                }
            }
        Display Intensity array
    end
```

Figure 2.1: The Z-Buffer Algorithm

"The A-Buffer, An Antialiased Hidden Surface Method" by L. Carpenter from *Proceedings of SIGGRAPH '84*, 1984, pages 103-108. Copyright 1984, Association for Computing Machinery, Inc., reprinted by permission.

The A-buffer, an Antialiased Hidden Surface Method

Loren Carpenter

Computer Graphics Project
Computer Division
Lucasfilm Ltd

Abstract

The A-buffer (anti-aliased, area-averaged, accumulation buffer) is a general hidden surface mechanism suited to medium scale virtual memory computers. It resolves visibility among an arbitrary collection of opaque, transparent, and intersecting objects. Using an easy to compute Fourier window (box filter), it increases the effective image resolution many times over the Z-buffer, with a moderate increase in cost. The A-buffer is incorporated into the REYES 3-D rendering system at Lucasfilm and was used successfully in the "Genesis Demo" sequence in Star Trek II.

CR CATEGORIES AND SUBJECT DESCRIPTORS: I.3.3 [**Computer Graphics**]: Picture/Image Generation - Display algorithms; I.3.7 [**Computer Graphics**]: Three-Dimensional Graphics and Realism - Visible line/surface elimination.

GENERAL TERMS: Algorithms, Experimentation.

ADDITIONAL KEY WORDS AND PHRASES: hidden surface, image synthesis, z-buffer, a-buffer, antialiasing, transparency, supersampling, computer imagery.

1. Introduction

There are many hidden surface techniques known to computer graphics. A designer of a 3-D image synthesis system must balance the desire for quality with the cost of computation. The A-buffer method, a descendant of the well-known Z-buffer, has proven to deliver moderate to good quality images at moderate cost. At each pixel, sufficient information is available to increase the effective resolution of the image several times over that of a simple Z-buffer.

2. Historical Perspective

The A-buffer belongs to the class of hidden surface algorithms called "scanline". The REYES (Renders Everything You Ever Saw) system, of which the A-buffer is a part, is a scanline renderer, but scanline order is not required by the A-buffer.

The first scanline algorithms[7] did perspective, clipping, sorting, visibility determination, and "filtering" all at the same time. They resolved visibility at one point per pixel, and aliased terribly, although our standards were different then. In 1974, E. Catmull described the Z-buffer method[2]. A Z-buffer is a screen-sized array of pixels and Z's. Objects, in no particular order, are examined to determine which pixels they cover. At each covered pixel, the perspective Z depth of the object is determined and compared with the Z in the array. If the new Z is closer, then the new Z, and the object's shade at this point, replaces the array's Z and pixel. This development started the trend toward modularizing the rendering process, as a Z-buffer could comprise the visibility section of almost any kind of renderer. Although extremely fast and simple, the Z-buffer aliases too much and cannot render transparent objects correctly.

The aliasing problems of the Z-buffer can be softened somewhat by modifying it from a point sampler to a line sampler so that visibility is determined over horizontal segments of scanlines[1]. In this way the line Z-buffer is very similar to the classical polygon algorithms of Watkins and others[7]. Polygons are sliced horizontally as in Watkins, but no X sorting is done. Instead, polygon segments conditionally overwrite others based on Z depth. The segment boundaries do not have to be coincident with pixel boundaries. This added information clears up aliasing of nearly vertical edges. However, nearly horizontal edges still alias and dropouts of small objects still occur.

In 1978, E. Catmull introduced the "ultimate" visibility method[3], a full polygon hidden surface process, based

on Weiler-Atherton[8], at each pixel. Dropouts are precluded, as every sliver is accounted for. The color of the resulting pixel is simply the weighted average of all the visible polygon fragments. This can be extremely expensive. It is so expensive that it's primary use is in 2-D animation of a few fairly large polygons. In that application, most pixels are completely covered by some polygon, where the hidden surface process has a trivial solution. Pixels needing the full power of the visibility resolver are rare, and so the total cost per frame is acceptable.

3. Goals and Constraints

The visibility techniques described above span a wide range of computational expense and image quality. What is needed is a method that combines the simplicity and speed of the Z-buffer with the two dimensional anti-aliasing benefits of Catmull's full polygon process at each pixel.

The method must support all conceivable geometric modeling primitives: polygons, patches, quadrics, fractals, and so forth. It must handle transparency and intersecting surfaces (and transparent intersecting surfaces). It must do all this while being fast enough for limited production using a DEC VAX 11/780.

4. Strategy

The rendering system (REYES) in which the visibility processor was to reside began to take shape in mid 1981. Adaptive subdivision[5] (splitting geometric primitives until "flat" *on the screen*) would produce a common intermediate form: polygons. Everything would be converted to polygons in approximately scanline order, as the picture developed. The polygons would be thrown away after the visibility resolver had finished with them and their memory space would be used for polygons to be created later. To reduce the scope and complexity of the visibility resolver, polygons would be clipped to pixel boundaries. The visibility resolver would only have to deal with one pixel at a time.

In a virtual memory computer, like the VAX, code space is not a serious limitation, so it was decided to optimize the algorithm for the common cases and write potentially voluminous code for the unusual situations.

5. Geometry inside the pixel

The geometric information inside a complex pixel is vital to the correct display of the pixel. Pictures produced by REYES had to be free of aliasing artifacts. The aliasing deficiencies of the simple Z-buffer precluded its use. More resolution inside the pixel was called for, but a full polygon intersector/clipper was too expensive. After some experimentation, a 4x8 bit mask (figure 1) was selected to represent the subpixel polygons. Clipping one polygon against another becomes a simple boolean operation. The mask is similar in several ways to the mask of Fiume, Fournier and Rudolph[4], although both were developed independently.

Silhouettes of objects still exhibited coarse intensity quantization effects, so the actual screen area of subpixel-sized polygons was kept with the mask. Whenever possible, the actual area is used instead of the bit count in the mask.

6. The A-buffer Algorithm

The A-buffer works with two different data types: "pixelstructs" (distinct from pixels) and "fragments". A pixelstruct is two 32-bit words (figure 2), one containing a Z depth and the other either a color or a pointer. A fragment (figure 3) is for the most part a polygon clipped to a pixel boundary. Pixelstructs occur in an array the size and shape of the final image (like the Z-buffer). In REYES, the array is paged in software to save virtual memory space. If a pixel is simple, i.e. completely covered, the Z value is positive and the pixelstruct contains a color. Otherwise, the Z value is negative and the pointer points to a list of fragments sorted front-to-back by frontmost Z.

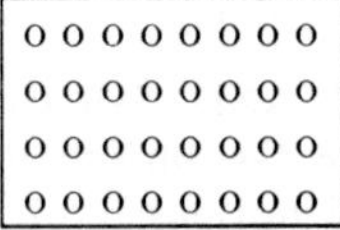

Figure 1. Pixel bit mask.

```
float           z;          /* negative Z */
fragment_ptr    flist;      /* never null */

                (or)

float           z;          /* positive Z */
byte            r, g, b;    /* color */
byte            a;          /* coverage */
```

Figure 2. Pixelstruct definition.

```
fragment_ptr  next;
short_int     r, g, b;       /* color, 12 bit */
short_int     opacity;       /* 1 - transparency */
short_int     area;          /* 12 bit precision */
short_int     object_tag;    /* from parent surface */
pixelmask     m;             /* 4x8 bits */
float         zmax, zmin;    /* positive */
```

Figure 3. Fragment definition.

The following discussion contains several symbols which we define here:

M	4x8 bit mask
A	area (0..1)
C	color (r, g, b)
Opacity	1 - transmission fraction
α	coverage, usually area times opacity[6]

Sorting in Z is necessary for two reasons. Proper calculation of transparency requires all visible transparent surfaces to be sorted in Z. The other benefit of a Z-sort is that fragments from the same geometric primitive tend to cluster together in the list and so can be merged. For example, a bicubic patch may be turned into several polygons. These polygons are all from the same continuous parent surface, but they may be chopped into fragments in an unpredictable order (depending on screen orientation, etc.) (figure 4). Merging two or more fragments simplifies the data structure and reclaims the space used by the merged-in fragments. If the result is opaque and completely covers the pixel we cannot with certainty reclaim hidden fragments, as they may be part of an incomplete intersecting surface.

The process of merging fragments is fairly straightforward. Fragments are merged if and only if they have the same object tag and they overlap in Z. This test is performed whenever a new fragment is added to a pixelstruct list. Object tags are integers assigned to continuous non-self-intersecting geometric primitive objects, like spheres and patches. The tag is augmented by a bit indicating whether the surface faces forward or backward, so as to prevent improper merging on silhouettes. If the fragments do not overlap on the screen ($\mathbf{M}_1 \cap \mathbf{M}_2 = \emptyset$) then the bitmasks are or'ed, the colors blended

$$\mathbf{C} = \mathbf{C}_1 \times \mathbf{A}_1 + \mathbf{C}_2 \times \mathbf{A}_2$$

and the areas added. If they overlap (which is highly abnormal), they are split into three parts.

$$\mathbf{M}_{\text{front-only}} = \mathbf{M}_{\text{front}} \cap \sim\mathbf{M}_{\text{back}}$$

$$\mathbf{M}_{\text{back-only}} = \mathbf{M}_{\text{back}} \cap \sim\mathbf{M}_{\text{front}}$$

$$\mathbf{M}_{\text{overlap}} = \mathbf{M}_{\text{front}} \cap \mathbf{M}_{\text{back}}$$

The contribution of the front fragment is computed,

$$\alpha_{\text{front}} = \mathbf{A}_{\text{front-only}} + \mathbf{Opacity}_{\text{front}} \times \mathbf{A}_{\text{overlap}}$$

the colors blended,

$$\mathbf{C} = \alpha_{\text{front}} \times \mathbf{C}_{\text{front}} + (1 - \alpha_{\text{front}}) \times \mathbf{C}_{\text{back}}$$

and the area computed.

$$\mathbf{A} = \mathbf{A}_{\text{front}} + \mathbf{A}_{\text{back}} \times \frac{\mathbf{A}_{\text{back-only}}}{\mathbf{A}_{\text{back-only}} + \mathbf{A}_{\text{overlap}}}$$

When no more fragments are to be sent to a pixelstruct, the pixelstruct's color is determined and written into the picture. Generally, the pixel will be fully covered by some object and a few pixel-sized fragments will remain. If any fragments are present, a recursive packing process is invoked.

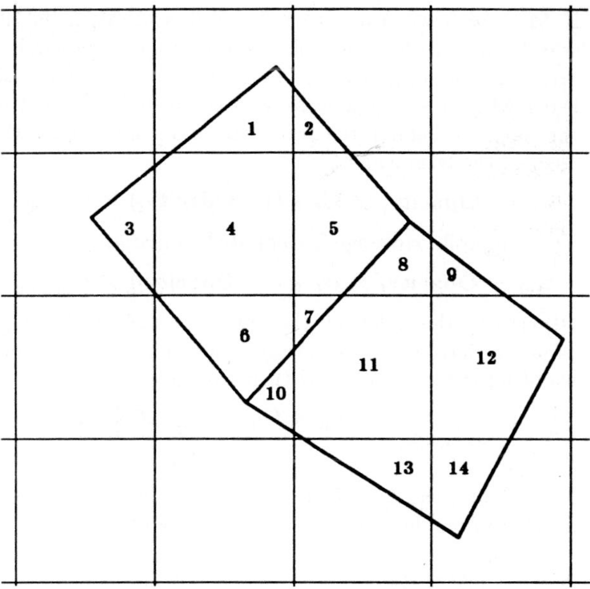

Figure 4. Typical fragment arrival order.

7. Packing fragments

Area-averaging means the color of a pixel is computed by the area-weighted average of the colors of the visible surfaces contained in the pixel. The problem is, then, how to determine the visible fragments and visible parts of fragments.

To understand the method used in the A-buffer, consider the following simplified example. Assume, for the moment, no transparency and no intersecting surfaces. If the fragment at the front of the list covers the pixel, we are done; otherwise, it covers part of the pixel. We divide the pixel into two parts, inside and outside, using the fragment's mask. The contribution of the inside part is the color of the fragment weighted by its area. The contribution of the outside part is some yet to be discovered color weighted by the complement of the fragment's area.

$$\mathbf{C} = \mathbf{C}_{\text{in}} \times \mathbf{A}_{\text{in}} + \mathbf{C}_{\text{out}} \times (1 - \mathbf{A}_{\text{in}})$$

The yet to be discovered color is found by recursively calling the packing routine with the outside mask to represent the rest of the pixel and a pointer to the next item in the fragment list.

We can now describe the method in more detail. We start the packing process with a full 32 bit search mask to represent the entire pixel. Fragments are considered only if they overlap the search mask. When all or part of a fragment is found within the search mask, the search mask part of the pixel is partitioned using the fragment mask.

$$\mathbf{M}_{\text{in}} = \mathbf{M}_{\text{search}} \cap \mathbf{M}_{\text{f}}$$

$$\mathbf{M}_{\text{out}} = \mathbf{M}_{\text{search}} \cap \sim\mathbf{M}_{\text{f}}$$

If $\mathbf{M_{out}} \neq 0$ we use a recursive call with $\mathbf{M_{out}}$ as the search mask to find the color of the rest of the searched area. If the fragment is transparent, a recursive call using $\mathbf{M_{in}}$ as a search mask is used to find the color of the surfaces behind the fragment to be filtered by the color of the fragment.

$$\mathbf{C_{in}} = \mathbf{Opacity_f} \times \mathbf{C_f} + (1 - \mathbf{Opacity_f}) \times \mathbf{C_{behind}}$$

The composite coverage is computed similarly.

$$\alpha_{in} = \mathbf{Opacity_f} \times \alpha_f + (1 - \mathbf{Opacity_f}) \times \alpha_{behind}$$

Otherwise, the color of the fragment suffices for $\mathbf{C_{in}}$. When we have the colors of the inside and outside regions we blend them weighted by their coverage.

$$\mathbf{C_{returned}} = \frac{\alpha_{in} \times \mathbf{C_{in}} + \alpha_{out} \times \mathbf{C_{out}}}{\alpha_{in} + \alpha_{out}}$$

For all but the first fragment on the list, we use the number of one bits in a mask to estimate area.

Now for intersections.

Pixels where intersecting surfaces are visible usually number in the dozens or hundreds in a typical 512x512 resolution picture. Also, the antialiasing along the line of intersection is not quite as critical as that on a silhouette, for example, because the contrast is often lower. These observations suggest we can get by with simple approximations.

Since no orientation information (vertices or plane equations) is kept in a fragment, we define an intersection to occur when the object tags differ and the fragments overlap in Z. This works satisfactorily in all but a few cases. Since we don't know exactly how much of the frontmost fragment is visible, we estimate it from the minimum and maximum Z values (figure 5).

$$\mathbf{Vis_{front}} = \frac{\mathbf{Zmax_{next}} - \mathbf{Zmin_{front}}}{(\mathbf{Zmax} - \mathbf{Zmin})_{front} + (\mathbf{Zmax} - \mathbf{Zmin})_{next}}$$

Since part of the front fragment obscures the next fragment and vice versa, we need to estimate the weighting factor to be used to blend the two fragment's colors.

$$\alpha_{in} = \mathbf{Vis_{front}} \times \mathbf{Opacity_{front}} + (1 - \mathbf{Vis_{front}}) \times (1 - \alpha_{next})$$

Figure 5. Visible fraction of front fragment.

```
Pack_under_mask (fragment_ptr, mask, r, g, b, a)

if this is the last fragment on the list
        return fragment's color and coverage
else
        find inside and outside masks
        if outside mask not empty
                find color and coverage of outside area
                        (recursive call with outside mask)
        if fragment is transparent or overlaps in Z with next on list
                find color and coverage of what's behind
                        (recursive call with inside mask)
        if nothing hidden behind the fragment affects its appearance
                return a blend of the fragment and the outside area
        else
                if Z's overlap with next fragment (maybe transparent)
                        estimate visibility ratio
                        estimate coverage of fragment
                        blend fragment with what's behind it
                        return blend of inside and outside
                else (just transparent)
                        blend fragment with what's behind it
                        return blend of inside and outside
end
```

Figure 6. Fragment packing procedure.

This is the sum of the unobscured part of the front fragment and the part of the front fragment filtered through the other fragment. Given these factors, we blend the front fragment with the other fragment within the inside mask.

$$C_{in} = \alpha_{in} \times C_{front} + (1 - \alpha_{in}) \times C_{next}$$

Then we blend the inside and outside part.

$$C_{returned} = \frac{\alpha_{in} \times C_{in} + \alpha_{out} \times C_{out}}{\alpha_{in} + \alpha_{out}}$$

A high level pseudocode description of the packer is given in figure 6.

8. Implementation details

The A-buffer is implemented in approximately 800 lines of C, including a substantial amount of debugging code. All arithmetic is done in fixed point (except for Z). There are two heavily used procedures inside the system that ought to be described in more detail.

The first is the bitmask constructor, which is designed to work correctly given arbitrary polygons. It begins with a polygon that has been clipped to a pixel boundary. The polygon bitmask is built up by exclusive or'ing together masks derived from the polygon's edges. Each polygon edge defines a trapezoid, bounded by the edge, the right side of the pixel, and the projection of the ends of the edge toward the right side of the pixel. (figure 7) The edge mask is constructed by or'ing together row masks taken from a table indexed by the quantized locations of the intercepts of the edge. The exclusive or of all these masks leaves one bits in the interior and zero bits elsewhere. All this sounds complicated, but it rarely involves more than eight boolean operations.

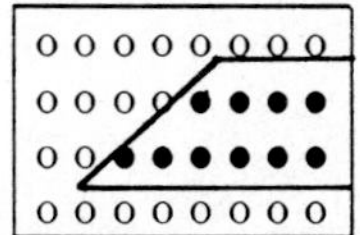

Figure 7. Polygon edge mask.

The other process computes the coverage ("area") of a polygon mask. Since the VAX has no bit counting instructions, the method is to strip off four bits at a time and look up the bit count in a table. The whole procedure can be put into a single C expression which generates efficient machine code.

9. Results

The REYES system, incorporating the A-buffer, has been used to make thousands of pictures. Figure 8 shows a magnified silhouette of the top of a teapot. Note the softness of the edge, even though the box filtering limits the edge intensity ramp to one pixel width. The Utah teapot, which appears in figures 8 and 9, is constructed so that its handle and spout penetrate its body. This is a common geometric modelling technique which avoids the explicit (and nearly intractable) calculation of the intersection curve. Figure 9 is a closeup of the upper part of the handle. The color of pixels through which the intersection curve passes is clearly a blend of the handle and body colors. Figure 10 is the "Genesis device". It is a collection of spheres, patches and polygons inside a partially transparent cylinder with quadrically modelled engines on the outside. Stars can be seen through the cylinder. All of figure 11, with the exception of the particle system grass plants, was rendered by REYES. The background of the picture was computed at 1024 lines and the foreground at 2048 lines resolution.

We have described a successful, relatively uncomplicated, anti-aliasing hidden surface mechanism. Like all visibility resolving methods, the A-buffer has its strengths, weaknesses, and limitations. It was designed to process the vast majority of pixels with minimum effort and maximum precision, spending compute time only on exceptional cases. On the other hand, the approximations used in the fragment intersection code can go astray if several surfaces intersect in the same pixel, and, of course, one cannot expect polygons smaller than the bitmask spacing to be sampled faithfully. Recognizing these limitations, we have found the A-buffer to be a practical, reliable means of producing synthetic images of high complexity.

References

1. CARPENTER, L., "A New Hidden Surface Algorithm," *Proceedings of NW76*, ACM, Seattle, WA, 1976.
2. CATMULL, E., *A Subdivision Algorithm for Computer Display of Curved Surfaces*, University of Utah, Salt Lake City, December 1974.
3. CATMULL, E., "A Hidden-Surface Algorithm with Anti-Aliasing," *Computer Graphics*, vol. 12, no. 3, pp. 6-11, ACM, 1978.
4. FIUME, E., A. FOURNIER, AND L. RUDOLPH, "A Parallel Scan Conversion Algorithm with Anti-Aliasing for a General-Purpose Ultracomputer," *Computer Graphics*, vol. 17, no. 3, pp. 141-150, ACM, July 1983.
5. LANE, J. M., L. C. CARPENTER, T. WHITTED, AND J. BLINN, "Scan-line methods for displaying parametrically defined surfaces," *Communications of the ACM*, vol. 25, no. 1, pp. 23-34, ACM, Jan. 1980.

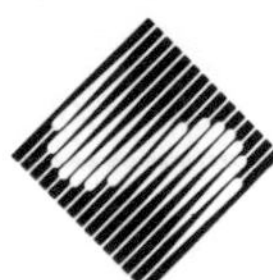

6. PORTER, T. AND T. DUFF, "Compositing Digital Images," *Computer Graphics*, vol. 18, no. 3, ACM, 1984.
7. SUTHERLAND, I. E., R. F. SPROULL, AND R. A. SCHUMACKER, "A characterization of ten hidden-surface algorithms," *Computing Surveys*, vol. 6, no. 1, pp. 1-55, ACM, March 1974.
8. WEILER, K. AND P. ATHERTON, "Hidden Surface Removal Using Polygon Area Sorting," *Computer Graphics*, vol. 11, no. 3, pp. 214-222, ACM, 1977.

Figure 8. Detail of teapot silhouette. (4×)

Figure 9. Detail of teapot handle intersection. (8×)

Figure 10. Genesis device. (4×)

Figure 11. Road to Point Reyes.

"Compositing 3-D Rendered Images" by T. Duff from *Proceedings of SIGGRAPH '85,* 1985, pages 41-44. Copyright 1985, Association for Computing Machinery, Inc., reprinted by permission.

Compositing 3-D Rendered Images

Tom Duff

Room 2C-425
AT&T Bell Laboratories
600 Mountain Avenue
Murray Hill, NJ 07974

ABSTRACT

The complexity of anti-aliased 3-D rendering systems can be controlled by using a tool-building approach like that of the UNIX(TM) text-processing tools. Such an approach requires a simple picture representation amenable to anti-aliasing that all rendering programs can produce, a compositing algorithm for that representation and a command language to piece together scenes. This paper advocates a representation that combines Porter and Duff's compositing algebra with a Z-buffer to provide simple anti-aliased 3-D compositing.

CR Categories and Subject Descriptors: I.3.3 [Picture and Image Generation] Display algorithms, Viewing algorithms, I.3.5 [Computational Geometry and Object Modelling] Curve, surface, solid and object representations, I.3.7 [Three-Dimensional Graphics and Realism] Visible line/surface algorithms

General Terms: Algorithms

Additional Keywords and Phrases: image synthesis, 3-D rendering, hidden-surface elimination, anti-aliasing, Z-buffer, compositing

1. Introduction

3-D rendering programs capable of dealing with detailed scenes are usually large and complex. For example, the version of REYES [1] used at Lucasfilm to create "The Adventures of André & Wally B." [12] is a 40,000 line C program. There are at most two people who understand it in its entirety.

There are several approaches to controlling this complexity. The NYIT Computer Graphics Laboratory has a set of special-purpose rendering programs that all use Z-buffer algorithms (see below) [4]. Each can initialize its Z-buffer with the results produced by the others and add objects to a scene. Thus, to produce a scene containing quadric surfaces, fractal terrain and polyhedra, three simple programs, each rendering one surface type can replace a combined quadric surface/fractal terrain/polyhedron rendering program.

Frank Crow at Ohio State University built a system that combines the output of heterogeneous rendering programs using a list-priority algorithm [3]. [15] describes a rendering test-bed that reduces objects on-the-fly to polygons, slices the polygons into spans the height of scan lines or smaller, and combines the spans using a Z-buffer (usually). The compositing algebra described in [10] is used at Lucasfilm to combine the output of many rendering tools (including REYES).

Their method is a list-priority algorithm with the list ordering worked out manually. A similar algorithm is used at most motion picture special effects houses, running on optical printers instead of digital computers [7].

All these systems have drawbacks. Z-buffer methods are hard to anti-alias, because their data representation is point-sampled (but note chapter 7 of [2]). The Lucasfilm and Ohio State systems require that all surfaces be linearly separable [9]. Even when it is possible to separate a scene by dicing it with cutting planes [5], the primitives in the diced scene may be more complex than in the original. It may even be impossible to find separating planes for scenes containing surfaces that intersect in non-planar curves.

Whitted and Weimer's approach requires that the various rendering sub-methods be connected by a complex polygon-span data structure. Considerable understanding of the system's internals is required to add new features. Anti-aliasing is difficult, but easier than with other Z-buffer style methods.

A similar complexity problem obtains with many document preparation systems and "integrated application environments." Emacs [6] is a text-editor with 450 commands, and more coming every day. Lotus 1-2-3 is a desk calculator with a 250 page instruction manual. The UNIX text processing tools [8] avoid this syndrome by cutting the text processing problem into many small sub-problems, with a small program to handle each piece. Because all the programs read and write a simple common data representation (ASCII character streams with end-of-line marked by a newline character) they can be wired together for particular applications by a simple command language. We would like to apply this philosophy to the problem of anti-aliased 3-D rendering. To do that, we need a simple picture representation that all our rendering programs can produce, a compositing algorithm for that representation and a command language with which to piece together scenes.

2. The rgbαz Representation

The **rgbαz** representation is a straightforward combination of the **rgbα** representation in [10] and a Z-buffer [2]. The hidden-surface algorithms for these representations are based on binary operators that combine a pair of images f and b pixel-by-pixel to produce a composite image $c = f$ **op** b. Applying the operator to a sequence of images in an appropriate order will produce the final image of the visible surfaces.

The Z-buffer operator f **zmin** b operates on a color value **rgb** and a depth coordinate **z** stored at each pixel in the frame buffer. The composite image has $\mathbf{rgb}_c = (\textbf{if } \mathbf{z}_f < \mathbf{z}_b \textbf{ then } \mathbf{rgb}_f \textbf{ else } \mathbf{rgb}_b)$, and $\mathbf{z}_c = \min(\mathbf{z}_f, \mathbf{z}_b)$ at each pixel. [13] categorizes this algorithm, along with the ray-tracing approach advocated by [14], as "brute-force image space" methods (although ray-tracing is usually done in object space), dismissing both as impractical. Ironically, they are the two most popular hidden surface algorithms in use today.

The **rgbα** compositing operator f **over** b operates on pixels containing

an **rgb** value and a value α between 0 and 1, which may be thought of as the fraction of the pixel that the object covers. Each component of **rgb** is between 0 and α (see [10] for details).

The operator **over** computes $\mathbf{rgb}_c = \mathbf{rgb}_f + (1-\alpha_f)\mathbf{rgb}_b$ and $\alpha_c = \alpha_f + (1-\alpha_f)\alpha_b$ at each pixel. The foreground $\mathbf{rgb}_f$ is unattenuated at each pixel, and $\mathbf{rgb}_b$ shows through more as α_f decreases. When $\alpha_f = 1$, $c = f$ and when $\alpha_f = 0$, $c = b$, since each component of $\mathbf{rgb}_f$ must be 0 when $\alpha_f = 0$. Using **over** with more than two elements requires knowledge of their front-to-back order, so that the operator can be applied to elements or previous composites that are adjacent in depth.

f **over** *b* is inherently anti-aliased (really area-sampled) if, as is usually the case, α_f and α_b are uncorrelated. It can make mistakes when, for example, two elements share an edge. The only apparent way to solve this problem is to store an unbounded amount of information inside each pixel. [1] is an example of such a method, but it runs slowly and is difficult to implement correctly.

zmin is commutative and associative; that is, the order in which objects are composed is irrelevant. Because the method is point-sampled, anti-aliasing is difficult. **over** trades commutativity for anti-aliasing. It doesn't care whether elements are composited front-to-back or back-to-front or some recursive combination of the two, but they must be adjacent in depth when they are combined.

The **rgbαz** algorithm's compositing operator **comp** combines the action of **zmin** and **over**. Each pixel contains **rgb** and α along with the **z** value at each corner. Corners that are not covered have **z** set to a value (called $+\infty$) larger than any legitimate **z** value. Since each **z** value is used in 4 pixels, we keep the upper left-hand corner **z** with its pixel and get the other values from adjacent pixels. (This means that we must store an extra column off-screen at the right, and a row off the bottom, whose **rgb** and α we never use.)

f **comp** *b* is computed by first comparing $\mathbf{z}_f$ to $\mathbf{z}_b$ at each corner of the pixel. There are $2^4 = 16$ possible outcomes. If the comparisons are not the same at all four corners, we say the pixel is *confused*. Along each pixel edge at whose ends the **z**'s compare differently, we linearly interpolate the **z**'s and find the point at which they are equal. Figure 1 shows how to divide the pixel in each case to compute the fraction β on which f is in front. Then $\mathbf{rgb}\alpha_c = \beta(f \textbf{ over } b) + (1-\beta)(b \textbf{ over } f)$, and $\mathbf{z}_c = \min(\mathbf{z}_f, \mathbf{z}_b)$.

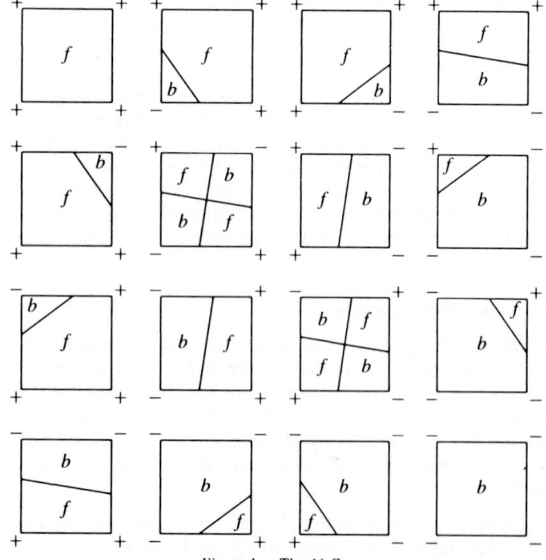

Figure 1 — The 16 Cases

Each square represents a pixel. The corners are marked with the sign of $\mathbf{z}_b - \mathbf{z}_f$. The label in each pixel fragment indicates which picture is visible in it. β is the total area of the fragments labeled *f*.

If $\mathbf{z}_f$ or $\mathbf{z}_b$ is $+\infty$ at some corner, we must pick an appropriate value to use as a surrogate in the comparisons and interpolations above. Currently, we circle the pixel clockwise and anticlockwise from the uncovered corner looking for two legitimate **z**'s and use their average.

Note that **comp** is commutative, since if we interchange f and b, β is replaced by $1-\beta$. For unconfused pixels, the result's **rgbα** is just *f* **over** *b* or *b* **over** *f*, as appropriate, and therefore the operation is associative in the unconfused case. This is almost good enough to let us combine pictures in any order. Since linearly separable objects have no confused pixels, **comp** performs just as well on them as **over**. For confused pixels associativity breaks down and mistakes can occur. For objects that legitimately intersect, the algorithm effectively computes a sub-pixel resolution polygonal curve that will be close to the intersection curve of the original objects and correctly mattes the objects together along the approximate curve. If an element q is between p and r, the pixels of *p* **comp** *r* can be confused with those of q, so elements cannot be composited in completely arbitrary order. Fortunately, the errors are usually small, so a cavalier attitude to compositing order is at least partially justified. If these errors are a problem, a group of elements can be composited all at once by sorting their pixels on their **z** coordinates and applying **comp** on adjacent elements. Then confusion-induced errors will only arise among elements whose confusion is intrinsic.

The **comp** algorithm may also encounter errors caused by the point-sampled **z** coordinates. In particular, small objects may be lost if they fall between the pixels. Furthermore, pixels are combined by area-sampling rather than convolution with a higher-order filter, which can introduce slightly scalloped intersection edges. **comp** shares with **over** the problem that errors can occur when its operands are not uncorrelated, as can happen in pixels crossed by many edges.

3. Examples

I have written a small set of programs to test these ideas. *3matte* executes the **comp** algorithm on a set of input pictures, producing an **rgbαz** output picture. *Quad* draws an anti-aliased rendition of a single quadric surface (figure 2), given the equation of its quadratic form. Using *3matte* to combine the output of multiple *quad* runs generates more complex surfaces, like the knobby-kneed robot of figure 3.

The *quad-3matte* combination is hardly a practical quadric-surface rendering system. It does show that with powerful compositing methods high quality renderings of significant objects can be produced using minimal tools.

Terrain generates anti-aliased perspective views of terrain from National Cartographic Information Center digital terrain data. Figure 4 is a view of central New Jersey, with the elevations exaggerated by a factor of 20. *Bg* generates background cards given the colors at the top and bottom of the screen. Figure 5 shows a small covey of flying saucers over New Jersey with a sky-colored background.

Figure 5 shows the sort of error that can be made when confused pixels are treated naively. Where a saucer passes behind the the rightmost foreground hill the silhouette of the hill is a little too dark near the peak.

Programs that do certain kinds of 2- and 3-dimensional image processing can operate on **rgbαz** pictures. For example, *hrot* rotates the hue of a picture, leaving alone its saturation and value [11]. The middle flying saucer of figure 5 was generated in the same colors as the one on the left, and had its hue rotated 30 degrees. *Fog* is a program that makes foggy images by mixing its input image with a fog color in an amount that depends on the **z** coordinates of the pixels. Figure 6 is the result of applying a purple haze to figure 5. The shadow-generation algorithm of [16] works on **rgbαz** pictures and could be enhanced to take advantage of the increased information available in the **rgbαz** representation.

These programs are all small and simple to write. *3matte* is 270 lines of C, *quad* is 428 lines, *terrain* is 339 lines, *bg* is 58 lines, *hrot* is 76 lines, and *fog* is 73 lines, for a total of 1244 lines.

Figure 5 is a frame from a short animated sequence produced using these programs. The sequence was 227 frames long, and took 34 hours and 26 minutes to compute (total wall-clock time, half on each of 2 VAX 11/750s, one with a floating-point accelerator and one without), or roughly 9 minutes per frame. Profiling the programs revealed that roughly 80% of their time was spent encoding and decoding the run-length encoded disk files in which the elements were stored. Not counting picture I/O, the time per frame was about 1.8 minutes. An extremely large frame buffer could eliminate picture I/O altogether.

4. Conclusions

The UNIX text-processing environment demonstrates that a suite of small programs acting on a common data representation, and bound together by a powerful command language, can be more powerful than a large integrated application program that tries to cover all eventualities. We believe that the same principle applies to image synthesis.

Experimentation is encouraged in an environment where little changes don't involve digging into, and possibly breaking, a huge monolithic program. New methods are easier to try out, and the consequences of failure are localized.

The **rgbαz** representation is easily produced by almost any rendering program and has a simple, fast anti-aliased compositing operation whose output is of high enough quality for all but the most exacting applications. The representation is the basis for a 3-D image synthesis toolkit. We expect that as we build more image synthesis and processing tools a rich 3-D graphics environment will emerge.

Acknowledgements

Don Mitchell designed the robot of figure 3. Rob Pike gave the paper a good critical reading.

References

[1] Loren Carpenter, "The A-buffer, an Antialiased Hidden Surface Method," *Computer Graphics*, Vol. 18, No. 3 (1984), pp. 103-108

[2] Edwin Catmull, *A Subdivision Algorithm for Computer Display of Curved Surfaces*, Ph.D. dissertation, Department of Computer Science, University of Utah, Salt Lake City, December 1974

[3] Frank Crow, "A More Flexible Image Generation Environment," *Computer Graphics*, Vol. 16, No. 3 (1982), pp. 9-18

[4] Tom Duff, *The Soid and Roid Manual*, NYIT Computer Graphics Laboratory internal memorandum, 1980

[5] Henry Fuchs, Zvi M. Kedem and Bruce F. Naylor, "On Visible Surface Generation By A Priori Tree Structures," *Computer Graphics*, Vol. 14, No. 3 (1980), pp 124-133

[6] James Gosling *UNIX Emacs*, CMU internal memorandum, August, 1982

[7] L. Bernard Happé, *Basic Motion Picture Technology*, Hastings House, New York, 1975

[8] Brian Kernighan and Rob Pike, *The UNIX Programming Environment*, Prentice-Hall, Englewood Cliffs NJ, 1984

[9] Martin E. Newell, "The Utilization of Procedure Models in Digital Image Synthesis," *University of Utah Computer Science Department*, UTEC-CSc-76-218, Summer 1975

[10] Thomas Porter and Tom Duff, "Compositing Digital Images," *Computer Graphics*, Vol 18, No. 3 (1984), pp. 253-259

[11] Alvy Ray Smith, "Color Gamut Transform Pairs," *Computer Graphics*, Vol 12, No. 3 (1978), pp 12-19

[12] Alvy Ray Smith, Loren Carpenter, Ed Catmull, Rob Cook, Tom Duff, Craig Good, John Lasseter, Eben Ostby, William Reeves, and David Salesin, "The Adventures of André & Wally B.," created by the Lucasfilm Computer Graphics Project. July 1984.

[13] Ivan Sutherland, Robert Sproull and R. A. Schumaker, "A Characterization of Ten Hidden Surface Algorithms," *Computing Surveys*, Vol. 6, No. 1 (1974), pp. 1-55

[14] Turner Whitted, "An Improved Illumination Model for Shaded Display," *Comm. ACM*, Vol. 23, No. 6 (June 1980), 343-349

[15] Turner Whitted and David Weimer, "A Software Test-Bed for the Development of 3-D Raster Graphics Systems," *Computer Graphics*, Vol. 15, No. 3 (1981), pp. 271-277

[16] Lance Williams, "Casting Curved Shadows on Curved Surfaces," *Computer Graphics*, Vol. 12, No. 3 (1978), pp. 270-274

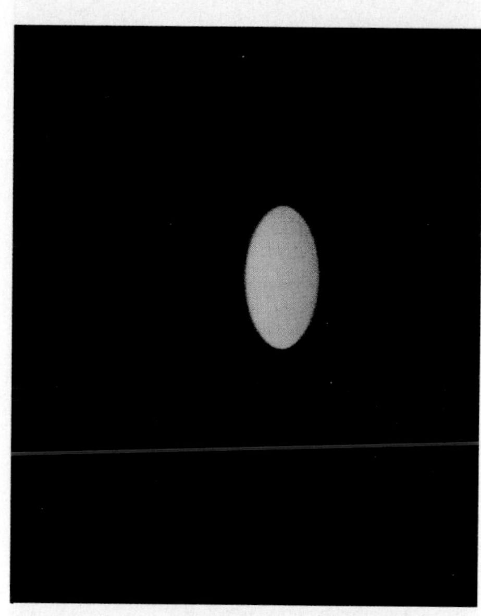

Figure 2 — Ellipsoid rendered by *quad*

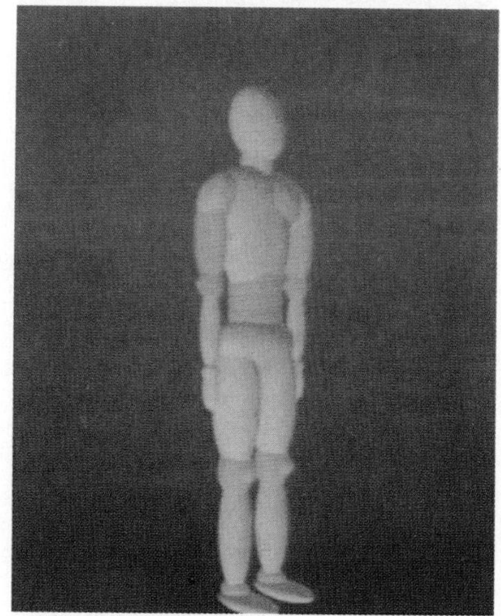

Figure 3 — Robot rendered by *quad*, *bg* and *3matte*

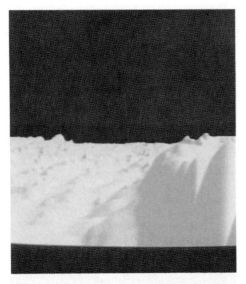

Figure 4 — New Jersey rendered by *terrain*

Figure 5 — Flying Saucers over New Jersey, rendered by *quad*, *bg*, *terrain* and *3matte*

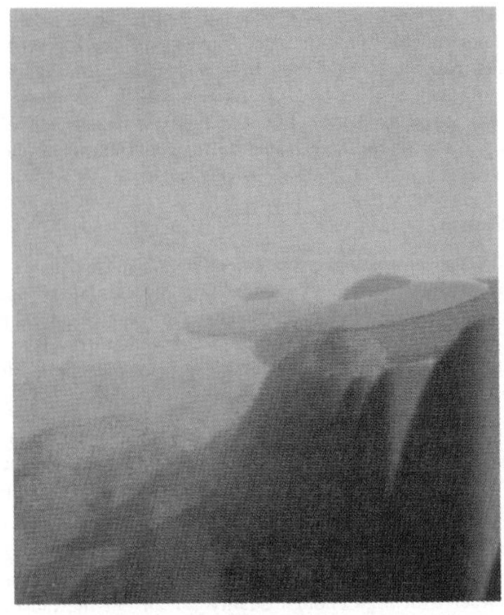

Figure 6 — Fog added to previous picture using *fog*

CASTING CURVED SHADOWS ON CURVED SURFACES

Lance Williams
Computer Graphics Lab
New York Institute of Technology
Old Westbury, New York 11568

Abstract

Shadowing has historically been used to increase the intelligibility of scenes in electron microscopy and aerial survey. Various methods have been published for the determination of shadows in computer synthesized scenes. The display of shadows may make the shape and relative position of objects in such scenes more comprehensible; it is a technique lending vividness and realism to computer animation.

To date, algorithms for the determination of shadows have been restricted to scenes constructed of planar polygons. A simple algorithm is described which utilizes Z-buffer visible surface computation to display shadows cast by objects modelled of smooth surface patches. The method can be applied to all environments, in fact, for which visible surfaces can be computed. The cost of determining the shadows associated with each light source is roughly twice the cost of rendering the scene without shadows, plus a fixed transformation overhead which depends on the image resolution. No extra entities are added to the scene description in the shadowing process. This comprehensive algorithm, which permits curved shadows to be cast on curved surfaces, is contrasted with a less costly method for casting the shadows of the environment on a single ground plane.

In order to attain good results, the discrete nature of the visible-surface computations must be treated with care. The effects of dither, interpolation, and geometric quantization at different stages of the shadowing algorithm are examined. The special problems posed by self-shadowing surfaces are described.

Key words: shadows, hidden surface algorithms, computer animation, computer graphics.

CR classification: 8.2

Introduction

The Z-buffer visible surface algorithm, first published by Catmull [1], was the first method to make possible computer generated shaded pictures of bicubic surface patches. The algorithm is extremely general and quite simple to implement but requires substantial memory.

A "frame buffer," in the current computer graphics parlance, is a memory that stores a complete digital picture. It may serve as an intermediary between the computer that produces the picture and a video driver which continuously refreshes a display. Some visible surface algorithms (e.g. [2]) require a frame buffer in order to compute an image. In this case, the frame buffer mediates the display process in a more substantial way.

The Z-buffer is an extension of this mass-memory approach to computer graphics which resolves the visible surfaces in a scene by storing depth (Z) values at each point in the picture. As objects are rendered, their Z values are compared at each point with the stored Z values to determine visibility. Since this determination requires only that a measure exist which orders the surfaces to be displayed, it is not too strong a statement to say that the Z-buffer algorithm provides a discrete solution to all scenes for which visible surfaces can be computed.

Z-buffer visible surface computation is of particular interest because it exhibits limiting-case properties [3]. The objects to be rendered do not have to be sorted beforehand, so indefinitely complex scenes can be handled. At the pixel level, the Z-buffer implicitly executes radix sorts in X and Y and simple indexing in Z. In X and Y, the sorts are bucket sorts, the special case of the radix sort where the radix encompasses the range of the keys, obviating all comparisons. In Z, the index of the sort is reduced to one, necessitating only a single comparison for each item.

Radix sorting is the only sorting method which grows only linearly in expense with the number of randomly-ordered items to be sorted, and the Z-buffer is the only visible surface algorithm the cost of which grows only linearly with the average depth complexity of the environment (that is to say, with the total screen area of all surfaces rendered, whether visible in the final image or not).

Thus the Z-buffer algorithm enjoys two key advantages over all other existing visible surface algorithms:

1. indefinitely large environments;

2. linear cost growth.

In addition, the final image computed has an associated Z partition, a "depth map" [4] of the scene. This extra information permits a great many interesting post-processes on a computed image. Such algorithms are noteworthy because their expense does not vary with the size or complexity of the environment, but depends only on the image resolution. The shadow algorithm described here is one attempt to exploit the Z partition.

Shadow Information

The display of shadows may make the shape and relative position of objects in computer generated scenes more comprehensible. Shadows emphasize and may serve to clarify the three dimensional nature of the forms displayed.

The shadows cast by a point source of light onto a flat surface represent, like a perspective transformation, a projection of the scene onto a plane. This simplified situation offers a convenient way of understanding the information that shadows convey. A scene rendered with shadows contains two views in one image. If we are content to cast shadows on a single wall or ground plane, these two views are simple projections. In general, of course, shadows may fall across any surface in the scene. Two views are still sufficient to compute the shadows, however, if they are Z-buffer views.

The proposed algorithm works as follows:

1. A view of the scene is constructed from the point of view of the light source. Only the Z values and not the shading values need be computed and stored.

2. A view of the scene is then constructed from the point of view of the observer's eye. A linear transformation exists which maps X,Y,Z points in the observer's view into X,Y,Z coordinates in the light source view. As each point is generated in the observer's view, it is transformed into the computed view in the light source space and tested for visibility to the light source before computing its shading value. If the point is not visible to the light source, it is in shadow and is shaded accordingly.

Step (2) as defined is the "correct" form of the proposed algorithm, but in the ensuing discussion and pictures a modified procedure is assumed. The complete scene is computed from the observer's viewpoint, and the point-by-point transformation to the light source space and consequent shadowing is undertaken as a post-process. This modified algorithm incorrectly shades the hilights in the scene, since they appear in the shading process and then are merely darkened if they are found to lie in shadow; hilights should not appear in shadowed areas at all. The modified algorithm may also suffer more severely from quantization problems, since the Z coordinates of the visible points will have been quantized to the resolution of the Z buffer (16 bits in the cases illustrated here) before transformation. On the other hand, the expense of the transformation in the modified version does not depend on the complexity of the scene, as it does when all points are transformed as they are computed. Operating as a post process, the transformation is applied only to the points that are visible in the final picture. The expense is thus dependent only on the resolution of the image. Like most point-by-point operations, expense increases with the square of the resolution.

Limitations of Image Space

The generalization to curved surfaces and the linear cost growth which distinguish the proposed algorithm are both attributable to the fact that all computations are performed in image space. This approach carries with it certain limitations, however, which must be weighed against the advantages.

Since shadow determination is based on transformation between two images, the user must take care to ensure that all objects which may cast a shadow in the observer's image be within the field of view of the light source image. The assumption is that points transformed into the light source space which lie outside the viewing volume of the light source are illuminated. Shadows may only be cast within the viewing volume of the light source.

While it is not precisely true that the light source must lie outside the observer's field of view, it can cast shadows only within its own field. If a light source within the observer's viewing volume is to cast shadows in all directions, its sphere of illumination must be sectored into multiple views as suggested by Crow [5]. Computing these views in the Z-buffer is only slightly more expensive than computing a single view containing all the objects in the scene. Transforming points from the observer's image into the light source space becomes more expensive, however. Either each point must be transformed into each light source view (the correct approach in computing shadows for multiple light sources), or clipped against the light source viewing volumes in the observer's space and transformed into the coordinates of the light source view in which it falls. The major difficulty with this method is the increased memory required.

Severe perspective, either in the observer's view or required by a light source close to the scene, may increase the quantization problems attendant in transforming from one image to the other. In any case, quantization and aliasing are the chief drawback of image space algorithms. The aliasing problem must be addressed vigorously whenever image space techniques are applied. This is a large and complicated issue, outside the scope of this paper; for a general treatment of aliasing and visible surface algorithms, see [1], [6], and especially [7]. [3] will treat the special topic of aliasing, geometric quantization and the Z-buffer.

Self-shadowing surfaces rendered by the proposed technique constitute an excellent case study in image space sampling problems. When we transform a point from a surface in the observer's space onto a surface in the light source space, it should ideally lie right on the surface of which it is a part. Due to the imprecision of machine arithmetic and more particularly to the quantization of Z-buffer surfaces, it will fall above or below the surface. Since we want the point to appear illuminated if it lies on a visible surface, we subtract a bias from

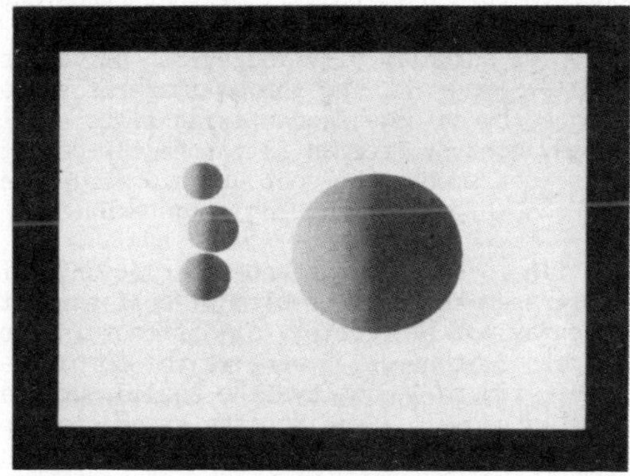

fig. 1
The observer's view of four spheres.

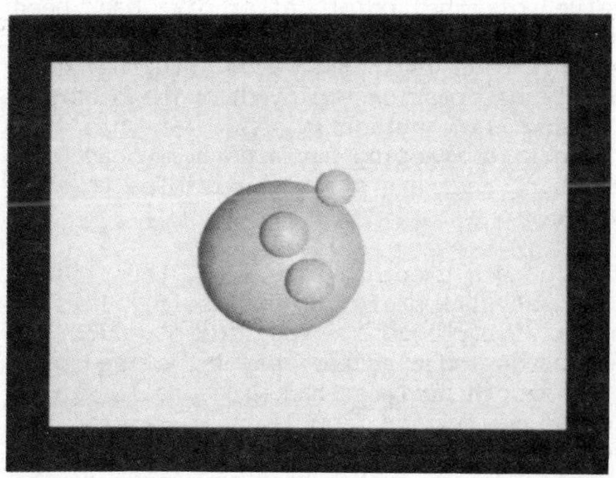

fig. 2
The four spheres viewed from the position of the light source.

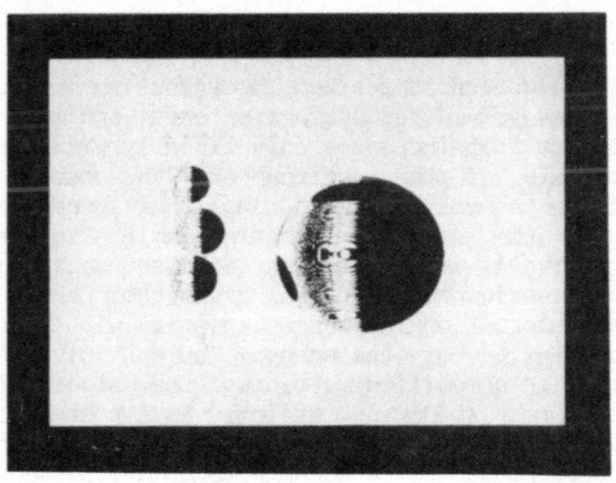

fig. 3
Shadow with reduced surface bias reveals quantization moire.

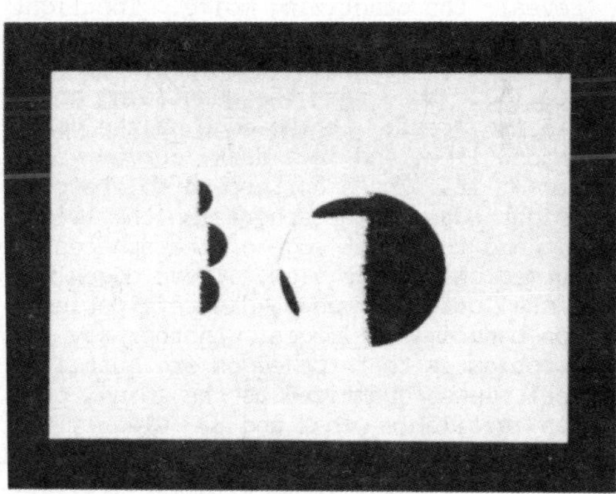

fig. 4
Increased bias and dither applied to shadow computation.

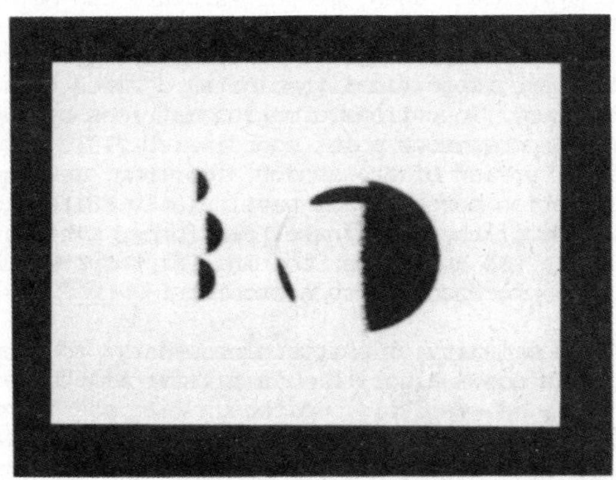

fig. 5
Low-pass filtering applied to shadow.

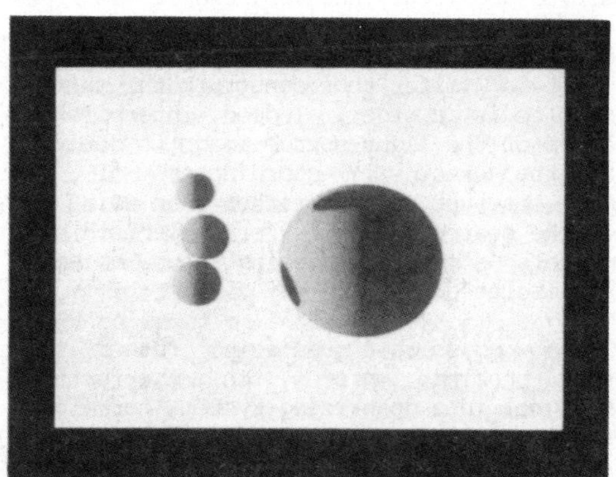

fig. 6
Shadow applied to the image of fig. 1

the Z value of the point after it has been transformed into the light source space (actually, of course, this bias is incorporated into the general linear transformation employed). The bias may move the shadow line slightly, but it has the desired effect of keeping surfaces from shadowing themselves where they are plainly visible to the light source.

As a surface curves smoothly away from the light, however, it must ultimately shadow itself. This is not a problem with polygons, the sharp edges of which make shadowing a rather sharply defined proposition. A smooth surface shadowing itself in a shallow curve may switch from light to dark on the strength of a least significant bit in the Z-buffer. Worse, it may switch back and forth as the quantizing error beats with the sampling grid, producing a vivid moire.

Figures 1 and 2 illustrate a simple scene from the point of view of an observer and from the point of view of the light source, respectively. The Z bias subtracted from the transformed points in computing the shadows of figure 3 has been deliberately reduced to reveal the quantizing moire. The light source is at infinity, rotated one hundred degrees about the vertical axis to the left of the observer's bearing. Note that the quantizing error is greatest in two areas: at the edge of the vertical solid shadow line, and in a dark curved band to the left of it. These correspond to, respectively, the right edge of the spheres in the light source view, and the right edge of the spheres in the untransformed observer's view. These edges are aliased in the original views, discrete periodic samples of non-bandlimited images. Another way of viewing the problem is that the edges are quantized in the original views, quantized to the nine bits of resolution available in X and Y. Clearly the problem is much greater than in Z, where sixteen bits are available. Unfortunately, extra lateral resolution is purchased at square law expense.

Bandlimiting the Z partition before sampling, if it were practical, would not improve matters. Z values at the edges of the spheres would be a smooth blend of the depth of the edge and the depth of the far clipping plane, meaningless points as far as the scene is concerned. The aliasing effects observed are local, however, and it is reasonable to treat the smooth surfaces within the ragged edges as correctly sampled. This assumption implies that a filter to reconstruct the surface between samples is in order. Indeed, interpolating the Z values of the light source image to derive Z values at the exact X,Y coordinates of the transformed observer points (rather than using the Z value of the nearest neighbor for comparison) improves matters somewhat, reducing shadow noise in the form of isolated pixels.

Treating shadow noise as a quantizing rather than an aliasing problem improves the image further. The error signal in a quantizing system correlates quite strongly with the signal. Addition of random noise in the range of a single quantum breaks up this correlation, reduces the resulting periodicities (moire) to which the human eye is so sensitive, and whitens the spectrum of the error. Figure 4 illustrates the sphere shadows with increased negative Z bias and bilinear interpolation of light source Z values to the X,Y of the transformed observer points, which have been dithered by the addition of normally distributed random values in the range -.5 to +.5. The shadow image is subsequently dejagged by an edge dequantizing filter similar to one advanced by Freeman [8], then low pass filtered to further smooth the contours and merge the dithered edge of self shadowing (figure 5).

As a final, not unimportant observation, figure 6 illustrates that the problem of self shadowing surfaces may not be terribly significant in practice. Figures 3 through 5 were of the computed shadows alone; figure 6 displays the shaded surfaces with their shadows. Shading the spheres according to the position of the light source casting the shadows causes a smooth shadow transition which obscures the quantization error. In practice, translucent shadows (their translucency corresponding to the additive "ambient" term in most surface shading formulations) generally look better than deep black shadows, and low pass filtering of the shadows before they are applied to the image subjectively approximates the soft penumbra cast by real light sources.

Conclusions

The algorithm described operates successfully on scenes of curved surface patches, and does so with a cost that increases only linearly with the complexity of the environment. The cost is roughly twice the cost of rendering the scene normally, plus the cost of transforming the points of the observer's image into the light source image. In the originally stated algorithm, the cost of transformation increases linearly with the depth complexity of the scene. The cost of transformation in a modified version of the algorithm which performs shadowing strictly as a post- process is fixed by the resolution of the screen, and corresponds to a scene with an average depth complexity of one. The rendering cost is only "roughly" twice the cost of rendering the scene normally, since the light source view requires no shading computation. Depending on the complexity of the shading rules applied [9], this may represent a substantial savings.

Speed does not directly correspond to "computational expense" when special hardware can be applied. The enormous interest in real-time graphics has led to the development of specialized transformation hardware, specifically, digital devices to multiply four by four transformation matrices by four element homogeneous point coordinates [10]. The modified version of the shadow algorithm, developed for animation purposes, is particularly suited to pipelining of the coordinate transforms. The intent at NYIT is to apply the Floating Point Systems AP120-B array processor to such problems.

The complexity of software necessary to implement the shadow algorithm is minimal if the necessary memory is available. Although it has long been suggested that two passes of a visible surface algorithm is sufficient to compute shadowing [5], relating the data provided by the two passes is very difficult for many algorithms. The Z-buffer provides a straightforward means of relating data in different views since the visible surfaces are three dimensional and hence subject to general three dimensional transformations.

The bright outlook for memory technology bodes well for mass-memory graphics. The shadow algorithm discussed here is one simple example of a wide class of extremely general algorithms which exhibit very desirable cost growth properties. The challenge of this approach to computer graphics is to cope successfully with the problems posed by the discrete nature of image space scene representations.

fig. 7a
3d smile sculpted by Alvy Ray Smith.

fig. 7b
evinces the shadow of a smile.

fig. 8
The robot casting his shadow on the wall and floor is composed of over 350 bicubic surface patches.

References

[1] Catmull, E., "A Subdivision Algorithm for Computer Display of Curved Surfaces," PhD. thesis, Dept. of Computer Science, University of Utah, 1974.

[2] Newell, M. G., Newell, R. G., and Sancha, T. L., "A Solution to the Hidden Surface Problem," Proceedings of the 1972 ACM National Conference.

[3] Williams, L., forthcoming PhD. thesis, University of Utah.

[4] For the application of this representation to scene analysis, see: Levine, M. D., O'Handley, D. A., and Yagi, G. M., "Computer Determination of Depth Maps," Computer Graphics and Image Processing, No. 2, 1973.

[5] Crow, F. C., "Shadow Algorithms for Computer Graphics," Siggraph 1977 Proceedings, Vol. 11, No. 2, Summer 1977.

[6] Blinn, J. F., "A Scan-Line Algorithm for the Display of Bicubic Surface Patches," PhD. thesis, Dept. of Computer Science, University of Utah, 1978.

[7] Crow, F. C., "The Aliasing Problem in Computer-Synthesized Shaded Images," PhD. thesis, Dept. of Computer Science, University of Utah, 1976.

[8] Freeman, H., "Computer Processing of Line Drawing Images," ACM Computing Surveys, Vol. 6, No. 1, March 1974.

[9] Blinn, J. F., "Models of Light Reflection for Computer Synthesized Pictures," Siggraph 1977 Proceedings, Vol. 11, No. 2, Summer 1977.

[10] Sutherland, I.E., "A Head-Mounted Three-Dimensional Display," Fall Joint Computer Conference 1968, Thompson Books, Washington, D.C., 757.

Especial thanks are due David DiFrancisco and Garland Stern for photographic assistance.

The Reyes Image Rendering Architecture

Robert L. Cook
Loren Carpenter
Edwin Catmull

Pixar
P. O. Box 13719
San Rafael, CA 94913

An architecture is presented for fast high-quality rendering of complex images. All objects are reduced to common world-space geometric entities called micropolygons, and all of the shading and visibility calculations operate on these micropolygons. Each type of calculation is performed in a coordinate system that is natural for that type of calculation. Micropolygons are created and textured in the local coordinate system of the object, with the result that texture filtering is simplified and improved. Visibility is calculated in screen space using stochastic point sampling with a z buffer. There are no clipping or inverse perspective calculations. Geometric and texture locality are exploited to minimize paging and to support models that contain arbitrarily many primitives.

CR CATEGORIES AND SUBJECT DESCRIPTORS: I.3.7 [**Computer Graphics**]: Three-Dimensional Graphics and Realism;

ADDITIONAL KEY WORDS AND PHRASES: image rendering, computer image synthesis, texturing, hidden surface algorithms, z buffer, stochastic sampling

1. Introduction

Reyes is an image rendering system developed at Lucasfilm Ltd. and currently in use at Pixar. In designing Reyes, our goal was an architecture optimized for fast high-quality rendering of complex animated scenes. By fast we mean being able to compute a feature-length film in approximately a year; high-quality means virtually indistinguishable from live action motion picture photography; and complex means as visually rich as real scenes.

This goal was intended to be ambitious enough to force us to completely rethink the entire rendering process. We actively looked for new approaches to image synthesis and consciously tried to avoid limiting ourselves to thinking in terms of traditional solutions or particular computing environments. In the process, we combined some old methods with some new ideas.

Some of the algorithms that were developed for the Reyes architecture have already been discussed elsewhere; these include stochastic sampling [12], distributed ray tracing [10, 13], shade trees [11], and an antialiased depth map shadow algorithm [32].

This paper includes short descriptions of these algorithms as necessary, but the emphasis in this paper is on the overall architecture.

Many of our design decisions are based on some specific assumptions about the types of complex scenes that we want to render and what makes those scenes complex. Since this architecture is optimized for these types of scenes, we begin by examining our assumptions and goals.

- **Model complexity.** We are interested in making images that are visually rich, far more complex than any pictures rendered to date. This goal comes from noticing that even the most complex rendered images look simple when compared to real scenes and that most of the complexity in real scenes comes from rich shapes and textures. We expect that reaching this level of richness will require scenes with hundreds of thousands of geometric primitives, each one of which can be complex.
- **Model diversity.** We want to support a large variety of geometric primitives, especially data amplification primitives such as procedural models, fractals [18], graftals [35], and particle systems [30, 31].
- **Shading complexity.** Because surface reflection characteristics are extremely varied and complex, we consider a programmable shader a necessity. Our experience with such a shader [11] is that realistic surfaces frequently require complex shading and a large number of textures. Textures can store many different types of data, including surface color [8], reflections (environment maps) [3], normal perturbation (bump maps) [4], geometry perturbation (displacement maps) [11], shadows [32], and refraction [25].
- **Minimal ray tracing.** Many non-local lighting effects can be approximated with texture maps. Few objects in natural scenes would seem to require ray tracing. Accordingly, we consider it more important to optimize the architecture for complex geometries and large models than for the non-local lighting effects accounted for by ray tracing or radiosity.
- **Speed.** We are interested in making animated images, and animation introduces severe demands on rendering speed. Assuming 24 frames per second, rendering a 2 hour movie in a year would require a rendering speed of about 3 minutes per frame. Achieving this speed is especially challenging for complex images.
- **Image Quality.** We eschew aliasing and faceting artifacts, such as jagged edges, Moiré patterns in textures, temporal strobing, and highlight aliasing.
- **Flexibility.** Many new image rendering techniques will undoubtedly be discovered in the coming years. The architecture should be flexible enough to incorporate many of these new techniques.

2. Design Principles

These assumptions led us to a set of architectural design principles. Some of these principles are illustrated in the overview in Figure 1.

1. **Natural coordinates.** Each calculation should be done in a coordinate system that is natural for that calculation. For example, texturing is most naturally done in the coordinate system of the local surface geometry (e.g., *uv* space for patches), while the visible surface calculations are most naturally done in pixel coordinates (screen space).
2. **Vectorization.** The architecture should be able to exploit vectorization, parallelism and pipelining. Calculations that are similar should be done together. For example, since the shading calculations are usually similar at all points on a surface, an entire surface should be shaded at the same time.
3. **Common representation.** Most of the algorithm should work with a single type of basic geometric object. We turn every geometric primitive into *micropolygons,* which are flat-shaded subpixel-sized quadrilaterals. All of the shading and visibility calculations are performed exclusively on micropolygons.
4. **Locality.** Paging and data thrashing should be minimized.
   a. **Geometric locality.** Calculations for a geometric primitive should be performed without reference to other geometric primitives. Procedural models should be computed only once and should not be kept in their expanded form any longer than necessary.
   b. **Texture locality.** Only the textures currently needed should be in memory, and textures should be read off the disk only once.
5. **Linearity.** The rendering time should grow linearly with the size of the model.
6. **Large models.** There should be no limit to the number of geometric primitives in a model.
7. **Back door.** There should be a back door in the architecture so that other programs can be used to render some of the objects. This give us a very general way to incorporate any new technique (though not necessarily efficiently).
8. **Texture maps.** Texture map access should be efficient, as we expect to use several textures on every surface. Textures are a powerful tool for defining complex shading characteristics, and displacement maps [11] can be used for model complexity.

We now discuss some of these principles in detail.

2.1. Geometric Locality.

When ray tracing arbitrary surfaces that reflect or refract, a ray in any pixel on the screen might generate a secondary ray to any object in the model. The object hit by the secondary ray can be determined quickly [20, 21, 34], but that object must then be accessed from the database. As models become more complex, the ability to access any part of the model at any time becomes more expensive; model and texture paging can dominate the rendering time. For this reason, we consider ray tracing algorithms poorly suited for rendering extremely complex environments.

In many instances, though, texture maps can be used to approximate non-local calculations. A common example of this is the use of environment maps [3] for reflection, a good approximation in many cases. Textures have also been used for refractions [25] and shadows [32, 36]. Each of these uses of texture maps represents some non-local calculations that we can avoid (principles 4a and 8).

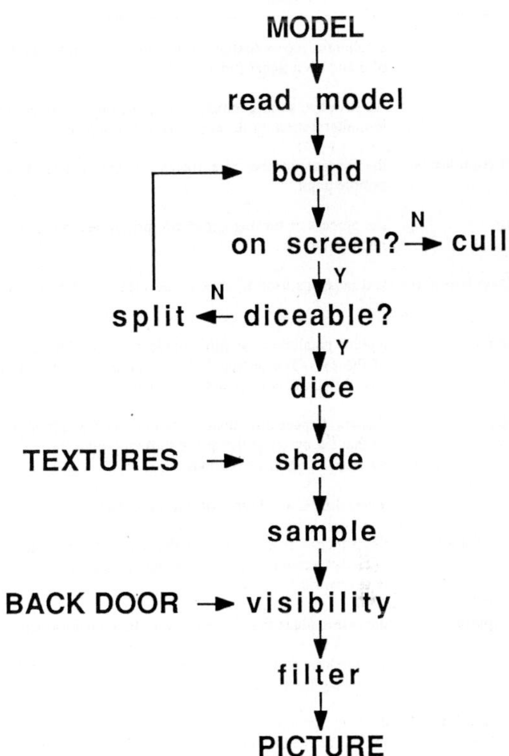

Figure 1. Overview of the algorithm.

2.2. Point sampling.

Point sampling algorithms have many advantages; they are simple, powerful, and work easily with many different types of primitives. But unfortunately, they have been plagued by aliasing artifacts that would make them incompatible with our image quality requirements. Our solution to this problem is a Monte Carlo method called *stochastic sampling,* which is described in detail elsewhere [12]. With stochastic sampling, aliasing is replaced with noise, a less objectionable artifact.

We use a type of stochastic sampling called *jittering* [12]. Pixels are divided into a number of subpixels (typically 16). Each subpixel has exactly one sample point, and the exact location of that sample point within the subpixel is determined by jittering, or adding a random displacement to the location of the center of the subpixel. This jittered location is used to sample micropolygons that overlap the subpixel. The current visibility information for each sample point on the screen is kept in a *z* buffer [8].

The *z* buffer is important for two reasons. First, it permits objects to be sent through the rest of the system one at a time (principles 2, 4, 5 and 6). Second, it provides a back door (principle 7); the *z* buffer can combine point samples from this algorithm with point samples from other algorithms that have capabilities such as ray tracing and radiosity. This is a form of 3-D compositing; it differs from Duff's method [15] in that the compositing is done before filtering the visible samples.

Glossary

CAT	a coherent access texture, in which *s* is a linear function of *u* and *t* is a linear function of *v*.
CSG	constructive solid geometry. Defines objects as the union, intersection, or difference of other objects.
depth complexity	the average number of surfaces (visible or not) at each sample point
dicing	the process of turning geometric primitives into grids of micropolygons.
displacement maps	texture maps used to change the location of points in a grid.
ε plane	a plane parallel to the hither plane that is slightly in front of the eye. The perspective calculation may be unreliable for points not beyond this plane.
eye space	the world space coordinate system rotated and translated so that the eye is at the origin looking down the $+z$ axis. $+x$ is to the right, $+y$ is down.
grid	a two-dimensional array of micropolygons.
geometric locality	the principle that all of the calculations for a geometric primitive should be performed without reference to other geometric primitives.
hither plane	the z=min plane that is the front of the viewing frustum.
jitter	the random perturbation of regularly spaced points for stochastic sampling
micropolygon	the basic geometric object for most of the algorithm, a flat-shaded quadrilateral with an area of about ¼ pixel.
RAT	a random access texture. Any texture that is not a CAT.
s* and *t	parameters used to index a texture map.
screen space	the perspective space in which the *x* and *y* values correspond to pixel locations.
shade tree	a method for describing shading calculations [11].
splitting	the process of turning a geometric primitive into one or more new geometric primitives.
stochastic sampling	a Monte Carlo point-sampling method used for antialiasing [12].
texture locality	the principle that each texture should be read off the disk only once.
u* and *v	coordinates of a parametric representation of a surface.
world space	the global right-handed nonperspective coordinate system.
yon plane	the z=max plane that is the back of the viewing frustum.

2.3. Micropolygons.

Micropolygons are the common basic geometric unit of the algorithm (principle 3). They are flat-shaded quadrilaterals that are approximately ½ pixel on a side. Since half a pixel is the Nyquist limit for an image [6, 26], surface shading can be adequately represented with a single color per micropolygon.

Turning a geometric primitive into micropolygons is called *dicing*. Every primitive is diced along boundaries that are in the natural coordinate system of the primitive (principle 1). For example, in the case of patches, micropolygon boundaries are parallel to *u* and *v*. The result of dicing is a two-dimensional array of micropolygons called a *grid* (principle 2). Micropolygons require less storage in grid form because vertices shared by adjacent micropolygons are represented only once.

Dicing is done in eye space, with no knowledge of screen space except for an estimate of the primitive's size on the screen. This estimate is used to determine how finely to dice, i.e., how many micropolygons to create. Primitives are diced so that micropolygons are approximately half a pixel on a side in screen space. This adaptive approach is similar to the Lane-Carpenter patch algorithm [22].

The details of dicing depend on the type of primitive. For the example of bicubic patches, screen-space parametric derivatives can be used to determine how finely to dice, and forward differencing techniques can be used for the actual dicing.

All of the micropolygons in a grid are shaded together. Because this shading occurs before the visible surface calculation, at a minimum every piece of every forward-facing on-screen object must be shaded. Thus many shading calculations are performed that are never used. The extra work we do is related to the *depth complexity* of the scene, which is the average number of surfaces at each sample point. We expect pathological cases to be unusual, however, because of the effort required to model a scene. Computer graphics models are like movie sets in that usually only the parts that will be seen are actually built.

There are advantages that offset the cost of this extra shading; the tradeoff depends on the particular scene being rendered. These are some of the advantages to using micropolygons and to shading them before determining visibility:

- **Vectorizable shading.** If an entire surface is shaded at once, and the shading calculations for each point on the surface are similar, the shading operations can be vectorized (principle 2).
- **Texture locality.** Texture requests can be made for large, contiguous blocks of texture that are accessed sequentially. Because shading can be done in object order, the texture map thrashing that occurs in many other algorithms is avoided (principle 4b). This thrashing occurs when texture requests come in small pieces and alternate between several different texture maps. For extremely complex models with lots of textures, this can quickly make a renderer unusable.
- **Texture filtering.** Many of the texture requests are for rectilinear regions of the texture map (principle 1). This is discussed in detail in the next section.
- **Subdivision coherence.** Since an entire surface can be subdivided at once, we can take advantage of efficient techniques such as forward differencing for patch subdivision (principles 1 and 2).
- **Clipping.** Objects never need to be clipped along pixel boundaries, as required by some algorithms.
- **Displacement maps** [11]. Displacement maps are like bump maps [4] except that the location of a surface can be changed as well as its normal, making texture maps a means of modeling surfaces or storing the results of modeling programs. Because displacement maps can change the surface location, they must be computed before the hidden surface calculation. We have no experience with the effects of large displacements on dicing.
- **No perspective.** Because micropolygons are small, there is no need to correct for the perspective distortion of interpolation [24]. Because shading occurs before the perspective transformation, no inverse perspective transformations are required.

2.4. Texture Locality.

For rich, complex images, textures are an important source of information for shading calculations [3, 8]. Textures are usually indexed using two parameters called *u* and *v*. Because *u* and *v* are also used for patch parameters, we will call the texture parameters *s* and *t* to avoid confusion. Surfaces other than patches may also have a natural coordinate system; we will use *u* and *v* for those surface coordinates too.

For many textures, *s* and *t* depend only on the *u* and *v* of the patch and can be determined without knowing the details of the shading calculations. Other textures are accessed with an *s* and *t* that are determined by some more complex calculation. For example, the *s* and *t* for an environment map depend on the normal to the surface (though that normal might in turn depend on a bump map that is indexed by *u* and *v*).

We accordingly divide textures into two classes: *coherent access textures* (CATs) and *random access textures* (RATs). CATs are textures for which s=**a**u+**b** and t=**c**v+**d**, where **a**, **b**, **c**, and **d** are constants. All other textures are RATs. Many CATs have $s=u$ and $t=v$, but we have generalized this relationship to allow for single textures that stretch over more than one patch or repeat multiple times over one patch.

We make this distinction because CATs can be handled much more easily and often significantly faster than RATs. Because *st* order is the same as *uv* order for CATs, we can access the texture map sequentially if we do our shading calculations in *uv* order (principles 1 and 4b). Furthermore, if micropolygons are created so that their vertices have *s* and *t* values that are integer multiples of powers of ½, and if the textures are prefiltered and prescaled and stored as resolution pyramids [36], then no filtering calculations are required at run time, since the pixels in the texture line up exactly with the micropolygons in the grid (principle 1). Figure 2 shows a primitive diced into a 4x4 grid and the corresponding texture map; notice how the marked micropolygon corresponds exactly to the marked texture region because we are dicing along *u* and *v*, the texture's natural coordinate system.

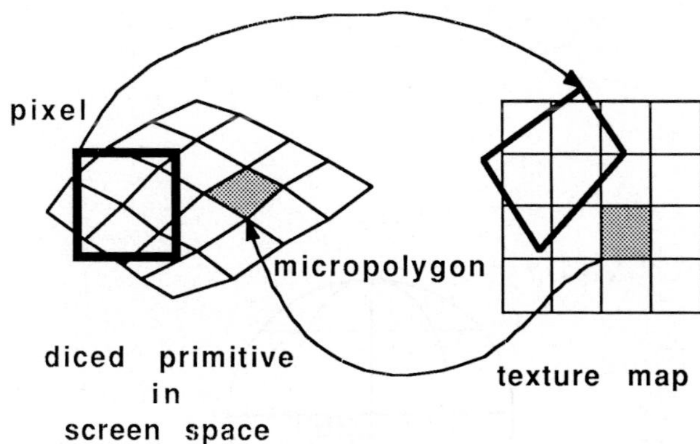

Figure 2. With CATs, micropolygons map exactly to texture map pixels. With the inverse pixel method, pixels map to quadrilateral areas of texture that require filtering.

By contrast, in the more traditional pixel texture access, the pixel boundary is mapped to texture space, where filtering is required. Filtering without a resolution pyramid gives good results but can be expensive [17]. Using a resolution pyramid requires interpolating between two levels of the pyramid, and the filtering is poor [19]. Summed area tables [14] give somewhat better filtering but can have paging problems.

RATs are more general than CATs, but RAT access is slower. RATs can significantly reduce the need for ray tracing. For example, reflections and refractions can frequently be textured onto a surface with environment maps. Environment maps are RATs because they are indexed according to the reflection direction. Another example of a RAT is a decal [2], which is a world-space parallel projection of a texture onto a surface, so that *s* and *t* depend on *x*, *y* and *z* instead of on *u* and *v*.

```
Initialize the z buffer.
For each geometric primitive in the model,
    Read the primitive from the model file
    If the primitive can be bounded,
        Bound the primitive in eye space.
        If the primitive is completely outside of the hither-yon z range, cull it.
        If the primitive spans the ε plane and can be split,
            Mark the primitive undiceable.
        Else
            Convert the bounds to screen space.
            If the bounds are completely outside the viewing frustum, cull the primitive.
    If the primitive can be diced,
        Dice the primitive into a grid of micropolygons.
        Compute normals and tangent vectors for the micropolygons in the grid.
        Shade the micropolygons in the grid.
        Break the grid into micropolygons.
        For each micropolygon,
            Bound the micropolygon in eye space.
            If the micropolygon is outside the hither-yon range, cull it.
            Convert the micropolygon to screen space.
            Bound the micropolygon in screen space.
            For each sample point inside the screen space bound,
                If the sample point is inside the micropolygon,
                    Calculate the z of the micropolygon at the sample point by interpolation.
                    If the z at the sample point is less than the z in the buffer,
                        Replace the sample in the buffer with this sample.
    Else
        Split the primitive into other geometric primitives.
        Put the new primitives at the head of the unread portion of the model file.
Filter the visible sample hits to produce pixels.
Output the pixels.
```

Figure 3. Summary of the algorithm.

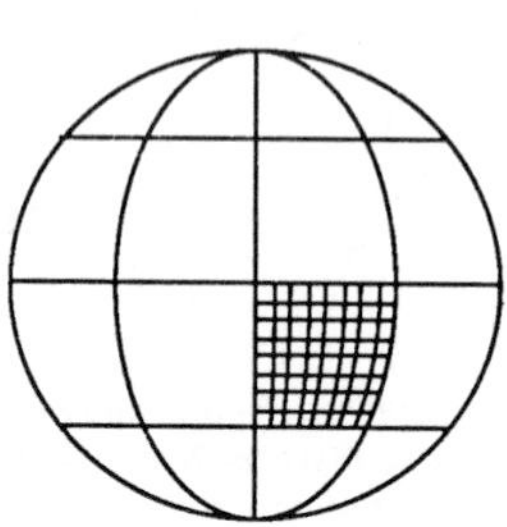

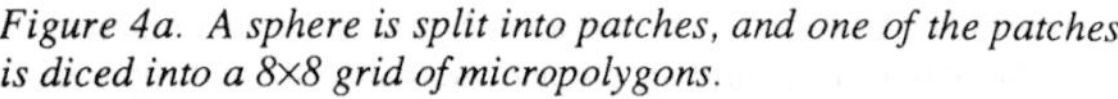

Figure 4a. A sphere is split into patches, and one of the patches is diced into a 8×8 grid of micropolygons.

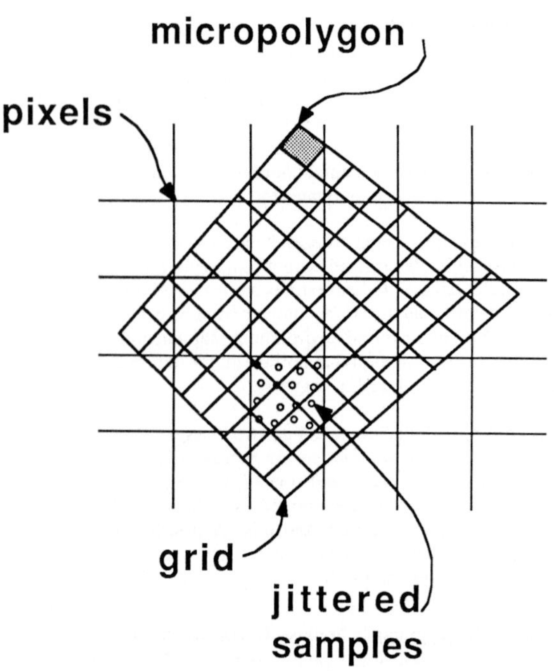

Figure 4b. The micropolygons in the grid are transformed to screen space, where they are stochastically sampled.

3. Description of the Algorithm

The algorithm is summarized in Figure 3. In order to emphasize the basic structure, this description does not include transparency, constructive solid geometry, motion blur, or depth of field. These topics are discussed later.

Each object is turned into micropolygons as it is read in. These micropolygons are shaded, sampled, and compared against the values currently in the z buffer. Since only one object is processed at a time, the amount of data needed at any one time is limited and the model can contain arbitrarily many objects.

Primitives are subdivided only in uv space, never in screen space. The first part of the algorithm is done in uv space and world space, and the second half is done in screen space. After the transformation to screen space, there is never any need to go back to world space or uv space, so there are no inverse transformations.

Each type of geometric primitive has the following routines:

- **Bound.** The primitive computes its eye-space bound; its screen-space bound is computed from the eye-space bound. A primitive must be guaranteed to lie inside its bound, and any primitives it is split into must have bounds that also lie inside its bound. The bound does not have to be tight, however. For example, a fractal surface can be bounded if the maximum value of its random number table is known [7, 18]. The fractal will be guaranteed to lie within this bound, but the bound probably will not be very tight. The effect of displacement maps must be considered in the calculation of the bound.
- **Dice.** Not all types of primitives need to be diceable. The only requirement is that each primitive be able to split itself into other primitives, and that this splitting eventually leads to primitives that can all be diced.
- **Split.** A primitive may split itself into one or more primitives of the same type or of different types.
- **Diceable test.** This test determines whether the primitive should be diced or split and returns "diceable" or "not diceable" accordingly. Primitives should be considered not diceable if dicing them would produce a grid with too many micropolygons or a large range of micropolygon sizes.

The bound, split, and dice routines are optional. If the diceable routine ever returns "diceable", the dice routine must exist; if the diceable routine ever returns "not diceable", the split routine must exist. If the bound routine exists, it is used for culling and for determining how finely a primitive should be diced in order to produce micropolygons of the correct size on the screen.

For example, consider one possible set of routines for a sphere. The sphere diceable routine returns "diceable" for small spheres and "not diceable" for large spheres. The sphere dice routine turns a sphere directly into micropolygons. The sphere split routine turns the sphere into 32 patches [16]. The patch dice routine creates a rectangular grid of micropolygons so that the vertices differ in u and v by integer multiples of powers of ½. This is done to obviate CAT filtering, but in this case it is also necessary for the prevention of patch cracks [9]. Figure 4a shows a sphere being split into patches and one of those patches being diced into an 8x8 grid of micropolygons. Figure 4b shows this grid in screen space with jittered sample locations in one of the pixels.

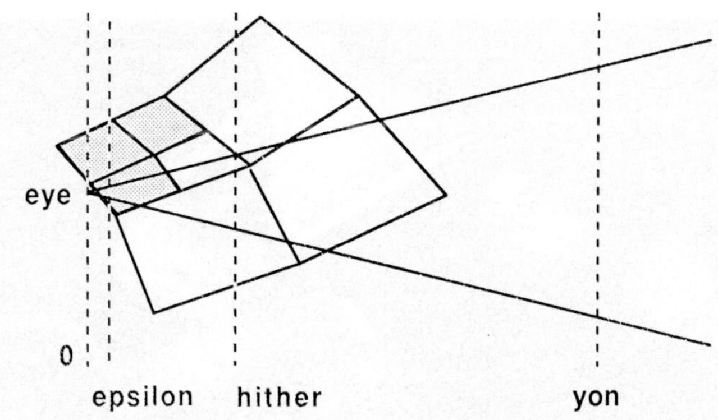

Figure 5. A geometric primitive that spans the ε and hither planes is split until its pieces can be culled or processed. The culled pieces are marked.

This algorithm does not require clipping. The viewing frustum consists of a screen space *xy* range and an eye space hither-yon *z* range. Objects that are known to be completely outside of this region are culled. Objects that are partly inside the frustum and partly outside are kept, shaded and sampled. Regions of these objects that are outside of the viewing frustum in the *x* or *y* directions are never sampled. Regions that are in front of or behind the viewing frustum may be sampled, but their hits are rejected if the sampled surface point lies outside the hither-yon *z* range. Note that if the filter that is used to sample the *z* buffer to produce pixels is wider than a pixel, the viewing frustum must be expanded accordingly because objects that are just off screen can affect pixels on the screen.

Sometimes an object extends from behind the eye to inside the viewing frustum, so that part of the object has an invalid perspective calculation and another part is visible. This situation is traditionally handled by clipping to the hither plane. To avoid clipping, we introduce the *ε plane*, a plane of constant *z* that lies slightly in front of the eye as shown in Figure 5. Points on the $z<\varepsilon$ side of this plane can have an invalid perspective calculation or an unmanageably large screen space *x* and *y* because of the perspective divide. If a primitive spans both the ε plane and the hither plane, it is considered "not diceable" and is split. The resulting pieces are culled if they are entirely outside of the viewing frustum, diced if they lie completely on the $z>\varepsilon$ side of the ε plane, and split again if they span both the ε plane and the hither plane. As long as every primitive can be split, and the splits eventually result in primitives with smaller bounds, then this procedure is guaranteed to terminate successfully. This split-until-cullable procedure obviates clipping. Objects that cannot be bounded can still be protected against bad perspective situations, since micropolygons are created in eye space. Their micropolygons can be culled or be run through a split-until-cullable procedure.

4. Extensions

Since this algorithm was first developed, we have found it easy to add a number of features that were not specifically considered in the original design. These features include motion blur, depth of field, CSG (constructive solid geometry) [1, 33], shadows [32] and a variety of new types of models. The main modification for transparency and CSG calculations is that each sample location in the *z* buffer stores multiple hits. The hits at each sample point are sorted in *z* for the transparency and CSG calculations. Motion blur and depth of field are discussed elsewhere in detail [10, 12, 13]. In the case of motion blur, micropolygons are moved for each sample point to a jittered time associated with that sample. For depth of field, they are moved in *x* and *y* according to a jittered lens location. Both motion blur and depth of field affect the bound calculations; the details are described elsewhere [13].

5. Implementation

We had to make some compromises to implement this algorithm on a general purpose computer, since the algorithm as described so far can require a considerable amount of *z* buffer memory. The screen is divided into rectangular buckets, which may be kept in memory or on disk. In an initial pass, each primitive is bounded and put into the bucket corresponding to the upper left corner of its screen space bound. For the rest of the calculations, the buckets are processed in order, left-to-right and top-to-bottom. First all of the primitives in the bucket are either split or diced; as primitives are diced, their micropolygons are shaded and put into every bucket they overlap. After all of the primitives in a bucket have been split or diced, the micropolygons in that bucket are sampled. Once a bucket is empty, it remains empty, so we only need enough *z* buffer memory for one bucket. The number of micropolygons in memory at any one time can be kept manageable by setting a maximum grid size and forcing primitives to be considered "not diceable" if dicing them would produce too large a grid.

We have implemented this revised version of the algorithm in C and have used it to make a number of animated films, including *The Adventures of André and Wally B.* [27], the stained glass man sequence in *Young Sherlock Holmes* [25], *Luxo Jr.* [28], and *Red's Dream* [29]. The implementation performs reasonably well, considering that the algorithm was designed as a testbed, without any requirement that it would run efficiently in C. For a given shading complexity, the rendering time is proportional to the number of micropolygons (and thus to screen size and to the number of objects).

An example of a image rendered with this program is shown in Figure 6. It is motion blurred, with environment maps for the reflections and shadow depth maps for the shadows [32]. The picture is by John Lasseter and Eben Ostby. It was rendered at 1024x614 pixels, contains 6.8 million micropolygons, has 4 light sources, uses 15 channels of texture, and took about 8 hours of CPU time to compute. Frames in *André* were 512x488 pixels and took less than ½ hour per frame. *Sherlock* frames were 1024x614 and took an hour per frame; *Luxo* frames were 724x434 and took 1½ hours per frame. Statistics on *Red's Dream* frames are not available yet. All of these CPU times are for a CCI 6/32, which is 4-6 times faster than a VAX 11/780.

Figure 6. 1986 Pixar Christmas Card by John Lasseter and Eben Ostby.

6. Discussion

This approach has certain disadvantages. Because shading occurs before sampling, the shading cannot be calculated for the specific time of each sample and thus cannot be motion blurred correctly. Shading after sampling would have advantages if the coherency features could be retained; this is an area of future research. Although any primitive that can be scan-converted can be turned into micropolygons, this process is more difficult for some primitives, such as blobs [5]. The bucket-sort version requires bounds on the primitives to perform well, and some primitives such as particle systems are difficult to bound. No attempt is made to take advantage of coherence for large simply-shaded surfaces; every object is turned into micropolygons. Polygons in general do not have a natural coordinate system for dicing. This is fine in our case, because bicubic patches are our most common primitive, and we hardly ever use polygons.

On the other hand, our approach also has a number of advantages. Much of the calculation in traditional approaches goes away completely. There are no inversion calculations, such as projecting pixel corners onto a patch to find normals and texture values. There are no clipping calculations. Many of the calculations can be vectorized, such as the the shading and surface normal calculations. Texture thrashing is avoided, and in many instances textures require no run time filtering. Most of the calculations are done on a simple common representation (micropolygons).

This architecture is designed for rendering exceedingly complex models, and the disadvantages and advantages listed above reflect the tradeoffs made with this goal in mind.

Acknowledgements

Thanks to Bill Reeves, Eben Ostby, David Salesin, and Sam Leffler, all of whom contributed to the C implementation of this algorithm. Conversations with Mark Leather, Adam Levinthal, Jeff Mock, and Lane Molpus were very productive. Charlie Gunn implemented a version of this algorithm in *chas*, the assembly language for the Pixar Chap SIMD processor [23]. Paul Heckbert helped analyze the texture quality, and Ricki Blau studied the performance of the C implementation.

References

1. ATHERTON, PETER R., "A Scanline Hidden Surface Removal Procedure for Constructive Solid Geometry," *Computer Graphics (SIGGRAPH '83 Proceedings)* **17**(3), pp. 73-82 (July 1983).
2. BARR, ALAN H., "Decal Projections," in *SIGGRAPH '84 Developments in Ray Tracing course notes* (July 1984).
3. BLINN, JAMES F. AND MARTIN E. NEWELL, "Texture and Reflection in Computer Generated Images," *Communications of the ACM* **19**(10), pp. 542-547 (October 1976).
4. BLINN, JAMES F., "Simulation of Wrinkled Surfaces," *Computer Graphics (SIGGRAPH '78 Proceedings)* **12**(3), pp. 286-292 (August 1978).
5. BLINN, JAMES F., "A Generalization of Algebraic Surface Drawing," *ACM Transactions on Graphics* **1**(3), pp. 235-256 (July 1982).
6. BRACEWELL, RONALD N., *The Fourier Transform and Its Applications*, McGraw-Hill, New York (1978).
7. CARPENTER, LOREN, "Computer Rendering of Fractal Curves and Surfaces," *Computer Graphics (SIGGRAPH '80 Proceedings)* **14**(3), pp. 9-15, Special Issue (July 1980).
8. CATMULL, EDWIN E., "A Subdivision Algorithm for Computer Display of Curved Surfaces," Phd dissertation, University of Utah, Salt Lake City (December 1974).
9. CLARK, JAMES H., "A Fast Algorithm for Rendering Parametric Surfaces," *Computer Graphics (SIGGRAPH '79 Proceedings)* **13**(2), pp. 7-12, Special Issue (August 1979).
10. COOK, ROBERT L., THOMAS PORTER, AND LOREN CARPENTER, "Distributed Ray Tracing," *Computer Graphics (SIGGRAPH '84 Proceedings)* **18**(3), pp. 137-145 (July 1984).
11. COOK, ROBERT L., "Shade Trees," *Computer Graphics (SIGGRAPH '84 Proceedings)* **18**(3), pp. 223-231 (July 1984).
12. COOK, ROBERT L., "Stochastic Sampling in Computer Graphics," *ACM Transactions on Graphics* **5**(1), pp. 51-72 (January 1986).

13. COOK, ROBERT L., "Practical Aspects of Distributed Ray Tracing," in *SIGGRAPH '86 Developments in Ray Tracing course notes* (August 1986).

14. CROW, FRANKLIN C., "Summed-Area Tables for Texture Mapping," *Computer Graphics (SIGGRAPH '84 Proceedings)* **18**(3), pp. 207-212 (July 1984).

15. DUFF, TOM, "Compositing 3-D Rendered Images," *Computer Graphics (SIGGRAPH '85 Proceedings)* **19**(3), pp. 41-44 (July 1985).

16. FAUX, I. D. AND M. J. PRATT, *Computational Geometry for Design and Manufacture,* Ellis Horwood Ltd., Chichester, England (1979).

17. FEIBUSH, ELIOT, MARC LEVOY, AND ROBERT L. COOK, "Synthetic Texturing Using Digital Filtering," *Computer Graphics* **14**(3), pp. 294-301 (July 1980).

18. FOURNIER, ALAIN, DON FUSSELL, AND LOREN CARPENTER, "Computer Rendering of Stochastic Models," *Communications of the ACM* **25**(6), pp. 371-384 (June 1982).

19. HECKBERT, PAUL S., "Survey of Texture Mapping," *IEEE Computer Graphics and Applications* (November 1986).

20. KAPLAN, MICHAEL R., "Space-Tracing, A Constant Time Ray-Tracer," in *SIGGRAPH '85 State of the Art in Image Synthesis seminar notes* (July 1985).

21. KAY, TIMOTHY L. AND JAMES T. KAJIYA, "Ray Tracing Complex Scenes," *Computer Graphics (SIGGRAPH '86 Proceedings)* **20**(4), pp. 269-278 (Aug. 1986).

22. LANE, JEFFREY M., LOREN C. CARPENTER, TURNER WHITTED, AND JAMES F. BLINN, "Scan Line Methods for Displaying Parametrically Defined Surfaces," *Communications of the ACM* **23**(1), pp. 23-34 (January 1980).

23. LEVINTHAL, ADAM AND THOMAS PORTER, "Chap - A SIMD Graphics Processor," *Computer Graphics (SIGGRAPH '84 Proceedings)* **18**(3), pp. 77-82 (July 1984).

24. NEWMAN, WILLIAM M. AND ROBERT F. SPROULL, *Principles of Interactive Computer Graphics (2nd ed.),* McGraw-Hill, New York (1979). pp. 361-363

25. PARAMOUNT PICTURES CORPORATION, *Young Sherlock Holmes,* Stained glass man sequence by Pixar and Lucasfilm Ltd. 1985.

26. PEARSON, D. E., *Transmission and Display of Pictorial Information,* Pentech Press, London (1975).

27. PIXAR, *The Adventures of André and Wally B.*, July 1984.

28. PIXAR, *Luxo Jr.*, July 1986.

29. PIXAR, *Red's Dream,* July 1987.

30. REEVES, WILLIAM T., "Particle Systems – A Technique for Modeling a Class of Fuzzy Objects," *ACM Transactions on Graphics* **2**(2), pp. 91-108 (April 1983).

31. REEVES, WILLIAM T. AND RICKI BLAU, "Approximate and Probabilistic Algorithms for Shading and Rendering Structured Particle Systems," *Computer Graphics (SIGGRAPH '85 Proceedings)* **19**(3), pp. 313-322 (July 1985).

32. REEVES, WILLIAM T., DAVID H. SALESIN, AND ROBERT L. COOK, "Shadowing with Texture Maps," *Computer Graphics (SIGGRAPH '87 Proceedings)* **21** (July 1987).

33. ROTH, S. D., "Ray Casting for Modeling Solids," *Computer Graphics and Image Processing*(18), pp. 109-144 (1982).

34. RUBIN, STEVEN M. AND TURNER WHITTED, "A 3-Dimensional Representation for Fast Rendering of Complex Scenes," *Computer Graphics (SIGGRAPH '80 Proceedings)* **14**(3), pp. 110-116 (July 1980).

35. SMITH, ALVY RAY, "Plants, Fractals, and Formal Languages," *Computer Graphics (SIGGRAPH '84 Proceedings)* **18**(3), pp. 1-10 (July 1984).

36. WILLIAMS, LANCE, "Pyramidal Parametrics," *Computer Graphics (SIGGRAPH '83 Proceedings)* **17**(3), pp. 1-11 (July 1983).

Chapter 3: Painter's Algorithms

Introduction

The painter's algorithm is one of the earliest visible-surface algorithms developed. The basic idea of this algorithm was first used by Schumacker et al. [Schu69] and by Newell et al. [Newe72]. The name "painter's algorithm" is based on an analogy to painting with opaque paint, where closer objects are painted over farther ones. In computer graphics, objects are first sorted with respect to distance from the viewpoint and then are painted sequentially into a frame buffer.

The first step in this algorithm is to sort all objects into a back-to-front order. It is required that if any object, "A," obscures any part of another object, "B," then object "B" must appear in the list before object "A." This condition is a partial order if no cycles of overlapping objects exist. If any cycles exist, then the ordering condition is inconsistent and the objects must be divided into pieces until no cyclic overlap occurs. Testing for this subdivision is described in Newell et al. [Newe72].

Many different sorting algorithms can be used to generate linear orders that satisfy the partial order. Newell et al. perform a straight forward sort by depth which is then adjusted until it satisfies the partial order. Fuchs et al. [Fuch80] (included in this chapter) describe a data structure, the Binary-Space-Partitioning (BSP) tree, that allows fast traversal, and generates a valid order from any viewpoint. This is a particularly flexible data structure that has applications outside of the painter's algorithm. Schumacker et al. [Schu69], Berlin [Berl85], and Garcia [Garc86] also organize the object database into a data structure that can be easily traversed in a sequence that satisfies the partial order from any viewpoint. Many systems, including Levoy [Levo77], Wallace [Wall81], Crow [Crow82], Porter and Duff [Port84] (included in this chapter), and Max [Max85], are referred to as "2½-dimensional," and assume that a valid order is known *a priori*. For some limited classes of objects, valid orders are easy to generate (see [Frie85]). Reeves [Reev83], in his particle systems, assumes that individual objects are small and far apart so that an approximate sorting into fixed-size buckets suffices.

Once an order has been established, each object, in back-to-front order, can then be scan converted and stored into the frame buffer. Each pixel that is covered by the object is overwritten with the value for the closer object. Figure 3.1 contains an outline of this algorithm.

This "simplest" version of the painter's algorithm has the drawback that shading calculations must be made for every pixel of every object regardless of the objects final visibility. Some shading calculations can be avoided by using a version of the painter's algorithm where the closest objects are painted first, then the farther objects are painted around and between those objects already painted. This adds a comparison at each pixel to tell if the pixel has been written. In this front-to-back painter's algorithm, a one-bit-per-pixel mask buffer is used to hold object-coverage information. The mask buffer is first initialized to all zeros and each object (in a front-to-back order) is then scan converted. If a pixel covered by the object does not have its mask bit set, shading calculations are performed and the value is stored into this pixel. If the mask bit is set, then the pixel contains a value from a closer object and is left unchanged. Figure 3.2 contains an outline of this algorithm.

These versions of the painter's algorithm have the serious drawback of requiring that a global order be established for drawing the objects. This ordering can be very expensive since it involves every object in the scene. Testing for cyclic overlap between objects is also very expensive. The painter's algorithm is generally not used for complex scenes unless some assumptions allow simplifications in or elimination of the sorting and overlap testing. Also, since the objects must be drawn sequentially into the frame buffer, opportunities to exploit parallelism on a per object basis are limited.

Early versions of the painter's algorithm, which made all-or-nothing overwriting decisions as described above, resulted in substantial aliasing artifacts. Antialiasing requires some partial overwriting of pixels along the edges of objects. Porter and Duff [Port84] (included in this chapter) formalized a technique to do this by calculating an extra channel of information for each pixel (the α channel), which contains partial transparency information for each pixel. This channel is used to smoothly blend foreground and background pixels and is an extension of previous work on transparency including that by Wallace [Wall81] and Stern [Ster79]. The technique works very well where object edges in the foreground and background are geometrically uncorrelated. In cases where object edges are correlated, the single alpha value does not contain enough information to specify the geometrical relationship between the foreground and background edges. This is not a problem if objects are correlated in known groups and if each set of correlated objects is rendered using an algorithm such as that of Crow [Crow82], or Carpenter [Carp84] (included in Chapter 2: Z-Buffer Algorithms), and the resulting uncorrelated images are then combined by using the painter's algorithm. The problem of detecting and handling correlated edges with antialiased versions of the painter's algorithm is addressed by Grant [Gran86]. Duff [Duff85] (included in Chapter 2: Z-Buffer Algorithms) extends the 2½-dimensional compositing techniques using RGBα rasters, into three-dimensional compositing by adding a depth (Z) channel yielding RGBαZ.

Reeves [Reev83] and Reeves and Blau [Reev85] (included in this chapter) have developed a modeling system based upon small particles that are suitable for rendering with the painter's algorithm. These particle systems are dynamic entities that can be created, extinguished, or moved, and which may change color, transparency, and shape over time. Reeves and Blau [Reev85] (included in this chapter), describe some approximate sorting algorithms for rendering tremendous numbers of tiny particles by using the painter's algorithm. Since the particles are small, there is little chance for cyclic overlaps. Since the locations of individual particles are largely determined by pseudorandom techniques, the particles will tend to obscure each other in an uncorrelated manner suitable for antialiased compositing using the techniques of Porter and Duff [Port84].

Other significant papers include the "slab method" of Voss [Voss83] for rendering clouds and the family of shadow mask sweep algorithms of Grant [Gran86]. These algorithms use the painter's algorithm to calculate both the direct illumination and the direct-image formation. Berlin [Berl85] and Garcia [Garc86] also have integrated planar mirror reflections into the painter's algorithm by utilizing a data structure similar to that of Fuchs et al. [Fuch80].

```
Painter's Algorithm
    Given
        List of polygons {P1, P2, ..., Pn }
        An array Intensity[x,y]
    begin
        for each polygon P in the polygon list do {
            for each pixel (x,y) that intersects P do {
                Intensity[x,y] = intensity of P at (x,y)
                }
            }
        Display Intensity array
    end
```

Figure 3.1: The Painter's Algorithm

```
Painter's Algorithm
    Given
        List of polygons {P1, P2, ..., Pn }
        An array mask[x,y] initialized to zero
        An array Intensity[x,y]
    begin
        for each polygon P in the polygon list do {
            for each pixel (x,y) that intersects P do {
                if mask[x,y] = 0 then {
                    Intensity[x,y] = intensity of P at (x,y)
                    mask[x,y] = 1
                    }
                }
            }
        Display Intensity array
    end
```

Figure 3.2: The Front-to-Back Painter's Algorithm

ON VISIBLE SURFACE GENERATION BY A PRIORI TREE STRUCTURES*

Henry Fuchs
University of North Carolina at Chapel Hill
Zvi M. Kedem
The University of Texas at Dallas
Bruce F. Naylor
The University of Texas at Dallas

ABSTRACT

This paper describes a new algorithm for solving the hidden surface (or line) problem, to more rapidly generate realistic images of 3-D scenes composed of polygons, and presents the development of theoretical foundations in the area as well as additional related algorithms. As in many applications the environment to be displayed consists of polygons many of whose relative geometric relations are static, we attempt to capitalize on this by preprocessing the environment's database so as to decrease the run-time computations required to generate a scene. This preprocessing is based on generating a "binary space partitioning" tree whose inorder traversal of visibility priority at run-time will produce a linear order, dependent upon the viewing position, on (parts of) the polygons, which can then be used to easily solve the hidden surface problem. In the application where the entire environment is static with only the viewing-position changing, as is common in simulation, the results presented will be sufficient to solve completely the hidden surface problem.

INTRODUCTION

One of the long-term goals of computer graphics has been, and continues to be, the rapid, possibly real-time generation of realistic images of simulated 3-D environments. "Real-time," in current practice, has come to mean creating an image in 1/30 of a second--fast enough to continually generate images on a video monitor. With this fast image generation, there is no discernable delay between specifying parameters for an image (using knobs, switches, or cockpit controls) and the image's appearance on the monitor's screen. Systems which can achieve this kind of performance are currently so expensive ($1M and up) that very few users can afford them. Users with more modest budgets have to be content with severely more limited performance--either a lower quality image ("wire frame" instead of solid-object modeling) or slower interaction (a time lag of several seconds to several minutes for a solid-object image).

---

*This research was partially supported by NSF under Grants MCS79-00168 and MCS79-02593, and was facilitated by the use of Theory Net (NSF Grant MCS78-01689).

PROBLEM STATEMENT

The problem to be solved is:

Given

1. a data base describing a 3-D environment in terms of, say, a few thousands tiles (polygons) describing the surfaces of the various objects in the environment, one or more light sources and
2. the (simulated) viewing position, orientation , and field of view,

Generate a color video image of the environment as it would appear from the given viewing position and orientation.

This image generation task consists, broadly, of the following three steps:

1. transforming points into the image space,
2. clipping away polygons outside the field of view,
3. generating the image from the polygons that remain. Generating the image consists of determining the proper color (intensities of red, green, and blue) for each of perhaps 250,000 picture elements (approximately 500 rows of dots, with 500 dots in each row). For each picture element ("pixel"),

   a) find the polygon closest to the viewing position. (This will be the visible polygon at this pixel, the

"On Visible Surface Generation by A Priori Tree Structures" by H. Fuchs, Z.M. Kedem, and B.F. Naylor from *Proceedings of SIGGRAPH '80*, 1980, pages 124-133. Copyright 1980, Association for Computing Machinery, Inc., reprinted by permission.

polygon which obstructs all others.)

b) given the visible polygon, determine the proper color for the pixel by evaluating a lighting model formula, see, e.g., (Newman and Sproull, 1979).

PROPOSED SOLUTION

Since current moderately-priced ($40-80k) real-time line-drawing systems (e.g. Evans and Sutherland Picture System 2, Vector General Model 3404) can easily perform steps 1 and 2, we shall concentrate on solutions to step 3. New solutions to this remaining step could then be combined with already available solutions to produce a complete system. Further, we believe step 3b can be effectively solved by distributing the individual pixel calculations among many small processors (Fuchs and Johnson, 1979). We thus concentrate in this paper on step 3a, determining the visible polygon at each pixel.

We propose an alternative solution to an approach first utilized a decade ago (Schumaker et al., 1969) but due to a few difficulties, not widely exploited. The general approach is based on the observation that in a wide variety of applications many images are generated of the same environment with only a change in the viewing position and orientation, but no change in the environment. For example, pilots in a simulator may practice many different landings at the same airport, with each landing generating thousands of new images. Similarly, an architect may "walk" through a newly designed house or housing development; a biochemist may rotate or move about a complicated protein molecule. To take advantage of such static environments, the data base is preprocessed once (for all time, or until the data base is changed) before any images are generated. In this preprocessing stage, certain geometric relationships are extracted which can then be used to speed up the visible polygon determination for each pixel, for all possible images.

It is important to note that although the development here is given only rigid objects and environments, these concepts can be extended to handle environments with some moving objects.

SOLUTION OVERVIEW

In order to determine the visible surface at each pixel, traditionally the distance from the viewing position to each polygon which maps onto that pixel is calculated. Most methods attempt to minimize the number of polygons to be so considered. Our approach eliminates these distance calculations entirely. Rather, it transforms the polygonal data base (splitting polygons when necessary) into a binary tree which can be traversed at image generation time to yield a <u>visibility priority</u> value for each polygon. These visibility priorities are assigned in such a way that at each pixel the closest polygon to the viewing position will be the one with the highest visibility priority. As we shall see, the visibility priorities are a function of the viewing position; they remain constant for all pixels in every image generated from the same viewing position. In cases for which these visibility priority numbers cannot be assigned to the original polygons (see, e.g., fig. 6) and some polygons need to be split, the splitting is done only once -- during the preprocessing phase -- never at image generation time.

PREPROCESSING PHASE

Let us now consider the set of polygons $P = \{p_1, p_2, \ldots, p_n\}$ which define the 3-D environment. Choose an arbitrary (for now) polygon p_k from this set. We note that the plane in which this polygon lies partitions the rest of 3-space into two half-spaces--call these S_k and $S_{\bar{k}}$. The two half-spaces are identified with the positive and negative sides of the polygon p_k. If p_k was defined with a "front" side, then that side is considered as the positive one; otherwise, one of the sides is arbitrarily chosen at this time to be the positive side.

What can we say about visibility priorities of these polygons? We know that if the viewing position is in one half-space, say in S_k, that no polygon within $S_{\bar{k}}$ can obstruct either polygon p_k or any polygon in S_k (see figure. 1).

Therefore, we split each of the polygons in $P - \{p_k\}$ along the plane of p_k, putting the polygons (or parts of them) which lie in S_k into one set and polygons which lie in $S_{\bar{k}}$ into another set. (Polygons coplanar with p_k can be put into either set.) We can represent the results of this splitting process by a binary tree (we'll call it a Binary Space Partitioning, or "BSP" tree) in which the root contains p_k and each branch's subtree contains the set of polygons associated with one of the half-spaces (Fig. 2).

We next consider one of the two new sets of polygons, say the one in S_k. We remove a polygon, say p_i and split the remaining polygons in S_i along the plane of p_i, putting those polygons (or parts thereof) lying on the positive side in one set ($S_{k,j}$) and those lying on the negative side in another set ($S_{k,\bar{j}}$). The overall tree after this step is shown in Fig. 3.

To complete the construction of the BSP tree we continue splitting sets until no non-null sets remain.

The entire preprocessing phase, then, consists of transforming the entire polygonal data base into a BSP tree by the following recursive procedure (stated in a simple pseudo-PASCAL):

```
PROC Make_tree(pl:polygon_list): tree;

BEGIN
k=Select_polygon (pl);
pos_list := null; neg_list := null;
/* pos refers to positive parts
   neg refers to negative parts */
FOR i := 1 TO Size_of(pl) DO
  BEGIN
  IF i <> k THEN
    BEGIN
    Split_polygon(pl[i], pl[k],
                  pos_parts,neg_parts);
    Add (pos_parts, pos_list);
    Add (neg_parts, neg_list)
    END
  END;
RETURN    Combine_tree(Make_tree(pos_list),
                  pl(k),
                  Make_tree(neg_list))
END;
```

We note again that this process is only performed once for all possible images from all viewing positions; the tree remains valid as long as the scene doesn't change.

IMAGE GENERATION PHASE

Calculating the visibility priorities, once the viewing position is known, is a variant of an in-order traversal of the environment's BSP tree (traverse one subtree, visit the root, traverse the other subtree). We wish, for example, to have an order of traversal that visits the polygons from those farthest away to those closest to the current viewing position. At any given node, there are two possibilities: positive side subtree, node, negative side subtree or negative side subtree, node, positive side subtree. We choose one of these two orderings based on the relationship of the current viewing position to the node's polygon. Specifically, we are interested in the side (positive or negative) of the node's polygon where the current viewing position is located. Let's call the two sides the "containing" side and the "other" side. The traversal for a back-to-front ordering is 1) the "other" side, 2) the node, and 3) the "containing" side. (This side-of-node-polygon determination is, of course, just a check of the sign of the Z component of the node polygon's normal vector after the usual transformation to the screen coordinate system.)

This notion of a traversal may be embodied in at least two different ways for visible surface image generation. One alternative is to assign priorities to polygons in the order that we visit them. Using the traversal order just described we will get a low-to-high visibility priority assignment. These values can then be used within a conventional visible surface display algorithm wherever visibility determinations need to be made. The other obvious alternative, which in fact is the one that we have implemented, does not assign explicit visibility priority values to polygons but uses the traversal to drive a "painter's" algorithm which paints onto the screen's image buffer each polygon as it is encountered in the traversal. Since higher priority polygons are visited later in the traversal and thus painter later, they will overwrite any overlapping polygons of lower priority. The following recursive procedure generates a visible surface image in the above-described manner.

```
PROC Back_to_front(eye:viewing_position;
                   t: BSP_tree);

BEGIN
IF Not_null (t) THEN
  IF pos_side_of (root [t],eye)
  THEN

    BEGIN
    back_to_front (eye, neg_branch [t]);
    Display_polygon (root [t]);
    Back_to_front (eye, pos_branch[t])
    END

  ELSE

    BEGIN
    Back_to_front (eye, pos_branch[t]);
    Display_polygon (root[t]);
    Back_to_front (eye, neg_branch[t])
    END
END
```

Figures 4,5,and 6 illustrate this visible surface algorithm. Since the display used had only one bit per pixel, the procedure Display_polygon painted the interior of the polygon the background shade and painted the outline of the polygon in the other shade.

The possible weakness of this approach is that the number of polygons in the tree may increase sharply. (Recall, every root polygon splits all crossing polygons in its list in order to put any polygon in one or the other of its subtrees.) We have attempted to limit this increase by selecting the root polygon at each stage to be the one whose plane splits the minimum number of polygons in its list. Table 1 indicates the performance of the system in limiting the number of polygons in the BSP tree. Figures 7 and 8 show the BSP tree for the environments of Figures 4 and 6, respectively.

Fig. no.	No. of Original Polygons	No. of Polygons in BSP Tree
4	11	11
5	72	100
6	3	5

Table 1: Number of polygons in tree versus original data base

We are currently examining a more sophisticated strategy for minimizing the number of polygons in the BSP tree. In addition to the just-described criterion of choosing a node polygon as one that minimizes the number of polygons that are split, a second criterion is also considered. This one maximizes the number of "polygon conflicts" eliminated. We define a polygon conflict as an occurrence between two polygons in one list in which the plane of one polygon intersects the other polygon. The hope is that these eliminated polygon conflicts will reduce the number of polygons which will need to be cut in the descendant subtrees. More precisely, if P is the set of polygons, then form the sets S_1, S_2, S_3 for each polygon p P as follows:

$S_1 \equiv \{q \in P \mid q$ is entirely in the positive half space of p$\}$

$S_2 \equiv \{q \in P \mid q$ is intersected by the plane of p$\}$

$S_3 \equiv \{q \in P \mid q$ is entirely in the negative half-space of p$\}$

We define a function

$$f(s_i, s_j) = \begin{cases} 1; & \text{polygon } s_j \text{ and the plane of } s_i \text{ intersect} \\ 0; & \text{otherwise} \end{cases}$$

and

$$I_{m,n} = \sum_{s_i \in S_m} \sum_{s_j \in S_n} f(s_i, s_j)$$

We then select the p such that for $S_1(p), S_2(p), S_3(p)$ the expression $[I_{1,3} + I_{3,1} - (|S_2| * \text{weight})]$ which is maximal.

FORMAL DEVELOPMENT

Let us now examine the nature of the binary space-partitioning (BSP) tree more closely. The construction can be carried, in essentially identical manner, for any dimension; nonetheless, it is only the three-dimensional version that is of major interest to us here. However, it is easier to explain its nature in the two-dimensional setting, as the various geometric structures arising can be clearly drawn; thus the discussion of the properties of the tree will be presented assuming a two-dimensional universe. Nonetheless, we encourage the reader, as the next section of the paper is read, to extrapolate the three-dimensional interpretation. In the latter portion of the paper, where combinatorial issues are examined, the results will be given for both two and three dimensions, since combinatorial complexity is dimension dependent. We now begin with some (slightly non-standard) terminology.

Segment - an oriented closed convex subset of a line, i.e., a finite segment, a ray, or a line, with a direction associated with it.

Region - a closed convex set of points of a plane. (A region is normally defined as an open connected set.)*

Extension of a Segment in a Region - given a segment s and a region R, define the extension of s in R to be the intersection of the line on which s lies with the region R, obtaining the segment $\hat{s}_R$. Assign to $\hat{s}_R$ the direction induced by s (we indicate this by pointing an arrow to the right)

Note that a region can be unbounded (a plane) "partially bounded" (e.g., a half-plane), or (completely) bounded (e.g., a finite polygon). The motivation for defining regions and segments in this manner is that in general we have no interest in distinguishing between the bounded, partially bounded, and unbounded sets. The 3-space analogies to segments

*A set is open if there is an "implicit boundary" which is not in the set. Formally, a set of points R in the plane is open if and only if $\forall x \in R$, $e > 0$ such that $\forall y[|x-y|<e \Rightarrow y \in R]$. A closed set is the complement of an open set (if bounded, the set includes the boundary). Formally, a set of points R in a plane is closed iff for every converging sequence $x \rightarrow x$, $\forall n[x \in R \Rightarrow x \in R]$.

and regions are polygons (or alternately, regions) and sectors (or volumes) respectively. The orientation of the polygons corresponds to the usual notion of the front and back sides. We are now ready to examine the general algorithm for construction of a labeled binary space-partitioning tree.

Algorithm I: Construction of a (2-space) BSP tree

<u>Input</u> - a region R and a set of segments Σ lying in R

<u>Output</u> - A BSP Tree

<u>Method</u> - call the function, BSPT, with R and Σ as parameters and $\hat{\Sigma} \leftarrow \Phi$.

<u>Procedure</u> - BSPT (R:region; Σ:set of segments) :node

<u>Begin</u>

<u>If</u> $\Sigma \neq \Phi$ <u>then</u>

<u>begin</u>

choose $s \in \Sigma$ and form $\hat{s}_R$

$\hat{\Sigma} \leftarrow \hat{\Sigma} \cup \{ \hat{s}_R \}$

Partition R and Σ by $\hat{s}_R$ into R_s, $R_{\bar{s}}$, Σ_{R_s}, $\Sigma_{R_{\bar{s}}}$ defined as:

$R_s \equiv \{ p \in R \mid p \in \hat{s}_R$ or p lies to the right of $\hat{s}_R \}$

$R_{\bar{s}} \equiv \{ p \in R \mid p \in \hat{s}_R$ or p lies to the left of $\hat{s}_R \}$

$\Sigma_{R_s} \equiv \{ B \cap R_s \mid B \in \Sigma - \{s\} \}$

$\Sigma_{R_{\bar{s}}} \equiv \{ B \cap R_{\bar{s}} \mid B \in \Sigma - \{s\} \}$

Create a new node v

leftson(v) :=BSPT($R_{\bar{s}}$,$\Sigma_{R_{\bar{s}}}$)

rightson(v) := BSPT (R_s,Σ_{R_s})

label(v) := s_R

return(v)

End

Else

Create a leaf ℓ

label(ℓ):=R

return(ℓ)

End BSPT

Let us look at an example before examining the properties of this algorithm.

Let R be a square and $\Sigma \equiv \{ a,b,c\}$, as in figure 9a.

If a is chosen first, we get figure 9b which creates figure 9c. If, next, $b_{R_{\bar{a}}}$ is chosen before c, the final result will appear as in figure 10.

Consider now the set $\hat{\Sigma}$ of segments, which of course lies wholly within the original R. It is easily seen that it partitions R into convex regions (polygons). Each such region, together with its boundary, will be referred to as an <u>area</u> (volume for 3-space). The set of all the areas created by the algorithm will be referred to as a <u>tessellation</u>. The areas may be thought of as the intersection of half-planes (half-spaces for 3-D) created by the lines on which the elements of Σ (or $\hat{\Sigma}$) lie. The purpose of orientation of the segments is to distinguish between the two half-planes. The subscripts of each region, generated by algorithm I, indicate the half-planes whose intersection forms the region. As an example, refer to figure 11 which is a BSP tree for the tessellation in fig. 10 where parentheses are used to indicate subscripting of regions.

<u>CHARACTERISTICS OF A BSP TREE</u>

It should be clear by now that the algorithm performs a recursive partitioning of the plane by the segments lying in it. However, observe that given a set of segments , that more than one tessellations can be generated by the algorithm depending upon the order in which segments are selected. Observe that in fig. 9, had the order of selection been c, b, a, fig. 12 would have been produced, which not only looks different from fig. 10, but has four areas, as opposed to five. Since a tessellation is formed by the extended segments, as opposed to the segments themselves and the length of an extended segment is dependent on the size of the region containing it at the time it is extended, selecting segments in different orders produces different regions, and thus the dependence of the tessellation on the order of selection.

It is also possible to have, for a given set of segments, more than one tree which describes the same tessellation. Assume that at some stage of the construction of the tree, we are examining the region R_k and the associated set of segments $\Sigma_{R_k} = \{s_1, s_2, ..., s_m\}$. If $\bigcup_{i=1}^{m} s_i = \bigcup_{i=1}^{m} \hat{s}_i$ with respect to R_k, then every permutation π on i= 1,2,...,m will result in a different subtree, where the subtree is generated by selecting segments in the order $s_{\pi(1)}, s_{\pi(2)},\ldots,s_{\pi(m)}$. Nonetheless, every subtree will describe the same tessellation of R_k. Consequently, there are distinct trees describing the same tessellation of the original region R. For example, in figure 13, either tree specifies the same tessellation.

An important special case occurs when the initial set of segments is equivalent to the extended set, i.e., $\cup\{s|s\varepsilon\Sigma\} = \cup\{\hat{s}|\hat{s}\varepsilon\hat{\Sigma}\}$. If in addition the initial region is a plane, all of the elements of Σ, would be lines. Since extension has no effect, the tessellation is fixed before the algorithm begins. We call such a tessellation a <u>maximum tessellation</u> because any set of segments lying on the same set of lines can produce only tessellations whose areas are the union of the areas of the maximum tessellation, as can be seen by comparing figures 10 and 12 with fig. 14. It follows that any set of segments has a corresponding maximum tessellation whose cardinality is the maximum of the number of areas produced by any tessellation resulting from the set. In general, the number of different tessellations that can be derived from a set Σ is, in some sense, the complement of the number of distinct trees which describe the same tessellations.

A BSP tree constructed by algorithm I contains nodes labeled with segments and nodes labeled with areas. The segment nodes are exactly the interior nodes of the tree and the "area" nodes are the leaves. The algorithm can be thought of as first generating a binary tree composed of only the segment nodes. There will then be segment nodes which have one or two empty sons. (Every node of a binary tree has potentially two sons, left and right. If a node does not have one or both sons, we refer to these as "empty sons.") At each empty son, an area node is added. The resulting tree is such that all segment nodes have both a left and a right son, either of which could be another segment node or an area node. Since binary trees of n nodes have n+1 empty sons, it follows that the number of area nodes is one more than the number of segment nodes, thus a tree of 2n-1 nodes is needed to represent a tessellation containing n areas.

Each subtree of a BSP tree represents some region R_i in the sense that the union of all the areas represented by the leaves of R_i equals R_i (the segments represented by the segment nodes of R_i are thus, also included in this union). For notational purposes we will designate the region represented by the entire tree as R_o. This, of course, is the original region from which the tessellation is formed. The extension of the segment s represented by the root q of a subtree partitions a region R_i, and the regions represented by the two subtrees of q are the two half-spaces formed from R_i by $\hat{s}$. If, upon traversing the tree one reaches q, then taking the left or right branch of q would have a geometric correspondence to selecting one of these two half-spaces. A path in the tree, then, reflects a successive selection of smaller and smaller portions of R_o. In fact the region represented by a subtree is the intersection of the half-spaces with respect to R_o formed by the extension of the segments which are on the path to the root of the subtree q (but not including q). It immediately follows that the area which is "added" at each empty son is exactly the intersection of the half-spaces with respect to R_o formed by the extension of segments whose nodes are on the path to the son.

It is easy to see how a BSP tree can be used to locate which area of the tessellation a point lies. Beginning at the root, determine on which side of a segment the point lies and proceed to the son representing the half-space corresponding to that side (points on the line being assigned arbitrarily to one of the two half-spaces). Repetition of this process will generate a path to a leaf node that represents the area in which the point lies, thus solving what might be called the "location problem" with respect to a tessellation.

<u>BSP Tree Used for Priority Ordering</u>

The ability of a BSP tree to be used for the generation of a priority ordering is based upon the principle that given in which half-space lies the point to which the ordering is relative (usually thought of as the "eye" or viewing position), all points in this same half-space will have priority over all points in the other half-space. Although this fact is fairly self evident for half-spaces, it is also true for any two convex regions.

To obtain a priority ordering from the tree, an inorder traversal is performed. The choice of taking the left or right branch of a node q representing segment s is always made in favor of the subtree which represents the region that is contained in the same half-space that the viewing position is in, this half-space having been formed by $\hat{s}$ with respect to R_o. It is easy to see that such a policy will result in the first area node to be reached being the one in which the viewing position lies, i.e. the solution to the location problem mentioned earlier. Priority is assigned to a node upon backing-up from it during the traversal.

Thus for each node q, all nodes of the chosen subtree receive higher priorities than q, and similarly, all nodes of the remaining subtree obtain a lower priority than q. The entire traversal of the tree will then produce a total ordering of the nodes, and this is precisely the visibility priority of the elements represented by the nodes. Note that it is requisite that R_0 be convex to guarantee this property. Since the partitioning of a convex object produces two convex objects, the convexity of R_0 implies the same property for all subsequent refinements of R_0 during the construction of the tree. Thus all areas are convex which is sufficient to guarantee the existence of a priority ordering of the areas.

Comparison of Uses of the BSP Tree

The first appearance of a BSP tree in the general literature was in Sutherland, et al. (1974) reviewing the work of Schumaker, et al. (1969), although the tree was not named and its general properties were not developed. The application presented was that in which invisible "dividing planes" were introduced to the data base. The method involved the designer of a simulation scene manually positioning "clusters" such as buildings, trees, mountains, etc., so that vertical dividing planes could be placed between the clusters to varying extents. This resulted, in terms of a BSP tree, in the generation of a tessellation of the surface by the dividing places which are represented by segment nodes, and each cluster was contained wholly within an area. Thus each cluster corresponded to an area node. A priority ordering could then be obtained on the clusters.

Additional power is available if the tessellation is a maximum tessellation. In this case, it is possible to compute off-line the priority ordering for each case of the viewing position being in a different area. This follows from the fact that since the areas are formed by a maximum tessellation, it is not possible for two different points in the same area to be on different sides of the extension of a segment with respect to R_0 (since in a maximum tessellation all segments are equal to their extensions with respect to R_0). Thus for each area the traversal of the tree is fixed. The Sutherland, *et al.*, presentation suggests taking advantage of this by pre-computing and storing for each area its inherent priority ordering on the clusters (since the dividing planes are not part of the scene they need not be included in the ordering). It was then sufficient to solve the location problem in order to obtain the priority ordering. Since this method requires n^2 storage space (where n is the number of clusters) and the traversal of the tree is O(n), it is not clear whether this approach is advantageous. Also since a maximum tessellation is required the tree will be the largest possible for a given set of clusters.

The application of BSP trees introduced in this paper is something of a complement to that presented in Sutherland, et al. Here those objects represented by the segment (or polygon) nodes constitute the visible data while the areas of the tessellation are of no importance. In fact, the function Make_tree presented earlier produces only the segment nodes. The area nodes are only implied by the empty sons. Also, Make_tree forms a BSP tree for three dimensions while the former method, although working in 3-D, forms a BSP tree for two dimensions, and Make_tree's tessellation in general is not maximal. Clearly the BSP tree can be used with dividing planes to divide 3-space into volumes, and a hybrid of polygons and dividing planes could also be developed. For instance, each area node of a tree constructed with dividing planes could be replaced with a BSP tree constructed of polygons for the cluster contained in the area.

Combinatorics of the BSP Tree

We will now examine the size of the BSP trees. The previous discussion was presented, for simplicity's sake, for the 2-D case; here we will derive some formulas both for the 2-D and 3-D BSP trees. Although we are most interested in the 3-D case, 2-D is important in the special 3-D case in which all of the objects "sit" on the ground and can be separated by vertical planes. This is equivalent to a 2-D BSP tree corresponding to the 2-D scene obtained by projecting the objects and the separating plane on the ground plane.

As noted previously, the BSP tree can be created by both infinite and finite objects. The infinite objects are planes for the 3-D case are lines for the 2-D case. The corresponding finite objects are non-intersecting convex polygons and segments. We will examine these two extremal cases in turn.

A d-dimensional BSP tree partitions the d-dimensional space by (d-1)-dimensional objects. We thus examine first, what is the maximum number $f_d(n)$ of volumes of a d-dimensional space that can be created by n (d-1)-dimensional planes. In the 2-D case we have been considering, this corresponds to the maximum tessellation of the plane using lines.

The general formula is

$$f_d(n) = \sum_{i=0}^{d} \binom{n}{i}.$$

As there is a one-to-one correspondence between the volumes and the leaves of the binary BSP tree, the number of the nodes of the BSP tree is $2f_d(n)-1$.

How many (d-1)-dimensional regions created from (d-1)-dimensional planes under the assumption that no 3 planes intersect along a single (d-2)-dimensional line? It can be shown that the number is

$$\sum_{i=0}^{d} i \binom{n}{1}.$$

In the other extremal case, where the objects given are n (d-1)-dimensional non-interpenetrating convex polygons, we examine the worst case, namely compute the maximum number of the (d-1)-dimensional regions that are obtained from the polygons by the intersection of the n (d-1)-dimensional planes on which they lie. It can be shown that the number is

$$\binom{n}{2} + n^{d-1}$$

We summarize the results in Table 2 for the two interesting cases d=2 and d=3.

	Volumes	Unbounded Objects	Bounded Objects
2-D:	$\frac{n^2+n}{2}+1$	n^2	$\frac{n^2+n}{2}$
3-D:	$\frac{n^3+5n}{6}+1$	$\frac{n^3-n^2+2n}{2}$	$\frac{n^3+3n^2+2n}{6}$

Table 2: Maximum possible nodes in BSP tree.

Conclusion

A solution has been presented to the visible surface problem which appears to be more efficient than previous solutions whenever many images are to be generated of the same static environment. The algorithm is easy to implement since both phases, the preprocessing and the image generation, can each be succinctly stated in a short recursive procedure. The major potential weakness, a large increase from the number of original polygons in the data base to the number in the BSP tree, has not occurred in any environment so far encountered.

Acknowledgement

We wish to thank Greg Abram for much needed and appreciated program development, Mike Cronin for numerous improvements to the narrative, and the referees for helpful and thorough reviews of the first draft of this paper.

References

Berman, G. and Fryer, K.D. Introduction to Combinatorics, (1972) Academic Press.

Fuchs, H. and Johnson, B. "An Expandable Multiprocessor Architecture for Video Graphics" Proc. 6th Annual Symp. on Computer Architecture, (1979) pp 58-67

Schumaker, R.A., Brand, B., Gilliland, M. and Sharp, W. "Study for Applying Computer-Generated Images to Visual Simulation," AFHRL-TR-69-14, U.S. Air Force Human Resources Laboratory (1969)

Sutherland, I.E., Sproull, R.F. and Schumaker, R.A. "A Characterization of Ten Hidden-Surface Algorithms", (1974) ACM Computing Surveys, 6 (1): 1-55

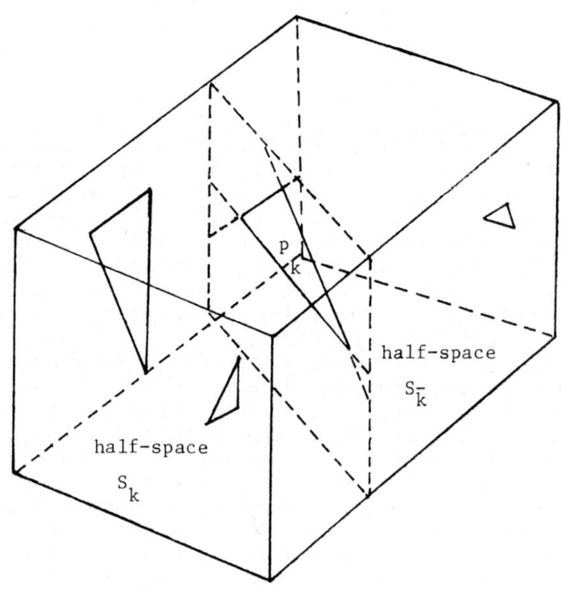

Figure 1: Environment split by plane of p_k

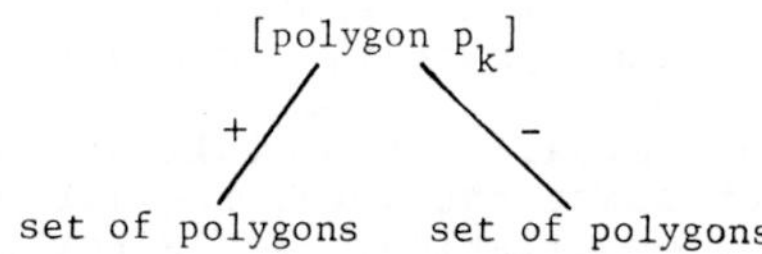

Figure 2: Beginning of BSP tree construction

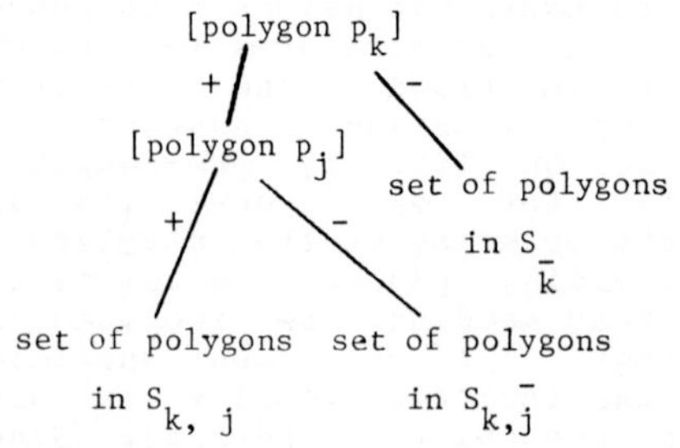

Figure 3: BSP tree after two steps

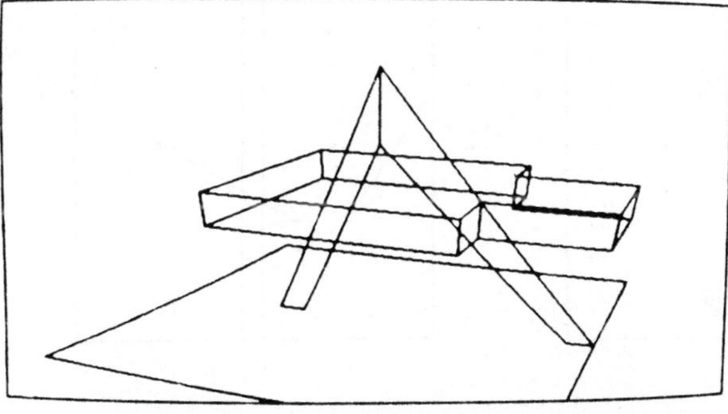

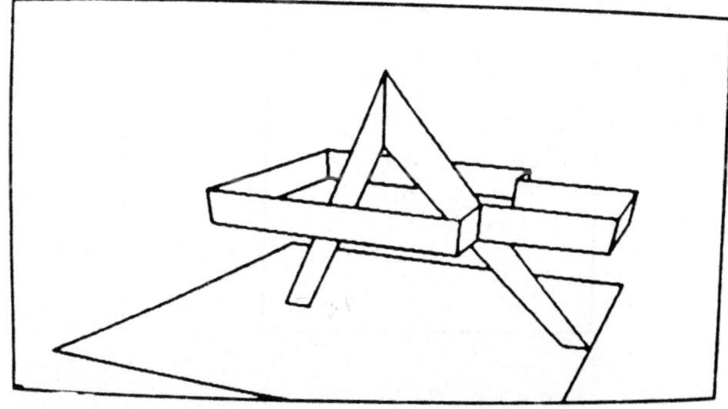

Figure 4: Wire-frame and visible line/surface images of same environment (11 original polygons; 11 in BSP tree)

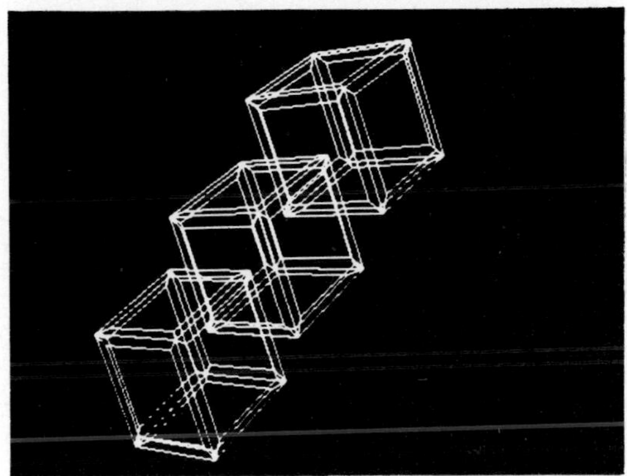

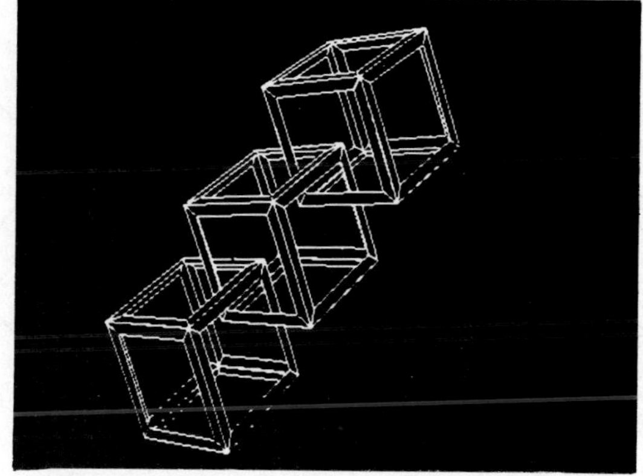

Figure 5: Wire-frame and visible line/surface images of same environment (72 original polygons; 100 polygons in BSP tree)

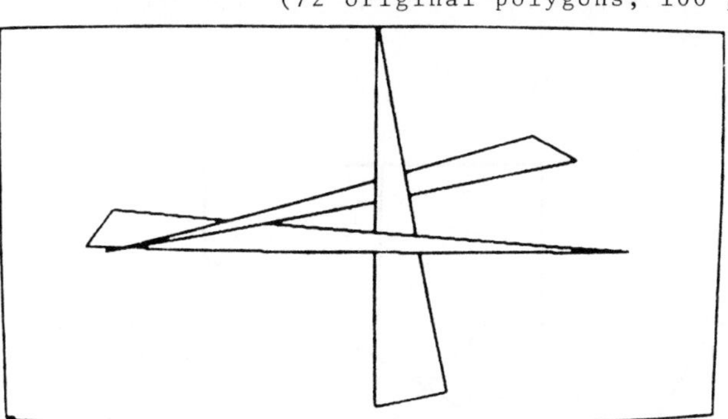

Figure 6: Visible line/surface image of simple object whose polygons cannot be directly assigned visibility priorities (some polygons here have been split during preprocessing)

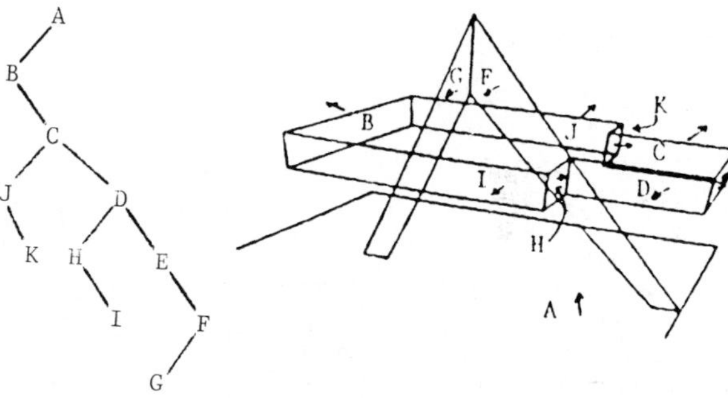

(left branches are positive)

(arrows on positive side of polygons)

Figure 7: BSP tree and polygons of Fig.4

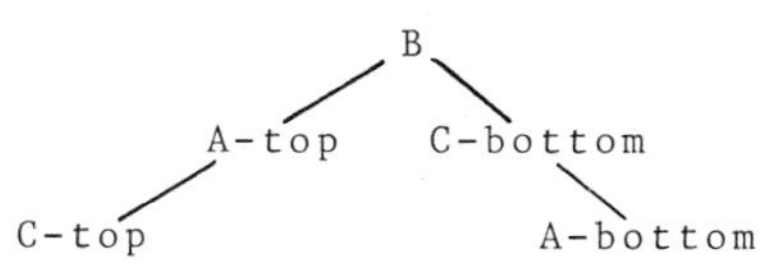

(left branches are positive; positive sides of all polygons are visible)

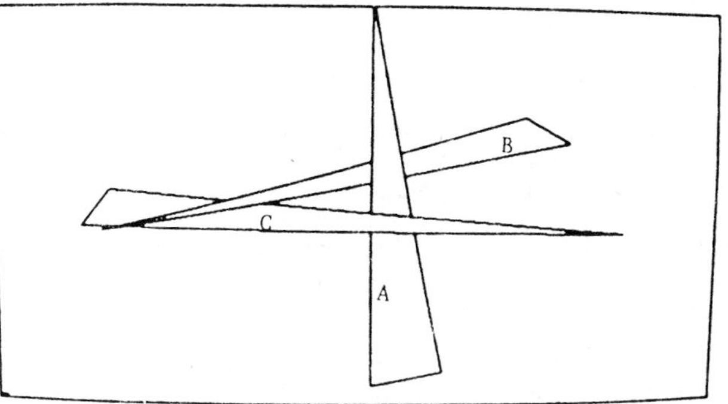

Figure 8: BSP tree and polygons of Fig. 6 (A and C have each been split into two parts by plane of polygon B)

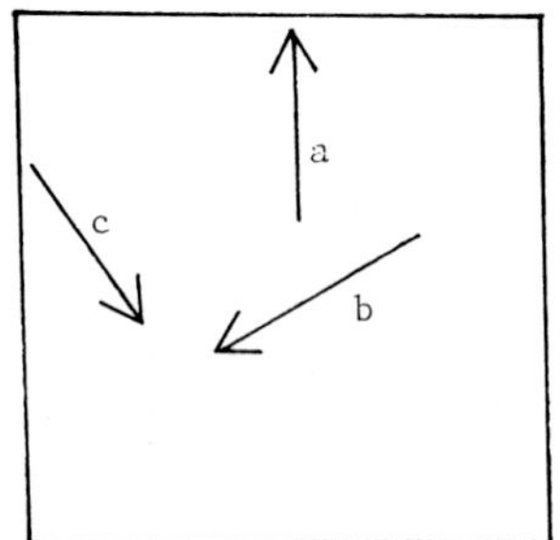

Figure 9a

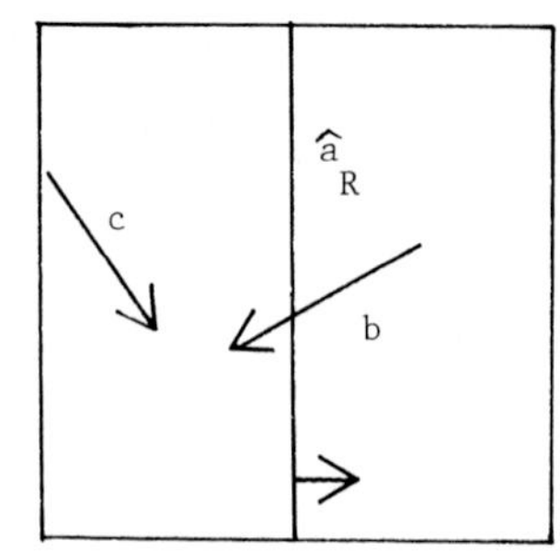

Figure 9b

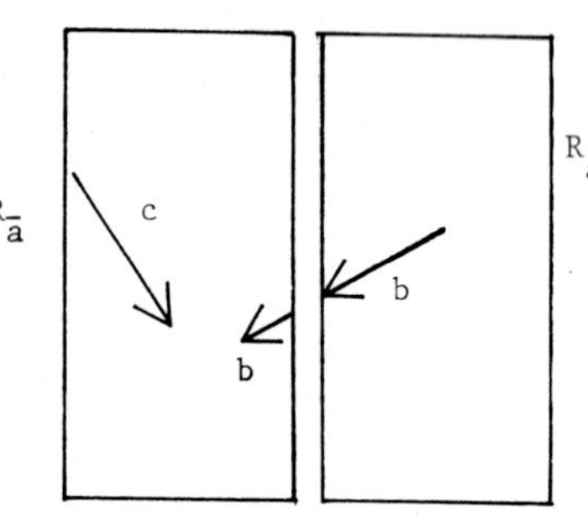

Figure 9c

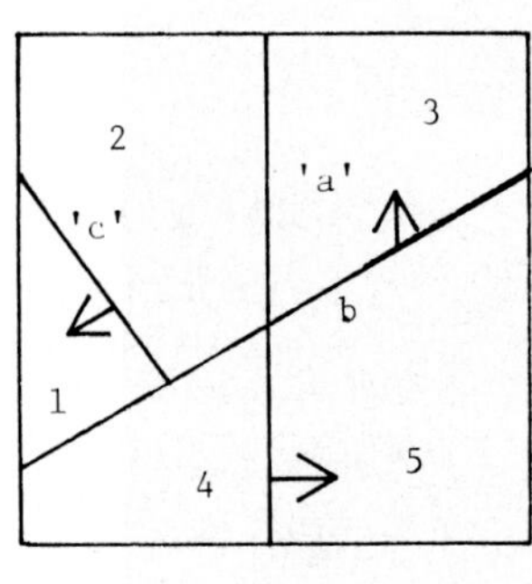

Figure 10

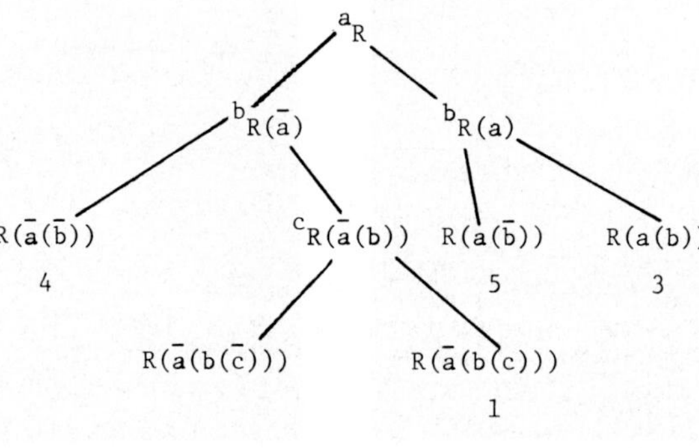

Figure 11

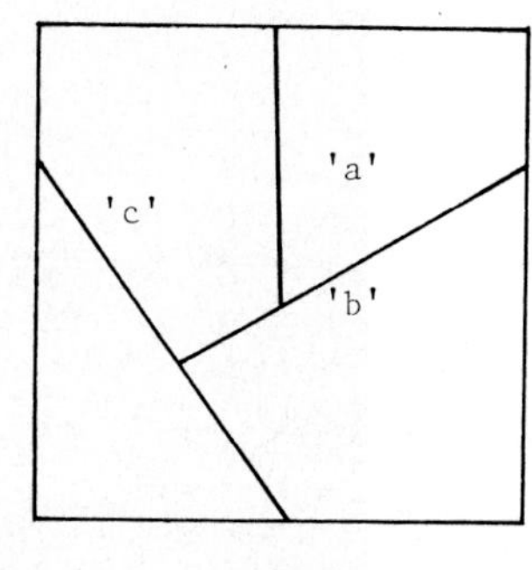

Figure 12

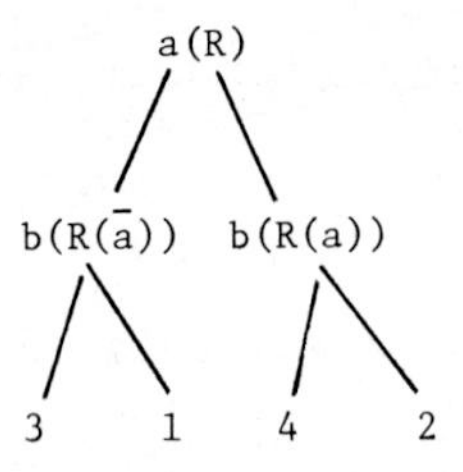

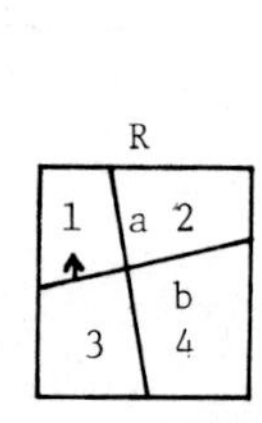

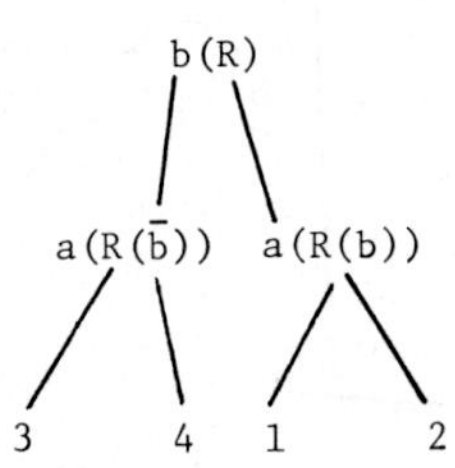

Figure 13

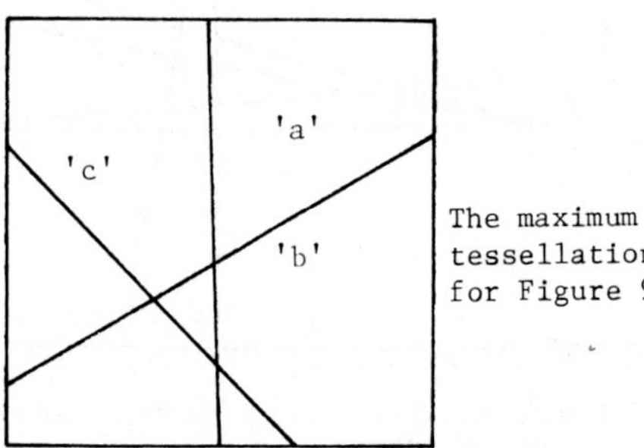

The maximum tessellation for Figure 9

Figure 14

(end)

"Compositing Digital Images" by T. Porter and T. Duff from *Proceedings of SIGGRAPH '84,* 1984, pages 253-259. Copyright 1984, Association for Computing Machinery, Inc., reprinted by permission.

Compositing Digital Images

Thomas Porter
Tom Duff †

Computer Graphics Project
Lucasfilm Ltd.

ABSTRACT

Most computer graphics pictures have been computed all at once, so that the rendering program takes care of all computations relating to the overlap of objects. There are several applications. however, where elements must be rendered separately, relying on compositing techniques for the anti-aliased accumulation of the full image. This paper presents the case for four-channel pictures, demonstrating that a matte component can be computed similarly to the color channels. The paper discusses guidelines for the generation of elements and the arithmetic for their arbitrary compositing.

CR Categories and Subject Descriptors: I.3.3 [**Computer Graphics**]: Picture/Image Generations — Display algorithms; I.3.4 [**Computer Graphics**]: Graphics Utilities — Software support; I.4.1 [**Image Processing**]: Digitization — Sampling.

General Terms: Algorithms

Additional Key Words and Phrases: compositing, matte channel, matte algebra, visible surface algorithms, graphics systems

† Author's current address: AT&T Bell Laboratories, Murray Hill, NJ 07974, Room 2C465

1. Introduction

Increasingly, we find that a complex three dimensional scene cannot be fully rendered by a single program. The wealth of literature on rendering polygons and curved surfaces, handling the special cases of fractals and spheres and quadrics and triangles, implementing refinements for texture mapping and bump mapping, noting speed-ups on the basis of coherence or depth complexity in the scene, suggests that multiple programs are necessary.

In fact, reliance on a single program for rendering an entire scene is a poor strategy for minimizing the cost of small modeling errors. Experience has taught us to break down large bodies of source code into separate modules in order to save compilation time. An error in one routine forces only the recompilation of its module and the relatively quick reloading of the entire program. Similarly, small errors in coloration or design in one object should not force the "recompilation" of an entire image.

Separating the image into *elements* which can be independently rendered saves enormous time. Each element has an associated *matte,* coverage information which designates the shape of the element. The *compositing* of those elements makes use of the mattes to accumulate the final image.

The compositing methodology must not induce aliasing in the image; soft edges of the elements must be honored in computing the final image. Features should be provided to exploit the full associativity of the compositing process; this affords flexibility, for example, for the accumulation of several foreground elements into an aggregate foreground which can be examined over different backgrounds. The compositor should provide facilities for arbitrary dissolves and fades of elements during an animated sequence.

Several highly successful rendering algorithms have worked by reducing their environments to pieces that can be combined in a 2 1/2 dimensional manner, and then overlaying them either front-to-back or back-to-front [3]. Whitted and Weimar's graphics test-bed [6] and Crow's image generation environment [2] are both designed to deal with heterogenously rendered elements. Whitted

and Weimar's system reduces all objects to horizontal spans which are composited using a Warnock-like algorithm. In Crow's system a supervisory process decides the order in which to combine images created by independent special-purpose rendering processes. The imaging system of Warnock and Wyatt [5] incorporates 1-bit mattes. The Hanna-Barbera cartoon animation system [4] incorporates soft-edge mattes, representing the opacity information in a less convenient manner than that proposed here. The present paper presents guidelines for rendering elements and introduces the algebra for compositing.

2. The Alpha Channel

A separate component is needed to retain the matte information, the extent of coverage of an element at a pixel. In a full color rendering of an element, the RGB components retain only the color. In order to place the element over an arbitrary background, a mixing factor is required at every pixel to control the linear interpolation of foreground and background colors. In general, there is no way to encode this component as part of the color information. For anti-aliasing purposes, this mixing factor needs to be of comparable resolution to the color channels. Let us call this an *alpha* channel, and let us treat an alpha of 0 to indicate no coverage, 1 to mean full coverage, with fractions corresponding to partial coverage.

In an environment where the compositing of elements is required, we see the need for an alpha channel as an integral part of all pictures. Because mattes are naturally computed along with the picture, a separate alpha component in the frame buffer is appropriate. Off-line storage of alpha information along with color works conveniently into run-length encoding schemes because the alpha information tends to abide by the same runs.

What is the meaning of the quadruple (r,g,b,α) at a pixel? How do we express that a pixel is half covered by a full red object? One obvious suggestion is to assign (1,0,0,.5) to that pixel: the .5 indicates the coverage and the (1,0,0) is the color. There are a few reasons to dismiss this proposal, the most severe being that all compositing operations will involve multiplying the 1 in the red channel by the .5 in the alpha channel to compute the red contribution of this object at this pixel. The desire to avoid this multiplication points up a better solution, storing the *pre-multiplied* value in the color component, so that (.5,0,0,.5) will indicate a full red object half covering a pixel.

The quadruple (r,g,b,α) indicates that the pixel is α covered by the color $(r/\alpha,\ g/\alpha,\ b/\alpha)$. A quadruple where the alpha component is less than a color component indicates a color outside the [0,1] interval, which is somewhat unusual. We will see later that luminescent objects can be usefully represented in this way. For the representation of normal objects, an alpha of 0 at a pixel generally forces the color components to be 0. Thus the RGB channels record the true colors where alpha is 1, linearly darkened colors for fractional alphas along edges, and black where alpha is 0. Silhouette edges of RGBA elements thus exhibit their anti-aliased nature when viewed on an RGB monitor.

It is important to distinguish between two key pixel representations:

$$black = (0,0,0,1);$$
$$clear = (0,0,0,0).$$

The former pixel is an opaque black; the latter pixel is transparent.

3. RGBA Pictures

If we survey the variety of elements which contribute to a complex animation, we find many complete background images which have an alpha of 1 everywhere. Among foreground elements, we find that the color components roll off in step with the alpha channel, leaving large areas of transparency. Mattes, colorless stencils used for controlling the compositing of other elements, have 0 in their RGB components. Off-line storage of RGBA pictures should therefore provide the natural data compression for handling the RGB pixels of backgrounds, RGBA pixels of foregrounds, and A pixels of mattes.

There are some objections to computing with these RGBA pictures. Storage of the color components premultiplied by the alpha would seem to unduly quantize the color resolution, especially as alpha approaches 0. However, because any compositing of the picture will require that multiplication anyway, storage of the product forces only a very minor loss of precision in this regard. Color extraction, to compute in a different color space for example, becomes more difficult. We must recover $(r/\alpha,\ g/\alpha,\ b/\alpha)$, and once again, as alpha approaches 0, the precision falls off sharply. For our applications, this has yet to affect us.

4. The Algebra of Compositing

Given this standard of RGBA pictures, let us examine how compositing works. We shall do this by enumerating the complete set of binary compositing operations. For each of these, we shall present a formula for computing the contribution of each of two input pictures to the output composite at each pixel. We shall pay particular attention to the output pixels, to see that they remain pre-multiplied by their alpha.

4.1. Assumptions

When blending pictures together, we do not have information about overlap of coverage information within a pixel; all we have is an alpha value. When we consider the mixing of two pictures at a pixel, we must make some assumption about the interplay of the two alpha values. In order to examine that interplay, let us first consider the overlap of two semi-transparent elements like haze, then consider the overlap of two opaque, hard-edged elements.

If α_A and α_B represent the opaqueness of semi-transparent objects which fully cover the pixel, the computation is well known. Each object lets $(1-\alpha)$ of the background through, so that the background shows through only $(1-\alpha_A)(1-\alpha_B)$ of the pixel. $\alpha_A(1-\alpha_B)$ of the background is blocked by object A and passed by object B; $(1-\alpha_A)\alpha_B$ of the background is passed by A and blocked by B. This leaves $\alpha_A\alpha_B$ of the pixel which we can consider to be blocked by both.

If α_A and α_B represent subpixel areas covered by opaque geometric objects, the overlap of objects within the pixel is quite arbitrary. We know that object A divides the pixel into two subpixel areas of ratio α_A:$1-\alpha_A$. We know that object B divides the pixel into two subpixel areas of ratio α_B:$1-\alpha_B$. Lacking further information, we make the following assumption: *there is nothing special about the shape of the pixel; we expect that object B will divide each of the subpixel areas inside and outside of object A into the same ratio* α_B:$1-\alpha_B$. The result of the assumption is the same arithmetic as with semi-transparent objects and is summarized in the following table:

description	*area*
$\overline{A}\cap\overline{B}$	$(1-\alpha_A)(1-\alpha_B)$
$A\cap\overline{B}$	$\alpha_A(1-\alpha_B)$
$\overline{A}\cap B$	$(1-\alpha_A)\alpha_B$
$A\cap B$	$\alpha_A\alpha_B$

The assumption is quite good for most mattes, though it can be improved if we know that the coverage seldom overlaps (adjacent segments of a continuous line) or always overlaps (repeated application of a picture). For ease in presentation throughout this paper, let us make this assumption and consider the alpha values as representing subpixel coverage of opaque objects.

4.2. Compositing Operators

Consider two pictures A and B. They divide each pixel into the 4 subpixel areas

B	A	*name*	*description*	*choices*
0	0	0	$\overline{A}\cap\overline{B}$	0
0	1	A	$A\cap\overline{B}$	0, A
1	0	B	$\overline{A}\cap B$	0, B
1	1	AB	$A\cap B$	0, A, B

listed in this table along with the choices in each area for contributing to the composite. In the last area, for example, because both input pictures exist there, either could survive to the composite. Alternatively, the composite could be clear in that area.

A particular binary compositing operation can be identified as a quadruple indicating the input picture which contributes to the composite in each of the four subpixel areas 0, A, B, AB of the table above. With three choices where the pictures intersect, two where only one picture exists and one outside the two pictures, there are $3\times2\times2\times1=12$ distinct compositing operations listed in the table below. Note that pictures A and B are diagrammed as covering the pixel with triangular wedges whose overlap conforms to the assumption above.

operation	quadruple	diagram	F_A	F_B
clear	(0,0,0,0)		0	0
A	(0,A,0,A)		1	0
B	(0,0,B,B)		0	1
A **over** *B*	(0,A,B,A)		1	$1-\alpha_A$
B **over** *A*	(0,A,B,B)		$1-\alpha_B$	1
A **in** *B*	(0,0,0,A)		α_B	0
B **in** *A*	(0,0,0,B)		0	α_A
A **out** *B*	(0,A,0,0)		$1-\alpha_B$	0
B **out** *A*	(0,0,B,0)		0	$1-\alpha_A$
A **atop** *B*	(0,0,B,A)		α_B	$1-\alpha_A$
B **atop** *A*	(0,A,0,B)		$1-\alpha_B$	α_A
A **xor** *B*	(0,A,B,0)		$1-\alpha_B$	$1-\alpha_A$

Useful operators include *A* **over** *B*, *A* **in** *B*, and *A* **held out by** *B*. *A* **over** *B* is the placement of foreground A in front of background B. *A* **in** *B* refers only to that part of A inside picture B. *A* **held out by** *B*, normally shortened to *A* **out** *B*, refers only to that part of A outside picture B. For completeness, we include the less useful operators *A* **atop** *B* and *A* **xor** *B*. *A* **atop** *B* is the union of *A* **in** *B* and *B* **out** *A*. Thus, ***paper* atop *table*** includes ***paper*** where it is on top of ***table***, and ***table*** otherwise; area beyond the edge of the table is out of the picture. *A* **xor** *B* is the union of *A* **out** *B* and *B* **out** *A*.

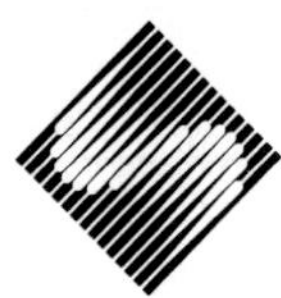

4.3. Compositing Arithmetic

For each of the compositing operations, we would like to compute the contribution of each input picture at each pixel. This is quite easily solved by recognizing that each input picture survives in the composite pixel only within its own matte. For each input picture, we are looking for that fraction of its own matte which prevails in the output. By definition then, the alpha value of the composite, the total area of the pixel covered, can be computed by adding α_A times its fraction F_A to α_B times its fraction F_B.

The color of the composite can be computed on a component basis by adding the color of the picture A times its fraction to the color of picture B times its fraction. To see this, let c_A, c_B, and c_O be some color component of pictures A, B and the composite, and let C_A, C_B, and C_O be the true color component before pre-multiplication by alpha. Then we have

$$c_O = \alpha_O C_O$$

Now C_O can be computed by averaging contributions made by C_A and C_B, so

$$c_O = \alpha_O \frac{\alpha_A F_A C_A + \alpha_B F_B C_B}{\alpha_A F_A + \alpha_B F_B}$$

but the denominator is just α_O, so

$$\begin{aligned} c_O &= \alpha_A F_A C_A + \alpha_B F_B C_B \\ &= \alpha_A F_A \frac{c_A}{\alpha_A} + \alpha_B F_B \frac{c_B}{\alpha_B} \\ &= c_A F_A + c_B F_B \qquad (1) \end{aligned}$$

Because each of the input colors is pre-multiplied by its alpha, and we are adding contributions from non-overlapping areas, the sum will be effectively pre-multiplied by the alpha value of the composite just computed. The pleasant result that the color channels are handled with the same computation as alpha can be traced back to our decision to store pre-multiplied RGBA quadruples. Thus the problem is reduced to finding a table of fractions F_A and F_B which indicate the extent of contribution of A and B, plugging these values into equation 1 for both the color and the alpha components.

By our assumptions above, the fractions are quickly determined by examining the pixel diagram included in the table of operations. Those fractions are listed in the F_A and F_B columns of the table. For example, in the *A* **over** *B* case, picture A survives everywhere while picture B survives only outside picture A, so the corresponding fractions are 1 and $(1-\alpha_A)$. Substituting into equation 1, we find

$$c_O = c_A \times 1 + c_B \times (1-\alpha_A).$$

This is almost the well used linear interpolation of foreground F with background B

$$B' = F \times \alpha + B \times (1-\alpha),$$

except that our foreground is pre-multiplied by alpha.

4.4. Unary operators

To assist us in dissolving and in balancing color brightness of elements contributing to a composite, it is useful to introduce a darken factor ϕ and a dissolve factor δ:

$$\textbf{darken}(A,\phi) \equiv (\phi r_A, \phi g_A, \phi b_A, \alpha_A)$$
$$\textbf{dissolve}(A,\delta) \equiv (\delta r_A, \delta g_A, \delta b_A, \delta\alpha_A)\ .$$

Normally, $0 \le \phi, \delta \le 1$ although none of the theory requires it.

As ϕ varies from 1 to 0, the element will change from normal to complete blackness. If $\phi > 1$ the element will be brightened. As δ goes from 1 to 0 the element will gradually fade from view.

Luminescent objects, which add color information without obscuring the background, can be handled with the introduction of a opaqueness factor ω, $0 \le \omega \le 1$:

$$\textbf{opaque}(A,\omega) \equiv (r_A, g_A, b_A, \omega\alpha_A)\ .$$

As ω varies from 1 to 0, the element will change from normal coverage over the background to no obscuration. This scaling of the alpha channel alone will cause pixel quadruples where α is less than a color component, indicating a representation of a color outside of the normal range. This possibility forces us to clip the output composite to the [0,1] range.

An ω of 0 will produce quadruples $(r,g,b,0)$ which do have meaning. The color channels, pre-multiplied by the original alpha, can be plugged into equation 1 as always. The alpha channel of 0 indicates that this pixel will obscure nothing. In terms of our methodology for examining subpixel areas, we should understand that using the **opaque** operator corresponds to shrinking the matte coverage with regard to the color coverage.

4.5. The PLUS operator

We find it useful to include one further binary compositing operator **plus**. The expression *A* **plus** *B* holds no notion of precedence in any area covered by both pictures; the components are simply added. This allows us to dissolve from one picture to another by specifying

$$\textbf{dissolve}(A,\alpha)\ \textbf{plus}\ \textbf{dissolve}(B,1-\alpha).$$

In terms of the binary operators above, **plus** allows both pictures to survive in the subpixel area AB. The operator table above should be appended:

operation	diagram	F_A	F_B
(0,A,B,AB) *A* **plus** *B*		1	1

5. Examples

The operations on one and two pictures are presented as a basis for handling compositing expressions involving several pictures. A normal case involving three pictures is the compositing of a foreground picture A over a background picture B, with regard to an independent matte C. The expression for this compositing operation is

$$(A \textbf{ in } C) \textbf{ over } B.$$

Using equation 1 twice, we find that the composite in this case is computed at each pixel by

$$c_O = c_A \alpha_C + c_B (1 - \alpha_A \alpha_C).$$

As an example of a complex compositing expression, let us consider a subwindow of Rob Cook's picture *Road to Point Reyes* [1]. This still frame was assembled from many elements according to the following rules:

Foreground = *FrgdGrass* **over** *Rock* **over** *Fence* **over** *Shadow* **over** *BkgdGrass*;

GlossyRoad = *Puddle* **over** (*PostReflection* **atop** (*PlantReflection* **atop** *Road*));

Hillside = *Plant* **over** *GlossyRoad* **over** *Hill*;

Background = *Rainbow* **plus** *Darkbow* **over** *Mountains* **over** *Sky*;

Pt.Reyes = *Foreground* **over** *Hillside* **over** *Background*.

Figure 1 shows three intermediate composites and the final picture.

Foreground = *FrgdGrass* **over** *Rock* **over** *Fence* **over** *Shadow* **over** *BkgdGrass*;

Hillside = *Plant* **over** *GlossyRoad* **over** *Hill*;

Background = *Rainbow* **plus** *Darkbow* **over** *Mountains* **over** *Sky*;

Pt.Reyes = *Foreground* **over** *Hillside* **over** *Background*.

Figure 1

Stars

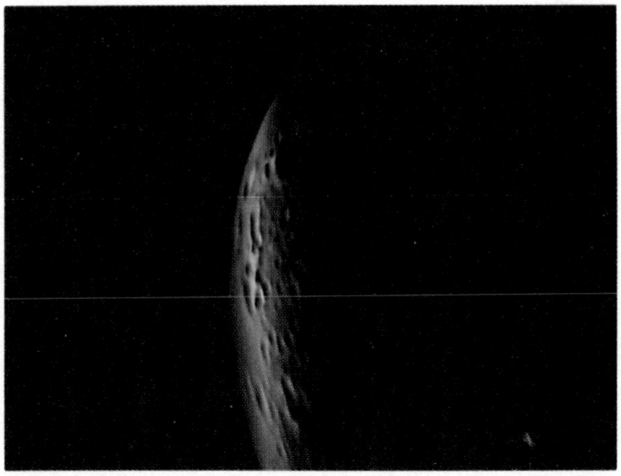

Planet

BFire

FFire

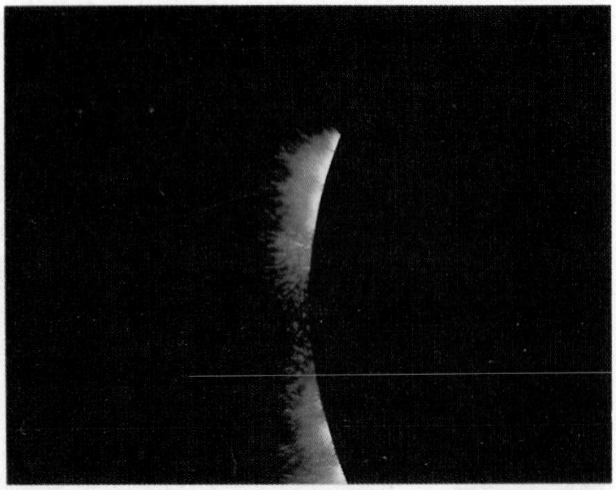

BFire **out** Planet

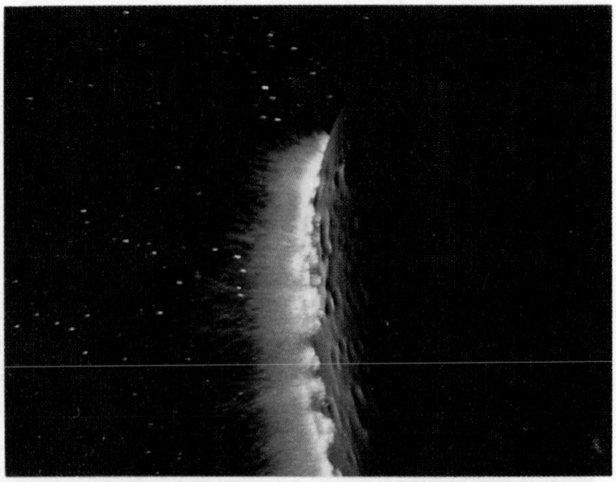

Composite

Figure 2

A further example demonstrates the problem of *correlated mattes.* In Figure 2, we have a star field background, a planet element, fiery particles behind the planet, and fiery particles in front of the planet. We wish to add the luminous fires, obscure the planet, darkened for proper balance, with the aggregate fire matte, and place that over the star field. An expression for this compositing is

(*FFire* **plus** (*BFire* **out** *Planet*))
over darken(*Planet*,.8) **over** *Stars* .

We must remember that our basic assumption about the division of subpixel areas by geometric objects breaks down in the face of input pictures with correlated mattes. When one picture appears twice in a compositing expression, we must take care with our computations of F_A and F_B. Those listed in the table are correct only for uncorrelated pictures.

To solve the problem of correlated mattes, we must extend our methodology to handle n pictures: we must examine all 2^n subareas of the pixel, deciding which of the pictures survives in each area, and adding up all contributions. Multiple instances of a single picture or pictures with correlated mattes are resolved by aligning their pixel coverage. Example 2 can be computed by building a table of survivors (shown below) to accumulate the extent to which each input picture survives in the composite.

FFire	BFire	Planet	Stars	Survivor
			•	Stars
		•		Planet
		•	•	Planet
	•			BFire
	•		•	BFire
	•	•		Planet
	•	•	•	Planet
•				FFire
•			•	FFire
•		•		FFire
•		•	•	FFire
•	•			FFire,BFire
•	•		•	FFire,BFire
•	•	•		FFire
•	•	•	•	FFire

6. Conclusion

We have pointed out the need for matte channels in synthetic pictures, suggesting that frame buffer hardware should offer this facility. We have seen the convenience of the RGBA scheme for integrating the matte channel. A language of operators has been presented for conveying a full range of compositing expressions. We have discussed a methodology for deciding compositing questions at the subpixel level, deriving a simple equation for handling all composites of two pictures. The methodology is extended to multiple pictures, and the language is embellished to handle darkening, attenuation, and opaqueness.

There are several problems to be resolved in related areas, which are open for future research. We are interested in methods for breaking arbitrary three dimensional scenes into elements separated in depth. Such elements are equivalent to clusters, which have been a subject of discussion since the earliest attempts at hidden surface elimination. We are interested in applying the compositing notions to Z-buffer algorithms, where depth information is retained at each pixel.

7. References

1. Cook, R. Road to Point Reyes. *Computer Graphics* Vol 17, No. 3 (1983), Title Page Picture.
2. Crow, F. C. A More Flexible Image Generation Environment. *Computer Graphics* Vol. 16, No. 3 (1982), pp. 9-18.
3. Newell, M. G., Newell, R. G., and Sancha, T. L.. A Solution to the Hidden Surface Problem, pp. 443-448. *Proceedings of the 1972 ACM National Conference.*
4. Wallace, Bruce. Merging and Transformation of Raster Images for Cartoon Animation. *Computer Graphics* Vol. 15, No. 3 (1981), pp. 253-262.
5. Warnock, John, and Wyatt, Douglas. A Device Independent Graphics Imaging Model for Use with Raster Devices. *Computer Graphics* Vol. 16, No. 3 (1982), pp. 313-319.
6. Whitted, Turner, and Weimer, David. A Software Test-Bed for the Development of 3-D Raster Graphics Systems. *Computer Graphics* Vol. 15, No. 3 (1981), pp. 271-277.

8. Acknowledgments

The use of mattes to control the compositing of pictures is not new. The graphics group at the New York Institute of Technology has been using this for years. NYIT color maps were designed to encode both color and matte information; that idea was extended in the Ampex AVA system for storing mattes with pictures. Credit should be given to Ed Catmull, Alvy Ray Smith, and Ikonas Graphics Systems for the existence of an alpha channel as an integral part of a frame buffer, which has paved the way for the developments presented in this paper.

The graphics group at Lucasfilm should be credited with providing a fine test bed for working out these ideas. Furthermore, certain ideas incorporated as part of this work have their origins as idle comments within this group. Thanks are also given to Rodney Stock for comments on an early draft which forced the authors to clarify the major assumptions.

"Approximate and Probabilistic Algorithms for Shading and Rendering Structured Particle Systems" by W.T. Reeves and R. Blau from *Proceedings of SIGGRAPH '85*, 1985, pages 313-322. Copyright 1985, Association for Computing Machinery, Inc., reprinted by permission.

Approximate and Probabilistic Algorithms for Shading and Rendering Structured Particle Systems

William T. Reeves

Computer Research and Development,
Lucasfilm Ltd

Ricki Blau

Computer Science Division, Dept. of Electrical Engineering and Computer Science,
University of California, Berkeley

Abstract

Detail enhances the visual richness and realism of computer-generated images. Our stochastic modelling approach, called *particle systems*, builds complex pictures from sets of simple, volume-filling primitives. For example, structured particle systems have been used to generate trees and a grass-covered forest floor. Particle systems can produce so much irregular, three-dimensional detail that exact shading and visible surface calculations become infeasible. We describe approximate and probabilistic algorithms for shading and the visible surface problem. Because particle systems algorithms generate richly-detailed images, it is hard to detect any deviation from an exact rendering. Recent work in stochastic modelling also enables us to model complex motions with random variation, such as a field of grass blowing in the breeze. We analyze the performance of our current algorithms to understand the costs of our stochastic modelling approach.

CR Categories and Subject Descriptors: I.3.3 [**Computer Graphics**]: Picture/Image Generation - Display algorithms; I.3.5 [**Computer Graphics**]: Computational Geometry and Object Modelling - Curve, surface, solid, and object representations - Modelling packages; I.3.7 [**Computer Graphics**]: Three-Dimensional Graphics and Realism - Animation - Colour, shading, shadowing, and texture

General Terms: Design, Algorithms, Performance Analysis

Key Words: stochastic modelling, approximation

1. Introduction

Natural, as opposed to man-made, objects exhibit an immense variety of irregular shapes and random variation in their detail. To represent this variety in synthetic images, we would like to have models that are not entirely deterministic. The use of *stochastic* models has recently been advanced as an approach to creating naturalistic detail in computer-generated images [5]. The idea of "data amplification" is fundamental to stochastic modelling algorithms, as well as to other classes of algorithms described by Smith [13]. A simple data base specifies the general characteristics of the modelled object, and detail is generated algorithmically to describe the object fully. A complicated image can be generated from a small data base, and the amount of detail can vary with the displayed size of the object.

The best-known examples of stochastic modelling are the *fractal* algorithms of Fournier, Fussell, and Carpenter [5], inspired by the mathematics of Mandelbrot [9], and the particle systems described by Reeves [12]. Particle systems represent objects as clouds of primitive particles that occupy their volumes, rather than using more classical surface-based representations such as polygons, patches, and quadric surfaces. A particle system is not a static entity, as its particles can move and change form with the passage of time. The position, orientation, attributes, and dynamics of each particle are defined by a set of constrained stochastic processes.

Particle systems are important for three reasons. First, because a particle is much simpler than most graphical primitives, many more can be drawn in a given amount of computation time. Hence, a more complex and detailed image can be generated. Second, particle systems are both procedural and stochastic. By employing data amplification techniques, they require less human design time than conventional modelling methods. Third, particle systems can be used to model objects that change form over a period of time. In our experience, it is more difficult to represent complex dynamics of this form with surface-based modelling techniques.

This paper presents several new results in particle systems that were left as future research in our previous paper [12]. These results were used in the film *The Adventures of André and Wally B.* [7] to generate three-dimensional background images of a forest and of grass covering its floor. An example is shown in Figure 1.

Our new algorithms generate more sophisticated particle systems with greater internal structure. The strength of these stochastic modelling algorithms is their ability to transform a small set of simple constraints into a complete description of complex objects. The problem is that they create so much irregular, three-dimensional detail that exact visible surface and shading calculations become infeasible. Our solution is to exploit the visual complexity of the models by adopting approximate and probabilistic algorithms. The rich detail in the images tends to mask deviations from an exact rendering. We also present some recent work in stochastic modelling that enables us to model more complex motions, such as a field of grass blowing in the breeze. Finally, we analyze the performance of our current algorithms and discuss the potential gains of hardware support for rendering particle systems.

Several other researchers have modelled and rendered images of trees and vegetation. Brooks et. al. [3] at MAGI extended a combinatorial geometry system to model simple trees. Marshall et. al. [10] from Ohio State University used a

Figure 1. Forest Scene from *The Adventures of André and Wally B.*

procedural technique to generate polygonal models of trees. Both of these early efforts produced deterministic models of individual trees, whereas our algorithms create large groups of trees with stochastic variation.

More recently, Aono and Kunii [1] developed geometric models that are based on botanical descriptions of trees and that exhibit accurate branching structures. Their research emphasizes issues in modelling; our work is more strongly oriented towards creating complex, coloured images. Gardner [6] has simulated scenes of trees and terrain using textured quadric surfaces; his approach is more efficient than ours, but it creates objects that are less highly detailed. Smith [13] described a modelling technique called *graftals* that represents plants using Lindenmayer systems. Bloomenthal [2] has created remarkably realistic images of trees, based on finely-detailed surface-oriented representations. Both Smith and Bloomenthal emphasize the detailed structure of individual plants, whereas we take a more global view of a forest environment.

2. Structured Particle Systems

Particle systems were first used to model a wall of fire in the Genesis sequence from the film *Star Trek II: The Wrath of Khan* [11]. The fire is modelled as particles of light that move in three-space. Each particle system resembles a miniature volcano from which many particles explode upwards, eventually falling to the planet's surface due to the pull of gravity. A frame from this sequence, such as Figure 2, displays the trajectories of the visible particles during the time that the imaginary camera shutter is open to record the frame. The trajectories are approximated by a sequence of straight line segments, one per frame. Thus, a motion-blurred line is drawn to represent each particle.

Associated with each fire particle is a set of parameters that describe its position and characteristics: the location from which it erupted, its initial velocity, and attributes such as colour and size. At generation time, the parameters are assigned initial values, drawn from a random distribution. Each particle is generated and transformed through time independent of all other particles.

The particle systems that model natural phenomena such as trees and grass are more structured, and, consequently, the particles are not independent. Each tree is drawn as a set of line segments, and possibly small circles, that constitutes its branches and leaves. Many complex relationships exist among the particles representing the branches and leaves of a tree, as together they must form a cohesive three-dimensional object. The rest of this section describes new techniques and types of controls for generating *structured* particle systems.

2.1 Trees

The first step in modelling a forest scene is to populate the forest with individual trees, creating a tree data base that contains the location and type of each tree. The specifications in this pre-computed data base are subsequently used to generate and render the trees, frame-by-frame, during a second stage of the computation.

2.1.1 Creating the Forest

Sometimes the scene designer wishes to place each tree exactly, perhaps to simulate some real environment. The designer positioned the trees in Figure 3 with an interactive model editor to ensure that they fit into the scene with other, separately-computed elements.

When a vast number of trees are to be modelled, as in Figure 4, it is more practical to generate their locations procedurally with special-purpose programs. Our tree placement program requires four types of input: a grid size that controls the spacing between trees, a parameter that specifies the minimum distance between any pair of trees, one or more regions on the horizontal plane that will be filled with trees, and a terrain map that provides the elevation of points on the plane. The program creates at most one tree per grid point, generating random displacements independently in the x and y dimensions to offset the actual location of the tree from the given point. Should parts of the forest become more crowded than the minimum spacing parameter allows, grid points are left empty.

The layout of a landscape can be controlled even when the placement algorithm is stochastic. For example, texture maps can direct the program to leave the terrain bare where meadows, streams, or other open areas exist. An even more sophisticated placement algorithm could be based on empirical forestry models and consider factors such as elevation, water drainage, and sunlight to determine the density of growth.

Tree type selection is performed at the same time as tree placement. Each tree is assigned a type (e.g., maple, spruce, or aspen) either interactively or procedurally. The stochastic methods used for Figure 4 distribute the deciduous trees more densely in the valleys and evergreen trees more densely on the hills. The probability that a tree is evergreen increases with the elevation; we use a random number to choose among the possible tree types.

2.1.2 Generating a Tree

The particle systems program processes the trees in the data base serially; it generates a complete model for each tree and then renders the model. Starting with the main trunk, the algorithm constructs the tree by recursively generating subbranches. The data structure for the model is a tree in which each node describes a branch segment.

Before invoking the recursive branch generation procedure, the algorithm stochastically assigns a set of initial characteristics and dimensions. Some of these dimensions are illustrated in Figure 5.

The values for these parameters are randomly drawn from distributions associated with the tree's type. For example, the following equation determines the height of a tree:

$$Height = MeanHeight + Rand() \times DeltaHeight$$

where Rand() is a procedure returning a pseudo-random number uniformly distributed between -1.0 and +1.0. *MeanHeight* and *DeltaHeight* are specified for the tree type; they represent the mean height and the maximum difference from the mean. If the height is distributed uniformly between a and b, then *MeanHeight* is $\frac{a+b}{2}$, and *DeltaHeight* is $\frac{|b-a|}{2}$. In Figure 3, the deciduous trees have a *MeanHeight* of 60 and a *DeltaHeight* of 12; the evergreen trees also have a *MeanHeight* of 60, but a *DeltaHeight* of 16.

One parameter may depend on another. For example, the global *width* controls the breadth of the primary branches; this parameter is stochastically set to a fraction of the tree's height according to the equation:

$$Width = Height \times (MeanWidth + Rand() \times DeltaWidth)$$

MeanWidth is 0.6 for the deciduous trees, and 0.5 for the evergreens. *DeltaWidth* is 0.05 for the deciduous trees, and 0.25 for the evergreens.

Figure 3. André's Forest

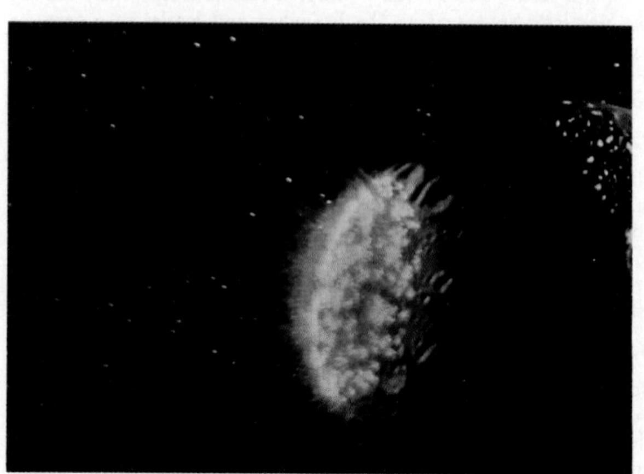

Figure 2. Frame from *Star Trek II: The Wrath of Khan*

Figure 4. Tree-covered Hills at Sunrise

The relationship between parameters need not be linear. For example, branches are tapered by decreasing the thickness as the distance d from the base of the branch increases, according to the equation:

$$thickness = thickness_b \times \sqrt{\frac{length - d}{length}}$$

where $length$ is the total length of the branch and $thickness_b$ is the thickness at its base.

The height of the lowest branch is stochastically set to a fraction of the tree's height. The distance between two sub-branches is drawn from a distribution that depends on the tree type and the thickness of the parent branch. Another control indicates whether branches occur singly or in whorls.

The parameters of the branch length distribution depend on the dimensions of the tree, as illustrated in Figure 5. An approximate bounding volume for the tree is computed from its height and width; its shape varies with the tree type, conical for evergreens and elliptical for deciduous trees. For each branch, we select a *branching angle* from a distribution associated with the tree type. We next compute *MeanLength*, the distance to the surface of the bounding volume from the position where the branch meets the trunk. The actual length of any branch is taken from a distribution centered on *MeanLength*.

A recursive algorithm generates sub-branches. We sample a distribution to obtain the ratio between the diameters of the parent and each sub-branch. The sub-branch inherits many parameters from its parent, but some controls are adjusted to the dimensions of the child. For example, sub-branches are spaced more closely together as the branch thickness decreases. The recursion stops either when a branch reaches a minimum thickness or at a specified maximum depth of recursion.

Characteristically, aspen trees, such as in Figure 3, have forked branches, but our evergreens do not. For each species, we specify a probability that a branch forks. A parent-child relationship exists between a branch and its sub-branch, but two forks of a branch have a sibling relationship and share probability distributions.

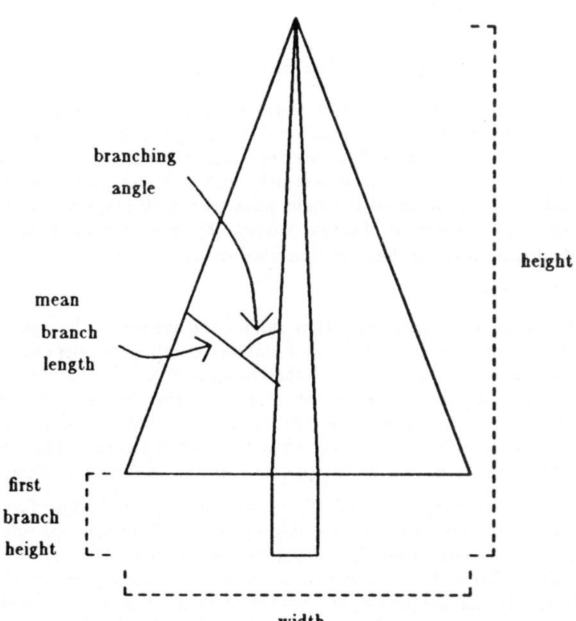

Figure 5. Dimensions Used in Tree Model

The colours in the image vary from tree to tree. The exact shades are offset by random amounts from mean values characteristic of the tree type. Two tables of colours are established for each tree, and the thickness of the branch determines which table is used. Colours for the trunk and main branches are taken from one table, and colours for the leaves from the other. Alternatively, one table may be used for old wood and the other for new.

The branch-generation algorithm produces trees with a regular structure, unlike real trees that have been affected by their environment and natural disasters. We simulate these effects by post-processing the three-dimensional description of the tree. Separate algorithms bend tree branches to simulate the effects of gravity, prevailing winds, and prevailing sunlight direction. Another algorithm randomly warps branches to simulate a form of catastrophe theory.

Finally leaves or needles are added to the branches that have no sub-branches. The stochastic parameters that control the placement and characteristics of leaves are: shape, orientation, spacing, density, colour, and location.

All of the random variables for the images in this paper were drawn from uniform distributions, as described above. In tuning the parameters, we concentrated more on visual results than on actual botanical data. Other, more accurate, distributions should be explored in the future.

Particle systems can be combined with elements computed using other techniques. For example, the tree trunks in Figure 3 were modelled as truncated, solid cones and rendered with conventional texture-mapping techniques.

Approximately 1.1 million particles compose the trees in Figure 3. Nearly sixty megabytes of binary data were generated from only twenty-one thousand bytes of input, resulting in a data amplification factor of over three thousand. The expansion factor is, naturally, less for scenes in which each object occupies only a small area of the screen. The input for the trees in Figure 4 was expanded by only a factor of four to generate fourteen megabytes of data; however, the input data base itself was generated procedurally from a much smaller specification.

2.2 Grass

The images of grass result from an extension of the work reported earlier by Reeves [12]. Clumps of grass are scattered randomly over the input terrain. A texture map, with a bird's-eye view of the terrain, optionally specifies the locations of bare spots or different types of grasses. Some stochastic parameters specify global parameters for an entire clump of grass: its position, orientation, area, density, and type.

Each clump contains many separate blades of grass. Both the structure of the clumps and the geometry of the individual blades are simpler than the models used for trees. Stochastic processes determine the number of blades within the clump and the characteristics for each blade: position, height, thickness, curvature, orientation, and colour. Short, straight-line particles approximate each blade's parabolic arc. Stochastic bends and kinks added to some blades of grass enhance the realism of the image. Simple flowers are created by adding yellow or blue particles to some blades of grass.

Eighteen thousand clumps of grass are visible in Figure 3. A total of 733,887 particles were drawn to render the grass.

3. Shading Models for Particle Systems

The fire particle systems require only simple shading calculations, because each particle is modelled as an independent light source[12]. Each fire particle is stochastically assigned an initial colour that changes over time according to a simple linear relationship that simulates cooling. The tree and grass particle systems reflect rather than emit light; they consequently require a more sophisticated shading model with ambient, diffuse, and specular shading components. For more realistic rendering, the shading algorithm also provides self-shadowing, external shadows, and coloured light sources.

A single tree may be composed of over one million independent particles. It would be a formidable task to shade each particle exactly, calculating whether it is in shadow and determining if it should be highlighted. In fact, unless the camera points directly at the sun from within the tree, it is almost impossible to tell whether or not any one leaf should be in shadow. Our solution is to use a probabilistic shading model for both the trees and the grass. For example, the particle's position and orientation determine the p-obability that it is in shadow. We calculate this probability and then use a random number to decide whether or not to render the particle as if it were in shadow.

3.1 Trees

Trees are self-shadowing, as branches and leaves of the tree shadow other parts of the same tree. In a forest, a tree is also shadowed externally by neighbouring trees. Our shading functions provide ambient, diffuse, and specular components and also approximate both forms of shadowing.

Highlights occur where the tree's branches or leaves are exposed directly to sunlight. This condition is most likely to exist close to the outer edge of the tree in the direction of the sun. Accordingly, the diffuse shading component for a particle varies with the distance into the tree from the light source, d_d, as shown in Figure 6. The diffuse component drops off exponentially as d_d increases according to the following equation:

$$D = e^{-\alpha d_d}$$

The parameter α controls the rate of the exponential dropoff. Random highlights are added by stochastically turning on a specular component whenever d_d is small and the cosine of the angle between the light direction and the branch direction is close to zero.

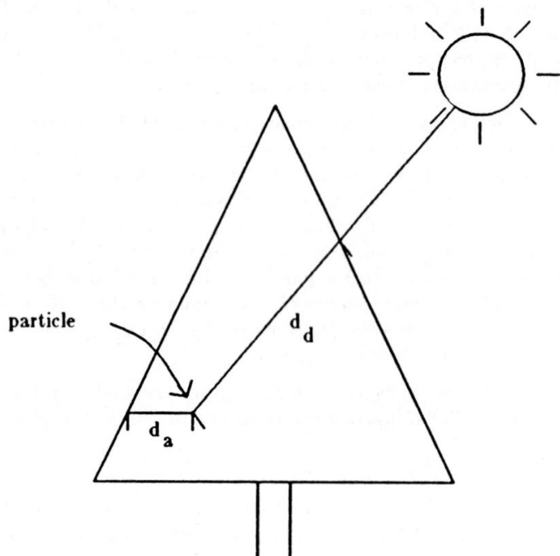

Figure 6. Distances Used by Tree Shading Algorithm

Self-shadowing is simulated primarily by controlling the ambient shading component. The ambient component for a particle drops off exponentially as the distance into the tree, d_a, increases. This distance, as shown in Figure 6, is independent of the position of the light source and represents the shortest distance from the particle to a point on the tree's bounding volume in a direction parallel to the ground. Another parameter, A_{min}, sets a minimum for the ambient component and guarantees that there is some light even in the deepest interior of the tree. The ambient component equation is therefore:

$$A = \max(e^{-\beta d_a}, A_{min})$$

A different problem is to add external shadows, those cast by other trees. Again, we use an approximation technique because exact computation of the shadows would be very expensive. The locations and heights of any trees positioned between a specified tree and the light source define a plane that skims the top of neighbouring trees and passes through the light source. An example is shown in Figure 7. Particles above this plane are in full sunlight, so the specular, diffuse, and ambient shading components all contribute to the shading calculation. The probability that sunlight reaches other parts of the tree decreases for particles located below the plane. If a particle is more than a specified distance below the plane, only the ambient shading component is used. For particles lying in between, a random number is selected to decide if the diffuse and specular components contribute to the shading.

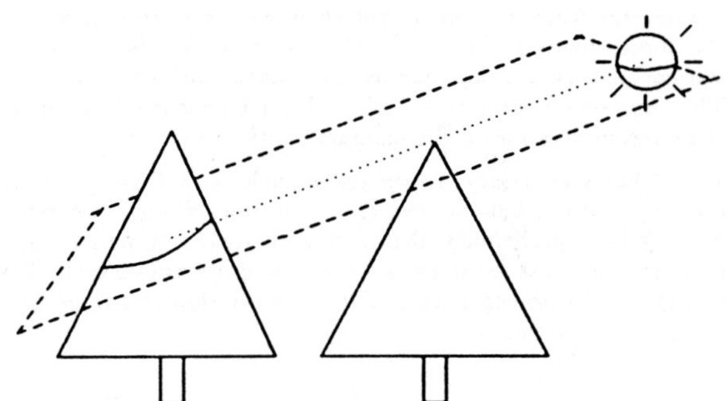

Figure 7. External Shadow Plane

To heighten the visual effect of the images in *André and Wally B.*, we used different colours for different types of light. A yellowish tinge to the diffuse and specular components produced an early morning sunrise warmth, and a bluish tinge to the ambient component of the light gave us a look inspired by the landscape artistry of Maxfield Parrish [8]. Figure 8 shows trees shaded with the techniques described in this section.

3.2 Grass

A similar stochastic algorithm shades the grasses. The contributions of both the diffuse and ambient components depend on the distance from the top of the clump of grass to the particle in question, decreasing exponentially as the depth increases. The difference between the two is that the diffuse component drops off much more quickly than the ambient component. As with trees, each lighting component can have a different colour.

The strongest visual effects are due to the shading function that casts tree shadows onto the grass. The principle idea behind our algorithm is a form of ray casting. We view the particle from the light source to see if it is visible through the trees. If the particle is not visible, it is in shadow. A simple and effective device for implementing this idea is the *shadow mask*. Our method is similar to a technique used by Lance Williams [15].

To create the shadow mask for a scene, we first compute an orthographic image of the trees from the direction of the light source. We then extract the silhouette information from this image and form a texture map. Before shading each particle of grass, we transform its position by this same orthographic transformation, effectively calculating a view of the particle from the light source. The calculated screen coordinates index into the shadow mask texture map to obtain a value that indicates how much the particle is in shadow. In the final colour computation, this value determines how much of the diffuse lighting component to use. If the particle is completely in shadow, only the ambient shading component is used. A single, pre-computed shadow mask is used for all frames in which the positions of the trees and of the light source remain constant. The shadow mask texture map in Figure 9 was used to shade the grass element in Figure 10.

The shadow mask technique effectively represents the shadows of trees on the grass because the trees are always between the grass and the sun. In general, the shadow mask technique works only if the objects casting the shadow are completely between the light source and the surface on which the shadow is cast. This limitation arises because the texture map that stores the shadow mask is only two-dimensional. Three-dimensional texture maps that store both depth and coverage information could solve this problem, but we have not explored this area.

4. Visible Surface Determination

Our previous research essentially ignored the visible surface problem with particle systems. The fires of *Star Trek II*, as shown in Figure 2, were composed of light-emitting particles. When several particles overlapped in a pixel, their colours were simply added together. With light-reflecting particles, such as those of the trees and grass, one particle can obscure another by being in front of it with respect to the selected camera position. We must now solve the visible surface problem.

The following sections describe two slightly different visible surface algorithms, one for the trees and one for the grass.

4.1 Trees

Consider a forest scene containing many trees. As we have seen, our stochastic generation algorithms usually attain a significant amount of data amplification. It is not feasible to generate particles for all trees in an image and then perform a traditional visible surface algorithm on them. Instead, we employ a painter's algorithm approach. We first sort all trees in the scene into a back-to-front order with respect to screen depth. Then, for each tree in turn, we generate a stochastic model, shade it, and render it into the image on top of any trees that have been previously rendered. As soon as a tree has been rendered, its data is discarded.

The accuracy of this back-to-front approach relies on the assumption that the bounding volumes of the trees do not intersect. While this assumption is inaccurate for forests in general, interesting images can be made with tree databases that conform to this restriction. The grass visible surface algorithm of the next section removes this non-intersecting restriction but is slightly more expensive.

Rendering each individual tree is not trivial either, as some branches of the tree obscure others. Within a tree we also apply a form of painter's algorithm that depends on a bucket sort. The bounding volume of the tree defines a set of buckets that are indexed by the eye space z distance of the particle — that is, by its depth into the scene. As a particle is generated, it is transformed into two-dimensional screen space and inserted into the bucket list corresponding to its average eye space z distance. After all particles have been generated, they are drawn in back-to-front bucket order on top of any particles that have already been rendered into the image. All particles are drawn as small, antialiased circles or short, antialiased straight line segments.

This bucket sort is another inexpensive but successful approximation. A completely accurate comparison sort of all the particles in a scene would require $O(n \log n)$ operations, where n is the number of particles. The approximate algorithm is linear in the number of particles, assuming that the trees have been sorted previously. Therefore, it requires only $O(m \log m + n)$ operations, where m, the number of trees, is much smaller than n. If we skipped the preliminary sort of the trees, a bucket sort of all particles could be accomplished with $O(n)$ operations, but the memory costs would be much greater. For our forest scenes, n typically ranges between 1.0 and 1.7 million. In contrast, m is usually less than 10,000, and, in close-up scenes such as Figure 11, it is only 195. We have never noticed any anomalies attributable to the bucket sort in any of our static or dynamic images. We commonly use about 2000 buckets. Even for a large tree, spanning fifty feet of depth, each bucket would cover a small area, about 0.3 inches. Since the images are so complex to start with, any imperfections are very difficult to detect as long as they are consistent from frame to frame.

4.2 Grass

We cannot create the appearance of a continuous carpet of grass without allowing clumps of grass to intersect. The visible surface algorithm for grass is more sophisticated than for trees because it permits intersecting clumps. The algorithm sorts the clumps of grass back-to-front and then calculates the bounding box of each clump in eye space. The clumps are generated in the back-to-front order, and the particles are entered into the bucket sort list. The difference is that the bucket list is not flushed and drawn at the end of each clump as it is at the end of each tree. Instead, only some of the buckets are drawn at the end of each clump. A bucket is drawn only if none of the bounding boxes from the remaining clumps overlaps it in eye-space z distance. Because the clumps are sorted, it is trivial to test for this condition.

Whenever the rear-most buckets are drawn, the range of the entire bucket list slides forward in eye-space z depth. Any undrawn particles remaining in the list may need to be reassigned to different buckets. This algorithm is more expensive than the non-intersecting tree algorithm because of two additional tasks – checking for overlapping buckets and reassigning particles when the range of the bucket list changes.

5. Complex Particle System Dynamics

The particle dynamics of the fires [11] were simple — each particle independently followed a parabolic trajectory. In the film *The Adventures of André and Wally B.*, the tree and grass elements were still. Since then, we have added realistic dynamics to depict a field of tall grasses blowing in the breeze. Stochastic models represent two phenomena, gusts of wind and the motion of wind-blown blades of grass.

The first step is to model wind. The scene designer specifies the terrain, a prevailing wind direction, and the average wind speed. A program generates wave fronts of particles that travel across the terrain. Each particle represents a small, localized gust of wind. The waves of particles display random variation, moving roughly parallel to the specified wind direction. New waves arrive at a rate that matches a specified wind gust frequency.

A *wind map* is a two-dimensional, top-down view of the terrain that specifies the wind intensity at discrete grid points. Letting the waves of particles move through time, we build a wind map for each frame of the animated sequence. The intensity of the wind at a particular location and time is determined by the number of wind gust particles close to the grid point.

Figure 8. Shaded Trees

Figure 11. Close-up Forest Scene

Figure 9. Shadow Mask

Figure 12. Still from Film of Blowing Grass

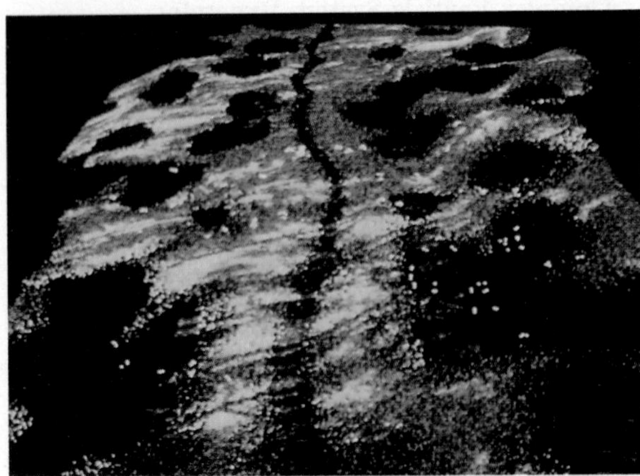

Figure 10. Grass Element Shadowed by Shadow Mask

Stochastic processes also model the reaction of the blade of grass as it is hit by a gust of wind. The simulated motion has the following key features:

- The blade bends around an axis that is perpendicular to the wind direction and passes through the blade's base.
- The amount of bending depends on the intensity of the gust of wind.
- The amount of bending increases with the distance from the ground, so that the blade is stiffest at its base.
- Over time and in the absence of other gusts, the blade returns to its original position following a damped sinusoidal motion called a *bending function*.
- The effects of successive gusts of wind are additive. At each frame, a bending function is generated and remembered for subsequent frames. The effective bending function at a given frame is the sum of all active bending functions.

The use of a two-dimensional wind map limits the motion of the wind to a plane. However, the algorithm achieves a three-dimensional look by tying each blade of grass to the ground and varying the degree of bending over the length of the blade.

Stochastic processes add further variation to the motion. For example, all blades do not bend exactly perpendicular to the wind direction, and blades close together use slightly different wind gust intensities. A blade of grass is bent by transforming the particles that represent it, taking care to keep them connected.

We can experiment with stochastic wind functions and wind maps, watching the wind patterns flow in real time on our vector display system. After adjusting the controls interactively, we can re-compute the motion in a few minutes to inspect the results. A short animated film of blowing grass has been computed. Figure 12 is one frame from the film.

6. Performance of Particle Systems Algorithms

In order to characterize the performance of particle systems algorithms, we measured the execution of four programs that produced different types of stochastic elements. All programs were run under Berkeley 4.2 UNIX† on an essentially idle VAX 11/750 with floating point accelerator and 4Mb of memory. The programs were written in C, except for some assembly-language routines for mathematical functions and matrix manipulation. We computed the elements twice, once storing the images in the virtual memory of the user process, as reported in Table 1, and once using a frame buffer with microcode line-drawing routines (which we call an *enhanced* frame buffer). All images were computed at 512 by 512 resolution.

Execution profiling explains where the cpu time is spent in the four programs. Table 2 shows the distribution of the user cpu time among three major phases of computation, described below:

1. generate,
2. shade and render, and
3. draw particles

The unaccounted time was consumed by global initialization, argument parsing, and sorting the data base. We also omit the time spent drawing trunks on the Near Trees, because they were not modelled by particle systems.

6.1 Generate

The details of model generation depend on the type of object being modelled. For example, one-fifth of the tree generation time is spent in the sin and cos routines, computing branch vectors based on the angle a branch makes with the trunk or parent branch. Simpler stochastic processes are used to generate the Fire element.

Model generation uses random numbers extensively. The incremental pseudo-random number generator in our math library takes about twenty-seven minutes to compute the twenty million random numbers used for the trees in Figure 4. In contrast, inline code accessing a pre-computed table of a few hundred random numbers takes less than four minutes. The table-driven approach creates satisfactory visual diversity and can provide, at approximately equal cost, random numbers drawn from any type of distribution. The visual success of this optimization has been observed by others [5,13].

6.2 Shade and Render

The second phase performs shading and perspective calculations, clips particles, and sorts them into screen-depth buckets. Perspective and clipping routines typically take between five and ten percent of the program's total running time. Shading also consumes about five to ten percent of the compute time for the trees and grass. Less time was spent shading the Far Trees than the Near Trees because simpler lighting models were used and external shadows were omitted. The least amount of time was spent on the shade and render phase for the Fire element, because it has the simplest shading models and requires no visible-surface calculations.

Floating point matrix and mathematical library routines accounted for about one-fifth of the total user time. These routines are called during both of the first two phases, but not in the final phase which uses only screen coordinates. Additional floating point operations are performed by in-line code in procedures outside the math and matrix libraries. For example, we examined a procedure that accounts for one-third of the tree generation time. More than three-fourths of the instructions in its inner loop were floating point instructions.

	Far Trees *Figure 4*	Near Trees *Figure 3*	Grass *Figure 3*	Fires *Figure 2*
number of frames	1	1	1	11
user cpu time (hh:mm:ss)	5:31:18	10:27:27	4:44:31	52:50
memory (Mb)	4.95	10.17	--	5.04
lines drawn (1000's)	592	1067	416	268
lines per frame (1000's)	592	1067	416	24

TABLE 1. Overall measurements for particle systems programs

	without frame buffer				with enhanced frame buffer			
	Far Trees	Near Trees	Grass	Fires	Far Trees	Near Trees	Grass	Fires
generate	32.5	11.4	13.8	28.3	47.6	18.6	25.0	37.9
shade and render	25.1	28.4	32.3	23.6	30.3	45.1	57.6	30.1
draw particles	33.2	49.9	51.6	41.0	14.8	19.6	13.2	23.6
total	90.8	89.7	97.7	92.9	92.7	83.3	95.8	91.6

TABLE 2. Percent of user time spent in each phase of computation

† UNIX is a trademark of Bell Laboratories.

6.3 Draw Particles

The final phase takes as input the description of particle primitives in two-dimensional screen coordinates and draws the primitives into the frame buffer. Our enhanced frame buffers have microcode routines for drawing anti-aliased lines and circles. The host provides the x and y coordinates for line endpoints, the width of the line, and its colour; the frame buffer then determines which pixels to modify. When a virtual frame buffer is used, both line-drawing calculations and address computation are performed in software, and drawing particles is the most expensive phase of the computation. As Tables 2 and 3 show, the frame buffer successfully takes over much of this work, leaving the host cpu to spend most of its time generating, shading, and rendering the model. Furthermore, the real frame buffer provides physical memory for the entire image and reduces the operating system costs for virtual memory management.

	Without frame buffer	With enhanced frame buffer	ratio with / without
Far Trees	5:31:18	4:06:05	.74
Near Trees	10:27:27	6:13:52	.60
Grass	4:44:31	2:34:42	.54
Fire	52:50	41:28	.78

TABLE 3. User time with and without a real frame buffer

An important advantage of the virtual frame buffer is its ability to store data of an arbitrary precision. The particle systems algorithm builds up a picture by repeatedly adding very small amounts of colour to a pixel. Experience indicates that eight bits per primary colour, while sufficient for displaying a finished image, are inadequate for computing some images. A real frame buffer with twelve to sixteen bits per colour and functions for drawing anti-aliased particle primitives would provide valuable hardware support for rendering particle systems.

Table 2 shows that Near Trees consumed proportionally more particle drawing time than Far Trees. Because the Near Trees particles appear larger on the screen, the line drawing calculations for each particle take longer.

6.4 Summary

Notably, no single phase of the computation dominates. Theoretical results obtained by Fournier show that the cost to compute a stochastic parametric surface by a fractal subdivision algorithm is linear in the number of points to be displayed [5]. He argues that if the subdivision algorithm is implemented efficiently, the time required to generate the model should be less than the time to transform, shade, and display it. From our measurements, we similarly conclude that the cost of creating an image with particle systems is not specifically due to the expense of generating the stochastic model, but is more generally explained by the inherent need to process a great deal of complexity in all phases of image creation. Even when we offload most of the costs of drawing primitives to the frame buffer, more time is typically required to manage, draw, and render the model than to generate it.

It is difficult to compare our measurements with the costs of creating synthetic images using traditional models. Images as complex as our forest scenes have rarely been modelled without using stochastic, or other algorithmic, methods to generate detail. When they have, the modelling effort must typically be measured in human design time. The costs of shading, visible surface calculations, and rendering are also difficult to compare with previous work, because few other measurements are available. Crow [4] and Whitted and Weimer [14] have published some measurements for pictures using conventional models, but their images were much simpler than ours. An interesting area for future work is the measurement and performance analysis of more general-purpose modelling and rendering software. We are currently investigating this area.

7. Conclusions

We have demonstrated that particle systems are able to model complex and structured objects. Simple primitives, given a set of relationships that bind them into a cohesive whole, can be used to produce complex models with extensive and varied detail. These relationships must specify the constraints by which millions of particles are dependent on one another. Because our new particle systems are more structured and dependent, we have developed more sophisticated algorithms to model their dynamics.

Particle systems were first used to model an amorphous phenomenon, fire, and it seemed natural to use a volume-filling representation. The tree and grass images demonstrate that volume-filling representations, such as particle systems, can effectively model solid objects. Such objects are conventionally modelled by surface-based techniques or solid geometry.

Procedural modelling techniques can be used to create models with more detail than a human designer could ever specify, and stochastic approaches can provide a rich variety of detail. Unfortunately, it is infeasible to compute exact solutions to the visible surface and shading problems for the enormous amount of detail that we can generate. Our algorithms are based on the belief that exact solutions are not always necessary in scenes with great visual complexity. We described an approximate painter's algorithm for visible surface determination and introduced probabilistic approaches to shading. Shadow masks, implemented as texture maps, simplified the task of adding shadows to the image.

Performance analysis shows that the computation is distributed relatively evenly among the three major phases of our particle systems algorithms: model generation, shading and rendering, and particle drawing. In particular, the cost of generating complex, structured models does not dominate the computation, as one might expect. Instead, the expense arises from the need to process a vast amount of three-dimensional detail throughout all phases of the computation in order to create the visual richness that we desire.

8. Acknowledgements

We would like to thank the members of the Computer Graphics Project of Lucasfilm Ltd for forming a stimulating and enjoyable working environment. John Lasseter contributed significantly to the visual design of the forest scenes and provided welcome encouragement. Eben Ostby developed special compositing software for the forest backgrounds. The shading algorithms profited from our discussions with Rob Cook. The work of the second author was supported in part by a State of California Microelectronics fellowship.

9. Bibliography

[1] Aono, M. and T. L. Kunii, Botanical tree image generation, *IEEE Computer Graphics and Applications 4*, 5 (May 1984), 10-34.

[2] Bloomenthal, J., Modeling natural trees with space curves, *SIGGRAPH 85, Computer Graphics 19*, 3 (July 1985).

[3] Brooks, J., R. Murarka, D. Onuoha, F. Rahn and H. Steingurg, An extension of the combinatorial geometry technique for modeling vegetation and terrain features, Contract report 159 for USA Ballistic Research Laboratories, Mathematical Applications Group, Inc., June 1974.

[4] Crow, F. C., A more flexible image generation environment, *SIGGRAPH 82, Computer Graphics 16*, 3 (July 1982), 9-18.

[5] Fournier, A., D. Fussell and L. Carpenter, Computer rendering of stochastic models, *Comm. ACM 25*, 6 (June 1982), 371-384.

[6] Gardner, G. Y., Simulation of natural scenes using textured quadric surfaces, *SIGGRAPH 84, Computer Graphics 18*, 3 (July 1984), 11-20.

[7] Lucasfilm Ltd, *The Adventures of André and Wally B.*, (film), Aug. 1984.

[8] Ludwig, C., *Maxfield Parrish*, Watson-Guptill, New York, 1973.

[9] Mandelbrot, B. B., *Fractals: Form, chance and dimension*, Freeman, San Francisco, 1977.

[10] Marshall, R., R. Wilson and W. Carlson, Procedure models for generating three-dimensional terrain, *SIGGRAPH 80, Computer Graphics 14*, 3 (July 1980), 154-162.

[11] Paramount, Genesis Demo from *Star Trek II: The Wrath of Khan*, in *SIGGRAPH Video Review Number 11*, June 1982.

[12] Reeves, W. T., Particle systems—A technique for modelling a class of fuzzy objects, *SIGGRAPH 83, Computer Graphics 17*, 3 (July 1983), 359-376.

[13] Smith, A. R., Plants, fractals, and formal languages, *SIGGRAPH 84, Computer Graphics 18*, 3 (July 1984), 1-10.

[14] Whitted, T. and D. M. Weimer, A software testbed for the development of 3d raster graphics systems, *Transactions on Graphics 1*, 1 (Jan. 1982), 43-58.

[15] Williams, L., Casting curved shadows on curved surfaces, *SIGGRAPH 78, Computer Graphics 12*, 3 (Aug. 1978), 270-274.

Chapter 4: Scan-Line Algorithms

Introduction

One of the earliest algorithms developed for image generation was the scan-line algorithm. This algorithm creates an image by processing the scene on a line-by-line basis, generating the picture by treating regions (windows) of the screen in turn, rather than treating each element of the scene. Windows are typically defined to be one scan line high, as wide as the screen, and are processed in a top-to-bottom fashion. Early scan-line algorithms were developed by Wylie et al. [Wyli67], Watkins [Watk70], Bouknight [Bouk70a] and Bouknight and Kelley [Bouk70b]. An excellent early survey is included in Sutherland et al. [Suth74].

The scan-line algorithm provides a generally fast method for image synthesis primarily because of the following: (1) the choice of the one-scan-line-high window allows a geometrical simplification of the processing, where visibility decisions can be made in a two-dimensional subset of three-dimensional space and (2) the *coherency* properties of an image can be exploited to speed the processing.

The geometrical simplification can be realized by considering the area described by a one-scan-line-high window to be a plane (with constant y value) in image space. The intersection of a polygon with this window can then be considered as a collection of line segments, and the visibility determination for the scan line can be carried out on these line segments, thus reducing a three-dimensional problem to a two-dimensional one. On a given scan line, a polygon is described in terms of its line segments and, most typically, by the endpoints of the segments.

The prototypical scan-line algorithm operates using three sorts: first, a y sort, then an x sort, and finally a z-depth sort to establish the visible element. This is illustrated in Figure 4.1. (We note that Sutherland et al. [Suth74] go into some depth discussing other sorting strategies.)

The purpose of the y sort is to limit the attention of the algorithm, on each scan line, to only those edges or faces that intersect the scan line. As processing for each scan line begins, the y-sorted structure is examined to find any new edges that enter on this scan line, and they are added to those already entered. Any edges that terminate on this scan line are discarded. This y-sorted structure is frequently implemented as an array of y buckets, one bucket per scan line.

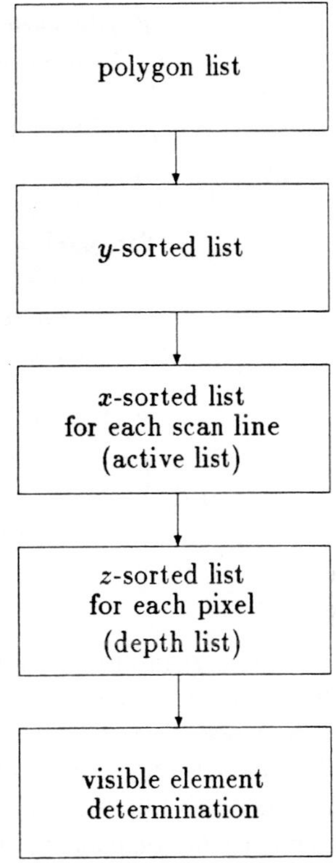

Figure 4.1: Flow in the Scan-Line Algorithm

The endpoints of line segments, which represent intersections of polygons and the scan line, are typically kept in an x-sorted structure, often called the "active list." This structure is modified whenever new polygons are entered from the y-sorted list (in which case new endpoints must be inserted into this list), whenever edges no longer intersect the plane representing the scan line (in which case, endpoints are removed from the list), and whenever incremental movement is made between scan lines. The x-sorted list can be retained from scan line to scan line by updating the endpoints to reflect the y value at the new scan line. This can be accomplished by a single addition, since edges of polygons are linear functions and the planes that represent the scan lines are a fixed distance apart. When the new x values are determined, they are resorted by increasing x. A bubble sort is often used, since it is optimal for the "nearly sorted" lists that result from the updating.

```
Scan Line Algorithm
    begin
    for each polygon P in the polygon list do {
        Insert P in a y-bucket according to its maximum y-value
        }
    for scanline = top_scanline to bottom_scanline do {
        if y-bucket[scanline] is not empty do {
            for each polygon P in y-bucket[scanline] {
                calculate the endpoints of P that intersect the scan line
                insert the endpoints onto the x-sorted list
                }
            }
        for pixel = left_pixel to right_pixel do {
            Construct z-depth list from the x-sorted list
            Construct the visible element(s) from the z-depth list
            Determine the pixel intensities from the visible element(s)
            }
        Update the x-sorted list for the next scanline
        }
    end
```

Figure 4.2: Basic Scan-Line Algorithm

The greatest variation in scan-line algorithms happens in the formation of the *z*-depth list. This list is formed from the *x*-sorted list. In the worst case, a *z*-depth list must be generated for each pixel to determine the visible element. In general, however, one can utilize characteristics of the scene to assist in reducing the computation time in this step. A general scan-line algorithm is given in Figure 4.2.

In the *x*-sorted list, the line segment between two consecutive endpoints is called a "span." If the objects in the scene do not penetrate each other, then we may assume that between the *x* values defining the span, only one object is visible. The processing of each sample span requires comparing the faces that fall within the span to determine which one is closest. This calculation can be performed completely with the *x* and *z* coordinates of the span, since the *y* coordinate is constant.

The basic differences between scan-line algorithms can usually be explained by stating how the algorithm handles the three sorted lists. For example, the *x*-sorted list may be used as input to a one-scan-line Z-buffer, thus avoiding the use of the *z*-depth list. One implementation that utilizes this is given by Fiume et al. [Fium83]. Crocker [Croc84] utilizes invisibility coherence (the fact that a primitive, invisible at one pixel, is also likely to be invisible at neighboring pixels) in the *x*-sorted list to substantially reduce the length of both the *x*-sorted and the *z*-depth list.

Whitted and Weimer [Whit82] (included in this chapter) explicitly calculate and store individual spans, with their illumination information, as a set of "span buffers." These span buffers can then be piped to different processes in the display pipeline to produce various image effects: spans that are obscured can be eliminated; spans can be tagged to make them selectively invisible; the image can be horizontally panned by translating the *x* coordinate of the spans; or, various illumination effects based upon the *z* coordinates of the span, can be generated.

Lane et al. [Lane80a] (included in this chapter) describe three algorithms used to render general bicubic patches: the Lane-Carpenter algorithm, the Whitted algorithm, and the Blinn algorithm.

The Lane-Carpenter algorithm utilizes the Bernstein-Bézier patch and its corresponding subdivision algorithm to recursively subdivide each patch until it is locally flat (within a set tolerance of being a four-sided planar polygon). In this case, they implement the *y*-sorted list as a set of *y* buckets, each bucket being a stack. As an entity *E* is popped from the stack, it can take one of two paths through the algorithm: (1) if E is a polygon, it is put onto the *x*-sorted list and (2) if E is a patch, it is subdivided into four subpatches. Each subpatch is tested for flatness and, if flat, is separated into two triangles (using the corners of the patch as vertices). The triangles are then pushed onto their corresponding *y* bucket. If the subpatch is not flat, it is pushed onto its corresponding *y* bucket and will pop out of the *y* buckets at a later time and be subdivided once again. This algorithm is outlined in Figure 4.3. In this manner, the *y*

```
Scan Line Algorithm for Procedural Entities
    begin
    for each entity E in the entity list do {
        Insert E in a y-bucket according to its maximum y-value
        }
    for  scanline = top_scanline to bottom_scanline do {
        while y-bucket[scanline] is not empty do {
            get entity E from y-bucket[scanline]
            if E is a polygon then {
                calculate the endpoints of P that intersect the scan line
                insert the endpoints onto the x-sorted list
                }
            }
                else {
                    Refine E into subentities E1, E2, ..., En
                    Insert each Ei in a y-bucket according to
                      its maximum y-value
                    }
            }
        for pixel = left_pixel to right_pixel do {
            Construct z-depth list from the x-sorted list
            Construct the visible element(s) from the z-depth list
            Determine the pixel intensities from the visible element(s)
            }
        Update the x-sorted list for the next scan line
        }
    end
```

Figure 4.3: Scan-Line Algorithm Extension for Procedural Entities

buckets can handle both polygonal entities and patch entities. Only the polygonal entities are inserted in the *x*-sorted list.

This algorithm generally works well, but it suffers from typical problems of subdivision in that it is possible to determine one patch flat and yet subdivide an adjoining patch (see Figure 4.4). This creates the possibility of a crack appearing in the surface. Lane and Carpenter [Lane79] have partially addressed this problem by using a method that guarantees flatness after a specified number of subdivisions.

This problem was also addressed by Clark [Clar79 (included in this chapter). Clark uses screen-space curvature as the primary consideration in the flatness test and a subdivision criterion based only upon the patch edges that avoids the cracks inherent in the straightforward subdivision method.

The visible-surface algorithm by Whitted (in [Lane80a]), subdivides bicubic patches by inserting internal edges at constant u and v values and at silhouette edges of the patch. The internal edges inserted in the patch define subpatches, each of which can be assumed to be nearly planar. These subpatches are then passed to the active list. Updating the edges of the entities in the active list is done by numerical iteration to insure accuracy. The Blinn algorithm (in [Lane80a]) passes non-polygonal entities (without subdivision) to the active list, updating the edges of the entities by numerical iteration. Care must be taken here to examine the normal to the surface and insert new endpoints for silhouette edges.

Atherton [Athe83] (included in this chapter) utilizes the scan-line paradigm to render scenes containing solid models derived from Boolean combinations of a limited set of primitives. This *Constructive-Solid-Geometry (CSG)*technique is widely used in the computer-aided-design area. This algorithm forms a *z*-depth list at each span endpoint. The ordered elements of this list are then evaluated versus the CSG tree to determine the visible element. If the visible elements calculated for two consecutive span endpoints agree, the visible element is thought to be visible throughout

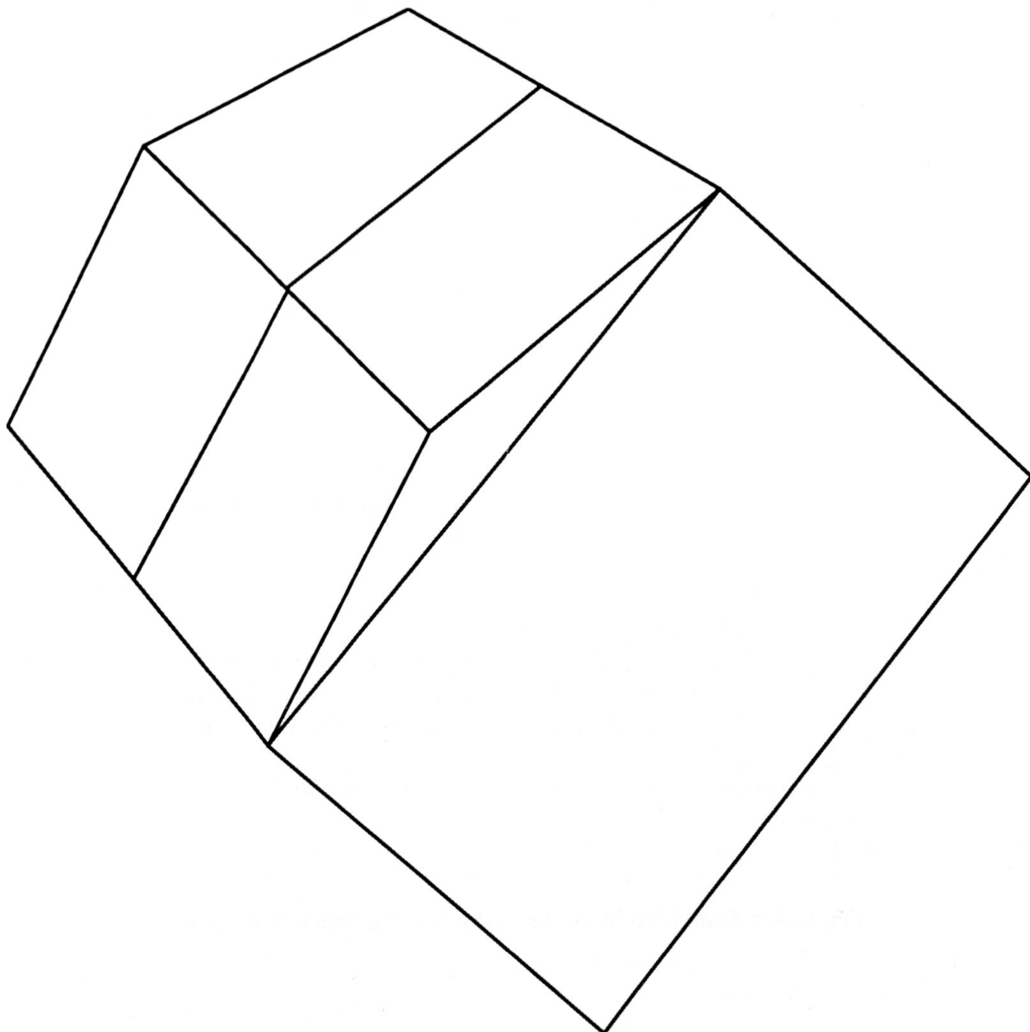

Figure 4.4: Cracks Caused by Subdivision

the span. If the visible elements at the endpoints do not agree, the span interval is subdivided, a new *z*-depth list is generated at the midpoint of the interval, and the process is repeated on each subinterval.

Shadows have been generated by using the scan-line paradigm by inserting special "shadow polygons" into the database. These polygons are generated by planes defined by contour edges of the objects in the scene and the light-source position. After forming the *z*-depth list, a counting method can be used to determine whether the visible point is in shadow. While this method was initially described by Crow [Crow77a], implementation details can be found in Bergeron [Berg86].

Max [Max86b] (included in this chapter) has developed a related scheme to determine shadows. In this work, the scan-line windows are generated radially from the light source, which guarantees that the shadows can be incrementally calculated upon the spans for each "scan line." The method also allows the calculation of intensity due to atmospheric scattering. Resampling of the data must occur in order to reconstruct a displayable image.

The fractal-generation algorithm of Fournier et al. [Four82] (included in this chapter) utilizes a small database and a stochastic-generation algorithm to enhance the database of polygons into a complex image. This algorithm can also be implemented with the Lane-Carpenter [Lane79] strategy by repeatedly pushing the stochastically subdivided pieces back into the *y* buckets until they are the desired size.

"A Softbed Test-Bed for the Development of 3-D Raster Graphics Systems" by T. Whitted and D.M. Weimer from *Proceedings of SIGGRAPH '81*, 1981, pages 271-277. Copyright 1981, Association for Computing Machinery, Inc., reprinted by permission.

A Software Test-Bed for the Development of 3-D Raster Graphics Systems

Turner Whitted
David M. Weimer
Bell Laboratories
Holmdel, New Jersey 07733

Abstract

We describe a set of utility routines for 3-D shaded display which allow us to create raster scan display systems for various experimental and production applications. The principal feature of this system is a flexible scan conversion processor that can simultaneously manage several different object types.

Communications between the scan conversion routine and processes which follow it in the display pipeline can be routed through a structure called a "span buffer" which retains some of the high resolution, three dimensional data of the object description and at the same time has the characteristics of a run length encoded image.

KEY WORDS AND PHRASES: computer graphics, shaded display, visible surface algorithms, graphics systems

CR CATEGORIES: 8.2

Design Philosophy

The most straightforward approach to shaded display of three dimensional objects has been to store all surface elements of a scene in main memory and produce images one scan line at a time. The advantage of this method is that all elements which are potentially visible at any point on the image are immediately accessible to the display process. In practice this means that anti-aliasing can be readily accomplished [5], and real-time performance is feasible [20,10]. Although main memory size appears to limit the complexity of the images that this method can produce, Crow [7] has demonstrated that appropriate tricks will enable the display of complex scenes.

Alternatively, one may process small parts of an object description one at a time, accumulating the final image in a frame buffer memory. If extra bits are provided in the frame buffer for depth values, then the object parts may be processed in any order using the z-buffer algorithm [4,13]. Otherwise they must be sorted in back-to-front order before being scan converted and written into a frame buffer [14]. The two advantages of this approach are linear growth of the processing time with respect to the complexity of the object description and the ability to manage object descriptions of unlimited complexity.

This technique of accumulating an image one part at a time has facilitated the development of "hybrid" display systems which can process more than one object type. Newell's use of procedure models [15] is a good example. The Computer Graphics Research Group at Ohio State developed a display system that incorporates lines and points as well as polygons as primitives [8] and includes procedure models for producing extremely complex object descriptions. The hybrid display system designed by Jim Blinn at JPL is capable of displaying higher order surfaces as well as polyhedra.

For a broad range of applications, no single approach to display system design will adequately meet the requirements of each application. Baecker [1] describes several display system configurations and points out their application specific strengths and weaknesses. Recognizing the drawbacks of a rigid approach, we have constructed a flexible tool for the development of 3-D raster display systems. It is designed to be a "test-bed" that can easily incorporate a variety of user defined techniques while remaining reasonably efficient. The test-bed can be assembled into the configurations previously mentioned, and is further capable of a configuration that allows images to be accumulated one part at a time, in any order, while retaining the information needed to perform anti-aliasing. In addition it can be arranged as a hybrid system that simultaneously processes a variety of object types in a single pass.

System Elements

The whole idea behind the test-bed is to minimize the amount of special programming required for new applications. Consequently, a variety of common routines are offered to the user to be assembled in a manner to suit the application.

Certain properties of the system are fixed - it generates an image in scan line order, and it requires that surfaces be ultimately reduced to planar convex polygons (although not necessarily prior to scan conversion). Its basic elements are also quite ordinary- a transformation and clipping front end, a scan conversion processor, and a shader. Data passed from the scan converter to the shader may be routed through a "span buffer". The advantages of this option are explained later in the section on span buffers and anti-aliasing.

The format for object descriptions is shown in figure 1. Each object is described in terms of polygons which in turn are described by edges which contain vertices. Any hierarchical organization at a level higher than single objects may be imposed by the user but isn't recognized by the display routines. In the default mode, the test-bed routines allocate only enough memory to store the object description being processed. An option exists for allocating additional memory to store polygons and edges which are created by procedure models during the course of scan conversion.

Each of the vertex elements except depth (z) is a 16-bit number. Fifteen bits of this resolution are used to define screen coordinates with $-16384 < x,y < 16384$ and $(x=0,y=0)$ at the center. Z is represented by a 32-bit number with the binary point in the middle. Since perspective transformations compress large, positive z values, this extra precision is required for determining the relative visibility of distant, closely spaced objects. These coordinates are completely independent of the display resolution. In fact, the display routines are written in such a manner that a user can specify any desired resolution between 2x2 and 16384x16384 by altering a single header file.

Transformation and clipping of conventional, passive polygonal object descriptions proceed in the following order: All rotation, translation and scaling are done first, followed by a clip against the near clipping plane. Then comes the perspective divide followed by clipping against the remaining clipping planes. The reason for this ordering is to avoid having the perspective divide wrap objects behind the viewer around to the front before clipping. This was the easiest scheme to implement, but it is currently being replaced by a routine to perform all clipping before the perspective divide. Parameters associated with the perspective and viewing transformations are kept as global variables throughout the display process so that they may be "undone" by those shaders which need to find the original object space coordinates of a point. (For an explanation of transformations associated with the display process, see the text by Newman and Sproull [16].)

The flexibility of the scan conversion routine stems from its facility for on-the-fly procedural expansion which is discussed in the next section. Otherwise it is conventional in the way that it processes polygon edges. For each scan line, any edge which is intersected first by that scan line is added to a list of active edges. The

Object description	
header	part identifier no. of polygons no. of edges no. of vertices head of poly list
polygons	poly identifier ptr to first edge storage mask
edges	forward list ptr backward list ptr interpolation mask ptr to polygon(1) ptr to polygon(2) ptr to vertex(1) ptr to vertex(2)
vertices	x (position) y (position) z (position) nx (normal) ny (normal) nz (normal) u (texture index) v (texture index)

Figure 1. Object description format

endpoints of each active edge are represented by at least an x-position, a z-position, and a shade value. Up to nine additional variables may be associated with each edge endpoint. The scan converter interpolates these variables along each edge using the familiar difference equation,

$$x_{n+1} = x_n + \Delta x$$

where

$$\Delta x = \frac{(x_2 - x_1)}{(y_2 - y_1)} \cdot \frac{32768}{resolution},$$

and (x_1,y_1,z_1) and (x_2,y_2,z_2) are, respectively, the upper and lower endpoints of the edge. Maintaining high resolution for the interpolated variables is necessary for anti-aliasing and makes variable resolution a little easier. As an edge is activated, the 16-bit quantities stored in the object description are placed in the upper half of a 32 bit number in the active edge descriptor (z is already a 32-bit number). By assigning the fractional part of each variable to the lower 16 bits of the number, the effects of round-off error in the interpolation are avoided. Since it would be wasteful to either store or interpolate meaningless data, storage and interpolation masks are included in the object description. The test-bed routines allocate memory in the active edge list according to bits set in the storage mask and interpolate active edge variables indicated by the interpolation mask. The scan converter can then be totally ignorant of the meaning of the variables that it interpolates, allowing the user to assign variables to such data as surface normal components, texture map indices, or reflected intensity values in a completely arbitrary manner. One could, for instance, simultaneously perform Gouraud [9] shading on specified polygons and Phong [17] shading on others. The shader need only check the interpolation mask to determine which technique applies for each polygon.

The list of active edges contains forward and backward pointers to allow the user to maintain the list in x-order. This ordering is required for visibility calculations using a Watkins [20] type algorithm, but isn't always necessary. We typically traverse the list of active polygons for each scan line to create spans which are passed to the shader. The shader then relies on either a z-buffer or a scan line depth sort to determine visibility.

Because of our interest in realism, we have had occasion to write several different shaders for various purposes. Two of them - a simple Gouraud shader and a Phong shader without bells and whistles - are provided as building blocks for users.

We recognize that many users are not interested in building display systems. In most cases they only need a mechanism for creating images from their own data bases. For such users, a "standard" system has been constructed. It stores all polygons prior to scan conversion, and it produces a 512 by 512 pixel Gouraud shaded monochrome image file. It is left to the user to convert his data to the proper object description format. For anything more complicated, we require the user to spend some time learning details of the test-bed.

A Generalized Scan Conversion Processor

A typical scan conversion routine that operates on a passive object description, i.e. a list of polygons and their edges, will begin its processing by performing a "bucket sort" on all of the edges in the object description based on the maximum y value of each edge. Each bucket corresponds to an individual scan line and contains a list of pointers to all edges that become active on that scan line.

For the raster test-bed, the scan converter is a generalization of one described by Lane and Carpenter [11] in which every scan line bucket is a stack. Elements that can be pushed onto the stack include not only polygon edges, but control points for bi-parametric surfaces, bounding boxes for procedurally defined surfaces, or whatever else the user specifies.

At every scan line, elements are popped off the stack until it is empty. As each element is popped, a subroutine corresponding to the element's type is called. With one exception, each of these routines results in new elements being pushed onto the current stack or the stack for a lower numbered scan line (i.e. a scan line whose y value is less than or equal to that of the current scan line). The exception is the routine that places polygon edges in the active edge list. This means, of course, that in order for all stacks to become empty, each type of element must ultimately be reduced to polygons. The process is outlined in figure 2. The particular patch splitter that we use is the Lane-Carpenter algorithm [12], although others [4,6] will work perfectly well.

```
procedure scan_convert
begin
    for each scan line do
    begin
        for each active edge do
        begin
            bump edge variable values
            if(edge no longer active)
            begin
                delete edge
                if(all edges of poly inactive)
                begin
                    delete poly
                end
            end
        end
        while stack not empty do
        begin
            pop(current scan line)
            if(type = edge) then
            begin
                add edge to active list
                if(poly not yet active)
                begin
                    add poly to active list
                end
            end
            else if(type = patch) then
            begin
                if(patch nearly planar) then
                begin
                    add approximating polygon
                        to object description
                end
                else
                begin
                    split into subpatches
                    push(ymax1) subpatch 1
                    push(ymax2) subpatch 2
                    push(ymax3) subpatch 3
                    push(ymax4) subpatch 4
                end
            end
            else if(type = ...) then
            begin
                ...
            end
        end
    end
end
```

Figure 2. Generalized scan conversion routine.

This on-the-fly expansion can be extended to any procedure that automatically produces a maximum y-value as part of the expansion. To take full advantage of the technique, the expansion procedures must also provide built-in garbage collection to prevent the accumulation of intermediate surface elements. For instance, once a procedurally generated edge is added to the active edge list it must be removed from the object description. When all edges of a procedurally generated polygon have been added to the active list, then the polygon description must be returned to free storage.

In addition to patch subdivision, we are currently incorporating a fractal surface subdivision procedure [3]. The test-bed has also been used to develop procedures for on the fly expansion of hierarchical object descriptions [18].

The prominent feature of this general purpose scan converter is its ability to process mixed object descriptions without either first sorting all objects by depth or maintaining a z-buffer for the entire image. Like other schemes that allow on-the-fly reduction to polygons, it can display complicated scenes without having to store all elements in the scene at once.

Span Buffers

The span buffer is a linked list of scan line segments formed when the edges of a surface element are intersected by a scan line. Use of this type of list to accumulate images which are being generated one part at a time is not new. The implementation of Newell, Newell, and Sancha's list priority algorithm [14] stored spans, called "beads", as a way of conserving memory. Hackathorn [8] describes a technique for accumulating run lengths in main memory to avoid frequent accesses to a bit map version of an image stored on disk. The spans referred to in this paper are similar to run length codes, but they contain considerably more three dimensional information.

For each span (figure 3) there are left and right edge intersection points such that each span is defined by its left x position, left z position, length in x, and $\Delta z/\Delta x$. If a Gouraud shader is used in the final display stage, then an intensity value, i, and $\Delta i/\Delta x$ are part of the span definition. Otherwise the three surface normal components and their rates of change are stored. Other quantities which can be interpolated across the span are texture map indices, direction to viewer, and direction to light source (for nearby light sources). As many or as few quantities as necessary may be included in each span definition.

Span buffer	
header	scan line number no. of spans no. of endpoints ptr to first span
spans	object id ptr to next span ptr to left endpoint ptr to right endpoint
endpoint	x (position) z (position) nx (normal) ny (normal) nz (normal) u (texture index) v (texture index) ....etc....

Figure 3. Span buffer format.

There are a variety of operations that can be performed on span buffers to produce useful effects. One of the simplest is to maintain the list in depth order while building up the image. Then all the properties of list-priority algorithms, including the ability to simulate transparency, are available without the need for an *a-priori* depth sort on polygons in the object description.

A second operation is garbage collection - i.e. the elimination of spans that are completely obscured by others. In its simplest form, this operation is merely a scheme for increasing the efficiency of the display process by minimizing the number of unnecessary operations performed by the shader. At its most complex it actually performs the visibility calculation by removing all but the visible spans.

A summary of the other operations follows:

Selective display - spans can be tagged to make them selectively invisible. This allows such operations as peeling the skin from a complex assembly to reveal the innards.

Horizontal panning - a crude way of moving the background portions of an image without recreating them. Movement involves only translating the x position of the span. Obviously, different parts can be moved at different rates. For 3-D animation this is not a very useful feature since better looking results can be obtained by applying all movement in the scene to the object description before generating the image. However, the span buffer can be applied to multi-plane (2-1/2 D) animation as well as the 3-D variety. Panning is a valuable multiplane technique.

Cyclic animation - a special case of selective display in which different spans are made visible in different frames to produce an effect like that of color map animation [19] but one that is more powerful.

Fast previewing - if several frames of animation are stored as span buffers, then the sequence may be rapidly previewed by using a fast, low quality shading technique. If the sequence is satisfactory, then it can be run through a high quality shader for filming or recording. Since the span buffer is the same in both cases, their is no need to redo any of the processing that preceded the shader.

Clearly, some care must be exercised when performing more than one span buffer operation at a time. For instance, indiscriminate garbage collection may interfere with the selective display feature.

As one might expect, span buffers require huge amounts of memory. Unless their advantages are important for a particular application their use is best avoided since they not only consume tens of megabytes of disk space, but require a corresponding amount of time for reading, updating, and writing.

Anti-aliasing

A small modification to the system elements provides an effective means of performing anti-aliasing with span buffer data. Spans can be thought of as the top and bottom edges of trapezoids that are created by clipping polygons against successive scan lines. The left and right edges of these trapezoids are implicitly defined by the span endpoints. Some polygons do not reduce to trapezoids when clipped against the scan lines (figure 4). If the notion of a span is generalized to include these edges which "fall between the cracks", then the span buffer will contain enough information to allow the use of an anti-aliasing tiler such as Catmull's [5].

The necessary addition to the span buffer is a number associated with each endpoint to denote the fractional y offset of the endpoint from the bottom scan line. For spans representing the tops and bottoms of trapezoids the number is zero. A change is also required in the edge activation procedure. When anti-aliasing is not performed, edges that fall between scan lines are discarded. For proper anti-aliasing, a subroutine is included that converts the edge to a properly formated span and adds it to the span buffer.

The most important feature of the span buffer is that it allows the image to be accumulated one piece at a time without losing the information needed for anti-aliasing.

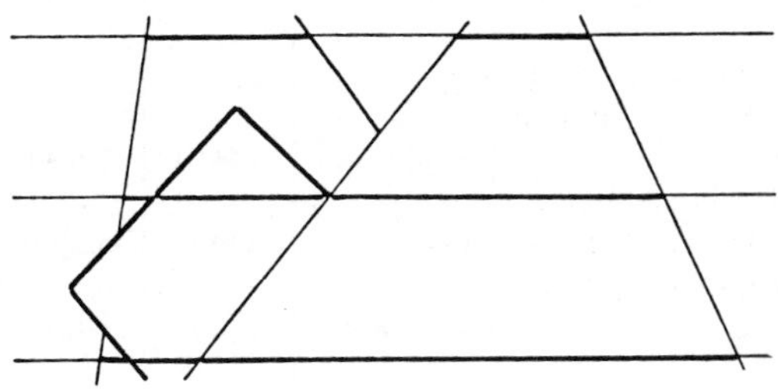

Figure 4. Strip between scan lines

Capabilities and Performance

We originally planned this system to be a development aid for several of our own projects involving a 3-D graphics editor, an animation language, further research on shaders, an the substitution of LSI circuits for parts of the display process. In addition we have made it available to people who needed a convenient mechanism for making pictures.

The entire test-bed is coded in the C language and has been tested on two machines (a PDP-11/45 and a VAX-11/780) running the UNIX operating system.[1] Because C allows the programmer to declare variables as either 16 or 32 bit integers independently of machine word length, identical code will run on either machine. We do find, however, that the larger addressing space of the 32 bit machine is necessary for conducting any really useful work.

So far our most intense area of activity has been shader development. Figure 6 is the product of a shader that incorporates shadows, transparency, and texture mapping. The shader uses Williams' shadow algorithm [23] and Blinn's bump mapping technique [2] for the texture mapped lettering. Three routines were assembled from test-bed elements to generate the texture map, to generate the shadow map, and to create the final image. For the case of the shadow map and the final image, both the curved and polygonal objects were displayed in a single pass through the scan conversion processor. The ability to simulate transparency is gained by maintaining a depth ordered span buffer.

Since the object description for figure 7 was too complex to process at one time, it was produced by multiple passes through the scan conversion processor and accumulated in a span buffer. Figure 8 is a combination of separate images of the chessmen, their reflections, and the chess board. The object in figure 9 is a fractal terrain model.

Figure 11 is representative of a simpler object description being used to measure the performance of hardware augmented z-buffer programs [22]. In this project the raster test-bed has actually been cannibalized to yield a bare bones display routine. The inner loop of the program is currently being transferred to a set of LSI chips.

Figure 5 summarizes some of the performance measurements taken from the test-bed while producing figures 6,7,9,10 and 11. Execution times given for the shader include z-buffer initialization and comparisons. Overall, we have found that the test-bed permits us to quickly try new ideas without writing much new code. While anything but the most naive use of the system requires some effort on the part of a potential user, we feel that this is small price when compared to the flexibility offered by the test-bed.

Acknowledgements

This system incorporates features that were suggested to us in conversations with a number of helpful people including Frank Crow of Ohio State University, Jim Blinn of JPL, Ed Catmull and Loren Carpenter of LucasFilm Ltd., Jeff Lane of Boeing, and Lance Williams of NYIT. We also wish to thank Steve Rubin for acting as our first user and main guinea pig. Experiments with span buffers are an extension of work [19] that was performed with support from the National Science Foundation, Grant MCS-75-06599.

[1] UNIX is a trademark of Bell Laboratories; PDP, and VAX are trademarks of Digital Equipment Corp.

Performance summary						
				percent time by routine		
picture	polys	edges	cpu time[1] (seconds)	scan convert	shade	misc
Figure 6	23554	70661	341	36	61	3
Figure 7	32000	44000	520	60	40	-
Figure 9	12492	19450	320	20	80	-
Figure 10	18188	28421	250	70	30	-
Figure 11	1800	2760	16	41	58	1

[1] all times are for 512x512 images without anti-aliasing.

Figure 5. Statistics for five pictures.

References

[1] Baecker, R., Digital video display systems and dynamic graphics, *Computer Graphics*, 13,2 (August 1979), 48.

[2] Blinn, J.F., Simulation of wrinkled surfaces, *Computer Graphics*, 12,2 (August 1978),286.

[3] Carpenter, L.C., and Fournier, A., and Fussell, D., Display of fractal curves and surfaces, to appear, *Comm. ACM*.

[4] Catmull, E., A subdivision algorithm for computer display of curved surfaces, PhD thesis, University of Utah, 1974.

[5] Catmull, E., A hidden surface algorithm with anti-aliasing, *Computer Graphics*, 12,3 (August 1978), 6.

[6] Clark, J.H., A fast algorithm for rendering parametric surfaces, supplement to *Computer Graphics* (distributed to SIGGRAPH '79 attendees), August 1979.

[7] Crow, F.C., Computer graphics in the entertainment industry, *Computer*, 11,3 (September 1977), 11.

[8] Csuri, C., Hackathorn, R., Parent, R., Carlson W., and Howard, M., Towards an interactive high visual complexity animation system, *Computer Graphics*, 13,2 (August 1979), 289.

[9] Gouraud, H., Continuous shading of curved surfaces, *IEEE Trans. Cmptrs*, C-20 (June 1971), 623.

[10] Jackson, J.H., Dynamic scan-converted images with a frame buffer display device, *Computer Graphics*, 14,3 (July 1980), 163.

[11] Lane, J.M., and Carpenter, L.C., A generalized scan line algorithm for the computer display of parametrically defined surfaces, *Computer Graphics and Image Processing*, vol. 11 (1979), 290.

[12] Lane, J.M., Carpenter, L.C., Blinn, J.F., and Whitted, T., Scan line methods for displaying parametrically defined surfaces, *Comm. ACM*, 23,1, (January 1980), 23.

[13] Myers, A.J., An efficient visible surface program, Report to National Science Foundation, Grant No. DCR74-00768 A01, Computer Graphics Research Group, Ohio State Univ., July 1975.

[14] Newell, M.E., Newell, G.S., and Sancha, T.L., A Solution to the hidden surface problem, Proc. of the ACM annual conference, 1973, 443.

[15] Newell, M.E., The utilization of procedure models in computer synthesized images, PhD thesis, University of Utah, 1975.

[16] Newman, W.M., and Sproull, R., *Principles of Interactive Computer Graphics*, McGraw-Hill, 1973.

[17] Bui-Tuong Phong, Illumination for computer generated pictures, *Comm. ACM*, 13,6 (June 1975), 311.

[18] Rubin, S.M., The representation and display of scenes with a wide range of detail, submitted for publication.

[19] Shoup, R., Color table animation, *Computer Graphics*, 13,2 (August 1979), 8.

[20] Watkins, G.S., A real-time hidden surface algorithm, PhD thesis, Univ. of Utah, 1970.

[21] Whitted, J.T., A processor for display of computer generated images, dissertation, North Carolina State University, August 1978.

[22] Whitted, T., Hardware enhanced 3-D raster display systems, Proceedings of Canadian Man-Computer Communication Conference, June 1981.

[23] Williams, L., Casting curved shadows on curved surfaces, *Computer Graphics*, 12,2 (August 1978), 270.

Figure 6. More bottles and glasses.

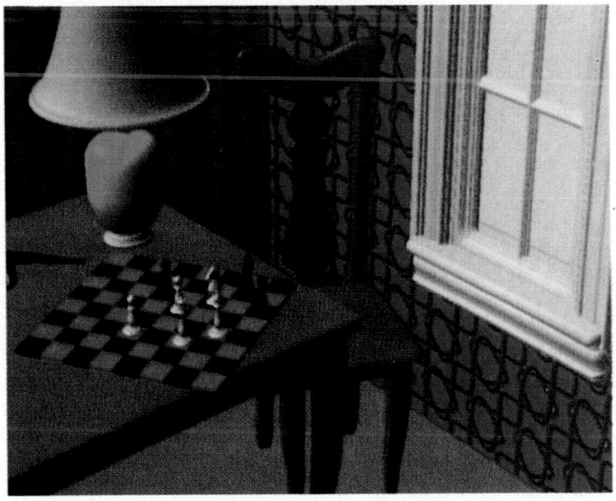

Figure 7. Room scene.

Figure 8. Foggy chessmen.

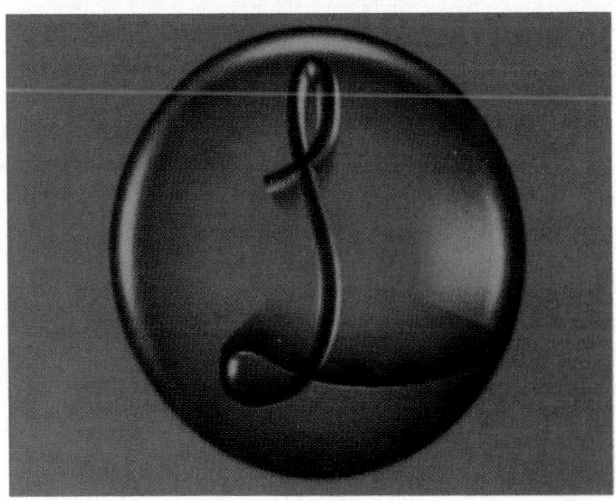

Figure 9. Logo.

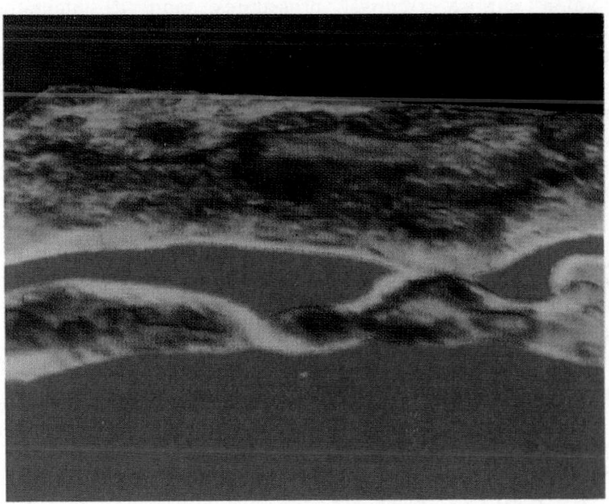

Figure 10. Fractal terrain.

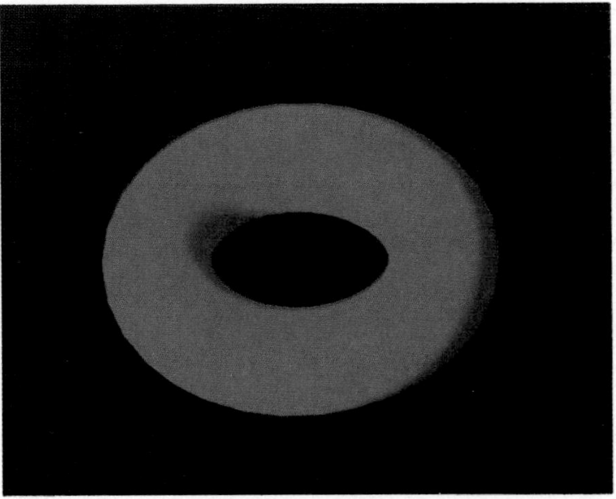

Figure 11. 30-sided torus.

"A Scan-Line Hidden Surface Removal Procedure for Constructive Solid Geometry" by P.R. Atherton from *Proceedings of SIGGRAPH '83*, 1983, pages 73-82. Copyright 1983, Association for Computing Machinery, Inc., reprinted by permission.

A SCAN-LINE HIDDEN SURFACE REMOVAL PROCEDURE FOR CONSTRUCTIVE SOLID GEOMETRY

Peter R. Atherton

General Electric Company
Corporate Research and Development
Schenectady, New York 12345

Abstract

This paper presents a new methodology for resolving visible surface images of solid models derived from Boolean combinations of volumetric building blocks. The algorithm introduced here is an extension of well-established scan-line hidden surface removal procedures, and it integrates knowledge of a Boolean construction tree in the surface resolution process. Several hidden surface coherence properties are discussed in terms of their possible exploitation in the intricate solid model visualization process. While many of the earlier coherence techniques depend on a polygon environment in which surfaces and volumes do not intersect, the Boolean process can not afford that luxury because it is inherently required to handle intersecting volumes and surfaces. Initial tests indicate that substantial performance improvements over previous methods can be achieved with the algorithm described in this paper, and that these improvements increase as model complexity increases.

An underlying philosophy of a dual solid modeling system is proposed in this paper. It suggests that two solid modelers are necessary to successfully satisfy both analytical precision requirements and user interface visualization requirements. The visual solid modeling task addressed in this paper provides greatly improved response capabilities, as compared to other systems, by striving to optimize the constructive solid model (CSG) solid model computations specifically for display purposes.

CR Categories: **I3.7** [Computer Graphics]: Three-Dimensional Graphics and Realism - Visible Line/Surface algorithm; **I3.5** [Computer Graphics]: Computational Geometry and Object Modeling — Curve, surface, solid and object representations; **I3.3** [Computer Graphics]: Picture/Image Generation — Display algorithms; **J.6** [Computer Applications]: Computer-aided Engineering — Computer-aided design (CAD), Computer-aided manufacture (CAM)

Key Words and Phrases: computer graphics, hidden-surface removal, hidden line removal, solid modeling, constructive solid geometry, computer-aided design

1. INTRODUCTION

In his book entitled *Emulation and Invention* [7], Brooke Hindle says of Samuel Morse

> "His great strength remained a quality of mind that permitted him to manipulate mental images of three-dimensional telegraph components as well as complete telegraphic systems, altering them at will and projecting various possibilities for change and development."

Few people possess the natural capability to mentally envision three-dimensional mechanical systems, particularly from someone else's description. Therefore, there is a very great opportunity for the application of computer graphics in solid modeling to assist the design, analysis, and manufacturing engineers with their spatial understanding of model structures. In concept, solid models can offer the designer more physically understandable building components, and computer graphics will afford him visual comprehension of the physical structures and the spatial relationships between those building blocks. In contrast to the views of some researchers in the solid modeling field [10, page 20], I feel that interactive graphics technology has a long way to go before it can offer all CAD/CAM users a tool that will provide three-dimensional visual insight equaling the natural abilities of someone like Samuel Morse.

The application of volumetric Boolean set operations to solid objects in order to represent more complex solid objects is commonly referred to as constructive solid geometry (CSG). The fundamental building blocks used in CSG are solid objects called primitives. Two primitives (for instance, A and B) can be combined to form a new solid object by applying one of the volumetric Boolean set operations defined as follows:

Union ($A \cup B$):	that volume of space found in either A or B
Intersection ($A \cap B$):	that volume of space found in both A and B
Difference (A-B):	that volume of space found in A but not found in B

The systematic application of the Boolean set operations is usually controlled by a binary tree data structure commonly referred to as a CSG tree (Figure 1). Each internal node of a CSG tree defines the Boolean set operation to be applied to

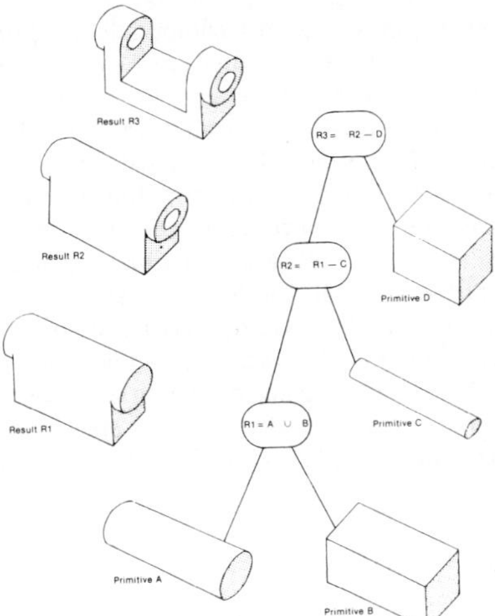

Figure 1. A CSG tree controls the systematic application of Boolean set operations

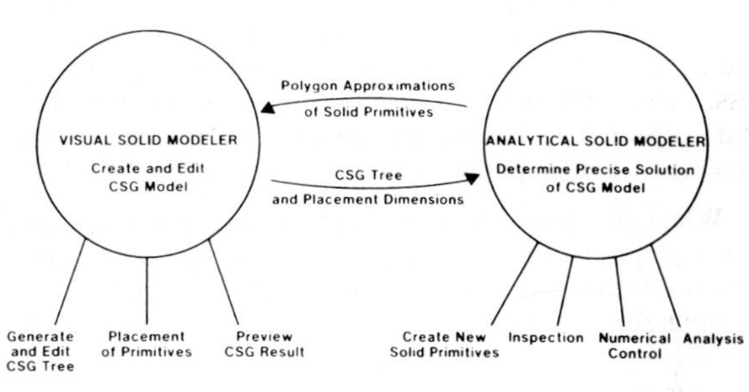

Figure 2. The Dual Solid Modeling Scenario

its two children. The leaves of the CSG tree contain information to indicate what solid primitives are to be used for Boolean processing. A CSG model includes both the CSG tree and the associated solid primitives. A new primitive can be created by geometrically evaluating the CSG model in order to produce a new solid object definition. A library of primitives can be built up from both original solid objects defined by some means other than CSG and the solid objects resulting from previous CSG evaluations.

For CAD/CAM applications, there are essentially two basic uses of a CSG model. In most manufacturing processes, a very precise evaluation of the CSG model is required. There is little concern for how much computing time is needed to derive this accurate definition as long as it is accomplished eventually. For example, numerical control engineers will normally refer to accuracy tolerances in terms of thousandths of an inch and run-times in terms of minutes or hours. On the other hand, most interactive visualization tasks such as design or robot programming need only enough accuracy and information about the CSG model to make a meaningful image of it. However, user interaction does require that images be generated rapidly in order to maximize user productivity. In the past, solid modelers have been developed with the intention of solving both the accuracy and interactive visualization tasks with essentially the same modeler. It is proposed here that these tasks can be better solved by deviating from the single modeler trend and analyzing each of these two tasks separately (Figure 2). Operating in the dual modeler scenario, a designer would create and edit a CSG model by interacting with the visual modeler at a design station. The analytical modeler would be invoked on a demand basis when exact model solutions are required for high-tolerance applications. The motivation behind this paper is to solve the visualization task efficiently, in order to provide informative shaded surface imagery of CSG models rapidly enough for effective interactive use.

As described in past literature there are two general approaches used to generate shaded surface images from CSG models:

1. Geometrically evaluate the CSG model in order to define the boundary surface model resulting from the application of volumetric Boolean processes to previously defined solid primitives. Subsequently, apply a hidden surface removal program to the resulting solid object boundary definition [1,4,5,8,13,14,17]. One class of hidden surface removal procedures that could be applied to boundary surface models is described in Section 3 of this paper.

2. Mathematically fire a ray through each image picture element into an environment composed of transformed primitives. For each ray, analyze the one-dimensional Boolean problem enough to resolve the first visible point along the ray [2,3,6,9,10,12,16,19]. The application of ray-firing is closely examined in Section 2.

Given that the "ultimate" user interface goal is real-time human interaction with the solid model, execution speed of the image generation task is a primary concern. In light of that goal, both approaches described above involve significant unnecessary computation. The first approach requires that a geometric solution to the CSG model be found before a display calculation can be made. As such, a great deal of the computation is wasted in resolving CSG results that the hidden surface removal process will hide. Also, calculation of the three-dimensional Boolean tasks (like surface intersections and data base changes) tends to be much more complex and time consuming than the subsequent hidden surface removal processing even for polygon based models or model approximations. Several commercial solid modelers do support polyhedral model approximations, but they utilize this time consuming two-step approach in order to generate CSG images. The ray-firing approach does simplify the Boolean calculations by operating in a one-dimensional space instead of three. It is significant to note that several CSG modelers that can produce a resultant boundary surface model from a CSG model use the ray-firing technique to produce shaded surface images [2,3]. Nonetheless, ray-firing does tend to be computationally expensive and time consuming in that distinct solutions are derived for every picture element. In other words, the general ray-firing approach is inefficient because it does not take advantage of coherence properties [12].

Based upon past analyses, shaded image generation of higher order surfaces can be made significantly faster by using polygonal approximation techniques [5]. In most engineering, manufacturing, inspection, and assembly applications, polygonal approximation of curved surfaces is either unacceptable in terms of accuracy or impractical in terms of the number of polygons necessary for reasonable tolerance limits. For a user display interface, however, the accuracy requirements are not nearly as rigorous. In addition, polygonal approximation computations of solid primitive surfaces can be performed as a preprocessing step to CSG interaction and need not be performed during the actual interaction process. Thus, interactive speed requirements seem to dictate that polygonal approximations be used for interactive image generation until superior methods are developed.

When the entire geometric model has been transformed into a polygonal form, a large body of existing hidden surface removal technology can be made available. To date, there is no publication known to the author that applies scan-line hidden surface removal techniques to the problem of generating shaded images directly from CSG models. The remainder of this paper will focus on the application of polygon-based scan-line techniques for visible surface processing of models composed of Boolean combinations of polygonal primitives. The next two sections provide a framework for the CSG scan-line hidden surface procedure by describing the fundamental ray-firing and scan-line hidden surface removal algorithms that will be applied. Following sections describe a specific CSG scan-line hidden surface procedure in detail, and how coherence techniques [14] can be applied to this more complex procedure. The paper concludes with a description of a CSG scan-line hidden surface implementation and a comparison to a corresponding ray-firing algorithm in terms of execution speed.

2. SOLVING ONE-DIMENSIONAL BOOLEAN TASKS USING RAY-FIRING

Ray-firing algorithms like those described by Roth [12] and Goldstein and Malin [6] apply a single procedure to every point on the viewing screen in order to resolve surface visibility while solving the required Boolean operations. This procedure determines the Boolean solution for a one-dimensional sample of the three-dimensional CSG model. A formalized classification of one-dimensional Boolean solutions in a polygon based environment has been proposed by Tilove [15]. The major significance of the ray-firing technique is that it does not require that a complete geometrical boundary surface solution of the CSG model be determined *a priori*. An iterative procedure for resolving the visible surface points from a CSG model using ray-firing might be structured as follows:

```
For each scan-line
  For each pixel in the scan-line
1.    For each surface
        Determine surface intersections with the
          visual ray
2.    Sort surface intersections by Z-depth
3.    Resolve the one-dimensional Boolean operations
        along the visual ray using the CSG tree
4.    Determine the first visible point along the
        ray from the Boolean solution
      Display point
```

Figure 3 illustrates the simplicity of solving Boolean operations in one dimension of the sampled space for two primitives. In addition to simplicity, this technique offers an attractive advantage for display — namely, the fact that the Boolean operations need only be solved as far as the first visible point. Unfortunately, that neat one-dimensional Boolean solution procedure must be precluded by expensive surface intersection and Z-sort computations. Furthermore, all four steps must be executed for every point on the screen. Roth does describe a culling procedure to somewhat reduce the number of surfaces to be considered for each picture element. The problem has changed little, however, because the surface intersection, Z-sort, Boolean, and visibility computations are still executed in the inner-most program loop for every pixel. Roth also describes a sampling/searching technique which will locate and display silhouette and surface intersection edges without having to analyze each display picture element. Unfortunately, that approach is not generalized for shaded surface display in that the higher level of sparseness of sampling that leads to speed improvement also leads to a higher potential for informational errors in the resulting image.

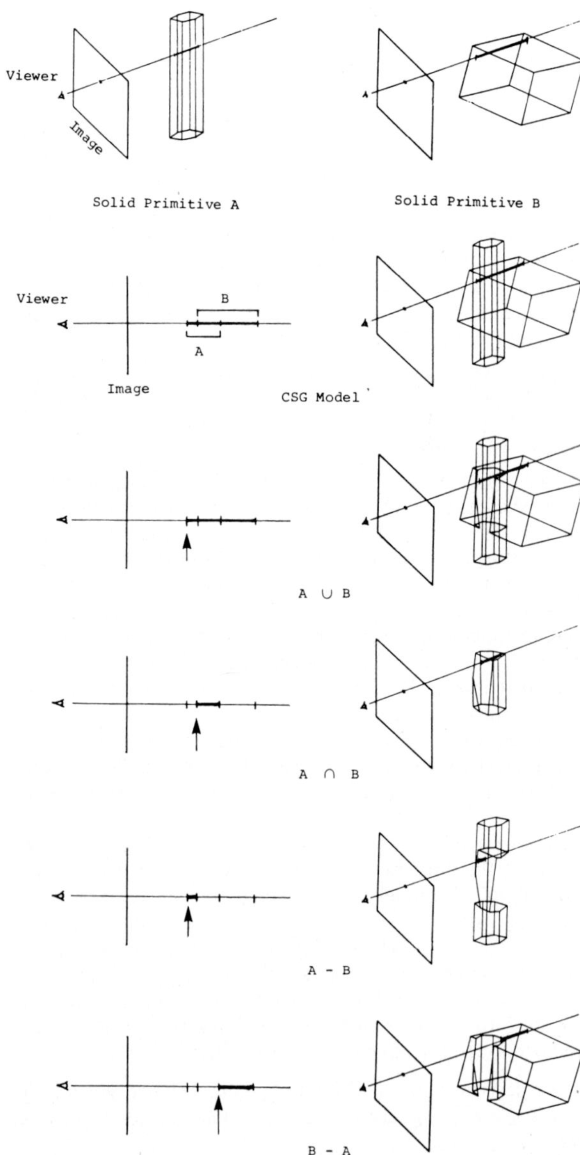

Figure 3. Ray-firing technique used to solve the one-dimensional Boolean problems for two solid primitives

3. OVERVIEW OF POLYGON SCAN-LINE HIDDEN SURFACE ALGORITHMS

A classification scheme for hidden surface removal algorithms was published in 1974 by Sutherland, Sproull and Schumacher [14]. Within this "taxonomy" of algorithms, Sutherland et al. classified three algorithms that sampled points in image space and resolved the visible surfaces based on depth priority. The three authors referenced by Sutherland et al. in this classification were Romney [11], Bouknight [1], and Watkins [17]. All three methods followed a similar sequence of operations that reflect an execution ordering of television-type raster devices. The four steps are described as follows:

1. Polygon edges are sorted by Y-vertex values typically using a bucket sort. For each scan-line, the Y-sorted list is utilized to determine which polygons should be considered for each scan-line, and where the associated scan-plane intersects each of those polygons. Sutherland et al. refer to the intersection of a scan-plane and a polygon as a segment.

2. For each scan-line that crosses one or more polygon surfaces in image space, an X-sorted list of related segments is determined in order to establish a sequential set of spans. A span is typically a continuous portion of a scan-line from which the visibility of a single segment can be resolved. Romney utilized a bucket sort to determine the X-ordering, whereas Bouknight and Watkins applied a bubble sort to update an X-sorted list between scan-lines, in order to capitalize on scan-line coherence properties.

3. In order to restrict further analysis to within the bounds of a span, all segments that enter the span are clipped to the span limits.

4. In most cases, visibility is then determined simply by searching for the segment portion that is closest to the viewer. Some additional complexity is encountered in the event that two visible segment portions cross within a span [1].

A typical scan-line program that utilizes the Y-X-Z order of sorting described above would have an iterative structure like the following:

```
1. For each polygon edge
      Bucket sort by the Y-vertex values
   For each scan-line
      For each active polygon
         Determine segment (intersection of
            scan-plane and polygon)
      Sort segments by X-vertex values
2.    Determine span boundaries
         For each span
3.          Clip active segments to span boundaries
4.          Resolve segment visibility within span by
               searching for the closest segment in Z
            Display segment
```

For each of the algorithms they studied, Sutherland et al. pointed out that the authors made crucial decisions in the selection of their sorting procedures and corresponding application of coherence properties. It is the judicious utilization of coherence that reduces the costly sorting computational requirements for these visible surface programs. The application of coherence becomes significantly more complex when a visible surface algorithm is extended to solve Boolean operations between solid primitives. Before the applications of coherence are dealt with in detail, it is appropriate to first describe a general scan-line hidden surface removal procedure for constructive solid geometry.

4. A GENERAL CSG SCAN-LINE HIDDEN SURFACE REMOVAL PROCEDURE

The hidden surface removal algorithm for CSG models that is to be presented utilizes a framework based on essentially the same four steps outlined by Sutherland et al. [14] for scan-line algorithms as described in the preceding section. The general CSG scan-line algorithm is achieved by integrating the efficient one-dimensional Boolean solution technique of the ray-firing approach into step (4) of the scan-line iterative structure. That is, for each span boundary, the one-dimensional Boolean problem is solved to the first visible point. Where the same surface is visible throughout a span, shading can be interpolated in between. The functional steps for the general CSG hidden surface removal procedure are structured as follows:

```
1. For each polygon edge
      Bucket sort by the Y-vertex values
   For each scan-line
      For each active polygon
         Determine segment (intersection of scan-plane
            and polygon)
      Sort segments by X-vertex values
2.    Determine span boundaries
         For each span
3.          Clip active segments to span boundaries
4.          Solve one-dimensional boolean operations
               to the first visible point as
               specified in the CSG tree
            If same Z-order of segments at boundaries
            Then
               Display segment
            Else
               Subdivide span at segment intersections
               and repeat steps (3) and (4) for each
               new span
```

Some complexity may be added where surface intersections take place between span boundaries. Note, however, that the image generation process need not have knowledge of those surface intersections that do not affect the resulting image.

A change in surface visibility within a span is detected by a difference in the order of segments encountered between the viewer and the first visible point at each span boundary. This order is determined as part of the one-dimensional Boolean calculation for both left and right sides of the span boundary. When needed, segment intersection decisions are made using this depth order with the understanding that all segments that fall within a span will completely traverse that span. After the intersection between two selected segments is determined, the X-component of the intersection is used to create another span boundary which subdivides the span under consideration. The two new spans formed by this subdivision are processed separately in a recursive manner. It is significant to recognize that in most practical cases, polygonal intersections are relatively rare occurrences. This characteristic is a coherence property which can be exploited to improve program efficiency and will be discussed further in the next section of this paper.

A simple example of this general scan-line procedure for generating visible surface imagery of a CSG model containing two primitives is illustrated in Figure 4. The two solid primitives found within the CSG model are a six-sided box (primitive A) and a four-sided pyramid (primitive B). A scan-plane that intersects each primitive and a volume of space common to both is illustrated in Figure 4-A. The seven end points of the resulting segments are sorted by their X-components and subsequently used to define six spans (Figure 4-B). Up to this point, the operations described are common to the scan-line hidden surface removal algorithms described earlier.

The ray-firing technique is applied to each span border in order to evaluate the one-dimensional Boolean problem up to the first visible point. Taken in Z-depth order, each segment intersection along the ray is examined to see if a CSG tree solution exists. If so, the first visible segment point is saved and all surface intersections encountered up to that point are maintained in a sorted list. The Boolean process must be solved on both the left and right sides of the span boundaries because a change in segment geometry may occur there. However, not all of the span boundaries are necessary to complete the processing for a scan-line because some do not represent any changes in surface visibility. Span boundaries that can be deleted from further consideration in the processing of a scan-line without affecting the resulting image exhibit one of the two following properties:

1. Boolean processing on each side of the span boundary resolves no visible points (as a result of subtraction or intersection operations).
2. Boolean processing resolves visible points from the same segment on both sides of the span boundary.

Figures 4-C through 4-F illustrate the four potential Boolean combinations of the two primitives. Pertinent span boundaries are labeled by the order of primitive surface intersections a visual ray would encounter on each side of the span boundary until the first visible point is found. Span boundaries that exhibit one of the two properties described above have been removed. Span boundaries that would be inserted as a result of segment intersections are included. Also illustrated are the outlines of the resulting images of each Boolean operation with the scan-plane intersections highlighted. Imagery can be produced for each scan-line in two forms. A hidden-line removed image can be produced on a sampled pixel basis by rendering each scan-line point that represents a visible segment endpoint or visible segment intersection. These points are produced as a result of the span boundary generation and deletion processes already described. If color and intensity information is maintained at each of the final span boundaries, shading values can be interpolated between in order to produce a faceted or smoothly shaded image. Examples of imagery produced in this manner can be found in Section 6 of this paper.

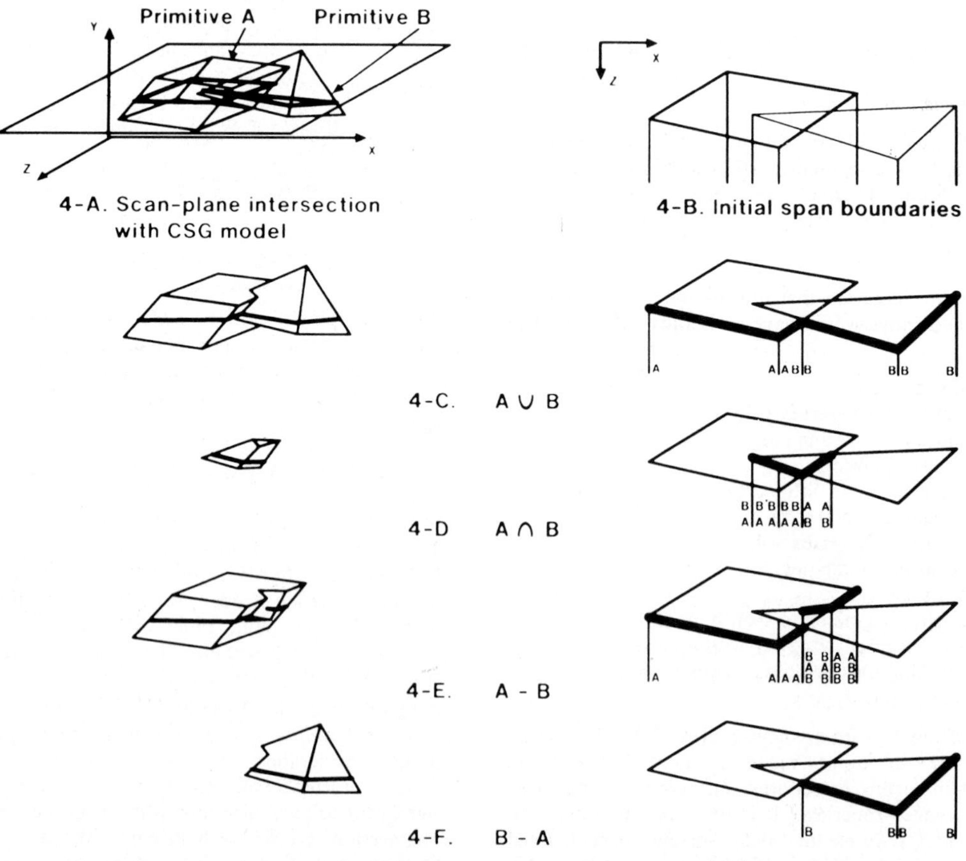

Figure 4. The CSG scan-line hidden surface removal process for two solid primitives

5. APPLICATION OF COHERENCE TECHNIQUES

Several coherence techniques for scan-line hidden surface removal algorithms have been previously published. Although the terminology may vary, the goal common to all is to reduce computation, particularly within inner program loops. The major categories of coherence techniques are listed below. Each of these will be examined for applicability to the CSG scan-line visible surface procedure.

A. *Span Coherence*: Only one surface is usually visible between initial span boundaries. The exception is necessary for intersecting surfaces.

B. *Visible Segment Coherence*: Where a segment is known to be visible across span boundaries, those boundaries need not be considered further [17].

C. *Scan-line Coherence*: There are relatively few changes between neighboring scan-lines.

  C.1 Intersections of adjacent scan-planes with a polygon model produce nearly the same set of segments [1,4,11,14,17].

  C.2 Sorted ordering of segments along the X-axis tends to be very similar for neighboring scan-lines [1,4,13,17].

  C.3 Sorted ordering of segments along the Z-axis tends to be very similar for neighboring scan-lines [4].

  C.4 Segment intersections have nearly the same X- and Z-components for neighboring scan-lines.

D. *Face Coherence*: The occurrence of intersecting surfaces is assumed to be relatively rare [4].

E. *Object Coherence*: Within its image space boundaries, the visibility status of a solid primitive changes little.

  E.1 Polygon connectivity can be applied to scan-line segments where no intersections exist [4,13].

  E.2 Where it is known that specific objects do not visibly intersect, silhouette boundaries of those objects can be used to determine visibility.

F. *Boolean Combination Coherence*: Simplifications can be devised from particular sequences of Boolean operations.

G. *Frame-to-frame coherence*: Image composition changes little between frames that are adjacent in time [8].

The coherence properties described in items (A) through (C) are specific to scan-line based algorithms whereas the properties represented by items (D) through (G) are more general in nature.

Several of these techniques were utilized to some extent in the general CSG scan-line algorithm described in the last section. Span coherence (A) can be considered as the first improvement over ray-firing algorithms. That is, where there is no change in surface visibility throughout a span, Boolean visibility computations need be executed only at the span boundaries. Shading can then be interpolated in between. Even when surface intersections require subdivision of an initial span, shading can be interpolated between the new subdivision span boundaries. Visible segment coherence (B) was established by a property that allowed for span boundaries where no visible point is resolved to be removed from further consideration in the processing of a scan-line. Note, however, that for both (A) and (B) to be applied in the CSG scan-line procedure, the depth order of all segments encountered up to the first visible point are necessary. Previous scanline hidden-surface algorithms need only be concerned with information relative to the single segment closest to the viewer since it would hide the other more distant segments.

Some applications of scan-line coherence property (C) can easily be added to the general CSG visible surface algorithm. Several people discovered that the straight polygon edges allow for a simplification of the scan-plane/polygon intersection calculation on successive scan-lines (C.1). That is, when each edge of a polygon is first encountered in the Y-bucket sorted list, the values dx/dy and dz/dy are found. While an edge remains active, segment endpoints for successive scan-lines can be determined using simple difference equations. Horizontal polygon edges are handled as a special case since they would result in a zero dy value. The X-sort scan-line coherence property (C.2) can be applied by maintaining the segment X-order information between successive scan-lines. Since the X-sort order generally changes very little between scan-lines, this coherence property can be utilized by applying a sorting algorithm that executes quickly on a list that is assumed to be nearly sorted. Several hidden surface program developers have found a bubble sort effective for maintaining the X-sort list from scan-line to scan-line [1,17].

Extension of other forms of scan-line coherence are not so easily applied to the CSG visible surface problem. The Z-sort coherence property (C.3) was first implemented by Hamlin and Gear [5] by combining the X- and Z-sort operations into a single "stack" procedure. Their execution statistics exhibited marginal improvement for geometric models that did not allow intersecting polygons. Extensions of the "stack" algorithm to handle intersecting polygons would increase program complexity, and execution speed could be adversely affected. The application of a segment intersection scan-line coherence property (C.4) appears to exhibit a similar efficiency weakness. For the application of constructive solid geometry, there is a potential for surface intersection at any screen location where primitives overlap. As such, the test for polygon intersection must be made at each span boundary where the visual ray penetrates more than one solid primitive regardless of the results from the previous scan-line.

Previous scan-line hidden surface algorithms that utilized face coherence (D) did so by providing a preprocessing step that would split up all intersecting polygons along their common borders. The major application for this approach would be for geometric models that were to be viewed from several positions, but whose internal components would not change relative to each other. In direct contradiction to that application, constructive solid modeling interaction demands relative movements between primitives be made with the potential of many surface intersections taking place. As Sutherland et al. pointed out [14], there is also a great probability of needlessly calculating intersections for portions of the model that would be hidden from view.

At least one form of object coherence, polygon connectivity (E.1), can easily be applied to the CSG hidden surface removal algorithm. For regions of image space where only one primitive resides, no Boolean or intersection solutions need be produced (Figure 5). For segments with visible points resolved from a single primitive, only the first point on each span boundary needs to be found, as in normal visible surface processing. Common span borders that resolve no visible points as a result of subtraction of intersection operations can be removed from further processing of a

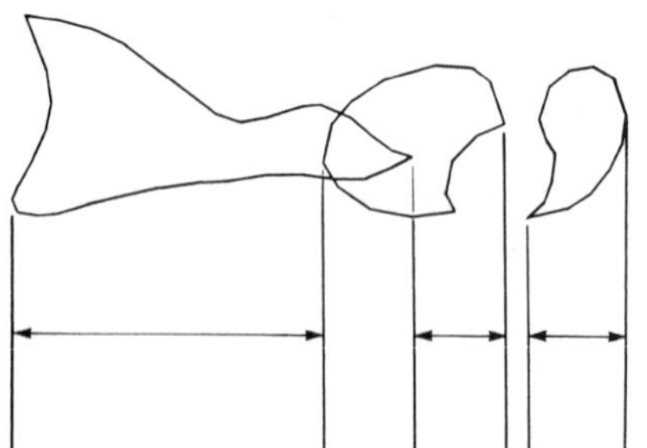

Figure 5. Object coherence properties can be used to define span boundaries where no Boolean operations need be resolved

scan-line. Uses of polygon connectivity coherence assume the common notion that surfaces bounding a primitive volume do not intersect. There appears to be potential for a similar application of polygon connectivity coherence at each level of the Boolean construction tree. At this point in time, the author has not found an efficient solution that compensates for the greatly increased complexity of this task.

There are several other potential areas of coherence application that could improve the efficiency of a CSG visible surface algorithm. Object coherence has often been applied to geometric models comprised of nonintersecting surfaces by determining visibility of primitives relative to each other using their visual silhouette border (E.2). Some extensions might be applied as special cases to the CSG model environment for nonintersecting primitives. An area not yet pursued is the application of rules characteristic to Boolean combinations that might provide some coherence benefits (F). An example of this would be where a region of the image space is covered by overlapping primitives that take part in only union operations. When this situation is detected in the Boolean tree, the visible surface task need only search for portions of the model nearest the viewer. This process is analogous to the standard scan-line hidden surface removal procedure (like that described in Section 3).

Perhaps the coherence techniques involving the most complicated application to the CSG visible surface problem are those that utilize knowledge maintained between image frames (G). This is because the CSG interactive editing process involves surface intersections and geometry changes which are not encountered in traditional frame-to-frame coherence applications. Several people have suggested local updating to only portions of an image that correspond to geometry changes. This approach is reasonable as long as the viewing transformations are consistent.

There remain several applications of coherence properties yet to be explored in the CSG visible surface task. The problems are significantly more complex than the traditional hidden surface removal problem; but the benefits to interactive solid modeling may result in significant future payoffs for CAD/CAM applications.

6. IMPLEMENTATION AND COMPARISONS

A Fortran implementation of the CSG scan-line hidden surface removal procedure described in Section 4 has been completed on a VAX 11/780 computer system. The CSG scan-line code is preceded by software that performs coordinate transformation, viewbox clipping, and perspective-divide operations. A transformation matrix can be allocated to each node of the CSG tree for relative scaling and placement of CSG model components.

The images in Figures 6 and 7 were generated by the CSG scan-line hidden surface removal program at 512 × 512 resolution. The images in Figure 6 were generated from simple CSG models, each containing the same three boxes. The top image in Figure 6 illustrates the relative placement of the three boxes before Boolean evaluation. The CSG model for the top image contained a single-node CSG tree for each primitive. The other two images represent CSG models with only one CSG tree apiece, utilizing all three primitives. New surfaces introduced by subtraction operations are highlighted in blue for better visualization.

The images in Figure 7 represent the two basic stages of a plastic coffee pot handle mold design, as produced using constructive solid modeling. During the first stage of design, solid primitives are either loaded from a library or created using in-house CAD systems. It is significant to point out that the coffee pot handle primitive was modeled using bicubic surface patches which have been approximated by polygons. Figure 7 illustrates some basic operations which a designer could use to create the bottom half of the mold cavity. In the first operation, a truncated cone is subtracted from the handle in order to provide space for a screw that will attach the handle to the rest of the coffee pot. This final representation of the plastic coffee pot handle is then subtracted from a metal block to form the bottom half of the mold.

In order to provide a basis of comparison in terms of program efficiency, a ray-firing CSG hidden-surface removal program has been implemented. The ray-firing program is a polygon-based implementation of the algorithm described in Section 2 of this paper, with extensions to use the culling-box technique suggested by Roth [12] in order to reduce computation. The CSG models depicted in Figures 6 and 7 were used as test cases and the results are summarized in Table 1.

Table 1

EXECUTION TIMING TEST RESULTS

Image	Number of Polygons	CPU seconds (Vax 11/780) Ray-Firing	CSG Scan-line
Figure 6:			
[(AuC) − B]	18	65.3	8.8
[(B − (AUC)]	18	64.6	9.1
Figure 7:			
[Handle − Cone]	1056	650.2	11.7
[Block − (Handle − Cone)]	1062	1143.6	18.8

The author found that the CSG scan-line program needed approximately 1/60th the CPU time required by the ray-firing program to derive shaded images from CSG models of similar complexity to the mold example. This is a very significant improvement when one considers the productivity increase a user might gain from waiting only 20 seconds for an image instead of 20 minutes. Initial tests indicate that the execution speed improvements exhibited by the CSG scan-line program over the ray-firing program increase with model complexity. In other words, the coherence techniques employed by the CSG scan-line program seem to dramatically improve relative performance with greater numbers of primitives and polygons.

It is significant to point out that existing CSG ray-firing programs normally do not use polygon approximations of primitive surface definitions. Rather, they typically restrict the user to a few relatively simple primitives (i.e., block, sphere, cylinder) for which straight-forward ray/surface intersections can be derived. The CSG scan-line hidden surface removal procedure described in this paper is intended to provide a general purpose solution for primitives bounded by any order of surface by using polygon approximations. For example, the coffee pot handle primitive shown in Figure 7 utilizes a third-order sculptured-surface definition that quadric level CSG modelers could not possibly duplicate. Approximation of curved surfaces with polygons may result in a significant increase in data space requirements, but that factor is becoming less pertinent each day as computer technology progresses; and the pay-offs in terms of geometric model generality and improved user interaction are great.

Work has begun on a workstation-based implementation of the CSG scan-line hidden surface removal procedure. It will utilize at least one microprocessor local to a frame buffer display system in order to improve user response, and will also serve to move some computational load from the host computer. This implementation will also provide a working tool for a dual solid modeling system as described in the Introduction of this paper.

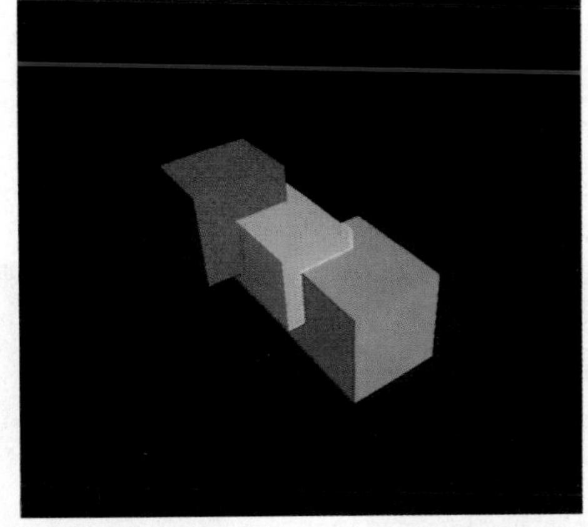

Positioning:
Block A : Green
Block B : Yellow
Block C : Blue

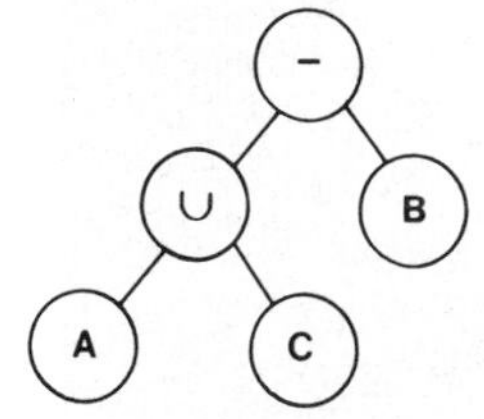

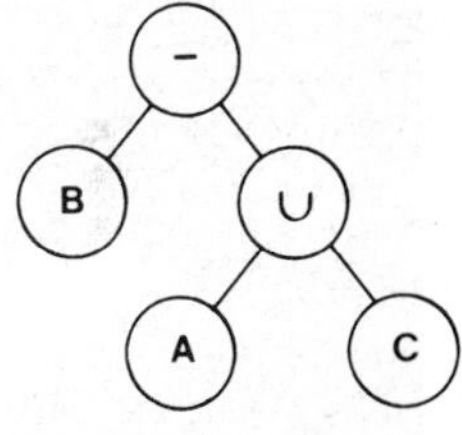

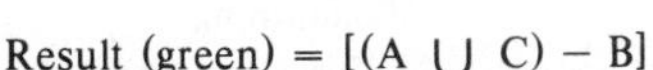

Result (yellow) = [B - (A ∪ C)]

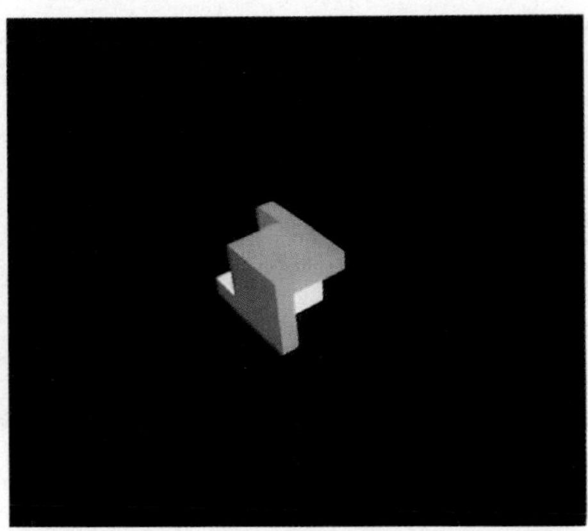

Figure 6. Three block example of output from the CSG scan-line hidden surface removal program

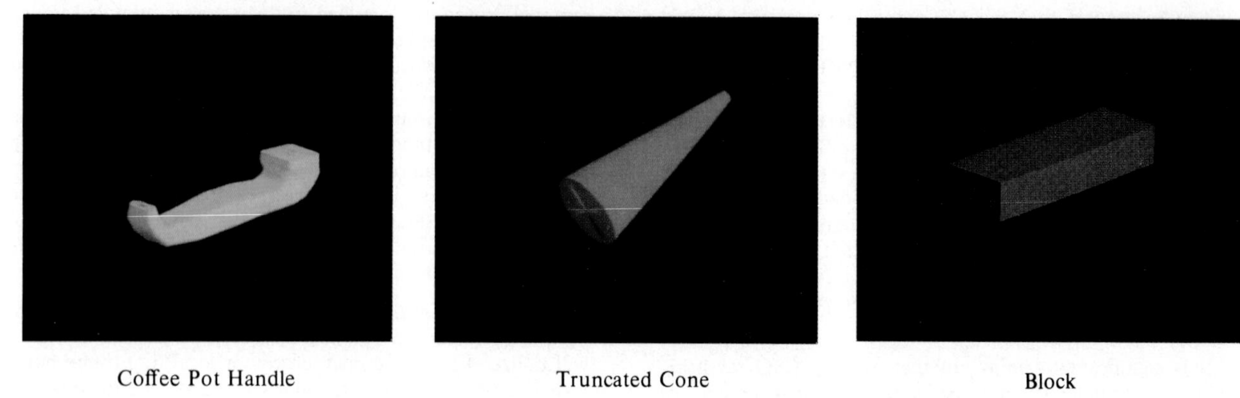

Coffee Pot Handle

Truncated Cone

Block

SOLID PRIMITIVES

Handle — Tcone

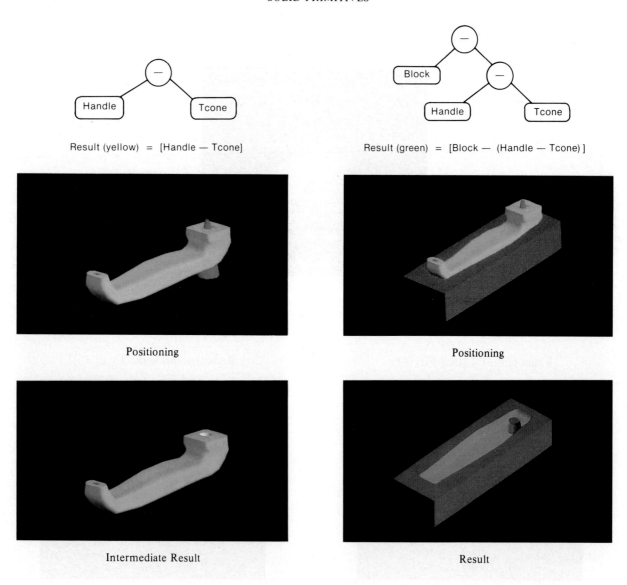

Result (yellow) = [Handle — Tcone]

Block — (Handle — Tcone)

Result (green) = [Block — (Handle — Tcone)]

Positioning

Positioning

Intermediate Result

Result

Figure 7. Mold design example of output from the CSG scan-line hidden surface removal program

7. CONCLUSION

A method for displaying visible surfaces of CSG models using a scan-line hidden surface removal procedure has been described. Implementations of this procedure demonstrate significant efficiency improvements over previous approaches. Initial tests indicate that these efficiency improvements increase with model complexity. These results indicate that a visual solid modeler based upon the CSG scan-line hidden surface removal procedure could be a truly interactive system. In addition to providing a vehicle for these dramatic speed improvements, the fundamental polygon basis of this procedure allows it to be a general purpose visualization tool for CSG model editing in that all higher order surfaces can be approximated to desired tolerances by polygons. There remain several coherence properties that could be further exploited in order to improve execution speed of the CSG hidden surface removal program even more. Further study is also necessary to understand what rendering techniques would provide the most information to the user at the least computational expense for the purpose of CSG model creation and editing.

A dual solid modeling system which serves to separate the functions of a "visual solid modeler" and an "analytic solid modeler" has been proposed. The CSG hidden surface removal algorithm presented in this paper is aimed at solving the interactive image generation requirements of the "visual solid modeler." A great deal of work remains in precisely defining the "analytical solid modeler" and the interrelationships between the analytical and visual solid modelers at a system level.

8. ACKNOWLEDGEMENTS

This paper incorporates a number of recommendations that were made by readers of earlier drafts. Of particular note were the comments made by Kevin Weiler who bathed my first draft with red ink. Recommendations by Lon Jones, Virg Lucke and three anonymous SIGGRAPH reviewers led to several clarifications and deletions of extraneous verbiage. The final proofreading, typesetting, photography and layout were accomplished by General Electric's Graphics Operation. The geometric models used for Figure 7 were provided by Jim Beck and John Hinds.

I would also like to thank Professor Wozny of Rensselaer Polytechnic Institute who is leading me in my Ph.D. effort of which this paper will play a major part.

9. REFERENCES

[1] Bouknight, W.J., "A Procedure for Generation of Three-Dimensional Half-Toned Computer Graphics Representations," *Comm. ACM*, Vol. 13, No. 9, September 1970.

[2] Boyse, J.W. and Gilchrist, J.E., "GMSolid: Interactive Modeling for Design and Analysis of Solids," *IEEE Computer Graphics and Applications*, Vol. 2, No. 2, March 1982, pp. 86-97.

[3] Brown, C.M., "PADL-2: A Technical Summary," *IEEE Computer Graphics and Applications*, Vol. 2, No. 2, March 1982, pp. 69-84.

[4] Hamlin, G. and Gear, C.W., "Raster-Scan Hidden Surface Algorithm Techniques," *Computer Graphics*, Vol. 11, 1977, No. 2, pp. 206-213.

[5] Foley, J.D. and VanDam, A., *Fundamentals of Interactive Computer Graphics*, Addison-Wesley, 1982.

[6] Goldstein, R.A. and Malin, L., "3D Modeling with the Syntha Vision System," First Annual Conference on Computer Graphics in CAD/CAM Systems, MIT, April 1979, pp. 244-247.

[7] Hindel, B., *Emulation and Invention*, New York University Press, 1981.

[8] Hubschman, H., and Zucker, S., "Frame-to-Frame Coherence and the Hidden Surface Computation: Constraints for a Convex World," *Computer Graphics*, Vol. 15, No. 3, August 1981, pp. 45-54.

[9] Myers, W., "An Industrial Perspective on Solid Modeling," *IEEE Computer Graphics and Applications*, Vol. 2, No. 2, March 1982, pp. 86-97.

[10] Requicha, A.A.G., and Voelcker, H.B., "Solid Modeling: A Historical Summary and Contemporary Asessment," *IEEE Computer Graphics and Applications*, Vol. 2, No. 2, March 1982, pp. 9-24.

[11] Romney, G.W., *Computer Assisted Assembly and Rendering of Solids*, Computer Science Department, University of Utah, TR-4-20, 1970.

[12] Roth, S.D., "Ray Casting for Modeling Solids," *Computer Graphics and Image Processing*, No. 18, 1982, pp. 109-144.

[13] Sechrest, S., and Greenberg, D.P., "A Visible Polygon Reconstruction Algorithm," *Computer Graphics*, Vol. 15, No. 3, August 1981, pp. 17-27.

[14] Sutherland, I.E., Sproull, R.F., and Schumacher, R.A., "A Characterization of Ten Hidden-Surface Algorithms," *ACM Computing Surveys*, Vol. 6, No. 1, March 1974, pp. 1-55.

[15] Tilove, R.B., "Set Membership Clarification: A Unified Approach to Geometric Intersection Problems," *IEEE Transactions on Computers,* Vol. C-29, No.10, October 1980.

[16] Voelcker, H.B., "Algorithms and Applications," Tutorial on Solid Modeling, SIGGRAPH '82 (ACM).

[17] Watkins, G.S., *A Real-Time Visible Surface Algorithm*, Computer Science Department, University of Utah, UTECH-CSC-70-101, June 1970.

[18] Wesley, M.A., Lozano-Perez, T., Lieberman, L.I., Lavin, M.A. and Grossman, D.D., "A Geometric Modeling System for Automated Mechanical Assembly," *IBM Journal of Research and Development*, Vol. 24, No. 1, January 1980.

[19] Wolfe, R., Fitzgerald, W., and Gracer, F., "Interactive Graphics for Volume Modeling," Procedings of the IEEE Eighteenth Design Automation Conference, pp. 463-470.

A Fast Algorithm for Rendering Parametric Surfaces

by
James H. Clark
NASA/Ames Research Center

ABSTRACT

An algorithm for rendering shaded pictures of parametric surfaces is presented. The algorithm recursively subdivides each surface element on the basis of its screen-space curvature until it is sufficiently close to bilinear to be scan-converted by conventional polygon rendering techniques. The mathematical basis used to carry out the subdivsion yields the curvature criterion as a coefficient so that the tests for termination of the subdivision process are extremely simple. In addition, a surface is subdivided only in the parametric direction in which its curvature deviates from the tolerance. The algorithm incorporates a very simple solution to the problem of separations between subpatches.

I. Introduction

Parametric curved surfaces provide a convenient alternative to dense polygonal coverings in describing smooth objects for subsequent rendering by computer. They allow a smooth object with no analytical definition to be approximated with a relatively small number of surface patches that join with tangent continuity, thereby saving considerable memory space in representing the object. Until the last several years, however, the only algorithm to successfully render these patches was that of Catmull(1), and although the pictures it generates are very realistic, it frequently consumes much computer time and storage.

In an attempt to reduce this computing time, several people have recently developed algorithms that render these patches in scan-line order. They have used two different approaches. Blinn(2) and Whitted(3) have used numerical techniques based upon Newton iteration to find the intersection of a curvilinear patch and successive scan planes. Although these approaches potentially converge very rapidly, they frequently suffer from stability problems and therefore may behave unpredictably. They also tend to be somewhat complex to implement.

A more fruitful approach has been taken by Carpenter and Lane. Using the Bernstein basis to represent the surfaces, they employ a subdivision algorithm similar to Catmull's. However, rather than subdividing patches until they are approximately the size of a pixel and writing the results into a depth buffer as in Catmull's algorithm, they subdivide the patch until it is within a tolerance of being geometrically flat. Their approach is similar to that of Nyddeger(5), except that his work was with bivariate analytic functions. Although this method prehaps converges more slowly than the Newton iteration methods, it has at least two significant advantages over them: it is not stability dependent and its output can be to conventional scan-line algorithms.

The algorithm presented here also takes the recursive subdivision approach, but it differs from the Carpenter/Lane work in three ways. The first is that they use the Bernstein basis, while the present algorithm employs central differencing as in Catmull's approach. Although the Bernstein basis is favorable because it is geometrically intuitive and exhibits the convex hull property(6), which the Carpenter/Lane algorithm makes use of, the number of arithmetic operations it requires is almost twice that of central differencing.

The second difference is that their algorithm performs a relatively time consuming set of dot products to test for geometric flatness, whereas the present work utilizes available coefficients to test immediately for parametric bilinearity. This test has a particularly simple form for cubics, but for arbitrary degree it results in about half the number of operations to test for termination of the recursive subdivision process. Also, since parametric, rather than geometric, curvature is used as the subdivision criterion, the boundaries of the generated bilinear elements form segments that approximate curves of constant parameter, thereby allowing textures to be mapped onto the surface.

Finally, their algorithm is subject to discontinuities in position between subpatches. These separations occur because in the subdivision process it sometimes occurs that one of two sibling patches is within the tolerance of planarity while the other is not and must be split along their common boundary. The result is a small separation that reveals itself only under certain viewing orientations. Therefore, an object in motion will exhibit occasional "cracks" in the surface caused by the separation. This is a very undesirable side effect of their implementation. The present algorithm gives a very simple solution to this problem. The solution can also be used in their implementation.

II. Subdivision Mathematics.

The surface formulation used in this work is based upon the Cartesian Product generalization of curve representations. This section briefly presents the mathematics of curve subdivision. The particular details of surface subdivision pertinent to this work are presented in the next section.

Bernstein Subdivision.

The subdivision operation for the Bernstein basis is most simply viewed as a reparametrization operation. A degree n curve is represented as a vector-valued parametric function of t:

$$f(t) = \sum_{i=0}^{n} B_{n,i}(t) \; p_i , \qquad (1)$$

where

$$B_{n,i}(t) = \binom{n}{i} t^i (1-t)^{n-i} , \qquad (2)$$

are the *Bernstein basis* (binomial distribution) functions and the p_i are 2 or 3 dimensional "control points", or points whose positions control the shape of the curve. The parameter t varies between 0 and 1. Each half of this curve can be reparametrized to the interval [0,1]. Because of the symmetry of the basis functions, only the first half is considered. The interval [0,1/2] is mapped onto the interval [0,1] with the substitution t=s/2 into equation (2), giving

$$B_{n,i}(t) =$$

$$B_{n,i}(s/2) = \binom{n}{i} s^i \; 2^{-n} \; (2-s)^{n-i}$$

$$= \binom{n}{i} s^i \; 2^{-n} \; (s + 2(1-s))^{n-i} ,$$

or

$$B_{n,i}(s/2) = \sum_{i=0}^{n} 2^{-k} \binom{k}{i} B_{n,k}(s),$$

where the quantity $(s + 2(1-2))^{n-i}$ has been expanded using the Binomial Theorem. Substituting this result into equation (1) and rearranging terms,

$$f(t) = \sum_{k=0}^{n} B_{n,k}(s) \left\{ \sum_{i=0}^{n} \binom{k}{i} p_i/2^k \right\} \qquad (3)$$

$$= \sum_{k=0}^{n} B_{n,k}(s) \qquad q_k , \quad s \quad [0,1]$$

where q_k is equal to the quantity in brackets. The q_k represent a new set of control points for the new parametrization of the curve. In other words, subdivision is accomplished by computing a new set of control points from the old set.

Central Differencing.

Another approach to splitting a curve into 2 subcurves can be obtained by expanding the polynomial f(t) in its algebraic form,

$$f(t) = \sum_{i=0}^{n} a_i \; t^i , \qquad (4)$$

in a Taylor Series about the point t in the following manner:

$$f(t+d) = f(t) + f'(t)\, d + E(t,d) + O(t,d)$$

and

$$f(t-d) = f(t) - f'(t)\, d + E(t,d) - O(t,d),$$

where E(t,d) is the composite of the remaining terms in the series with even powers in d and O(t,d) is the composite of the odd terms. The constant d is the half width of the subdivision interval. Adding these two equations

$$f(t+d) + f(t-d) = 2 f(t) + 2 E(t,d),$$

from which is obtained

$$f(t) = (f(t+d) + f(t-d))/2 - E(t,d). \qquad (5)$$

Therefore, the value of the function at the midpoint t of the interval [t-d,t+d] is found by averaging its value at the endpoints and subtracting the value of the function E(t,d) evaluated at the midpoint. Since E(t,d) is itself a polynomial of degree 2 less than the original polynomial, its value at the midpoint of the interval can be computed from a similar expression. The same holds for all successively reduced polynomials until finally the remaining polynomial E(t,d) is a constant (possibly 0).

Subdivision of Cubic and Quintic Curves.

Cubic curves are adequate for most computer graphics applications and quintics suffice for most geometric design applications. Hence, in this section specific comparisons between the subdivision approaches for cubics and quintics are presented.

The expression in brackets of equation (3) is normally computed(6) using the recursive equation

$$q_m^{n+1} = (q_m^n + q_{m+1}^n)/2,$$

where

$q_j^0 = p_j$ are the original control points,

$a_i = q_0^i$,

and

$b_i = q_i^{n-i}$.

These equations require a total of k(k+1)/2 adds and divides by 2 to compute the control points a_i and b_i of the two subcurves, where k is the degree of the original curve. Assuming adds and divides by 2 require the same amount of computing time, T, a cubic requires 12T units and a quintic requires 30T. For example, the subdivision equations for cubics are

$$a_0 = p_0,$$

$$b_3 = p_3,$$

$$a_1 = (p_0+p_1)/2,$$

$$b_2 = (p_2+p_3)/2,$$

$T = (p_1+p_2)/2,$

$a_2 = (a_1+T)/2,$

$b_1 = (T+b_3)/2,$

$b_0 = (a_3+b_1)/2,$

$a_3 = b_0,$

where the equal sign represents the assignment operation.

The central difference approach requires fewer operations. From equation (5), the difference equations for cubics are

$$f(t) = (f(t+d) + f(t-d)) / 2 - g(t,d), \quad (7)$$

and

$$g(t,d) = (g(t+d,d) + g(t-d,d)) / 2,$$

where

$$g(t,d) = f''(t)\ d^2/2.$$

The last of these equations implies that

$$g(t,d^n) = g(t,d^{n-1})\ d^2,$$

where n is the level of subdivision. This equation expresses the change in g(t,d) between successive levels of subdivision, e.g. between level 1 and level 0, since d=1/2,

$$g(t,1/2) = g(t,1)/4.$$

Therefore letting f0, g0, f1, g1 be the initial respective values f(0), g(0,1), f(1), g(1,1), the cubic is subdivided according to the following equations, where the equal sign is the assignment operation:

$$\begin{aligned} f0 &= f0 \\ g0 &= g0/4 \\ g(1/2) &= (g0+g1)/8 \\ f(1/2) &= (f0+f1)/2 - g(1/2) \quad (8) \\ g1 &= g1/4 \\ f1 &= f1. \end{aligned}$$

The corresponding equations for quintic subdivision are

$$\begin{aligned} f0 &= f0 \\ g0 &= g0/4 \\ h0 &= h0/16 \\ h(1/2) &= (h0+h1)/32 \\ g(1/2) &= (g0+g1)/8 - 6h(1/2) \\ f(1/2) &= (f0+f1)/2 - g(1/2) - h(1/2) \quad (9) \\ h1 &= h1/16 \\ g1 &= g1/4 \\ f1 &= f1, \end{aligned}$$

where the initial values are

$$g0 = f''(0)/2,$$

$$h0 = f^{[4]}(0)/4!$$

$$g1 = f''(1)/2!,$$

and

$$h1 = f^{[4]}(1)/4!.$$

Therefore from these equations only 7T units are required for cubic and 14T are required for quintic subdivision, where it has been assumed that multiplications require the same amount of time as shifts and adds. This is roughly half the number required with the Bernstein basis.

Since the values of g0 and g1 are divided by 4 each time the recursive application of these equations is made, and since g(1/2) is the average of g0 and g1 divided by 4, it is clear that the curvature that g(t,d) measures rapidly goes to zero with successive application of these equations. The h values in equation (9) go to zero even more rapidly. Therefore, it is clear from both sets of equations that the value of f(1/2) very rapidly becomes just the average of the endpoints of the curve, i.e. the curve becomes flat over the smaller intervals. These values can be used to test just how linear the curve becomes, and after some point need not be subtracted from f(1/2) any longer. This is discussed more in the context of terminating the subdivision.

III. The Algorithm

Since cubics are sufficient for modelling surfaces that join with continuous tangent, there is usually little demand in computer graphics for higher degree algorithms. The work presented here implements only cubic subdivision, and the criteria given below for termination, although they also hold for higher degree, are based upon the geometric properties of the cubic curve in the Bernstein representation.

Subdivision Criteria.

Figure 1 shows a cubic curve with the control points p_i of the original curve, the control points a_i of the [0,1/2] subcurve and b_i of the [1/2,1] subcurve. The control polygon of the original curve is shown a solid lines, and the subcurves' control polygons are shown as dashed lines. The vectors v_1 and v_2 represent the portions "clipped" from the corners of the original polygon in performing the subdivision.

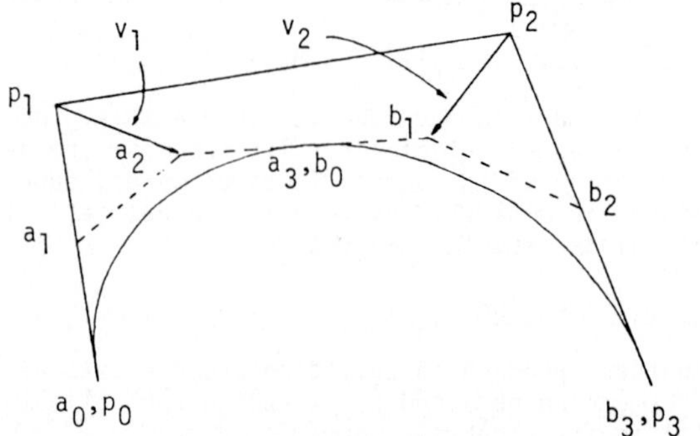

Figure 1. A cubic curve with control points p_i and points a_i and b_i of its subcurves.

The quantities v_1 and v_2 are constant multiples of the curvature of f(t) at their respective endpoints. This is easily verified by differentiating equation (1) with n=3. Therefore, from equation (7), v_1 and v_2 are proportional to g0 and g1 at each level of subdivision. Since g0 and g1 are each reduced by a factor of 1/4 at each level of subdivision, v_1 and v_2 clearly go to zero in the limit of infinitely many subdivisions. Therefore g0 and g1, or v_1 and v_2, provide a good measure of the flatness of a cubic curve. A similar argument may be made for the g0, g1, h0, h1 functions for quintics.

The level of subdivision should also be based upon the resolution of the destination display device(7). It is possible that v_1 or v_2 is very large in object space coordinates and yet very small relative to pixel distances. This screen space test is done by first dividing each of g0 and g1 by the depth coordinate of f0 and f1 respectively. By proper choice of the tolerance against which these are tested, the number of generated polygons, or bilinear elements, will be just sufficient to yield a smooth rendering of the surface. In this way, a curve or surface will be "optimally" subdivided according to a combination of the screen area it covers and its curvature.

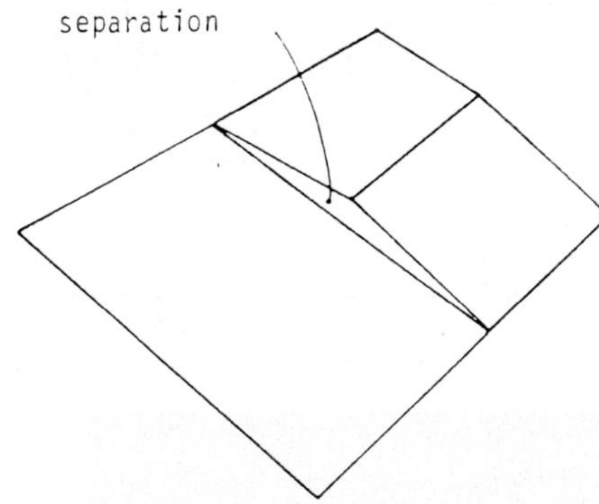

Figure 2. An exaggerated illustration of the separation resulting from subdividing one sibling patch and not the other.

To illustrate the simplicity of the subdivision termination tests, it is worth explicitly considering the tests implemented. In the surface formulation, each corner of a patch has associated with it four values,

$$f(u,v) = \sum_i \sum_j a_{i,j} \; u^i \; v^j ,$$

$$dfu(u,v) = [d^2 f(u,v)/du^2]/2,$$

$$dfv(u,v) = [d^2 f(u,v)/dv^2]/2,$$

$$dfuv(u,v) = [d^4 f(u,v)/dv^2 du^2]/4,$$

where each of u and v assumes the value 0 or 1, giving a total of 16 vector-valued quantities for the patch. The computations of equation 8 are carried out on one parameter at a time. In the following sequence, a polygon is output for rendering only if all of the tests are passed.

1. Are both the u=1 and u=0 boundary curves of the patch "flat"? If not, subdivide in the v direction, and recursively test the new subpatches generated. That is, for the u=1 curve, are all of the components of both dfv(1,0) and dfv(1,1) less in magnitude than the tolerance. Similarly for the u=0 curve.

2. Are both the v=1 and v=0 boundary curves of the patch "flat"? If not, subdivide in the u direction, and recursively test the new subpatches generated.

3. Is the middle of the patch "flat"? If not, subdivide in the u direction (arbitrary), and recursively test the new subpatches generated. This test is done on the magnitudes of the components of dfuv(u,v), for u,v=0,1.

Discontinuities.

Algorithms that recursively subdivide on the basis of the local curvature of a surface experience continuity problems. The problems result from subdividing one part of a surface along a boundary shared with a part needing no subdivision, thereby causing a "crack", or separation, along this boundary. This is illustrated in exaggerated form in Figure 2. Both Nyddeger and Carpenter and Lane experienced this problem. Nyddeger solved it by adding tiny "filler" polygons to the generated cracks. The Carpenter/Lane algorithm does not address the problem.

The present algorithm solves the problem by first considering only the boundary curves in determining if a patch requires further subdivision, as outlined above; if they exceed the tolerance, then the patch does and it is subdivided. Once a boundary is deemed "flat", however, then the quantity g(1/2) in equation (8) is subsequently not subtracted from (fo+f1)/2. Therefore, even it the patch requires further subdivision along this boundary for reasons other than the boundary's effect on it, the boundary is assumed to be a straight line(i.e., the midpoint is simply the average of the two endpoints) so that no separation occurs.

This technique applies as well to surfaces of any degree. Once a boundary curve becomes sufficiently linear, E(t,d) in equation (5) is simply not subtracted if the subcurve must subsequently be subdivided.

Results.

Figure 3 is a line drawing of the control polygons for 12 bicubic surface patches. The patches are arranged in this pattern to illustrate all of the features of the subdivision algorithm.

A line drawing of the 261 polygons output by the algorithm applied to this set of patches is shown in Figure 4a. For clarity, a side view of half of the object is shown in Figure 4b. Note that the cylindrically shaped region is subdivided only in the direction of curvature. This region, which is composed of two surface patches, is joined to two more patches which comprise the "elbow" portion of the surface. In this elbow region, subdivision occurs in both directions since there is curvature in both directions. Blending this region into the flat portion of the surface at the end are four surface patches. Note that tey are subdivided to the same limit as the "elbow" where they join to it, yet they are subdivided very little near the planar region. Finally, the four planar patches are not subdivided at all.

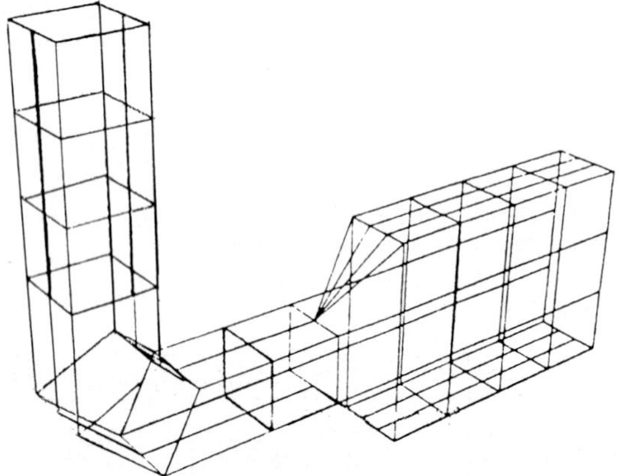

Figure 3. A line drawing of the control polygons for the object appearing in all subsequent figures.

A shaded rendering of this object is shown in Figure 5. This picture was produced by applying an algorithm described by Catmull(8) to the polygons shown in Figure 4. This algorithm reduces the effects of aliasing by averaging the portions of the polygons visible within each pixel weighted by their respective intensities. The results were shaded using a method described by Phong(9).

IV. Conclusions.

A significant motivation for generating polygons as output of any curved surface rendering algorithm is that they can be input to conventional scan-line algorithms, and therefore all of the techniques known for rendering polygons can be applied. Because of its inherent simplicity and stability over other numerical techniques, recursive subdivision is a very desirable means to generate these polygons.

The subdivision algorithm described dynamically subdivides a surface patch on the basis of its screen space curvature. As a result, for a fixed geometry, the number of polygons it generates depends upon the screen area that the surface covers; the minimum number of polygons it generates is equal to the number of surface patches used in defining the object. However, the algorithm is also useful for statically generating polygonal data bases for smooth objects. That is, objects defined by surface patches may be subdivided only on the basis of object space curvature, and the results can be used as a data base for existing polygon based algorithms.

The central difference basis simplifies the arithmetic required to subdivide the surfaces and yields as a byproduct a set of coefficients that

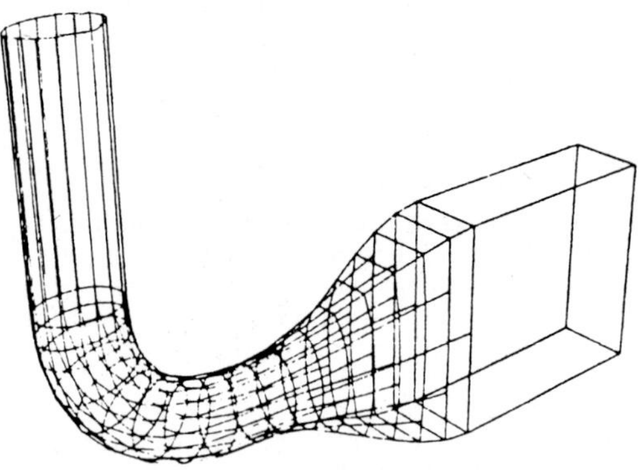

Figure 4a. A line drawing of the polygons resulting from the subdivision algorithm.

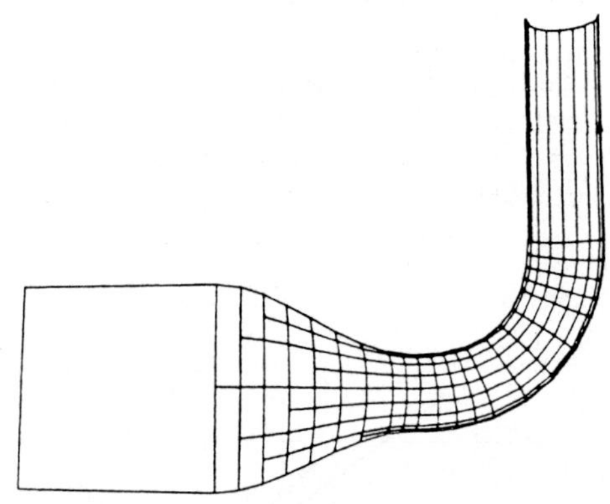

Figure 4b. Half of the object appearing in Figure 4a.

Figure 5. A shaded picture of the object created by standard polygon rendering techniques.

measure the parametric bilinearity of the subpatches created. In addition, it leads to a very simple solution to the very serious problem of separations, which other subdivision algorithms have not adequately addressed.

The sequence of tests applied in the present work to determine the need for further subdivision may also be applied using the Bernstein basis. The key notion is that the criteria for subdividing the boundary curve shared between two sibling patches should be based only upon the properties of that curve. Once it is within the tolerance of being linear, any subsequent subdivisions of it are accomplished by treating it as though it were exactly linear, thereby eliminating the physical separations between surfaces. Using the central difference basis, this simply means that its endpoints are averaged to get the midpoint.

Acknowledgments

The author would like to thank Ed Catmull and Jeff Lane for discussions of their algorithms that led to enhancements in the present algorithm.

References

1. Catmull, E. E., A Subdivision Algorithm for Computer Display of Curved Surfaces, University of Utah, UTEC-CSc-74-133, 1974.
2. Blinn, J. F., A Scan Line Algorithm for Computer Display of Curved Surfaces, Proc. SIGGRAPH 78, to appear, CACM.
3. Whitted, T., A Scan Line Algorithm for Displaying Parametrically Defined Surfaces, Proc. SIGGRAPH 78, to appear, CACM.
4. Carpenter, L. and Lane, J. , private communication, to appear, CACM.
5. Nyddeger, R. A Data Minimization Algorithm of Analytical Models for Computer Graphics, Masters Thesis, Dept. of Computer Science, University of Utah, 1972.
6. Lane,J. and Riesenfeld, R., A Theoretical Development for the Computer Generation and Display of Piecewise Polynomial Surfaces, to appear, IEEE TPAMI.
7. Clark, J. H. , Hierarchical Geometric Models for Visible Surface Algorithms, CACM 19, Oct. 1976.
8. Catmull, E. E., A Hidden-Surface Algorithm with Anti-Aliasing, SIGGRAPH 79, pp. 6-10.
9. Phong, B. T., Illumination for Computer Generated Images, CACM 18, June 1975, pp. 311-317.

"Scan Line Methods for Displaying Parametrically Defined Surfaces" by J.M. Lane, L.C. Carpenter, T. Whitted, and J.F. Blinn from *Communications of ACM*, Volume 23, Number 1, January 1980, pages 23-34. Copyright 1980, Association for Computing Machinery, Inc., reprinted by permission.

Scan Line Methods for Displaying Parametrically Defined Surfaces

Jeffrey M. Lane
Boeing Commercial Airplane Company

Loren C. Carpenter
Boeing Computer Services

Turner Whitted
Bell Laboratories

James F. Blinn
Caltech/JPL

Turner Whitted's work was performed at North Carolina State University, Raleigh, N.C., and was supported in part by the National Science Foundation under grant MCS 75-06599.

Authors' present addresses: J.F. Blinn, Jet Propulsion Laboratory, 4800 Oak Grove Dr., 125-104, Pasadena, CA 91103; L.C. Carpenter and J.M. Lane, Mail Stop 35-02, The Boeing Company, P.O. Box 3707, Seattle, WA 98124; T. Whitted, Bell Telephone Labs., Room 4F621, Holmdel, NJ 07733.

This paper presents three scan line methods for drawing pictures of parametrically defined surfaces. A scan line algorithm is characterized by the order in which it generates the picture elements of the image. These are generated left to right, top to bottom in much the same way as a picture is scanned out on a TV screen. Parametrically defined surfaces are those generated by a set of bivariate functions defining the *X*, *Y*, and *Z* position of points on the surface. The primary driving mechanism behind such an algorithm is the inversion of the functions used to define the surface. In this paper, three different methods for doing the numerical inversion are presented along with an overview of scan line methods.

Key Words and Phrases: computer graphics, scan line algorithm, shaded graphics display, parametric surfaces

CR Categories: 5.12, 5.13, 8.1, 8.2

Graphics and Image Processing — J.D. Foley, Editor

1. Introduction

Computer aided design has long been concerned with the design of parametrically representable surfaces. Such surfaces are those defined by three bivariate functions:

$$X = X(u, v)$$
$$Y = Y(u, v)$$
$$Z = Z(u, v)$$

As the parameters vary between 0 and 1, the functions sweep out the surface in question. The mathematical representation of these surfaces provides shapes with pleasing properties of continuity and smoothness. Until recently, the only method for drawing shaded pictures of such a surface has been to divide it into many polygonal facets and to apply any of several polygon drawing algorithms. A few years ago, Catmull [3] devised one of the first algorithms for drawing bicubic parametric surfaces directly from the mathematical surface formulation. While this algorithm generates images of superior quality, it still has some drawbacks. These have to do with speed and memory requirements and the ease of performing anti-aliasing operations. These drawbacks are eliminated by the class of algorithms known as scan line algorithms. Such algorithms generate the picture elements in order from left to right, top to bottom on the screen, much as a television might scan them out. The algorithms described here are scan line based algorithms for generating such images which remove some of the difficulties of Catmull's algorithm without substantial sacrifice in picture quality. Before presenting the new methods, however, it will be useful to review scan line techniques for polygonal objects.

2. Scan Line Algorithms

Each of the new algorithms is a generalization of more conventional scan line algorithms for drawing polygonal objects. It is therefore worthwhile to examine conceptually what is happening during a scan line algorithm for polygons. It is assumed for both the polygonal case and the parametric curve case that the objects to be drawn have been transformed to a screen space with X going to the right, Y going up, and Z going into the screen. Furthermore, the perspective transformation is assumed to have been performed on all objects as described in [6, 14] so that an orthographic projection of X and Y onto the screen is appropriate. In the case of parametric curved surfaces this serves to alter the form of the functions somewhat but the processing performed upon those functions remains the same.

A scan line algorithm basically consists of two nested loops, one for the Y coordinate going down the screen and one for the X coordinate going across each scan line of the current Y. For each execution of the Y loop, a plane is defined by the eyepoint and the scan line on the screen. All objects to be drawn are intersected with this plane. The result is a set of line segments in XZ, one (or more) for each potentially visible polygon on that scan line. These line segments are then processed by the X scan loop. For each execution of this loop a scan ray is defined by the eyepoint and a picture element on the screen. All segments are intersected with this ray to yield a set of points, one for each potentially visible polygon at that picture element. These points are then sorted by their Z position. The point with the smallest Z is deemed visible and an intensity is computed for it. The processing during the X scan is, then, fundamentally the same as the processing during the Y scan except for the change in dimensionality. During the Y scan, 3D polygons are intersected with a plane to produce 2D line segments. During the X scan, 2D line segments are intersected with a line to produce 1D points.

Many enhancements must be added to the basic scheme to make it practical. Most of these are referred to as taking advantage of the "coherence" of the picture. This basically means that many of the calculations are made incremental rather than absolute. The opportunity to do this is, indeed, much more the reason for generating pictures in scan line order in the first place. For example, the Y scan is responsible for constructing a list of all potentially visible segments which will be processed by the X scan. Rather than construct this list from scratch for each Y coordinate, it is usual to keep the list around between scan lines and update it according to how it has changed. Changes to this "active segment list" take three forms. As the scan plane drops below a vertex of the polygon which represents a local maximum, a new segment must be created and added to the list, Figure 1(a). As the scan plane drops below a vertex which represents a local minimum, a segment must be deleted from the list, Figure 1(b). Finally, for those segments which remain in the list, XZ coordinates of the endpoints of the segments must be updated to reflect their new position, Figure 1(c).

This latter operation can also be computed incrementally. The endpoint of an active segment is generated by the intersection of an edge of the polygon (a straight line segment) with the scan plane. The amounts of change in X and Z for a unit step in Y are constants along the entirety of the edge. The increments can be computed once when the edge first becomes active and just added to the XZ position for each step in Y.

Editor's Note: This is a combination of three individual papers previously accepted for publication in *Communications of the ACM*. The papers were "A Scan Line Algorithm for the Computer Display of Parametrically Defined Surfaces" by J. Lane and L. Carpenter, "A Scan Line Algorithm for Displaying Parametrically Defined Surfaces" by J. Blinn, and "A Scan Line Algorithm for Computer Display of Curved Surfaces" by T. Whitted. The latter two papers were presented at SIGGRAPH '78. The section editor is grateful to J. Blinn for suggesting that the papers be merged, and to J. Lane for managing the production of the new paper.—J.D. Foley

Fig. 1. Incremental scan line operations.

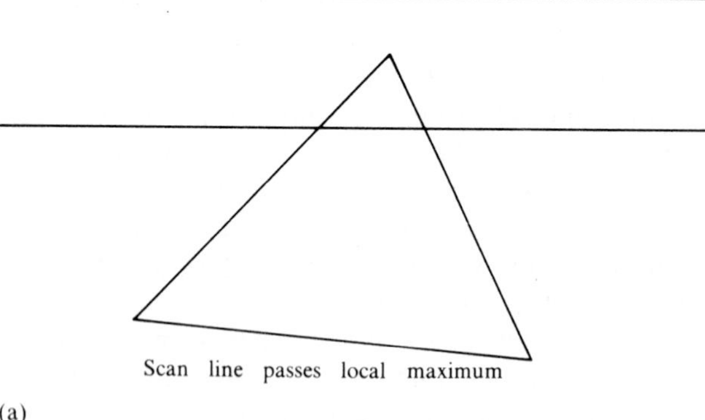

(a)

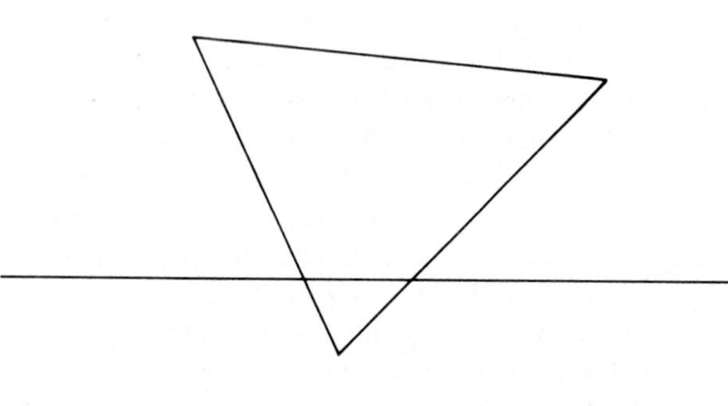

(b)

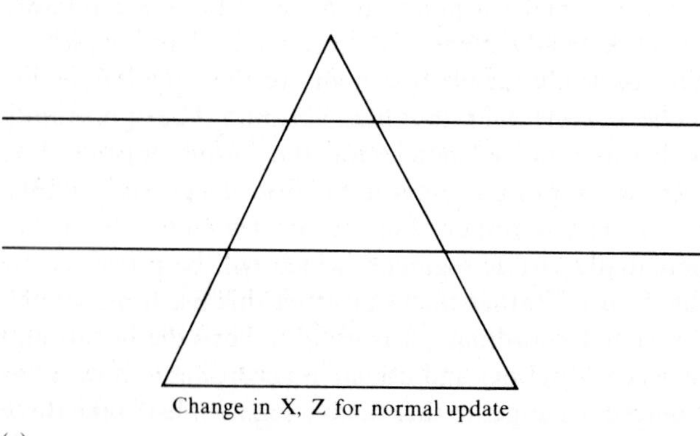

(c)

The computation for the Y loop then reduces to the following processes. All endpoints are initially sorted in Y to determine the order in which they will pass through the Y scan plane. For each new Y, the X and Z coordinates of all existing segments are updated. If any polygon vertices have been passed, new segments are created or old ones deleted according to the type of vertex. The calculations are analogously made incremental for the X scan. As it proceeds, it maintains its own "active point list" of intersections. We consider the X scan process in more detail in the next section.

2.1 *X-Z* Plane Processing

Each of the algorithms described here, like polygon algorithms, generates a list of sample points in the X-Z plane for every scan line. The sample points are linked in pairs by straight lines to form scan line segments, which are a piecewise linear approximation to the curve of intersection between the X-Z scanning plane and the surface element being displayed. The ways in which these segments are formed varies considerably between the various algorithms. The further processing of these segments, i.e., the transformation from segments to pixels, makes use of common shading techniques which can be applied to any of the algorithms. We will discuss shading techniques further in Section 2.2.

The visible surface algorithm scans line segments to resolve the two final unknowns in the display process: (1) which scan line segments or portions of segments are visible, and (2) what intensity value must be applied to each pixel along a visible segment.

2.1.1 *Z* before *X* sorting. Conceptually, visibility is easy to determine: Whatever surface lies closest to the viewer at any given point is the visible one. One way to actually calculate the visibility is to sort all surfaces with respect to their distance from the viewer and assign a priority to each surface based on the order of the sorted list [3]. If the priority cannot be resolved, then the surfaces must be subdivided until an unambiguous ordering is found. Then at each point along a scan line, the segment belonging to the highest priority surface is the visible one. A simpler technique is to wait until after the list of scan line segments has been generated to determine priority. Then the sort can be made in the X-Z plane with less chance of ambiguities.

Alternatively, an algorithm may paint each scan line segment into a pixel buffer, starting with the farthest segment and ending with the nearest. If any segment overlaps another that has been previously written, it will overwrite the previous one. In this way the nearest surface will be visible in the final image. To display transparent surfaces, near surfaces only partially overwrite the background. This priority technique has the disadvantage that each scan line segment must be painted whether it is visible or not.

When displaying opaque surfaces, it is not necessary to know the entire ordering of segments; it is sufficient to know just which one has the highest priority. A simple way of determining this uses a "z-buffer" (an array containing as many locations as the scan line does pixels) [1, 4]. The z-buffer is initialized to the depth of the far clipping plane. Then as each segment is processed, its depth is compared to the value stored in the z-buffer. If the new depth is greater than the currently visible one, the new segment is not visible at that point. If the new depth is less than the currently visible one, the new depth value is written into the z-buffer and the intensity value calculated for the current segment at that point overwrites the previous value. In this manner the nearest segment will always be visible regardless of the order in which segments were processed.

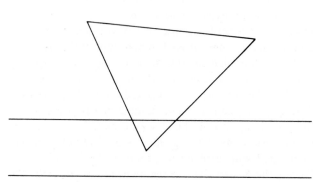

2.1.2 *X* before *Z* sorting. Instead of sorting segments according to depth (*Z* dimension), it is sometimes more convenient to sort according to the *X* value of the left-most endpoint and let the processing move from left to right along the scan line. The shading processor will add a segment to its active list as soon as the *X* value of its left endpoint is less than the *X* value of the current pixel. If the new segment is in front of the currently visible segment, then the new one is declared visible. It remains visible until it intersects another active segment or is obscured by a newly active segment. By processing segments in this order, the shader considers only the visible surfaces and saves a considerable amount of time.

2.1.3 Scan line coherence. An alternative to sorting in *X* and *Z* is to simply write each segment into a scan line *z*-buffer, where a pixel is overwritten only if the new *z* value is in front of the old *z* value as in [10]. *X* before *Z* sorting is employed in the first algorithm below, *Z* before *X* is employed in the second, and the third algorithm uses the scanline *z*-buffer technique.

The above discussion refers to the order of processing, and to visibility calculations. The remaining processing, called shading, will assign an intensity value to each point once it is declared visible.

2.2 Intensity Computation

It is known that the reflected light received by an observer from any point on an object depends on the angle between the direction of sight and the reflected light vector at that point. This dependency may be modeled in many different ways in synthetic images. Gouraud [5] determined intensity at a point on a surface by

(2.2.1) $\quad \text{Intensity} = s(L \cdot N)$

where s is a reflectance factor, L is the unit light source vector, N is the unit normal vector, and $\cdot$ denotes the vector "dot" product. Phong [7] improved this model to approximate highlights

(2.2.2) $\quad \text{Intensity} = s(L \cdot N) + g(V \cdot N)^n$

where V is a unit virtual light source direction, g is a measure of the glossiness, and $n \geq 1$. Further work on mathematical models for intensity calculation has been done by Blinn [1].

Blinn noted that the proportion of specular reflection g varies with the direction of the light source, and the direction of maximum reflection is not always exactly along V. In his model Blinn assumes the surface being simulated is composed of a collection of highly reflective microfacets oriented randomly on the surface. His mathematical model for intensity then becomes

(2.2.3) $\quad \text{Intensity} = s(L \cdot N) + g(1 - s)$

where

$$g = \frac{DGF}{(N \cdot E)},$$

- D is the distribution function of the directions of the microfacets of the surface,
- G is the amount by which the facets shadow and mask each other,
- E is the eye direction, and
- F is the Fresnel reflection law.

The Gouraud model was used in shading the figures in Section 5, the Phong model was used in Section 4, and the Blinn model in Section 3.

3. Blinn Algorithm

This algorithm generalizes the concept of scanning a polygon to scanning a surface patch. The relevant properties of polygons which make them scannable are:

(a) We can determine *Y*-maxima/minima from the corner points and sort on *Y* coordinate.
(b) We can track edges as functions of *Y*.
(c) Each scan line segment is scannable in *Z* as a function of *X*.

Parametric surfaces have none of these properties. The *Y*-maxima/minima can occur on the boundary or the interior of the patch, and we need to distinguish between local and global maxima/minima. Not only do we need to track the boundary edges, but we need to track silhouette edges as well. For smooth surfaces the silhouette edges correspond to curves in the surface where the *Z*-component of the normal is zero. (See Figure 2.) These curves may or may not intersect the boundary of the patch. Neither the boundary nor the silhouette edges need be monotonic in *Y*, or representable as a function of *Y*. Similar problems exist for each *X* scan.

Although for parametric surface patches the *Y*-maxima/minima and edge information is not readily available, one can approximate this data with iterative techniques [14]. The relevant systems of equations are:

For determining boundary curve interactions with the current scan line (*Y* scan):

(a) $Y(0, v) = Yscan,$
(b) $Y(1, v) = Yscan,$
(c) $Y(u, 0) = Yscan,$
(d) $Y(u, 1) = Yscan.$

For determining silhouette edge intersections with the current scan line:

$$Y(u, v) = Yscan$$
$$Zn(u, v) = 0$$

where $Zn(u, v)$ is the Z component of the normal equation of the patch.

For determining local Y maxima/minima:

$$Yu(u, v) = 0$$
$$Yv(u, v) = 0$$

Fig. 2. Two Types of Edges for Curved Surfaces.

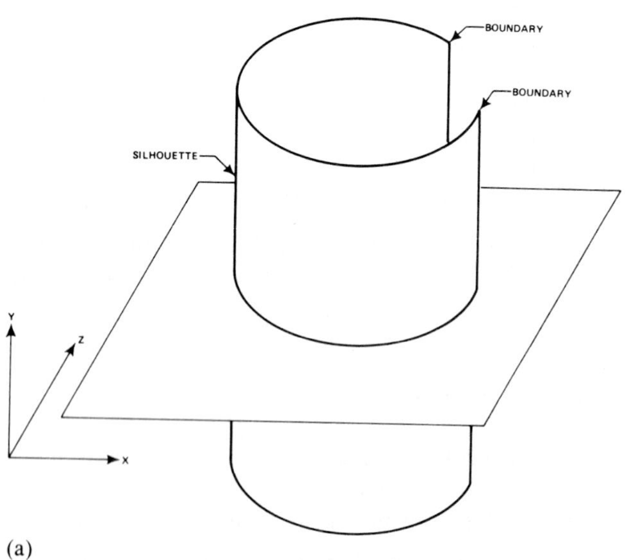

(a)

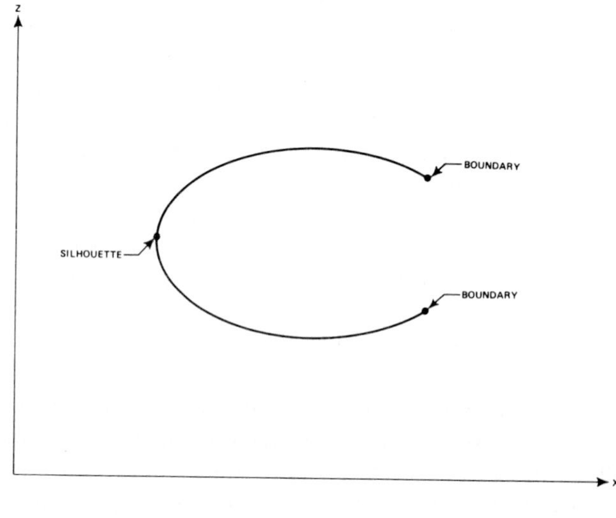

(b)

where Yu and Yv are the partials with respect to u and v.

For determining segments of the x scan:

$$Y(u, v) - Y\text{scan} = 0$$
$$X(u, v) - X\text{scan} = 0.$$

Newton iteration is a useful technique for solving each of these systems [14]. In particular, since Newton iteration requires an initial guess at a solution, a type of coherence can be built into the tracking mechanism if we use the previous (u, v) solution as a guess for the current scan line. As with polygons, edges are created at Y maxima and at the intersection of boundary and silhouette edges. Similarly, edges are deleted at Y minima and intersections with boundary edges. By inserting silhouette edges and partitioning all edges with Y maxima/minima, we have effectively partitioned the surface patch itself into pieces which are monotonic decreasing in Y and singularly valued in Z. This information is used during the X scan to produce the front most point on the surface for any (X scan, Y scan) point.

Problems with this approach would appear to be numerous. Singularities or cusps in the patch and its derivatives can occur even though the surface is analytic as a function of (u, v). For these cases Newton iteration is not appropriate and other iterative or heuristic approaches have to be used. There can be many types of Y maxima/minima such as saddle points, which induce the creation of additional edges, and the problem of resolving multiple condition points, such as a silhouette edge starting at a boundary point where a maxima also occurs, are always present. More details on special cases can be found in [1]. However, for most models of three-dimensional shapes the surface pieces tend to be well-behaved, and for these surfaces this algorithm has proven robust and relevant.

4. Whitted Algorithm

A second algorithm for surface display is also a generalization of polygon type algorithms. In it, patches are described in terms of edges, which in this case are cubic curves instead of straight lines. These edges are intersected by successive scanning planes to form the endpoints of scan line segments that are passed to the shader.

This approach fails naturally, if the surface element contains a silhouette on its interior or if it is excessively curved. To circumvent this problem the processor that generates edges also detects silhouettes and divides the patch along the silhouette curve. If a patch is excessively curved, the edge generator can produce additional curves on the interior of the patch to improve the accuracy of the image.

4.1 Edge Description of Patches

Bicubic surface patches have four natural edge curves: $E_0 = f(u, 0)$, $E_1 = F(0, v)$, $E_2 = f(u, 1)$, and $E_3 = f(1, v)$, each of which is cubic in one variable. If, as in the case of excessively curved patches, it is necessary to specify additional "edges" on the interior of the patch, these edges (parametric curves on the surface) are also cubic curves of one variable, defined by either $E_u = f(k_u, v)$ or $E_u = f(u, k_u)$. The addition of two such interior edges, specified by $k_u = 0.5$ and $k_v = 0.5$, has the effect of dividing the patch into four subpatches, as shown in Figure 3.

A third type of edge is the patch silhouette, i.e., the curve on the surface for which the z component of the normal vector is zero. In general, the order of the silhouette curve is greater than the cubic, but it is approximated here by a piecewise cubic interpolant so that the silhouette can be treated the same as any other edge. If the

Fig. 3.

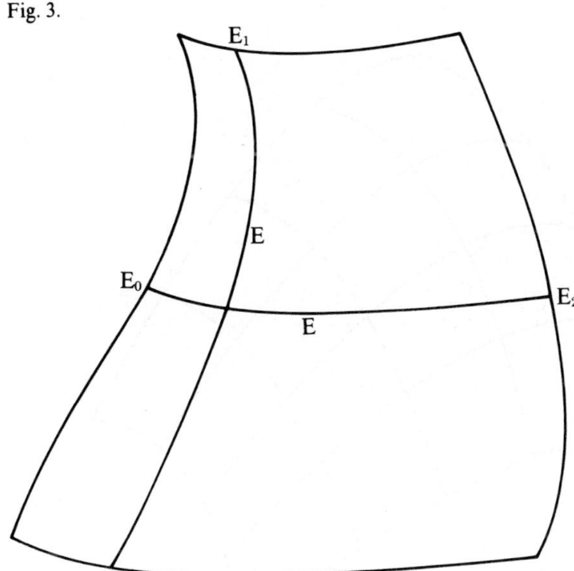

silhouette curve passes through a patch, $f(u, v)$, there are two points (u_a, v_a) and (u_b, v_b), each on an edge of the patch such that $N_z(u_a, v_a) = 0$ and $N_z(u_b, v_b) = 0$ where N_z is the z component of the normal vector. At each of these points a plane tangent to the surface is defined by the two vectors df/du and df/dv. Since any vector tangent to the surface must lie in this plane, the derivative of the silhouette curve can be expressed as a linear combination of the two vectors that define the plane. Then a hermite interpolant joining the two endpoints can be specified by:

$$p(x) = [t^3\ t^2\ t\ 1]\ M\ P$$

where

$$M = \begin{bmatrix} 2 & -2 & 1 & 1 \\ -3 & 3 & -2 & -1 \\ 0 & 0 & 1 & 0 \\ 1 & 0 & 0 & 0 \end{bmatrix}$$

and

$$P = \begin{bmatrix} f(u_a, v_a) \\ f(u_b, v_b) \\ \alpha_u df(u_a, v_a)/du + \alpha_v df(u_a, v_a)/dv \\ \beta_u df(u_b, v_b)/du + \beta_v df(u_b, v_b)/dv \end{bmatrix}$$

The accuracy of the resulting silhouette curve depends on the number of cubic segments used in the piecewise approximation and on the choice of α and β. Since each cubic segment spans the area between endpoints on the edges of a patch, the specification of additional edges on the interior of the patch containing the silhouette will improve the result. After the patch is subdivided by adding internal edges, the silhouette generator examines each subpatch in turn to see if its edges are intersected by the silhouette and produces an approximating segment that spans the two endpoints. This approach to approximating the silhouette is similar to the one described in [9]. If the silhouette crosses the boundaries of a subpatch just once, or more than twice, or crosses any one boundary more than once, or if it is contained entirely within the subpatch, then the silhouette generator defaults and an error occurs on the visible portion of that subpatch.

The choice of α and β terms in the interpolation formula determine both the direction and magnitude of the endpoint derivative vector. Since excessively curved patches are typically subdivided by the insertion of internal edges, one may assume that each subpatch examined by the silhouette generator is reasonably close to planar. Then a very simple approximation will suffice for α and β. First let

$$(|\alpha_u^1|/|\alpha_v^1|) = (|u_2 - u_1|/|v_2 - v_1|)$$

with

$$|\alpha_v^1| = 1 - |\alpha_u^1|$$

Then the first expression can be rewritten as

$$|\alpha_u^1| = 1/(1 + |v_2 - v_1|/|u_2 - u_1|)$$

To adjust for the arclength of the interpolant

$$|\alpha_u| = |\alpha_u^1|\ \sqrt{(u_2 - u_1)^2 + (v_2 - v_1)^2}$$
$$|\alpha_v| = |\alpha_v^1|\ \sqrt{(u_2 - u_1)^2 + (v_2 - v_1)^2}$$

with signs given by

$$\mathrm{sgn}(\alpha_u) = \mathrm{sgn}(u_2 - u_1)$$

and

$$\mathrm{sgn}(\alpha_v) = \mathrm{sgn}(v_2 - v_1)$$

Finally, let $\beta_u = \alpha_u$ and $\beta_v = \alpha_v$. Figure 4 shows the resulting silhouette approximation superimposed on a set of sectional curves.

The definition of a cubic edge requires 12 coefficients: four each for the x, y, and z components. In addition, surface normal information along each edge must be provided for use by both the shader and the silhouette detector. If only an orthogonal view is required in the

Fig. 4.

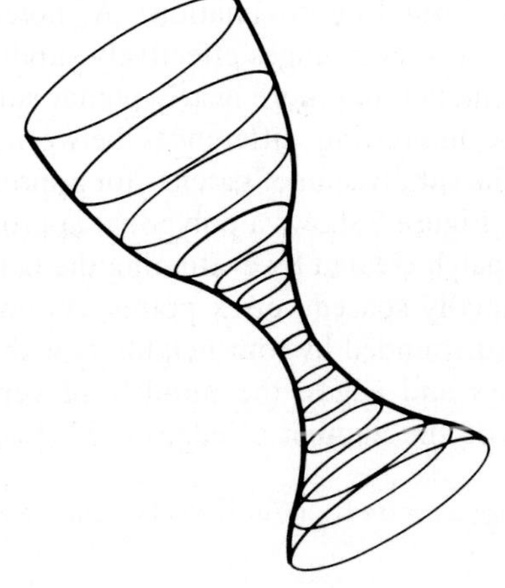

Fig. 5.

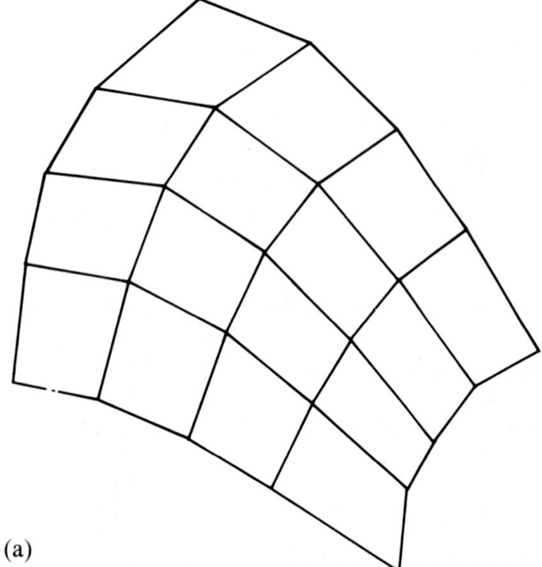
(a)

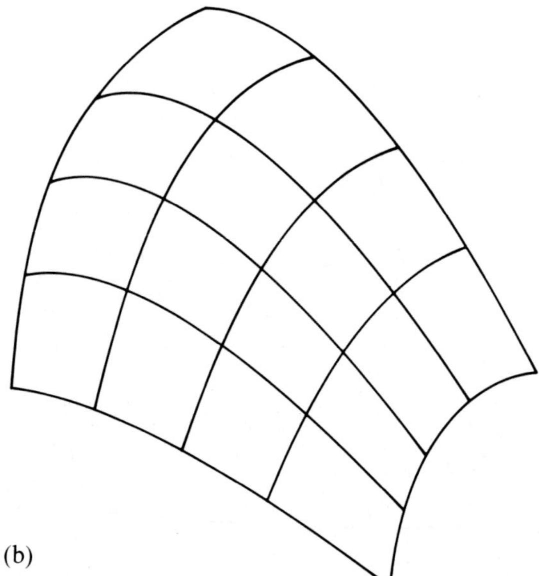
(b)

final display, all of the required information can be obtained from the coefficients of the derivative with respect to the constant parameter along each edge.[1] The derivative with respect to the variable parameter (the curve's tangent vector) can be derived readily from the curve coefficients. The cross-product of these two derivatives yields an exact normal at each point on the edge.

Ordinarily a perspective view is required. A technique described by Catmull [3] uses a bicubic equation to approximate the cubic normal function along each edge. The perspective view of the surface is generated by transforming the control points for the surface and using the resulting control points to form an approximation to the transformed bicubic surface. The bicubic normal approximation is not passed through the perspective transform since proper shading depends on preserving the object space illumination direction. Use of the approximate normal function has the added advantage of speeding the scan conversion process since it is not necessary to calculate cross-products at every intersection point on the edge to find the surface normal.

Edges are stored in a y-sorted list of modules, each containing 24 coefficients (12 for the edge curve and 12 for the cubic normal approximation). As noted before, the inclusion of interior edges effectively subdivides the surface into smaller and more nearly planar subpatches.

There are interesting differences between this approach and the subdivision of patches for approximation by polygons. Figure 5 shows a polygonal approximation of a bicubic patch created by evaluating the patch equation at 25 equally spaced vertex points. Assuming that the patch is surrounded by four neighbors with which it shares vertices and edges, the number of vertices per patch is 16 and the number of edges is 32. Each vertex is defined by six coefficients (three for position and three for the surface normal) and each edge description requires two pointers (one to each of the endpoint vertices). The total number of words required per patch is 160. Figure 5 shows the same patch in terms of its boundary curves and six internal edges. Assuming that the boundaries are shared, the total number of edges per patch is eight, requiring 192 words of memory. In general, if a patch is subdivided M times in the u direction and N times in the v direction and represented by quadrilateral polygons, the number of edges required is $2MN$ per patch. For the approach given here only $M + N$ cubic edges are required. (In Figure 5, $M = 4$ and $N = 4$). Furthermore, every cubic edge lies entirely on the surface (except for the silhouette approximation) whereas if a polygonal approximation is used, the edges coincide with the surface only at the vertices.

4.2 Intersection Processor

The intersection (scan conversion) processor is the heart of this algorithm; it operates on the edge list and outputs scan line segments in reverse order of visibility.

The first stage of the procedure examines each edge to insure that it is monotonic in y, segmenting those that are not, and avoiding the problem of finding multiple intersections of the edge with a single scan line. The presence of extrema along an edge can be detected rapidly by examining the coefficients of the y component of the edge curve, and since the derivative of the curve is quadratic, their location is found using the quadratic formula to solve for zeros of the derivative.

The equation $E_y(t) = y_n$ where y_n is the y value of scan line number and $E_y(t)$ is the y component of the edge curve is solved using Newton's iteration to yield t_n. In turn, $E_x(t_n)$, $E_z(t_n)$, and the components of the normal vector at that point on the edge are computed. Making

[1] On the edge $E_u = f(u\ k_v)$, df/dv is a cubic function with respect to u.

use of scan line coherence, a first order estimate of the solution for the next scan line,

$$t_{n+1} \approx t_n - (y_n - y_{n+1})/E_y^1(t_n)$$

results in rapid convergence of the next solution, usually in the first iteration. Because it is restricted to the (0, 1) interval, Newton's method will occasionally fail to converge. In this case the scan conversion routine resorts to a brute force binary search for the solution.

Because the internal edges and concavities lead to multiple pairs of intersection points, edges of a given patch must be sorted into ascending x order to insure the generation of proper segments. Note that this is a relatively cheap sort since a patch is typically intersected only a few times on any given scan line. As each segment is formed, it is inserted into a depth ordered list of all segments for the current scan line. In the interest of high speed processing, the depth separator test is limited to comparing the average depth of segment endpoints to establish the priority of segments. The test is performed in two dimensions instead of three and involves only scan line segments rather than entire objects or patches. Z ordering of the segments is included to enable the simulation of transparency, but it can be eliminated if only opaque surfaces are considered, since final visibility is established by z-buffer comparisons that are incorporated into the shader.

5. Lane-Carpenter Algorithm

In this section we present a scan line algorithm for the computer display of curved surfaces which makes use of a subdivision technique similar to that of Catmull [3] combined with a polygon display algorithm. The approach is quite simple:

The Display Algorithm

Step 1. Patches are sorted by maximum possible Y value.

Step 2. As each scan line is processed, patches with this maximum possible Y value are subdivided until:

- (a) Any one piece no longer overlaps the scan line and therefore is placed in the inactive patch list; or
- (b) The patch is within a set tolerance of being a four-sided planar polygon, at which time it may be processed as with a polygon scan line algorithm.

The algorithm is essentially a polygon algorithm in which the active list of displayable elements consists of four-sided polygons, while the inactive list now has parametric patches as elements. However, the active elements are also parametric patches, and full use of the information in the definition can be used to blend adjoining subpatches with arbitrary smoothness in intensity. Step 1 can be done with a radix sort which runs in linear time. Note: If in 2b we set the tolerance to be less than one raster, the silhouette is guaranteed to be smooth in appearance.

A brief discussion of the Catmull subdivision algorithm for parametric bicubic patches will make this algorithm more readily understood. A parametric cubic curve may be defined as:

$$P(t) = \sum_{i=0}^{3} fi(t)Pi$$

for t in [0, 1] and Pi in R^3, where $\{fi(t)\}$ is a basis for cubic polynomial functions. Typically $fi(t) = t^i$, the power basis. Surfaces are defined by taking the tensor product of the curve methods. For bicubics we have

$$P(u, v) = \sum_{i=0}^{3} \sum_{j=0}^{3} fij(u, v)Pij,$$

for (u, v) in $[0, 1] \times [0, 1]$, $fij(u, v) = fi(u)fj(v)$, and Pij in R^3. The subdivision problem for curves is to determine for $t0$ in [0, 1], the sets of coefficients $Q0$, $Q1$, $Q2$, $Q3$ and $R0$, $R1$, $R2$, $R3$ such that

$$P(t \cdot t0) = \sum_{i=0}^{3} fi(t)Qi$$

and

$$P((1 - t0)t + t0) = \sum_{i=0}^{3} fi(t)Ri,$$

for t in [0, 1]. The analogous problem for surfaces is, for $(u0, v0)$ in $[0, 1] \times [0, 1]$, determine sequences $\{Qij\}$, $\{Rij\}$, $\{Sij\}$, and $\{Tij\}$ such that

$$P(u \cdot u0, v \cdot v0) = \sum_{i=0}^{3} \sum_{j=0}^{3} fij(u, v)Qij,$$

$$P(u \cdot u0, (1 - v0)v + v0)) = \sum_{i=0}^{3} \sum_{j=0}^{3} fij(u, v)Rij,$$

$$P((1 - u0)u + u0), v \cdot v0) = \sum_{i=0}^{3} \sum_{j=0}^{3} fij(u, v)Sij,$$

and

$$P((1 - u0)u + u0), (1 - v0)v + v0)) = \sum_{i=0}^{3} \sum_{j=0}^{3} fij(u, v)Tij$$

for (u, v) in $[0, 1] \times [0, 1]$. Since the subdivision of bicubic patches is a direct extension of the method for cubic curves, we can direct our attention to the curve methods here.

Because subdivision in Catmull's algorithm proceeds until patches are pixel size, high speed is essential. The choice of basis $\{fi(t)\}$ is therefore important. Catmull derived the following basis which allowed him to compute the new coefficients for a cubic split at $t0 = \frac{1}{2}$ with only three adds (assuming fixed shifts can be hardwired):

$$f0(t) = 1 - t$$
$$f1(t) = t^3/3 + t^2 - 2t/3$$
$$f2(t) = t^3/3 - t/3$$
$$f3(t) = t$$

In matrix notation for the curve we have

$$P(t) = [t^3 t^2 t\, 1] \begin{bmatrix} 0 & -\frac{1}{3} & \frac{1}{3} & 0 \\ 0 & 1 & 0 & 0 \\ -1 & -\frac{2}{3} & -\frac{1}{3} & 1 \\ 1 & 0 & 0 & 0 \end{bmatrix} \begin{bmatrix} P0 \\ P1 \\ P2 \\ P3 \end{bmatrix}$$

Note $P(0) = P0$ and $P(1) = P3$. It is easily verified for the choice $t0 = \frac{1}{2}$ that

$$\begin{aligned} Q0 &= P0 &,\quad R0 &= Q3, \\ Q1 &= P1/4 &,\quad R1 &= Q2, \\ Q2 &= (P1 + P2)/8 &,\quad R2 &= P2/4, \\ Q3 &= (P0 + P3)/2 - (P1 + P2)/8 &,\quad R3 &= P3. \end{aligned}$$

To the authors' knowledge there is no faster method to subdivide a parametric cubic polynomial at $t = \frac{1}{2}$ than with the Catmull basis. However, the subdivision algorithm for display requires a subdivision of the patch and test for convergence. There does not seem to be a quick and accurate test for convergence with the Catmull basis which does not nullify the speed of the subdivision. For this reason we chose to use the Bernstein basis [3] for representing parametric cubics and bicubics.

The cubic Bernstein basis is given by

$$\begin{aligned} f0(t) &= (1 - t)^3 \\ f1(t) &= 3t(1 - t)^2 \\ f2(t) &= 3(1 - t)t^2 \\ f3(t) &= t^3 \end{aligned}$$

In matrix notation for the curve we have

$$P(t) = [t^3 t^2 t\, 1] \begin{bmatrix} -1 & 3 & -3 & 1 \\ 3 & -6 & 3 & 0 \\ -3 & 3 & 0 & 0 \\ 1 & 0 & 0 & 0 \end{bmatrix} \begin{bmatrix} P0 \\ P1 \\ P2 \\ P3 \end{bmatrix}$$

As with Catmull's basis, $P(0) = P0$ and $P(1) = P3$. It can be verified for the choice $t0 = \frac{1}{2}$ that

$$\begin{aligned} Q0 &= P0 &,\quad R0 &= Q3 \\ Q1 &= (P0 + P1)/2 &,\quad R1 &= (P1 + P2)/4 + R2/2 \\ Q2 &= Q1/2 + (P1 + P2)/4 &,\quad R2 &= (P2 + P3)/2 \\ Q3 &= (Q2 + R1)/2 &,\quad R3 &= P3 \end{aligned}$$

Thus with the Bernstein basis, subdivision of a cubic requires 6 adds. However, a very accurate and rapid convergence test is possible with this basis. Note that the basis functions $fi(t)$ are positive and sum identically to 1, i.e.,

$$fi(t) \geq 0, \text{ for all } i \text{ and } \sum_{i=0}^{3} fi(t) = 1,$$

for t in [0, 1]. That is, every point of the curve lies within the convex hull of the coefficients Pi (see Figure 6). Thus the maximum Y of the curve (surface) is bounded by the maximum Y of the Pi (Pij). From [11] we know that the sequence of new coefficients converges to the curve (surface) as we continue to subdivide. Therefore we can use the length (area) of the convex hull of these points to bound the length (area) of the curve (surface) segment (see Figure 7).

Fig. 6. Subdivision of cubic Bernstein polynomial.

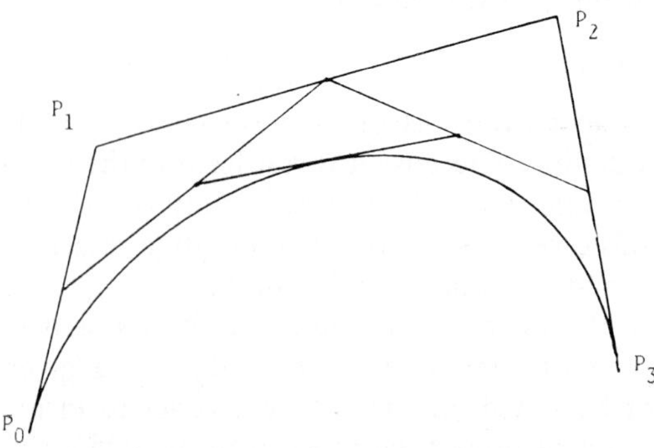

We are now ready to discuss the implementation of the Display Algorithm. All surface patches are represented in terms of the appropriate tensor product Bernstein basis. Then Steps 1 and 2(a) are easily accomplished by testing the subpatch coefficients. The "flatness" test in Step 2(b) reduces to testing the "flatness" of the enclosing convex hull, both for the boundary curves being linear and the patch interior being planar. Lane and Riesenfeld have shown in [11] that this convergence to linear polynomial form must take place. A simple flatness test for curve boundaries is to measure the distance of interior points on the convex hull to the line segment joining the end points. A similar test for surface flatness is to compute the distance of the convex hull points to the plane of any three corner points.

When the convex hull of the coefficients is planar within a given tolerance, the patch Y maxima and minima occur at corner points and the edges may be treated as linear. In short, the geometry of the patch may be treated as a four-sided polygon, yet we still have the true coefficients of the patch. These can be used to calculate the correct intensities for each point of the patch.

This algorithm produces smooth looking pictures while offering distinct advantages over previously published methods. The pictures have smoother silhouettes than can be generated with a priori polygon approximation, while the time and memory requirements are comparable to that of the polygon scan line algorithms. Numerical and heuristic methods are avoided by employing the subdivision techniques and theorems of [11]. By orienting the initial surfaces and maintaining the same orientation on the subpatches, we are able to cull back facing patches, thereby saving considerable processing time. Due to the independent splitting of subpatches, it is possible that cracks in the surface can occur during the scanning process. This problem can be effectively controlled by lowering the tolerance of the approximation to less than one raster.

6. Summary

Each of the hidden surface algorithms presented here has its advantages, which are directly related to the type of polygon algorithm generalization which has been made.

Fig. 7. Successive Subdivision Showing Convergence to Surface.

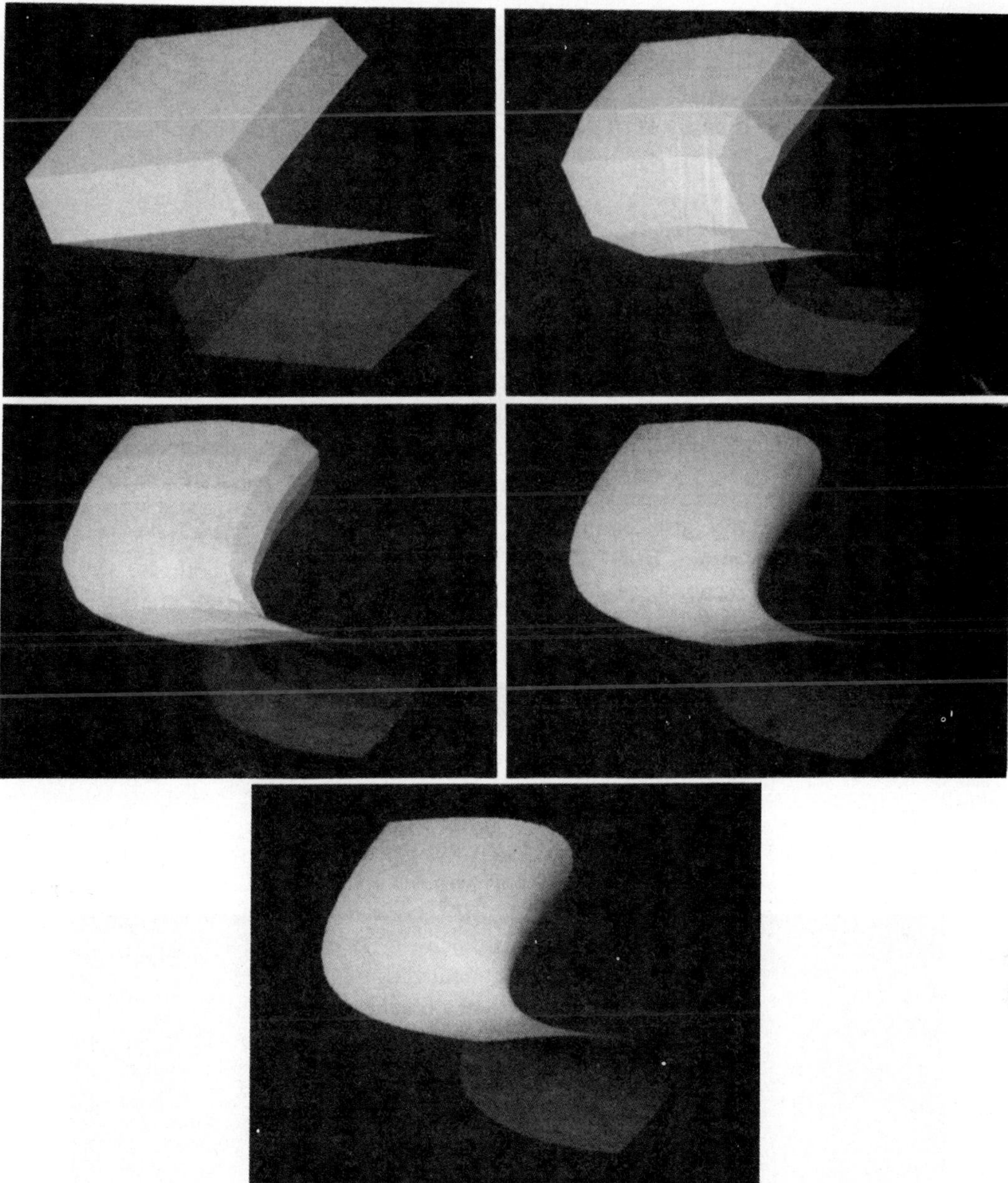

The Whitted algorithm generalizes the technique for handling surface pieces bounded by straight line segments to a method for handling surface pieces bounded by cubic curve segments. If a bicubic patch is a priori represented as curved polygon elements, this algorithm produces images void of polygonal silhouettes, a distinct advantage. Disadvantages are the inability to pick up internal silhouettes and the use of numerical techniques for tracking edges, although for polynomials these can be made to always converge [12]. Figure 9 was produced with this algorithm.

The Carpenter/Lane algorithm approximates curved surface patches with surface pieces bounded by straight line segments, where the approximation is made only as good as the view necessitates. Further, the approximation is not made a priori, but as the image is being scanned out, thus minimizing the amount of storage necessary to represent the scene. The algorithm depends upon recursive subdivision which yields easy access to the bounds and flatness properties of the subpatches. A disadvantage of the algorithm are the "holes" that can occur in the image generated due to the representation of the boundaries of "tileable" patches by straight lines. Figure 10 was made with the Carpenter/Lane algorithm.

Figure 8 was produced with the Blinn algorithm. The Blinn algorithm is more general than either of the previous two, in that no priori fit with polynomial surface patches need be made to nonpolynomial surfaces. Further, shading can be accomplished by working with numerical techniques on the original function, thus the continuous tone image may be more faithful. A disadvantage of the Blinn technique is its dependence on

Fig. 8. Blinn Algorithm.

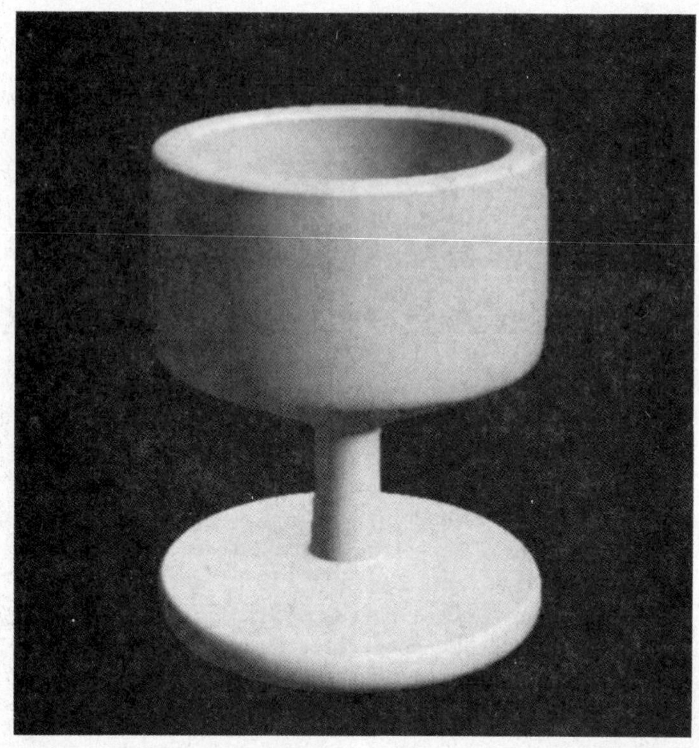

Fig. 9. Whitted Algorithm.

Fig. 10. Lane/Carpenter Algorithm.

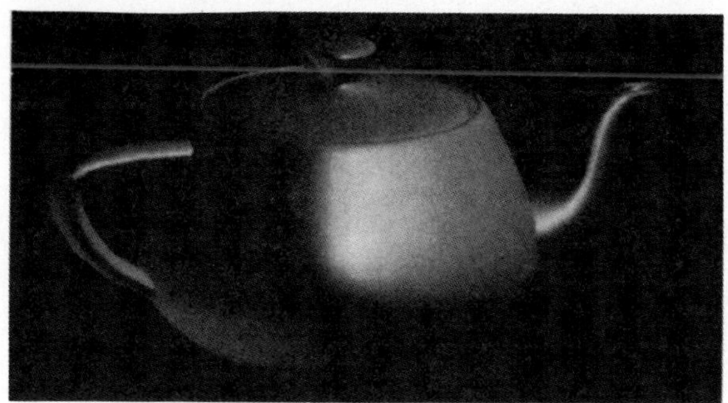

Teapot (28 bicubic patches)

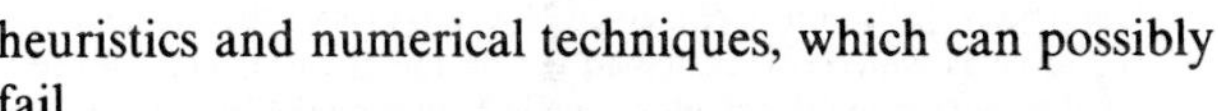

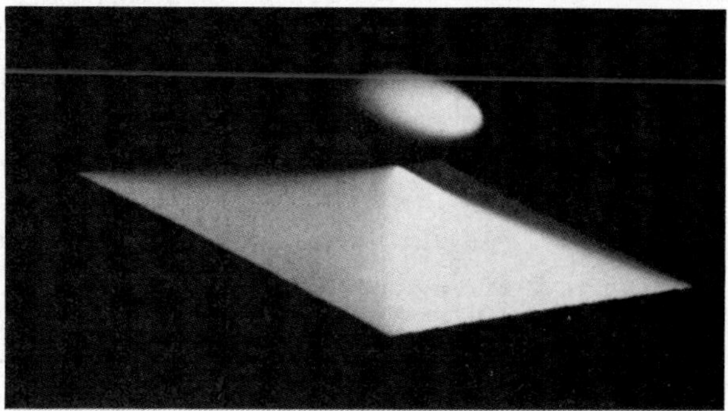

Knot (1 bicubic patch)

heuristics and numerical techniques, which can possibly fail.

A new algorithm, derived from insights gained in writing this paper, combines the advantages of each of the above algorithms while avoiding their disadvantages. The algorithm is essentially a Carpenter/Lane algorithm, except that active elements are now surface elements with curved edges (polynomial), as in the Whitted algorithm, and the inactive list is composed of surface pieces, where the surface pieces are represented procedurally [16], in terms of the parameter range of, and pointer to, the initial surface. The necessary information to generate and place subpatches is then derived procedurally from the initial surface as in the Blinn algorithm. The new algorithm is currently being implemented by two of the authors, Carpenter and Lane.

Acknowledgments. The authors wish to thank the referees for the care with which they reviewed the paper and for their constructive comments and suggestions. L.C. Carpenter and J.M. Lane would like to especially thank R. Lovestedt for software support and the University of Utah Computer Graphics group for the use of their excellent graphics laboratory.

Received June 1979; accepted October 1979; revised November 1979

References

1. Blinn, J.F. Computer display of curved surfaces. Th., Comptr. Sci. Dept., U. of Utah, Salt Lake City, Utah, 1978.
2. Blinn, J.F. Simulation of wrinkled surfaces. Proc. 5th Conf. Computer Graphics and Interactive Techniques, Atlanta, Ga., 1978, pp. 286–292.
3. Catmull, E.E. Computer display of curved surfaces. Proc. IEEE Conf. Computer Graphics, Pattern Recognition and Data Structures, Los Angeles, Calif., May 1975, p. 11.
4. Dahlquist, G., Bjorck, A., and Anderson, T. *Numerical Methods.* Prentice-Hall, Englewood Cliffs, N.J., 1974.
5. Gouraud, H. Continuous shading of curved surfaces. *IEEE Trans. Comptrs. C-20* (June 1971), 623.
6. Newman, W.M., and Sproull, R.F. *Principles of Interactive Computer Graphics.* McGraw-Hill, New York, 1973.
7. Phong, B-T. Illumination for computer generated pictures. *Comm. ACM 18,* 6 (June 1975), 311.
8. Whitted, J.T. A scan line algorithm for computer display of curved surfaces. Proc. 5th Conf. Computer Graphics and Interactive Techniques, Atlanta, Ga., 1978, p. 26.
9. Yoshimura, S., Tsuda, J., and Hirano, C. A computer animation technique for 3-D objects with curved surfaces. Proc. of the 10th Ann. UAIDE Meeting, Stromberg Datagraphix, 1971, pp. 3.140–3.161.
10. Myers, A.J. An efficient visible surface algorithm. Rep. to NSF, DCR 74-00768 AO1, 1975.
11. Lane, J.M., and Riesenfeld, R.F. A theoretical development for the computer generation and display of piecewise polynomial surfaces. To appear in IEEE Trans. on Pattern Analysis and Machine Intell.
12. Lane, J.M., Riesenfeld, R.F. Bounds on a polynomial. Submitted for publication.
13. Prenter, P.M. *Splines and Variational Methods.* Wiley Interscience, New York, 1975.
14. Ortega, J.M., and Rheinboldt, W.C. *Interactive Solution of Nonlinear Equations in Several Variables.* Academic Press, London and New York, 1971.

Atmospheric Illumination and Shadows

Nelson L. Max
Lawrence Livermore National Laboratory

Abstract

The shadow volume algorithm of Frank Crow was reorganized to provide information on the regions of illuminated space in front of each visible surface. This information is used to calculate the extra intensity due to atmospheric scattering, so when the atmosphere is partly in shadow, columns of scattered light will be visible. For efficiency in sorting the shadow edges, the image is computed in polar coordinates.

Key Words

Shadows, atmospheric scattering, Watkins hidden surface algorithm, polar coordinates, shadow polygon.

Introduction

Sunlight scattering from water or dust in the air causes the atmosphere to glow. This glow is particularly visible in beams or columns of light in an otherwise shadowed environment. The goal of this work is to simulate these atmospheric shadow effects.

To compute the glow from the scattering along a ray from the eye, one must know which parts of the ray are illuminated and which are in shadow. The hidden-surface/shadow algorithm must be able to provide the extra information.

There are five basic types of shadow algorithms in current use.

(1) ***Z buffer*** (Williams [1]). Compute the light-source and viewpoint images by depth buffer algorithms. Transform the viewpoint image to the light-source image and compare depths. If the visible point at a pixel is farther from the light than the corresponding depth in the light-source image, it is in shadow.

(2) ***Area subdivision*** (Atherton and Weiler [2]). In both the viewpoint and light-source projections, divide the image into polygonal regions in which a single surface is visible. Transform the illuminated regions in the light source view into object space and paint them as surface detail before the viewpoint projection is rendered.

(3) ***Shadow volumes*** (Crow [3]). Create shadow polygons, which, together with the polygons in the original data base, bound the volume of space shadowed by each object. The new shadow polygons lie in planes joining the light source to edges in the data base. Include these shadow polygons in the z sort of a scan-line hidden-surface algorithm, and count the parity of the shadow polygons in front of a visible surface to see if it is in shadow.

(4) ***Preprocessing*** (Nishita, Okamura, and Nakamae [4], Bouknight and Kelly [5]). Compare a given object to every other, to get a list of objects which can cast shadows on the given object. Use this list to determine the shadows while rendering the objects in scan line order.

(5) ***Ray tracing*** (Whitted [6], Cook, Porter, and Carpenter [7]). At each sampled surface point, trace a ray towards the light source and see if it hits any other objects first.

The first three methods can readily provide the necessary information for atmospheric shadow effects. To use the first method, transform the ray from the eye into the light-source view, and as it crosses each pixel, compare its depth with that in the Z buffer to see whether it is in shadow. As in the original cast-shadow application, there are aliasing problems which are aggravated because the sampling in the two views does not correspond. In general, the Z-buffer algorithms are not good at anti-aliasing, but have the advantage of handling diverse object types easily. Every pixel on each transformed ray must be considered, which makes the atmospheric shadow computation of order n^3, if the two views are n by n.

To use the second method, the ray is again transformed to the light-source view and compared in depth to the plane equation of each subdivided polygon it crosses in that view, in order to determine the regions of illumination. There are now no sampling problems, because the area subdivision is defined with floating point accuracy instead of at some image resolution. There is also some coherency from the polygons crossed by the transformed ray, so the computation is not necessarily of order n^3, but depends instead on the complexity of the scene. It is a challenging computational geometry problem for future research to create a data structure for the area subdivision which can be efficiently intersected with the transformed rays.

The first two methods both require a finite, flat, light-source view, which may not be possible if the light source is inside the window visible from the viewpoint.

I have chosen to implement the third method, modified by reorganizing the sorting and scan line processing to provide the atmospheric shadow information more efficiently.

Although the last two methods are capable of rendering the penumbras from area light sources, the information necessary for atmospheric shadows is not readily available.

1. Polar coordinate scan lines

I wanted to render forest scenes with shadows of many small leaves. In such scenes, every line segment on a leaf edge generates a shadow polygon, and there are no savings from considering only contour edges as suggested by Crow [3]. In the usual orientation, most of the leaves are at the top half of the frame, and their shadow polygons extend past the bottom. Therefore, for a horizontal scan line in the lower half of a scene containing N leaf edges, all N shadow polygons must be considered and sorted in x and in z. Normally, a scan-line algorithm gains efficiency because in a complex scene with many small polygons, most polygon edges can be expected to cross only a few scan lines. This expected efficiency is negated by the situation described above.

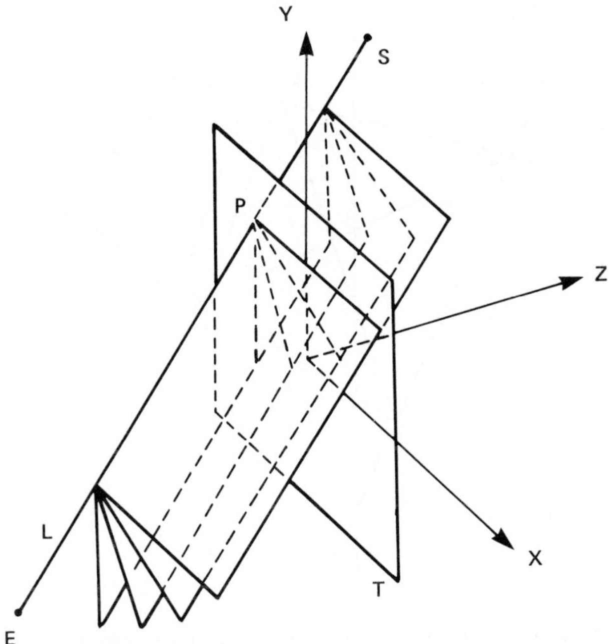

Figure 1. Four scan planes, meeting at the line L between the eye E and the light source S. They intersect the picture plane T in four lines, meeting at the point P, which is the projection of the light source.

However, if the sun is directly overhead and the picture plane is vertical, the efficiency can be regained by using vertical scan lines. The scan planes corresponding to these scan lines all meet in a vertical line through the viewer's eye. Since the sun direction also lies in this vertical line, the shadow polygon generated by an edge will cross only those scan planes that the edge itself crosses.

It is possible to generalize this situation by using radial scan lines in polar coordinates. Consider the line L between the eye E and the light source S, or in the direction of an infinite light source. As shown in Figure 1, this line intersects the picture plane T in a point P, and a family of scan planes meeting in the line L intersect T in a family of lines meeting at P. As above, since each scan plane contains both the eye and the light source, the only shadow polygons intersecting a scan plane come from edges which also intersect that scan plane. This technique greatly simplifies the sorting of shadow polygons and should be useful even if atmospheric shadows are not required.

The point P is the origin for a system of polar coordinates on the image, with radial scan lines. P may lie inside or outside the image window. The case just discussed, where the sun is exactly overhead, is a degenerate one where P is at infinity because the line L is parallel to T, and is not handled in the implementation reported here.

2. The θ-r (z, shadow) sort

My algorithm is a polar coordinate modification of an existing Watkins hidden-surface algorithm available at LLNL (see Watkins [8], Newman and Sproull [9], Rogers [10] and the acknowledgment section below). It sorts first in θ, next in r, and then separately and simultaneously in z and a shadow distance parameter.

The angular coordinate θ goes counterclockwise and edges are sorted into buckets according to the greatest θ of their two endpoints. Scan lines are processed by decreasing θ in analogy to the standard video scan with decreasing y. If P lies outside the image window, there is an interval of possible θ values, but if P lies inside, there is a whole circle of values. In this latter case, scan line processing starts at $\theta = \pi$ and ends at $\theta = -\pi$. Edges which cross from positive to negative θ must be broken into two parts, one extending from $\theta = \pi$ to the endpoint with positive θ, and one from the other endpoint until $\theta = -\pi$. They are thus entered into two different θ buckets.

A further problem exists if a polygon's projection contains P in its interior. If P is inside the polygon, an extra edge surrounding P must be created, going from $\theta = \pi$ to $\theta = -\pi$, with r = 0. The depth and shading attributes at P are found by intersecting the line L of Figure 1 with the polygon, and are entered at both endpoints of the new edge.

The endpoint depth and shading information for each edge are converted to integers and packed efficiently into the 64-bit words of the Cray-1. They are unpacked when the edges are removed from the bucket sort and placed in the appropriate entries in the data blocks for scan line processing of the scan-plane/polygon intersection segments. These *segment blocks* contain r, depth, and shading information for the left and right edges of the segment, as shown in Table 1, and various pointers discussed below.

Segment block data structure

1. **Pointer to previous segment block in r sort.**
2. **Pointer to next segment block in r sort.**
3. **Polygon number.**
4. **Pointer to next segment in active segment list.**
5. **Pointer to next segment on test list.**
6. **Left edge data for θ, r, z, color, normals, and u, v texture parameters.**
7. **Right edge data for θ, r, z, color. . .etc.**
8. **Left shadow edge block.**
   a. shadow sort parameter
   b. shadow polygon plane equation
   c. pointer to next 0/many change
   d. pointer to next 0/1/many change
   e. value (0, 1, or 2) of current shadow multiplicity
9. **Right shadow edge block (same data as for left edge).**
10. **Bit which is 1 if the polygon is front lit.**
11. **Name of texture map.**
12. **U and V partial derivative vectors, for bump mapping.**
13. **Plane equation of polygon with sun on positive side.**

Table 1.

Since a straight polygon edge projection in the picture plane T intersects the radial polar coordinate lines in a non-linear way, the r, z, and shading information cannot be updated from one scan line to the next by the usual incremental addition. Instead, the edge's intersection with each scan line is computed explicitly, and the other data are interpolated from their values at the edge endpoints. The hidden-surface processing then proceeds as in the Watkins algorithm, with the r sort taking the place of the traditional x sort, and the scan plane x − z sort turning into an r − z sort. An r sorted list of segment blocks is maintained from one scan line to the next, using pointers (items 1 and 2 in Table 1). The scan line is rendered as a sequence of *spans*, along which a single polygon is known to be visible. Polygons potentially affecting the current span are kept in an *active segment list* (item 4 in Table 1). For further details on the Watkins algorithm, see [8], [9], or [10].

3. The shadow sort

Every polygon edge defines a shadow plane containing it and the light source, and a semi-infinite *shadow polygon* in this plane. (See Crow [3].) The shadow polygons intersect a given scan plane in

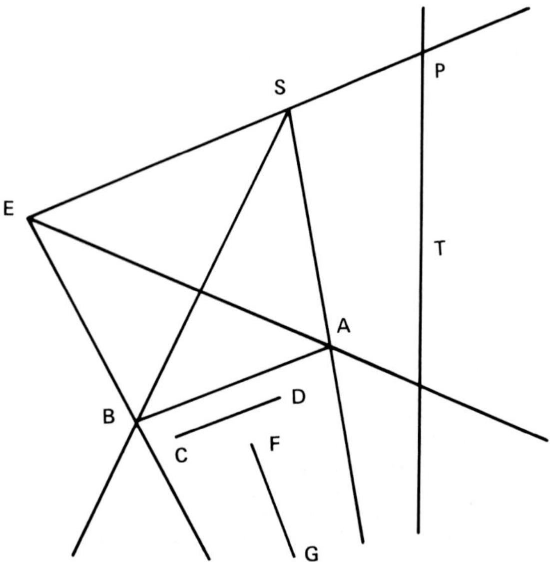

Figure 2a. A scan plane through the viewpoint E and the light source S, intersecting the view plane in line T, and three polygons in segments AB, CD, and FG. The light source is in front of the viewpoint.

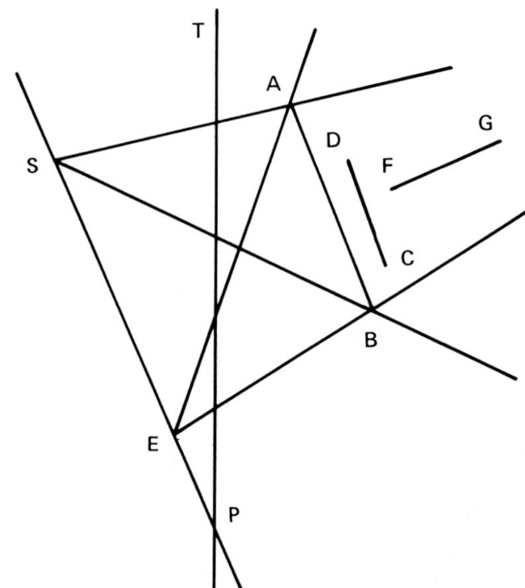

Figure 2b. Same data as in Figure 2a, rotated so that the light source is behind the viewpoint.

shadow edges, and the plane equations for the shadow polygons are stored in *shadow edge blocks*, which are physically part of the segment blocks, but are also linked into separate lists. (See Table 1, items 8 and 9.)

In order to compute the atmospheric shadows, these shadow edges must be sorted in the order of increasing distance from the eye. Since the shadow edges are all parallel, or all radiate from the light source, they never cross except (possibly) at the light source. Therefore they can be sorted in an order which remains valid from one viewing ray to the next along a scan plane.

When the light source is at infinity, the parameter for the shadow sort is the perpendicular distance between the shadow edge and the eye. If the light source is finite, the extended shadow edge passes through it, and the sort parameter is the angle between the shadow edge direction and the line L from the light source to the eye. The shadow edges are linked into the shadow sort list by a separate shadow sort pointer, which identifies the shadow edge block with the next highest sort parameter marking a transition between light (0 shadows) or darkness (1 or more shadows). (See Table 1, item 8c.)

We can think of the scan plane as made up of a collection of rays from the eye, ordered by the r sort in increasing angles away from the sun direction. Along these rays are regions in shadow, bounded at the shadow sort parameters of the shadow edges. These regions determine the shadowed surfaces when rendering a span, and also the shadowed regions in the atmosphere.

At the appropriate time, as discussed below, each polygon in turn must have its shadow edges merged into the shadow sort. This could result in no change, if the new shadow region is already in shadow, or in one or two new shadow edges, depending on the overlap with existing shadows. Old shadow edges overlapped by the new region are unlinked from the sort list, which can thus grow shorter. If care is taken to join shadow regions which exactly abut, then after a network of polygons defining a continuous surface has been processed, the result in the shadow sort is the same as if only shadow polygons for the profile edges had been entered. (See Crow [3].)

Consider the scan plane through the eye E and the light source S, as shown in Figures 2a and 2b. In Frank Crow's algorithm, the shadow edges would be considered together with the polygon segments during the two-dimensional sort constituting the hidden surface algorithm on this plane. Here, we treat the shadow edges separately, in the simpler one-dimensional merge/sort just described, which accounts only for the sort parameter of a shadow edge, and not the position at which it begins.

In order for this to work, the scan plane must be swept out in order by rays from the eye making increasing angles α with the light source direction, so that before a polygon is rendered, all polygons which could cast shadows on it have been considered and merged into the shadow sort.

In the case shown in Figure 2a, the light source is in front of the viewer, and increasing α corresponds to increasing r, so the Watkins algorithm proceeds in the order of increasing r. However, in the case of Figure 2b, where the light source is behind the viewer, the situation is reversed, and the algorithm must proceed in the order of decreasing r.

Suppose segment AB is the current span to be rendered. In both Figures 2a and 2b, any polygon which can cast a shadow on AB must interest the triangle SAB. By the time this current span is reached, any polygons contained in the semi-infinite angle SEA have already been merged into the shadow sort. But we must treat carefully polygons intersecting the angle AEB, and in particular, the segment AB itself.

We say a polygon is *front lit* if the side facing the viewer also faces the light source, as is true for polygon AB in the figures. In this case, the segment AB is merged into the shadow sort only after the r processing has completely passed it; otherwise it would shadow itself. The neglected shadows caused by this delay will not affect the final picture, because segments like CD and EF, which should have been shadowed by AB, are hidden by AB.

It is also necessary to refrain from merging segments CD and EF until AB has been rendered, otherwise they will cast backwards shadows onto AB. Since CD is front lit, it is delayed by the rule already mentioned for AB. Back lit segments like FG are merged when one of the following conditions becomes true: (a) the segment FG overlaps the span to be rendered and lies at least partly on the sunlit side of the polygon visible in the span, (b) the segment FG is itself about to be rendered, or (c) the r processing has completely passed FG.

When a polygon is entered into the active segment list, its plane equation is computed and entered into its segment block, as coefficients of an affine function which is positive on the side of the polygon containing the light source. (See item 13 in Table 1.) Also a bit (item 10) is set to 1 if the viewpoint is on the positive side of this plane, so that the polygon is front lit. Segments with this bit set are merged into the shadow sort at the time they are removed from the active segment list.

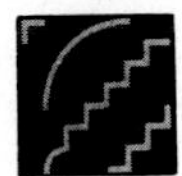

Not-yet-merged back lit active segments are linked into a sublist called the test list (item 5 in Table 1), to facilitate checking conditions (a), (b), and (c) before each span is rendered. The test for (a) uses the plane equation (item 13) for the currently visible segment.

4. Translucency

In a forest, the leaves are translucent and light falling on the sunlit side causes the other side to glow. (A shadow is still cast, however, because the light is scattered in all directions, rather than being partially transmitted along a unique refracted direction.) To get this effect, I could not merely delay entering back lit translucent segments into the shadow sort, to prevent them from shadowing themselves, because they must still shadow other polygons.

Instead, I maintain a "0/1/many" shadow counter, which is 0 for regions with no shadows, 1 for a single shadow, and 2 (representing many) for regions blocked from the sun by more than one polygon. In each shadow edge block is an entry for the count of the region beyond that shadow edge (item 8e in Table 1). The shadow sort pointer discussed above treats 2 the same as 1 in deciding how to merge a new segment into the sort, so I call this the "0/many" list. If a scene has any translucent polygons, a separate 0/1/many list pointer (item 8d) is maintained for the potentially longer sort of 0/1/many shadow regions, and all segments are merged into both linked lists. To do both merges at once, the merge subroutine traces through the 0/many pointers until the 0/many region containing the first shadow edge of the new segment has been found. It then follows the 0/many and 0/1/many pointers separately from this point, and adjusts the lists accordingly. If the 0/many list has N entries, the first search step takes time of order N.

Translucent polygons add 1 to the count of the regions they shadow. When the back lit side of a translucent segment is rendered, 1 is subtracted from the count to determine which regions are glowing. Opaque polygons and front lit translucent polygons add 2 to the count and are thus more likely to shorten the 0/1/many list.

When a visible segment of a polygon is rendered, its endpoints define a region of the shadow sort list, whose counts are used to determine the shadows on the segment. During the sequential search for this region in the 0/many list, the plane equations for all shadow polygons up to and including this region are copied into linearly ordered data arrays. These arrays are then used by the Cray-1 in a vectorized ray/plane intersection computation to determine the illuminated intervals along each ray from the eye. Since this ordered data is needed, a more sophisticated search taking time of order log N cannot be used.

5. Atmospheric illumination

We must now calculate the integrated atmospheric glow along a ray from the eye. This computation varies depending on whether the distance to the light source is finite or infinite.

First, assume the light source, like the sun, is at infinity. In Figure 3, U is a unit vector from the eye along a viewing ray R, with the eye at the origin O, and H is a height above which no data in the model extends. Also, V is a unit vector in the direction of the sun, φ is the angle between the sun direction and the vertical and θ is the angle between the ray R and the vertical. We wish to compute the scattered light reaching the eye from a non-shadowed interval AB on the ray R. We first consider the absorption of the sunlight due to the haze above a point P on the interval AB.

Assume that the haze has constant density and absorbs a fraction b dr of the light along an infinitesimal length dr of the ray R. If I(r) is the intensity at distance r through the haze, then $[d\,I(r)]/I(r) = -b\,dr$, and by integration $I(r) = I(0)\exp(-br)$. Let I_o represent the sunlight intensity at altitude H. In Figure 3, the z coordinate at P is $s\cos\theta$, so the distance r from P to T is $r = PG\sec\varphi = (H - s\cos\theta)\sec\varphi$, and the intensity reaching P is $I_o\exp[-b(H - s\cos\theta)\sec\varphi]$.

In this paper, we assume a single scattering model for light diffusion through haze, as described in Blinn [11] and Max [12]. (For a more sophisticated model of light scattering, see Kajiya [13].) According to the single scattering model, the dust particles or water droplets in the air will scatter an amount ρds of the light at P towards the eye. The scattering coefficient ρ depends on the density and albedo of the particles, and on the scattering angle (see Blinn [11]). The point P is at a distance s from the eye, so this scattered light is further attenuated by a factor $\exp(-bs)$. Therefore, the light reaching the eye, scattered from the infinitesimal ray segment of length ds at P, is $\rho I_o\exp[-b(H - s\cos\theta)\sec\varphi]\exp(-bs)\,ds$.

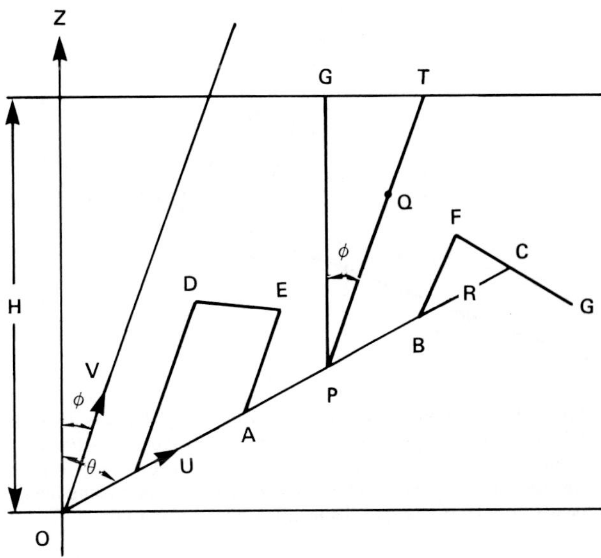

Figure 3. A vertical plane through a ray R between the eye at O and a first polygon intersection point C. For clarity, the figure shows the case when the unit direction vector V to the sun lies in the same vertical plane, so the parallel lines making an angle of φ with the vertical all represent sun rays or shadow edges. The ray R makes an angle of θ with the vertical and U is a unit vector along the ray. DE and FG represent polygon segments casting shadows, and AB is an illuminated interval on the ray between the shadows. $P = sU$ is a typical point in this interval. $Q = sU + tV$ is a typical point on the ray from P towards the sun.

The total light reaching the eye, scattered from the interval between $A = s_iU$ and $B = s_{i+1}U$ is

$$\int_{s_i}^{s_{i+1}} \rho I_o \exp[-bH\sec\varphi - bs(1 - \cos\theta\sec\varphi)]\,ds$$

$$= \rho I_o \exp(-bH\sec\varphi)\int_{s_i}^{s_{i+1}} \exp[-bs(1 - \cos\theta\sec\varphi)]\,ds$$

$$= \rho I_o \exp(-bH\sec\varphi)\left.\frac{\exp[-bs(1 - \cos\theta\sec\varphi)]}{-b(1 - \cos\theta\sec\varphi)}\right|_{s_i}^{s_{i+1}}$$

which is of the form $C\{\exp[-D(s_{i+1})] - \exp[-D(s_i)]\}$.

The constants C and D depend on the ray, but not on the distances s_i, so the sum of the scattered light reaching the eye from all the illuminated intervals on a ray can be computed in a vectorizable loop, using a vectorized exponential function.

This calculation can be generalized for the case of layered fog, whose density b(z) is a function of only the altitude z above sea level. Perlin [14] suggests that the integral $g(z) = \int_0^z b(u)\,du$ be precomputed and tabulated. Then, to find the total density between the eye and the point $P = sU$ in Figure 3, we need only look up $g(s\cos\theta)$ and multiply by $\sec\theta$.

Assume that the scattering coefficient ρ satisfies $\rho = \beta b(z)$, with the constant β depending only on the angle between the viewing ray and the sun direction. Then, because of the lucky identity

$$d/dz\,\{\exp[-g(z)]\} = -dg/dz\,\{\exp[-g(z)] = -b(z)\exp[-g(z)]\},$$

it turns out that the analysis above for constant density can be repeated for layered fog, giving a total scattering intensity of the form $C\sec\theta\,\{\exp[-Dg(s_{i+1}\cos\theta)] - \exp[-Dg(s_i\cos\theta)]\}$ with C and

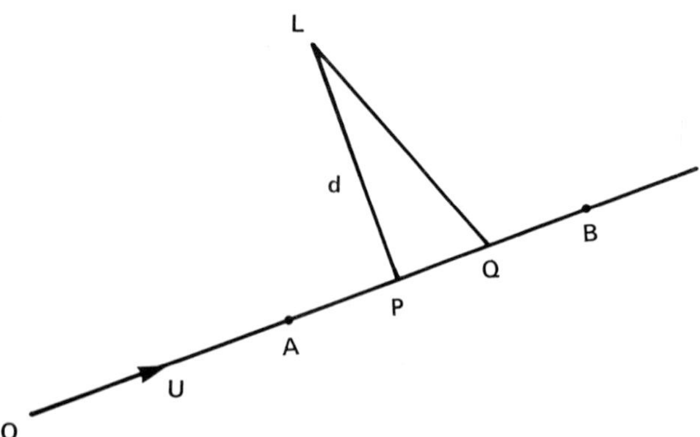

Figure 4. An illuminated interval AB on a ray. The eye is at the origin O, and the light source L is at a finite distance. The line LP is perpendicular to the ray, meeting it at P. The length d of LP is the shortest distance from L to the ray. If U is a unit vector along the ray, then P = s_oU, where s_o is the length of the segment OP.

D depending on φ, H, and β.

In the case of a finite light source, we must take into account the inverse square law, and I only have an easy answer for the case of constant density, no absorption, and constant albedo independent of the angles, which now change even along a single ray. Suppose a point source is at position L, as shown in Figure 4, and a ray from the eye approaches its closest distance d to L at point P = s_o U. Let Q = sU be any other point on the ray. The distance from Q to L is $\sqrt{d^2 + (s - s_o)^2}$. By the inverse square law, assuming no absorption, the intensity at Q is $K/[d^2 + (s - s_o)^2]$.

So the intensity along an interval between A = s_i U and B = s_{i+1} U is

$$\int_{s_i}^{s_{i+1}} \frac{K\,ds}{d^2 + (s - s_o)^2} = \frac{K}{d} \int_{s_i}^{s_{i+1}} \frac{\frac{ds}{d}}{1 + \left(\frac{s - s_o}{d}\right)^2}$$

$$= \frac{K}{d} \int_{t_i}^{t_{i+1}} \frac{dt}{1 + t^2} = K\left[\tan^{-1}(t_{i+1}) - \tan^{-1}(t_i)\right]/d$$

where $t_i = (s_i - s_o)/d$.

Using any of the above methods, the total scattered energy, E, is found by adding up the integrals from each of the illuminated segments along the ray from the eye to a surface point.

6. Composite colors and their cubic interpolation

The final composite color of a surface as influenced by the haze along a ray depends on several quantities: the total scattered energy E as computed above, the surface color (s_r, s_g, s_b) as determined from the illumination and surface shading models, and a haze transmission factor T. The use of a "fog factor" T is already common in computer imagery. If the fog has constant density, with absorption coefficient b, then the transmission factor is T = exp (–bs) where s is the distance from the eye to the surface. For layered fog, T = exp [–sec θ g (s cos θ)], where θ is as shown in Figure 3, and g is the integral of the fog density along a vertical line as discussed above.

Even if the ray is entirely in shadow, the fog still imparts a color (h_r, h_g, h_b) from its ambient illumination. In this case, the standard method for finding the output color (f_r, f_g, f_b) is

$$(f_r, f_g, f_b) = T\,(s_r, s_g, s_b) + (1 - T)\,(h_r, h_g, h_b).$$

Now let (i_r, i_g, i_b) represent the color of the haze when illuminated, so that (e_r, e_g, e_b) = (i_r, i_g, i_b) – (h_r, h_g, h_b) is the extra glow. Then if a ray is partly illuminated, the output color is

$$(f_r, f_g, f_g) = T(s_r, s_g, s_b) + (1 - T)(h_r, h_g, h_b) + E(e_r, e_g, e_b),$$

where E is the total scattering energy computed in section 5. (Care must be taken so that this extra term does not cause the color to exceed the displayable range.)

The output of the hidden-surface/shadow algorithm is a collection of visible surface segments, separated into illuminated or shadowed intervals. Each color component f_c, for c = r,g,b, must be interpolated across every interval as a function of the radius parameter r along a radial scan line. These functions may be highly non-linear since s_r, s_g, s_b, T, and E all vary across the surface, and the perspective projection and exponential absorption are non-linear.

The functions $f_c(r)$ must be accurately approximated, or else the color may change suddenly where a new polygon or shadow edge interrupts a longer interval from the previous scan line. I chose to approximate the f_c using a hermite cubic interpolation polynomial t_c, which matches the values of f_c and its derivatives at the interval end points. (See Mortenson [15], Rogers and Adams [16].)

At a division point between a region of shadow and light on the same visible surface, only s_r, s_g, and s_b change suddenly. T and E remain continuous, and need be computed only once. Their derivatives are estimated from finite differences, by evaluating T and E at nearby points.

The endpoint color components and their derivatives are used to calculate the interpolated values $t_c(1/2)$ of the hermite polynomials at the interval midpoint using the identity $t_c(1/2) = f_c(0)/2 + f_c(1)/2 + f'_c(0)/8 - f'_c(1)/8$.

The actual colors at the interval midpoint are also computed by evaluating T, E, and (s_r, s_g, s_b). If all three actual colors agree with their interpolated values to within a specified tolerance, the corresponding hermite polynomial is used for the interval. Otherwise, the interval is subdivided recursively using the actual values found at the midpoint (and at a nearby point for the finite difference) until the tolerance criterion is met or the maximum permitted recursion level is reached.

7. Scan conversion with anti-aliasing

This polynomial shading information must now be scan converted into a standard rectilinear image. If the data were sampled at discrete radial points into a polar coordinate array, it could be resampled by the methods of Catmull and Smith [17]. But this would mean sacrificing the extra accuracy available in the continuous radial direction. Instead, I have used gaussian filtering on an image which is black except on the infinitely thin radial scan lines, where the intensity is given by the polynomials. An explanation of this filtering will appear in a forthcoming paper [18].

8. Clipping

For a perspective view without shadows, all polygons are usually clipped to a view volume, as shown in Figure 5.

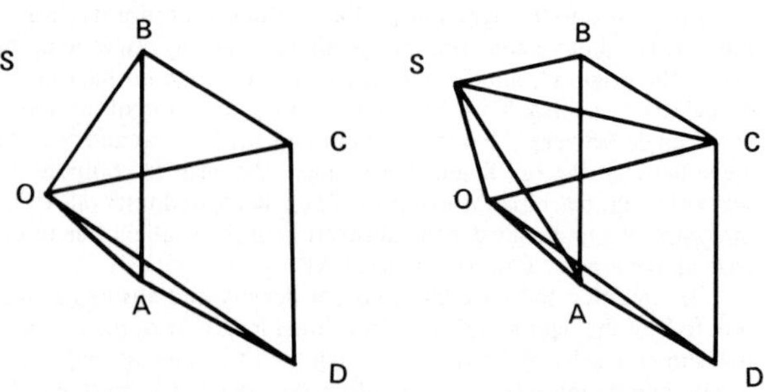

Figure 5. Left: A view pyramid, bounded by four slanted triangles, and a far clipping plane ABCD. From the point of view of the light source S, only faces OAB and OBC are visible, and the profile is the broken line OCBAO. Right: The larger clipping volume for shadows is formed by removing faces OAB and OBC, and adding faces SOC, SCB, SBA, and SAO. The removed planes OAB and OBC, and the near clipping plane, will later be used to separate off the visible polygons.

This eliminates polygons which are invisible and prevents vertices behind the eye from being incorrectly projected. For a view with shadows, such clipping might eliminate polygons which could cast shadows on visible ones. Unless the light source is within the view volume, a larger shadow-casting volume must be found, which includes all polygons which could cast shadows into the view volume.

The planes bounding the shadow casting volume come from two lists: a) the faces of the view volume whose outward normal points away from the light source, and b) planes formed by joining the light source direction to profile edges of the view volume. The profile edges can be identified as those which appear exactly once among the edges of the faces in list a). A third list c) contains the faces of the view volume not in list a), as well as a near clipping plane used to avoid division by zero.

All polygons are clipped to the planes in lists a) and b) to remove polygons or parts of polygons which are irrelevant to the image. Then the planes in list c) are used to break the resulting polygons into two groups: the visible polygons and the shadow-only polygons.

The shadow-only polygons are entered into the θ bucket sort. They need not be entered into the Watkins r − z sort, but they must be merged together as non-translucent segments in the shadow sort lists, before the r − z sort is started.

9. Summary

Put all edges into θ buckets.
For all buckets, in order of decreasing θ:
- Enter all edges from bucket θ into r sort segment blocks.
- Merge all shadow-only segments into shadow sort.
- For each visible span generated by the Watkins r − z sort:
  - Merge back lit polygon segments which satisfy conditions (a), (b), or (c) of section 3 into shadow sort.
  - Find intervals of light and shade on the visible span.
  - For each interval, approximate color functions by recursively defined piecewise cubic polynomials, and scan convert each piece into rectilinear pixel array.
  - Merge front lit polygon segments which end during the span into shadow sort.
- Remove edges which terminate at this θ from active r sort.
- Update edges for next radial scan line.

Output final picture.

10. Results

Figure 6 shows a jack-o-lantern, lit by a candle inside it. The finite light source is within the view volume. It took approximately 20 seconds to compute on the Cray-1, at 512 by 512 resolution. Figure 7 shows vertical columns of light coming through a hole in the clouds. The sun is at infinity directly overhead, and the methods of Max [12] were used to compute the atmospheric shadows from the partially transparent clouds.

Figure 8 shows three polygons casting shadows on each other, on the ground below, and in the atmosphere. The contrast in the atmospheric illumination is most apparent where there is a shadow polygon almost parallel to the line of sight. The light is at infinity above and behind the viewer, so the atmospheric shadows appear smaller near the ground, due to the perspective forshortening. Figure 9 shows several trees, designed by Jules Bloomenthal (see [19]), with shadow-mapped bark (see [20]).

These results show that it is possible to integrate atmospheric illumination efficiently into a scan line hidden-surface algorithm, if radial scan lines are used.

Acknowledgments

This work was performed under the auspices of the U.S. Department of Energy by Lawrence Livermore National Laboratory (LLNL) under contract number W-7405-ENG-48.

The algorithm was adapted in incremental fashion from a direct descendant of the original Fortran program written by Gary Watkins to test his proposed hardware hidden surface algorithm. It was rewritten by Mike Achuleta at LLNL and later modified by Bruce Brown, Paul Renard, and Gene Cronshagen. I found incremental changes to an existing program easier than planning a new algorithm from scratch, because I could use the pictures to debug each new feature. I wish to thank Jules Bloomenthal for the tree trunk data and bark texture, Maria Lopez for typing this paper, and Charles Grant for carefully reading and commenting on it.

References

[1] Williams, Lance, "Casting Curved Shadows on Curved Surfaces," SIGGRAPH '78 proceedings, pp. 270–274.

[2] Atherton, Peter, Weiler, Kevin, and Greenberg, Donald, "Polygon Shadow Generation," SIGGRAPH '78 proceedings, pp. 275–281.

[3] Crow, Franklin, "Shadow Algorithms for Computer Graphics," SIGGRAPH '77 proceedings, pp. 242–248.

[4] Nishita, Tomoyuki, Okamura, Isao, and Nakamae, Eihachiro, "Shading Models for Point and Linear Sources," ACM Transactions on Graphics, Vol 4 no. 2 (1985), pp. 124–146.

[5] Bouknight, J., and Kelly, K., "An algorithm for producing half-tone computer graphics presentations with shadows and movable light sources," SJCC, AFIPS, Vol 36 (1970), pp. 1–10.

[6] Whitted, Turner "An Improved Illumination Model for Shaded Display," Communications of the ACM, Vol 23 (1980), pp. 343–349.

[7] Cook, Robert, Porter, Thomas, and Carpenter, Loren, "Distributed Ray Tracing," SIGGRAPH '84 proceedings, pp. 137–145.

[8] Watkins, Gary, "A real-time visible surface algorithm," Ph.D. Thesis, University of Utah (1970) UTECH-CSc-70-101.

[9] Sproull, Robert, and Newman, William, "Principles of Interactive Computer Graphics" (first edition is better on this subject), McGraw Hill, New York (1973).

[10] Rogers, David, "Procedural Elements for Computer Graphics," McGraw Hill, New York (1985).

[11] Blinn, James, "Light Reflection Functions for Simulation of Clouds and Dusty Surface," SIGGRAPH '82 proceedings, pp. 21–29.

[12] Max, Nelson, "Light Diffusion through Clouds and Haze," Computer Vision Graphics, and Image Processing, Vol 33 (1986), pp. 280–292.

[13] Kajiya, James, and Von Herzen, Brian, "Ray Tracing Volume Densities," SIGGRAPH '84 proceedings, pp. 165–174.

[14] Perlin, Ken, "State of the Art in Image Synthesis '85 Course Notes," ACM SIGGRAPH '85, course 11.

[15] Mortenson, Michael, "Geometric Modelling," John Wiley and Sons, New York (1985).

[16] Rogers, David, and Adams, J. A., "Mathematical Elements for Computer Graphics," McGraw Hill, New York (1976).

[17] Catmull, Ed, and Smith, Alvey Ray, "3-D Transformations of Images in Scanline Order," SIGGRAPH '80 proceedings, pp. 279–285.

[18] Max, Nelson "Anti-Aliasing Scan Line Data" to be submitted to IEEE Computer Graphics and Applications.

[19] Bloomenthal, Jules, "Modelling the Mighty Maple," SIGGRAPH '85 proceedings, pp. 305–311.

[20] Max, Nelson, "Shadows for Bump Mapped Surfaces," in Advanced Computer Graphics: Proceedings of Computer Graphics Tokyo '86, T. L. Kunii, ed., Springer Verlag, Tokyo (1986), pp. 145–156. To be revised and submitted to The Visual Computer.

Figure 6. A jack-o-lantern, lit by a candle.

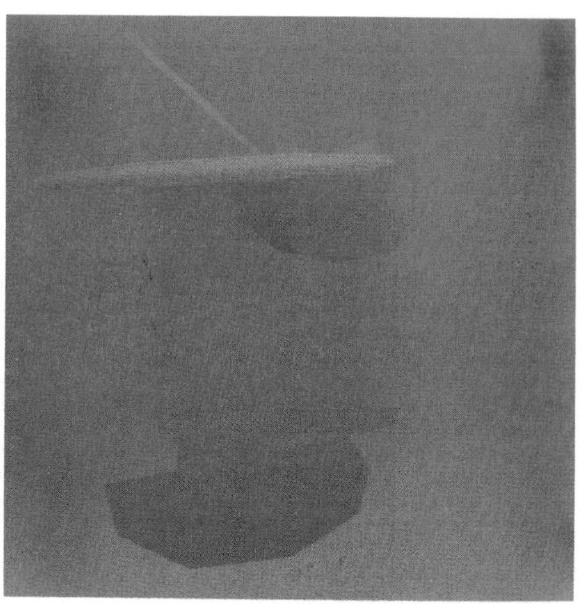

Figure 8. Three polygons casting atmospheric shadows.

Figure 7. Sunlight coming through a break in the clouds.

Figure 9. Several trees.

"Computer Rendering of Stochastic Models" by A. Fournier, D. Fussell, and L. Carpenter from *Communications of ACM*, Volume 25, Number 6, June 1982, pages 371-384. Copyright 1982, Association for Computing Machinery, Inc., reprinted by permission.

Graphics and Image Processing

James Foley*
Editor

Computer Rendering of Stochastic Models

Alain Fournier
University of Toronto

Don Fussell
The University of Texas at Austin

Loren Carpenter
Lucasfilm

A recurrent problem in generating realistic pictures by computers is to represent natural irregular objects and phenomena without undue time or space overhead. We develop a new and powerful solution to this computer graphics problem by modeling objects as sample paths of stochastic processes. Of particular interest are those stochastic processes which previously have been found to be useful models of the natural phenomena to be represented. One such model applicable to the representation of terrains, known as "fractional Brownian motion," has been developed by Mandelbrot.

The value of a new approach to object modeling in computer graphics depends largely on the efficiency of the techniques used to implement the model. We introduce a new algorithm that computes a realistic, visually satisfactory approximation to fractional Brownian motion in faster time than with exact calculations. A major advantage of this technique is that it allows us to compute the surface to arbitrary levels of details without increasing the database. Thus objects with complex appearances can be displayed from a very small database. The character of the surface can be controlled by merely modifying a few parameters. A similar change allows complex motion to be created inexpensively.

B. Mandelbrot, on whose work this paper is based, has raised certain objections which will be published in a subsequent issue.

This paper reports the results of two independent research efforts—one by Carpenter and the other by Fournier and Fussell. They both submitted papers to the 1980 SIGGRAPH conference, and through the conference to *CACM*. Both papers were accepted for *CACM* with the understanding that the authors would consolidate their work into a single integrated and definitive piece.—J. Foley.

* Former editor of Graphics and Image Processing. Robert Haralick is the current editor of this department, which has recently been renamed Image Processing and Computer Vision (see April '82 *Communications*, pp 311–312.)

Alain Fournier and Don Fussell's work was performed at The University of Texas at Dallas, and was partially supported by NSF Grant MCS-79-01168 and facilitated by the use of the Theory Net, NSF Grant MCS-78-01689. Loren Carpenter's work was performed while at Boeing Computer Services.

Authors' Present Addresses: A. Fournier, Computer Systems Research Group, 121 St Joseph St, University of Toronto, Toronto, Ontario M5S 1A1; D. Fussell, Department of Computer Science, The University of Texas at Austin, Austin, Texas 78712; L. Carpenter, Lucasfilm, P. O. Box 2009, San Rafael, California 94912.

CR Categories and Subject Descriptors: I.3.3. [**Computer Graphics**]: Picture/Image Generation—*display algorithms*; I.3.5. [**Computer Graphics**]: Computational Geometry and Object Modeling—*curve, surface, solid, and object representation*;I.3.7 [**Computer Graphics**]: Three Dimensional Graphics and Realism—*color, shading, shadowing, and texture.*

General Term: Algorithms

Additional Key Words and Phrases: fractals, terrain models, stochastic models

1. Introduction

Traditional modeling techniques used in computer graphics have been based on the assumption that objects are essentially a collection of smooth surfaces which can be mathematically described by deterministic functions. The simplest such technique assumes that objects are collections of polygons whose surfaces are obviously described by linear functions. Greater flexibility is achieved by the use of surfaces which are described by higher-order polynomials, as with Bezier [1] or B-spline surface patches [12].

These techniques have been quite successful in rendering realistic images of artificial objects, with their relatively simple macroscopic characteristics and their regularly periodic surface features. Natural objects, such as stones, clouds, trees, terrain, etc. are characterized in general by no such regular features or simple macroscopic structures, and these methods have been less effective in modeling them.

Macroscopic features of natural objects are often represented explicitly using large amounts of data. In the case of terrain, the information is usually obtained from contour maps, and in some fashion transformed into a surface represented by a large number of polygons [11]. Similarly, smoke has been modeled as volumes containing very large numbers of points distributed according to certain theoretical functions used in the study of smoke formation [8]. In both cases, capturing the macroscopic features to be modeled involves significant time and/or space requirements and the use of specialized techniques that are not generally applicable to other types of natural features. The problem is that these conceptually simple objects require a large number of modeling primitives (points, polygons, or patches) because they are visually quite complex. On the other hand, a conceptually or technologically complex object, like an airplane, can be very effectively modeled with a smaller number of such primitives.

Using a completely different approach, small-scale textures of natural objects have generally been modeled by some single repetitive texture function mapped onto all patches comprising such an object. However, the regularity of the effect detracts considerably from a natural appearance.

A fundamental limitation of these approaches is that objects are modeled at a predetermined, fixed scale regardless of its suitability for any particular viewing distance. Thus, from sufficiently far away, all but the most large-scale changes in terrain modeled by a fixed set of polygons may be invisible, rendering a large portion of the database and the processing required to display it superfluous. Likewise, a view of such terrain from very close up may reveal no more than a flat, featureless portion of a polygon, lacking any cues that it does indeed represent terrain. The latter problem may be alleviated somewhat by texture mapping, but with the usual static texture definitions it is still possible to get too close for the resolution of the texture pattern.

In many applications in which natural phenomena are to be represented, one is primarily interested in achieving sufficient realism in the representation of the objects for their nature to be easily recognizable. The specific features of any such objects on all but the most macroscopic scale are of secondary importance. For example, in a computer-generated animated sequence we may wish to have a mountain range which is obviously a mountain range but which is not intended to correspond to any particular real-world mountains. In such a case, we are interested only in the general size, shape, and position of the mountain range as specific features to be modeled explicitly. In order to make such an "object" recognizable as a mountain range, we would like to generate the macroscopic features that any typical mountain range would have. It would be advantageous to have a technique that would allow us to do this without the use of a large database to represent the object. In applications where one wishes to display real-world data, the addition of suitable information at various scales may be used to enhance realism. For example, in flight simulators, various types of terrain are represented by a few large polygons whose color, shape, and position provide vague cues as to their nature. If a pseudo-random rocky texture could be added to surfaces representing mountainous terrain, much more realistic images could be generated. The use of an extremely large, detailed database for such purposes would be prohibitive, while the use of traditional, deterministic texture mapping techniques would not be fully satisfactory.

The representation of motion in computer graphics systems has suffered, less obviously, from a similar limitation. Previous attempts to represent turbulent motion have been limited by the apparent complexity of the task. An effective means of generating an irregular surface with an irregular motion in a flexible way will allow the solution of such problems as realistically modeling a waterfall, rapids, or ocean waves, all of which present serious challenges to computer graphics researchers [19], [24].

All of the drawbacks mentioned above result primarily because most traditional models of real-world phenomena in computer graphics are totally deterministic in philosophy. There have been some exceptions, however. Early work by Mezei et al. [20] generated textures and irregular shapes by random techniques, and Blinn [2] improved the realism of previous shading methods by using a model based on probabilistic assumptions. Also, research in image analysis and pattern recognition has produced a body of results on the statistical analysis of texture as well as some interesting examples of image synthesis using stochastic techniques [10], [23], [21].

We propose to extend the flexibility of the mathematical modeling techniques in computer graphics by generalizing the assumptions made about the characteristics of an object's surface and of its motion. Our basic approach is to model both primitives and their motion as a combination of both deterministic and stochastic features. Thus the surface of an object may be a polynomial function of a set of predetermined locations, or it may be a stochastic function of those locations, or both. Likewise, the motion of an object may be described as a smooth function interpolating its initial and final positions, or it may vary irregularly along the way. In this paper, we introduce simple and efficient techniques for rendering a large class of stochastic models which can be used to represent a variety of natural phenomena.

2. Stochastic Models

In a traditional graphics system, the modeling system is the part where the objects are defined in terms of the basic building blocks: the modeling primitives. The modeling primitives mainly used have been points, lines, polygons, and parametric patches. We define here a new kind of modeling primitive.

A stochastic model of an object (or more generally of a phenomenon, to extend the concept of an object to include possibly a time parameter), is defined to be a model where the object is represented by a sample path (a realization) of some stochastic process of one of more variables.

Stochastic objects can be made from several stochastic modeling primitives just as traditional deterministic objects are built from, for example, polygons or parametric patches. Also, since the class of stochastic processes properly includes the deterministic functions, the definition of stochastic models includes all previously used primitives.

Table I. Possible Applications of Stochastic Models.

Dimension of Primitive	Dimension of Stochastic Process (number of parameters)			
	One-D Process	Two-D Process	Three-D Process	Four-D Process
1	Intensity on a line, Intensity in time	Scalar field	Intensity in 3-D space	Intensity in 3-D space in time
2	Direction on a plane, Surface in time	2-D vector on a surface	Intensity and altitude on a surface	Intensity and altitude on a surface in time
3	Direction in space in time, Color in time	Normal to a surface, Color on a surface	Color in space, Vector field in 3-D space	Color in space in time, Moving vectors

At the level of resolution normally used, the natural objects to be modeled can be taken to be continuous and will need continuous stochastic processes to model them. Since ultimately the models will be used for display on discrete devices, it is very convenient to have a means of computing a discrete sample of the continuous model at the rate required by the resolution of the image. This would usually correspond to the Nyquist rate, but if anti-aliasing is needed the rate of sampling can be chosen to be higher.

It is now clear that the three elements required for stochastic modeling are: (1) an appropriate object (phenomenon) to be modeled; (2) a stochastic process to model it with; (3) an algorithm to compute the sample paths of this process.

Objects that have features with stochastic properties that are strong enough so that appreciable savings in both storage and processing are obtained by replacing the stored values for the stochastic features by the few parameters needed by the definition of the stochastic process are likely to be represented most effectively using stochastic models. To use signal processing terminology, an object which has a high noise/signal ratio is a good candidate. It should be noted, however, that the stochastic process might model what at first appears to be signal, as will be seen in the example given below.

The stochastic process to be used can have two kinds of origin.

—It can be a legitimate mathematical model of the phenomenon to be modeled. A model in computer graphics is not normally required to be a mathematical model, but, of course, it does not hurt if it is. The example given for terrain falls into this category.

—The stochastic process can be empirically chosen, with the parameters determined to fit a particular application. Techniques need to be developed which employ some sort of canonical stochastic processes, to be used in stochastic approximation the same way power functions, for example, are used in curve fitting.

Since the stochastic process used can be analytically defined, many traditional algorithmic techniques can be considered as means to compute the sample paths. One of the most effective for display purposes is the recursive subdivision technique, introduced by Catmull [5] for parametric patches, and most notably used by Clark [7] and Lane et al. [13]. The same technique can be used in the context of stochastic modeling, and the advantages are even more important here.

—The depth of the recursion will be controlled by the on-screen resolution, giving two important benefits. We never run out of details, since the process can always generate new data as we close in. We never produce more details than necessary, therefore the computational effort is always commensurate with the on-screen image complexity.

—The basic computational step in the recursive subdivision uses an interpolation formula. Interpolation formulas are in general much easier to compute than incremental ones, especially those for midpoint interpolation, therefore further lowering the computational cost.

Depending upon the phenomenon being modeled, the stochastic process will have dimensions from 1–4, and the computed sample path, or more exactly the stochastic element computed from the sample path will have dimensions from 1–3. The various possibilities are in Table I, and some of the applications are indicated. Since in addition the stochastic element can be composed with various deterministic modeling primitives, the development of a wide range of new modeling techniques will be required, and some new computational issues will be raised.

The following sections address these issues in the context of one particularly useful and interesting stochastic model.

3. Fractals: A Stochastic Terrain Model

Perhaps the most common natural phenomenon to be represented in current applications of computer graphics is terrain. Since terrain is generally characterized by randomly distributed features that are recognizable by their overall properties as opposed to specific macroscopic features (as in the case of the mountain range example), its strong stochastic properties make it a good choice for the application of a stochastic model.

As noted above, we require a stochastic process that is appropriate for modeling terrain and an algorithm for computing sample paths of the process. In the following section we describe a suitable process for modeling terrains as well as a variety of other natural phenomena. We will then proceed in the subsequent section to develop new techniques for rendering the sample paths and for the construction of stochastic primitives which are especially suited for use in computer graphics.

3.1 Fractional Brownian Motion

In 1968, Mandelbrot and van Ness introduced the term "fractional Brownian motion" (which will be abbreviated to fBm) to denote a family of one-dimensional Gaussian stochastic processes which provide useful models for many natural time series [14]. Since then, multidimensional extensions of fBm have been studied by Mandelbrot as models of a wide range of natural phenomena, including in particular terrains (in two dimensions) and the isosurfaces (positions in space at which some parameter has equal value) of turbulent fluids [16].

We give a brief description of fBm. Let u be a real parameter such that $-\infty < u < \infty$, and let w be the set of all values of a random function taken from a sample space **W**. Ordinary Brownian motion, $B(u, w)$ is a real random function with independent Gaussian increments such that $B(u + \Delta, w) - B(u, w)$ has mean zero and variance σ^2 and $B(u_2, w) - B(u_1, w)$ is independent of $B(u_4, w) - B(u_3, w)$ whenever the intervals (u_1, u_2) and (u_3, u_4) do not overlap. Let H be a real parameter such that $0 < H < 1$ and let b_0 be an arbitrary real number. The random function $B_H(u, w)$, called reduced fractional Brownian motion, is defined by

$$B_H(0, w) = b_0$$

$$B_H(u, w) - B_H(0, w) = [1/\Gamma(H + 0.5)]$$

$$\left\{\int_{-\infty}^{u} [(u - s)^{H-0.5} - (-s)^{H-0.5}]\, dB(s, w) + \int_{0}^{u} (u - s)^{H-0.5}\, dB(s, w)\right\}$$

Thus $B_H(u, w)$ is a moving average of $B(u, w)$ weighted by $(u - s)^{H-0.5}$. Note that $B_{0.5}(u, w) = B(u, w)$, so when $H = 0.5$ we obtain ordinary Brownian motion. Thus we have a family of random functions whose values at any value of u depend upon all past values of u.

As for ordinary Brownian motion, the increments of fBm are stationary. Typical sample paths for $H = 0.5$ (ordinary Brownian motion), $H = 0.3$, and $H = 0.7$ are given in Figs. 1, 2, and 3.

A Fourier analysis of samples of such functions shows no dominant frequency, but rather a range of frequencies at all orders of magnitude. Fractional Brownian motions are members of the class of "1:f noises" [14], that is, those signals in which the contribution of each frequency to the power spectrum is nearly inversely proportional to the frequency. Additionally, the increments of fBm are statistically self-similar. This means formally that $B_H(u + \Delta u, w) - B_H(u, w)$ and $h^{-H}[B_H(u + h\Delta u, w) - B_H(u, w)]$ have the same finite joint distribution functions. Intuitively these features of fBm indicate that we may observe a sample of one of these functions at any scale and perceive identical statistical features. A surface generated using fBm would thus possess macroscopic features up to the order of magnitude of the overall surface generated, corresponding to the lowest possible frequencies in the Fourier spectrum of the sample, as well as arbitrarily small surface detail, corresponding to the higher frequencies in the Fourier spectrum.

Fig. 1. Ordinary Brownian Motion ($H = 0.5$).

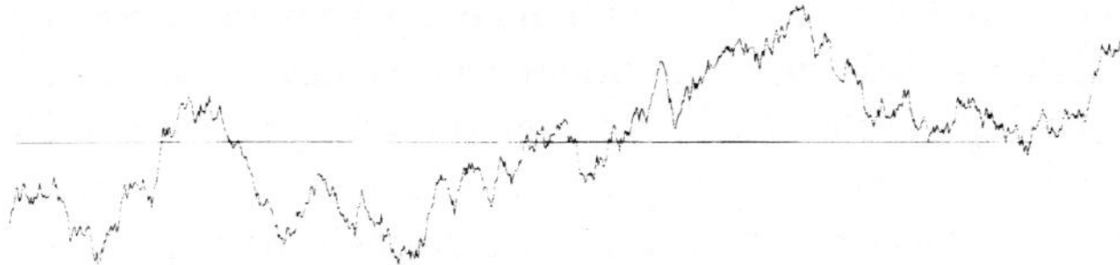

Fig. 2. Fractional Brownian Motion ($H = 0.3$).

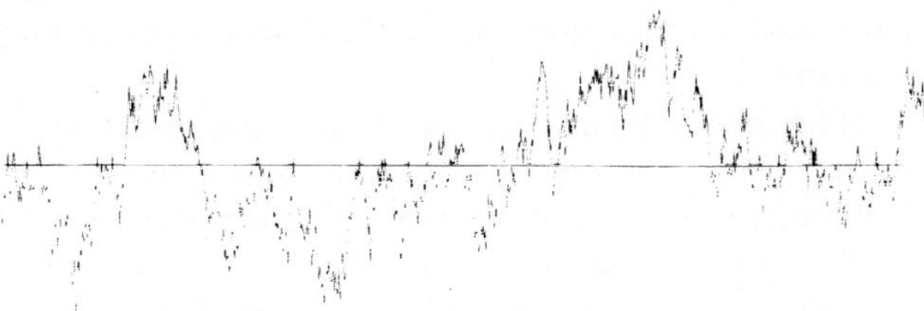

Fig. 3. Fractional Brownian Motion ($H = 0.7$).

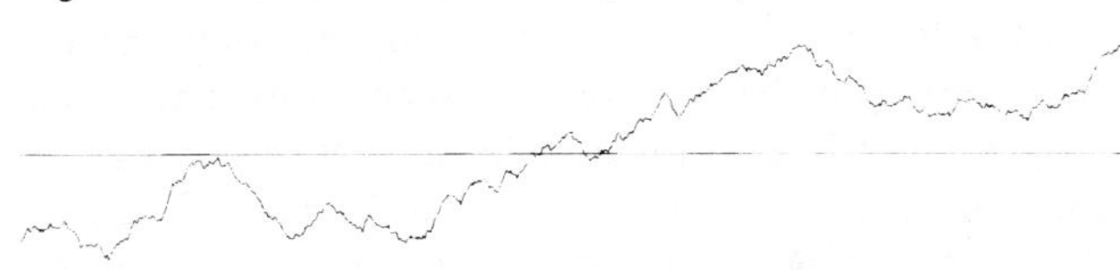

3.2 Algorithms For Realizing Models Based On FBm

3.2.1 Algorithmic Requirements

In order for fractional Brownian motion to be generally useful for modeling in computer graphics, appropriate algorithms for computing its sample paths must be found. Since high quality images of complex scenes typically require that on the order of 10^6 sample points be generated, the efficiency of any such algorithm is obviously of critical importance. Not only should the asymptotic complexity of the algorithm be linear in the number of sample points generated, but the amount of computation involved in generating each sample point must also be as small as possible.

Although it is important, efficiency alone is not sufficient to make a sample path generating algorithm appropriate for use in graphics. In order to achieve the flexibility of deterministic models used in graphics, objects should be modeled piecewise as collections of stochastic primitives. Any modeling primitives in computer graphics must have two properties in order to be useful. The first of these, which we call *internal consistency*, is the reproducibility of the primitive at any position in an appropriate coordinate space and at any level of detail. That is, a modeling primitive should be rendered in such a way that its features do not depend on its position or orientation in space. In addition, the features visible when the primitive is rendered at high magnification should be consistent with those rendered at a coarser scale. For deterministic primitives of any type, scale consistency is easily maintained on smooth curves or surfaces. Likewise, positional consistency (modulo the aliasing problem) is easy to maintain for primitives such as points, lines, or polygons, and for higher-order curves and surfaces has been achieved through the use of parametric definitions. Internal consistency of either type is, however, more difficult to maintain for stochastic sample paths and requires more care in the design of generating algorithms.

The other crucial property of modeling primitives is what we term *external consistency*. This refers to the continuity properties of adjacent modeling primitives. If modeling primitives are intended to share a common boundary, it must be possible to ensure that they are indeed continuous across this boundary at any scale at which they may be rendered. Additional consistency constraints such as derivative or higher-order surface continuity may be required in some cases, and other properties such as color may be subject to consistency constraints across primitives. As with internal consistency, this property has been easily maintained in the rendering of first-order primitives, although it has presented a serious research concern in the design of efficient algorithms for rendering higher-order deterministic curves and surfaces [7], [13]. Again, the problem of maintaining external consistency promises to be an even more serious concern in the design of algorithms for rendering stochastic primitives.

Let us again note here that when rendering any continuous analytically defined curve or surface, we are actually calculating a discrete set of sample points from the surface. These points are generally only approximations to the surface since even for deterministic functions the limited word size of a computer allows only for approximate representation of arbitrary real numbers. In computing sample paths of stochastic functions, it is often the case that only approximations can be calculated efficiently or at all, even leaving aside the numerical problems just mentioned. Nevertheless, such approximations are acceptable provided they are sufficiently good, which in computer graphics means that they meet visual criteria of indistinguishability from the actual sample paths. Indeed, since the process we are applying is a good model of terrain only on the basis of empirical statistical tests and not because they are derived from a theoretical model of terrain formation, any approximation which is sufficiently good to pass our visual test may itself be likely to be an equally good model by these statistical tests. In any case, visual acceptability as opposed to statistical criteria will be the basis on which we judge the quality of an approximation algorithm for graphical use.

3.2.2 Previous Algorithms

Mandelbrot has published a number of methods for calculating discrete approximations to fBm in various dimensions. These involve three basic approaches: a shear displacement process, a modified Markov process, and an inverse Fourier transformation.

The first uses the fact that fBm is the limit of a fractional Poisson field [17]. A fractional Poisson field in n-dimensions is a scalar field where at each point $\mathbf{P}$ the value of $F(\mathbf{P})$ is the sum of an infinite collection of steps (in the case of terrain, these steps can be seen as straight faults) whose directions, locations, and amplitudes are three sequences of mutually independent random variables. This method was used by Mandelbrot to generate the first computer simulation of a fractional Brownian surface. While it has solid theoretical foundations and has been used to produce striking pictures, it is not suitable for our applications, both for its $O(N^3)$ time complexity for surfaces, and for the fact that it is not clear that it could be adapted to our boundary constraints.

The second method is based on an algorithm to compute an approximation to discrete fractional Gaussian noise, which is the increment of fBm [15]. The algorithm computes what Mandelbrot called fast fractional Gaussian noise (ffGn) as a sum of a low frequency term and a high frequency term. The high frequency term is a Markov–Gauss process. The low frequency term is a weighted sum of M Markov–Gauss processes, M being a number proportional to $\log(N)$. The fast fractional Gaussian noise algorithm represents a considerable improvement in the computation of linear fBm, since its time complexity is $O(N\log(N))$ and its parameters can be adjusted to suit the observed time series if it is to be used in statistical analysis. Although some objection to the use of a two-dimensional extension to this method may be made on the grounds that its time complexity is greater than linear, a much more serious objection is that it appears that there is no valid extension of the method to two dimensions. Also, there seems to be no obvious method to adjust the computation to the needed resolution while maintaining any consistency.

The third approach, which also gives an $O(N\log(N))$ time complexity involves the generation of Gaussian white noise, in which all frequencies are equally represented, and then filtering it using fast Fourier transform techniques in order to force the different frequencies to fall off as required by the value of the parameter H for the particular fractional Gaussian noise desired. Fourier techniques were used by R. Voss to illustrate [18].

Each of the methods discussed above has its own theoretical and practical advantages. However, they have in common the drawbacks that their time complexity is greater than linear and that the basic operations involved in their computation are costly (involving transcendental functions). We will now present our own method for computing an approximation to fBm which avoids these drawbacks.

3.2.3 A Recursive Subdivision Algorithm

We have noted above the three basic requirements that an approximation algorithm appropriate for stochastic modeling must meet, and we have discussed the advantages of the recursive subdivision algorithms for rendering models of any type in computer graphics. We now present such a recursive algorithm for generating approximations to the sample paths of one-dimensional fBm.

In order to be able to use this type of algorithm, the crucial requirement is that the distribution of the process for which samples are to be computed can be interpolated from the boundary points of the sample. Since one of the features of fBm is an infinite span of interdependence, it is not *a priori* obvious that such an approach would be successful. However, two facts help design an approximation algorithm.

—Fractional Brownian motion is self-similar. This means, as stated above, that the increments of $B_H(u)$ (for simplicity of notation, we will henceforth use $B_H(u)$ instead of $B_H(u, w)$) are such that $B_H(u + \Delta u) - B_H(u)$ and $B_H(u + h\Delta u) - B_H(u)$ have the same distribution if the latter is rescaled by a factor of h^{-H}, H being the self-similarity parameter.

—A formula exists [14] for the conditional expectation of $B_H(u)$, $0 \leq u \leq 1$, knowing $B_H(0) = 0$ and $B_H(1) = 1$: $E[B_H(u) | B_H(1)] = \frac{1}{2}(u^{2H} + 1 - |u - 1|^{2H})$. When $u = \frac{1}{2}$, the right-hand side becomes $\frac{1}{2}$ independently of H.

These two properties give an estimate of the expected value and the variance of the increment of the process, which is all that is needed, since the process is Gaussian.

An algorithm designed using these properties is given below in Pascal. The function GAUSS(seed, index) returns a Gaussian random variable with zero mean and unit variance. It uses the variable "seed" as its seed. Explicit control over this seed is given in order to allow for external consistency as discussed below.

```
Declarations in main program:
  type result = array [0..maxsize] of real;
  var maxlevel, seed, i:integer; scale, h:real; Fh:result;
Procedure called:
  procedure fractal (maxlevel, seed:integer; h, scale:real);
  var first, last:integer;
     ratio, std:real;
  procedure subdivide (f1, f2:integer; std:real);
     var fmid:integer; stmid:real;
     begin
       fmid:= (f1 + f2) div 2;
       if (fmid <> f1) & (fmid<> f2) then
          begin
          Fh [fmid] := (Fh [f1] + Fh [f2])/2.0 + gauss (seed, fmid)*
            std;
          stdmid := std * ratio;
          subdivide (f1, fmid, stdmid);
          subdivide (fmid, f2, stdmid)
          end
     end; /* subdivide */
  begin
     first := 0;
     last := 2↑maxlevel;
     Fh [first] := gauss (seed, first) * scale;
     Fh [last] := gauss (seed, last) * scale;
     ratio := 2↑ - h;
     std := scale * ratio;
     subdivide (first, last, std)
  end; /* fractal */
```

Fig. 4. Computation of a Scalar Value by Subdivision.

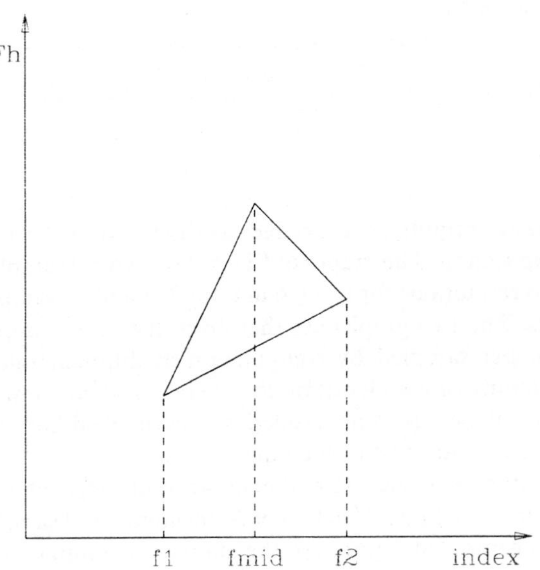

The algorithm recursively subdivides the interval [first, last] and generates a scalar value at the midpoint which is proportional to the current standard deviation times the scale or "roughness" factor (see Fig. 4). h is a parameter which determines the "fractal dimension" of the sequence output by the algorithms. (For a definition and discussion of fractal dimension, see [18].) It is equivalent to the H of fBm and can take on values between 0 and 1. Maxlevel determines the level of recursion needed. This algorithm is suitable for parametric applications since the recursion subdivides a parameter space into equal intervals. A similar algorithm which operates directly in a two-dimensional object space is given below. This algorithm is particularly suited for nonparametric subdivision.

```
procedure fractal(t1, t2, epsilon, h, scale:real; seed:integer);
  var f1, f2, ratio, std:real;
  procedure subdivide (f1, f2, t1, t2, std:real);
    var tmid, fmid:real;
    begin
      if (t2 - t1) > epsilon then
        begin
           tmid := (t1 + t2)/2.0;
           fmid := (f1 + f2)/2.0
                 + std*gauss(seed, tmid);
           std := std*ratio;
           subdivide (f1, fmid, t1, tmid, std);
           subdivide(fmid, f1, tmid, t1, std)
        end
      else output (f1, t1, f2, t2)
    end /* subdivide */
  begin
      f1 := gauss(seed, t1) scale;
      f2 := gauss(seed, t2) scale;
      ratio := 2↑ - h;
      std := scale*ratio;
      subdivide (f1, f2, t1, t2, std)
  end; /* fractal */
```

The sequence of scalar displacements generated gives an approximate sample path of one-dimensional fBm of parameter R. Unlike fBm, this approximation is neither stationary, isotropic, nor self-similar, as pointed out by B. Mandelbrot. This sample path can be used to create

Fig. 5. Typical Curve Obtained at Two Resolutions. h = 0.8, 17, and 257 sample points.

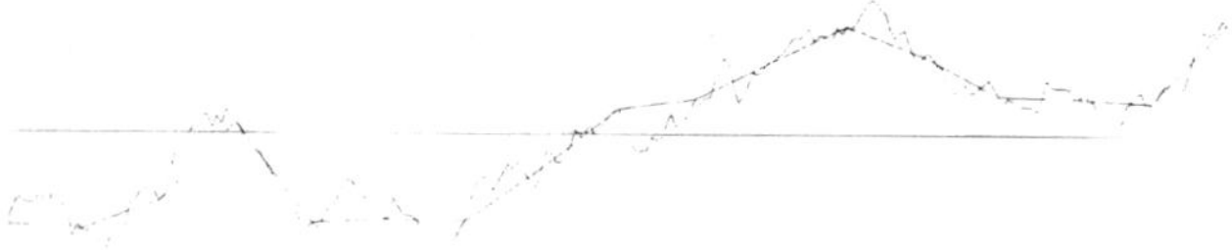

stochastic primitives as needed, as discussed in the following section. The graphs of Fig. 5 show typical samples at two resolutions for h = 0.6 and for 257 and 17 sample points. The two graphs are then from the same sample paths, but sampled by computation at different rates. This ability of the algorithm to generate discrete sample paths only at the rate needed makes it ideal for the purposes of stochastic modeling.

It is easy to see that the number of steps in the algorithm is a linear function of N, the number of sample points computed. Moreover, the amount of computation required to generate each sample point is small, requiring in the second case only 4 real additions, 1 subtraction, 3 real multiplications, and two divisions by 2 in addition to the generation of the pseudo-random variable. This makes it superior to the methods discussed above in terms of efficiency. By tying the random numbers generated at the endpoints to the values of t1 and t2, external consistency can be ensured since any adjacent sample paths generated with this algorithm would have the same endpoints. Internal consistency with respect to scale is assured by tying the seeds of the random number generator to the positions of the points calculated. Of course, internal consistency with respect to position is violated in this case unless t1 and t2 are assumed to be parametric variables and hence not subject to positional change. This can be avoided by using point-specific indices to compute the seed instead of the position, and using t1, t2 only for recursion control.

4. Applications of the Model

4.1 Creation of Stochastic Primitives

The most generally useful application of a stochastic model in graphics is in the construction of stochastic modeling primitives, which can be used for piecewise construction of objects with stochastic features. We describe in this section the construction of one and two-dimensional modeling primitives based on our recursive fBm sample path generator. We also discuss appropriate applications for these primitives and give examples.

4.1.1 One-Dimensional Primitives

The algorithm given in Sec. 3 for generating our approximations to fBm can be viewed as the construction of a "fractal polyline" primitive from an initial deterministic line segment. Of course, all displacements generated can either be viewed as offset vectors in the y direction of a two-dimensional coordinate system as

Fig. 6. Using the Scalar Value to Compute a Curve in the Plane.

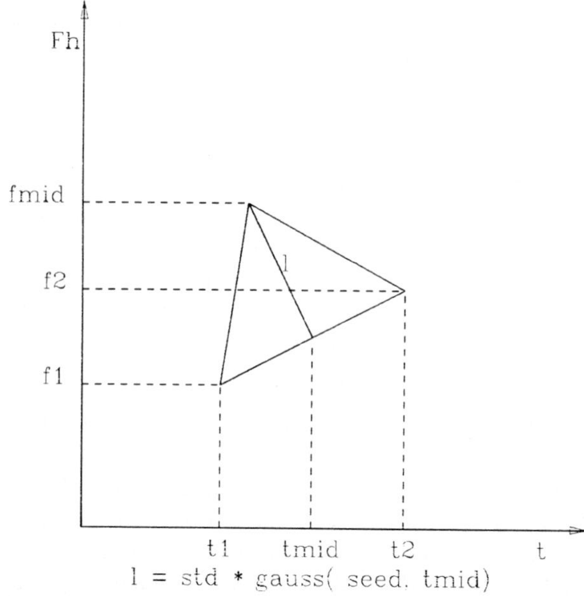

indicated in Fig. 4 or simply as scalar displacements as mentioned above. In the former case, rather unsatisfactory primitives are generated since displacements are tied to the coordinate system rather than the line segment from which the displacement occurs. To eliminate this coordinate system dependency, it is better to take the scalar displacement of the midpoint at each step in the recursion, and use it as an offset from that midpoint along a vector normal to the original line segment. This construction is illustrated in Fig. 6. The only inherent directionality in the resulting curve is that imparted by the slope of the original line segment at the highest level of detail. Figure 7 shows a typical curve resulting from such a procedure, with h = 0.5, with 2, 5, and 257 points.

In order to construct continuous curves from these fractal polylines the displacements of the endpoints of

Fig. 7. Typical Curve Obtained. h = 0.5, 0, 3, and 255 interpolated points.

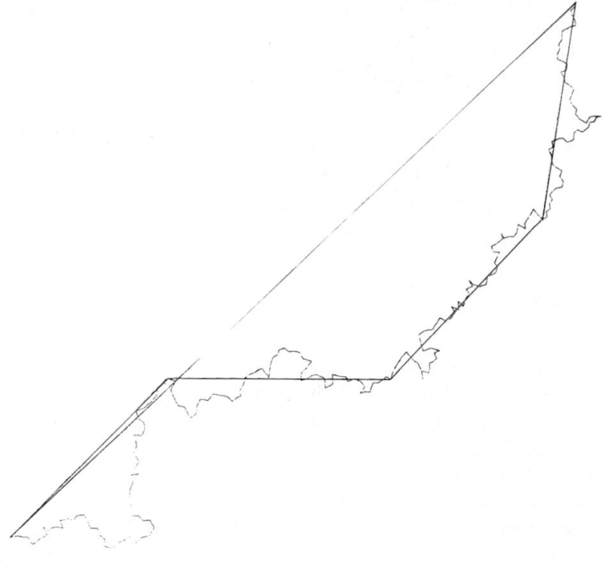

Fig. 8. Construction for a Parametric Curve.

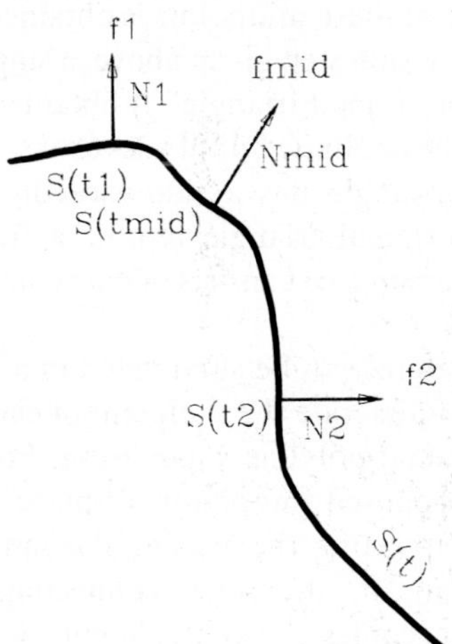

the initial line segment should be fixed at 0. This makes it trivial to guarantee the zero-order continuity of the curve produced. Higher orders of continuity of the fractal surface are meaningful only in a statistical sense since fBm has no derivative at any point [14]. It may be desirable to construct fractal curves based on smooth curves rather than the perimeters of polygons. In this case, the initial curve can be constructed piecewise, for instance, from either interpolating or approximating splines [12]. In this way, various statistical orders of continuity can be assured for this curve with derivative continuity being the most interesting. The scalar sequence generated by the subdivision process can be considered as displacements along vectors normal to the base curve at the appropriate midpoints in parameter space of the curve, as shown in Fig. 8. A more expensive alternative is to let the original spline curve be subdivided into two new spline curves with the original midpoint in parameter space becoming their common boundary and a new set of control points being generated. This common point is then displaced the generated random scalar distance along the common normal to the two curves at their boundary by displacing the adjacent end control points of the curves appropriately.

Any of the fractal polyline primitives constructed in these ways can be combined in arbitrary ways to construct representations of natural phenomena. For instance, the course of an imaginary river as it appears on a map could be generated using an appropriate value of h and level of scale. The instantaneous configuration of a bolt of lightning is also an appropriate candidate, as illustrated in the film *Vol Libre* [4]. An imaginary coastline on a map can also be created from fractal polylines like those of Fig. 7.

A more interesting application allows fractal primitives based on real data to be constructed using a technique we will call "stochastic interpolation." For instance, consider the polygon of Fig. 9 whose 8 vertices are sample points digitized from a map of Australia. The polygon is obtained as a linear interpolation of the positions of adjacent pairs of endpoints. However, it is

Fig. 9. Australia: 8 Sample Points.

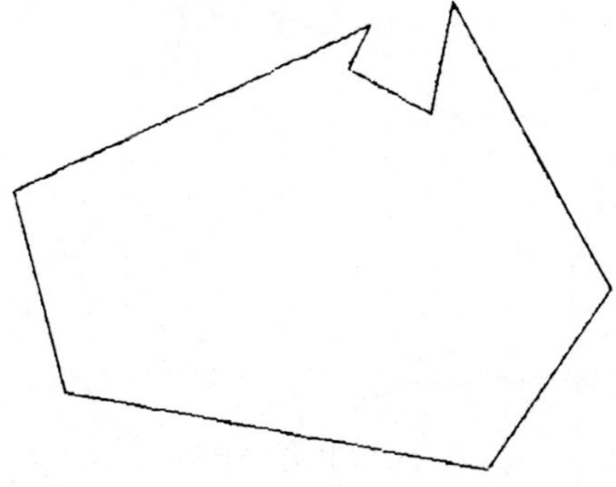

Fig. 10. Stochastic Interpolation. 8 original points and 8 × 127 interpolated points (h = 0.5).

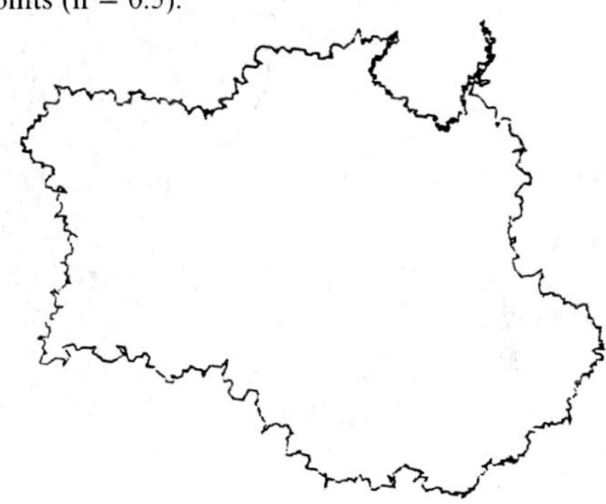

Fig. 11. Stochastic Interpolation. (h = 0.7).

well known that the coastline of Australia is very irregular when viewed at most any magnification, and so the regular polygon, although maybe recognizable as Australia by its overall shape, is not very realistic and looks nothing like the representation of the coastline presented on any reasonably accurate map. Moreover, empirical data suggests that the stochastic characteristics of Australia's coastline are nearly identical to those of one-dimensional fBm with $H = 0.87$ [18], [22]. Figures 10–13 show fractal polylines generated from the line segments of Fig. 9, with various values of h. All of them are much more realistic than Fig. 9, and Fig. 12 looks so real that those of us ignorant in geography would have difficulty arguing that this is not in fact the coastline of Australia traced from a map. Note that h in Fig. 12 is very close to the empirically measured value.

The visual evidence just cited provides a very strong argument that coastlines are best represented by curves

Fig. 12. Stochastic Interpolation. (h = 0.87).

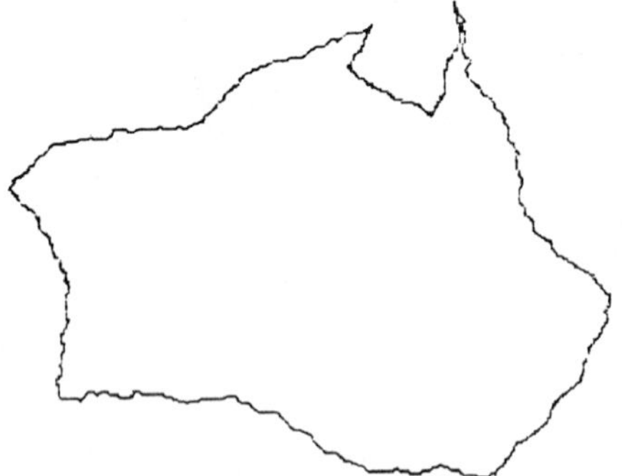

Fig. 13. Stochastic Interpolation (h = 1.0).

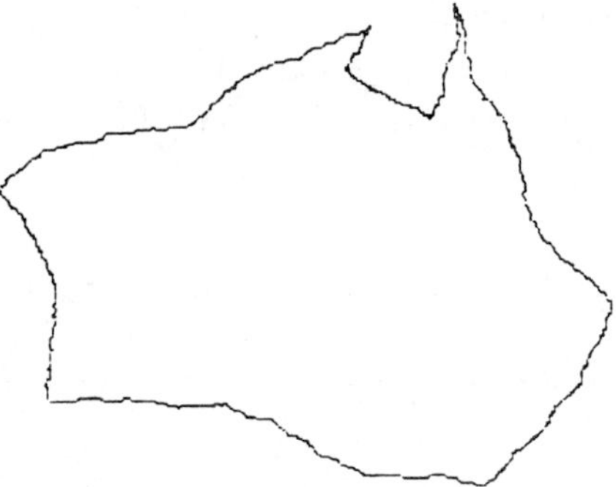

with matching stochastic properties. All the real data obtained by digitizing the map is present in all of Figs. 9–13 since the endpoints of the line segments are not displaced in any case, but the stochastic interpolated curves give a much truer picture of Australia's coastline than a polygon does. In general, for natural phenomena with random, irregular characteristics, it can be argued that the quality of an interpolation between real sample points obtained from that phenomenon should be judged by the correspondence of its stochastic properties with those of the real sample itself.

4.1.2 Two-Dimensional Primitives

One of the most useful applications of a stochastic model in a three-dimensional environment is the representation of irregular surfaces, in this case, terrains. As in one-dimensional modeling, we wish to define a surface which is stochastic rather than deterministic, which at the same time maintains all the nice properties of the surface models currently most useful in computer graphics. We present two somewhat different approaches to the construction of two-dimensional fractal surface primitives. The first is based on a subdivision of polygons to create "fractal polygons" similar to the fractal polylines described above. The second is to define a stochastic parametric surface.

4.1.2.1 Polygon Subdivision. Consider a scene in which all surfaces consist of triangles. This type of model is very commonly used to represent real-world data which has been acquired automatically [11]. Each triangle can be subdivided into four smaller triangles by connecting the midpoints of the sides of the triangles. If the positions in three-space of these midpoints is obtained by a fractal polyline subdivision step given above, a single step in the rendering of a "fractal triangle" is obtained. These subdivisions can be continued until a level of scale is reached in which no triangle has a side exceeding a specified length. The original triangle is now a fractal triangle whose irregular surface consists of many small triangular facets.

A quadrilateral can be subdivided in a slightly more complex way. Generate the midpoint of each of the four sides using fractal polyline subdivision. For each of the two pairs of opposed midpoints, displace the midpoint of the line connecting them using the same procedure. The midpoint of the line connecting these two "midpoints" becomes the center point of the quadrilateral subdivision and four smaller quadrilaterals are generated. This process is continued as with triangles until the desired resolution is obtained, resulting in a fractal quadrilateral whose surface is composed of many quadrilateral facets.

If a scene is modeled by a mesh of triangles or quadrilaterals which are to be rendered as stochastic primitives using polygon subdivision, some care must be taken to ensure internal and external consistency. Internal consistency with respect to position requires that the seeds of the random number generator be indexed by some sort of invariant point identifiers rather than by functions dependent on the positions of the points. Internal consistency with respect to scale requires that the same random numbers be generated in the same order at each level of the subdivision, as before. External consistency is a bit trickier. Since adjacent polygons share a common boundary which must be subdivided, this subdivision must generate the same points on that boundary for both polygons. An obvious requirement is that the same random displacements must be generated on each boundary, which can be accomplished again by tying the seeds of the random number generator to identifers of points on the boundary, making certain that the same identifiers are assigned to the corresponding points in the representation of each polygon's boundary. However, if these displacements are allowed to be in a direction normal to the surface of the original polygon, problems arise when the adjacent polygons are not coplanar, as is generally the case. This is illustrated in Fig. 14. A solution is to calculate the normal of each point in the mesh as the average of the normals of the polygons containing it. Points randomly displaced along these normals will coincide when calculated for adjacent polygons, as desired. Of course, a similar problem exists for every new point calculated in the subdivision, even those completely internal to an original polygon. This can either be solved the same way, calculating the normals during the subdivision, or, less expensively, by letting all displacements be in a direction normal to the original polygon instead of averaging the normals of adjacent polygons created by subdivision.

Fig. 14. Gap Created by Tangent Discontinuity at the Boundary Between Two Polygons (0 original points, × interpolated points).

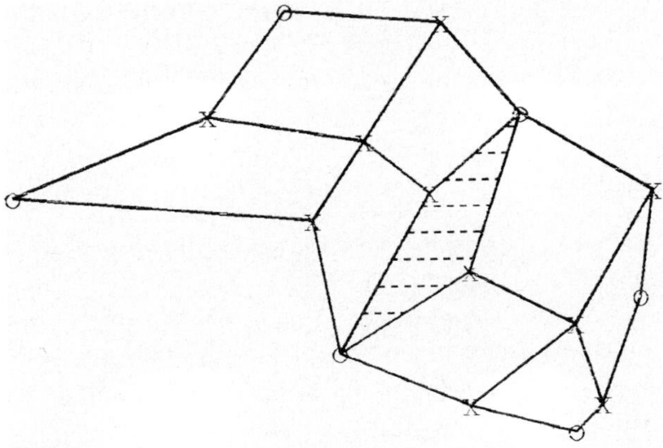

The primary advantage to this approach is the speed with which calculations can be done since only linear functions need be used. It does generate a surface which is self-similar within the range of scale covered by the subdivision and which does have a fractal dimension when carried to the limit. Thus its statistical properties are similar to those of two-dimensional fBm [14], although a better method for approximating fBm is given below. One important difference is that the surface generated in the limit is Markovian (for two-dimensional continuous processes, this means the values of opposite sides of an arbitrary boundary are independent given the boundary), while fBm, in which all sample points are correlated with all others, is not Markovian. As we have stated, however, our primary criterion is visual, and these methods can produce striking pictures of many terrains. The foreground of the cover picture, for instance, was produced using triangle subdivision. The most serious pitfall in using this method to produce good pictures is that derivative discontinuities across adjacent polygons can be annoyingly obvious in pictures that are not smooth shaded if the roughness factor used in the subdivision is not carefully chosen. (Note that smooth shading pictures of rugged terrain has a tendency to destroy the character of the surface.) The Markovian nature of the process, with no correlation between non-neighboring points, also tends to lead to the occasional generation of new polygons with radically divergent normals relative to other neighboring polygons during the subdivision process unless the random number generator is carefully constrained. Another way to obtain smooth surfaces is to use the computed stochastic points as control points of parametric patches, as was done to produce Fig. 15.

4.1.2.2 Stochastic Parametric Surfaces. Stochastic surface primitives can be created by extending deterministic parametric primitives as well as by polygon subdivision. In this case, we wish to define a surface description which is stochastic in nature rather than deterministic, which at the same time maintains the nice properties of the models currently most useful to represent complex objects in computer graphics. It is natural then, to consider functions of the form $\mathbf{X}(u, v) = \mathbf{P}(u, v) + \mathbf{R}(u, v, w)$,

Fig. 15. Surface Produced Using the Stochastically Interpolated Points as Control Points for a B-spline Surface.

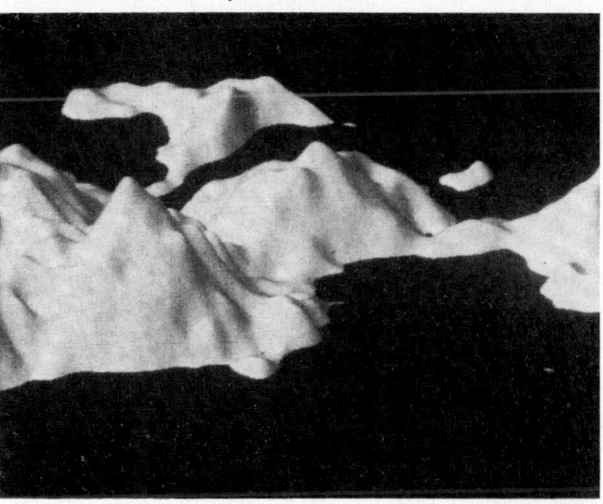

where $\mathbf{P}(u, v)$ is a vector-valued polynomial in u and v, and $\mathbf{R}(u, v, w)$ is a vector-valued random function on the sample space space $\mathbf{W}$, $w \in \mathbf{W}$. Thus $\mathbf{X}(u, v)$ is a two-dimensional stochastic process which we call *a stochastic surface function.* Intuitively, $\mathbf{P}(u, v)$ provides a way of defining the overall position of the surface while $\mathbf{R}(u, v, w)$ causes a stochastic variation in that position over the range of the parameters u and v.

$\mathbf{P}(u, v)$ can be any deterministic parametric function of two dimensions such as a bicubic or bilinear patch. $\mathbf{R}(u, v, w)$ is a vector normal to $\mathbf{P}(u, v)$ whose length is a random scalar $r(u, v, w)$. The calculation of $\mathbf{P}(u, v)$ and its normal are well-understood procedures for many surfaces which are useful in graphics [1], [5], [12]. We are interested in methods for generating $\mathbf{R}(u, v, w)$ as a two-dimensional extension of our fBm approximation algorithm.

The most straightforward approach is to use a method identical to the quadrilateral subdivision given above. This retains the drawbacks of that method, with the exception that normal averaging is unnecessary for those deterministic functions that assure derivative continuity across patch boundaries. If we compute the vector normal along with each subdivision, what is really needed is a non-Markovian approach which provides a better approximation to fBm across the surface of a patch. Of course, since we compute each patch separately, the overall surface cannot be strictly a fBm surface. If the parametric surface definition of the object has the proper stochastic properties globally, however, the approximation of the stochastic surface to fBm will be reasonable. An alternative would be to generate the entire stochastic surface at once, but this is impractical in most situations. Note that this difficulty, caused by the nonlocal character of fBm, does not arise in other stochastic processes of interest, making such computations easier.

To introduce the needed interdependence between points in the two-dimensional approximations to fBm, we will use the following scheme. First we compute the

Fig. 16. Order of Computation for Grid in Two Dimensions. (Order is 0, 1a, 1b, 2a, 2b, $\cdots$) * indicates points interpolated from boundary values only.

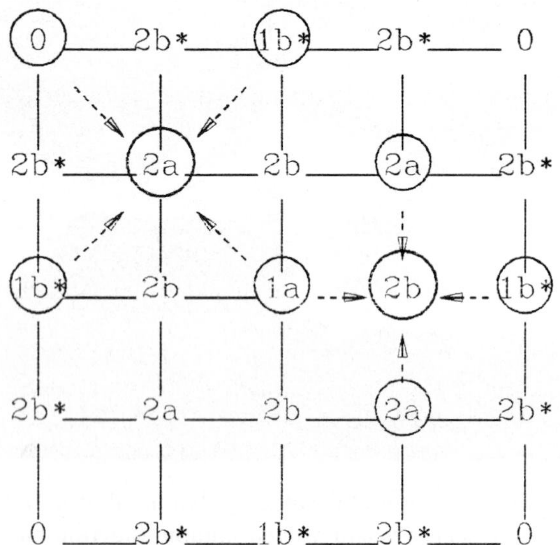

boundary of the patch, using the one-dimensional version of the algorithm to the level desired. We then fill the square for each level, computing the centers, then the sides, using at each step the four neighbors (diagonally for the centers, horizontally and vertically for the sides). At each step the new point is computed as a Gaussian pseudo-random variable, whose expected value is the mean of the four neighbors at this level, and whose standard deviation is $c^{-\ell H}$, with ℓ the level, H the self-similarity parameter, and c a constant to be adjusted to fit the application (see illustration in Fig. 16).

Figures 17–19 show a planet that has been generated with this technique using 10 bicubic Bezier patches. The "land" is made of patches with stochastic surfaces and the "sea" is made of the same patches with no stochastic component. The "coastlines" are then the zerosets of the two-dimensional fBm generated. Note that we used a depth-buffer algorithm to compute these intersections, but we could just as well have added the texture only

Fig. 18. Planets at Different World Space Resolutions but Similar Screen Space Resolutions.

Fig. 17. Planets at Different Resolutions (coastlines are from depth-buffer computations).

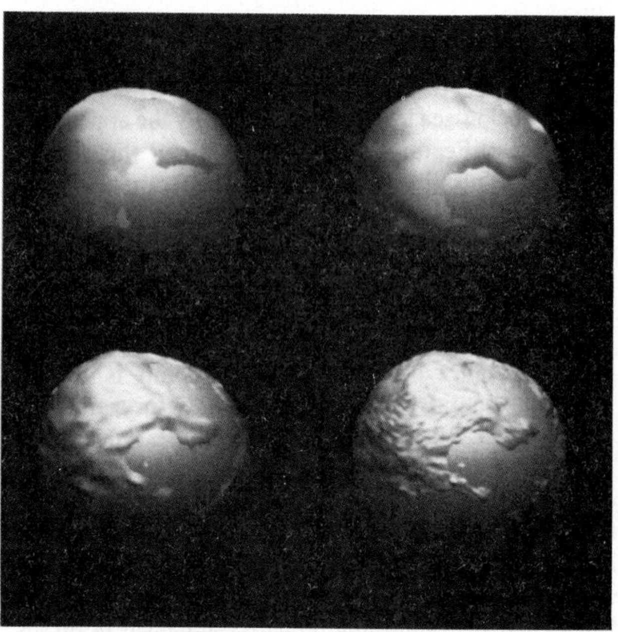

where the displacement is positive and obtained the same "coastlines." The value of h has been chosen to be 0.6 since it is close to the empirical value obtained from actual measurements of geographic features [22]. The altitude has been exaggerated to give a more dramatic effect (the altitude of the highest peaks is about 10 percent of the radius of the planet). The subdivision has been stopped at a fairly low resolution, to illustrate the properties of the method, and the patches are actually processed as polygons (triangles to be specific) by the display system.

Figure 17 shows different resolutions for the planet at the same screen coordinate size, with the level of recursion being 2, 3, 4, and 5. At this on-screen size, though the overall appearance is similar, details, espe-

Fig. 19. Zooming in to the Planet.

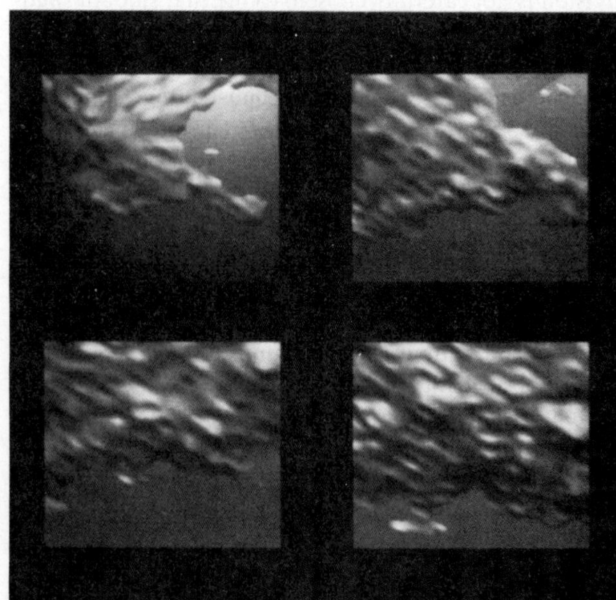

cially for coastlines, are obviously different. This is due to the fact that the screen coordinate distance between computed points on the surface is much more than one pixel (about 20 pixels for the first planet of Fig. 17), and at the next level of computation the midpoint can be above or below sea level, changing locally the appearance of the coast. Features whose size is about the distance between points (in screen coordinates) can be significantly altered. For this reason in normal practice this distance should be kept at or below the size of a pixel.

Figure 18 shows the four objects together at sizes such that the on-screen resolution is the same. Observe that even though we are still above the pixel level (the average distance between computed points is about 2 pixels), the quality of the picture is satisfactory, and there are no noticeable differences in the appearance of the four planets. Considering that the whole database for the planet consists of only 90 three-dimensional points (defining the 10 Bezier patches), the comparison with a picture produced from a real terrain database which could require several 10,000 triangles for a comparable visual complexity is highly favorable. Of course, if the reproduction of a specific set of surface features obtained from cartographic data, for example, were required, it would still be necessary to model these features deterministically to the level of detail desired, and the database would grow accordingly.

Figure 19 illustrates how the process can be continued to zoom in to the surface to any desired level of detail, while keeping the same on-screen resolution. On the upper left is an easily recognizable part (the lower left corner) of the planet. On each of the other views, the central area is enlarged about twice. The main features of each view carry over to the next one, while new details appear. Here the average distance between computed points is about 6 pixels. This process can be continued further, still *with no modification* of the database, until we are arbitrarily close to the surface. Care has to be taken, however, because as the differences between two neighboring points become very small, the computation of the surface normals and the comparisons of the depth values in the Z-buffer can become inaccurate. The zooming in and out process can be repeated as often as desired since the particular stochastic surface generated is fixed and reproducible.

Parametric techniques will generally require somewhat more computation than polygon subdivision since the nonlinear deterministic functions involved require more computation for the rendering of points. In addition, since the recursive subdivision is done in parameter space, it is difficult to tie the depth of the recursion to the final distances apart in world or screen coordinates of the sample points generated. On the other hand, most of the difficulties cited for polygon subdivision are solved using this method. In particular, a surface is generated which has non-Markovian properties very close to those of fBm, and thus provides a much closer approximation. As a result, the value of h in the subdivision corresponds closely to H of fBm, so that empirical determinations of this value can be directly employed to generate terrain representations with characteristics similar to the measured surface, alleviating much experimental "twiddling" of parameters. Also, the higher correlations between points on the patch eliminate the need for tight control of the random number generator to avoid the glitches mentioned above.

The cost of the computation of the surface is a linear function of the number of points *displayed*. The cost of computation of the stochastic variables can be lowered using table lookup techniques (note that the numbers used do not need to pass very stringent tests for randomness). This indicates that the increase in computational cost will be small relative to the cost of the usual transformations and shading algorithms.

These algorithms share the general advantages of subdivision algorithms. They allow continuing the computation of the texture down to the pixel level, or even the subpixel level if some anti-aliasing is needed, while at the same time keeping the level of surface details constant as the object gets larger or smaller in screen space.

At the other end of the range in screen space, if the object is much larger than the screen size, the texture should be computed to the highest level of detail only for the portion of the patch or polygon that is not clipped out. Since such a subpatch or subpolygon cannot be computed solely on the basis of local information, some points outside of the displayed area are needed. It can be shown [9] that the total number of sample points to be computed is bounded by a linear function of the number of points to be displayed. So this algorithm allows "zooming" in and out on the surface, keeping the same displayed level of complexity (within one binary order of magnitude), while the time and space complexity grows only linearly as a function of the number of points actually displayed. This is then an implementation of a truly hierarchical approach to surface modeling, the importance of which was pointed out by Clark [6].

Another interesting feature of the algorithm for practical applications is that it is easy to change the value of the parameter h at any level of the computation. Therefore a terrain that looks very rugged from a distance (a low value of h), can become rather smooth at a higher scale (a high value of h). This models what happens if valleys are filled with sediments, for instance. This is a particular example of a general technique, namely changing the characteristic of the stochastic process, or even the stochastic process itself, according to the recursion level.

In our planet example, the nonstochastic components of the stochastic surface are the patches defining a close approximation of the sphere. As a result, the macroscopic features of the land masses are not predetermined. In most applications, however, the macroscopic features would be known, and some points of the surface would have the actual measured coordinates. In this case, it is better (and easy) to force the stochastic component to be zero at these points. Thus the stochastic surface will interpolate these points, and we have a method for stochastic interpolation in two dimensions. Of course, the polygon subdivision methods generate no displacements at the original vertices and thus always produce stochastic interpolations of these vertices.

5. Further Applications of the Model

5.1 Other Stochastic Surface Properties

We have thus far only considered the application of fBm and other stochastic models to the creation of primitives whose surface position has stochastic characteristics. Other properties of a surface, such as its color, might also be allowed to vary stochastically. For instance, another instance of two-dimensional fBm with a high value of H and a low roughness factor could be used to determine the color of the surface of the planet. Of course, this property should also be continuous across patch boundaries. Another technique for color variation which can be used with polygon subdivision requires that a color be initially assigned to each vertex of the polygon to be subdivided. When a midpoint is computed for a side of the polygon, its color becomes that of one of the endpoints of the side. Which endpoint is chosen is decided according to a Boolean random function. When the subdivision is complete, the color of each facet's surface can simply be taken as the average of the colors of its vertices. This technique was used in generating the color variations and snow cap on the mountain range in the foreground of the cover picture.

5.2 Motion

Although various effective techniques have been developed for creating a series of images of a scene in which smooth, continuous motions of objects in the scene are depicted, these tend not to be very effective in handling complex irregular motions such as the path of a lightning bolt or the motion of a leaf in the wind. Stochastic techniques can provide powerful means of modeling motion which would have been difficult or impossible to represent otherwise. Consider, for instance, the action of unfolding a crumpled piece of paper. Figure 20 is four frames from a sequence representing such an action. These frames were generated using Bezier patches mapped with approximations to fBm with varying values of h. As h is changed from 0.3 to 0.9, the patch is rescaled to keep its surface area constant.[1] Thus a complex motion that would have been very expensive to generate previously is modeled very easily with stochastic

Fig. 20. Motion by Variation of h(h = 0.3, 0.5, 0.7, 0.9).

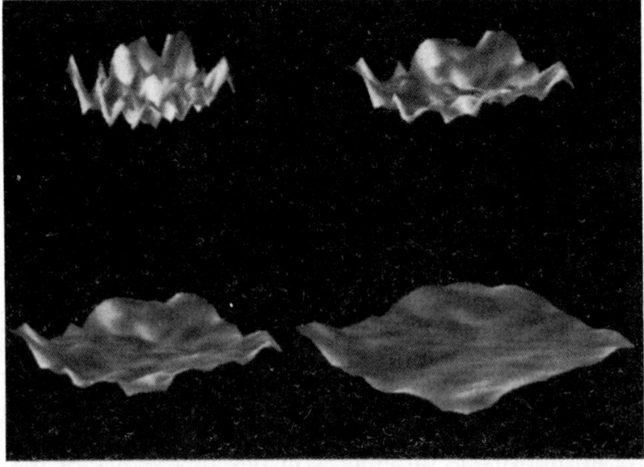

techniques. Another example is the motion of a simple lightning bolt. The path of the lightning bolt can be represented as a fBm function from one dimension into three, like Brownian motion of a molecule in three-space. By simply changing the random numbers generated, while keeping the endpoint displacements fixed at 0, a sequence of instantaneous positions of the lightning bolt is created. Generating the same number of sample points in each instance, and allowing the motion of each sample point to interpolate the positions of that point in each of the "key frames" generated above, the motion of the lightning can be generated. Note that the interpolated path of each sample point can be created using either a deterministic or a stochastic technique. The lightning in the film *Vol Libre* [4] was generated in this way.

6. Conclusion

We suggest that recognition of the importance of the stochastic properties of the real world will lead to greatly increased flexibility in the modeling techniques used in computer graphics, just as probabilistic models have contributed significantly to the development of several related disciplines. We have applied Mandelbrot's fBm model for terrain and other natural phenomena and have developed efficient and appropriate sample path generating algorithms. We have shown several methods for creating stochastic modeling primitives of one and two-dimensions based on these algorithms and have demonstrated the use of stochastic interpolation of real sampled data points to create realistic representations of sampled phenomena. These methods constitute very natural and compact hierarchical object descriptions which are applicable to the modeling of various natural phenomena at a small fraction of the cost of deterministic methods of comparable quality, when these exist at all.

The techniques presented here barely scratch the surface of the possibilities of the stochastic approach to modeling. The most immediate extensions of this work are to use the same techniques to modify surface char-

[1] Note that a real fBm surface has infinite area, although our discrete approximations to it are, of course, finite. See [18].

acteristics other than position, for example, to create stochastic color patterns as has subsequently been done in the movie *Peak* by Mark Snilily, or to render small scale texture by stochastic variation of surface normals analogous to Blinn's method [3]. In contrast to these one and two-dimensional stochastic methods, the study of three and four-dimensional stochastic models should lead to interesting techniques for the representation of complex volumes and motions.

As indicated above, there are two general sources of stochastic models that may be of use in graphics. Although in this paper we have illustrated a mathematical model useful in representing terrain, there might be many natural objects for which it is unlikely that one will find a suitable mathematical model. Techniques which allow the empirical determination of parameters of a flexible canonical stochastic model which fit specific natural objects would be very useful in this regard. Research in the development of such techniques holds the promise of rich rewards for computer graphics.

Acknowledgments. The first two authors would like to thank Zvi Kedem for his many helpful suggestions and overall support, and Henry Fuchs, who taught them how to make pictures with computers. We thank Benoit Mandelbrot for providing inspiration through his book, and for his kindness and encouragement. We also thank Martin Tuori and Martin Taylor of DCIEM in Toronto, who helped in producing Figures 17 to 20.

Received 3/80; revised 12/81; accepted 2/82.

References

1. Bezier, P. Mathematical and practical possibilities of UNISURF. In Barnhill, R.E. and Riesenfeld, R.F. (Eds.). *Computer Aided Geometric Design*, Academic, (1974).

2. Blinn, J.F. Models of light reflection for computer synthesized pictures. In *Proceedings of SIGGRAPH '77.* Also published as *Comput. Graphics, 11,* 2, (Aug. 1977), 192–198.

3. Blinn, J.F. Simulation of wrinkled surfaces. In *Proceedings of SIGGRAPH '77.* Also published as *Comput. Graphics, 12,* 3, (Aug. 1978), 286–292.

4. Carpenter, L.C. *Vol Libre.* Computer generated animated movie. First Showing at SIGGRAPH '80 (July 1980).

5. Catmull, E. Computer display of curved surfaces. In *Proc. IEEE Conference on Computer Graphics, Pattern Recognition and Data Structure.* (May 1975).

6. Clark, J.H. Hierarchical geometric models for visible surface algorithms. *Comm. ACM, 19,* 10, (Oct. 1976), 547–554.

7. Clark, J.H. A fast algorithm for rendering parametric surfaces. In *Proceedings of SIGGRAPH '79.* Also published as *Computer Graphics, 13,* 2 (Aug. 1979), 174.

8. Csuri, C., Hackathorn, R., Parent, R., Carlson, W., and Howard, M. Toward an interactive high visual complexity animation system. In *Proceedings of SIGGRAPH '79.* Also published as *Comput. Graphics, 13,* 2, (Aug. 1979), 289–299.

9. Fournier, A. *Stochastic Modeling in Computer Graphics.* Ph.D. Dissertation, University of Texas at Dallas, (1980).

10. Fu, K.S. Syntactic image modeling using stochastic tree grammars. *Computer Graphics and Image Processing, 12,* (1980), 136–152.

11. Fuchs, H., Kedem, Z.M., and Uselton, S.P. Optimal surface reconstruction from planar contours. *Comm. ACM, 20,* 10, (Oct. 1977), 693–702.

12. Gordon, W.J. and Riesenfeld, R.F. B-spline curves and surfaces. In Barnhill, R.E. and Riesenfeld, R.F. (Eds.), *Computer Aided Geometric Design*, Academic, (1974).

13. Lane, J.M., Carpenter, L.C., Whitted, T., and Blinn, J. Scan-line methods for displaying parametrically defined surfaces. *Comm. ACM, 23,* 1, (Jan. 1980), 23–34.

14. Mandelbrot, B.B. and Van Ness, J.W. Fractional Brownian motions, fractional noises and applications. *SIAM Review, 10,* 4, (Oct. 1968), 422–437.

15. Mandelbrot, B.B.. A fast fractional Gaussian noise generator. *Water Resources Research, 7,* 3, (June 1971), 543–553.

16. Mandelbrot, B.B. On the geometry of homogeneous turbulence, with stress on the fractal dimension of iso-surfaces of scalars. *J. Fluid Mechanics, 72,* 2, (1975), 401–416.

17. Mandelbrot, B.B. Stochastic models for the earth's relief, the shape and fractal dimension of coastlines, and the number area rule for islands. *Proc. Nat. Acad. Sci. USA, 72,* 10, (Oct. 1975), 2825–2828.

18. Mandelbrot, B.B. *Fractals: Form, Chance and Dimension.* Freeman, San Francisco, (1977).

19. Max, N. Vectorized procedural models for natural terrains: Waves and islands in the sunset. In *Proceedings of SIGGRAPH '81.* Also published as *Comput. Graphics, 15,* 3, (Aug. 1981), 317–324.

20. Mezei, L., Puzin, M., and Conroy, P. Simulation of patterns of nature by computer graphics. *Information Processing* 74, 52–56.

21. Modestino, J.W., Fries, R.W., and Vickers, A.L. Stochastic image models generated by random tessellations in the plane. *Computer Graphics and Image Processing, 12,* (1980), 74–98.

22. Richardson, L.F. The problem of statistics of deadly quarrels. *General Systems Yearbook, 6,* (1961), 139–187.

23. Schachter, B. and Ahuja, N. Random pattern generation process. *Computer Graphics and Image Processing, 10,* (1979), 95–114.

24. Schachter, B. Long crested wave models. *Computer Graphics and Image Processing, 12,* (1980), 187–201.

Chapter 5: Ray-Tracing Algorithms

Introduction

Ray-tracing methods employ the principles of geometric optics. For each pixel on the screen, a ray of infintesimal width is traced from the specified eyepoint through the pixel, into object space. The ray is tested against each object in the database, and the object (if any) for which this intersection is the closest to the eyepoint is used to calculate the intensity of the pixel on the screen.

The ray-tracing method has its roots in the works of Appel [Appe68], who used it in the calculation of his "quantitative invisibility" and the work of Goldstein and Nagel [Gold71], who utilized only the basic step in their implementation of the SYNTHAVISION system. Kay and Greenberg [Kay79] considered an extension to the algorithm that included refraction, but it was Whitted [Whit80] (included in this chapter) who made the primary breakthrough by utilizing the ray-tracing method to integrate shadows, reflection, and refraction under a common shading model.

Whitted's extension is very simple. Whenever it is determined that a ray intersects a surface, a secondary ray is first traced from the intersection point toward a point-light source. If the ray encounters an object between surface and light source, the intersection point can be considered to be in shadow and the intensity of the pixel diminished according to the illumination model. A ray can also be traced in the direction of reflection. If the "reflected" ray intersects a surface, the closest surface intersected by this ray is determined, and a portion of the illumination from this second surface is then used in determining the total intensity of the pixel. This adds a level of recursion to the algorithm in that a reflected ray generates additional shadow rays and possible other reflected rays. A similar method is used to calculate refraction from transparent surfaces.

Algorithms, which consider shadows, reflection, and refraction, generate a tree of rays at each pixel, with the edges of the tree indicating the ray-tracing process and the nodes of the tree holding illumination information. To calculate the intensity of the pixel, a tree search is made to gather all illumination information together that influences the intensity.

The ray-tracing algorithm as described by Whitted is very easy to implement (an outline is given in Figure 5.1), and, being based upon the principles of geometric optics, a wide variety of visual effects can be incorporated into the algorithm. However, the algorithm as presented suffers from two primary difficulties: aliasing, which occurs because of the inherent point sampling nature of the algorithm; and the large number of ray/surface-intersection tests, which form a bottleneck in the computational aspects of the algorithm.

The sampling problems of ray tracing can be controlled by simply tracing additional rays per pixel and distributing these rays spatially to find a distribution of intensities over the pixel. The actual intensity displayed can then be a weighted average of the calculated subintensities. Whitted [Whit80] initially recognized this fact and compensated for the sampling problems by tracing additional rays when the intensity variance for rays traced at the corners of a pixel was too large.

Cook et al. [Cook84a] (included in this chapter) developed the method of "distributed ray tracing," in which rays are not only distributed spatially throughout the pixel but can be distributed independently in multi-dimensional space. For example, this allows the generation of motion blur effects, (by distributing the rays in time), depth-of-field effects, (by distributing the rays about the eyepoint), and soft-shadow effects, (by distributing the rays about the light source). Cook [Cook86] and Dippé and Wold [Dipp85b] present stochastic methods by which this sampling can be done. Lee et al. [Lee85] have given an adaptive sampling technique that creates additional samples depending on the variance of previous samples generated.

The ray/surface-intersection calculation is the bottleneck for the time complexity of the ray-tracing algorithm. A ray/sphere intersection test is fairly simple, as is a ray/cylinder test (which is why one sees early ray-traced pictures consisting mostly of spheres, cylinders, and large polygons). However, the calculation becomes much more complex for other primitives. Blinn [Blin82a] has defined a class of algebraic surfaces (usually denoted *blobbies*), and has given a numerical method of calculating the intersection of rays with these surfaces. Hanrahan [Hanr83] has illustrated a ray/surface-intersection test for surfaces that can be written as polynomial functions of the spatial coordinates, which includes planes and quadric surfaces. Kajiya [Kaji83](included in this chapter) has detailed a variety of

```
Ray Tracing Algorithm
    begin
    for each pixel P do {
        form a ray R in object space through the camera
            position and the pixel
        Intensity = trace ( R )
        use Intensity to color the pixel P
        }
    end

    procedure trace ( Ray ) giving Intensity
        begin
            for each entity E in the scene {
                calculate the intersections of E and the Ray (if any)
                }
            if the Ray hits no entity then {
                    return ( background intensity )
                    }
                else {
                    Find the entity E with the closest intersection
                    calculate the intensity I at the intersection point
                    return ( Illumination_model ( I, trace ( reflection_ray ), trace ( refraction_ray ))
                    }
        end
```

Figure 5.1: The Ray-Tracing Algorithm without Shadows

methods for the ray/surface-intersection test for prisms, surfaces of revolution, and fractals. Roth [Roth82] has given a method by which ray tracing can be extended to CSG (Constructive-Solid-Geometry) models. Sederberg and Anderson [Sede84] have developed methods for calculating the ray/surface intersection for Steiner patches (which are specific types of quadratic polynomial parametric patches). Techniques for calculating the intersection between a ray and a surface generated by sweeping methods have been developed by van Wijk [vanW84,vanW85]. Kajiya [Kaji82], Toth [Toth85], Sweeney and Bartels [Swee86], and Joy and Bhetanabhotla [Joy86] (included in this chapter) have all developed methods for the ray/surface-intersection test with bicubic patches. Many of these tests are quite complex and time consuming (for example, the methods of several authors [Blin82a, vanW84, vanW85, Toth85, Joy86] include some numerical calculations for each ray).

Several methods have been developed to limit the attention of the algorithm to only surfaces that lie near the ray. Hierarchical-bounding-box tests were initially studied because they allow a quick test of a ray against a bounding box of a procedural entity. If the ray misses the box, then it can be assumed to miss the entire object. Algorithms of this type were presented by Rubin and Whitted [Rubi80], Weghorst et al. [Wegh84], Kajiya [Kaji83] and Kay and Kajiya [Kay86].

Spatial-subdivision techniques, which subdivide the object space into disjoint cells, were also developed for this purpose. The cells are then utilized as buckets, each holding a list of the surfaces that intersect the cell. The development of a fast algorithm, which allows an ordered enumeration of the cells that lie in the path of a ray, will then allow the ray/surface-intersection test to be accomplished only against those objects that lie in the direct path of the ray—substantially eliminating much of the cost of the calculation. Fujimoto et al. [Fuji86] (included in this chapter) accomplish this by surrounding the primitives in object space with a regular grid of cells, each of which holds a list of objects that intersect the cell. A three-dimensional version of Bresenham's algorithm [Bres65] is utilized to "trace" the rays through the set of cells. Glassner [Glas84] (included in this chapter) has developed a similar algorithm that uses an octree decomposition of the space (a bintree version of this algorithm has also been developed by Kaplan [Kapl85]). Naylor and Thibault [Nayl86] have developed a BSP-tree

bounding box

subdivision technique in which a ray is tested against the tree by examining the subtree closest to the eyepoint before examining the object in the current node and then the further subtree. Joy and Bhetanabhotla [Joy86] also utilize a subdivision method similar to that of Kaplan but determine the subdivision level by the operational characteristics of a numerical intersection test.

Arvo and Kirk [Arvo87] (included in this chapter) have developed an algorithm that classifies rays, which have five degrees of freedom, into unique hypercubes, depending on the spatial coordinates of the ray origin and two spherical angles defining the direction of the ray. Each hypercube contains a sorted list of objects, which potentially intersects any ray classified into the hypercube. This limits the number of cells in the subdivision that need be examined.

Several authors have expanded on the ray-tracing concept to produce algorithms that attempt to trace large numbers of similar rays in a computationally efficient fashion. Algorithms in this class include those by Amanatides [Aman84], who developed a method of ray tracing cones of light; Potmesil and Chakravarty [Potm81] who used similar methods to develop a lens camera model for image synthesis; Heckbert and Hanrahan [Heck84], who have presented a method of ray tracing polygonal scenes by tracing polygonal beams of light; Müller [Mull86], who developed methods of grouping rays by their direction; and Shinya et al. [Shin87], who adapted an algorithm to trace a "pencil" of rays.

"An Improved Illumination Model for Shaded Display" by T. Whitted from *Communications of ACM*, Volume 23, Number 6, June 1980, pages 343-349.

Graphics and Image Processing — J.D. Foley, Editor

An Improved Illumination Model for Shaded Display

Turner Whitted
Bell Laboratories
Holmdel, New Jersey

To accurately render a two-dimensional image of a three-dimensional scene, global illumination information that affects the intensity of each pixel of the image must be known at the time the intensity is calculated. In a simplified form, this information is stored in a tree of "rays" extending from the viewer to the first surface encountered and from there to other surfaces and to the light sources. A visible surface algorithm creates this tree for each pixel of the display and passes it to the shader. The shader then traverses the tree to determine the intensity of the light received by the viewer. Consideration of all of these factors allows the shader to accurately simulate true reflection, shadows, and refraction, as well as the effects simulated by conventional shaders. Anti-aliasing is included as an integral part of the visibility calculations. Surfaces displayed include curved as well as polygonal surfaces.

Key Words and Phrases: computer graphics, computer animation, visible surface algorithms, shading, raster displays

CR Category: 8.2

Introduction

Since its beginnings, shaded computer graphics has progressed toward greater realism. Even the earliest visible surface algorithms included shaders that simulated such effects as specular reflection [19], shadows [1, 7], and transparency [18]. The importance of illumination models is most vividly demonstrated by the realism produced with newly developed techniques [2, 4, 5, 16, 20].

Author's address: Bell Laboratories, Holmdel, NJ 07733.

The role of the illumination model is to determine how much light is reflected to the viewer from a visible point on a surface as a function of light source direction and strength, viewer position, surface orientation, and surface properties. The shading calculations can be performed on three scales: microscopic, local, and global. Although the exact nature of reflection from surfaces is best explained in terms of microscopic interactions between light rays and the surface [3], most shaders produce excellent results using aggregate local surface data. Unfortunately, these models are usually limited in scope, i.e., they look only at light source and surface orientations, while ignoring the overall setting in which the surface is placed. The reason that shaders tend to operate on local data is that traditional visible surface algorithms cannot provide the necessary global data.

A shading model is presented here that uses global information to calculate intensities. Then, to support this shader, extensions to a ray tracing visible surface algorithm are presented.

1. Conventional Models

The simplest visible surface algorithms use shaders based on Lambert's cosine law. The intensity of the reflected light is proportional to the dot product of the surface normal and the light source direction, simulating a perfect diffuser and yielding a reasonable looking approximation to a dull, matte surface. A more sophisticated model is the one devised by Bui-Tuong Phong [8]. Intensity from Phong's model is given by

$$I = I_a + k_d \sum_{j=1}^{j=ls} (\bar{N} \cdot \bar{L}_j) + k_s \sum_{j=1}^{j=ls} (\bar{N} \cdot \bar{L}'_j)^n, \tag{1}$$

where

I = the reflected intensity,
I_a = reflection due to ambient light,
k_d = diffuse reflection constant,
$\bar{N}$ = unit surface normal,
$\bar{L}_j$ = the vector in the direction of the jth light source,
k_s = the specular reflection coefficient,
$\bar{L}'_j$ = the vector in the direction halfway between the viewer and the jth light source,
n = an exponent that depends on the glossiness of the surface.

Phong's model assumes that each light source is located at a point infinitely distant from the objects in the scene. The model does not account for objects within a scene acting as light sources or for light reflected from object to object. As noted in [6], this drawback does not affect the realism of diffuse reflection components very much, but it seriously hurts the quality of specular reflections. A method developed by Blinn and Newell [5] partially solves the problem by modeling an object's environment and mapping it onto a sphere of infinite radius. The technique yields some of the most realistic computer generated pictures ever made, but its limitations preclude its use in the general case.

In addition to the specular reflection, the simulation of shadows is one of the more desirable features of an illumination model. A point on a surface lies in shadow if it is visible to the viewer but not visible to the light source. Some methods [2, 20] invoke the visible surface algorithm twice, once for the light source and once for the viewer. Others [1, 7, 12] use a simplified calculation to determine whether the point is visible to the light source.

Transmission of light through transparent objects has been simulated in algorithms that paint surfaces in reverse depth order [18]. When painting a transparent surface, the background is partially overwritten, allowing previously painted portions of the image to show through. While the technique has produced some impressive pictures, it does not simulate refraction. Kay [17] has improved on this approach with a technique that yields a very realistic approximation to the effects of refraction.

2. Improved Model

A simple model for reflection of light from perfectly smooth surfaces is provided by classical ray optics. As shown in Figure 1, the light intensity, I, passed to the viewer from a point on the surface consists primarily of the specular reflection, S, and transmission, T, components. These intensities represent light propagated along the $\bar{V}$, $\bar{R}$, and $\bar{P}$ directions, respectively. Since surfaces displayed are not always perfectly glossy, a term must be added to model the diffuse component as well. Ideally the diffuse reflection should contain components due to reflection of nearby objects as well as predefined light sources, but the computation required to model a distributed light source is overwhelming. Instead, the diffuse term from (1) is retained in the new model. Then the new model is

$$I = I_a + k_d \sum_{j=1}^{j=ls} (\bar{N} \cdot \bar{L}_j) + k_s S + k_t T, \tag{2}$$

where

S = the intensity of light incident from the $\bar{R}$ direction,
k_t = the transmission coefficient,
T = the intensity of light from the $\bar{P}$ direction.

The coefficients k_s and k_t are held constant for the model used to make pictures in this report, but for the best accuracy they should be functions that incorporate an approximation of the Fresnel reflection law (i.e., the coefficients should vary as a function of incidence angle in a manner that depends on the material's surface properties). In addition, these coefficients must be carefully chosen to correspond to physically reasonable values if realistic pictures are to be generated. The $\bar{R}$ direction is determined by the simple rule that the angle

Fig. 1.

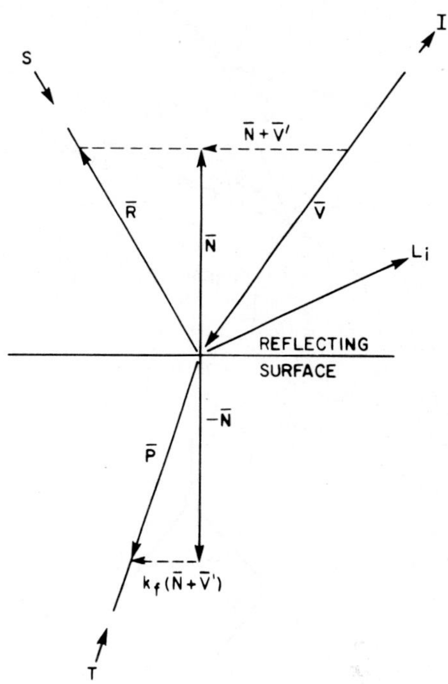

of reflection must equal the angle of incidence. Similarly, the $\bar{P}$ direction of transmitted light must obey Snell's law. Then, $\bar{R}$ and $\bar{P}$ are functions of $\bar{N}$ and $\bar{V}$ given by

$$\bar{V}' = \frac{\bar{V}}{|\bar{V} \cdot \bar{N}|},$$
$$\bar{R} = \bar{V}' + 2\bar{N},$$
$$\bar{P} = k_f(\bar{N} + \bar{V}') - \bar{N},$$

where

$$k_f = (k_n^2 |\bar{V}'|^2 - |\bar{V}' + \bar{N}|^2)^{-1/2},$$

and

k_n = the index of refraction.

Since these equations assume that $\bar{V} \cdot \bar{N}$ is less than zero, the intersection processor must adjust the sign of $\bar{N}$ so that it points to the side of the surface from which the intersecting ray is incident. It must likewise adjust the index of refraction to account for the sign change. If the denominator of the expression for k_f is imaginary, T is assumed to be zero because of total internal reflection.

By making k_s smaller and k_d larger, the surface can be made to look less glossy. However, the simple model will not spread the specular term as Phong's model does by reducing the specular exponent *n*. As pointed out in [3], the specular reflection from a roughened surface is produced by microscopic mirrorlike facets. The intensity of the specular reflection is proportional to the number of these microscopic facets whose normal vector is aligned with the mean surface normal value at the region being sampled. To generate the proper looking specular reflection, a random perturbation is added to the surface normal to simulate the randomly oriented microfacets.

Fig. 2.

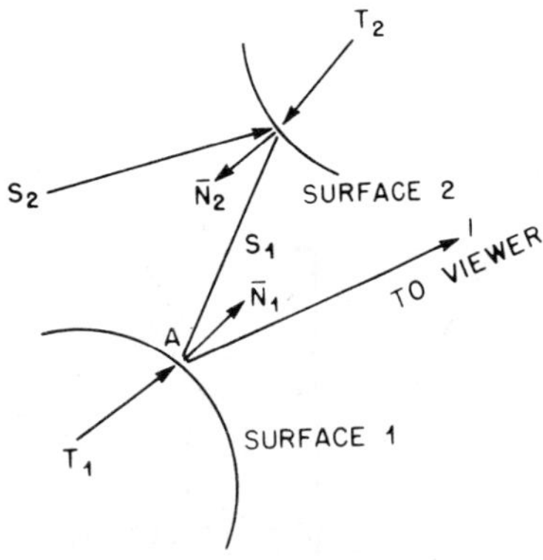

Fig. 3.

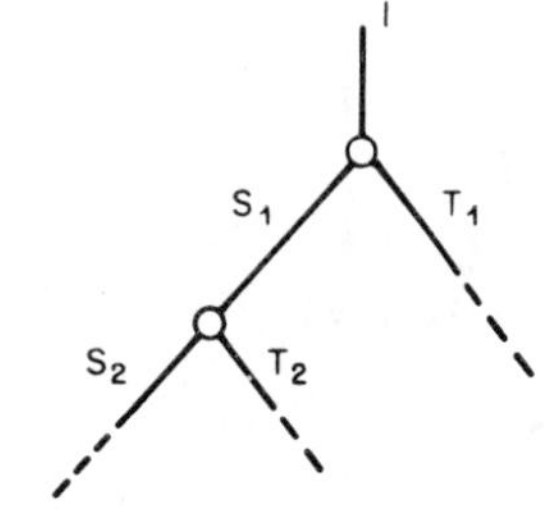

(A similar normal perturbation technique is used by Blinn [4] to model texture on curved surfaces.) For a glossy surface, this perturbation has a small variance; with greater variances the surface will begin to look less glossy. This same perturbation will cause a transparent object to look progressively more frosted as the variance is increased. While providing a good model for microscopic surface roughness, this scheme relies on sampled surface normals and will show the effects of aliasing for larger variances. Since this scheme also requires entirely too much additional computing, it is avoided whenever possible. For instance, in the case of specular reflections caused directly by a point light source, Phong's model is used at the point of reflection instead of the perturbation scheme.

The simple model approximates the reflection from a single surface. In a scene of even moderate complexity light will often be reflected from several surfaces before reaching the viewer. For one such case, shown in Figure 2, the components of the light reaching the viewer from point A are represented by the tree in Figure 3. Creating this tree requires calculating the point of intersection of each component ray with the surfaces in the scene. The calculations require that the visible surface algorithm (described in the next section) be called recursively until all branches of the tree are terminated. For the case of surfaces aligned in such a way that a branch of the tree has infinite depth, the branch is truncated at the point where it exceeds the allotted storage. Degradation of the image from this truncation is not noticeable.

In addition to rays in the $\bar{R}$ and $\bar{P}$ direction, rays corresponding to the $\bar{L}_j$ terms in (2) are associated with each node. If one of these rays intersects some surface in the scene before it reaches the light source, the point of intersection represented by the node lies in shadow with respect to that light source. That light source's contribution to the diffuse reflection from the point is then attenuated.

After the tree is created, the shader traverses the tree, applying eq. (2) at each node to calculate intensity. The intensity at each node is then attenuated by a linear function of the distance between intersection points on the ray represented by the node's parent before it is used as an input to the intensity calculation of the parent. (Since one cannot always assume that all the surfaces are planar and all the light sources are point sources, square-law attenuation is not always appropriate. Instead of modeling each unique situation, linear attenuation with distance is used as an approximation.)

3. Visible Surface Processor

Since illumination returned to the viewer is determined by a tree of "rays," a ray tracing algorithm is ideally suited to this model. In an obvious approach to ray tracing, light rays emanating from a source are traced through their paths until they strike the viewer. Since only a few will reach the viewer, this approach is wasteful. In a second approach suggested by Appel [1] and used successfully by MAGI [14], rays are traced in the opposite direction—from the viewer to the objects in the scene, as illustrated in Figure 4.

Unlike previous ray tracing algorithms, the visibility calculations do not end when the nearest intersection of a ray with objects in the scene is found. Instead, each visible intersection of a ray with a surface produces more rays in the $\bar{R}$ direction, the $\bar{P}$ direction, and in the direction of each light source. The intersection process is repeated for each ray until none of the new rays intersects any object.

Because of the nature of the illumination model, some traditional notions must be discarded. Since objects may be visible to the viewer through reflections in other objects, even though some other object lies between it and the viewer, the measure of visible complexity in an image is larger than for a conventionally generated image of the same scene. For the same reason, clipping and eliminating backfacing surface elements are not applicable with this algorithm. Because these normal preprocessor stages that simplify most visible surface algorithms cannot be used, a different approach is taken. Using a technique similar to one described by Clark [11], the object description includes a bounding volume for each item in the scene. If a ray does not intersect the bounding volume of an object, then the object can be eliminated from further processing for that ray. For simplicity of representation and ease of performing the intersection calculation, spheres are used as the bounding volumes.

Since a sphere can serve as its own bounding volume, initial experiments with the shading processor used spheres as test objects. For nonspherical objects, additional intersection processors must be specified whenever a ray does intersect the bounding sphere for that object. For polygonal surfaces the algorithm solves for the point of intersection of the ray and the plane of the polygon and then checks to see if the point is on the interior of the polygon. If the surface consists of bicubic patches, bounding spheres are generated for each patch. If the bounding sphere is pierced by the ray, then the patch is subdivided using a method described by Catmull and Clark [10], and bounding spheres are produced for each subpatch. The subdivision process is repeated until either no bounding spheres are intersected (i.e., the patch is not intersected by the ray) or the intersected bounding sphere is smaller than a predetermined minimum. This scheme was selected for simplicity rather than efficiency.

The visible surface algorithm also contains the mechanism to perform anti-aliasing. Since aliasing is the result of undersampling during the display process, the most straightforward cure is to low-pass filter the entire image before sampling for display [13]. A considerable amount of computing can be saved, however, if a more economical approach is taken. Aliasing in computer generated images is most apparent to the viewer in three cases: (1) at regions of abrupt change in intensity such as the silhouette of a surface, (2) at locations where small objects fall between sampling points and disappear, and (3) whenever a sampled function (such as texture) is mapped onto the surface. The visible surface algorithm looks for these cases and performs the filtering function only in these regions.

For this visible surface algorithm a pixel is defined in the manner described in [9] as the rectangular region whose corners are four sample points as shown in Figure 5(a). If the intensities calculated at the four points have nearly equal values and no small object lies in the region between them, the algorithm assumes that the average of the four values is a good approximation of the intensity over the entire region. If the intensity values are not nearly equal (Figure 5(b)), the algorithm subdivides the sample square and starts over again. This process runs recursively until the computer runs out of resolution or until an adequate amount of information about the detail within the sample square is recovered. The contribution of each single subregion is weighted by its area, and all such weighted intensities are summed to determine the intensity of the pixel. This approach amounts to performing a Warnock-type visibility process for each pixel [19]. In the limit it is equivalent to area sampling, yet it remains a point sampling technique. A better method, currently being investigated, considers volumes defined by each set of four corner rays and applies a containment test for each volume.

Fig. 4.

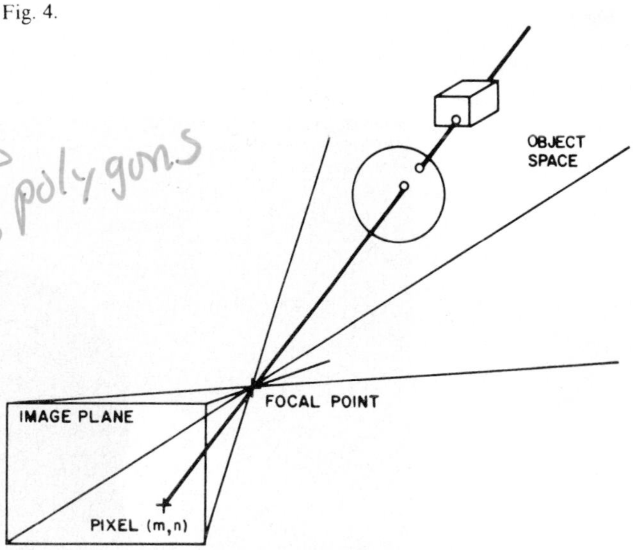

OBJECT SPACE

FOCAL POINT

IMAGE PLANE

PIXEL (m,n)

Fig. 5.

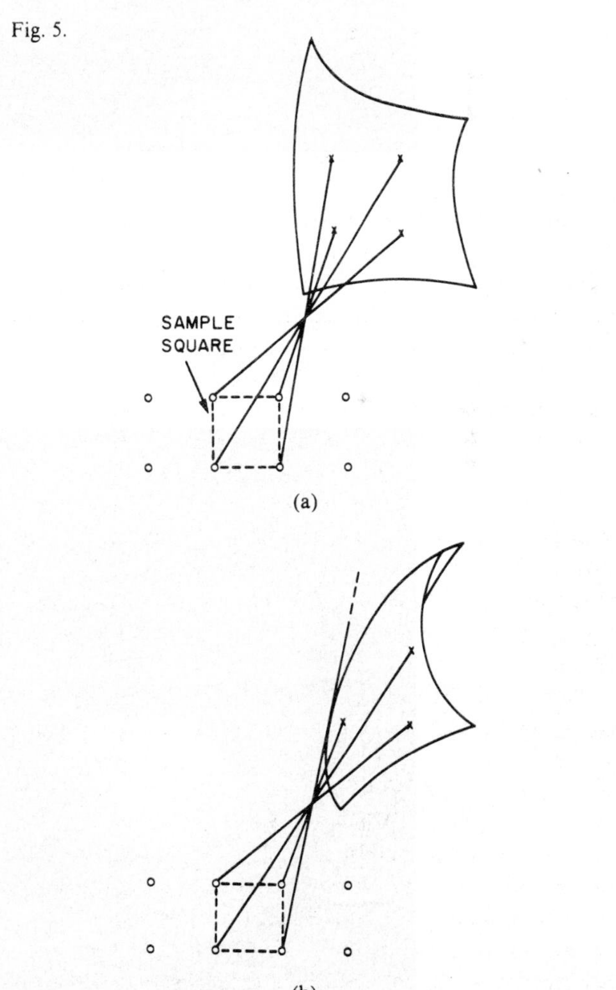

To ensure that small objects are not lost, a minimum radius (based on distance from the viewer) is allowed for bounding spheres of objects. This minimum is chosen so that no matter how small the object, its bounding sphere will always be intersected by at least one ray. If a ray passes within a minimum radius of a bounding sphere but does not intersect the object, the algorithm will know to subdivide each of the four sample squares that share the ray until the missing object is found. Although

Fig. 6.

Fig. 7.

Fig. 8.

Fig. 9.

adequate for rays that reach the viewer directly, this scheme will not always work for rays being reflected from curved surfaces.

4. Results

A version of this algorithm has been programmed in C, running under UNIX[1] on both a PDP-11/45 and a VAX-11/780. To simplify the programming, all calculations are performed in floating point (at a considerable speed penalty). The pictures are displayed at a resolution of 480 by 640 pixels with 9 bits per pixel. Originally color pictures were photographed from the screen of a color CRT so that only three bits were available for each of the three primary colors. Ordered dither [15] was applied to the image data to produce 111 effective intensity levels per primary. For this report pictures are produced by a high-quality color hardcopy camera that exposes each color separately to provide eight bits of intensity per color.

For the scenes shown in this paper, the image generation times are

Figure 6: 44 minutes,
Figure 7: 74 minutes,
Figure 8: 122 minutes.

All times given are for the VAX, which is nearly three times faster than the PDP-11/45 for this application. The image of Figure 6 shows three glossy objects with shadows and object-to-object reflections. The texturing is added using Blinn's wrinkling technique. Figure 7 illustrates the effect of refraction through a transparent object. The algorithm has also been used to produce a short animated sequence. The enhancements provided by this illumination model are more readily apparent in the animated sequence than in the still photographs.

A breakdown of where the program spends its time for simple scenes is:

Overhead—13 percent,
Intersection—75 percent,
Shading—12 percent.

For more complex scenes the percentage of time required to compute the intersections of rays and surfaces increases to over 95 percent. Since the program makes almost no use of image coherence, these figures are actually quite promising. They indicate that a more efficient intersection processor will greatly improve the algorithm's performance. This distribution of processing times also suggests that a reasonable division of tasks between processors in a multiprocessor system is to have one or more processors dedicated to intersection calculations with ray generation and shading operations performed by the host.

[1] UNIX is a trademark of Bell Laboratories.

5. Summary

This illumination model draws heavily on techniques derived previously by Phong [8] and Blinn [3–5], but it operates recursively to allow the use of global illumination information. The approach used and the results achieved are similar to those presented by Kay [16].

While in many cases the model generates very realistic effects, it leaves considerable room for improvement. Specifically, it does not provide for diffuse reflection from distributed light sources, nor does it gracefully handle specular reflections from less glossy surfaces. It is implemented through a visible surface algorithm that is very slow but which shows some promise of becoming more efficient. When better ways of using picture coherence to speed the display process are found, this algorithm may find use in the generation of realistic animated sequences.

Received 12/78; revised 1/80; accepted 2/80

References

1. Appel, A. Some techniques for shading machine renderings of solids. AFIPS 1968 Spring Joint Comptr. Conf., pp. 37–45.
2. Atherton, P., Weiler, K., and Greenberg, D. Polygon shadow generation. Proc. SIGGRAPH 1978, Atlanta, Ga., pp. 275–281.
3. Blinn, J.F. Models of light reflection for computer synthesized pictures. Proc. SIGGRAPH 1977, San Jose, Calif., pp. 192–198.
4. Blinn, J.F. Simulation of wrinkled surfaces. Proc. SIGGRAPH 1978, Atlanta, Ga., pp. 286–292.
5. Blinn, J.F., and Newell, M.E. Texture and reflection in computer generated images. *Comm. ACM 19*, 10 (Oct. 1976), 542–547.
6. Blinn, J.F., and Newell, M.E. The progression of realism in computer generated images. Proc. of the ACM Ann. Conf., 1977, pp. 444–448.
7. Bouknight, W.K., and Kelley, K.C. An algorithm for producing half-tone computer graphics presentations with shadows and movable light sources. AFIPS 1970 Spring Joint Comptr. Conf., pp. 1–10.
8. Bui-Tuong Phong. Illumination for computer generated images. *Comm. ACM 18*, 6 (June 1975), 311–317.
9. Catmull, E. A subdivision algorithm for computer display of curved surfaces. UTEC CSc-74-133, Comptr. Sci. Dept., Univ. of Utah, 1974.
10. Catmull, E., and Clark, J. Recursively generated B-spline surfaces on arbitrary topological meshes. *Comptr. Aided Design 10*, 6 (Nov. 1978), 350–355.
11. Clark, J.H. Hierarchical geometric models for visible surface algorithms. *Comm. ACM 19*, 10 (Oct. 1976), 547–554.
12. Crow, F.C. Shadow algorithms for computer graphics. Proc. SIGGRAPH 1977, San Jose, Calif., pp. 242–248.
13. Crow, F.C. The aliasing problem in computer-generated shaded images. *Comm. ACM 20*, 11 (Nov. 1977), 799–805.
14. Goldstein, R.A. and Nagel, R. 3-D visual simulation. *Simulation* (Jan. 1971), 25–31.
15. Jarvis, J.F., Judice, C.N., and Ninke, W.H. A survey of techniques for the display of continuous tone pictures on bilevel displays. *Comptr. Graphics and Image Proc. 5* (1976), 13–40.
16. Kay, D.S. Transparency, refraction, and ray tracing for computer synthesized images. Masters thesis, Cornell Univ., Ithaca, N.Y., January 1979.
17. Kay, D.S., and Greenberg, D. Transparency for computer synthesized images. Proc. SIGGRAPH 1979, Chicago, Ill., pp. 158–164.
18. Newell, M.E., Newell, R.G., and Sancha, T.L. A solution to the hidden surface problem. Proc. ACM Ann. Conf., 1972, pp. 443–450.
19. Warnock, J.E. A hidden line algorithm for halftone picture representation. Tech. Rep. TR 4-15, Comptr. Sci. Dept., Univ. of Utah, 1969.
20. Williams, L. Casting curved shadows on curved surfaces. Proc. SIGGRAPH 1978, Atlanta, Ga., pp. 270–274.

"Distributed Ray Tracing" by R.L. Cook, T. Porter, and L. Carpenter from *Proceedings of SIGGRAPH '84*, 1984, pages 137-145. Copyright 1984, Association for Computing Machinery, Inc., reprinted by permission.

Distributed Ray Tracing

Robert L. Cook
Thomas Porter
Loren Carpenter

Computer Division
Lucasfilm Ltd.

Abstract

Ray tracing is one of the most elegant techniques in computer graphics. Many phenomena that are difficult or impossible with other techniques are simple with ray tracing, including shadows, reflections, and refracted light. Ray directions, however, have been determined precisely, and this has limited the capabilities of ray tracing. By distributing the directions of the rays according to the analytic function they sample, ray tracing can incorporate fuzzy phenomena. This provides correct and easy solutions to some previously unsolved or partially solved problems, including motion blur, depth of field, penumbras, translucency, and fuzzy reflections. Motion blur and depth of field calculations can be integrated with the visible surface calculations, avoiding the problems found in previous methods.

CR CATEGORIES AND SUBJECT DESCRIPTORS: I.3.7 [**Computer Graphics**]: Three-Dimensional Graphics and Realism;

ADDITIONAL KEY WORDS AND PHRASES: camera, constructive solid geometry, depth of field, focus, gloss, motion blur, penumbras, ray tracing, shadows, translucency, transparency

1. Introduction

Ray tracing algorithms are elegant, simple, and powerful. They can render shadows, reflections, and refracted light, phenomena that are difficult or impossible with other techniques[11]. But ray tracing is currently limited to sharp shadows, sharp reflections, and sharp refraction.

Ray traced images are sharp because ray directions are determined precisely from geometry. Fuzzy phenomenon would seem to require large numbers of additional samples per ray. By distributing the rays rather than adding more of them, however, fuzzy phenomena can be rendered with no additional rays beyond those required for spatially oversampled ray tracing. This approach provides correct and easy solutions to some previously unsolved problems.

This approach has not been possible before because of aliasing. Ray tracing is a form of point sampling and, as such, has been subject to aliasing artifacts. This aliasing is not inherent, however, and ray tracing can be filtered as effectively as any analytic method[4]. The filtering does incur the expense of additional rays, but it is not merely oversampling or adaptive oversampling, which in themselves cannot solve the aliasing problem. This antialiasing is based on an approach proposed by Rodney Stock. It is the subject of a forthcoming paper.

Antialiasing opens up new possibilities for ray tracing. Ray tracing need not be restricted to spatial sampling. If done with proper antialiasing, the rays can sample motion, the camera lens, and the entire shading function. This is called *distributed ray tracing.*

Distributed ray tracing is a new approach to image synthesis. The key is that no extra rays are needed beyond those used for oversampling in space. For example, rather than taking multiple time samples at every spatial location, the rays are distributed in time so that rays at different spatial locations are traced at different instants of time. Once we accept the expense of oversampling in space, distributing the rays offers substantial benefits at little additional cost.

- Sampling the reflected ray according to the specular distribution function produces gloss (blurred reflection).
- Sampling the transmitted ray produces translucency (blurred transparency).
- Sampling the solid angle of the light sources produces penumbras.

- Sampling the camera lens area produces depth of field.
- Sampling in time produces motion blur.

2. Shading

The intensity I of the reflected light at a point on a surface is an integral over the hemisphere above the surface of an illumination function L and a reflection function R[1].

$$I(\phi_r,\theta_r) = \int_{\phi_i}\int_{\theta_i} L(\phi_i,\theta_i)R(\phi_i,\theta_i,\phi_r,\theta_r)\,d\phi_i d\theta_i$$

where

(ϕ_i,θ_i) is the angle of incidence, and

(ϕ_r,θ_r) is the angle of reflection.

The complexity of performing this integration has been avoided by making some simplifying assumptions. The following are some of these simplifications:

- Assume that L is a δ function, i.e., that L is zero except for light source directions and that the light sources can be treated as points. The integral is now replaced by a sum over certain discrete directions. This assumption causes sharp shadows.
- Assume that all of the directions that are not light source directions can be grouped together into an ambient light source. This ambient light is the same in all directions, so that L is independent of ϕ_i and θ_i and may be removed from the integral. The integral of R may then be replaced by an average, or ambient, reflectance.
- Assume that the reflectance function R is a δ function, i.e., that the surface is a mirror and reflects light only from the mirror direction. This assumption causes sharp reflections. A corresponding assumption for transmitted light causes sharp refraction.

The shading function may be too complex to compute analytically, but we can point sample its value by distributing the rays, thus avoiding these simplifying assumptions. Illumination rays are not traced toward a single light direction, but are distributed according to the illumination function L. Reflected rays are not traced in a single mirror direction but are distributed according to the reflectance function R.

2.1. Gloss

Reflections are mirror-like in computer graphics, but in real life reflections are often blurred or hazy. The distinctness with which a surface reflects its environment is called *gloss*[5]. Blurred reflections have been discussed by Whitted[11] and by Cook[2]. Any analytic simulation of these reflections must be based on the integral of the reflectance over some solid angle.

Mirror reflections are determined by tracing rays from the surface in the mirror direction. Gloss can be calculated by distributing these secondary rays about the mirror direction. The distribution is weighted according to the same distribution function that determines the highlights.

This method was originally suggested by Whitted[11], and it replaces the usual specular component. Rays that reflect light sources produce highlights.

2.2. Translucency

Light transmitted through an object is described by an equation similar to that for reflected light, except that the reflectance function R is replaced by a transmittance function T and the integral is performed over the hemisphere behind the surface. The transmitted light can have ambient, diffuse, and specular components[5].

Computer graphics has included transparency, in which T is assumed to be a δ function and the images seen through transparent objects are sharp. Translucency differs from transparency in that the images seen through translucent objects are not distinct. The problem of translucency is analogous to the problem of gloss. Gloss requires an integral of the reflected light, and translucency requires a corresponding integral of the transmitted light.

Translucency is calculated by distributing the secondary rays about the main direction of the transmitted light. Just as the distribution of the reflected rays is defined by the specular reflectance function, the distribution of the transmitted rays is defined by a specular transmittance function.

2.3. Penumbras

Penumbras occur where a light source is partially obscured. The reflected intensity due to such a light is proportional to the solid angle of the visible portion of the light. The solid angle has been explicitly included in a shading model[3], but no algorithms have been suggested for determining this solid angle because of the complexity of the computation involved. The only attempt at penumbras known to the authors seems to solve only a very special case[7].

Shadows can be calculated by tracing rays from the surface to the light sources, and penumbras can be calculated by distributing these secondary rays. The shadow ray can be traced to any point on the light source, not just not to a single light source location. The distribution of the shadow rays must be weighted according the projected area and brightness of different parts of the light source. The number of rays traced to each region should be proportional to the amount of the light's energy that would come from that region if the light was

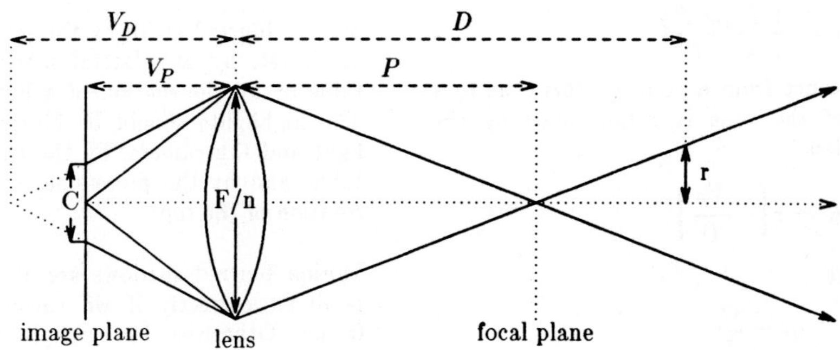

Figure 1. Circle of Confusion.

completely unobscured. The proportion of lighted sample points in a region of the surface is then equal to the proportion of that light's intensity that is visible in that region.

3. Depth of Field

Cameras and the eye have a finite lens aperture, and hence their images have a finite depth of field. Each point in the scene appears as a circle on the image plane. This circle is called the circle of confusion, and its size depends on the distance to the point and on the lens optics. Depth of field can be an unwanted artifact, but it can also be a desirable effect.

Most computer graphics has been based on a pinhole camera model with every object in sharp focus. Potmesil simulated depth of field with a postprocessing technique. Each object is first rendered in sharp focus (i.e., with a pinhole camera model), and later each sharply rendered object is convolved with a filter the size of the circle of confusion[8]. The program spends most of its time in the focus postprocessor, and this time increases dramatically as the aperture decreases.

Such a postprocessing approach can never be completely correct. This is because visibility is calculated from a single point, the center of the lens. The view of the environment is different from different parts of the lens, and the differences include changes in visibility and shading that cannot be accounted for by a postprocessing approach.

For example, consider an object that is extremely out of focus in front of an object that is in focus. Visible surface calculations done with the pinhole model determine the visibility from the center of the lens. Because the front object is not in focus, parts of the focused object that are not visible from the center of the lens will be visible from other parts of the lens. Information about those parts will not available for the postprocessor, so the postprocessor cannot possibly get the correct result.

There is another way to approach the depth of field problem. Depth of field occurs because the lens is a finite size. Each point on the lens "looks" at the same point on the focal plane. The visible surfaces and the shading may be different as seen from different parts of the lens. The depth of field calculations should account for this and be an integral part of the visible surface and shading calculations.

Depth of field can be calculated by starting with the traditional ray from the center of the lens through point p on the focal plane. A point on the surface of the lens is selected and the ray from that point to p is traced. The camera specifications required for this calculation are the focal distance and the diameter of the lens $\frac{F}{n}$, where F is the focal length of the lens and n is the aperture number.

This gives exactly the same circle of confusion as presented by Potmesil[8]. Because it integrates the depth of field calculations with the shading and visible surface calculations, this method gives a more accurate solution to the depth of field problem, with the exception that it does not account for diffraction effects.

Figure 1 shows why this method gives the correct circle of confusion. The lens has a diameter of $\frac{F}{n}$ and is focused at a distance P so that the image plane is at a distance V_P, where

$$V_P = \frac{FP}{P-F} \text{ for } P>F .$$

Points on the plane that is a distance D from the lens will focus at

$$V_D = \frac{FD}{D-F} \text{ for } D>F$$

and have a circle of confusion with diameter C of[8]

$$C = |V_D - V_P| \frac{F}{nV_D}$$

For a point I on the image plane, the rays we trace lie inside the cone whose radius at D is

$$r = \frac{1}{2}\frac{F}{n}\frac{|D-P|}{P}$$

The image plane distance from a point on this cone to a point on the axis of the cone is r multiplied by the magnification of the lens.

$$R = r\left(-\frac{V_P}{D}\right).$$

It is easily shown that

$$R = \frac{C}{2}.$$

Hence any points on the cone have a circle of confusion that just touches the image point I. Points outside the cone do not affect the image point and points inside the cone do.

4. Motion Blur

Distributing the rays or sample points in time solves the motion blur problem. Before we discuss this method and how it works, let us first look in more detail at the motion blur problem and at previous attempts to solve it.

The motion blur method described by Potmesil[9] is not only expensive, it also separates the visible surface calculation from the motion blur calculation. This is acceptable in some situations, but in most cases we cannot just calculate a still frame and blur the result. Some object entirely hidden in the still frame might be uncovered for part of the the time sampled by the blur. If we are to blur an object across a background, we have to know what the background is.

Even if we know what the background is, there are problems. For example, consider a biplane viewed from above, so that the lower wing is completely obscured by the upper wing. Because the upper wing is moving, the scenery below it would be seen through its blur, but unfortunately the lower wing would show through too. The lower wing should be hidden completely because it moves with the the upper wing and is obscured by it over the entire time interval.

This particular problem can be solved by rendering the plane and background as separate elements, but not all pictures can easily be separated into elements. This solution also does not allow for changes in visibility within a single object. This is particularly important for rotating objects.

The situation is further complicated by the change in shading within a frame time. Consider a textured top spinning on a table. If we calculate only one shade per frame, the texture would be blurred properly, but unfortunately the highlights and shadows would be blurred too. On a real top, the highlights and shadows are not blurred at all by the spinning. They are blurred, of course, by any lateral motion of the top along the table or by the motion of a light source or the camera. The highlights should be blurred by the motion of the light and the camera, by the travel of the top along the table, and by the precession of the top, but not by the rotation of the top.

Motion blurred shadows are also important and are not rendered correctly if we calculate only one shade per frame. Otherwise, for example, the blades of a fan could be motion blurred, but the shadows of those blades would strobe.

All of this is simply to emphasize the tremendous complexity of the motion blur problem. The prospects for an analytic solution are dim. Such a solution would require solving the visible surface problem as a function of time as well as space. It would also involve integrating the texture and shading function of the visible surfaces over time. Point sampling seems to be the only approach that offers any promise of solving the motion blur problem.

One point sampling solution was proposed by Korein and Badler[6]. Their method, however, point samples only in space, not in time. Changes in shading are not motion blurred. The method involves keeping a list of all objects that cross each sample point during the frame time, a list that could be quite long for a fast moving complex scene. They also impose the unfortunate restriction that both vertices of an edge must move at the same velocity. This creates holes in objects that change perspective severely during one frame, because the vertices move at drastically different rates. Polygons with edges that share these vertices cannot remain adjoining. The algorithm is also limited to linear motion. If the motion is curved or if the vertices are allowed to move independently, the linear intersection equation becomes a higher order equation. The resulting equation is expensive to solve and has multiple roots.

Distributing the sample points in time solves the motion blur problem. The path of motion can be arbitrarily complex. The only requirement is the ability to calculate the position of the object at a specific time. Changes in visibility and shading are correctly accounted for. Shadows (umbras and penumbras), depth of field, reflections and intersections are all correctly motion blurred. By using different distributions of rays, the motion can be blurred with a box filter or a weighted filter or can be strobed.

This distribution of the sample points in time does not involve adding any more sample points. Updating the object positions for each time is the only extra calculation needed for motion blur. Proper antialiasing is required or the picture will look strobed or have holes[4].

5. Other Implications of the Algorithm

Visible surface calculation is straightforward. Since each ray occurs at a single instant of time, the first step is to update the positions of the objects for that instant of time. The next is to construct a ray from the lens to the sample point and find the closest object that the ray intersects. Care must be taken in bounding moving objects. The bound should depend on time so that the number of potentially visible objects does not grow unacceptably with their speed.

Intersecting surfaces are handled trivially because we never have to calculate the line of intersection; we merely have to determine which is in front at a given location and time. At each sample point only one of the surfaces is visible. The intersections can even be motion blurred, a problem that would be terrifying with an analytic method.

The union, intersection, difference problem is easily solved with ray tracing or point sampling[10]. These calculations are also correctly motion blurred.

Transparency is easy even if the transparency is textured or varies with time. Let τ be the transparency of a surface at the time and location it is pierced by the ray, and let R be the reflectance. R and τ are wavelength dependent, and the color of the transparency is not necessarily the same as the color of the reflected light; for example, a red transparent plastic object may have a white highlight. If there are n-1 transparent surfaces in front of the opaque surface, the light reaching the viewer is

$$R_n\prod_{i=1}^{n-1}\tau_i + R_{n-1}\prod_{i=1}^{n-2}\tau_1 + \cdots + R_2\tau_1 + R_1 = \sum_{i=1}^{n} R_i \prod_{j=1}^{i-1} \tau_j.$$

If the surfaces form solid volumes, then each object has a τ, and that τ is scaled by the distance that the transmitted ray travels through that object. The motion blur and depth of field calculations work correctly for these transparency calculations.

The distributed approach can be adapted to a scanline algorithm as well as to ray tracing. The general motion blur and depth of field calculations have been incorporated into a scanline algorithm using distributed sampling for the visible surface calculations. Special cases of penumbras, fuzzy reflections, and translucency have been successfully incorporated for flat surfaces.

6. Summary of the Algorithm

The intensity of a pixel on the screen is an analytic function that involves several nested integrals: integrals over time, over the pixel region, and over the lens area, as well as an integral of reflectance times illumination over the reflected hemisphere and an integral of transmittance times illumination over the transmitted hemisphere. This integral can be tremendously complicated, but we can point sample the function regardless of how complicated it is. If the function depends on n parameters, the function is sampled in the n dimensions defined by those parameters. Rather than adding more rays for each dimension, the existing rays are distributed in each dimension according to the values of the corresponding parameter.

This summary of the distributed ray tracing algorithm is illustrated in Figure 2 for a single ray.

- Choose a time for the ray and move the objects accordingly. The number of rays at a certain time is proportional to the value of the desired temporal filter at that time.

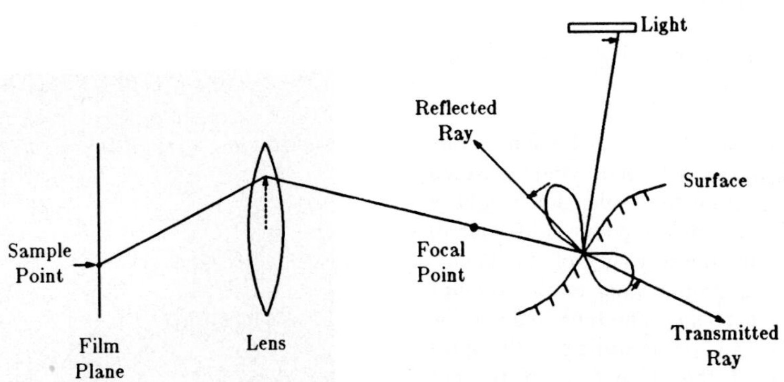

Figure 2. Typical Distributed Ray Path

- Construct a ray from the eye point (center of the lens) to a point on the screen. Choose a location on the lens, and trace a ray from that location to the focal point of the original ray. Determine which object is visible.
- Calculate the shadows. For each light source, choose a location on the light and trace a ray from the visible point to that location. The number of rays traced to a location on the light should be proportional to the intensity and projected area of that location as seen from the surface.
- For reflections, choose a direction around the mirror direction and trace a ray in that direction from the visible point. The number of rays traced in a specific direction should be proportional to the amount of light from that direction that is reflected toward the viewer. This can replace the specular component.
- For transmitted light, choose a direction around the direction of the transmitted light and trace a ray in that direction from the visible point. The number of rays traced in a specific direction should be proportional to the amount of light from that direction that is transmitted toward the viewer.

7. Examples

Figure 3 illustrates motion blurred intersections. The blue beveled cube is stationary, and the green beveled cube is moving in a straight line, perpendicular to one of its faces. Notice that the intersection of the faces is blurred except in in the plane of motion, where it is sharp.

Figures 4 and 5 illustrate depth of field. In figure 4, the camera has a 35 mm lens at f2.8. Notice that the rear sphere, which is out of focus, does not blur over the spheres in front. In figure 5, the camera is focused on the center of the three wooden spheres.

Figure 6 shows a number of moving spheres, with motion blurred shadows and reflections.

Figure 7 illustrates fuzzy shadows and reflections. The paper clip is illuminated by two local light sources which cast shadows with penumbras on the table. Each light is an extended light source (i.e., not a point light source) with a finite solid angle, and the intensity of its shadow at any point on the table is proportional to the amount of light obscured by the paper clip. The table reflects the paper clip, and the reflection blurs according to the specular distribution function of the table top. Note that both the shadows and the reflection blur with distance and are sharper close to the paper clip.

Figure 3. Motion Blurred Intersection.

Figure 4. Depth of Field.

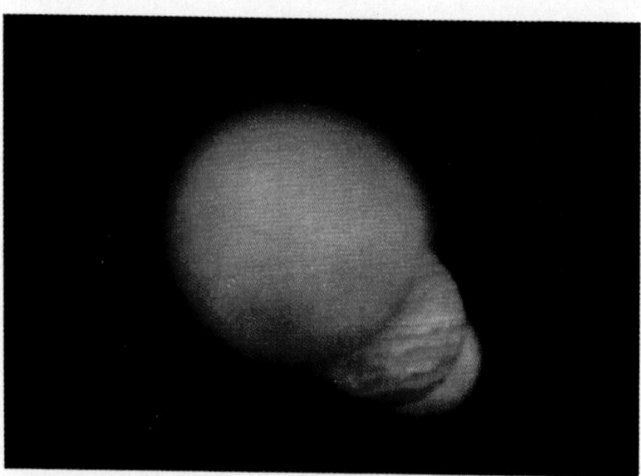

Figure 5. Depth of Field.

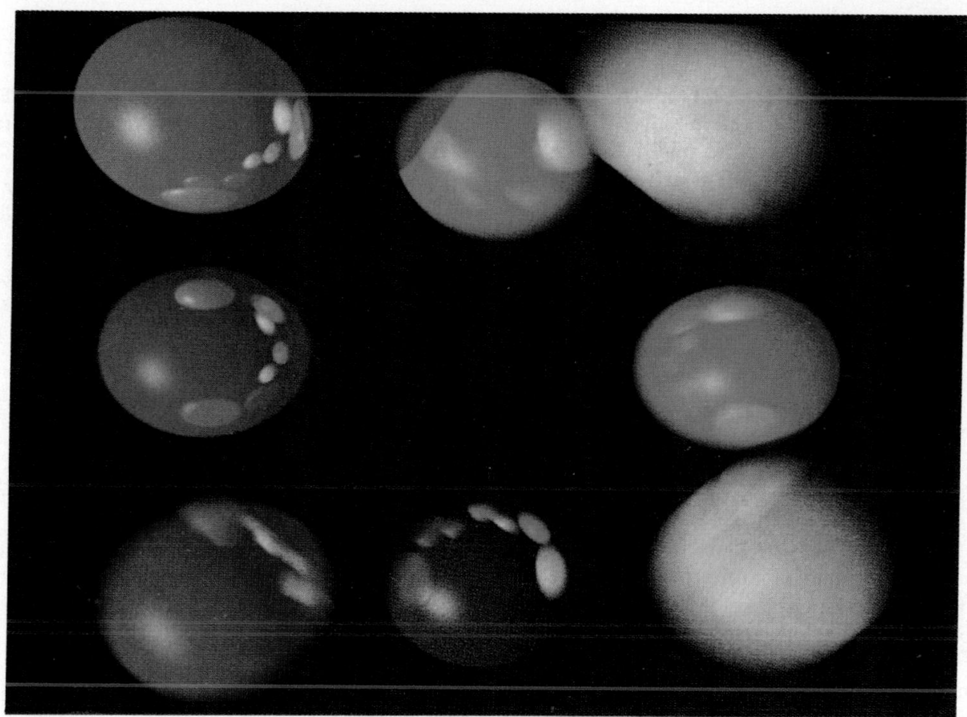

Figure 6. Balls in Motion.

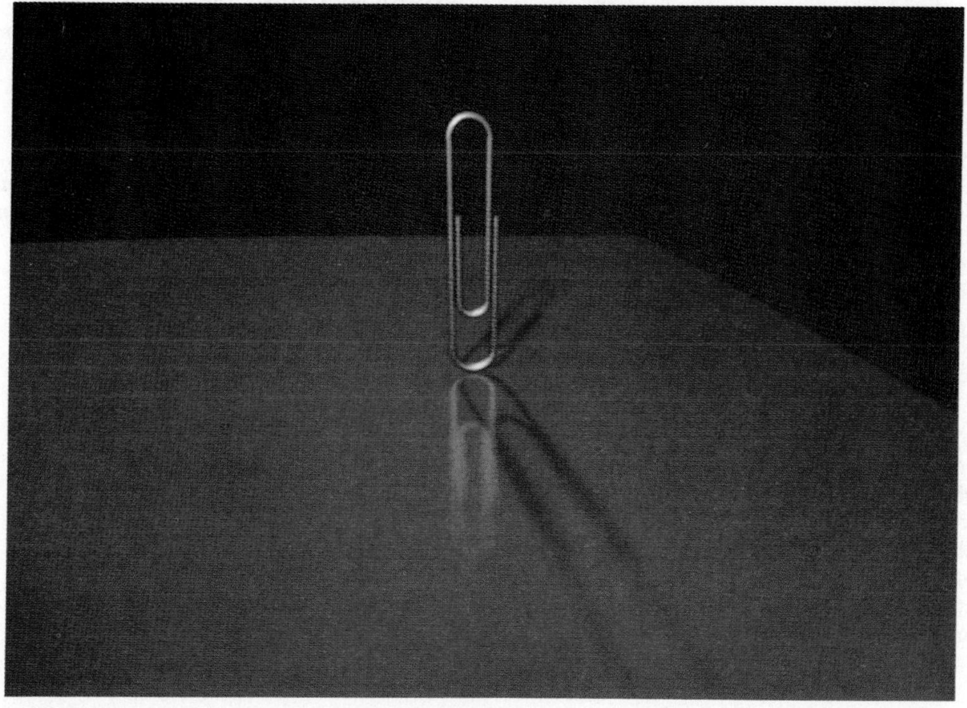

Figure 7. Paper Clip.

Figure 8 shows 5 billiard balls with motion blur and penumbras. Notice that the motion is not linear: the 9 ball changes direction abruptly in the middle of the frame, the 8 ball moves only during the middle of the frame, and the 4 ball only starts to move near the end of the frame. The shadows on the table are sharper where the balls are closer to the table; this most apparent in the stationary 1 ball. The reflections of the billiard balls and the room are motion blurred, as are the penumbras.

Figures 3, 5, and 7 were rendered with a scanline adaptation of this algorithm. Figures 4, 6, and 8 were rendered with ray tracing.

8. Conclusions

Distributed ray tracing a new paradigm for computer graphics which solves a number of hitherto unsolved or partially solved problems. The approach has also been successfully adapted to a scanline algorithm. It incorporates depth of field calculations into the visible surface calculations, eliminating problems in previous methods. It makes possible blurred phenomena such as penumbras, gloss, and translucency. All of the above can be motion blurred by distributing the rays in time.

These are not isolated solutions to isolated problems. This approach to image synthesis is practically no more expensive than standard ray tracing and solves all of these problems at once. The problems could not really be solved separately because they are all interrelated. Differences in shading, in penumbras, and in visibility are accounted for in the depth of field calculations. Changes in the depth of field and in visibility are motion blurred. The penumbra and shading calculations are motion blurred. All of these phenomena are related, and the new approach solves them all together by sampling the multidimensional space they define. The key to this is the ability to antialias point sampling.

9. Acknowledgements

Rodney Stock proposed the approach to antialiased point sampling that formed the basis of the paradigm explored in this paper. John Lasseter drew the environment map of the pool hall for "1984". Ed Catmull worked with us in the image synthesis working group and helped develop and refine these ideas. He and Alvy Ray Smith provided invaluable suggestions along the way. Tom Duff wrote the ray tracing program that we adapted to distributed ray tracing.

References

1. COOK, ROBERT L., TURNER WHITTED, AND DONALD P. GREENBERG, *A Comprehensive Model for Image Synthesis.* unpublished report
2. COOK, ROBERT L., "A Reflection Model for Realistic Image Synthesis," Master's thesis, Cornell University, Ithaca, NY, December 1981.
3. COOK, ROBERT L. AND KENNETH E. TORRANCE, "A Reflection Model for Computer Graphics," *ACM Transactions on Graphics,* vol. 1, no. 1, pp. 7-24, January 1982.
4. COOK, ROBERT L., "Antialiased Point Sampling," Technical Memo #94, Lucasfilm Ltd, San Rafael, CA, October 3, 1983.
5. HUNTER, RICHARD S., *The Measurement of Appearance,* John Wiley & Sons, New York, 1975.
6. KOREIN, JONATHAN AND NORMAN BADLER, "Temporal Anti-Aliasing in Computer Generated Animation," *Computer Graphics,* vol. 17, no. 3, pp. 377-388, July 1983.
7. NISHITA, TOMOYUKI, ISAO OKAMURA, AND EIHACHIRO NAKAMAE, *Siggraph Art Show,* 1982.
8. POTMESIL, MICHAEL AND INDRANIL CHAKRAVARTY, "Synthetic Image Generation with a Lens and Aperture Camera Model," *ACM Transactions on Graphics,* vol. 1, no. 2, pp. 85-108, April 1982.
9. POTMESIL, MICHAEL AND INDRANIL CHAKRAVARTY, "Modeling Motion Blur in Computer-Generated Images," *Computer Graphics,* vol. 17, no. 3, pp. 389-399, July 1983.
10. ROTH, S. D., "Ray Casting for Modeling Solids," *Computer Graphics and Image Processing,* no. 18, pp. 109-144, 1982.
11. WHITTED, TURNER, "An Improved Illumination Model for Shaded Display," *Communications of the ACM,* vol. 23, pp. 343-349, 1980.

Figure 8. 1984.

Reprinted from *IEEE Computer Graphics and Applications*, April 1986, pages 16-26.

ARTS: Accelerated Ray-Tracing System

Takayuki Tanaka and Kansei Iwata
Graphica Computer Corporation

In this article we propose algorithms that address the two basic problems encountered in generating continuous-tone images by ray tracing speed and aliasing. We examine previous approaches to the problem and then propose a scheme based on the coherency of an auxiliary data structure imposed on the original object domain. After investigating both simple spatial enumeration and a hybrid octree approach, we developed 3DDDA, a 3D line generator for efficient traversing of both structures.

3DDDA provides an order of magnitude improvement in processing speed compared to other known ray-tracing methods. Processing time is found to be virtually independent of the number of objects involved in the scene. For large numbers of objects, this method actually becomes faster than scan-line methods. To remove jags from edges, a scheme for identifying edge orientation and distance from pixel center to true edge has been implemented. The time required for antialiasing depends on the total length of the edges encountered, but it is normally only a fractional addition to the time needed to produce the scene without antialiasing.

In recent years a rendering technique known as ray tracing has firmly established itself as a tool of the computer graphics community.[1-7] For those who are not familiar with the technique, Rogers[8] can be recommended as an excellent introduction.

Ray tracing is currently well known for providing the highest quality of image synthesis. The superior image quality achieved by ray tracing—which uses a global illumination model rather than the local illumination models used by traditional scan-line algorithms—is perhaps most evident when corresponding images produced by the different algorithms are compared.[5] Despite the impressive images, however, many improvements can still be made to further upgrade the image quality. These improvements include more realistic illumination models,[3] antialiasing,[3,9] fuzzy shadows and dull reflections,[10] and diffuse reflection from distributed light sources.[11] Hence much of the research effort in ray tracing is devoted to these problems.

However, in a cost/performance comparison with traditional, mostly scan-line methods, ray tracing appears to be seriously handicapped. Roth[6] noted that many experts in the CAD/CAM field have doubts about the sufficiency of ray casting and consider it an impractical, brute-force method. The calculation speed of the ray-tracing method is undoubtedly one of the basic problems that must be dealt with. Until we solve this problem, we cannot expect ray tracing to achieve the widespread use that the scan-line methods enjoy, even though the latter produce far inferior images.

Why is ray tracing so computationally expensive?

The main cause was clearly identified at the very moment ray tracing first entered the field of computer graphics. According to Whitted,[2] for simple scenes 75 percent of the total time is spent on calculating intersections between rays and objects. For more complex scenes the proportion goes as high as 95 percent. The time that must be spent calculating the intersections is directly related to the number of objects involved in the scene.

Scan-line efficiency is achieved by well-established methods such as incremental calculation of geometry based on object and/or image coherency.[12-18] Various forms of coherency commonly exploited in other rendering methods unfortunately are not easy to exploit in the case of ray tracing. In general each ray is traced independently without taking advantage of the information calculated previously for its neighbors.

Much recently reported research has concentrated on speeding up the computations involved in ray tracing. The attack has been concentrated mainly on reducing the complexity of intersection calculation. (The present article is no exception in this respect.) It is perhaps worthwhile to emphasize that virtually all the published approaches are based on a single common notion, which is that of associating a bounding volume or extent with each object in the scene.

To reduce the number of surfaces that must be checked against a given ray, the ray is first checked against gross volumes, or extents, that bound the objects. Extents have been in use since ray tracing was first introduced,[2,6] and have usually been specified in the hierarchical data structures describing the environment. This method, initiated by Rubin and Whitted,[2] has now become common practice in ray tracing.

The differences among the various approaches based on the application of extents stem from the following aspects:

- shapes of the extents
- hierarchical relations between extents
- level of coherency that is exploited

These aspects are naturally interrelated: Certain shapes preclude the use of certain hierarchies and certain hierarchies preclude the use of certain forms of coherency. A discussion of variously shaped extents and the advantages of each shape can be found, for example, in Hall and Greenberg.[3]

Most of the early developments were based on (1) object coherency, using a hierarchical object description, or (2) hierarchical clustering of objects, either provided by the application or automatically generated during the rendering process.[3] This approach produced certain improvements in calculation speed, but it did not represent the kind of breakthrough that could reduce the rendering time to the level achieved by traditional image synthesis methods.

A hierarchy based on the octree data structure in a form suitable for ray tracing was first advocated by Fujimura et al.[19] and almost simultaneously by Matsumoto and Murakami.[20] It was later also used by Glassner.[21] Recently Kaplan[7] has used a data structure called BSP but having essentially the same fundamental properties as the octree. The results presented in these papers show that exploiting octree coherency yields much better results than previous methods in which the hierarchy was based directly on object coherence. In general, an improvement in speed of an order of magnitude has been achieved.

Identifying and exploiting various forms of coherency is one of the most fundamental aspects of computer graphics. Practice shows that it is a basic precondition for efficient execution of computer graphics programs. Exploiting coherency in its ultimate form leads to algorithms based on an incremental application of very simple operations that in many cases can use "integer logic" to replace time-consuming floating-point arithmetic. Incremental techniques, by nature very elegant and simple, are generally made feasible in computer graphics by the existence of various forms of coherency.

We felt that the previously published results did not yet represent the maximum level to which the coherency of an octree hierarchy could be exploited. As a next step in this direction we proposed a new, totally incremental tool for traversing the octree structure: Three Dimensional Digital Differential Analyser, or 3DDDA.

We also felt that the octree structure, while being a function of object shape and scene topology, is not necessarily the form of auxiliary structure that provides the optimum degree of coherency. This is because ray tracing in an octree involves complex processing for traversal of the tree structure. This led us to adopting and investigating the structure we call SEADS (Spatially Enumerated Auxiliary Data Structure). The structure of SEADS is actually completely independent of object shape and topology and thus fails to take any advantage of object coherency. On the other hand, the level of coherency of this auxiliary structure corresponds to the level of coherency that the raster grid provides for a conventional DDA (Digital Differential Analyser) line generator.

SEADS provides an environment for ray tracing that outpaces the hybrid octree approaches . . . by an order of magnitude.

Various experiments have proved that the combination of 3DDDA and SEADS provides an environment for ray tracing that outpaces the hybrid octree approaches presented in previous papers by an order of magnitude. Various experimental results have shown that the rendering time is virtually independent of the number of objects in the scene. When the number of objects is very large, ray tracing—despite its reputation for inefficiency—actually becomes faster than other rendering methods.

3DDDA

The purpose of this section is to describe 3DDDA, the basic tool for traversing SEADS. The extension of 3DDDA that enables it to traverse the octree will be discussed after the octree structure is introduced.

We start with the remark that SEADS can be thought of as a 3D extension of the raster grid, with pixels becoming voxels. Voxels in SEADS are orthogonal cuboidal cells. The inherent 2D coherency of a raster grid is thus naturally extended to 3D. Such an extension of a data structure calls for an extension of the tool that traverses it—the line generator. As described in any introductory text on computer graphics, a line generator can be thought of as a very efficient tool for identifying rectangular pixels pierced by a 2D line placed on a raster grid. Modifying the basic algorithms in order to identify not some but all pixels pierced by the line is fairly straightforward. The extension of this notion to the identification of SEADS voxels pierced by a ray (3D line) is obvious and does not require further elaboration. We proceed directly

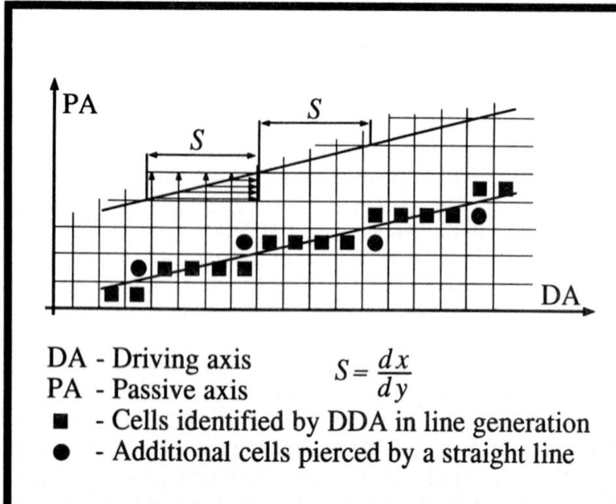

Figure 1. DDA (Digital Differential Analyzer) for line generation in two dimensions.

to technicalities.

The line generator can be implemented in many ways (see Rogers,[8] pp.30-39, and Fujimoto and Iwata[22]), but it works basically as follows: During the process of generating each consecutive pixel's coordinates, the coordinate corresponding to the driving axis (DA) is unconditionally incremented by one unit. The DA (or "axis of the greatest movement") is determined by the slope of the line and is one of the coordinate axes (Figure 1). At the same time a control term—an "error term" which is traditionally measured perpendicular to the DA—is updated by subtracting from it the slope value and then checking whether it is still smaller than half the pixel size. When this test fails, a unit increment (or decrement) of the coordinate perpendicular to the DA is performed. The control term is corrected by adding the value corresponding to one pixel whenever underflow occurs.

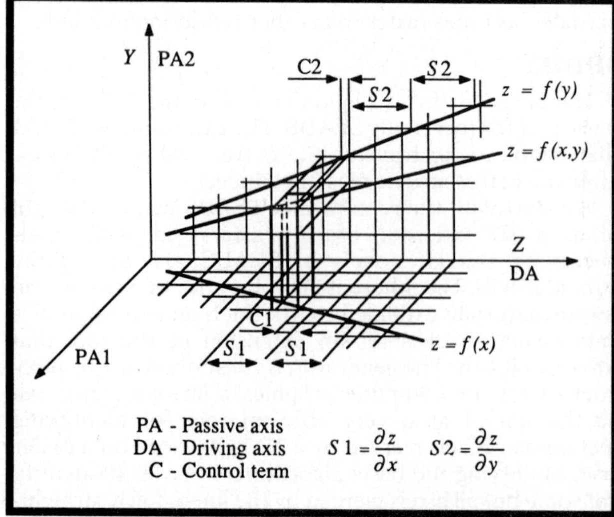

Figure 2. 3DDDA (Three-Dimensional Digital Differential Analyzer) for ray tracing in three dimensions.

The process described above generates the center coordinates of those pixels in closest proximity on the left or right side of the mathematical line. The objective of a DDA used for line generating is to enumerate those pixels that lie close to the true line. While a line may be displayed using many different pixel configurations, one configuration is usually preferred. The configuration corresponding to the optimal line is influenced by factors such as uniform pixel intensity or brightness.[22] In general the pixels representing the optimal line, in addition to being the closest to the true line, also satisfy a condition that only one pixel is generated for each vertical column (Figure 1).

On the other hand, the objective of a DDA used for cell identification purposes is to enumerate those cells that are pierced by the straight line (Figure 1). Two rather simple modifications are necessary to convert the above scheme into one that can identify the pixels through which the line passes. First, movement perpendicular to the DA, which in the standard DDA is coupled with that of the DA, must be separated from it in order to ensure that the DDA always goes from one pixel to an adjacent one without skipping any on its way. Second, the threshold value against which the control term is checked must be made zero instead of half of the pixel size. With these modifications the DDA, instead of generating pixel coordinates closest to the center line, will generate the coordinates of all the pixels through which the line passes.

The above scheme, however, will work only if the traced ray's origin and end point are located at the centers of cells. This obviously is not generally the case. Here we cannot overemphasize the proper initialization of DDA. In Fujimoto and Iwata[22] such initialization was necessary to provide higher addressability, going beyond that of the raster memory resolution; here it is essential for proper cell identification. Notice that the control term can also be measured in the direction parallel to the DA (Figure 1). Its units will then correspond to pixel units, and the range of the control term will correspond to the inverse value of the slope. Actually this approach was adopted to generate smooth vectors,[22] when a control term measured directly in gray-scale units along the DA was used for generating the pixel's coordinates and intensity (for antialiasing). In the present application, however, measuring the control term along the DA is vital because it corresponds to the cell size unit. This control term is essential in providing the proper order of cell entry in the case of the 3D cuboidal grid. Before explaining that, let us first extend the notion of the DDA to three dimensions.

One way to realize 3DDDA is to use two synchronized DDA's working in mutually perpendicular planes that intersect along the DA (Figure 2). In each plane the modified DDA explained above pursues the projection of a 3D line onto that plane. Now, since both control terms are measured along the same DA in units of the cuboid size, it is clear that it is possible to provide proper identification of the string of cells pierced by 3DDDA simply by first processing that plane on which the smaller control term is generated. Later we shall see that expressing the control term in cell-sized units is also essential in efficient 3DDDA traversal of the octree. 3DDDA works very much like the two-dimensional DDA. After an unconditional step in the DA direction is executed, control terms in both planes are processed, and movement to the neighboring cell is performed if necessary. A special situation arises when such movement is necessary in both planes simultaneously (Figure 2). This means that on a particular step, both passive indices of a cell must be updated. If this operation is performed in the wrong order, an erroneous cell will be identified. The code for initialization and for the main part of the algorithm is very similar to the one presented in Fujimoto and Iwata.[22] The only difference is that the control term is initialized and calculated not in gray-scale units but in cell-size units.

3DDDA is applied along the ray direction, and it directly identifies all three indices of the cell. Calculation of coordinates of the intersection with the cell mesh could easily be added, but it is not necessary for cell identification. Because incremental logic is inherent to 3DDDA, all intersections (with the exception of initialization) are processed without any multiplication or division.

Each time the 3DDDA hits any of the planes, the next cuboid representing a mesh element is identified and checked for being in HETERO state. If this is the case, then all of the segments it contains are checked for possible intersection with the ray. If an intersection is found, either ray spawning is performed or the particular branch of the shade tree is terminated, depending on the control parameters and/or model attributes. Otherwise (if HOMO or ray does not intersect any of the segments within the cuboid) 3DDDA continues pursuing the ray in the same direction until some object is intersected or until it leaves the mesh domain.

In conventional ray-tracing programs, increasing the complexity of the model or the number of objects usually results in a situation where a single ray pierces a considerable number of objects. This in turn requires searching for the surface nearest to the observer, or possibly to a spawned ray's origin. This is one of the factors contributing to the well-known phenomenon of ray tracing: Calculation time exhibits exponential growth with the complexity and number of objects in the scene. Here, it is worth noting that 3DDDA traces only the relevant extents (cuboids), and it traces them in the appropriate consecutive order. No global sorting for hidden points is necessary. Local sorting with a rather limited number of items is occasionally necessary when more than one segment is hit within a single cuboid. In general, though, the number of cells containing more than one element will tend to decrease with increasing resolution of the mesh.

The octree

The octree[10,23-26] encoding scheme is similar to the cell decomposition (spatial enumeration) method explained above. The information contained in the octree-encoded representation of a scene is identical to that available in the cell decomposition. From the storage point of view, however, the data are stored in a hierarchical tree structure with nodes representing disjoint cuboids of geometrically decreasing size. Each node of the tree corresponds to a region of the scene and has one or more values that define the region. If the value of the node completely describes the region, it is a terminal or a leaf. If not, an ambiguity exists and the node points to the eight children that represent eight subregions or octants of the parent node (Figure 3). In general the octree representation can be expected to take advantage of the spatial coherence found in most objects.[25]

In this context let us analyze more closely the situation presented in Figure 3, which is actually a 2D quadtree. In this particular case it is evident that the total number of nodes in the quadtree encoding and the number of cells in simple spatial enumeration happen to be equal up to the level 3. This observation is important because in general it is more time-consuming to retrieve information from or traverse the octree than it is with the cell-decomposed structure. In this particular case it is evident that the difference between the total numbers of nodes and cells is expected to become more and more significant as the resolution is increased. However, even if it is assumed that this is generally the case, it will be difficult to predict the resolution at which the octree-encoded structure becomes superior to that of simple cell decomposition.

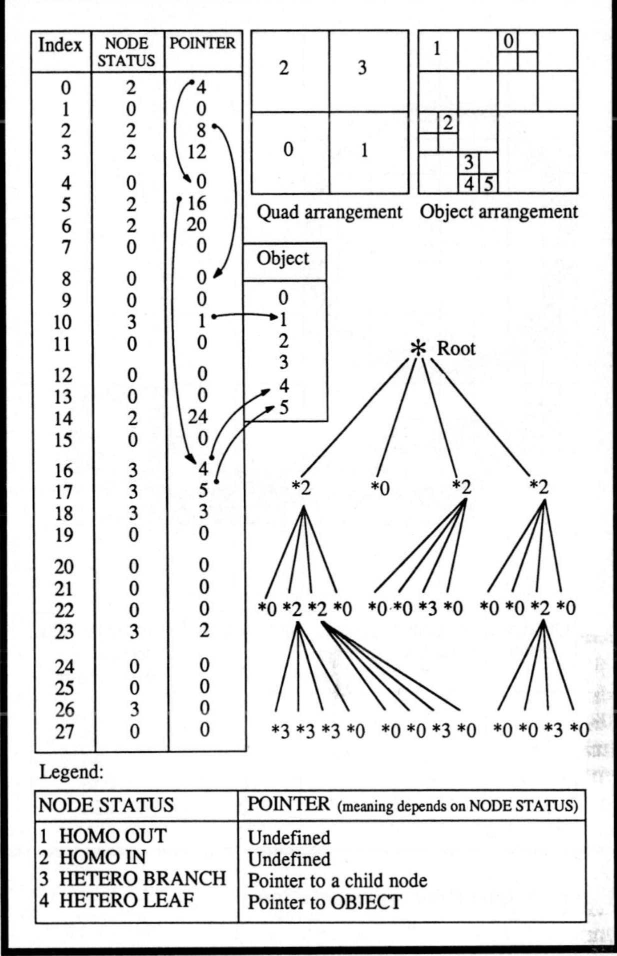

Index	NODE STATUS	POINTER
0	2	4
1	0	0
2	2	8
3	2	12
4	0	0
5	2	16
6	2	20
7	0	0
8	0	0
9	0	0
10	3	1
11	0	0
12	0	0
13	0	0
14	2	24
15	0	0
16	3	4
17	3	5
18	3	3
19	0	0
20	0	0
21	0	0
22	0	0
23	3	2
24	0	0
25	0	0
26	3	0
27	0	0

NODE STATUS	POINTER (meaning depends on NODE STATUS)
1 HOMO OUT	Undefined
2 HOMO IN	Undefined
3 HETERO BRANCH	Pointer to a child node
4 HETERO LEAF	Pointer to OBJECT

Figure 3. Quadtree division for a cluster of objects.

What resolution can we reasonably afford? Meagher,[25] advocating usage of the pure octree, points out that the main disadvantage of the encoding technique is the large memory requirement. He presents proof that the quantity of memory required to store a 2D quadtree object is of the order of the perimeter of the object. Similarly, the memory and processing computation for a 3D object is on the order of the surface area of the object. Depending on the object and the resolution, this can still represent a large storage requirement. Several million bytes of node storage may be necessary to represent realistic situations.[25] Such memory size will not always be justified or even feasible.

The seriousness of this problem was also recognized by Kunii et al.[19] The octree is an approximation of a smooth-surfaced object by small cuboids, so it is inevitable that

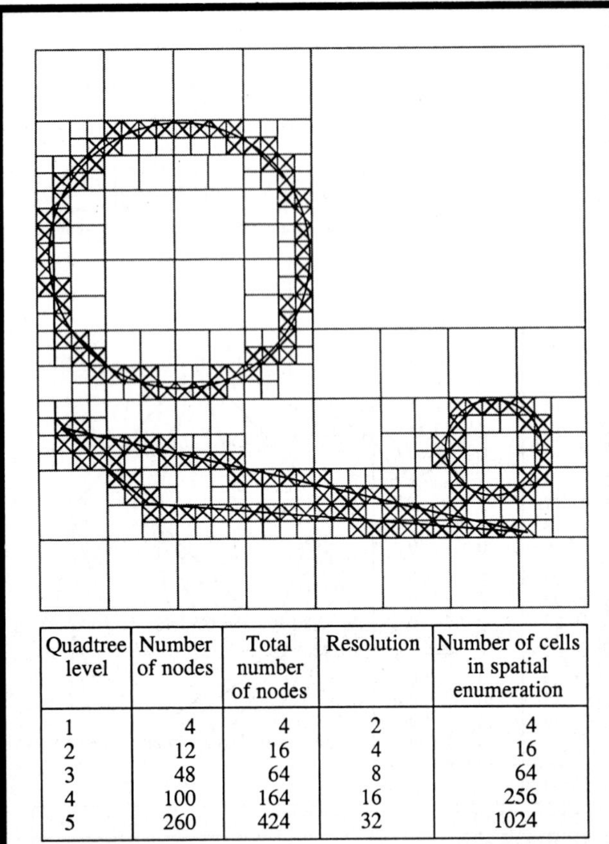

Quadtree level	Number of nodes	Total number of nodes	Resolution	Number of cells in spatial enumeration
1	4	4	2	4
2	12	16	4	16
3	48	64	8	64
4	100	164	16	256
5	260	424	32	1024

Figure 4. Quadtree representation.

the encoded object acquires some notched surfaces. In order to avoid displaying a jagged surface, the object must be represented by a very deep octree. A complex object with reasonably high resolution, then, requires enormous data storage and a high-speed processor. This means the most important advantages of the octree, namely processing speed and memory economy, are lost.[19] The solution proposed by Kunii et al. is basically hybrid. Instead of using a pure octree structure, they proposed combining the octree representation with the surface model.

Another example of a hybrid approach to tree encoding, applied to FEM mesh generation, is presented by Yerry and Shephard.[10] The hybrid approach is also adopted in the present paper: CSG versus octree (and cell decomposition). The hybrid approach appears at least for the time being to be more realistic than pure octree encoding or simple cell decomposition. However, the question of how much resolution can be justified still remains. A general representation depicting a solid body as a 3D array typically occupies 1000 × 1000 × 1000 cells.[23] The maximum level value used by Kunii et al.[19] was 10. This results in a similar resolution ($2^{10} = 1024$). Superiority of the octree over simple cell decomposition will be decided by experiment. However, even at high resolution it is possible to envisage a scene with many objects and low homogeneity for which the octree structure will not necessarily be justified.

Octree encoding. The tree structure encoding will be explained by an example (Figure 4). For simplicity a quadtree is used in the example. Extension to the case of an octree is trivial. The scene consists of six objects numbered 0 to 5. The node arrangement and the corresponding tree levels are shown on the upper part of the figure. The legend below explains the meaning of the node status code. Information concerning the encoded tree structure is arranged in two one-dimensional arrays: NODE_STATUS and POINTER. POINTER, depending on NODE_STATUS of the particular entry, can contain either (1) a pointer to another entry in array POINTER itself, as is the case for a HETERO-BRANCH node, or (2) a pointer to array OBJECT, as is the case for the nonhomogeneous terminating node HETERO-LEAF. For HOMO nodes the contents of array POINTER are irrelevant. This arrangement enables 3DDDA to traverse the structure quickly, as will be explained in the next section.

Traversing the octree. In optimizing traversal of the octree structure by 3DDDA, special attention must be paid to the ordering of the octants of a node. The order adopted in this paper deviates from the conventional definition and follows instead the systematic order proposed by Yamaguchi et al.[26] and shown in Figure 5. In this arrangement each digit of the binary node number corresponds to a cell index in the cell decomposition of a node. Since for a single node there exist exactly two octants in each principal direction x,y,z, all three indices satisfy the condition $0 \leq i, j, k \leq 1$. 3DDDA traverses a single node exactly as it traverses the cell-decomposed structure. When moving from one cell to an adjacent cell, it updates one of the three indices. Changing an index results directly in producing the number of the adjacent octant entered by 3DDDA.

The above description concludes the explanation of how the 3DDDA traverses octants in a node. Since this traversing takes place on a single level, let us call it a horizontal traversal. Horizontal traversal will be terminated when any of the three indices overflows or underflows. This corresponds to the situation when a ray leaves a node. In order to identify the adjacent node it is necessary to ascend the tree. This will be termed vertical traversing of the octree. Vertical traversing can also take place in the form of descending the tree, which is necessary each time 3DDDA identifies a HETERO-BRANCH

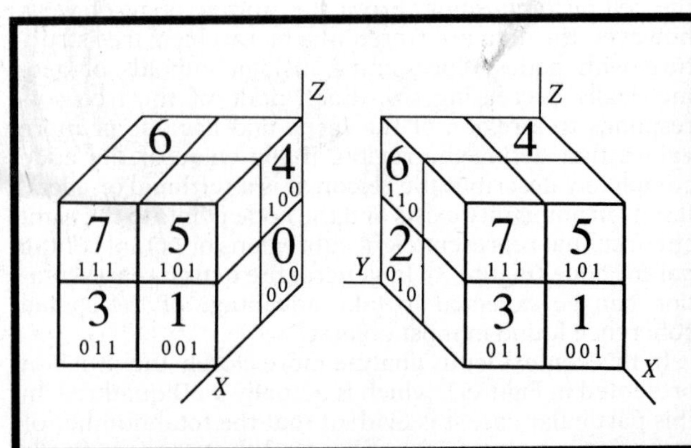

Figure 5. Systematic order of octants.

node. The octree must be traversed downwards (sometimes for several levels) until a HETERO-LEAF or HOMO node is reached.

Due to space limitations it is impossible to explain here all the details concerned with the vertical traversing of the octree. The important fact is that vertical traversing of the octree is performed by making use of the 3DDDA byproducts. During descent of the tree corresponding pointers from array POINTER (Figure 4) are recorded in a separate short working array. The length of this array is equal to the number of levels in the tree. The pointer array is not linked backwards (upwards) and the pointers recorded in the working array are very helpful in ascending the tree. 3DDDA execution is suspended during vertical traversal. During descent of the tree the current values of its variables—specifically both control terms, the inverse slopes, and the octant size—determine which child of the node has to be entered. These values must be multiplied or divided by two on each vertical movement from one level to the next, but in fixed-point arithmetic this operation is simpler than, for example, an addition.

In summary we can conclude that, during horizontal traversal of the octree, 3DDDA automatically generates all necessary variables without floating-point division or multiplication, exactly as it does when traversing the SEADS. Thus, no modifications in 3DDDA are necessary for the octree. Horizontal traversal is identical to the case of simple cell decomposition and vertical traversal is realized by making use of 3DDDA byproducts.

Results. All algorithms explained in the previous sections have been implemented in FORTRAN 77. Initial experiments were performed on a Digital Equipment Corporation VAX 11/750 (4M-byte CPU) under the VMS operating system.

3DDDA. For 3DDDA, the computational cost of moving from one cell to another was initially 72.3 microseconds. After further optimization—which involved removal of all subroutine calls, dimension declarations, and indices, and introduction of integer logic into the main part of the algorithm—this cost was further decreased to 20.6 microseconds. Our current 3DDDA is thus able to identify the cell index more than 13 times faster than Glassner's proposed traversal algorithm[21] can find coordinates to a next cell. (We implemented Glassner's simple spatial enumeration algorithm for comparison purposes, and it requires 276.2 microseconds for that operation.)

When 3DDDA is used it has to be initialized once for each ray, a process requiring 0.591 milliseconds. For 512 × 512 resolution, it will take less than three minutes to initialize 3DDDA for all pixels in the screen. (See the starting point of line A in Figure 6.) Line A shows the total overhead time, which varies with the number of cells. It should be obvious that this time is not dependent on the number of objects, or on the shape of the objects, or on the degree of coherency of the objects in the scene.

On the other hand, overhead time for the octree is quite heavily dependent on all these factors. To compare the overhead time for octree encoding and spatial enumeration, the total number of cells generated by the octree encoding program was recalculated to find the average number of cells along one axis. All the overhead times indicated in Figure 6 are for the situation in which all rays are traced throughout the encoded domain without terminating on pierced objects. Line C in Figure 6 represents overhead time for the original object (see Figure 7). Line G corresponds to the scene in which all 7011 atoms of the original model have been dispersed uniformly by the use

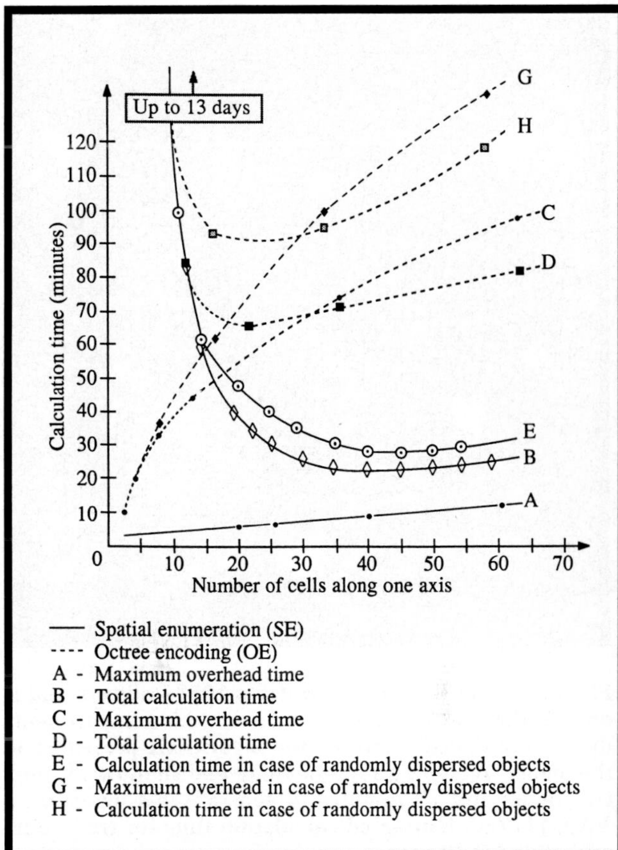

Figure 6. Calculation times for the image in Figure 7.

Figure 7. Antialiased spherical DNA containing 7011 atoms of various kinds. Almost all the rays were spawned, and a concave spherical surface behind the model is magnifying some of the atoms. The shadow of the molecule is cast on the spherical surface. It took two hours to produce this image on a VAX 11/750 using ARTS. Estimated calculation time for traditional ray tracing is one month.

Figure 8. "CG Tokyo 85" contains 10584 objects and is one of the many models used for timing experiments during the development of the algorithms presented in this paper. Including ray spawning and shadows, it took two hours and 15 minutes to generate this image on a VAX 11/750. Estimated calculation time for traditional ray tracing is 40 days.

of random numbers.

It is clear from the above results that the octree structure is very sensitive to lack of coherency and is put at a further disadvantage in comparison to spatial enumeration. It was expected that traversing of the octree structure would be more expensive than spatial enumeration. However, it was also expected that octree encoding would have an advantage for cases where high scene coherency results in a large percentage of empty areas. (The object in Figure 7 occupies less than 9 percent of the hexahedron domain in which it is embedded. In spatial enumeration it is possible to tailor the overall domain dimensions to fit the shape of the scene. This will result in a smaller number of cells. However, for comparison purposes the same hexahedron domain is used for spatial enumeration and octree encoding.) In octree encoding smaller cells are converging to the object surface[25] and empty areas are encoded in bigger cells. This means that in comparison to spatial enumeration a ray can reach the surface of an object by traversing fewer cells, and the probability of hitting an object within the HETERO cell is bigger. Experimental results, however, suggest that all this was outpaced by the cost of vertical traversing of the octree. As was noted in the previous section, vertical traversing must be performed after at most four cells are identified through 3DDDA during horizontal traversing. But the average frequency of vertical traversing is much higher, for it may be needed as soon as one horizontal step is performed. Depending on the depth of the octree, it may quite often be necessary to perform several steps of ascending and descending the octree.

From the above discussion it should be clear that, with respect to speed of calculation, the overhead time precludes any advantage of octree over spatial enumeration. This was confirmed by experiment. (Compare lines B and E with D and H in Figure 6.) Experiments have shown that there exists a clear optimum number of cells in spatial enumeration and an optimum number of levels for octree encoding for which the calculation time reaches its minimum. This minimum happens to correspond to a relatively limited number of cells that can be handled easily by most of the contemporary minicomputers or workstations. We performed a considerable number of experiments in order to find how this optimum number of cells is affected by such factors as scene coherency, object size, and number of objects. It is impossible to present all timing results here, but the results presented in Figure 6 were found to be fairly representative. In particular we have found that although scene coherency to some extent influences the overall calculation time—as does the object size—it does not influence the optimum number of cells. This optimum is slightly influenced by the number of objects and goes to the left (smaller number of cells) with decreasing numbers of objects.

The above experiments provide an important hint to those who advocate a pure octree with a considerable number of levels. Unless the octree-encoded structure can be traversed rapidly enough, pure octree encoding may not necessarily speed up the calculations. (It should be stressed here that we are limiting ourselves to ray-tracing applications. Each ray is traced independently, one for each pixel on the screen.) In the present application the hybrid approach proved essential in obtaining considerable speed improvement. Obviously traversing speed is influenced by more than just the efficiency of the algorithm. It can be assumed that when the same program is run on a supercomputer or special-purpose hardware, a more than proportional improvement in speed would result; the overhead time decrease would move the optimum further to the right, resulting in better performance.

Enumeration. When comparing SEADS with the octree approach, we should also discuss the encoding time. This time is an order of magnitude shorter when SEADS is used. Encoding the DNA model shown in Figure 6 took 17 seconds in SEADS, while octree encoding took over three minutes (207 seconds). In both cases reencoding is necessary only when the topology of the objects changes; reencoding is not necessary when the whole scene undergoes rigid body transformations (rotation and translation) or when the viewpoint is changed. Nevertheless, even when encoding has to be performed, the time required by SEADS can be virtually ignored; it is just a fraction of the rendering time even for very large numbers of objects.

B-reps. Further experiments have shown that the calculation time is only very slightly influenced by the number of objects in the scene, as illustrated by Figure 8. (Actually, this was the goal of the present research.) As a next step in evaluating the proposed algorithm and data structure, a comparison with scan-line method was performed. The popular general-purpose computer graphics package MOVIE.BYU was used. Objects were changed from spheres to hexahedrons. (MOVIE.BYU works with the boundary representation scheme, so approximating the sphere by a number of polygons would put it at a disadvantage.) Results are presented in Figure 9. Unfortunately, the internal limitations of MOVIE.BYU are such that, unless the number of bits in certain data structures is increased, it cannot handle more than 8192 polygons. This corresponds to 1365 hexahedrons. From simple extrapolation, however, it can be deduced that the technique presented here, Accelerated Ray Tracing (ART), is as fast as MOVIE.BYU when the number of objects in the scene approaches 1600. Beyond that limit, ART actually becomes faster. For example, 16,000 hexahedrons are calculated within 17 minutes by ART, whereas it would take about two hours to calculate the same scene using MOVIE.BYU.

The experimental results above suggest that ART can be used for fast rendering of models approximated by polygonal facets or tiles, as in the B-rep (boundary representation) method. This kind of representation is actually used in the majority of solid modelers used in commercial CAD/CAM systems. In order to make direct rendering of B-reps possible, we have implemented a nonsolid primitive: polygon.

A B-rep model of one of the newest cars made by Mazda, the RX-7, has been used for timing experiments. This model is approximated by 46,000 polygons (Figure 10). Less than one-and-a-half minutes was needed to enumerate this amount of data in SEADS using a VAX 11/785. It took 25 minutes for our ART system to synthesize the image. It should be noted here that rendering one object (polygon) that covers approximately the same area on the screen requires about 7.5 minutes.

Unfortunately, we are unable to provide any experimental comparison, since none of our scan-line-based rendering programs can handle this amount of data. (MOVIE.BYU, for example, can handle only a fraction of it.) However, some comments are in order here. When an object involving tens of thousands of polygons is displayed on a relatively low-resolution screen (512 × 512 in this example), most of its individual polygons affect very few pixels—very often only one—and there are some cases where the polygons are simply too small to be displayed. In such a situation, it becomes virtually impossible to make use of object coherency: Various increments are calculated for each polygon but never used, or used so few times that incremental calculation cannot be justified at all. For this reason we expect that it would be difficult for any renderer based on an incremental method to reach the performance cited here.

We are aware of the fact that the above-cited timing data must be modified if calculation is performed for higher resolution. Our results on antialiasing, however, suggest that there is hardly any need to go to a resolution higher than 512 × 512, at which all images presented in this article were calculated and displayed. In the section on antialiasing we noted that processing for antialiasing is in general proportional to the total length of the edges. This might suggest that in our particular example involving 46,000 polygons, the total length of the edges will be so great that the processing time for antialiasing becomes intolerable, but this is not in fact the case. An edge as processed by our antialiasing algorithm does not necessarily correspond to the edge of the geometric entity; an edge is detected only where the change in intensity is greater than a certain threshold at which perceptible aliasing occurs. In our example most of the actual geometric edges are simply not processed, because the difference in shade level between adjacent polygons is too small to produce a perceptible aliasing effect. In practice very few edges other than those corresponding to the outline of the car had to be antialiased.

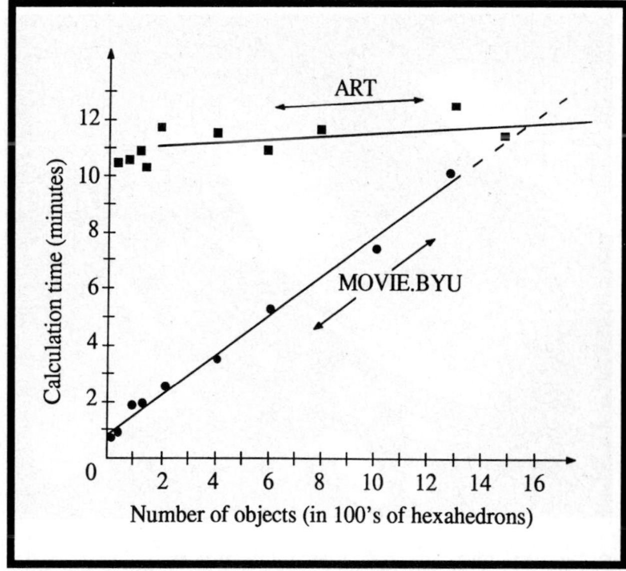

Figure 9. A comparison of the calculation times for ART and MOVIE.BYU.

Figure 10. "Brain" is a density cloud created using the DNA model in Figure 6. Density for each individual electron was represented by Gaussian bump. Note that the colors representing different types of atoms are also fused. Preprocessing time was eight seconds and rendering time was 45 minutes on a VAX 11/785.

The model in Figure 11 was rendered without smooth shading in order to make the polygon tiles visible. When smooth shading is applied,[29] it is possible to achieve basically the same visual effect by approximating the car with far fewer polygons. However, having a virtually constant rendering time can be significant for rendering free-form surfaces. Much of the recent research effort in ray tracing has concentrated on speeding up the intersection calculation for surface patches, which is known to be especially expensive. In spite of significant improvements in calculation speed, the process of rendering patches is generally so slow that it is practically excluded from practical applications. The above cited timings suggest that ART can be used for efficient rendering of free-form

Figure 11. This model of Mazda's RX-7 sports car contains 46,000 (mostly four-sided) polygons. Preprocessing took 2.5 minutes and rendering took 26 minutes on a VAX 11/785.

patches approximated to the desired tolerance by polygon tiles.

Metaball. Various primitives have been used in experiments to show the universality of the proposed method. The concept of a complex primitive called metaball or density cloud was first introduced by Nishimura[27] (the Links ray-tracing system). In the English-language literature it was later introduced by Blinn[28] as a result of independent development.

The model of a density cloud used in our experiments contained all 7011 of the atoms displayed in Figure 7 as simple spheres. The complex surface shown in Figure 11 corresponds to a certain threshold of electron density distribution resulting from a fusion of intensity distribution of the individual atoms. Calculation of the intersection of a ray and such a surface is generally far more expensive than it is in the case of ordinary primitives. The intersection cannot be found algebraically; numerical calculation is required. (Regula falsi and Newton iteration are used.)

The problem is aggravated by the number of atoms in the cloud. The intensity distribution of each atom is defined as a Gaussian bump.[28] It reaches its maximum at the center of the atom and becomes zero at an infinite distance from this center. Since the intensity distribution of each atom spreads to infinity, the resulting intensity at an arbitrary point in space becomes influenced by each atom. So for a model containing more than a few atoms, the summation of a function over all the atoms is computationally out of the question. However, we can economize considerably by using in the calculation only those atoms "close" to the point being considered. The term close means in practice that the density influence of a particular atom is above a certain allowable error threshold which can be defined by the user. Such a threshold will result in enclosing each atom in a sphere of influence. This information is used during the enumeration phase and, with any particular atom, only those voxels that happen to be interior to such a sphere are culled and enumerated.

To achieve a similar effect, Blinn[28] has implemented a scheme using three levels of culling. The first level is introduced in the outer loop corresponding to the y direction when moving from one scan line to the next. The second level is performed in the x direction when moving from one pixel (ray) to another. The final level is in the inner loop in the z direction, along the ray. Since culling is performed during rendering, in the inner loop, the total rendering time was significantly influenced. For a small number of atoms (timing figures are presented only for the case of 64 atoms) the time spent for culling is less than 30 percent of the total rendering time. However, increasing the number of atoms will inevitably present us with the situation where the renderer spends most of its time culling.

In the present algorithm, this culling is first of all not performed during the rendering process. Rather, it is naturally incorporated in the enumeration phase. Enumeration time for the model shown in Figure 11 is virtually the same as for the model in Figure 7. Even for a significant number of objects this time (less than 10 seconds) corresponds to a negligible fraction of the rendering time (less than one hour). As noted before, the intersection calculation for density clouds is expensive because the Gaussian bump used for expressing the density function necessitates numerical calculation. We expect to improve the calculation speed of the density cloud primitive still further, by implementing a polynomial function such as the biquadratic. Clouds defined using this function will not require numerical solution for the intersection calculation.

Antialiasing

The main problem with antialiasing for ray tracing is that not enough information is associated with a single ray.[29] Rays allow us to sample at the one point in the center of the pixel. Without firing additional rays, there is no way of knowing or calculating what else is visible in the neighborhood surrounding the sample point.

In classical ray tracing, antialiasing is usually done by adaptive subdivision of pixels near large intensity changes or small objects.[2,9] This method, now almost universally employed, attempts to use heuristic criteria to probe the image frequently enough that small details will not be overlooked. Depending on the criteria, it will sometimes subdivide too little, resulting in aliasing, or too much, in which case processing time will be wasted. Heckbert and Hanrahan have proposed a different approach,[9] in which a polygon scan converter with a pixel integrator is adopted. This method of antialiasing is sometimes used in scan-line algorithms for continuous-tone images. However, it was possible for Heckbert and Hanrahan to adopt it because the beam-tracing approach they were presenting uses a polygon renderer for scan conversion to form the final image. Polygon edges are determined during scan conversion so that information can be used directly for antialiasing.

It is sometimes argued that the only way to antialias within standard ray tracing is to go to a higher resolution.[29] The approach presented in this article shows that this is not exactly the case. The Adjustable Fourier Window Technique reported previously showed that high-quality antialiasing can be performed with a very low computational cost.[22] More recently it has been shown that it can also be used successfully for antialiasing with subpixel resolution.[12] Objects smaller than a pixel can be properly rendered. At the same time it was shown that full information about the antialiased edge (position and slope) was not necessary for its antialiasing. What is essentially needed is the distance to the edge from a neighboring pixel measured perpendicular to the Driving Axis. Whether the DA is the x-axis or the y-axis can be determined in 75 percent of cases by simple comparison of the difference of generated pixel intensity, both vertically and horizontally. In the remaining 25 percent of cases an additional ray must be fired to resolve the ambiguity. After the DA is determined, the position of the edge intersection measured perpendicular to the DA can be determined with sufficient precision (one-eighth of pixel size) after firing only three rays. In general not more than four additional rays have to be fired to antialias an edge.[12,22]

Conclusions

This article has introduced a general method of improving the computational speed of the ray-tracing method to a level where the image synthesis time is practically constant, and thus independent of the number of objects in the scene. Experimental results show that for a very large number of objects the rendering process is actually executed faster than in other currently used methods. It has also been shown that the proposed method can efficiently handle both models defined by the use of B-reps and models defined as unions of solid primitives.

This is achieved essentially by creating an environment where the number of objects that have to be checked against each ray is limited to an insignificant fraction of the total number of objects involved in the scene. This fraction very often corresponds to a single object.

The above scheme is realized by imposing on the object an auxiliary structure characterized by a high level of coherency (SEADS), and developing a traversing tool in the form of a line generator (3DDDA) that takes advantage of this coherency in a very efficient manner based on incremental integer logic. ■

Acknowledgments

We would like to express our gratitude to Mr. Christopher G. Perrott, chief engineer at Graphica Computer Corporation, for his advice and fruitful critical remarks concerning the content of this article; for his help in optimizing the code; and finally for proofreading the article. We also extend our gratitude to Dr. Nelson Max from Lawrence Livermore Laboratory. It was he who suggested that our accelerated ray tracing could efficiently handle a complex primitive such as the density cloud, and encouraged us to implement it. Dr. Max also provided us with various DNA models that were very helpful in testing our algorithms.

References

1. Steven M. Rubin and Turner Whitted, "A 3-Dimensional Representation for Fast Rendering of Complex Scenes," ACM 0-89791-021-4/80/0700-0110, 1980, pp.110-116.
2. Turner Whitted, "An Improved Illumination Model for Shaded Display," *Comm. ACM,* Vol. 23, No. 6, June 1980, pp.343-349.
3. Roy A. Hall and Donald P. Greenberg, "A Testbed for Realistic Image Synthesis," *IEEE CG&A,* Vol. 3, No. 8, Nov. 1983, pp.10-20.
4. Hank Weghorst, Gary Hooper, and Donald P. Greenberg, "Improved Computational Methods for Ray Tracing," *ACM Trans. Graphics,* Vol. 3, No. 1, Jan. 1984, pp.51-69.
5. Naoki Hashimoto and Edward Lau, *TIPS-1 77 Version System Manual,* Computer Aided Manufacturing-International, Inc., Ithaca, NY, Apr. 1981.
6. S.D. Roth, "Ray Casting for Modelling Solids," *Computer Graphics and Image Processing,* No. 18, 1982, pp.104-109.
7. Michael R. Kaplan, "Space-Tracing, a Constant Time Ray-Tracer," SIGGRAPH 85 tutorial, San Francisco, July 1985.
8. David F. Rogers, *Procedural Elements for Computer Graphics,* McGraw-Hill, 1985, pp.236-305,363-380.
9. Paul S. Heckbert and Pat Hanrahan, "Beam Tracing Polygonal Objects," *Computer Graphics* (Proc. SIGGRAPH 84), Vol. 18, No. 3, July 1984, pp.119-127.
10. Mark A. Yerry and Mark S. Shephard, "A Modified Quadtree Approach to Finite Element Mesh Generation," *IEEE CG&A,* Vol. 3, No. 1, Jan./Feb. 1983, pp.39-46.
11. Tomoyuki Nishita and Eihachiro Nakamae, "Half-tone Representation of 3-D Objects Illuminated by Area Sources of Polyhedron Sources," *Proc. IEEE Compsac,* Chicago, Nov. 1983, pp.237-242.
12. Akira Fujimoto, Christopher G. Perrott, and Kansei Iwata, "A 3-D Graphics Display System with Depth Buffer and Pipeline Processor," *IEEE CG&A,* Vol. 4, No. 6, June 1984, pp.11-23.
13. Paolo Sabella and Michael J. Wozny, "Toward Fast Color-Shaped Images of CAD/CAM Geometry," *IEEE CG&A,* Vol. 3, No. 8, Nov. 1983, p.65.
14. G. Hamlin, Jr., and C.W. Gear, "Raster Scan Hidden Surface Algorithm Techniques," *Computer Graphics* (Proc. SIGGRAPH 77), Vol. 11, No. 2, pp.206-213.
15. I.E. Sutherland, R.F. Sprout, and R.A. Schumacker, "A Characterization of Ten Hidden Surface Algorithms," *Computing Surveys,* Vol. 6, No. 1, Mar. 1974, pp.1-55.
16. W. Jack Bouknight, "A Procedure for Generation of Three-dimensional Half-tones," Computer Graphics Presentations, *Comm. ACM,* Sept. 1970, pp.292-301.
17. Henri Gourand, "Continuous Shading of Curved Surfaces," *IEEE Trans. Computers,* June 1971, pp.302-308.
18. Bui Tuong Phong, "Illumination for Computer Generated Pictures," *Comm. ACM,* Vol. 18, No. 6, June 1975, pp.311-317.

19. K. Fujimura, H. Toriya, K. Yamaguchi, and T.L. Kunii, "An Enhanced Oct-tree Data Structure and Operations for Solid Modeling," Technical Report 83-01, Dept. of Information Science, University of Tokyo, Jan. 1983.
20. Hitoshi Matsumoto and Kouichi Murakami, "Ray-Tracing with Octree Data Structure" (in Japanese), *Proc. 28th Information Processing Conf.*, Tokyo, 1983, pp.1535-1536.
21. Andrew S. Glassner, "Space Subdivision for Fast Ray Tracing," *IEEE CG&A*, Vol. 4, No. 10, Oct. 1984, pp.15-22.
22. Akira Fujimoto and Kansei Iwata, "Jag-Free Images on Raster Displays," *IEEE CG&A*, Vol. 3, No. 9, Dec. 1983, pp.26-34.
23. Louis J. Doctor and John G. Torborg, "Display Techniques for Octree-Encoded Objects," *IEEE CG&A*, Vol. 1, No. 3, July 1981, pp.29-38.
24. Chris L. Jackins and Steven L. Tanimoto, "Oct-Trees and Their Use in Representing Three-Dimensional Objects," *Computer Graphics and Image Processing*, 14, 1980, pp.249-270.
25. Donald Meagher, "Geometric Modeling Using Octree Encoding," *Computer Graphics and Image Processing*, 19, 1982, pp.129-147.
26. K. Yamaguchi, T.L. Kunii, K. Fujimura, and H. Toriya, "Octree-Related Data Structures and Algorithms," *IEEE CG&A*, Vol. 4, No. 1, Jan. 1984, pp.53-59.
27. Osaka University CG Group, "LINKS-1" (in Japanese), *PIXEL 83*, 5-6, No. 12, May/June 1983, pp.73-92.
28. James F. Blinn, "A Generalization of Algebraic Surface Drawing," *ACM Trans. Graphics*, Vol. 1, No. 3, July 1982, pp. 255-256.
29. John Amanatides, "Ray Tracing with Cones," *Computer Graphics* (Proc. SIGGRAPH 83), Vol. 18, No. 3, July 1983, pp. 129-135.

Additional Readings

Atherton, Peter R., "A Method of Interactive Visualization of CAD Surface Models on a Color Video Display," *Computer Graphics* (Proc. SIGGRAPH 81), Vol. 15, No. 3, Aug. 1981, pp.279-287.

Atherton, Peter R., "A Scan-Line Hidden Surface Removal Procedure for Constructive Solid Geometry," *Computer Graphics* (Proc. SIGGRAPH 83), Vol. 17, No. 3, July 1983, pp.73-83.

Cook, Robert L., Thomas Porter, and Loren Carpenter, "Distributed Ray Tracing," *Computer Graphics* (Proc. SIGGRAPH 84), Vol. 18, No. 3, July 1984, pp.137-144.

Davis, Jon, Michael J. Bailey, and David C. Anderson, "Projecting Realistic Images of Geometric Solids," *Computers in Mechanical Engineering*, Aug. 1982.

Dippe, Mark, and John Swensen, "An Adaptive Subdivision Algorithm and Parallel Architecture for Realistic Image Synthesis," *Computer Graphics* (Proc. SIGGRAPH 84), Vol. 18, No. 3, July 1984, pp.149-158.

Hanabusa, Kenetsu, "Animation with CRAY-1," (in Japanese), *PIXEL '83*, 7-8, No. 13, July/Aug. 1983, pp.161-162.

Jones, C.B., "A New Approach to the 'Hidden Line' Problem," *The Computer Journal*, Vol. 14, No. 3.

Liang, You-Dong, and Brian A. Barsky, "A New Concept and Method for Line Clipping," *ACM Trans. Graphics*, Vol. 3, No. 1, Jan. 1984, pp.1-22.

Max, Nelson L., "Computer Representation of Molecular Surfaces," *IEEE CG&A*, Vol. 3, No. 5, Aug. 1983, pp.21-29.

Murakami, Kouchi, and Hitoshi Matsumoto, "Method for Rendering CSG" (in Japanese), Proc. 27th Information Processing Conf., Tokyo, 1983, pp.1533-1534.

Rogers, David F., and Linda M. Ryback, "On an Efficient Line-Clipping Algorithm," *IEEE CG&A*, Vol. 5, No. 1, Jan. 1985, pp.82-86.

Sears, Ken H., and Alan E. Middledtich, "Set-Theoretic Volume Model Evaluation and Picture-Plane Coherence," *IEEE CG&A*, Vol. 4, No. 3, Mar. 1984, pp.41-46.

Yamamoto, Tsuyoshi, *Personal Computer Graphics* (in Japanese), CQ Publishing Corp., Tokyo, 1983, pp.47-90.

Akira Fujimoto, formerly Wieslaw Romanowski, is a chief engineer with the Software Research Division of the Graphica Computer Corporation, a company that produces computer graphics and image processing systems. His research interests include computer graphics for raster-scan devices, applications of computer graphics in scientific and engineering analysis, and CAD.

Fujimoto received an ME in mechanical engineering from the Technical University Szczecin (Poland) and from the University of Tokyo, where he subsequently obtained his PhD. He is a member of the Society of Naval Architects of Japan, the Computer Graphics Society (GCS), and the GKS Japan Committee of GCS.

Takayuki Tanaka is an analyst-programmer in the Software Research Division of Graphica Computer Corporation. His research interests include operating systems, high-level languages, artificial intelligence, and computer graphics algorithms. He has taken part in the development of a number of image-rendering software packages for Graphica Computer Corporation.

Tanaka was graduated from Sundai Electronic Institute in 1984.

Kansei Iwata is president of Graphica Computer Corporation, which he founded in 1975. From 1970 to 1975, he was employed by Iwatsu Electronic Company, Ltd., where he was chief of the Electronic Circuit Research Laboratory at the Technical Institute in 1974 and 1975. His research interests are related to pulse transmission and electronic circuit design.

Iwata received his BA and PhD in electrical engineering from Tohoku University in Sendai, Japan. He is a member of the IEEE and the ACM.

The authors' address is Graphica Computer Corporation, 6-21-6 Nagayama Tami-shi, Tokyo 206, Japan.

Speed up ray-tracing techniques by reducing the number of time-consuming object-ray intersection calculations that have to be made. You'll be able to handle large databases considerably faster.

Space Subdivision for Fast Ray Tracing

Andrew S. Glassner
University of North Carolina at Chapel Hill

Speed up ray-tracing techniques by reducing the number of time-consuming object-ray intersection calculations that have to be made. You'll be able to handle large databases considerably faster.

Reprinted from *IEEE Computer Graphics and Applications*, October 1984, pages 15-22.

Space Subdivision for Fast Ray Tracing

Andrew S. Glassner
University of North Carolina at Chapel Hill

The most powerful general image synthesis method used today is referred to generically as ray tracing. Ray tracing was first described by Appel[1] and later by Bouknight and Kelley[2] and Kay.[3] The algorithm used by most ray-tracing programs is described by Whitted.[4] This paradigm is attractive because of its very elegant implementation and the wide range of natural phenomena it models.

Although ray tracing as it stands is not the final word in image synthesis, it is probably the most realistic technique we have today. This realism is further enhanced by the technique of distributed ray tracing described by Cook, Porter, and Carpenter.[5] Unfortunately, ray tracing is also very slow. Ray-tracing algorithms are famous for the large amounts of computer time they consume to create even one picture of moderate complexity. It is this slowness that prevents more people from using the powerful ray-tracing methods.

Previous work in speeding up the picture-generation process has concentrated on screen-space solutions and hardware solutions. Roth[6] has described a method for examining a rough rendering of a scene and investigating those areas of the screen where additional work seems to be necessary. Ullner[7] describes hardware solutions that consist of multiple microprocessors in various configurations, with each processor handling a subset of either rays or objects. Both of these approaches use the basic ray-tracing algorithm as described by Whitted and attempt to draw pictures faster by either running the algorithm in parallel or running it less often for a complete picture.

A different approach toward speeding up the process is explored in this article: we decrease the time required by the algorithm to render a given pixel. To do this, we first need to determine what are the most time-consuming portions of the algorithm.

Whitted reports that ray-object intersections can require over 95 percent of the total picture-generation time. A synopsis of the ray-tracing technique with a qualitative breakdown of where time is spent is also given in Glassner.[8] Kajiya[9] has shown, with a simple skeleton of the ray-tracing process, that these intersections comprise an "inner loop" of the algorithm. He demonstrates that each ray must be checked against each object in the scene so that the number of intersection calculations is linear with respect to the product of the number of rays traced and the number of objects in the entire picture. Doubling the number of objects in a scene (about) doubles the rendering time; doubling both the objects and the rays takes four times longer to render the image.

Recent work has concentrated on the ray-object intersection problem for various classes of objects (Kajiya[10,11] and Hanrahan[12]). These algorithms show that the intersection operation can require any amount of floating-point operations—from just a few to many thousands.

If we want to reduce the time spent on ray-object intersections, we have at least two choices. We can speed up the intersection process itself, possibly with specialized hardware. Alternately, we can reduce the number of ray-object intersections that must be made to fully trace a given ray; this is the approach followed in this article.

Overview of the new algorithm

The new algorithm is based on a simple observation. To make this observation, let us divide the space in a three-dimensional scene into small compartments, keeping a list of all the objects that reside in each of these compart-

EH0281-6/88/0000/0160$01.00 © 1984 IEEE

ments. We can then speed up the ray-tracing process in the following way.

Start a ray and determine in which compartment it originated. Follow the ray and compare it against only the objects it hits in that compartment. If one or more objects in the compartment are pierced, find the closest pierced object and return its color as the value of the ray. We are then finished tracing that ray, for we have found the first object the ray hit. If the ray does not hit an object in this compartment, project the ray into the next compartment and repeat the process.

If each compartment contains a small number of objects, we can process that compartment quickly. If we're lucky and find right away that the ray has hit an object, we have only a small number of object intersections to process. If we're very unlucky and find the ray has hit nothing until we hit the world sphere (Kajiya[8]), we are still better off because we probably have checked fewer objects than there are in the entire scene. Therefore, unless the overhead of getting from compartment to compartment is very high, we will always save time relative to intersecting every object in the entire database.

Fortunately, a very good scheme for breaking up space into such compartments is available. This octree technique is described extensively in Jackins and Tanimoto[13] and Meagher.[14] An octree structure allows us to dynamically subdivide space into cubes of decreasing volume until each cube (called a voxel) contains less than a maximum number of objects. Octrees are normally used to define the shapes of objects that are difficult to model with primitive surfaces. In that context, each cell of the tree is either occupied by that object, or it is empty. Each occupied cube may contain some information about color, density, or some other attribute of the object, but the cube itself is considered to be either fully filled by the object or empty of it.

Here, we use each cell of the octree to hold a list, not a piece of an object. The list describes all the objects in the scene that have a piece of their surface in that cell.

Usually when we synthesize images we are interested only in the surfaces of the objects in our scene. The assumption is that the inside of a transparent or translucent object is either empty or else described by other, independently defined objects. For example, when we test a ray against a sphere, we care only about those points on the sphere where the ray pierces the sphere's surface. It's unimportant to know if a given point on the ray is inside or outside the sphere. Thus, for this algorithm, we subdivide space into an octree, associating a given voxel with only those objects whose *surfaces* pass through the volume of the voxel. See Figure 1.

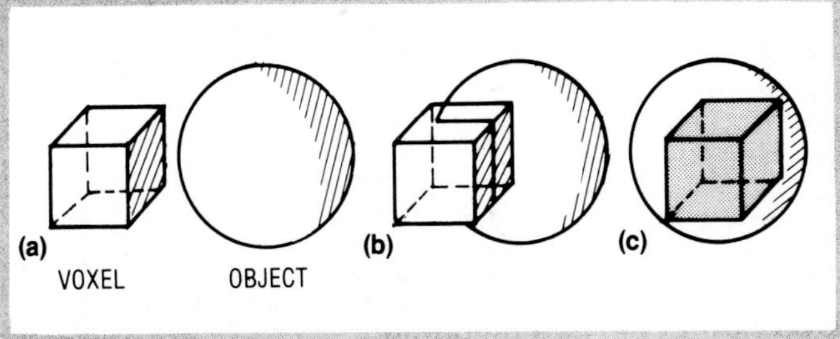

Figure 1. Space subdivision. An object is considered associated with a voxel if and only if some of the object's surface exists within the voxel. (a) shows an object not associated with the voxel; (b) shows an object that is associated with the voxel; and (c) illustrates the voxel within an object (the object is not associated with the voxel).

The next two sections of this article present the techniques central to the new algorithm. The first section describes the process of building and maintaining the octree and a technique for obtaining fast access to any node. The second section describes the mechanism for finding the next node intersected by a ray when it has hit nothing in the current node.

Octree building and storage

The arguments for using octrees as the spatial compartments mentioned above are that octrees are well studied and understood and that they allow dynamic spatial resolution. Volumes with high object complexity can be recursively subdivided into smaller and smaller volumes, generating new nodes in the tree for only these new volumes.

When a ray fails to hit any objects in a given node, it must move on to another node in space. As we will see in the next section, the algorithm works by finding a point guaranteed to be in the next node encountered by the ray and then determining the particular node containing that point. In this section we address the process of finding the node.

A very economical octree storage technique has been described by Gargantini.[15] We use a slight variation here to speed up the time required to find a given node.

The parent node (which just encloses the world sphere) is labeled node 1. When we subdivide a node, it passes its name as a prefix to all its children, which are numbered 1 through 8, as shown in Figure 2. Thus, the eight children of the parent node are nodes 11 through 18. The children of node 13 are nodes 131 through 138, and so on. Now we need a way to address a node of a given name.

If we subdivide the parent node twice, we find the largest node name possible is 188. Clearly, we don't want to allocate 188 nodes when we start the program; for example, we might find that nodes 131-138 never need to be created. The dynamic resolution of the octree scheme suggests a dynamic allocation of memory, creating a new node only when we need it. But then we return to the problem of finding a given node. If we just ask the operating system for a chunk of memory to be used when it's time to create (say) node 173, then how do we find node 173 later on?

There are two extremes in the continuum of answers to this question. At one extreme we could create a table with an entry for every possible node name that contains that node's address. This possibility would require vast amounts of storage (more than for a straightforward eight-pointers-at-a-node scheme!), but it would also have the advantage of extreme speed in finding the address of a node with a given name. At the other extreme, we could create a large linked list of all the nodes in the octree, which we would have to scan from the beginning each time we want to locate a given node. This provision would have the advantage of requiring very little memory beyond that needed for the nodes themselves, but it would slow the operation to search the list each time we must look for a particular node.

An attractive compromise is to mix the two ideas using a hashing scheme. We can hash the name of a node into some small number and then follow a linked list of all nodes that hash into that number starting at a given point in a table. By changing the size of the table, we can pick any point in the continuum described above. Thus we trade speed for memory consumption and vice versa. A very simple hashing function, which merely returns the node name modulo the table size, seems to work fine.

Here we see the difference between the original numbering scheme proposed by Gargantini and the one used here. Gargantini suggested numbering the nodes 0 through 7, which had the advantage of assigning an octal number to each node. However, consider the case of subdividing node 0: one of the nodes created would have the name 00. To a computer, the number 00 is the same as the number 0, and we would have no way of differentiating the two. Similarly, 005 would be the same as 05, and so on. A solution to this problem would be to keep the name of each node as a character string. This would keep node 0 different from 000, but the string representation is bulkier than an integer, as well as slower in comparing it against another of its own type.

The modification presented here is to number the children from 1 to 8. Numbering the nodes this way loses the octal purity of the original scheme, but it allows us to name the nodes with numbers instead of character strings. Thus, node 1 could never be confused with node 111, and similarly node 15 is distinct from node 1115.

We can then find the name of a node containing a point (x,y,z) with the scheme presented in Figure 3.

Once we have a node name, we must search through the appropriate linked list for its entry and associated object list. Clearly the fewer nodes there are to be searched through, the faster (on the average) we will find the node we're looking for. We can use another observation to reduce the number of nodes stored as entries in the table/linked list structure by a factor of eight.

Each time we subdivide a node (because it contains too many objects, or more precisely, too many surfaces), we create all eight children at once. When we want to allocate memory for these eight children, we can ask the memory allocator for one large block of memory big enough to hold all eight nodes. We then use the first eighth for the first child node, the second eighth for the second child node, and so on. Now we need to store only the first child in the hash table/linked list structure. The other children are easily found by adding the right number of node lengths to the first node's address; i.e., add one node length for node 2, add two node lengths for node 3, and so on. This scheme is illustrated in Figure 4.

As we subdivide nodes, we keep a record of the smallest node created anywhere in space. This record can just be the length of the side of the smallest node; we will see why we want this information when we look at the algorithm for moving the ray from voxel to voxel.

Let's now look at the structure of an octree node. It consists of four members: a name, a subdivision flag, center and size data, and an object-list pointer. The name is an integer that is the name of this node. The subdivision flag is set if this node has been subdivided. The center and size information may be omitted to conserve memory space and derived on the fly from just the node name (this is another time-space trade-off). The object-list pointer points to the start of a list of integers in a dynamically

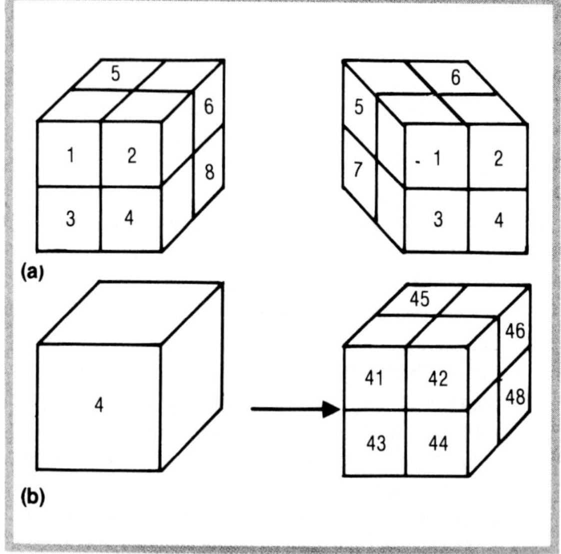

Figure 2. Space subdivision. (a) Subnodes are labeled 1-8; (b) a parent voxel passes its name as a prefix to its children.

```
                    LISTING 1

findnode(x,y,z) {
    node = 1;
    WHILE ( node_subdivided  is TRUE ) {
        IF (x > node_center_x)
            IF (y > node_center_y)
                IF (z > node_center_z)
                        node = (node*10) + 6;
                ELSE    node = (node*10) + 2;
            ELSE
                IF (z > node_center_z)
                        node = (node*10) + 8;
                ELSE    node = (node*10) + 4;
        ELSE
            IF (y > node_center_y)
                IF (z > node_center_z)
                        node = (node*10) + 5;
                ELSE    node = (node*10) + 1;
            ELSE
                IF (z > node_center_z)
                        node = (node*10) + 7;
                ELSE    node = (node*10) + 3;
    }
    RETURN ( node )
}
```

Figure 3. Node-finding scheme.

allocated array. The integer indicated by this pointer is the number of the first object in this node. Subsequent integers continue to represent other objects, until some illegal object number (say -1) is encountered, signalling the end of the object list for this node.

Now we know how to generate the octree so we can easily and quickly find a node of interest knowing only a point in the node. Let's now look at the process of deciding whether or not to subdivide a given node as we build the tree.

What we're interested in doing now is looking at the list of objects that have surfaces that pass through the parent node of the node under consideration. We will include each of these objects in the list of objects for this child if its surface also passes through the child's volume. When we have done this for each child, we can consider how many objects are contained in each child. If any child has too many objects (and we have room to create new nodes), we may then subdivide each overfull node recursively.

The algorithm used to determine whether an object's surface passes through a voxel treats convex objects (particularly spheres) with more efficiency than arbitrary objects.

In general, we intersect the object with each of the six planes that bound the voxel. Should any of these points of intersection lie within the square region of the plane that is the side of the voxel, the object is kept. Otherwise, some point within the object must be examined. If that interior point is within the voxel, the object is kept; otherwise, it is discarded. A very efficient formulation of this algorithm for the special case of polygons is found in Sutherland and Hodgman.[16]

Movement to the next voxel

Two important facts guide us in designing the algorithm to get to the next voxel. First, because the space is dynamically resolved when we build the octree, we don't know how large (or small) any voxel in space is with the exception of the current one. The second fact is that the movement operation must be accomplished as fast as possible. Certainly, the movement must be minimally fast enough that we don't lose the time we save by cutting down ray-object intersections by giving that time to voxel-movement operations.

The general idea behind the voxel-movement algorithm is to find a point that is guaranteed to be in the next voxel, whatever its size. This point is then used to derive a voxel name (and its associated size and object list) according to the schemes presented in the previous section.

In the following, the term current node refers to the node that has yielded no intersections; it is the node we are leaving for greener pastures. We will refer to points on the ray being traced with the parameter t. The value of t increases as we move away from the origin, where t has the value 0.

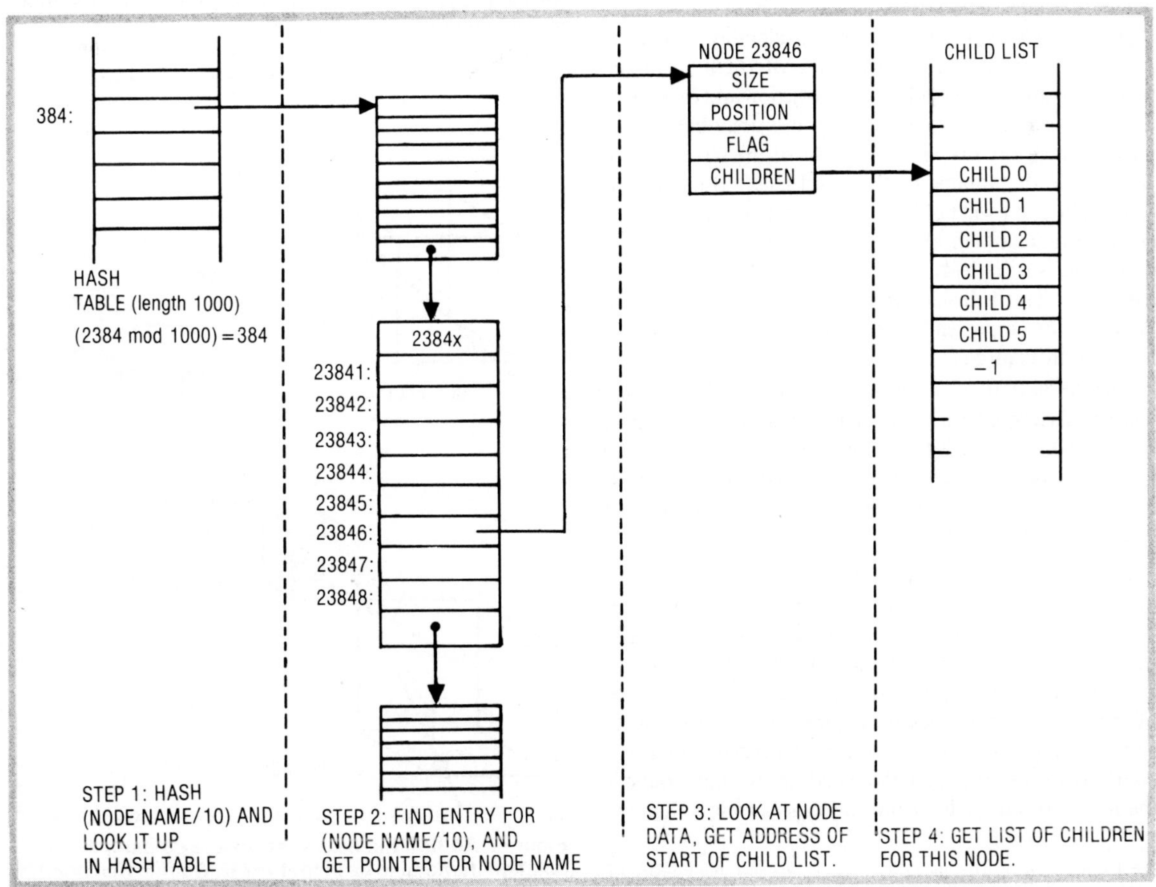

Figure 4. Sample hash table/linked list. Here, we want information for node 23846.

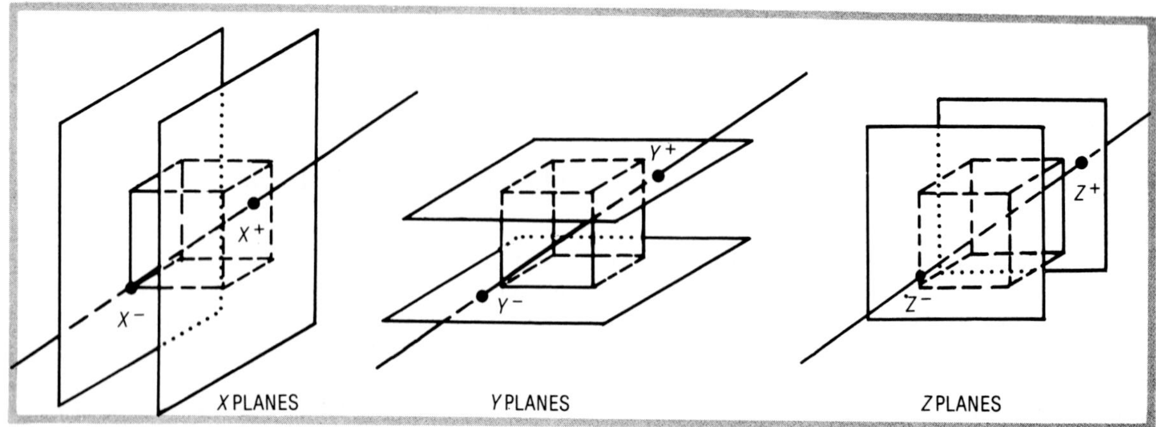

Figure 5. To find the endpoints of the ray segment within a voxel we first intersect that ray with the six bounding planes of the voxel, noting the ray's t value at each intersection.

We know that the voxel we want to examine next will contain points on the ray with t values greater than the ray may attain in the current node. Thus the first step is to find the largest value of t the ray may assume while still in the current node.

Let's designate this value of t as $t+$. We can find $t+$ by intersecting the ray with the six planes that bound the current voxel.* Two of these intersections give us bounds on t parallel to the x axis, two others parallel to the y axis, and the remaining two parallel to the z axis. We can find t values for all six of these points as shown in Figure 5. Each plane is parallel to two of the three coordinate axes, a fact that simplifies its plane equation considerably. It is inexpensive to intersect a ray with one of these "simple" planes because it costs only one subtraction and one divide operation per plane. Note that the points describing the intersections of the ray with the planes of the voxel may lie far outside the volume of the voxel itself. But certainly some values of t will hold for all three ranges: these are exactly the values of t inside the voxel. The intersection of the three ranges of t yields those values of t that the ray may assume while it is inside the box. The value of $t+$ is the value of the upper end of this range of t values, as illustrated in Figure 6.

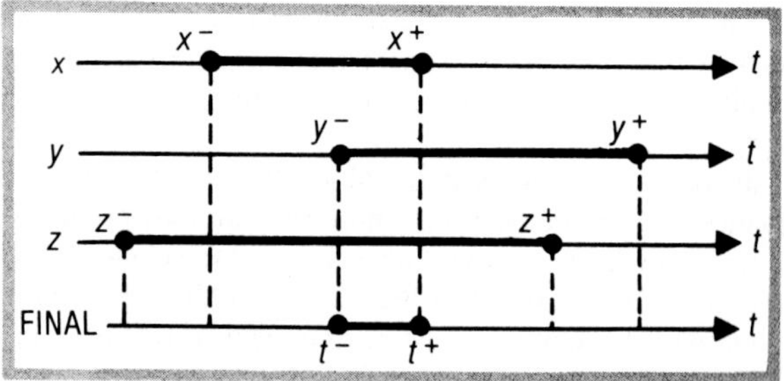

Figure 6. To find the values of t that a ray may assume within a voxel, we find the intersection of the three ranges determined in Figure 5.

The resolution of space in the next voxel to be encountered cannot be any finer than the finest resolution we reached when we built the octree. Now we see the reason we kept a record of the minimum-sized voxel when we built the tree. Let us call the length of the side of this smallest voxel Minlen.

Figure 7 illustrates that we can find the next voxel by merely moving perpendicularly to the face of the voxel that contains $t+$. If $t+$ is on an edge, we must travel perpendicularly to both faces sharing the edge, and similarly we must travel in three directions if $t+$ is on a corner of the voxel. These movement operations are trivial to compute and perform because each is perpendicular to a coordinate axis. We are guaranteed not to move outside the next voxel if we limit our movement to less than the

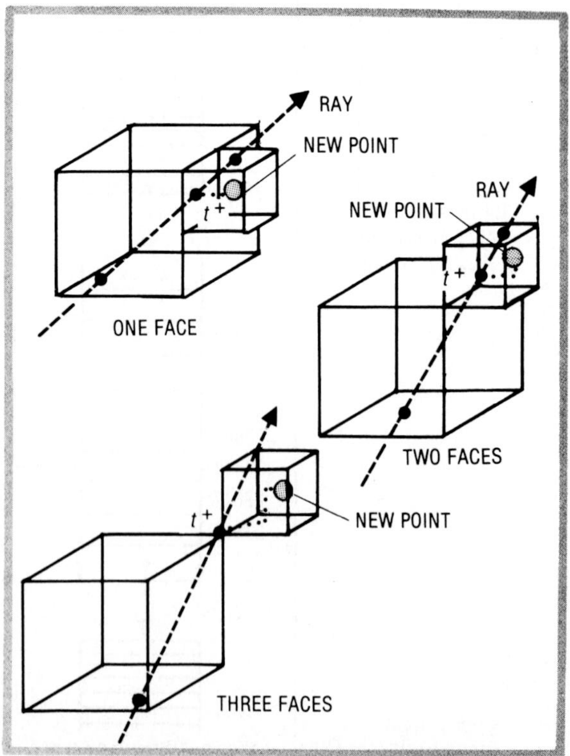

Figure 7. To find the next voxel in a ray's path, we find a point guaranteed to be in that voxel. We find that point by moving the distance Minlen/2 perpendicular to each face in which t^+ lies.

* It is sufficient to intersect the ray with only four planes, but I suggest the additional code necessary to determine which four outweigh the advantages of eliminating two intersections.

Table 1. Timing statistics for old and new ray-tracing algorithms.

	CHECKER-BOARDS AND BALLS	SPIRALS	RECURSIVE PYRAMID	GEODESIC CUBE	SINC FUNCTION	GREAT CIRCLES
NUMBER OF OBJECTS	53	401	1,025	1,536	3,656	7,681
NUMBER OF RAYS TRACED	884,413	532,036	352,322	597,245	448,177	466,524
CHILDREN PER VOXEL	8	20	30	8	30	25
NUMBER OF VOXELS	105	169	473	2,889	2,897	3,009
OLD NUMBER OF INTERSECTIONS	46,830,111	212,713,658	320,825,000	915,439,104	1,636,286,600 (ESTIMATE)	3,553,061,000 (ESTIMATE)
NEW NUMBER OF INTERSECTIONS	6,149,864	13,789,597	9,008,077	9,848,255	10,615,831	17,298,843
AVERAGE INTERSECTIONS PER RAY	6.9	25.9	25.6	16.5	23.7	37.1
OLD TIME (HR:MIN)	8:22	8:53	17:41	42:12	≈63:00 (ESTIMATE)	≈141:00 (ESTIMATE)
OCTREE BUILD TIME (HR:MIN)	0:04	0:02	0:02	0:08	0:12	0:21
NEW TIME (HR:MIN)	2:23	0:40	2:25	2:49	3:22	4:44

Figure 8. Two perfectly reflecting, intersecting spheres sit between a pair of checkerboards.

Figure 10. A procedurally generated model, similar to a kite designed by Alexander Graham Bell.

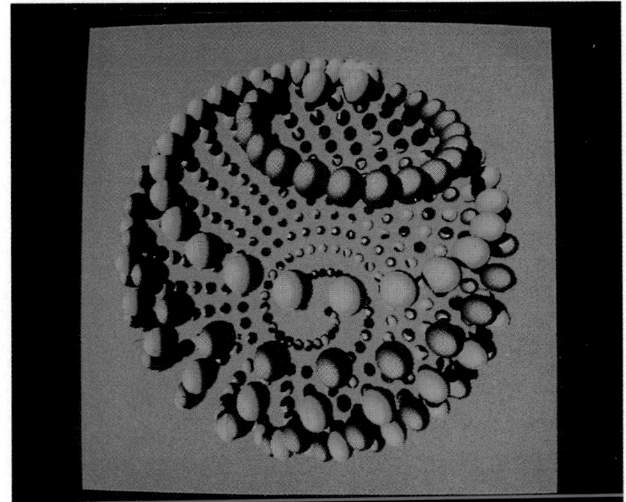

Figure 9. Two interweaving spirals of spheres. Note the shadows on the distant balls.

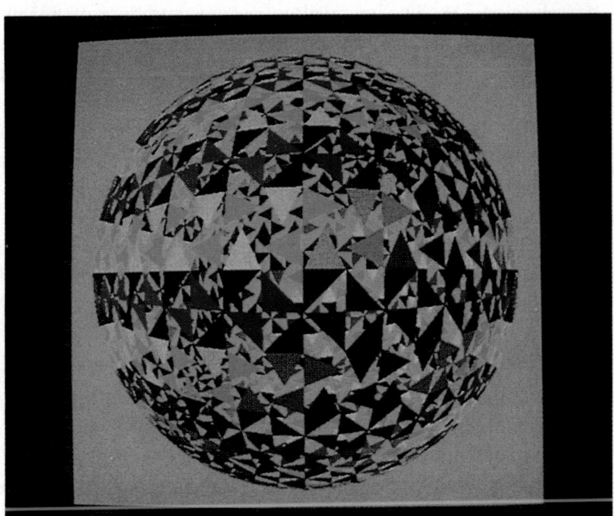

Figure 11. Two different (4, 4, 3), tilings of a geodesically projected cube share the surface of a sphere.

minimum length of the side of that box. That minimum length is Minlen, as stored when we built the octree.

Thus, if we travel some fraction of Minlen (say Minlen/2) from $t+$ in each necessary direction, perpendicularly to the faces of the current voxel, we have a point within the next voxel encountered by the ray.

As long as we know that the point we finally end up with is within this smallest possible voxel, we're guaranteed that it is within the smallest voxel on the other side whatever the resolution over there might be. For if the resolution isn't fine enough to have created this smallest voxel, it is certainly within the volume of the voxel that would have been its parent, or the parent of that voxel, and so on.

Timing and sample pictures

The timing figures in Table 1 are based on statistics gathered from runtime profilers and timers. The timing statistics are used with code written in C, executed under the Unix operating system, and run on a Vax-11/780.

All the measurements were made running the same code. The old technique measurements were made using the new technique and just one huge voxel containing everything; thus there was a very slight amount of additional overhead (less than 0.01 percent). The overall execution time for the new algorithm is the sum of the octree-creation time and the image synthesis time. Of course, once the octree is built, multiple points of view can be generated without performing another setup. Note that due to the nature of naive ray-tracing techniques, the order in which the database is created (and thus the order in which the objects are intersected) can heavily influence the number of intersections necessary to render a complete picture with the traditional method.

The code runs the reflection model introduced by Cook and Torrance.[17] All color calculations are produced on a 16-wavelength visible light spectrum and are converted first to the CIE color coordinates XYZ and then to monitor RGB values when the final picture is displayed.

Figures 8-13 show ray-traced pictures of increasing complexity. Each scene was illuminated with ICI standard illuminant A. The light yellow, orange, and dark purple objects posess the spectral characteristics of a desaturated-yellow gladiolus petal, bright orange gladiolus petal, and wine-colored gladiolus petal, respectively. The red objects reflect as red felt, and the green objects are leaf green. All these colors are found in Evans.[18] The blue backgrounds are different shades of Carolina Blue, the usual color of the sky in Chapel Hill.

Figure 8 demonstrates reflection and shadowing in a standard ray-tracing test environment. Figures 9 and 10 show shadowing from large numbers of spheres and polygons.

Figure 11 was made by subdividing a cube and then projecting it onto the surface of a sphere.[19] Each resulting patch of the sphere was tiled with one of two patterns made of four triangles.

Figure 12 shows several thousand spheres following the function $\sin(x) / x$, or sinc, rotated about the y axis.

Figure 13 is also a projected, subdivided cube. In this case, the tiling consisted of an over-and-under pattern, which was rotated and colored appropriately for each level of subdivision. The result is a set of bands that surround the sphere.

Note that the octree needs to be created only once per static database. Thus we need only make the octree once to produce multiple pictures from different points of view. Another point to note is that most machines have a restriction on the number of digits we can store in an integer. If a node is heavily populated and has used all the digit resolution the machine can afford, the node name can be split into low and high fields with a separate integer for each. This step requires extra work, but shrewd programming can keep the extra computing down to only those nodes with expanded names.

Figure 12. A large number of spheres follow the function sin(x)/x for several half-periods.

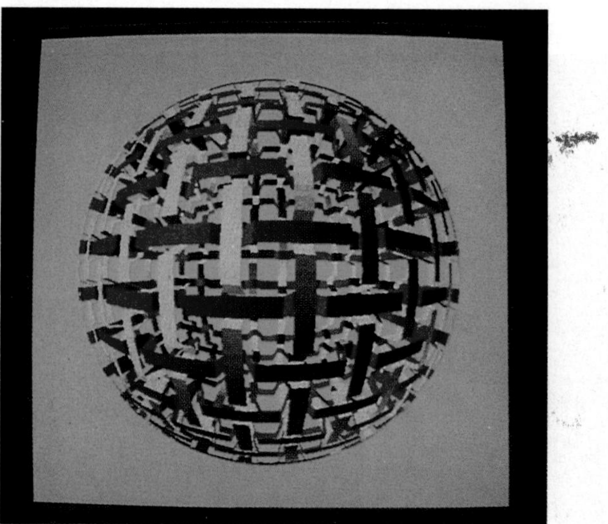

Figure 13. A single overlap pattern recursively applied to a subdivided cube of frequency 3 and then projected onto a sphere.

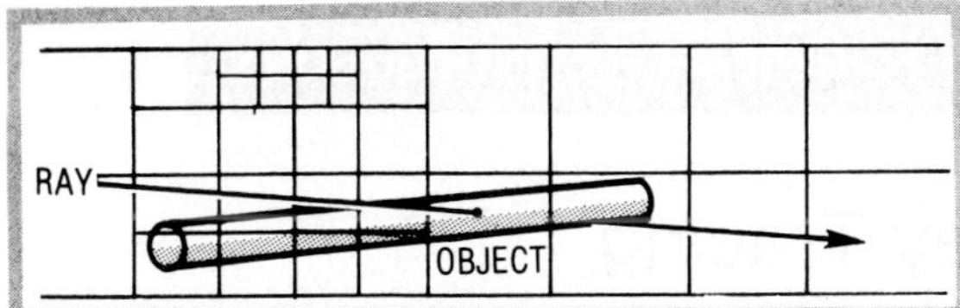

Figure 14. It is possible that a given ray may be tested against the same object several times.

In contrast to the naive techniques, it is possible that a particular ray may have to be tested against a single object several times. This uncommon event is pictured in Figure 14.

Conclusions

We have seen that the infamous slowness of ray-tracing techniques is caused primarily by the time required for ray-object intersection calculations. We have also seen a new way of tracing the ray through small subsets of space at a speed that reduces the number of ray-object intersections that must be made, thereby cutting the overall ray-tracing time considerably.

This new algorithm makes possible the ray tracing of complex scenes by medium- and small-scale computers. It is hoped that this will enable the power of ray tracing to be embraced by more people, helping them generate pictures at the leading edge of computer graphics. ■

Acknowledgments

I am grateful to Professor Frederic Way III of Case Western Reserve University who provided the opportunity and freedom to pursue this work. Thanks also go to Arch Robison and Ben Pope for helping me with algorithms to determine if particular objects were within arbitrary voxels.

Critical reviews of this paper were provided by Mark Boenke and Clayton Elwell, and editorial help was received from Ed Levinson. The recursive pyramid picture is very similar to an image produced by Alan Norton, who consented to its use as test data and an example image. Jim Weythman and Linda Laird of Bell Communications Research provided the opportunity and facilities to prepare the final text, and Tom Duff of Bell Labs helped produce early versions of the pictures in record time.

References

1. A. Appel, "Some Techniques for Shading Machine Renderings of Solids," *AFIPS Conf. Proc.*, Vol. 32, 1968, pp. 37-45.
2. W. K. Bouknight and K. C. Kelley, "An Algorithm for Producing Half-Tone Computer Graphics Presentations with Shadows and Movable Light Sources," *AFIPS Conf. Proc.* Vol. 36, 1970, pp. 1-10.
3. D. S. Kay, "Transparency, Refraction, and Ray Tracing for Computer Synthesized Images," master's thesis, Cornell University, Ithaca, N.Y., Jan. 1979.
4. T. Whitted, "An Improved Illumination Model for Shaded Display," *Comm. ACM*, Vol. 23, No. 6, June 1980, pp. 343-349.
5. Robert L. Cook, Thomas Porter, and Loren Carpenter, "Distributed Ray Tracing," *Computer Graphics* (Proc. Siggraph), Vol. 18, No. 3, pp. 137-145.
6. S. D. Roth, "Ray Casting for Modeling Solids," *Computer Graphics and Image Processing*, Vol. 18, 1982.
7. M. K. Ullner, "Parallel Machines for Computer Graphics," PhD thesis, California Institute of Technology, Pasadena, Calif., 1983.
8. A. Glassner, *Computer Graphics User's Guide*, Howard W. Sams & Co., Indianapolis, 1984.
9. J. T. Kajiya, "Siggraph 83 Tutorial on Ray Tracing," *Proc. Siggraph*, Course 10 notes, 1983.
10. J. T. Kajiya, "Ray Tracing Parametric Patches," *Computer Graphics* (Proc. Siggraph), Vol. 16, No. 3, 1982, pg. 255.
11. J. T. Kajiya, "New Techniques for Ray Tracing Procedurally Defined Objects," *Computer Graphics* (Proc. Siggraph), Vol. 17, No. 3, 1983, pp. 91-99.
12. P. Hanrahan, "Ray Tracing Algebraic Surfaces," *Computer Graphics* (Proc. Siggraph), Vol. 17, No. 3, 1983, pp. 83-89.
13. C. L. Jackins and S. L. Tanimoto, "Octtrees and Their Use in Representing Three-Dimensional Objects," *Computer Graphics and Image Processing*, Vol. 14, No. 3, p. 249-270.
14. D. Meagher, "Geometric Modelling Using Octtree Encoding," *Computer Graphics and Image Processing*, Vol. 19, No. 2, 1982, pp. 129-147.
15. I. Gargantini, "Linear Octtrees for Fast Processing of Three-Dimensional Objects," *Computer Graphics and Image Processing*, Vol. 20, No. 4, 1982, pp. 265-274.
16. I. E. Sutherland and G. W. Hodgman, "Reentrant Polygon Clipping," *Comm. ACM*, Vol. 17, No. 1, Jan. 1974, pp. 32-42.
17. R. L. Cook and K. E. Torrance, "A Reflection Model for Computer Graphics," *ACM Trans. Graphics*, Vol. 1, No. 1, 1982, pp. 7-24.
18. R. Evans, *An Introduction to Color*, John Wiley & Sons, New York, 1948.
19. R. Buckminster Fuller, *Synergetics: Explorations in the Geometry of Thinking*, MacMillan, New York, 1975.

Andrew S. Glassner is a graduate student with the Department of Computer Science at the University of North Carolina at Chapel Hill and a consultant in computer graphics for Bell Communications Research. He has worked on graphics at the New York Institute of Technology's Computer Graphics Lab, the IBM Thomas J. Watson Research Center, and Bell Communications Research. His research interests include raster-based computer graphics, novel input/output devices, digital sound synthesis, topology, language design, and the creative use of computers.

Glassner is the author of *Computer Graphics User's Guide*, a tutorial of computer graphics techniques for artists and other nonprogrammers. He received the BS in computer engineering from Case Western Reserve University and is a member of the ACM.

Questions about this article may be directed to the author at the University of North Carolina at Chapel Hill, Department of Computer Science, Chapel Hill, NC 27514.

New Techniques for Ray Tracing Procedurally Defined Objects

JAMES T. KAJIYA
California Institute of Technology

We present new algorithms for efficient ray tracing of three procedurally defined objects: fractal surfaces, prisms, and surfaces of revolution. The fractal surface algorithm performs recursive subdivision adaptively. Subsurfaces which cannot intersect a given ray are culled from further consideration. The prism algorithm transforms the three-dimensional ray-surface intersection problem into a two-dimensional ray-curve intersection problem, which is solved by the method of strip trees. The surface-of-revolution algorithm transforms the three-dimensional ray-surface intersection problem into a two-dimensional curve-curve intersection problem, which again is solved by strip trees.

Categories and Subject Descriptors: I.3.3 [**Computer Graphics**]: Picture/Image Generation; I.3.5 [**Computer Graphics**]: Computational Geometry and Object Modeling; I.3.7 [**Computer Graphics**]: Three-Dimensional Graphics and Realism.

General Terms: Algorithms

Additional Key Words and Phrases: Raster graphics, ray tracing, fractal surfaces, procedural modeling, strip trees, stochastic models, surfaces of revolution, solid modeling, image synthesis

1. INTRODUCTION

Of all synthetic images, those rendered by ray tracing are unsurpassed for realism [1, 11, 17]. Ray tracing has been criticized by some because of its large appetite for floating-point computation. Yet despite the fact that ray tracing is conceded to be the slowest of all methods for rendering computer imagery, no other technique has a performance envelope quite as large. The combined effects of hidden surfaces, shadows, reflection, and refraction can be handled by ray tracing with a simplicity and elegance unmatched by its competitors.

This paper is about novel ways of performing the key computational step in rendering procedural objects through ray tracing. We present new ways of computing the intersection of a ray and certain procedurally defined objects. The

This is a revised version of a paper originally delivered at the 1983 SIGGRAPH Conference, and printed in the Proceedings of that conference (ACM, New York, 1983).

Author's address: California Institute of Technology, Pasadena, CA 91125.

ACM Transactions on Graphics, Vol. 2, No. 3, July 1983, Pages 161–181.

use of procedural objects is not new to ray tracing—Whitted [17] and Rubin and Whitted [16] have advocated their use. Indeed, we intend to show that the natural organization for ray tracing programs is one using procedural objects.

In Section 2 we present a method which efficiently computes the intersection of a ray with a fractal surface. In the course of the development of this algorithm we present a number of results useful to other fractal rendering techniques. We also analyze the complexity of the new technique. In Section 3, we give an algorithm for intersecting a ray with a surface defined by translating a plane curve orthogonally. We call a surface of this type a *prism*. In Section 4, we treat surfaces of revolution. The algorithm works efficiently even for radius curves defined by thousands of points.

Algorithms for efficient rendering of prisms and surfaces of revolution are of immediate importance to computer-aided design and manufacture applications. Combined with well-known methods for ray tracing Boolean combinations of primitives [11, 15], the above techniques facilitate rendering of models described by constructive solid geometry (CSG). Indeed, most of the objects in CSG are combinations of prisms and surfaces of revolution [4, 14]: the so-called swept volumes.

In Section 5 we present the results of our algorithms, and in Section 6, discuss directions for further work.

It is likely that the locus of ideas exposed here will be applicable to other types of objects exhibiting a high degree of symmetry and/or a hierarchical organization. These ideas suggest a rich variety of techniques applicable to many procedural objects which has heretofore gone unsuspected.

2. FRACTAL SURFACES

The so-called method of fractals [10, 12] has generated models of startling realism. One would conjecture that applying a ray tracing rendering algorithm to objects modeled by this technique would yield very interesting images indeed. Unfortunately, practical considerations prevent one from doing this directly.

Though it is a simple algorithm, the fractal modeling technique generates models that are of visual interest because of their great geometric complexity. A typical fractal surface consists of polygons whose numbers may reach easily into the six figure range. As we shall see below, naive ray tracing is simply too slow to feasibly render a complex fractal surface.

The method we present here overcomes this problem. It does so by evolving the fractal surface in concert with the rendering of it. We generate only those parts of the surface which are likely to intersect the ray being traced. In this way, each ray need be compared with only a handful of polygons instead of the large collection of polygons making up the entire fractal surface. We compute a certain polytope, that is, an *extent*, which completely encloses the surface ultimately evolved with a high degree of certainty. If a ray intersects this extent we must inspect its contents more closely. If not, the extent is pruned from further consideration, thus saving much computation. We mention that this method is essentially the adaptive subdivision technique mentioned in [10], translated to the ray tracing context.

2.1 The Recursive Subdivision Method

We use the subdivision method for generating fractals [5, 9, 10]. In what follows we give a brief review of the technique as presented in the references above.

The recursive subdivision technique proceeds as follows.[1] The surface is modeled as a large number of triangles. The x- and y-coordinates of the triangle vertices are set on an isometric grid (see Figure 1), while their z-coordinates are generated recursively as follows.

Once the displacements z_i, $i = 1, 2, 3$, for a given level of recursion are determined, generate three new independent random variables ξ_i, $i = 1, 2, 3$, with mean given by the equation

$$E\xi_i = \frac{z_j + z_k}{2},$$

and variance

$$var(\xi_i) = \left(\frac{l_i}{2}\right)^{2H},$$

where l_i is the length of the side of a traingle and H is the "fractal dimension." That is, z_i is the height of the vertex i of a triangle and the ξ_i is the displacement over the bisector of its opposite edge. These are summed to make z_i' the vertices of triangles at the next level of recursion.

2.2 The Rendering Algorithm

The rendering algorithm is very simple. Instead of instantiating the surface in its entirety, we evolve a piece at a time. There are several advantages to this.

In the ray tracing method, the intersection computation is the most time-consuming step. If we were to fully evolve the fractal surface, we would need to determine the intersection point of the current ray with every polygon.[2] As a typical scene requires tracing on the order of a million rays, and as a fractal surface may contain the same order of magnitude of polygons, the intersection computation under the naive method would require a trillion ray–polygon intersections. Clearly this is impractical.

By evolving only a piece of the fractal surface at a time, we can cut down the number of intersections which must be computed.

The computation must intersect a ray r with a recursively defined surface. Suppose that we are able to enclose each part of the surface with an *extent*, that is, a volume which is guaranteed to contain a segment of the fully evolved surface. The fractal surface is represented by a tree t of branching ratio four. At each node n of t we associate a pair (p, e) where p is a polygon, called a *facet*, representing the surface at the level of recursion indexed by the depth of n, and e is an extent which encloses the surface given by the subtree at n. The leaf nodes

[1] We restrict ourselves to the case of triangularized surfaces. See Carpenter [5] and Fournier and Fussell [9] for other models.

[2] One of the reviewers has pointed out that a fractal surface can never be *fully* evolved but only approximated to a certain level of detail.

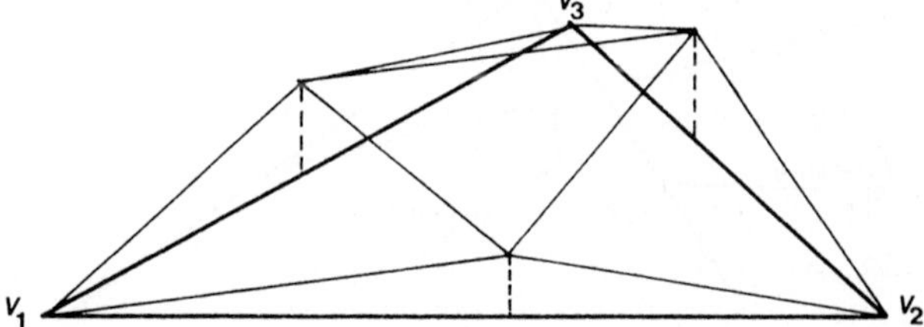

Fig. 1. Fractal subdivision. The midpoint of each edge of the triangle (V_1, V_2, V_3) is displaced in z by a random variable.

of the tree correspond to the fully evolved fractal surface. The polygon corresponding to a leaf node shall be called a *primitive facet.*

An object A is said to *shadow* a node $n(p, e)$ with respect to a ray r if the ray intersects A at a point closer to the ray origin than the intersection with e. A node $n(p, e)$ is said to be *active* if its extent e intersects the ray and no primitive facet shadows it. Note that an inactive node can never contain the closest intersection of the ray with the fully evolved surface.

The algorithm maintains a list of active nodes which are to be traced by the current ray r. With each node is associated a *distance* d from the origin of the ray to the closest intersection with its extent.

The algorithm proceeds as follows.

Choose the closest node n and remove it from the active node list.

Intersect with the four extents e_i, $i = 1, \ldots, 4$, associated with the children n_i, $i = 1, \ldots, 4$ of the node n.

If no e_i intersects r then there are no new active nodes. Start over.

Else, add the nodes whose extents e_i intersect the ray to the active node list.

If the new nodes contain primitive facets p_i and the facets intersect the ray then cull from the active node list the nodes shadowed by the closest p_i. (Simply compare the distance of each node to the distance of the facet intersection point).

It may be conjectured that a node ought to be rendered inactive whenever it is shadowed by any facet (not necessarily primitive). Certainly this holds in the two-dimensional case (see Figure 2a). Figure 2b, however, shows that this is false in the three-dimensional case. The facet for node n shadows its neighboring extent but contains no primitive facet doing so.

2.3 Computing Extents

The key to the performance of the above algorithm lies in the specification of extents. Beyond the necessary conditions for an extent—that it enclose the actual surface segment corresponding to a node—there are two additional desiderata which extents should satisfy. First, extents should be *tight,* that is, they should enclose the actual surface snugly. Consider the case when extents are not tight, as when an extent is the whole of space. Then no pruning will ever take place: the algorithm degenerates to the naive method. As extents become more and more snug, opportunity to prune surfaces arises. Thus tight extents improve the asymptotic complexity of the algorithm. The second desideratum for an extent is that it be easily intersected with a ray. That is, one should not expend undue

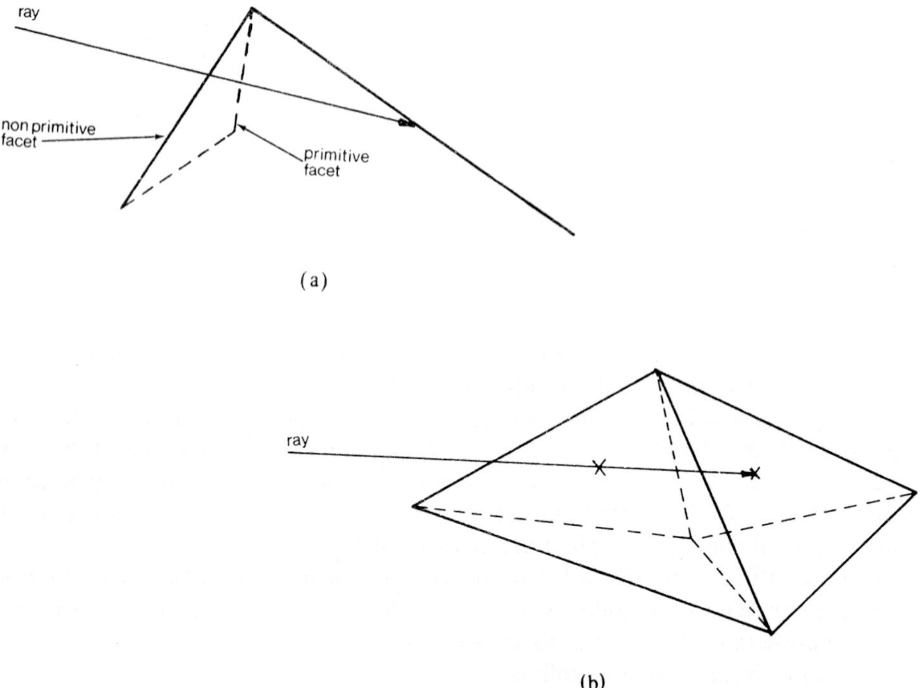

Fig. 2. Shadowing by nonprimitive facets: (a) In the two-dimensional case, nonprimitive facets shadowing other facets is a sufficient condition to cull them from further consideration; (b) In the three-dimensional case a nonprimitive facet may shadow another at a given stage of evolution, but later stages (shown as dotted lines) may uncover the shadowed facet.

amounts of computation in determining whether a ray intersects an extent or not. This criterion determines the not insignificant multiplier in the complexity of the algorithm.

By the second criterion, an ideal extent for ray tracing is the sphere. Among all bounding surfaces it is the easiest to intersect with a ray. However, it fails with respect to the first criterion. Spheres do not contain fractal surfaces very snugly.

We have chosen the extent which is shown in Figure 3. This extent is formed by taking the convex hull of the facet translated in z by a distance $\pm \eta$. Because of its shape we have called this object a *cheesecake extent.* Given that η is of minimum value, this extent is relatively tight. Because it is formed from triangles and rectangles, it is easy to determine ray intersections.

How can we determine the value of η? A fractal surface is stochastically defined. Thus it is not possible to predict with complete certainty how it will vary. On the other hand, because the statistical properties of the surface are well known, we can chose η so that there is an overwhelming probability that a cheesecake encloses the fully evolved surface.

There are two approaches we may take. The first uses the Chebyshev inequality [7]: Let X be a random variable with $E|X| < \infty$ and variance σ_X^2. Then

$$P\{|X - EX| \geq a\} \leq \frac{\sigma_X^2}{a^2}, \qquad a > 0.$$

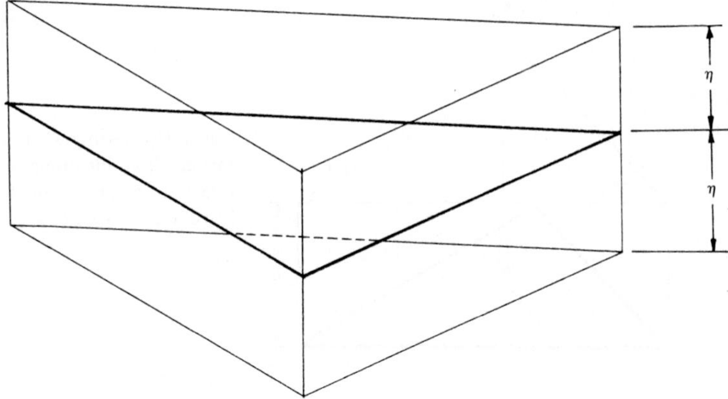

Fig. 3. A cheesecake extent. This extent is formed by the volume swept out by a facet in z by $\pm\,\eta$.

Now, if $S(x, y)$ is a generalized Levy surface [12], the variance of

$$\Delta S = S(x_1, y_1) - S(x_2, y_2)$$

is simply a function of the distance d between the points (x_1, y_1) and (x_2, y_2):

$$var(\Delta S) = d^{2H} V_H,$$

where V_H is a constant depending on the fractal dimension H, (see Corollary 3.4 of Mandelbrot and van Ness [13]).

The point of maximum distance from all the vertices of a triangle with sides of length l is the center. This distance is $l\sqrt{3}/3$. If we use the expression for unconditional variance (it is clear that conditioning can only make the variance go down), then the variance is given by:

$$\sigma = \left(\frac{1\sqrt{3}}{3}\right)^{2H} V_H.$$

Choosing η to be 10σ guarantees a 99 percent chance of the cheesecake enclosing the fully evolved surface.

If, as is usual, we know the surface follows a Gaussian distribution then we can do much better than the Chebyshev inequality. The probability that the center point extends beyond the cheesecake is then simply twice the tail of the distribution. For example, choosing η to be 3σ gives $P = 0.9974$. Carpenter has pointed out that if the random numbers ξ_i are generated via table lookup, then extents may be calculated with total certainty [6].

2.4 Analysis of the Algorithm

To analyze this algorithm we note that there are three cases of ray intersection: (1) the ray does not intersect the top level cheesecake; (2) the ray intersects the top level but not the surface; and (3) the ray intersects the surface.

If the ray does not intersect the top level cheesecake then one intersection computation is sufficient to prune the fractal. Assuming extensive self-shadowing

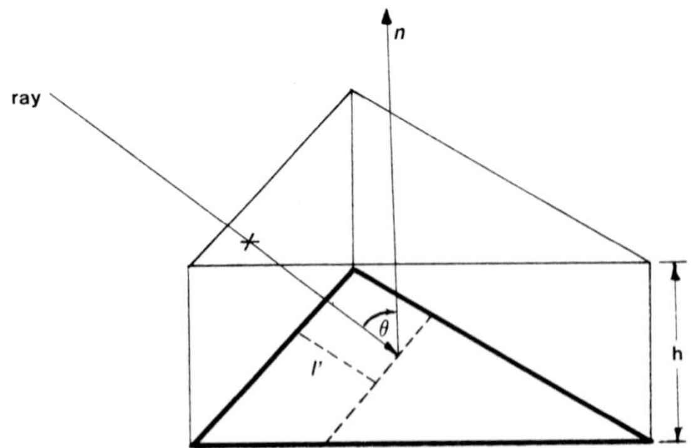

Fig. 4. Estimating wasted computations. If an incoming ray strikes a facet at a small enough angle θ, it will miss the sides.

does not occur, the number of rays which hit the cheesecake (but not necessarily the fractal) is roughly the same as the number of pixels in which the fractal is visible.

The number of rays of the second case is small if the extents are at all tight; to be conservative we treat these rays as if they were of the third case.

The algorithm chooses active nodes to process on the basis of distance. In the best case, only those nodes contained in the path from the root to the primitive facet are chosen. At each step, new nodes are spawned and added to the active node list.

Each step computes intersections with four cheesecakes and may either discard or add the new nodes to the active node list. When the primitive facet is finally encountered the entire rest of the list is culled. Thus the number of intersection computations which must be done is $4 \log_4 n$. The number of node generation steps is the same. Generating each new node is relatively cheap compared to the intersection computation.

Thus in the best case, the number of intersection calculations is

$$(\text{number of visible pixels}) \times 4 \log_4 n.$$

In the worst case, the extents are able to do no pruning at all. Then we degenerate to the naive case: nm where n is the number of primitive triangles and m is the number of rays for the scene.

It has been our experience that the average case with real data possesses the same asymptotic complexity as the best case. We present some preliminary computations indicating why this should be so. In general, however, evaluating the average case complexity is problematical.

We would like to calculate the probability that a ray striking a triangular facet with a given set of angles will strike neighboring cheesecakes first, thus causing unnecessary intersection computations to be performed. In the following analysis we assume that ray strike points are distributed uniformly across a facet.

Let a ray strike a triangular facet with angle θ to the facet normal (see Figure 4). It must then be at a distance of less than l' from the boundry in order to strike a neighboring cheesecake, where

$$l' = h \tan \theta.$$

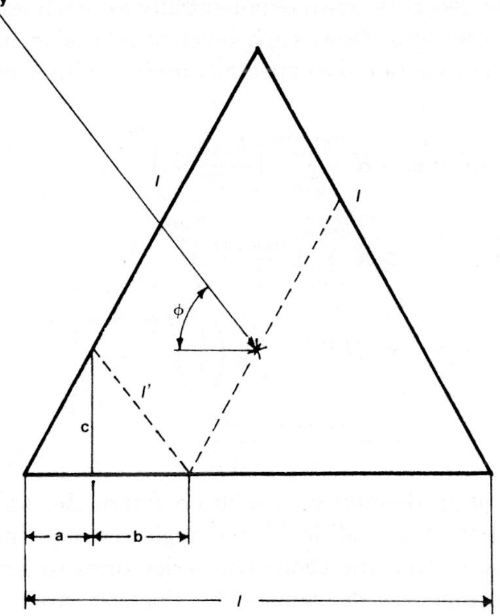

Fig. 5. Estimating wasted computations. This figure shows a top view of Figure 4. We use it to calculate the area of the shaded region.

Now, projecting the ray onto the facet plane gives Figure 5.

The ratio of the area of the entire triangular facet to the area of the shaded region gives the probability that a random ray will strike a neighboring cheesecake first. This ratio may be computed by noting that the following equations hold:

$$c = l' \sin \phi$$

$$a = \frac{c}{\tan \frac{\pi}{3}} = \frac{c}{\sqrt{3}}$$

$$b = l' \cos \phi.$$

The ratio of the areas is the ratio of $a + b$ to l or

$$\begin{aligned} Prob &= \frac{l'}{l}\left(\cos \phi + \frac{\sqrt{3}}{3} \sin \phi\right) \\ &= \frac{h \tan \theta}{l}\left(\cos \phi + \frac{\sqrt{3}}{3} \sin \phi\right), \end{aligned}$$

where h is determined as the cheesecake height of the previous section, say 4σ. So the probability of at least an extra intersection computation occuring given a certain set of angles for the incoming ray is thus:

$$\begin{aligned} P\{\text{Extra Computation} \mid \theta, \phi\} &= 4\left(\frac{\sqrt{3}}{3}\right)^{2H} V_H \tan \theta \\ &\times\left(\cos \phi + \frac{\sqrt{3}}{3} \sin \phi\right) \frac{l_{\text{neighbor}}^{2H}}{l_{\text{triangle}}} \\ &= K l_{\text{neighbor}}^{2H}. \end{aligned}$$

The probability given a set of angles goes down exponentially for each level of recursion of the neighboring cheesecakes. Now, each level of recursion halves l_{neighbor}. We sum the geometric series to obtain the expected number of intersection computations required.

$$\text{Number of computations} = K \sum_{n=0}^{\text{max level}} \left(\frac{l_{\text{neighbor}}}{2^n}\right)^{2H}$$

$$\leq K \sum_{n=0}^{\infty} \left(\frac{l_{\text{neighbor}}}{2^n}\right)^{2H}$$

$$= K l_{\text{neighbor}}^{2H} \sum_{n=0}^{\infty} \left(\frac{1}{2}\right)^{2Hn}$$

$$= K \frac{(2l_{\text{neighbor}})2H}{2^{2H} - 1}.$$

The key observation to be made about the above calculation is that the number of expected superfluous computations for small incidence angles is very small—much less than for the worst case. In fact, the geometric series sums to a small constant making the asymptotic complexity the same as for the best case.

To find the expected number of superfluous computations we use the theorem of total probability. But here the evaluation of the number of computations becomes problematical. The distribution of angles is not a simple uniform distribution. Figure 6 shows that a facet relatively far from the ray source sees a distribution of angles which is highly peaked about the viewing angle. When shadowing and reflection occur, the distribution is far from uniform.

The general character of the average performance observed in practice is very good. For example, when the level of recursion was increased from 5 to 6—quadrupling the number of polygons from 1024 to 4096—the runtime of the algorithm increased by some 12 percent.

No effort has been made to cache calculated subtrees. Each ray intersection must evolve the surface anew from the top node. Whitted has suggested that caching the subtree computations would be a very useful optimization [16].

3. PRISMS

A box is formed by moving a rectangle orthogonally in space, and a cylinder is formed by so moving a circle. In general, we define a *prism* to be a volume formed by translating a plane curve along a vector n for a distance d. The curve is defined in a plane P whose normal vector is n.

Many objects can be defined as collections of prisms; among them, block letters, machine parts formed by extrusion, simple models of urban architecture, and surfaces with "ridges" on a plane which embellish the texture of a surface.

These objects can always be modeled as collections of polygons. We consider the case where the plane curves defining these surfaces are complex, that is, having thousands of vertices. Ray tracing such prisms, defined as collections of polygons, would be extremely expensive.

The technique we describe here illustrates a general technique which will be used again later. We take advantage of the essential symmetries characterizing these surfaces to reduce the intersection problem from three to two dimen-

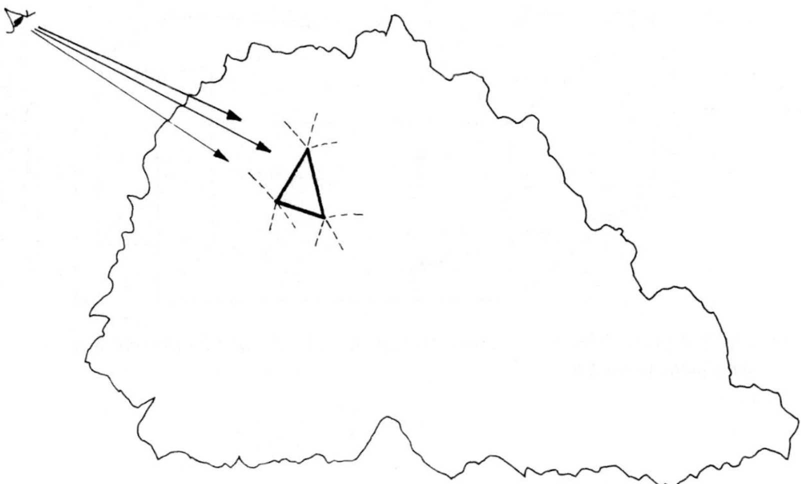

Fig. 6. Estimating wasted computations. Under typical viewing conditions, the angle of ray–facet intersections is hardly uniformly distributed.

sions. We then solve this two-dimensional ray tracing problem by using a representation for plane curves, known as *strip trees,* which is popular in computational geometry [2].

A prism is defined as the union of three parts. The first part is the set of *sides* of the prism given by the locus of points $tn + \gamma(s)$, where $\gamma(s)$ is a curve embedded in a plane P known as the *baseplane*, n is the unit normal of P, and $0 < t < h$ where h is the *height* of the prism. The second and third parts of the prism are known as the *base* and *cap.* The base B is the set of points interior to the curve $\gamma(s)$ in P, the cap is simply the set $B + hn$.

We now give the algorithm for intersecting a ray with a prism. First find the intersection point of the ray with the base and cap planes and project these points down onto the base plane. Then project the ray itself onto the base plane. We have now reduced the problem to a two-dimensional one because of the following proposition (see Figure 7).

PROPOSITION. To intersect a ray $r(t) = o + tv$ with a prism $(B, h, \gamma(s))$, let the ray–base plane strike point be at $t = t_0$. Let the base plane projection of the ray–cap plane strike point be $t = t_1$. Then r strikes the prism iff (1) the base plane projection $r'(t)$ of $r(t)$ intersects the curve $\gamma(s)$ at a point $t = t'$ and

$$0 < |t' - t_0| v \cdot n < h,$$

where n is the unit normal of the baseplane B, or (2) $r'(t_0)$ or $r'(t_1)$ is in the interior of $\gamma(s)$.

This proposition then suggests the following algorithm.

Find the ray strike points $t = t_0$ and $t = t_1$ with the base plane B and with the cap plane $B + hn$, respectively.

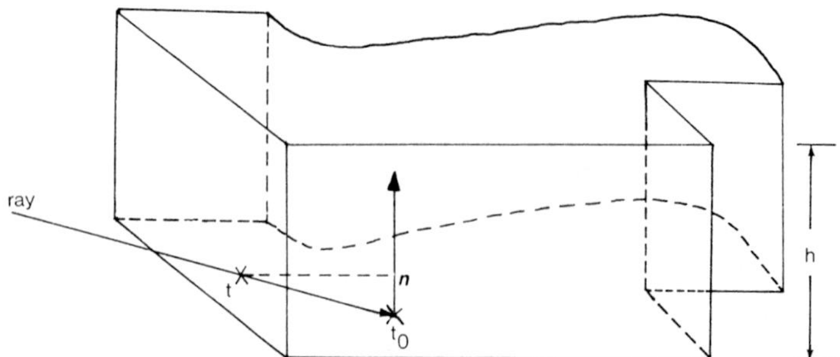

Fig. 7. A prism. The ray is shown striking the side of a prism of height h with base plane normal n.

Project the ray r down into the base plane to give the two-dimensional ray r'.

Find all the intersections of the ray r' with $\gamma(s)$. (We discuss how this will be done after the algorithm.)

Sort the intersections by distance t from the ray origin o.

Scan the sorted list and perform the actions conditioned by the following cases: (1) Cap plane strike point: if inside $\gamma(s)$ then stop else proceed. (2) Base plane strike point: if inside $\gamma(s)$ then stop else proceed. 3) A $\gamma(s)$ intersection: if the intersection point $t = t'$ is such that $0 < |t' - t_0| v \cdot n(B) < h$ then stop else proceed.

How is the intersection of the two-dimensional ray r' with an arbitrary plane curve $\gamma(s)$ to be done? We use the method of strip trees. Strip trees are presented in [2] as generalizations of structures computed in a curve digitization algorithm invented by Duda and Hart [8]. A strip tree is a hierarchical structure which represents the curve at varying resolutions.

The strip tree associated with a curve $\gamma(s)$ is a tree t with nodes $n(e, c)$, where c is a portion of $\gamma(s)$ and e is an extent which completely encloses c. An extent e is shown in Figure 8; it is a triple $e = (b, w_1, w_2)$ consisting of a *baseline b*, and two widths w_1, w_2. The baseline is a line segment of arbitrary orientation. Geometrically, the extent is a rectangle whose edges are determined by the baseline and widths. The extent rectangle is chosen in such a way as to enclose the minimum area containing the curve segment c. Thus each edge of e touches at least one point of c (see Figure 9). The subtrees of node n subdivide c on a point which touches the edge.

We now give an algorithm for generating a strip tree associated with any plane curve $\gamma(s)$.

Choose as a baseline the line segment connecting the first and last point of the curve. Now scan the curve for the maximum and minimum signed distance away from the baseline. These set the widths of the root triangle. Divide the curve at one of these points and compute the subtrees recursively.

It is evident that this is an $n \log n$ computation. A linear time algorithm is also available [2].

It is now a simple matter to efficiently intersect a two-dimensional ray with a plane curve defined by a strip tree. First test for intersection with the root extent.

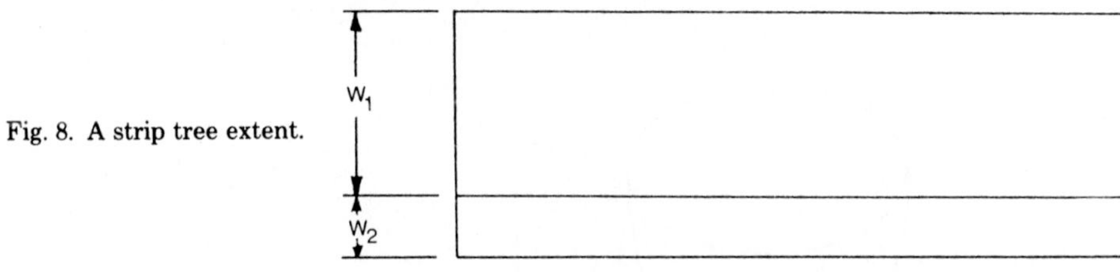

Fig. 8. A strip tree extent.

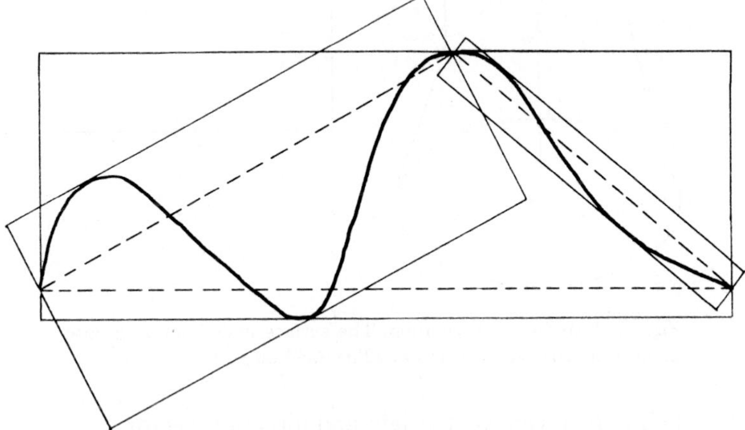

Fig. 9. A strip tree. Rectangular extents completely enclose the bold curve.

If there is an intersection then intersect with each of the subtrees, if not, there is no intersection with the ray. Continue recursively.

Given the above algorithms we are now able to calculate the intersection point of the ray with the prism. Calculating the normal of the surface at the intersection point is simple. If the ray strikes either the base or the cap plane then the normal is the plane normal. Otherwise, it strikes the sides. The three-space normal is then a simple linear transformation of the two-space normal which is given by the strip tree baseline equation. This linear transformation is determined by the base plane normal.

4. SURFACES OF REVOLUTION

Polygon or patch methods may serve as approximations of the surfaces of revolution described in this section. However, this technique can model complex surfaces which would require dozens of patches or hundreds of polygons. The tracing time of such patches or polygon collections would be high. The method described here takes advantage of the high degree of symmetry available in the model. As ray tracing algorithms go, it is relatively fast.

A surface of revolution is defined via a 3-tuple $(b, a, \rho(s))$, where b is a point called the *base point*, a is the *axis vector*, and $\rho(s)$ is the *radius function* (see Figure 10).

Figure 11 shows the geometrical interpretations of the following definitions. We define the *cut plane* as the plane parallel to the axis of revolution containing

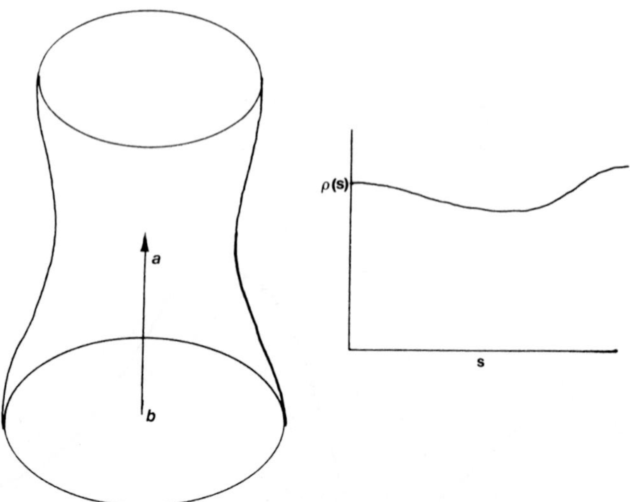

Fig. 10. A surface of revolution. The surface is defined by a base point b, an axis vector a, and a radius function $\rho(s)$.

the ray. Let the ray be given as an origin and direction vector:

$$r(t) = o + tv.$$

Then the cut plane normal c is given by

$$c = a \times v.$$

The plane contains the ray origin o. Define d to be the perpendicular distance of the base point b to the cut plane.

The algorithm first reduces the problem of intersecting a ray r with a surface of revolution to the problem of intersecting a two-dimensional ray r' with two plane curves γ^1, γ^2 formed by intersecting the cut plane with the surface of revolution.

Define a coordinate system in the cut plane as follows. The origin of the plane is the projection b' of the base point. The y-axis vector is the projection of the axis of revolution a, the x-axis unit vector is given by $a \times c$.

The algorithm now attempts to intersect the two-dimensional ray with the two curves γ^1, γ^2 representing the surface meeting the cut plane. But how are these two plane curves to be determined? Figure 12 shows how the curves depend on the radius function $\rho(s)$ and the distance d:

$$\gamma^i_x = \pm\sqrt{\rho^2_x - d^2}$$

$$\gamma^i_y = \rho_y.$$

If the quantity under the root is negative then the curve disappears altogether.

Since the radius curve $\rho(s)$ may contain thousands of points, it would be extremely expensive to calculate the plane curves γ^i for every ray using the above

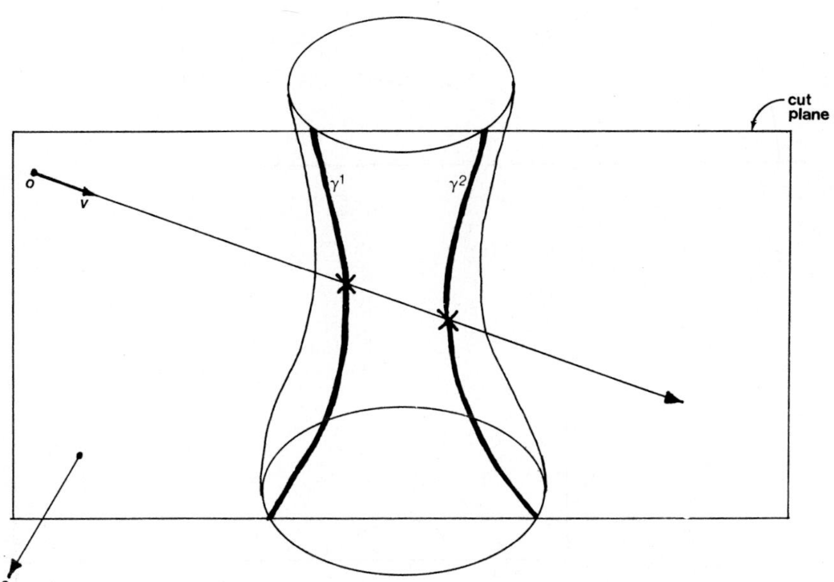

Fig. 11. Computing the intersection. The cut plane contains the ray and is parallel to the axis of revolution. It cuts the surface into two curves.

relation. Even if we do, the choice of a particular algorithm to intersect the curves with the ray remains open. Of course, we intend to use strip trees. But if we do so directly then we would be forced to recalculate the bounding extents at each intersection computation. This is because the plane curves change radically for each different ray. Such a scheme would be impractically slow. Strip trees only yield advantages if their extents can be precalculated and reused for each ray trace.

The solution to this problem is to trace in a different space. Specifically, we trace not in (x, y)-space but in (x^2, y)-space, where the equation defining the two plane curves appears as:

$$\gamma_x = \rho_x - d^2$$

$$\gamma_y = \rho_y.$$

The original radius curve ρ is defined as the square of the actual radius curve. The plane curve γ is simply translated by the square of the distance d of the cut plane from the base point.

Figures 13a and 13b show examples of this transformation. As the distance of the cut plane from the axis grows, more of the curve lies below the axis. Note that we are now tracing curved rays that bounce off the origin. Thus the parts of curves below the axis are inaccessible to the ray. To trace curved rays we use a slightly different ray equation. Instead of tracing rays defined as

$$r = o + tv,$$

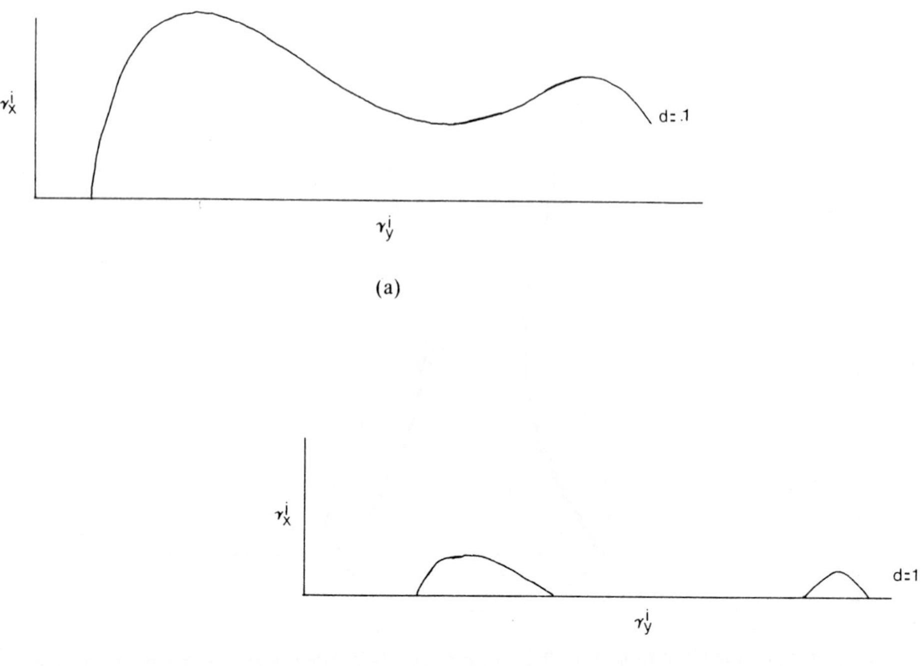

Fig. 12. Intersection curves. The cut plane intersection curves vary dramatically in shape with the cut plane to base point distance.

we now trace rays defined as

$$r_x = (o_x + tv_x)^2$$

$$r_y = o_y + tv_y.$$

We must now intersect a curved ray (as defined above) with an arbitrary plane curve. Fortunately, this plane curve is translated by d so that now it is a simple matter to use strip trees. We recursively intersect the curved ray with an extent box. Each extent intersection is easily accomplished by straightforward solution of a polynomial in t with at most quadratic degree. Solving for t gives the distance from the ray origin. Substituting into the original vector form for the ray gives the exact intersection point.

The above algorithm then determines the intersection point of a ray with a surface of revolution. To complete the ray tracing process we need to compute the surface normal. This is done in two steps, the first of which is to translate the slope of the plane curve in bent (x^2, y)-space back into a plane normal in flat (x, y)-space. We do this by using the following equations. Let i_x be the x-coordinate of the intersection (in flat two-space), and l_x, l_y the components of the normal vector in bent two-space given by the baseline line equation in the strip tree definition. The normal vector (n_x, n_y) expressed in flat two-space

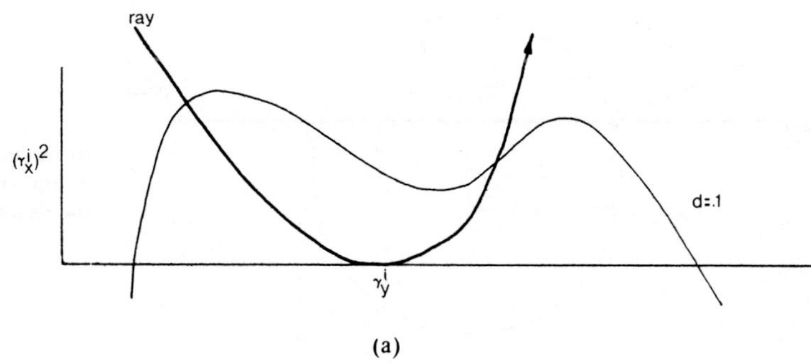

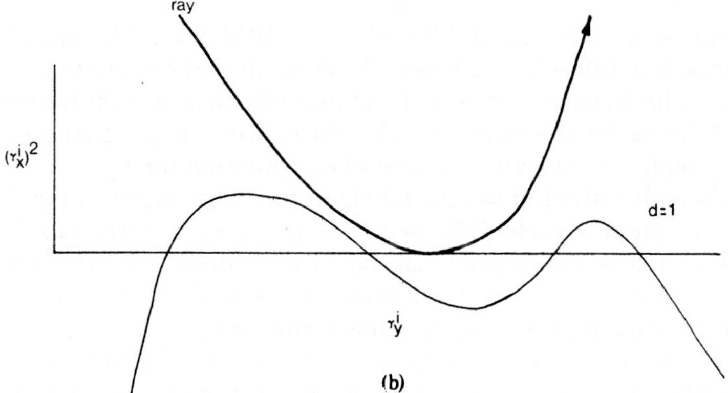

Fig. 13. Intersecting a ray in bent space: (a) The bent space ray is now curved. The two intersection points represent intersections with different γ_x^i; (b) Changing the cut plane to base point distance simply translates the radius curve.

coordinates is then:

$$n_x = \frac{2l_x i_x}{\sqrt{(2l_x i_x)^2 + l_y^2}}$$

$$n_y = \frac{l_y}{\sqrt{(2l_x i_x)^2 + l_y^2}}.$$

The second step is to translate the plane normal into a space normal using the geometry shown in Figure 14. The space normal is given by:

$$n = n_x i_x c \times a + n_x(-d)c + |x| n_y a.$$

We have now calculated the intersection point and the normal to the surface at that intersection point for a surface of revolution. This is all that is required for rendering the surface.

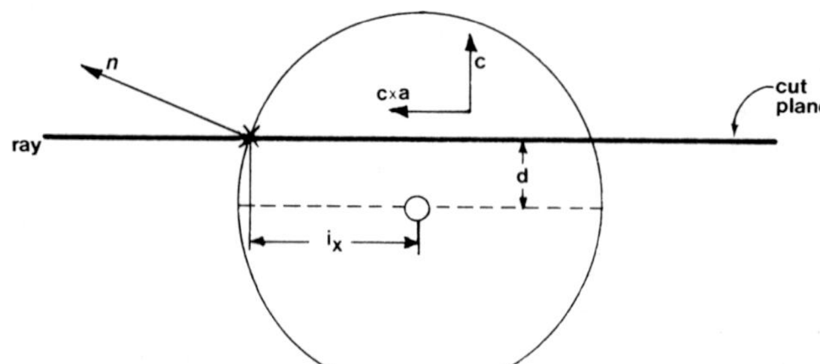

Fig. 14. Calculating the three-space normal. This is a top view looking down the axis vector.

5. RESULTS

The above algorithms were coded in FORTRAN on a IBM-4341. The actual fractal algorithm performed differs from the one presented in that no selection of closest extents occurs. The facets are expanded and pruned in a strict depth-first manner with fixed ordering for the four subnodes. Evidently, the programmed algorithm is slightly simpler at the cost of increased computation time.

Figure 15 shows a sample output of the fractal algorithm. The fractal "valley" is evolved from a single initial triangle with vertices $(-1, -\sqrt{3}/3, 0.5)$, $(1, -\sqrt{3}/3, 0.5)$, $(0, \sqrt{3}/2, 0)$. Note that the mountain can be seen to shadow itself. This image, computed at a resolution of 512×512 pixels, consumed 450 minutes of CPU time. There are 262,144 primitive facets defining this surface.

Figure 16 shows an example of the prism algorithm. In this scene, a curve with four fingers is translated along the z-axis. This image was produced with 50 minutes of CPU time.

An example of the surface-of-revolution algorithm is shown in Figure 17. This scene shows a wine glass resting on a single triangle. The wine glass is defined as a base point b on the surface of the triangle, an axis of revolution coincident with the z-axis, and a radius curve of only 9 points. This points out an interesting feature of the algorithm. Because the radius curve is defined in bent two-dimensional space, straight lines translate into parabolas. Thus the curvature of the glass is due entirely to the curvature of the coordinate system. This image, computed at a resolution of 256×256 pixels, consumed 20 minutes of CPU time on a DECSYSTEM-2060.

6. FURTHER WORK

There are several obvious extensions of the above algorithms which allow for other primitives. A modification of the fractal rendering algorithm will work for arbitrary *deterministic* height fields defined on triangular grids. Many objects in computer graphics may be so defined: human faces, digitized terrain, planar polygons with detailed surface features, injection-molded objects, etc. In fact, this algorithm is applicable to scan-line rendering methods as well as ray tracing.

A *subdivision tree* is constructed by recursively subdividing the height field. Each node of the tree stores an extent enclosing a section of the field. Once such a tree has been constructed, we use the fractal rendering algorithm. The algorithm operates in exactly the same manner as above except that the tree is fully

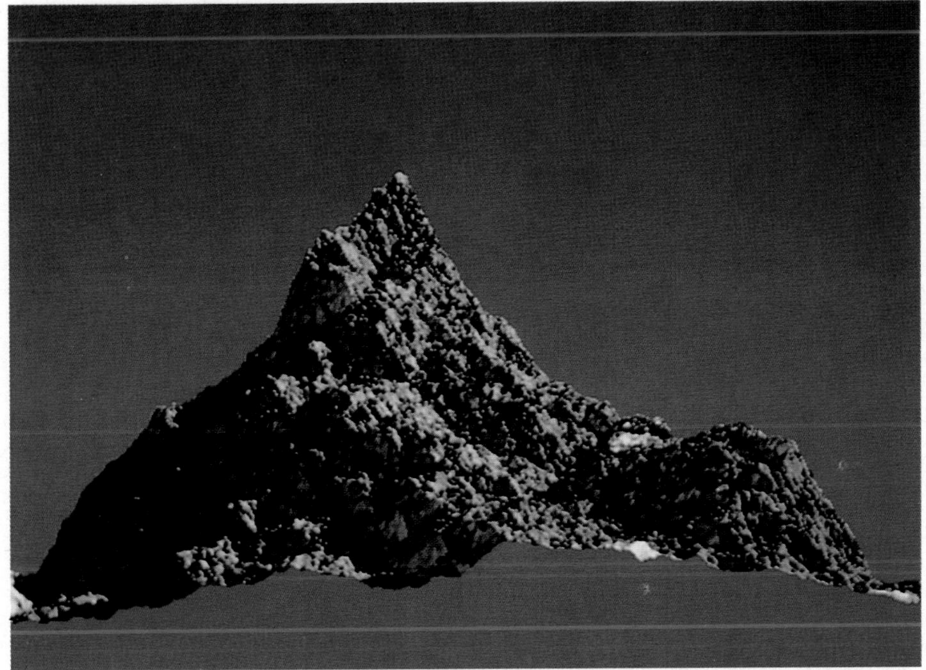

Fig. 15. A fractal surface. Note that the surface can be seen to be shadowing itself.

instantiated before rendering. Generating the subdivision tree is similar to the strip tree algorithm.

Recursively execute the following step:

Scan the surface defined by the domain triangle, searching for the point of maximum and minimum distance η_1, η_2 to the triangle containing the vertices. Store the extent cheesecake with distance η_1, η_2. Subdivide the domain triangle into four subtriangles.

Note that the complexity of constructing this tree is $n \log_4 n$, where n is the number of points in the height field. A linear time algorithm which computes somewhat larger cheesecake extents is also possible by constructing the tree in a bottom-up fashion. Both of these algorithms construct bivariate analogs of strip trees and essentially mimic the strip tree algorithms [2].

A further modification of the height field algorithm follows from the observation that objects other than polygons can serve as leaf nodes in the tree. Such a tree, with extents given by procedural definitions, is easily seen to be an elaboration of the well-known method of Rubin and Whitted [16].

It may well be that extents other than cheesecakes would be more effective for the fractal rendering algorithm. For example, it is easy to argue that ellipsoids would be tighter extents than cheesecakes. The conditional variance of a fractal segment is greatest in the center of the fractal and diminishes as it approaches the vertex of a facet. Ellipsoids also exhibit this behavior but cheesecakes do not.

To construct an ellipsoid extent, one would choose two of the three ellipsoid principal axes to be in the plane of the triangle. The principal lengths would be

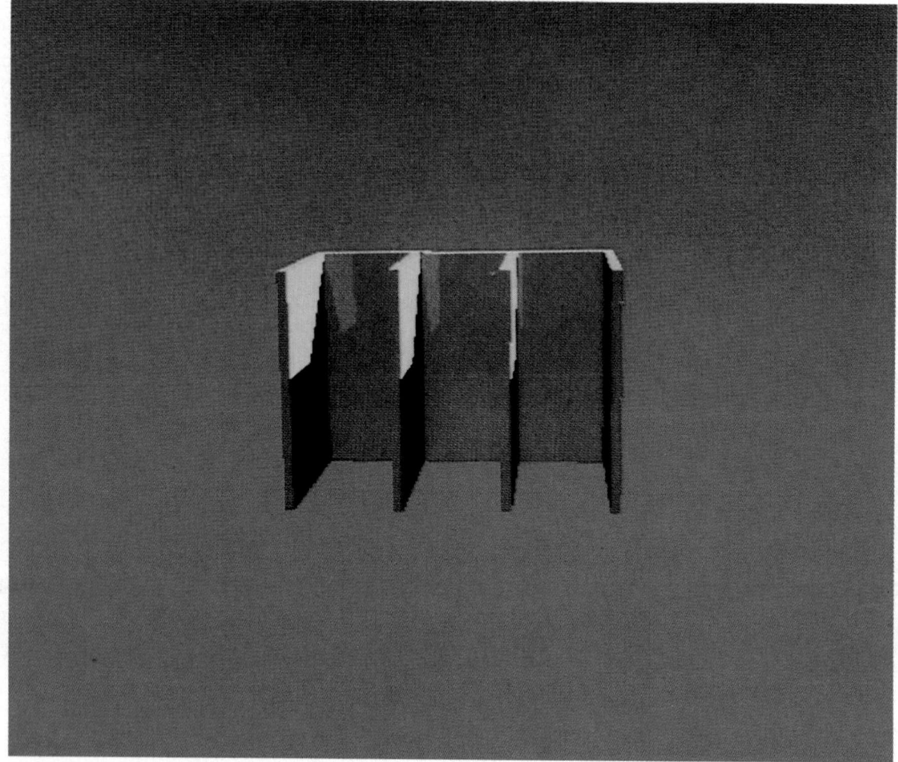

Fig. 16. A prism.

set to cover the vertices. The third principal axis should be vertical with principal length sufficient to cover $\pm\eta$ in the center of the ellipsoid.

It should be easy to calculate intersection points between a ray and an extent. And, certainly, intersecting a ray with an ellipsoid is almost as easy as intersecting one with a sphere. Let the matrix A be formed using the principal axes as rows. Intersecting a ray r with an ellipsoid is equivalent to intersecting a ray $A^{-1}r$ with a sphere.

The prism and surface-of-revolution algorithms may be extended in a number of ways. One such extension is to allow curves other than simple line segments to reside in the leaves of the strip tree. There are two requirements that such new leaf curves should satisfy. First, they should be completely enclosed by a suitable rectangular extent. Second, it should be relatively easy to intersect a ray with primitive curves. Useful primitives are: circular arcs, parabolas, and algebraic curves.

Both algorithms may also be generalized by linearly transforming the incoming ray. In this way surfaces of revolution may have elliptical instead of circular cross sections. In addition, this technique can model skewed surfaces of revolution and skewed prisms.

Note also that the methods presented here may be applied in a mutually recursive manner to efficiently render objects of potentially high complexity. We

Fig. 17. A surface of revolution. This glass is defined by only 18 real numbers.

can best explain what we mean by an example. Suppose the task is to model an office building. One way to do this would be to model it as a prism where each face of the prism is the base plane of a collection of smaller prisms each of whose faces is, say, a deterministic height field. The rendering of this building would recursively invoke the algorithms presented above.

Of course, the normal computation of the surface is subject to the now standard techniques of Phong smoothing, and Blinn perturbation mapping. The prism and surface-of-revolution algorithms also allow a cheaper version of these techniques to be applied to the two-dimensional normals as well. Thus it is possible to generate, say, smoothly reflecting and refracting prisms even though the boundary curves may be coarsly polygonal.

ACKNOWLEDGMENTS

I would like to thank Howard Derby for many discussions and much help during the course of this investigation. I also thank the SIGGRAPH and *TOG* reviewers for suggesting many useful changes.

REFERENCES

1. APPEL, A. Some techniques for shading machine renderings of solids. In *Proc. Spring Joint Computer Conference* (Atlantic City, April 30–May 2, 1968), AFIPS Press, Arlington, Va., pp. 37–45.
2. BALLARD, D.H. Strip trees: A hierarchical representation for curves. *Commun. ACM 24*, 5 (May 1981), 310–321.
3. BLINN, J.F. Simulation of wrinkled surfaces. *Comput. Gr. 12* (Aug. 1978), 286–292.
4. BRAID, I.C. Designing with volumes. Ph.D. dissertation, Cambridge University, Cambridge, U.K. (1973).

5. CARPENTER, L.C. Computer rendering of fractal curves and surfaces. In *SIGGRAPH '80 Conference Proceedings Supplement* (Aug. 1980), ACM, New York, pp. 9–15.
6. CARPENTER, L.C. Private communication (1983).
7. CHOW, Y.S., AND TEICHER, H. *Probability Theory: Independence, Interchangeability, Martingales.* Springer-Verlag, New York (1978).
8. DUDA, R.O. AND HART, P.E. *Pattern Classification and Scene Analysis.* Wiley-Interscience, New York (1973).
9. FOURNIER, A., AND FUSSELL, D. Stochastic modelling in computer graphics. In *Proc. SIGGRAPH '80 Conference Proceedings Supplement* (August 1980), ACM, New York, pp. 1–8.
10. FOURNIER, A., FUSSELL, D. AND CARPENTER, L. Computer rendering of stochastic models. *Commun. ACM* 25, 6 (June 1982), 371–384.
11. GOLDSTEIN, E. AND NAGLE, R. 3D visual simulation. *Simulation 16* (Jan. 1971), 25–31.
12. MANDELBROT, B. *Fractals: Form, Chance, and Dimension.* W.H. Freeman, San Francisco (1977).
13. MANDELBROT, B. AND VAN NESS, J. Fractional Brownian motions, fractional noises and applications. *SIAM Rev. 10,* 4 (Oct. 1968), 422–437.
14. REQUICHA, A.A.G. Representations for rigid solids: theory, methods, and systems. *Comput. Surv.* 12, 4 (Dec. 1980), 437–464.
15. ROTH, S.D. Ray casting for modeling solids. *Comput. Gr. Image Process. 18,* 2 (Feb. 1982), 109–144.
16. RUBIN, S. AND WHITTED, T. A three-dimensional representation for fast rendering of complex scenes. *Comput. Gr. 14* (1980), 110–116.
17. WHITTED, T. An improved illumination model for shaded display. *Commun. ACM 23,* 6 (June 1980), 343–349.

Received March 1983; revised July 1983; accepted August 1983

"Ray Tracing Parametric Surface Patches Utilizing Numerical Techniques and Ray Coherence" by K.I. Joy and M.N. Bhetanabhotla from *Proceedings of SIGGRAPH '86*, 1986, pages 279-285. Copyright 1986, Association for Computing Machinery, Inc., reprinted by permission.

Ray Tracing Parametric Surface Patches Utilizing Numerical Techniques and Ray Coherence

Kenneth I. Joy
Murthy N. Bhetanabhotla

Signal and Image Processing Laboratory
Computer Science Division
Department of Electrical and Computer Engineering
University of California, Davis

Abstract

A new algorithm for ray tracing parametric surface patches is presented. The method uses quasi-Newton iteration to solve for the ray/surface intersection and utilizes ray-to-ray coherence by using numerical information from adjoining rays as initial approximations to the quasi-Newton algorithm. Techniques based upon object space subdivision are used to insure convergence to the correct intersection point. Examples are given of the use of the algorithm in scenes containing Bézier surface patches. Results show that a significant number of ray/surface intersections on these parametric surface patches can be found using very few iterations, giving a significant computational savings.

Categories and Subject Descriptors: I.3.3 [**Computer Graphics**]: Picture/Image Generation; I.3.5 [**Computer Graphics**]: Computational Geometry and Object Modeling ; I.3.7 [**Computer Graphics**]: Three-Dimensional Graphics and Realism

General Terms: Algorithms

Additional Key Words and Phrases: Computer graphics, ray tracing, visible-surface algorithms, parametric surfaces, quasi-Newton methods.

1. Introduction

Ray Tracing is a powerful yet simple approach to image generation. It has its roots in the works of Appel [1] and Bouknight and Kelley [4], but most current implementations are based upon the results of Whitted [28], who specified a method to accurately determine the light propagation throughout a scene, including reflections, refractions from transparent surfaces and shadows. The method has become the primary vehicle from which highly realistic imagery is generated.

The primary computational burden of the algorithm is the calculation of the intersection of a ray and a surface. Typically, for complex scenes modeling complex lighting effects, anti-aliasing or motion blur [6, 9, 21], this calculation must be performed millions of times. Direct methods of calculation have been found for several surface types, including spheres, polygons [28], cylinders and volumes of revolution [20], Steiner Patches [22] and bicubic surface patches [19]. Numerical techniques have been employed in the calculation for certain algebraic surfaces [3, 16] and for parametric surface patches [26, 25].

Reducing the number of ray/surface intersection calculations has been addressed by several authors [8, 13, 14, 18, 24, 27, 28]. Object space subdivision [8, 13, 14, 18] divides the scene into cells, each holding information as to the surfaces that intersect the cell. A fast method is then given for tracing the rays through the cells, only performing intersections with those objects which are contained in the intersected cells. Hierarchical definition of the data using bounding volumes [27] has also been shown to be useful.

This paper also focuses on numerical techniques to calculate the intersection of a ray and surface, specifically quasi-Newton methods. These methods accelerate the steepest-descent technique for function minimization by using computational history to generate a sequence of approximations. We describe this technique in section 2. Section 3 describes the application of the quasi-Newton algorithm to the process of ray tracing and develops a minimal set of information that is needed in the iteration. The integration of this "computational history" into a ray coherence scheme is discussed in section 4 and an adaptation of an object space subdivision scheme used to implement the ray coherence is given in section 5. Implementation details and Examples are contained in sections 6 and 7.

2. Quasi-Newton Methods

Given a non-negative function $F : \mathbf{R}^n \dashrightarrow \mathbf{R}$ and an initial approximation $x^{(0)}$, Newton's method for finding a local minimum of $F(\mathbf{x})$ generates a sequence of points,

$$\mathbf{x}^{(k+1)} = \mathbf{x}^{(k)} - s^{(k)} \left[\mathbf{J}^{(k)}\right]^{-1} \mathbf{g}^{(k)}$$

where

- $\mathbf{g}^{(k)} = \nabla F(\mathbf{x}^{(k)})$, the gradient of F at $\mathbf{x}^{(k)}$,
- $\mathbf{J}^{(k)} = \nabla^2 F(\mathbf{x}^{(k)})$, the Hessian matrix of F evaluated at $\mathbf{x}^{(k)}$, and
- $s^{(k)}$ is a scalar satisfying

$$s^{(k)} = \min_{s} \left(F(\mathbf{x}^{(k)} - s \left[\mathbf{J}^{(k)}\right]^{-1} \mathbf{g}^{(k)}) \right)$$

The convergence of the method is better than linear (i.e. *superlinear*), and under certain, very strict, conditions on the structure of the function F and its derivatives, second order convergence can be achieved (see [7]).

This method, unfortunately, exhibits two main computational bottlenecks. First, methods or formulas must be supplied by which $\mathbf{J}^{(k)}$ can be evaluated and inverted at each iteration. Second, the calculation of $s^{(k)}$, which is usually accomplished by a "line search" (see [7]), must be exact in order to achieve superlinear convergence. These problems can be avoided in the class of *quasi-Newton methods*. These methods use an initial estimate and computational history to generate a symmetric, positive definite, estimate $\mathbf{H}^{(k)}$ to $[\mathbf{J}^{(k)}]^{-1}$ at each step rather than performing the computation work of evaluating and inverting $\mathbf{J}^{(k)}$. Thus, given an initial approximation $\mathbf{x}^{(0)}$ and an initial estimate $\mathbf{H}^{(0)}$ of the inverse Hessian, the quasi-Newton methods generate a sequence of points

$$\mathbf{x}^{(k+1)} = \mathbf{x}^{(k)} - s^{(k)}\mathbf{H}^{(k)}\mathbf{g}^{(k)} \tag{1}$$

and a sequence of updates to the approximate inverse Hessian

$$\mathbf{H}^{(k+1)} = \mathbf{H}^{(k)} + \mathbf{D}^{(k)}$$

where the correction $\mathbf{D}^{(k)}$ is derived from information collected during the last iteration. We note that this is a generalization of the *simple Newton Iteration* discussed by Toth [26], which can be obtained by setting $s^{(k)} = 1$ and $\mathbf{H}^{(k)} = \mathbf{H}^{(0)}$ in equation (1). This method clearly has computational advantages over the conventional Newton's method in that only first derivatives are required, and no matrix inversions need be calculated.

Procedures for updating the approximate inverse Hessian $\mathbf{H}^{(k)}$ have been a active topic of research in nonlinear optimization theory for a number of years. The update used in this research, and found to work well in practice, was developed independently by Broyden [5], Fletcher [11], Goldfarb [15] and Shanno [23] and is referred to as the *BFGS update*. It is given by the following:

Theorem (BFGS)

Let $\mathbf{y}^{(k)} = \mathbf{g}^{(k+1)} - \mathbf{g}^{(k)}$, $\sigma^{(k)} = \mathbf{x}^{(k+1)} - \mathbf{x}^{(k)}$, and

$$r = \frac{(\sigma^{(k)})^T\mathbf{y}^{(k)}}{(\sigma^{(k)})^T\mathbf{y}^{(k)} + (\mathbf{y}^{(k)})^T\mathbf{H}^{(k)}\mathbf{y}^{(k)}}$$

and define

$$\begin{aligned}\mathbf{H}^{(k+1)} = \mathbf{H}^{(k)} &+ \frac{(\sigma^{(k)} - r\,\mathbf{H}^{(k)}\mathbf{y}^{(k)})(\sigma^{(k)} - r\,\mathbf{H}^{(k)}\mathbf{y}^{(k)})^T}{(\sigma^{(k)} - r\,\mathbf{H}^{(k)}\mathbf{y}^{(k)})^T\mathbf{y}^{(k)}} \\ &+ (r-1)\frac{\mathbf{H}^{(k)}\mathbf{y}^{(k)}(\mathbf{y}^{(k)})^T\mathbf{H}^{(k)}}{(\mathbf{y}^{(k)})^T\mathbf{H}^{(k)}\mathbf{y}^{(k)}}\end{aligned} \tag{2}$$

Then, $\mathbf{H}^{(k+1)}$ is positive definite and symmetric, and the quasi-Newton iteration (1) converges superlinearly. In fact, the iteration converges superlinearly even with inexact line searches.

Proof : See [5, 11, 15, or 23], or for a more general treatment see [7]

The fact that superlinear convergence is achieved with inexact line searches implies that exhaustive searches for the exact minimum on the line are not needed. In practice results have also shown the value of taking the full Newton step ($s^{(k)} = 1$) when close to the actual solution. Therefore line searches used with quasi-Newton iteration have evolved to the following form (see [7, 23]).

Let $f(s) = F(\mathbf{x}^{(k)} - s\,\mathbf{H}^{(k)}\mathbf{g}^{(k)})$, and set α to a small positive value, then

- If $f(1) < f(0) + \alpha f'(0)$, then set $s^{(k)} = 1$.
- if $f(1) \geq f(0) + \alpha f'(0)$, then fit a cubic polynomial to the four values $f(0)$, $f(1)$, $f'(0)$, and $f'(0)$, find the unique minimizer $\hat{s}$ of this cubic, and set $s^{(k)} = \hat{s}$

This minimizer can be calculated by the following procedure. Let

$$a = f'(0) + f'(0) - 2f(1) - 2f(0)$$
$$b = 3f(1) + 3f(0) - 2f'(0) - 2f'(0)$$

then

$$\hat{s} = \frac{-b + \sqrt{b^2 - 3af'(0)}}{3a}$$

This search takes a maximum of only two function evaluations and two derivative evaluations. In general, the cubic fit is usually done only once to get the algorithm "on track". The full Newton step is then done on subsequent iterations.

In general, these quasi-Newton methods have been shown to perform better than Newton's method. The total number of iterations to reach a solution may be greater in the quasi-Newton case, but the decreased number of function evaluations allow a better overall performance.

3. Applying Quasi-Newton Methods to Ray Tracing

Given the parametric surface

$$\mathbf{S}(u,v) \; : \; \begin{cases} x(u,v) \\ y(u,v) \\ z(u,v) \end{cases}$$

and a ray, defined by the anchor $\mathbf{P} = (x_p, y_p, z_p)$, and the unit direction $\mathbf{R} = \langle x_r, y_r, z_r \rangle$, we obtain the square of the distance from the surface to the ray by

$$F(u,v) = |\mathbf{V}|^2 - (\mathbf{V}\cdot\mathbf{R})^2$$

where

$$\mathbf{V} = \mathbf{S}(u,v) - \mathbf{P}$$

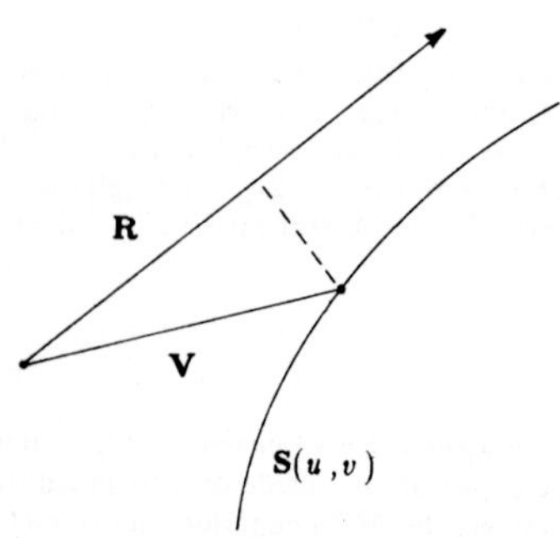

Distance from a Point on the Surface to a Ray
Figure 1

In a more verbose form, this becomes

$$F(u,v) = (x(u,v) - x_p)^2 + (y(u,v) - y_p)^2 + (z(u,v) - z_p)^2 - t^2$$

where t, the distance along the ray to the point where the minimum is achieved, is given by $\mathbf{V}\cdot\mathbf{R}$, i.e.

$$t = x_r(x(u,v) - x_p) + y_r(y(u,v) - y_p) + z_r(z(u,v) - z_p)$$

If a local minimum of F is zero, then this corresponds to a point where the ray intersects the surface. Those points where F is a minimum, but where $F > 0$, indicate that the ray misses the surface by a finite distance. This is actually desirable in that the algorithm will still converge near "silhouette edges" of surface, but will give a non-zero minimum.

Given an initial estimate $(u^{(0)},v^{(0)})$ to the closest point of intersection, we can use a quasi-Newton iteration, with a BFGS update procedure, to solve for the point where the minimum of F exists. We have $\mathbf{g}^{(k)} = \begin{pmatrix} \frac{\partial F}{\partial u} \\ \frac{\partial F}{\partial v} \end{pmatrix}$, where The partial of F with respect to u is given by

$$\frac{\partial F}{\partial u}(u,v) = 2\left(\frac{\partial \mathbf{S}}{\partial u}\cdot\mathbf{V} - t\frac{\partial \mathbf{S}}{\partial u}\cdot\mathbf{R}\right)$$

$$= 2\frac{\partial \mathbf{S}}{\partial u}\cdot\left(\mathbf{V} - t\,\mathbf{R}\right)$$

$$= 2\frac{\partial \mathbf{S}}{\partial u}\cdot\left(\mathbf{S} - (\mathbf{P} + t\,\mathbf{R})\right)$$

and, similarly, the partial of F with respect to v is given by

$$\frac{\partial F}{\partial v}(u,v) = 2\frac{\partial \mathbf{S}}{\partial v}\cdot\left(\mathbf{S} - (\mathbf{P} + t\,\mathbf{R})\right)$$

and the iteration proceeds as

- Assume $\mathbf{H}^{(0)}$ and $\begin{bmatrix} u^{(0)} \\ v^{(0)} \end{bmatrix}$ are given.
- Iterate the following
  - Set $\mathbf{d}^{(k)} = -\mathbf{H}^{(k)}\mathbf{g}^{(k)}$
  - Calculate an acceptable value for $s^{(k)}$, by using a line search in the direction $\mathbf{d}^{(k)}$
  - Set $\sigma^{(k)} = s^{(k)}\mathbf{d}^{(k)}$
  - if $|\sigma^{(k)}| < \epsilon$, where ϵ is some preset tolerance, then terminate the algorithm and return $\mathbf{x}^{(k)}$ as the solution.
  - Set $\mathbf{x}^{(k+1)} = \mathbf{x}^{(k)} + \sigma^{(k)}$
  - Update $\mathbf{H}^{(k)}$ by the BFGS update of equation (2)

We note that $\mathbf{H}^{(k)}$ is a 2×2 symmetric matrix. Thus it requires only 5 real numbers, including $u^{(0)}$, $v^{(0)}$, and 3 values for the approximate inverse Hessian, to be stored and updated to perform the quasi-Newton iteration. Each iteration requires one function evaluation and one gradient evaluation, plus the number of evaluations in the line search, and the few sums and multiplications that are needed to update the approximate inverse Hessian.

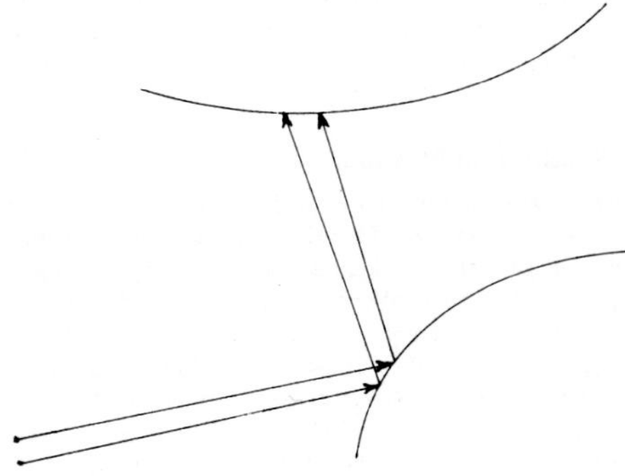

Ray Coherence
Figure 2

4. Utilizing Ray Coherence

The use of coherence in ray tracing algorithms has been discussed by several authors [28, 27, and 24]. It can be observed that in most scenes, groups of rays follow nearly the same path from the eye, striking the same objects. When calculating the ray/surface intersections, the probability is high that two adjoining rays coming from the eyepoint will strike the same surface, and will intersect the surface in the same general area. The same is true for adjoining reflected (refracted) rays that hit the same surface (see Figure 2). Therefore, in a large number of cases, the ray/surface intersection calculations should be nearly identical.

If it can be determined that a ray potentially strikes a parametric surface S, we can exploit ray coherence by setting the initial approximation $(u^{(0)},v^{(0)})$ and $\mathbf{H}^{(0)}$ in the quasi-Newton iteration to be the the parametric values (u,v) and approximate inverse Hessian $\mathbf{H}$ calculated on the final iteration by the quasi-Newton algorithm for the last ray to hit the surface. If we require the two rays to be at the same relative position in the ray tree, originate from the same surface, and intersect S in the same neighborhood, then (u,v) should be an excellent approximation to the minimum of F required by the ray/surface intersection calculation In addition, $\mathbf{H}$ should be an accurate approximation to the inverse Hessian at the intersection point, and convergence of the quasi-Newton method should be rapid.

Unfortunately, even if adjoining rays satisfy the above properties, we cannot insure that the iteration converges to the

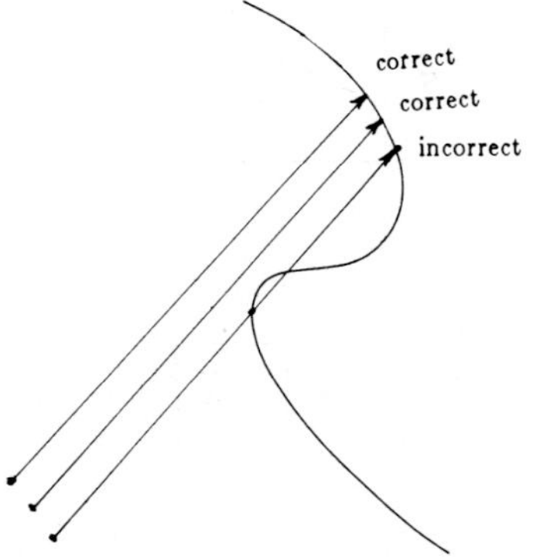

Iteration to an Incorrect Intersection.
Figure 3

correct solution (see Figure 3). In order to solve this problem, we resort to a space subdivision technique to restrict the ray coherence utilization to a limited area of object space and to insure that two rays that are "close" intersect the surface in the same general neighborhood.

5. Space Subdivision Methods

Object space subdivision methods have been recently developed [14, 13, 18, 8] for the purpose of limiting the ray/surface intersection calculations by restricting the calculations to only those objects that lie near the ray. As a preprocessing step, object space is subdivided into a set of cells, each cell acting as a bucket containing information as to the objects in the space that intersect the cell. A fast method is then used to determine an ordering of the cells that intersect the ray. The ray can then be tested against each object in the relevant cells until an object is intersected, or no intersection is found. The use of such algorithms can significantly reduce the number of ray/surface intersections that must be calculated.

The algorithms of Glassner [14] and Kaplan [18], which are essentially equivalent, are most appropriate for use in restricting the ray coherency. These algorithms subdivide the space into an octree of cells and can proceed to an arbitrary tree depth. This data base of cells, created to limit the number of ray/surface intersection calculations, can also be utilized to assist the ray coherence usage of the quasi-Newton iteration.

We classify the 3-tuples ($\mathbf{S}$, C_1, C_2) according to the ray/surface intersection calculation for rays that are anchored in cell C_1, pass through cell C_2, and are to be tested against surface $\mathbf{S}$. This 3-tuples are classified into the following types (see Figure 4).

- Type 1 -- For any ray that is anchored in C_1 and passes through C_2, it can be determined that equation (4) has a unique minimum for the portion of the surface $\mathbf{S}$ contained in the cell.
- Type 2 -- For some ray anchored in C_1 that passes through C_2 a silhouette edge exists on the surface $\mathbf{S}$ with respect to the ray, and it can be determined that equation (4) has either a single minimum, with $F > 0$, or two local minima, each with $F = 0$, for all rays with anchor in C_1 and passing through C_2.
- Type 3 -- This type includes all rays that cannot be classified as either type 1 or 2.

These 3-tuples are classified only if a ray encounters a cell that contains one or more parametric surfaces, and no classification has previously been calculated.

Within cells with rays of Type 1, the algorithm uses the ray coherence to assist in the calculation of the intersection. Within cells with rays of type 2, there may be two intersections to choose from. Ray coherence can again be used, but extra checking must be done to insure that the numerical algorithm does not calculate an incorrect intersection. This can be done by examining the normal vector to the surface at each point calculated and comparing it with previous values. Within cells of type 3, the ray coherency cannot be used, and an alternate intersection algorithm must be utilized. As rays move across adjacent cells, ray coherency can still be utilized if the adjacent cells are of the same type.

The calculations to classify a ray are expensive, but only need to be calculated infrequently. We have implemented a subdivision technique that works adequately, but is somewhat slow. In order to minimize the number of type 3 classifications, we require the preprocessing step to continue to subdivide cells that contain surfaces until the curvature of the surface multiplied by the diagonal of the cell is less than a preset tolerance.

6. Implementation Issues

As with all numerical based algorithms care must be taken to insure the validity of the information used by the iteration. In particular, it is possible that the smallest eigenvalue of the matrix $\mathbf{H}^{(k)}$ will approach zero. In this case, if the eigenvalue is too small, the matrix can be replaced with the identity matrix and the iteration can continue. Similar action is taken if truncation errors cause the matrix $\mathbf{H}^{(k)}$ to become non-positive definite. In this case, one of the eigenvalues becomes negative. Detection of these problems is simple in that $\mathbf{H}^{(k)}$ is a 2×2 matrix, and the eigenvalues are trivial to determine.

There are fairly intricate relationships between the many tolerances needed to implement this algorithm. If the cell size is too large, then virtually all cell/surface 3-tuples are of type 3, and no ray coherency may be used. If the tolerance used to stop the quasi-Newton algorithm is too small, then the algorithm may take many iterations to converge, negating the benefits of ray coherence. We have found the following tolerances to be acceptable

- The quasi-Newton algorithm continues until

$$|\sigma^{(k)}| < .00001 * diag(O)$$

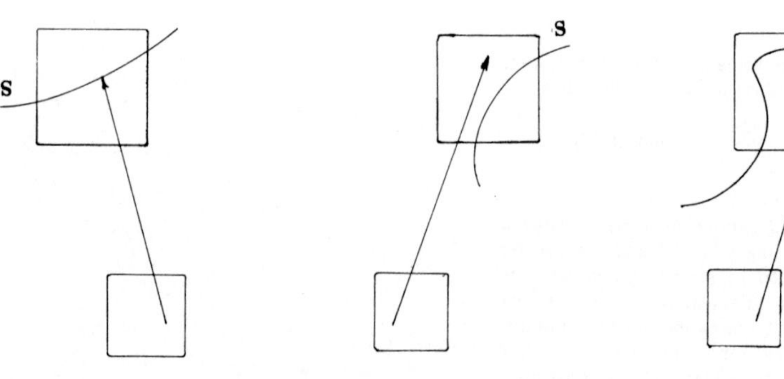

Figure 4

where $diag(O)$ is the length of the diagonal of a box surrounding the object space.

- When determining the octree of cells, cells that contain parametric surfaces continue to be subdivided until

$$| K | * diag(cell) < .01$$

where K is the maximum curvature of the surface in the cell (see [10]).

- Two rays are "close" if the angle between the direction vectors is less than 5 degrees and the anchors lie in the same cell.

For rays that are classified in cell/surface 3-tuples of type 3, we currently have implemented a variation of Toth's algorithm [26] to calculate the intersections. This method is also used if the numerical calculations fail to converge after 10 iterations.

7. Examples

Figures 5, 6 and 7 illustrate the use of the algorithm on scenes containing several Bézier patches. Statistics for the renderings are given in Tables 1 and 2.

Figure 5 consists of 60 shiny spheres reflected in a surface consisting of 16 Bézier patches. The picture was generated at 512×512 resolution, with no anti-aliasing. Figure 6 consists of a lamp generated using 310 Bézier surface patches. The picture was generated to a resolution of 512×512 using supersampling to produce an anti-aliased image. Figure 7 consists of the lamp, rendered with full reflection, refraction and shadows. Four point light sources (three representing the light bulb) were used to illuminate the scene. Supersampling was again utilized to produce the anti-aliased image.

We note that in all cases over 90% of the ray/surface intersection calculations performed with the quasi-Newton method converge in less than three iterations. The algorithm also performed significantly better on the supersampled images.

8. Conclusions

In this paper, we have introduced methods of applying quasi-Newton iteration to the problem of intersecting a ray with an arbitrary, parametrically defined surface patch. The method takes minimal storage, and converges rapidly to a solution even near silhouette edges. The BFGS updating formula gives a method by which previously calculated inverse Hessian matrices, $\mathbf{H}^{(k)}$, can be utilized to give excellent initial approximations for the iteration for adjoining rays. Thus we can utilize ray coherence by using calculated values from one ray as initial approximations for the quasi-Newton iteration at an adjoining ray. Convergence has been shown to be excellent, with over 90% of the intersection calculations accomplished in two iterations or less.

The ray-cell classification scheme is an integral part of the algorithm. Currently it has been implemented by subdivision techniques, and faster algorithms are currently being investigated. Better classification schemes should yield additional improvements to the algorithm.

9. Acknowledgments

The authors would like to thank the Computer Research Group and the Computer Graphics Group at Lawrence Livermore National Laboratory for their support. Nelson Max, Chuck Grant, Brian Cabral and Mike Gwilliam made many helpful comments on an early version of this paper.

This research was supported in part by a grant from Lawrence Livermore National Laboratory, Contract 5607805.

10. Bibliography

[1]. Appel, A., "Some Techniques for Shading Machine Renderings of Solids," *Proc. AFIPS Spring Joint Computer Conf.*, Vol. 32, 1968, 37-49.

[2]. Blinn, J.F., "Computer display of curved surfaces," Ph.D. dissertation, Department of Computer Science, University of Utah, December 1978.

[3]. Blinn, J.F., "A generalization of algebraic surface drawing," *ACM Trans. on Graphics*, Vol 1, No. 3, July 1982, 236-256.

[4]. Bouknight, J., and K. Kelley, "An Algorithm for Producing Half-Tone Computer Graphics Presentations with Shadows and Movable Light Sources," *Proc. AFIPS Spring Joint Computer Conf.*, Vol. 36, 1970, 1-10.

[5]. Broyden, C.G., "The convergence of a class of double-rank minimization algorithms," Parts I and II, *J.I.M.A. 6*, 76-90, 222-236.

[6]. Cook, R.L., T. Porter and L. Carpenter, "Distributed ray tracing," *Computer Graphics 18*, No. 3, (Proceedings of SIGGRAPH/84), July 1984, 137-144.

	Figure 5	Figure 6	Figure 7
Rays Traced	1,600,000	1,200,000	4,750,000
Patch Intersections	463,000	480,000	1,808,000
Convergence in			
1 Iteration	59.2%	69.1%	74.2%
2 Iterations	34.9%	26.7%	21.8%
3 Iterations	3.0%	2.3%	1.5%
4 Iterations	0.4%	0.1%	0.2%
5 Iterations	0.2%	0.1%	0.2%
6 Iterations	0.1%	0.1%	0.1%
>6 Iterations	0.3%	0.2%	0.2%
Alternate Method Required	1.9%	1.7%	1.8%

(Percentages given are of total patch intersections)

Numerical Statistics

Table 1

	Figure 5	Figure 6	Figure 7
Total Number of Cells	3116	5145	5145
Cell Classification			
Type 1	96.0%	87.6%	88.4%
Type 2	3.8%	12.2%	11.4%
Type 3	0.2%	0.2%	0.2%

Cell Classification

Table 2

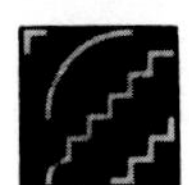

[7]. Dennis, J.E., and R.B. Schnabel, *Numerical Methods for Unconstrained Optimization and non-Linear Equations* Prentice-Hall, Englewood Cliffs, NJ, 1983.

[8]. Dippé, M.A.Z., and J. Swensen, "An adaptive subdivision algorithm and parallel architecture for realistic image synthesis," *Computer Graphics 18,* No. 3, (Proceedings of SIGGRAPH/84), July 1984, 149-158.

[9]. Dippé, M.A.Z. and E.H. Wold, "Antialiasing through stochastic sampling," *Computer Graphics 19,* No. 3, (Proceedings of SIGGRAPH/85), July 1985, 69-78.

[10]. Faux, I.D., and M.J. Pratt, *Computational Geometry for Design and Manufacture* Ellis Horwood, Chichester, 1982.

[11]. Fletcher, R., "A new approach to variable metric algorithms," *Computer Journal 13,* 317-322.

[12]. Fletcher, R., *Practical Methods of Optimization,* John Wiley & Sons, Chichester, England, 1980.

[13]. Fujimoto, A., T. Tanaka and K. Iwata, "ARTS: Accelerated Ray Tracing System," *IEEE Computer Graphics and Applications* Vol. 6, No. 4, April 1986, 16-26.

[14]. Glassner, A.S., "Space subdivision for fast ray tracing," *IEEE Computer Graphics and Applications 4,* No. 10, November 1984, 15-22.

[15]. Goldfarb, D., "A family of variable metric methods derived by variational means," *Math. Comp. 24,* 23-26.

[16]. Hanrahan, P., "Ray tracing algebraic surfaces," *Computer Graphics 17,* (Proceedings of SIGGRAPH/83), No. 3, July 1983, 83-86.

[17]. Joy, K.I., "On the use of quasi-Newton methods in ray tracing parametric surface patches," Technical Report CSE-85-10, Computer Science Division, Department of Electrical and Computer Engineering, University of California, Davis, October, 1985.

[18]. Kaplan, M.R., "Space tracing: a constant time ray tracer," 1985 SIGGRAPH Tutorial on State of the Art in Image Synthesis, July, 1985.

[19]. Kajiya, J.T., "Ray tracing parametric patches," *Computer Graphics 16,* (Proceedings of SIGGRAPH/82) (3), 1982, 245-254.

[20]. Kajiya, J.T., "New techniques for ray tracing procedurally defined objects," *ACM Trans. on Graphics 2,* No. 3, July 1983, 161-181.

[21]. Lee, M.E., R.A. Redner and S.P. Uselton, "Statistically optimized sampling for distributed ray tracing," *Computer Graphics 19,* No. 3, (Proceedings of SIGGRAPH/85), 61-68.

[22]. Sederberg, T.W., and D.C. Anderson, "Ray tracing of Steiner patches," *Computer Graphics 18,* No. 3, (Proceedings of SIGGRAPH/84), July 1984, 159-164.

[23]. Shanno, D.F., "Conditioning of quasi-Newton methods for function minimization," *Math. Comp. 24,* 657-664.

[24]. Speer, L.R., T.D. DeRose and B.A. Barsky, "A theoretical and empirical analysis of coherent ray-tracing," *Proceedings of Graphics Interface 85,* May, 1985, 1-8.

[25]. Sweeney, M.A.J. and R.H. Bartels, "Ray Tracing Free-Form B-Spline Surfaces", *IEEE Computer Graphics and Applications* Vol. 6, No. 2, February 1986, 41-49.

[26]. Toth, D.L., "On ray tracing parametric surfaces," *Computer Graphics 19,* (Proceedings of SIGGRAPH/85), No. 3, July 1985, 171-179.

[27]. Weghorst, H., G. Hooper and D.P. Greenberg, "Improved computational methods for ray tracing," *ACM Trans. on Graphics 3,* No. 1, January 1984, 52-69.

[28]. Whitted, T., "An improved illumination model for shaded display," *CACM,* Vol. 23, No. 6, June 1980, 343-349.

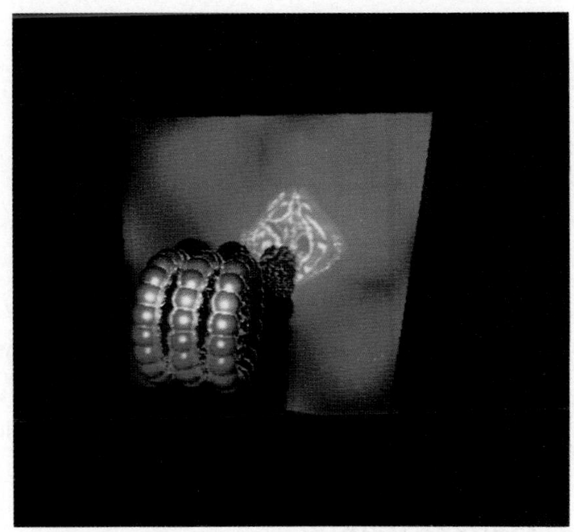

Figure 5

Figure 7

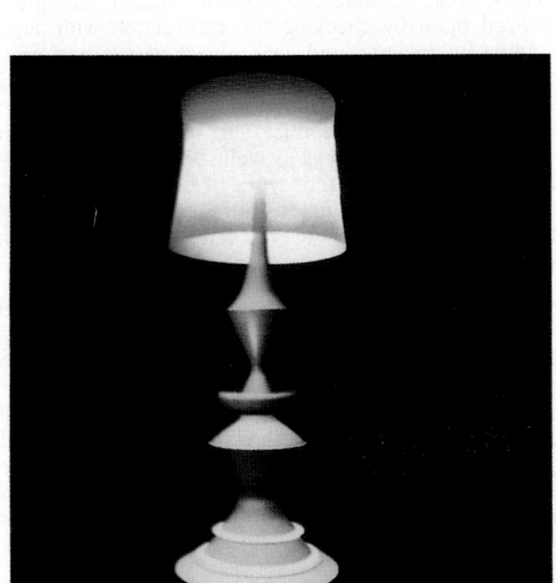

Figure 6

Fast Ray Tracing by Ray Classification

James Arvo
David Kirk

Apollo Computer, Inc.
330 Billerica Road
Chelmsford, MA 01824

Abstract

We describe a new approach to ray tracing which drastically reduces the number of ray-object and ray-bounds intersection calculations by means of 5-dimensional space subdivision. Collections of rays originating from a common 3D rectangular volume and directed through a 2D solid angle are represented as hypercubes in 5-space. A 5D volume bounding the space of rays is dynamically subdivided into hypercubes, each linked to a set of objects which are candidates for intersection. Rays are classified into unique hypercubes and checked for intersection with the associated candidate object set. We compare several techniques for object extent testing, including boxes, spheres, plane-sets, and convex polyhedra. In addition, we examine optimizations made possible by the directional nature of the algorithm, such as sorting, caching and backface culling. Results indicate that this algorithm significantly outperforms previous ray tracing techniques, especially for complex environments.

CR Categories and Subject Descriptors:
I.3.3 [**Computer Graphics**]: Picture/Image Generation;
I.3.7 [**Computer Graphics**]: Three-Dimensional Graphics and Realism;

General Terms: Algorithms, Graphics

Additional Key Words and Phrases: Computer graphics, ray tracing, visible-surface algorithms, extent, bounding volume, hierarchy, traversal

1. Introduction

Our goal in studying algorithms which accelerate ray tracing is to produce high-quality images without paying the enormous time penalty traditionally associated with this method. Recent algorithms have focused on reducing the number of ray-object intersection tests performed since this is typically where most of the time is spent, especially for complex environments. This is achieved by using a simple-to-evaluate function to cull objects which are clearly not in the path of the ray.

1.1 Previous Work

Rubin and Whitted [14] developed one of the first schemes for improving ray tracing performance. They observed that "exhaustive search" could be greatly improved upon by checking for intersection with simple bounding volumes around each object before performing more complicated ray-object intersection checks. By creating a hierarchy of bounding volumes, Rubin and Whitted were able to reduce the number of bounding volume intersection checks as well. Weghorst, et. al. [17] studied the use of different types of bounding volumes in a hierarchy, and discussed how ease of intersection testing and "tightness" of fit determine the bounding volume's effectiveness in culling objects.

The object hierarchy of Rubin and Whitted made the crucial step away from the linear time complexity of exhaustive search but still did not achieve acceptable performance on complex environments. This was due in part to the top down search of the object hierarchy required for every ray. Another factor was the difficulty of obtaining a small bound on the number of ray-object intersection tests and ray-bounds comparisons required per ray since this depended strongly on the organization of the hierarchy.

Another class of algorithms employs 3D space subdivision to implement culling functions. The initial candidates for intersection are associated with a 3D volume containing the ray origin. Successive candidates are identified by regions which the ray intersects. Concurrently and independently, Glassner [4], and Fujimoto, et. al. [3] pursued this approach. Glassner investigated partitioning the object space using an octree data structure, while Fujimoto compared octrees to a rectangular linear grid of 3D voxels. Kaplan [7] proposed a similar scheme and observed that a binary space partitioning tree could be used to accomplish the space subdivision. A drawback common to all of these approaches is that a ray which misses everything must be checked against the contents of each of the regions or voxels which it intersects.

None of these algorithms made use of the coherence which exists between similar rays. Speer, et. al. [15] examined the concept of "tunnels" as a means of exploiting ray-tree coherence. Speer attempted to construct cylindrical "safety regions" within which a ray would miss all objects, but observed that despite considerable coherence, the cost of constructing and using the cylindrical tunnels negated the benefit of the culling they accomplished.

Kay and Kajiya [8] introduced a new type of bounding volume, plane-sets, and a hierarchy traversal algorithm which is able to check objects for intersection in a particular order, regardless of the locality of the bounding volume hierarchy. This algorithm had the key advantage over previous object hierarchy schemes that objects could be checked for intersection in approximately the order that they would be encountered along the ray length.

1.2 A New Approach

Our ray classification approach differs significantly from previous work in that it extends the idea of space subdivision to include ray direction. The result is an extremely powerful culling function that is, empirically, relatively insensitive to environment complexity.

A key feature of the algorithm is that a single evaluation of its culling function is capable of producing a small but complete set of candidate objects, even if the ray misses everything. This is accomplished by adaptively subdividing the space of all relevant rays into equivalence classes, E_1, E_2, ..., E_m, and constructing candidate object sets C_1, C_2, ..., C_m, such that C_i contains all objects which the rays in E_i can intersect. Evaluating the culling function reduces to classifying a given ray as a member of an equivalence class and retrieving the associated candidate set. The algorithm strives to keep $| C_i |$ small for all i, and several new techniques are employed which lessen the impact of those sets for which it fails to do so.

2. 5-Space and Ray Classification

In many ray tracing implementations, rays are represented by a 3D origin coupled with a 3D unit direction vector, a convenient form for intersection calculations. However, geometrically a ray has only five degrees of freedom, as evidenced by the fact that the same information can be conveyed by only five values: for instance, a 3D origin and two spherical angles. Consequently, we can identify rays in 3-space with points in 5-space, or, more precisely, with points in the 5-manifold $\mathbf{R}^3 \times \mathbf{S}^2$, where $\mathbf{S}^2$ is the unit sphere in $\mathbf{R}^3$. It follows that any neighborhood of rays, a collection of rays with similar origins and directions, can be parametrized by a subset of $\mathbf{R}^5$. We shall use such parametrizations in constructing a culling function which makes use of all five degrees of freedom of a ray.

The ray classification algorithm can be broken into five subtasks. All but the last operate at least partly in 5-space. These are:

[1] *5D Bounding Volume:*
Find a bounded subset, $E \subset \mathbf{R}^5$, which contains the 5D equivalent of every ray which can interact with the environment.

[2] *5D Space Subdivision*:
Select subsets E_1, ..., E_m which partition $E \subset \mathbf{R}^5$ into disjoint volumes.

[3] *Candidate Set Creation*:
Given a set of rays represented by a 5D volume E_i, create a set of candidates, C_i, containing *every* object which is intersected by one of the rays.

[4] *Ray Classification*:
Given a ray corresponding to a point in E, find a set, E_i, of a partitioning, E_1, ..., E_m, which contains the point, and return the associated candidate set C_i.

[5] *Candidate Set Processing*:
Given a ray and a set of candidate objects, C_i, determine the closest ray-object intersection if one exists.

For each ray that is intersected with the environment, [4] is used to retrieve a set of candidate objects and [5] does the actual ray-object intersections using this set. As we shall see, [1] is carried out only once while [2] and [3] incrementally refine the partitioning and candidate sets in response to ray classification queries in [4]. Ideally we seek a partitioning in [2] such that corresponding candidate sets created in [3] contain fewer than some predetermined number of objects. These subtasks are described in detail in sections 3 through 7.

2.1 Beams as 5D Hypercubes

Because much of the algorithm involves 5D volumes it is important to choose volumes which have compact representations and permit efficient point-containment queries and subdivision. For these reasons we use 5D axis-aligned parallelepipeds, or hypercubes. These are stored as five ordered pairs representing intervals along the five mutually orthogonal coordinate axes which we label X, Y, Z, U, and V.

Each hypercube, representing a collection of rays, has a natural 3D manifestation which we call a *beam*. This is the unbounded 3D volume formed by the union of semi-infinite lines, or rays in the geometrical sense, defined by the points of the hypercube. Beams play a central role in candidate set creation since they comprise exactly those points in 3-space which are reachable by a set of rays. Given the importance of this role it is essential that hypercubes define beam volumes which are easily represented, such as convex polyhedra. This geometry is completely determined by the way we identify rays with 5D points.

2.2 Rays as 5D Points

In this section we describe the means of associating a unique point in $\mathbf{R}^5$ with each distinct ray in $\mathbf{R}^3$. As mentioned earlier, a ray can be mapped to a unique 5-tuple, (x,y,z,u,v), consisting of its origin followed by two spherical angles. Unfortunately the beams associated with hypercubes under this mapping are not generally polyhedra. To remedy this, we piece together several mappings which have the desired properties locally, and together account for the whole space of rays.

Consider the intersection of a ray with an axis-aligned cube of side two centered at its origin. Each distinct ray direction corresponds to a unique intersection point on this cube. A 2D coordinate system can be imposed on these points by normalizing the ray direction vector, **d**, with respect to the ∞-norm, as shown in Equation 1, and extracting (u,v) from the result, as shown in Equation 2.

$$\mathbf{w} = \frac{\mathbf{d}}{\|\mathbf{d}\|_\infty} = \frac{(d_x, d_y, d_z)}{\mathrm{MAX}(|d_x|, |d_y|, |d_z|)} \quad [1]$$

$$(u, v) = \begin{cases} (w_y, w_z) \text{ if } w_x = \pm 1, \text{ or else} \\ (w_x, w_z) \text{ if } w_y = \pm 1, \text{ or else} \\ (w_x, w_y) \text{ if } w_z = \pm 1 \end{cases} \quad [2]$$

This establishes a one-to-one correspondence between $[-1,1]\times[-1,1]$ and rays passing through a single face of the cube. By partitioning the rays into six dominant directions defined by the faces of the cube, and restricting the mapping to each of these domains, we obtain six bicontinuous one-to-one mappings. We associate each with a *dominant axis*, denoted +X, -X, +Y, -Y, +Z, or -Z. The inverse mappings, or parametrizations, define an atlas of $\mathbf{S}^2$, covering the set of ray directions with images of $[-1,1]\times[-1,1]$. This is trivially extended to $\mathbf{R}^3\times\mathbf{S}^2$. In order to meet our requirement of a global one-to-one correspondence, however, we index into six "copies" of $[-1,1]\times[-1,1]$ using the dominant axis of a ray. For a given ray, this axis is determined by the axis and sign of its largest absolute direction component.

Intervals in U and V together define pyramidal solid angles through a single cube face while intervals in X, Y, and Z define rectangular 3D volumes. Hypercubes then define beams which are unbounded polyhedra with at most nine faces. This is shown in Figure 1b along with a 2D analogy as an aid to visualization in Figure 1a.

3. The 5D Bounding Volume

The first step of the ray classification algorithm is to find a bounded subset of $\mathbf{R}^5$ containing all rays which are relevant to the environment. We start by finding a 3D bounding box, B, which contains all the objects of the environment. Such a box is easily obtained from individual object extents. The desired bounding volume can then be built from six copies of the hypercube $B\times[-1,1]\times[-1,1]$, each corresponding to a unique dominant axis and accounting for directions covering one sixth of the unit sphere, $\mathbf{S}^2$.

The 3D bounding box, B, also serves another purpose. If the eye point is outside of B, then every first-generation ray must be checked for intersection with it. If there is no intersection, we know the ray hits nothing in the environment. Otherwise, the ray must be moved into the 5D bounding volume by resetting its origin to the point of intersection.

Other bounding volumes can be used in place of B for this second purpose. For instance, plane-sets [8] can produce a much tighter bound, thereby identifying more rays which miss all the objects in the environment. Another advantage lies in ray re-origining. By pushing the rays up to the boundary of the tighter volume, we reduce the space of rays, making the space subdivision task more efficient.

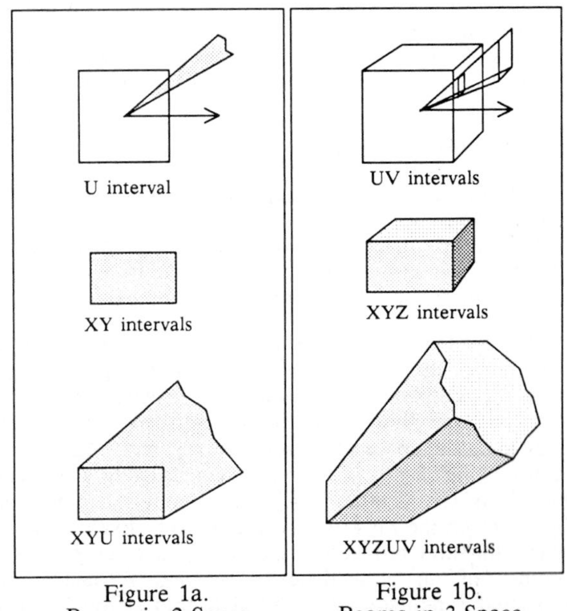

Figure 1a. Beams in 2-Space.

Figure 1b. Beams in 3-Space.

4. 5D Space Subdivision

When intersecting a ray with the environment we need only consider the set of objects whose bounding volumes are intersected. The purpose of tasks [1] through [4] in section 2 is to produce a set of objects containing these, and few others, for any ray in the environment. This is done efficiently by exploiting scene coherence, which ensures that similar rays are likely to intersect similar sets of objects. Due to the continuity of our ray parametrizations, this implies that decreasing the diameter of a hypercube increases the likelihood that the rays of its beam behave similarly. The role of 5D space subdivision is to produce hypercubes which are sufficiently small that the rays of each corresponding beam intersect approximately the same objects. This allows us to share one set of candidate objects among all the rays of a beam.

We use binary space subdivision to create a hypercube hierarchy, dividing intervals exactly in half at each level, and repeatedly cycling through the five axes. Any ray can be contained in a hypercube of arbitrarily small diameter by this mechanism. Given that we use only a sparse subset of the potential rays, however, it is unnecessary to finely subdivide the entire 5D bounding volume. Instead, we confine subdivision to occur in those regions populated with rays generated during ray tracing. We subdivide only on demand, when the 5D coordinates of a ray are found to reside in a hypercube which is too large. Thus, beginning with the six bounding hypercubes, we construct the entire hierarchy by lazy evaluation.

When a ray causes new paths to be formed in the hypercube hierarchy, two heuristics determine when subdivision terminates. We stop if either the candidate set or the hypercube falls below a fixed size threshold. A small candidate set indicates that we have achieved the goal of making the associated rays inexpensive to intersect with the environment. The hypercube size constraint is imposed to allow the cost of creating a candidate set to be amortized over many rays.

5. Candidate Set Creation

Given a hypercube, the task of creating its candidate set consists of determining all the objects in the environment which its rays can intersect. This is done by comparing each object's bounding volume with the beam defined by the hypercube. If the volumes intersect, the object is *classified* as a candidate with respect to that hypercube and is added to the candidate set.

The six bounding hypercubes are assigned candidate sets containing all objects in the environment. As subdivision proceeds, candidate sets are efficiently created for the new hypercubes by making use of the hierarchy. Only those objects in an ancestor's candidate set need be reclassified.

For space efficiency, we need not create a candidate set for every intermediate hypercube in the hierarchy. When a hypercube is subdivided along one axis, the beams of the resulting hypercubes usually overlap substantially, and are quite similar to the parent beam. Consequently, a single subdivision eliminates few candidates. This suggests performing several subdivisions before creating a new candidate set. A strategy which we have found to be effective is to subdivide each of the five axes before creating a new candidate set. While this allows up to 2^5 hypercubes to derive their candidate sets from the same ancestor, the reduction in storage is significant. Also, due to lazy evaluation of the hierarchy, it is rare that all descendants are even created.

5.1 Object Classification

The object classification method used in candidate set creation is critical to the performance of the ray tracer. A very fast method may be too conservative, creating candidate sets which are much too large. This causes unnecessary overhead in both candidate set creation and processing. A classifying method which performs well in rejecting objects may be unacceptable if it is too costly. As with object extents used for avoiding unnecessary ray-object intersection checks, there must be a compromise between the cost of the method and its accuracy [17]. In the following subsections we discuss the tradeoffs of three object classification techniques which can be used independently or in combination.

5.1.1 Classifying Objects with LP

The first object classification method we describe employs linear programming to test for object-beam intersection, and requires objects to be enclosed by convex polyhedra. A polyhedral bounding volume is conveniently represented by its vertex list, or hull points, and can be made arbitrarily close to the convex hull of the object. Since the beam is itself a polyhedron, the object classification problem reduces to testing for intersection between two polyhedra. This is easily expressed as a linear program using the hull points [12] and then solved using the simplex method [13]. The result is an exact classification scheme for this type of bounding volume. That is, an object is classified as a candidate of a hypercube if and only if some ray of the beam intersects its bounding polyhedron.

Unfortunately, our experience has shown that the computation required to solve the linear program is prohibitively high, precluding its use as the primary object classification method. It is overly complex for handling the very frequent cases of objects which are either far from the beam or inside it. Nevertheless, it is a useful tool for testing and evaluating the effectiveness of approximate object-classification methods.

5.1.2 Classifying Objects with Planes

The linear programming approach rejects an object from the candidate set if and only if there exists a separating plane between the beam and the object's bounding polyhedron. This suggests a simpler approach which tests several planes directly, classifying an object as a candidate if none of the planes are separators.

For every beam there are several planes which are particularly appropriate to test, each with the entire beam in its positive half-space. Four of these planes are parallel to the faces of the UV pyramid, translated to the appropriate XYZ extrema of the hypercube. Up to three more are found "behind" the beam, containing faces of the XYZ hypercube extent. If all of the vertices of an object's bounding polyhedron are found to be in the negative half-space of one of these planes, the object is rejected. The half-space tests are greatly simplified by the nature of these planes, since all are parallel to at least one coordinate axis.

This method is fast and conservative, never rejecting an object which is actually intersected by the beam. It is also approximate, since objects will be erroneously classified as candidates when, for example, their bounding polyhedra intersect both a U and a V plane without intersecting the beam.

5.1.3 Classifying Objects with Cones

Another approach to object classification uses spheres to bound objects and cones to approximate beams. This is similar to previous uses of cones in ray tracing. Amanatides [1] described the use of cones as a method of area sampling, providing accurate and inexpensive anti-aliasing. Kirk [9] used cones as a tool to calculate proper texture filtering apertures, and to improve anti-aliasing of bump-mapped surfaces. In our context, cones prove to be very effective for classifying objects bounded by spherical extents.

To create a candidate set for a hypercube we begin by constructing a cone, specified by a unit axis vector, **W**, a spread angle, θ, and an apex, **P**, which completely contains the beam of the hypercube. If this cone does not intersect the spherical extent of an object, the object is omitted from the candidate set. The details of the cone-sphere intersection calculation are given in both [1] and [9]. We describe the construction of the cone below with the aid of function **F** in Equation 3, which defines inverse mappings of those described in section 2.2.

$$\mathbf{F}(u, v) = \begin{cases} (1, u, v) & \text{if } +X \text{ is dominant} \\ (-1, u, v) & \text{if } -X \text{ is dominant} \\ (u, 1, v) & \text{if } +Y \text{ is dominant} \\ (u, -1, v) & \text{if } -Y \text{ is dominant} \\ (u, v, 1) & \text{if } +Z \text{ is dominant} \\ (u, v, -1) & \text{if } -Z \text{ is dominant} \end{cases} \quad [3]$$

The cone axis vector, **W**, depends only on the dominant axis of the hypercube and its U and V intervals, (umin,umax) and (vmin,vmax). It is constructed by bisecting the angle between the vectors **A** and **B**, which are given by Equations 4 and 5.

$$\mathbf{A} = \mathbf{F}(\text{umin}, \text{vmax}) \quad [4]$$

$$\mathbf{B} = \mathbf{F}(\text{umax}, \text{vmin}) \quad [5]$$

To find the cone spread angle we also construct vectors **C** and **D** using Equations 6 and 7. We then compute θ as shown in Equation 8.

$$\mathbf{C} = \mathbf{F}(\text{umin}, \text{vmin}) \quad [6]$$

$$\mathbf{D} = \mathbf{F}(\text{umax}, \text{vmax}) \quad [7]$$

$$\theta = \text{MAX}(\mathbf{A}\angle\mathbf{W}, \mathbf{B}\angle\mathbf{W}, \mathbf{C}\angle\mathbf{W}, \mathbf{D}\angle\mathbf{W}) \quad [8]$$

Once the axis and spread angle are known, the apex of the cone, **P**, is determined by the 3D rectangular volume, R, defined by the XYZ intervals of the hypercube. The point **P** is located by displacing the centroid of R in the negative cone axis direction until the cone exactly contains the smallest sphere bounding R. The resulting expression for **P** is given in Equation 9, where $\mathbf{R}_0$ and $\mathbf{R}_1$ are the min and max extrema of R.

$$\mathbf{P} = \frac{\mathbf{R}_0 + \mathbf{R}_1}{2} - \mathbf{W}\frac{\| \mathbf{R}_0 - \mathbf{R}_1 \|_2}{2 \text{ SIN } \theta} \quad [9]$$

The cone is used to classify all potential candidates of the hypercube and is constructed only once per hypercube. The comparison between the cone and the object's bounding sphere is fast, making the cost of a distant miss low. This reduces the penalty of infrequent candidate list creation, the space saving measure discussed in section 5.

A linear transformation, M, applied to an object can also be used to modify its bounding sphere. By transforming the center of the sphere by M and scaling its radius by $\| M \|_2$, we obtain a new sphere which is guaranteed to contain the transformed object. The matrix 2-norm is given by $\sqrt{\rho(M^T M)}$ [11], where ρ, the spectral radius, is the largest absolute eigenvalue of a matrix. If $M^T M$ is sparse, the eigenvalue calculation is quite simple. An iterative technique like the power method can be used for the remaining cases [5].

6. Ray Classification

Every ray-environment intersection calculation begins with ray classification, which locates the hypercube containing the 5D equivalent of the ray. This entails mapping the ray into a 5D point and traversing the hypercube hierarchy, beginning with the bounding hypercube indexed by the dominant axis of the ray, until we reach the leaf containing this point. Due to lazy evaluation of the hierarchy, this traversal may have the side effect of creating a new path terminating at a sufficiently small hypercube containing the ray if such a path has not already been built on behalf of another ray. If the candidate set associated with the leaf hypercube is empty, we are guaranteed that the ray intersects nothing. Otherwise, we process this set as described in the next section.

7. Candidate Set Processing

Once ray classification has produced a set of candidate objects for a given ray, this set must be processed to determine the object which results in the closest intersection, if one exists. To optimize this search we continue to make use of object bounding volumes for coarse intersection checks. We also reject objects whose bounding volumes intersect the ray beyond a known object intersection. This can further reduce the number of ray-object intersection calculations, but still requires that the ray be tested against all bounding volumes of the candidate set.

We can remove this latter requirement by taking advantage of the fact that all rays of a given beam share the same dominant axis. By sorting the objects of the candidate sets by their minimum extents along this axis, then processing them in ascending order, we can ignore the tail of the list if we reach a candidate whose entire extent lies beyond a known intersection. This is an enormous advantage because it can drastically reduce the number of bounding volume checks in cases where the ray intersects an object near the head of the list. For example, in Figure 2 only the first two objects are tested because all subsequent objects are guaranteed to lie beyond the known intersection. By sorting the candidate sets of the six bounding hypercubes along the associated dominant axes before 5D space subdivision begins, the correct ordering can be inherited by all subsequent candidate sets with no additional overhead. Object bounding boxes provide the six keys used in sorting these initial candidate sets.

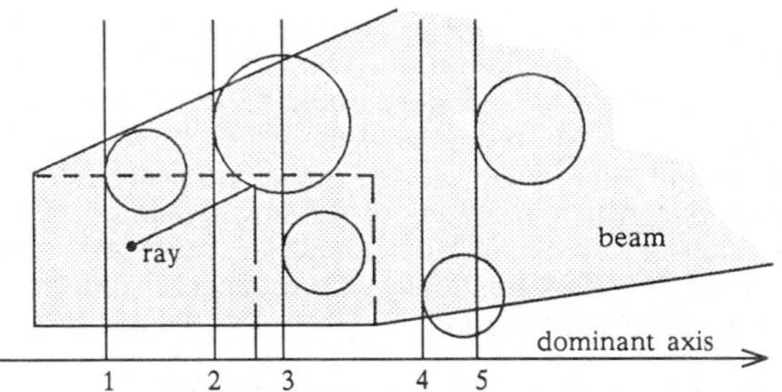

Figure 2. Sorted candidates.

8. Backface Culling

Though backface culling is a popular technique in the field of computer graphics [10], it has previously been of very limited use in ray tracing since polygons which are not in the direct line of sight can still affect the environment by means of shadows, reflections, and transparency. When creating the candidate set of a hypercube, however, it is appropriate to eliminate those polygons which are part of an opaque solid and are backfacing with respect to *every* ray of its beam. When classifying with cones, this latter criterion is met if Equation 10 is satisfied, where **N** is the front-facing normal of the polygon, **W** is the cone axis, and θ is the cone spread angle.

$$\mathbf{N} \bullet \mathbf{W} > \mathrm{SIN}\ \theta \qquad [10]$$

Using this technique, rays headed in opposite directions through the same volume of space may be tested against totally disjoint sets of polygons. By eliminating nearly half the candidates of most hypercubes, backface culling greatly accelerates both the creation and processing of candidate sets.

9. Image Coherence and Caching

Due to image coherence, two neighboring samples in image space will tend to produce very similar ray trees. This implies that successive rays of a given generation will tend to be elements of the same beam. We use this fact to great advantage by caching the most recently referenced hypercubes of each generation and checking new rays first against this cache. If a ray is contained, it is a cache hit, and the previous candidate set is returned immediately, without re-traversing the hypercube hierarchy. Otherwise, we classify the ray by traversal and update the cache with the new hypercube and candidate set. Although hierarchy traversal is very efficient, verifying that a point lies within a hypercube requires only ten comparisons, a considerable shortcut.

A related caching technique is used exclusively for shadows. Rays used for sampling light sources are special because there is no need to compute the closest intersection. It suffices to determine the existence of an opaque object between the ray origin and the intersection with the light source. If a given point in 3-space is in shadow, nearby points are likely shadowed by the same object. The shadow cache simply records the last object casting a shadow with respect to each light source and checks that object first, as part of the next shadow calculation.

10. Candidate Set Truncation

Because we cannot decide when one object occludes another based on bounding volumes alone, a candidate set must contain all objects whose bounding volumes intersect the beam. Thus, even extremely narrow beams can produce candidate sets which are large. This poses no problem for candidate set processing because sorting insures that far-away occluded objects will never be tested. This does increase storage requirements, however, by increasing the number of candidate sets which contain a given object.

We can drop far-away objects from a candidate set at the expense of a slight penalty incurred by rays which are not blocked by the nearer objects. This is done by truncating a sorted candidate set at a point where the remaining objects are outside the XYZ extent of the hypercube and marking this point with a *truncation plane* orthogonal to the dominant axis. For example, in Figure 2 this could occur just before the fourth object. We process a truncated candidate set differently only when no object intersection is found in front of the truncation plane. See Figure 3. In this case we re-position the ray to the truncation plane, re-classify, and process the new candidate set. Though this is similar to previous 3D space subdivision techniques [3][4][7], we retain the distinct advantages of sorting and backface culling within the truncated candidate sets, as well as the ability to pass rays through unobstructed regions of space with virtually no work.

We reduce the cost of occasional re-classification steps by adding a cache dimension indicating the number of times a ray has been reclassified. This allows most re-classifications to be done without traversing the hypercube hierarchy. Moreover, re-reclassifying a ray often results in a net gain by narrowing the included volume as we proceed further away from the original ray origin. See Figure 4.

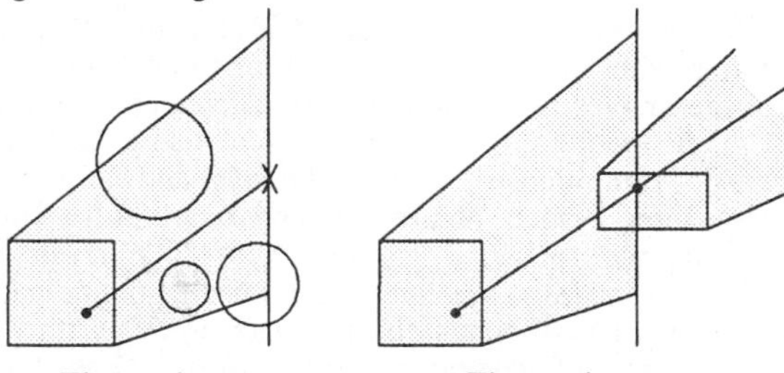
Figure 3. Set truncation.

Figure 4. Beam narrowing.

11. First-Generation Rays

First-generation rays have only two degrees of freedom, making them easy to characterize, and frequently outnumber all other rays, making them important to optimize. Many ray tracing implementations obviate the need for first-generation rays altogether by means of more conventional scan-line or depth-buffer algorithms. For extremely complex environments, however, the value of these methods diminishes, since they are forced to expend some effort on every object, even those which do not contribute to the final image. It is therefore worthwhile to examine ray tracing techniques which can perform superlinearly on these rays.

The ray classification algorithm benefits in a number of ways from the special nature of first-generation rays. Because they originate from a degenerate 3D volume, the eye point, first-generation rays can be classified using u and v alone. This increases the efficiency of ray classification by simplifying the traversal of the hypercube hierarchy, which becomes a hierarchy of 2D rectangles. Candidate set creation also benefits because the beams associated with the degenerate hypercubes are non-overlapping pyramids. Candidate sets are therefore cut in half, on average, with every subdivision. This makes it feasible to obtain smaller candidate sets, thereby speeding up candidate set processing as well. The result of these optimizations for first-generation rays is an image-space algorithm which closely resembles the 2D recursive subdivision approach introduced by Warnock [16].

12. Summary

We have described a method which accelerates ray tracing by drastically reducing the number of ray-object and ray-bounds intersection checks. This is accomplished by extending the notion of space subdivision to a 5D scheme which makes use of ray direction as well as ray origin. Rays are classified into 5D hypercubes in order to retrieve pre-sorted sets of candidate objects which are efficiently tested for intersection with each ray. The computational cost of intersecting a ray with the environment is very low because similar rays share the benefit of culling far-away objects, thereby exploiting coherence. This technique can be used to accelerate all applications which rely upon ray-environment intersections, including those which perform Monte Carlo integration [2][6]. Empirical evidence indicates that performance is closer to constant time than previous methods, especially for very complex environments.

13. Results

All test images were calculated at 512 by 512 pixel resolution with one sample per pixel for timing purposes. All of the images in the figures were calculated at 512 by 512 pixel resolution and anti-aliased using adaptive stochastic sampling with 5x5 subpixels and a cosine-squared filter kernel. Figures 5a and b are false color images of the recursive pyramid with four levels of recursion, from [8]. The hue of the false color indicates the number of ray-bounds checks which were performed in the course of computing each pixel. The scale proceeds from blue for 0 bounding volume checks to red for 50 or more. Figure 5a depicts the performance of the ray classification algorithm without the first-generation ray optimization, and Figure 5b shows how performance improves when this optimization is enabled.

The same basic model is instanced to ten levels of recursion in Figure 5c. This environment contains over four million triangles and was ray traced in 1 hour and 28 minutes (see table in Figure 6).

Figure 7 is a reflective teapot on a checkerboard, and Figure 8 shows the original five Platonic Solids and the newly discovered Teapotahedron.

Figure 9a shows the Caltech tree with leaves as they might appear rather late in the year. Figure 9b is a false color rendering with the same scale as described above. The fine yellow and red lines at the edge of the dark blue shadows in the false color image indicate shadow calculations which required processing a candidate set. The interior areas of the shadows are dark blue, indicating very few bounding volume checks, due to the shadow cache optimization.

The same tree is shown in Figure 10 rendered in false color without leaves. Even though there are fewer primitives, the number of ray-bounds checks is not much different from that of the tree with leaves. This is due to the difficulty of accurately classifying long arbitrarily oriented cylinders.

Figure 11a is a true color image of a grove of 64 instanced trees with leaves. This environment contains 477,121 objects and was ray traced in 4 hours and 53 minutes. Figure 11b is a false color rendering of the grove of trees.

We wish to compare the performance of our algorithm with that of previous methods. Due to the generosity of Tim Kay at Caltech, we were able to run benchmarks using the same databases used in [8]. Since we did not have access to a Vax 11/780 for our benchmarks, we chose an Apollo DN570, which has roughly the same level of performance. Kay and Kajiya compared the performance of their program on the recursive pyramid of Figure 9 with the performance reported by Glassner [4]. Glassner's program took approximately 8700 Vax 11/780 seconds to render the scene, while Kay's program took approximately 2706 seconds, which translates roughly to a factor of 2.6 improvement after accounting for differences in the scene. Our program took approximately 639 seconds on an Apollo DN570, representing a further factor of 4.2 improvement.

Acknowledgements

We would like to thank Rick Speer, both for organizing an informal ray tracing discussion group at the 86 SIGGRAPH conference, and for directing the discussion toward coherence and directional data structures. Pat Hanrahan deserves credit for supplying the insight that directional classification of rays need not be tied to objects. Thanks to Christian Bremser, John Francis, Olin Lathrop, Jim Michener, Semyon Nisenzon, Cary Scofield, and Douglas Voorhies for their diligent critical reading of early drafts of the paper. Special thanks to Olin Lathrop and John Francis for help in defining and implementing the "ray tracing kernel", the testbed used for this work, and to Jim Michener for his many helpful technical comments. Resounding applause to Tim Kay for making his pyramid and tree databases available. Last but by no means least, thanks to Apollo Computer and particularly to Christian Bremser and Douglas Voorhies for making time available to perform this work.

References

[1] Amanatides, John., "Ray Tracing with Cones," Computer Graphics, 18(3), July 1984, pp. 129–135.

[2] Cook, Robert L., Thomas Porter, and Loren Carpenter., "Distributed Ray Tracing," Computer Graphics 18(3), July 1984, pp. 137–145.

[3] Fujimoto, Akira,, and Kansei Iwata., "Accelerated Ray Tracing," Proceedings of Computer Graphics Tokyo '85, April 1985.

[4] Glassner, Andrew S., "Space Subdivision for Fast Ray Tracing," IEEE Computer Graphics and Applications, 4(10), October, 1984, pp. 15–22.

[5] Johnson, Lee W., and Riess, Dean R., "Numerical Analysis," Addison-Wesley, 1977.

[6] Kajiya, James T., "The Rendering Equation," Computer Graphics 20(4), August 1986, pp. 143–150.

[7] Kaplan, Michael R., "Space Tracing: A Constant Time Ray Tracer," ACM SIGGRAPH '85 Course Notes 11, July 22–26, 1985.

[8] Kay, Timothy L. and James Kajiya., "Ray Tracing Complex Scenes," Computer Graphics, 20(4), August 1986, pp. 269–278.

[9] Kirk, David B., "The Simulation of Natural Features using Cone Tracing," Advanced Computer Graphics (Proceedings of Computer Graphics Tokyo '86), April 1986, pp. 129–144.

[10] Newman, William M., and Robert F. Sproull., "Principles of Interactive Computer Graphics," 1st edition, McGraw-Hill, New York, 1973.

[11] Ortega, James M., "Numerical Analysis, A Second Course," Academic Press, New York, 1972.

[12] Preparata, Franco P., and Michael I. Shamos., "Computational Geometry, an Introduction," Springer-Verlag, New York, 1985.

[13] Press, William H., Brian P. Flannery, Saul A. Teukolsky, William T. Vetterling., "Numerical Recipes," Cambridge University Press, Cambridge, 1986.

[14] Rubin, Steve, and Turner Whitted., "A Three-Dimensional Representation for Fast Rendering of Complex Scenes," Computer Graphics 14(3), July 1980, pp. 110–116.

[15] Speer, L. Richard, Tony D. DeRose, and Brian A. Barsky., "A Theoretical and Empirical Analysis of Coherent Ray Tracing," Computer-Generated Images (Proceedings of Graphics Interface '85), May 27–31, 1985, pp. 11–25.

[16] Warnock, John E., "A Hidden-Surface Algorithm for Computer Generated Half-tone Pictures,", Ph.D. Dissertation, University of Utah, TR 4-15, 1969.

[17] Weghorst, Hank, Gary Hooper, and Donald Greenberg., "Improved Computational Methods for Ray Tracing," ACM Transactions on Graphics, 3(1), January 1984, pp. 52–69.

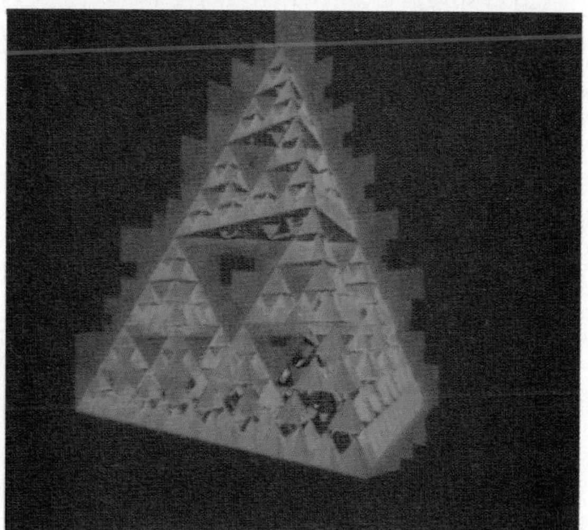

Figure 6: Run–time Statistics

All pixel, ray, and classify counts are in thousands

	Pyramid **4	Pyramid **10	Tree Branches	Tree Leaves	Grove 64 Trees	Teapot	Platonic Solids
Objects	1024	4.2E6	1272	7455	477,121	1824	1405
Pixels	262	262	262	262	262	262	262
Shading Rays	262	262	262	262	262	262	262
Shadow Rays	37	28	133	150	128	187	224
Total Rays	299	290	395	412	390	534	515
Rays that hit	43	30	149	191	213	206	240
Beam/Object Classifies	10.50	117.06	16.01	17.02	46.46	47.71	10.41
Object Intersections	188	288	989	716	1884	523	4896
CPU Time, DN570 sec.	639	5335	2194	3230	17607	3100	2474
(sec/ray)	0.002	0.018	0.006	0.008	0.045	0.006	0.008
(sec/ray that hit)	0.015	0.178	0.015	0.017	0.083	0.015	0.010

Figure 7. Reflective Teapot

Figure 8. Platonic Solids

Figure 9a. Autumn Tree

Figure 9b. False Color Tree with Leaves

Figure 10. Leafless Tree

Figure 11a. Grove of Trees

Figure 11b. False Color Grove of Trees

Chapter 6: Continuous Algorithms

Introduction

The ray-tracing, Z-buffer, and painter's algorithms provide image data only at discrete points, and scan-line algorithms provide data only along discrete scan lines. In contrast, continuous algorithms determine the regions of the image in which a single surface is visible. If the objects are modeled by polygons, these visible regions will also be polygons and can be specified to the floating-point precision of the computer. This has several benefits.

First, most images have area coherence. That is, if a polygon is visible at a pixel, the same polygon is likely to be visible at an adjacent pixel. By computing the visible regions explicitly, we take full advantage of this area coherence. Thus, the visible-surface computation time varies with the complexity of the subdivision of the image area into visible regions and is independent of the final output resolution.

Second, a "polygons in, polygons out" visible-surface algorithm can also be used for shadows, as described in the papers by Atherton and Weiler [Weil77, Athe78]. The algorithm is applied from the point of view of each light source. Visible regions are the ones directly illuminated by the light source, and hidden regions are in shadow. The shadow polygons can be projected back into the three-dimensional model as detail polygons, with illumination modified if the polygon was determined to be in shadow.

Third, a hidden-line view suitable for a vector display, can be generated by drawing the polygonal outlines of the visible regions.

Finally, the exact subdivision of the image into visible regions is useful for antialiasing. If the shading on these regions is specified as a function of x and y, the image is determined everywhere, and the integrals needed for antialiasing can be evaluated accurately.

Warnock [Warn69] devised an early algorithm by using area coherence, based on recursive subdivision of the image area into quarters. At each stage, the polygons overlapping the current area are compared to see if there is a "blocking" polygon that surrounds the area and is in front of all other polygons, or if only a single polygon overlaps the area. In these simple cases, the single visible polygon can be rendered directly into the area. Otherwise, the area is divided into quarters and each quarter is treated recursively. It is not necessary to test all the input polygons for overlap during the recursion since only polygons that overlap an area can overlap any of its quarters, and polygons that surround an area surround each quarter. Warnock proposed terminating the recursion when the current area reached the size of a single pixel and using a default color if it were still not a simple case. This termination condition means that the visible regions are not specified to floating-point accuracy. For more accurate antialiasing, it is useful to continue the recursion until the area is some fraction of a pixel.

Another early area-based algorithm was devised by Knowlton and Cherry [Know77] for chemical models consisting of spheres and cylinders. The visible regions from such a model will be bounded by pieces of circles, straight lines, and conic-section curves (usually ellipses). Knowlton and Cherry approximated the conic sections by circles so that the visible regions were bounded by line segments and circular arcs. This simple description makes it practical to modify a visible region iteratively as the occlusion or intersection with each object is considered in turn.

The paper by Weiler and Atherton [Weil77] (included in this chapter) presents a true "polygon in—polygon out" algorithm. This algorithm recursively divides the image area using the polygon boundaries from the model instead of using an array of squares or rectangles as Warnock did. Thus superfluous vertical and horizontal edges are not introduced. An initial clipping polygon is chosen (preferably one close to the viewer) and the image area is divided into two regions, one inside and one outside this polygon. All other polygons are clipped into two lists, one for each region. If either region is covered by a single blocking polygon, it becomes one of the output visible regions. Otherwise, another clipping polygon is chosen, and the region is subdivided recursively. Even if all input polygons are convex, they may become concave or have holes chopped into them during the clipping process, so a polygon clipper was developed, which could handle concave polygons with holes.

Since each polygon is used at most once as a clipping polygon, the recursion must terminate and will thus determine all the visible regions with floating-point precision. This argument for termination assumes that if a collection of clipped polygons all project onto the same region, one of them must be in front. This assumption is only valid if the polygons do not intersect, which is a restriction on the input to this algorithm.

Although the cost of this visible region determination is independent of the image resolution, it grows as n^2, where n is the number of polygons in the input, because each polygon must be compared to or used to clip every other polygon. Weiler and Atherton suggest ameliorating this n^2 growth by dividing the image area into rectangular windows, clipping each polygon into every window that it overlaps, and processing each window separately. In his antialiasing algorithm, Catmull [Catm78] carries this to an extreme, using windows the size of a single pixel. This may be somewhat inefficient, since moderate sized polygons will overlap many windows. On the other hand, if a window is small, it is more likely to be covered by a single blocking polygon and require no further subdivision. Franklin [Fran80] (included in this chapter) has analyzed the tradeoff between these two effects and found an optimal size for the windows based on the number and size of the input polygons. He shows that if the input polygons are randomly distributed in space, his choice of window size will result in an expected computation time, which is linear in the number of input edges. This claimed performance has been disputed by people who doubt that in polygonal models in actual use the polygons will ever be appropriately random. For example, surfaces are often modeled from many small adjacent polygons, and adjacent polygons are correlated, not random. However, in this case, several polygons on a frontmost surface may join together in a network to cover a window, and Franklin's use of blocking polygons could be generalized to blocking networks. This idea is essentially the "head sort" of Catmull [Catm84].

Another family of area-based algorithms are the scan-plane-sweep algorithms. As in the scan-line algorithms, a horizontal plane is scanned from the top to the bottom of the image, intersecting the visible regions in visible segments. However, instead of stopping at each output scan line, the scan plane stops only at special positions, called "events," where the topological arrangement of the visible segments could change. Assuming that the input polygons do not intersect, events can occur only at vertices or at points where two projected edges cross. A list of potential next events is maintained, and the scan plane stops at the closest one. For efficiency, a list of edges, which intersect the scan plane, is also maintained, sorted from left to right. Then to find the next crossing event for an edge, it need only be intersected with its left or right neighbors. Hamlin and Gear [Haml77] propose a table-based method for adjusting the topology of the visible segments (or equivalently, the list of visible edges) as each event is passed. For example, if a "middle edge" (an edge common to two polygons with otherwise disjoint projections) crosses in front of another edge, no change of visibility occurs, but if it crosses behind a non-middle edge, a change can occur.

The implementation of Hamlin and Gear gives only the visible edges. Sechrest and Greenberg [Sech81] and Séquin and Wensley [Sequ85] both give methods of connecting these edges to form the polygons bounding the visible regions.

For smooth surfaces approximated by a network of polygons, there is another type of coherence since a middle edge cannot change the visibility of other edges, as pointed out above. Hornung [Horn81] presents an algorithm that first considers only the non-middle edges and determines the visible regions of the whole surface network. These regions are then subdivided by the middle edges into the visible regions of the individual polygons. This increases efficiency because there are many fewer edges involved in the initial surface-visibility step.

When visible polygons are returned at the floating-point precision of the machine, this may still not be sufficient to calculate their topology correctly. One method of solving this problem is to convert all input to exact rational numbers, using multiple-word numerators and denominators, and to carry out all calculations with exact rational arithmetic. In principle, such exact methods can be extended to visibility calculations for algebraic surfaces, by using techniques such as those in [Arno83].

In the field becoming known as "computational geometry" [Mehl84, Prep85], researchers are trying to solve geometrical problems with minimal computer time and memory space by using sophisticated data structures, such as balanced binary trees, for the geometric sorting. For the visibility problems discussed here, the resources needed are strongly dependent on the arrangement of the input polygons, as mentioned above in connection with Franklin's paper [Fran80].

Nurmi [Nurm85] has shown that the scan-plane-sweep algorithm can be implemented by using time and space proportional to $(n + k) \log n$, where n is the number of edges in the input data and k is the number of edge intersections in the picture plane. In the worst case example, the number k of intersections can be proportional to n^2, and since all these intersections are visible, n^2 is also the complexity of the output. McKenna [McKe87] has presented a similar algorithm, which takes time and space proportional to n^2 and is, therefore, optimal for the worst case.

HIDDEN SURFACE REMOVAL USING POLYGON AREA SORTING

by

Kevin Weiler and Peter Atherton

Program of Computer Graphics

Cornell University

Ithaca, New York 14853

ABSTRACT

A polygon hidden surface and hidden line removal algorithm is presented. The algorithm recursively subdivides the image into polygon shaped windows until the depth order within the window is found. Accuracy of the input data is preserved.

The approach is based on a two-dimensional polygon clipper which is sufficiently general to clip a concave polygon with holes to the borders of a concave polygon with holes.

A major advantage of the algorithm is that the polygon form of the output is the same as the polygon form of the input. This allows entering previously calculated images to the system for further processing. Shadow casting may then be performed by first producing a hidden surface removed view from the vantage point of the light source and then resubmitting these tagged polygons for hidden surface removal from the position of the observer. Planar surface detail also becomes easy to represent without increasing the complexity of the hidden surface problem. Translucency is also possible.

Calculation times are primarily related to the visible complexity of the final image, but can range from a linear to an exponential relationship with the number of input polygons depending on the particular environment portrayed. To avoid excessive computation time, the implementation uses a screen area subdivision preprocessor to create several windows, each containing a specified number of polygons. The hidden surface algorithm is applied to each of these windows separately. This technique avoids the difficulties of subdividing by screen area down to the screen resolution level while maintaining the advantages of the polygon area sort method.

COMPUTING REVIEWS CLASSIFICATION: 3.2, 4.9, 4.40, 4.41

KEYWORDS: Hidden Surface Removal, Hidden Line Removal, Polygon Clipping, Polygon Area Sorting, Shadowing, Graphics

INTRODUCTION

A new method for the computation of visible surfaces for environments composed of polygons is presented. The output of the method is in the form of polygons, making it useful in a variety of situations including the usual display applications. The primary components of the method consist of a generalized algorithm for polygon clipping and a hidden surface removal algorithm. The polygon clipper is sufficiently general to clip a concave polygon with holes to the area of a concave polygon with holes. The hidden surface algorithm operates on polygon input which has already been transformed and clipped to the final viewing space. The X and Y axis of this viewing space are thus parallel to the display surface and the Z axis is parallel to the line of sight.

Many visible surface algorithms have been developed, each with unique characteristics and capabilities. A survey presented by Sutherland et al [11] provides a method of categorization as well as a statistical comparison of many of the polygon based algorithms.

Their classification divides the algorithms into three types: object space, image space and list-priority algorithms. The "object space" methods perform the hidden surface computations for potentially visible polygons within the environment to an arbitrary precision usually limited only by machine precision. The "image space" methods are performed to less resolution and determine what is visible within a prescribed area on the output display, usually a raster dot. The "list-priority" algorithms work partially in each of these two domains.

The performance of "object space" methods (Roberts [8], Appel [1], Galimberti [4]) and "list-priority" methods (Newell, Newell and Sancha [7], Schumacher [9]) is dependent on the complexity of the environment. Since all of these algorithms make comparisons between items (objects, polygons, edges), the number of sorting steps required can rise exponentially with the number of input items. However, the computational time is independent of the resolution or size of the image.

In contrast, the "image-space" algorithms make polygon to screen area comparisons (Warnock [12], Watkins [13], Bouknight [3], and depth map or Z-buffer algorithms). Therefore, the number of sorting steps is possibly linear with the number of input polygons, but can vary exponentially with the resolution required.

The algorithm presented qualifies as an object space algorithm since all of its calculations are performed to arbitrary precision. The sorting methods used include a preliminary partial depth sort, an x-y polygon sort, and a conclusive depth sort which may involve recursive subdivision of the original area.

The algorithm probably most closely resembles the Warnock (image space) algorithm in its method of operation. The major difference between them is that the Warnock algorithm performs the x-y sort by screen area, while the new algorithm does the x-y sort by polygon area. Polygon area coherence across the surface of the polygon is preserved as much as possible thereby reducing the number of lateral sorts required. Both algorithms use the techniques of recursive subdivision when necessary. The Warnock algorithm will subdivide until a solution or a preset resolution level has been reached. The new algorithm continues to subdivide only until the proper depth order has been established.

Computation times of the new algorithm vary with both environmental complexity and the visible complexity of the image, and partially depend on the validity of the initial depth sort. For an environment consisting of a number of polygons entirely obscured by a single forward polygon, with a correct initial depth sort, the number of lateral comparisons required is linearly related to the number of input polygons. For environments where every polygon may be partially obscured, but is visible as one piece, the number of lateral comparisons is related to one half the square of the number of input polygons. If few polygons are entirely obscured and many are split into several visible pieces, the relationship to the number of input polygons can be worse than n^2. In practice, the relationship is usually better. Additions to the algorithm as described later may be used to limit the effects of exponential growth rates.

The characteristics of the algorithm allow several options not always available in existing approaches. Of particular importance is the capability for generating perspective images with shadows. Translucency and surface detailing are also possible.

Figure 1. Dice with shadows and surface detail.

Because the output of the algorithm is in the form of polygons as opposed to a raster format, and because the output data does not overlay itself on the image plane, the algorithm effectively solves for hidden lines as well as hidden surfaces. Additional line visibility information can also be stored to enhance CRT displays by eliminating double brightness lines.

HIDDEN SURFACE ALGORITHM

In general, the algorithm selects a polygon shaped area in the x-y plane from the vantage point of the observer and solves the hidden surface problem in that area completely before going on to any other area. This area may itself be subdivided recursively if there is an error in the initial depth sort. Output from the algorithm never overlaps on the x-y plane since each visible area has had all polygons behind it removed. The algorithm proceeds from front to back across the transformed object space, producing portions of the final image along the way and temporarily reversing direction only when an initial depth sort error is detected.

The hidden surface algorithm involves four steps:

a) a preliminary rough depth sort,

b) an x-y polygon area sort to the area of the currently most forward polygon,

c) a depth sort by removal of polygons behind the current forward polygon, and

d) a conclusive depth sort by recursive subdivision when necessary.

The initial sorting step attempts to place the list of input polygons into a rough depth priority order, from those closest to the observer to those furthest away. Any reasonable criterion for a sorting key, such as ordering on the nearest Z value of each polygon, is acceptable. This step is not mandatory but greatly increases the efficiency of the algorithm in later stages. The initial depth sorting operation is only performed once at the beginning of processing and is not repeated.

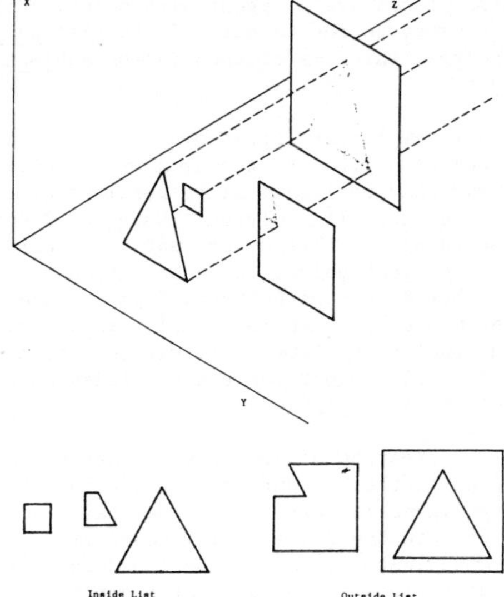

Figure 2. Example of an X-Y clip of a polygon environment by the triangle (leftmost). Two output lists are generated. One list consists of polygons inside the clipping volume created by the X-Y clip to the triangle. The other list consists of polygons outside the clipping volume. Note that non-convex polygons and polygons with holes can be generated by the clipping process.

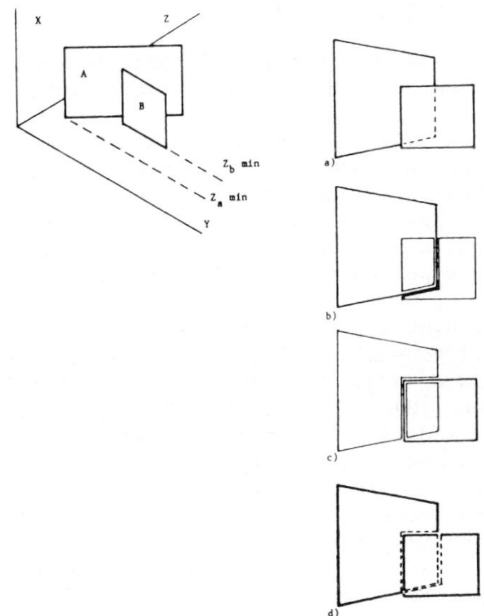

Figure 3. Recursive subdivision caused by initial depth sort error. Polygon A is in front of polygon B by Z-minimum sort but B obscures A.
a) View of scene from observer position.
b) Clip by polygon A. Inside piece of B in front - recursion is performed.
c) Clip of inside list by polygon B, piece of A behind B is removed.
d) Final display.

The first polygon on the sorted input list is then used to clip the remainder of the list into new lists of polygons inside and outside of the clip polygon (Figure 2). In essence, this x-y clipping subdivision is equivalent to lateral area sorting.

The process now examines the inside list and removes any polygons located behind the current clip polygon since they are hidden from view.

Next, if any remaining polygons on the inside list are located in front of the clip polygon, an error in the initial depth sort has been discovered and the algorithm recursively subdivides the region of interest by repeating the clipping process with the offending polygon as the clip polygon and the current inside list as the input list (Figure 3). Finally, when the recursive subdivision has been completed, the inside list is displayed and the algorithm repeats the entire process using the outside list as input. The process is continued until the outside list is exhausted.

It is important to note that the clip polygon actually used as the clipping template is a copy of the original polygon rather than several pieces of its remainder. While keeping a copy of the original increases the storage requirements, the number of clipping edges and the number of clips to perform can be minimized. In this way computation time can be substantially reduced.

After obscured polygons have been removed and before recursive subdivision, a check must be made for the case of cyclic overlap where a single polygon lies both in front of and behind a polygon (Figure 4a). A stack is kept of polygon names which have been used as clipping polygons for this screen area, but have not finished processing because of recursive subdivision. If the algorithm is ready to make a recursive subdivision because a polygon is in front of the current clip polygon, a check is made to see if the name of that polygon is on the stack. If it is, a case of cyclic overlap exists and no additional recursion is necessary since all material behind that polygon has already been removed. This cyclic overlap condition occurs as a result of clipping to the original copy of polygons instead of their remainders. The reduction in the number of clips required outweighs the disadvantage of the simple check required for cyclic overlap. Note that another case of cyclic overlap involving several polygons is implicitly handled by the algorithm (Figure 4b).

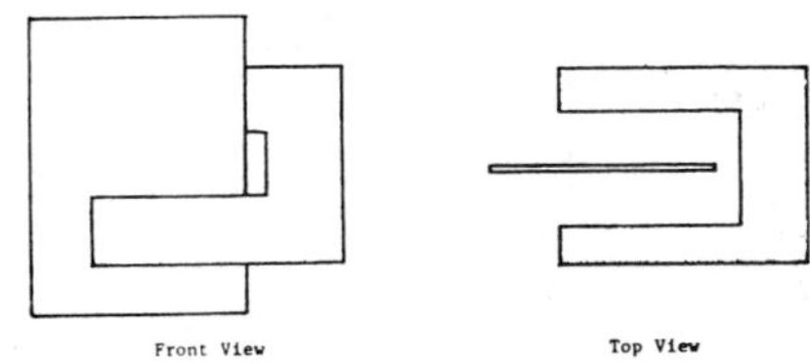

Figure 4a. Cyclic overlap with single polygon.

Figure 4b. Cyclic overlap with several polygons.

POLYGON CLIPPING ALGORITHM

Two dimensional polygon clipping is central to the hidden surface removal approach presented.

If only convex polygons were allowed in a scene, clipping a scene by the convex areas of the polygons could quickly yield non-convex areas and holes (Figure 2). Thus even for a restricted environment, a polygon clipper capable of handling concave polygons with holes is necessary.

A clipping algorithm capable of clipping concave polygons with holes to the inside portion of a convex area has been described by Sutherland and Hodgman [10]. The algorithm has the merit of simplicity and is particularly useful for screen subdivision and viewbox clipping. A modified version of this algorithm would clip polygons to a plane and create output polygons on each side of the clipping plane. This version could be used to clip to the borders of a convex polygon yielding intact inside and outside polygons if the planar clip was applied against each edge of the convex clipping polygon. The entire exterior space would then be clipped by infinite planes; however, the effects of each border clip would not be localized and many new exterior polygons would be created. Since this is undesirable in a situation where computational complexity may increase greatly with the number of polygons, another method of clipping has been developed which minimizes the number of polygons created during the clipping process (Figure 5) [14].

The polygon clipper presented is a generalized x-y polygon clipper which is capable of clipping a concave polygon with holes to the borders of concave polygons with holes. Clipping is performed to the borders of the <u>clip polygon</u>. The polygon which is clipped is the <u>subject polygon</u>.

Any new borders created by the clipping of the subject polygon to the area of the clip polygon need only be identical to portions of the borders of the clip polygon. Using this concept, no new edges not already present in either the clip or subject polygon need be introduced and the number of output polygons from the process can be minimized. While the clip is a two-dimensional clip, depth information can be preserved in all output for use by hidden surface calculations.

The creation of new polygons due to intersections of the boundaries of the clip and subject polygons is performed by partial transversals of both boundaries. If the outside borders of the subject polygon are followed in a clockwise direction, the borders of the newly clipped output polygons can be found by making a right turn at each place the two polygons intersect. The process continues until the starting point is arrived at again (Figure 6). The inner or hole borders of the subject polygon must be followed in a counter-clockwise manner in order to use this right turn rule. Note that the borders of the clip polygon used to complete the new polygons must be traversed twice, once in each direction.

Additional techniques are necessary to deal with cases where the borders of the clip polygon do not intersect with borders of the subject polygon but lie completely inside the area of the subject polygon.

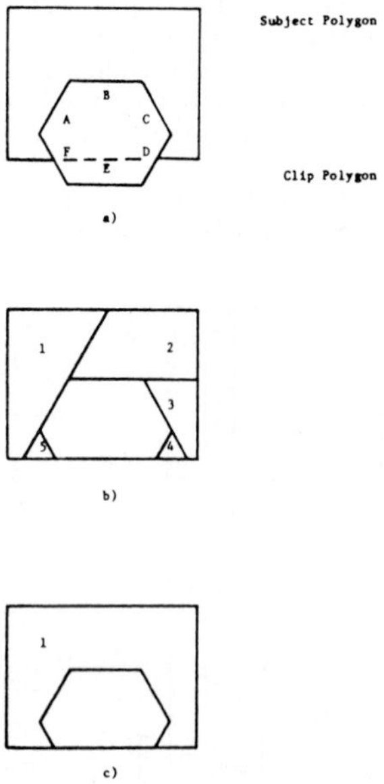

Figure 5. Results of clipping a subject polygon (square) by a clip polygon (hexagon) using different clipping algorithms
a) Subject polygon and clip polygon
b) Result of clipping with infinite planes starting clockwise with edge A
c) Result of general polygon clipper

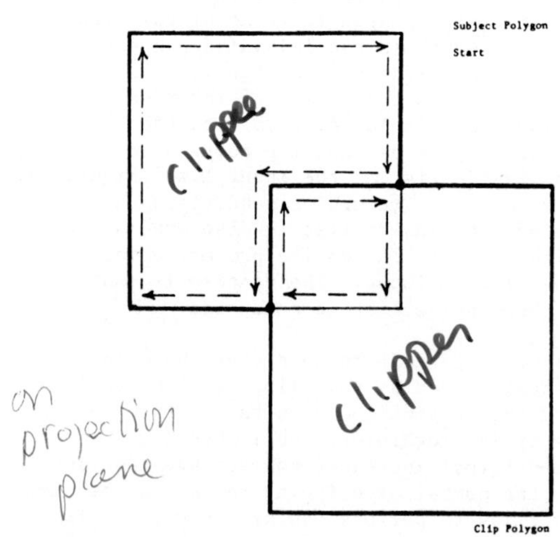

Figure 6. Clipped output polygons caused by intersecting contours can be traced out by following the borders of the subject polygon in a clockwise manner and making a right turn at every intersection of the contours. Note that the borders of the clip polygon are traversed twice in order to form the two output polygons.

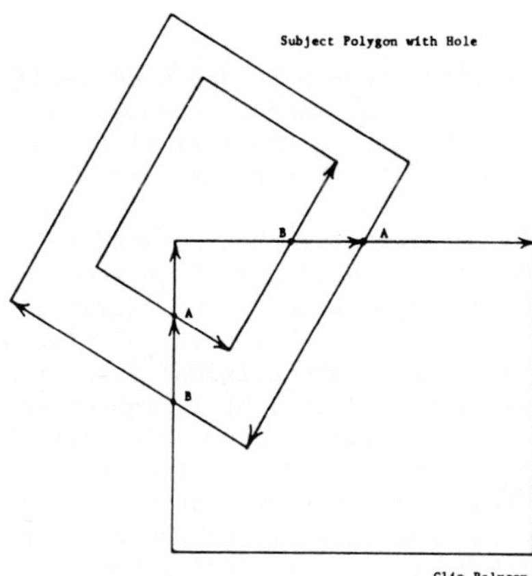

Figure 7. The two types of intersections are based on the directionality of the contours. Note that outside contours are clockwise and holes are counterclockwise.
a) Clip polygon border passes to the left (outside) of the subject polygon border.
b) Clip polygon border passes to the right (inside) of the subject polygon border. Note that types alternate along any contour.

A more detailed description of the clipper follows:

A polygon is defined as an area enclosed by a series of edges consisting of straight lines. These edges may touch upon one another at single non-contiguous points. There are no intrinsic limits as to the number of edges or holes a polygon may have. Contours are the edges or boundaries of a polygon. The term main contour refers to the exterior boundaries of a polygon, while hole contour refers to the interior boundaries of a polygon.

The algorithm represents a polygon as a circular list of vertices, one list for the main contour and one list for each of the holes. The vertices of the main contour are linked in clockwise order and the holes in counter-clockwise order. Using this order, as one follows along the chain of vertices of a polygon, the outside is always to the left while the interior of the polygon is always to the right (Figure 7).

The clip polygon remains the same after the clipping process as before. The subject polygon may be fragmented by the clipping process. The results of the clipping process are two lists of polygons, one of polygons inside the clip polygon area and one of polygons outside the clip polygon (Figure 2). The clipping process is as follows:

1. The borders of the two polygons are compared for intersections. At each intersection a new false vertex is added into the contour chain of each of the two polygons. The new vertices are tagged to indicate they are intersection vertices. A link is established between each pair of new vertices, permitting travel between two polygons wherever they intersect on the x-y plane. If care is taken in placement of intersections where the subject and clip polygon contours are identical in the x-y plane, no degenerate polygons will be produced by the clipping process.

2. Contours which have no intersections are now processed. Each contour of the subject polygon which has no intersections is placed on one of two holding lists. One holding list is for contours inside of the clip polygon; the other is for contours outside of it. Clip polygon contours outside of the subject polygon are ignored. Clip polygon contours inside of the subject polygon in effect cut a hole in the subject polygon, producing two new contours. In this case two copies of the clip polygon contour are made (one in reverse order); one copy is placed on each of the holding lists.

3. Two lists of intersection vertices found on all of the subject polygon contours are formed. The first list contains only those intersections where the clip polygon border passes to the outside of the subject polygon (from the point of view of the subject polygon this occurs whenever the clip polygon passes to the left) (Figure 7). The second list contains those intersections where the clip polygon border passes to the inside (to the right). These two types of intersections will be found to alternate along any given contour and the number of intersections will always be even. This means only one determination of intersection type is necessary per contour.

4. The actual clipping is now performed (Figure 8):

a) An intersection vertex is removed from the first intersection list to be used as a starting point. If the list is exhausted, the clipping is complete; Go to step 5.

b) Follow along the subject polygon vertex chain until the next intersection is reached.

c) Jump to the clip polygon.

d) Copy the chain of polygon vertices until the next intersection vertex is reached.

e) Jump back to the subject polygon.

f) Repeat steps "b" to "e" until the starting point has been reached. At this point the contour of a new inside polygon has just been closed.

The outside polygons can be created by a second pass if the contour vertex chain is double-linked (bi-directional). This is accomplished by starting at intersection vertices from the second intersection vertex list and following the reverse links during traversal of the clip polygon. Otherwise the contours of the outside polygons must be closed during the first pass. This can be done by making a second copy of the vertex chain during the clip polygon traversal (step 4d) in reverse order and attaching its "loose" ends to the unused intersection points at its begin and end locations. A second pass is still needed to find out where these outside contours are. All polygons created are placed on the proper holding lists.

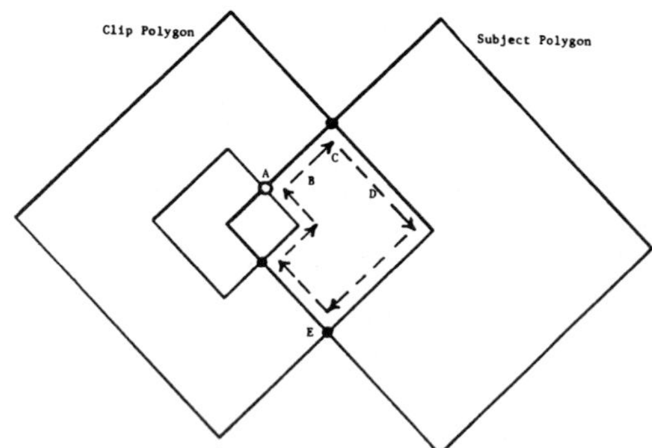

Figure 8. Example of creation of an inside polygon during the clipping process.
a) Intersection vertex starting point of subject polygon
b) Follow subject polygon until next vertex intersection
c) Jump to clip polygon
d) Copy chain of clip polygon vertices
e) Jump back to the subject polygon

5. All holes on the holding lists are attached to the proper main contours. There are several methods of determining which polygons are hole contours. The conceptually simplest method is to test directionality of the contours since main contours will always be clockwise and hole contours will always be counterclockwise. A more efficient method is based on using the highest of a precedence of types of intersections located on a contour. The types used in this precedence are related to the cause of the intersection, such as a main contour intersecting a hole contour, a hole contour intersecting a hole contour, etc. The clipping process is now complete.

EXTENSIONS

Several extensions to the hidden surface algorithm allow greater versatility and efficiency. Of those described below, surface detail, shadowing, and screen subdivision have been implemented.

Surface Detail

Polygons that describe information such as color differences or designs within the boundaries of a planar polygon are referred to here as surface detail. Since they do not affect the boundaries of the polygon to which they belong, they cannot affect hidden surface calculation and should not be included in it. Instead, whenever a polygon is output from the hidden surface computations, the surface detail belonging to the original source of that polygon is clipped to the area of the output polygon. Any of the surface detail within the bounds of the output polygon is then output at this time. This technique can greatly simplify the hidden surface problem for those situations in which surface detail might have otherwise been specified as regular polygons involved in the hidden surface removal process.

Shadowing

The polygon area sort approach lends itself to the generation of shadows because the output of the algorithm is in the form of polygons which are suitable for further processing.

Shadow creation is then reduced to the problem of producing a hidden surface removed view of a scene from the position of the light source. Visible polygons from this point of view are transformed back to the original space and are treated as surface detail of a lighter shade on their source polygons. After this initial shadowing, a normal hidden surface removed view can be taken from any viewpoint to create a correctly shadowed scene. Multiple light sources may be represented using the same process.

Since full machine precision of the output is possible, this particular technique shows promise of being useful not only for display purposes, but also for engineering applications such as energy analyses related to solar heat gain [2].

Translucent Polygons

Translucent polygons can be represented with a slight modification of the depth culling portion of the algorithm. When a translucent polygon becomes the clip polygon, polygons which are behind it should not be removed, but instead tagged and identified as being obscured by that particular translucent polygon. When a polygon is obscured by several translucent polygons, the effect can be accumulated. Since display output is not made for a given area until after the hidden surface removal process for that area is complete, images can be correctly rendered. Partial shadows and shades cast by translucent planes would be handled by the shadowing process in the same manner as normal shadows.

Screen Subdivision

Reducing the exponential rate of the number of sorting steps required for visible surface computation is highly desirable. Some mechanism for dealing with large numbers of polygons or polygons with large numbers of edges which exceed the capacity of main storage should also be provided. The benefits of the polygon area sort approach should be maintained.

By taking the approach of a Warnock style screen area subdivision, the image can be divided into areas each containing a specified maximum number of polygons. Each of these areas can then be processed by the hidden surface removal system separately. This method keeps the number of polygons within storage capacities, while effectively reducing the number of lateral sorting steps to an almost linear relationship with the number of polygons. This is accomplished by reducing the range of the exponential growth factors of the hidden surface removal to the maximum number of polygons allowed within each screen subdivision. The overall number of lateral sorting steps for hidden surface removal is then almost linear to the number of polygons. The screen subdivision process itself follows an n log n growth rate.

Note that it is possible that the polygons can also be subdivided along the Z axis if their depth exceeds the specified limit. An example would be a large number of screen-sized polygons parallel to the display. Two methods can be used to deal with this case.

The first solution, valuable only for hidden surface removal, uses a technique similar to the frame buffer overlay technique of Newell, et al [7]. The image is subdivided along the Z axis into several "boxes" of space containing a specific number of polygons. The boxes are ordered from back to front and each box is separately solved. The results are output to a frame buffer in order, with the results from each succeeding box overlaying previous results. This technique, while sufficient for most display purposes and quicker than the one presented in the next paragraph, loses some of the advantages of the polygon area sort algorithm and cannot produce fully shadowed images or hidden line removed images.

A more general solution is to divide the scene by Z subdivisions into boxes as before. The farthest box is then solved, and the solution of this last box is treated as surface detail on the plane of a distant polygon parallel to the screen and with the same x-y limits as the box (such surface detail, while associated with the "backdrop" plane for hidden surface removal, can still maintain all depth information for three dimensional output)(Figure 9). This newly created polygon is then added to the next to last box and that box is solved. The process repeats until all of the boxes have been solved. The techniques of surface detail and of consolidation (described later) are used here to reduce the numbers of polygons involved in the hidden surface problem. This solution has the same effect as the first method visually, but is different in that no external overlay techniques are used in order that the solution be entirely expressed in terms of polygons. This difference in the two solutions illustrates one of the primary differences between the Newell, et al, approach and the hidden surface algorithm presented here.

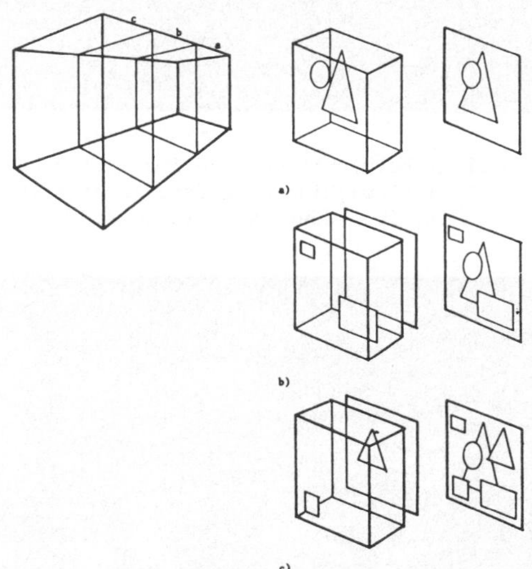

Figure 9. Z subdivision example. The space is divided into 3 "boxes" by Z subdivision to reduce the number of polygons to be solved in the visible surface problem at any one time. The last box (a) is solved and the solution is expressed as a single "backdrop" plane with surface detail. This new plane is solved together with the next box (b) to produce a new backdrop plane, and so on, until the entire space has been solved.

Consolidation

While the hidden surface algorithm takes advantage of polygon area coherence, even greater gains can be achieved by taking advantage of object coherence where several related polygons obscure objects behind them [11]. An example is the case where solid objects are represented as a series of polygons.

Consolidation can be accomplished by creating a new silhouette polygon exactly encompassing all the polygons of the group. Individual component polygons can then be represented as surface detail of the new polygon (Figure 10). This technique is particularly valuable for convex polyhedra, where it is known that the component polygons do not overlap each other after removal of the backward facing polygons.

The advantage of consolidation is that one polygon replaces several polygons in the hidden surface computations, thus reducing the number of polygon clips and depth tests required. Furthermore, since the number of sorting steps required is related to the number of polygons, any method of reducing the number of polygons

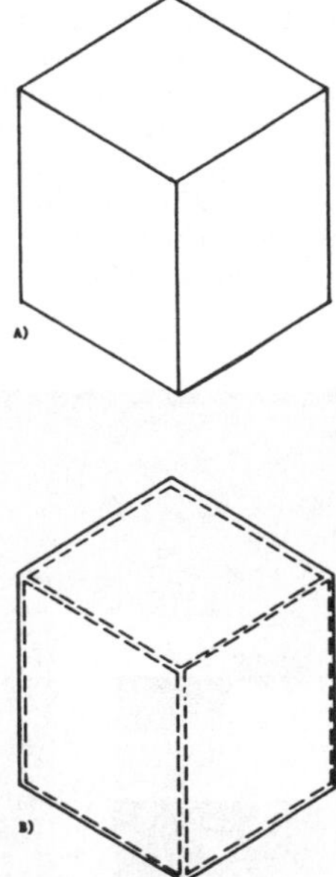

Figure 10. Consolidation of 3 polygons representing a cube (a) into a single polygon with 3 surface detail polygons (shown dotted) (b)

offers the greatest potential in reducing overall computation time.

IMPLEMENTATION

The hidden surface and hidden line removal system described has been implemented at Cornell's Laboratory for Computer Graphics [5]. The program was written in FORTRAN IV and runs on a PDP 11/50 with a floating point processor under the RSX-11M operating system. The available display equipment includes both static and dynamic vector displays, as well as a video frame buffer and color monitor. Some sample photographs of several environments are shown in Figures 1 and 11.

The system was designed as a flexible subroutine package for use in a variety of applications programs. Complete matrix transformation, viewbox clipping, and backplane removal facilities are provided. Once the input data has been defined in an input data file it may be repeatedly transformed for an unlimited number of views as specified by a matrix file. A filming capability for the generation of long sequences of images is also provided.

The system is organized as four separate tasks including the user's task, a data preparation task, the hidden surface removal task, and a monitor task. This system reduces the complexities of user interface requirements and increases the flexibility of the runtime configuration in terms of sequential or concurrent execution and of core usage. All communication between tasks is limited to file access and system messages. System dependent functions are contained only in top level control routines in each task.

The user task is not required to be aware of the details of the configuration or that any file system exists; all interaction takes place through interface routines provided by the hidden surface removal system. Sufficient information is provided in all output files so that any file may be displayed on any vector or raster output device without prior knowledge of the contents of the output file.

CONCLUSION

A hidden surface and hidden line removal algorithm using polygon area sorting has been presented. A generalized polygon clipper, capable of clipping concave polygons with holes to concave polygons with holes, is incorporated allowing polygon format to be maintained for both the input and output. Calculation times are primarily related to the visible complexity of the final image.

Inherent characteristics of the polygon area sorting algorithm give rise to both positive and negative features. Disadvantages are the relative complexity of the clipping and the need to render polygons separately as contrasted to generating the output on a scan line basis. Advantages include flexible polygon representations which can provide for the creation of complex environments and arbitrary output precision. Perhaps the primary advantage is the similarity between the output and input forms, enabling shadow generation and surface details to be treated in a manner consistent with the entire hidden surface removal process.

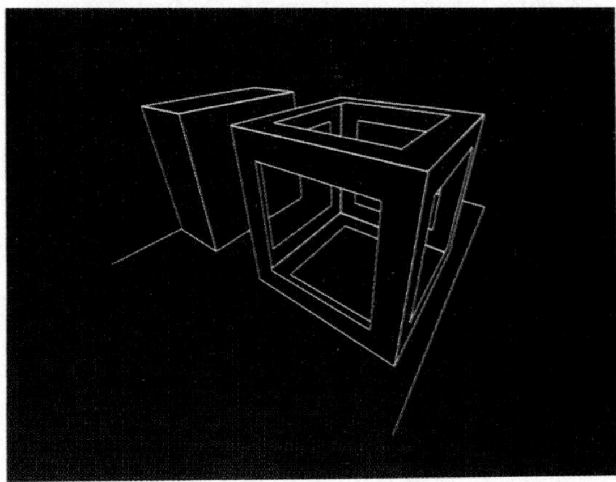

Figure 11. (above) Hidden line image of cubes.
(below) Hidden surface image of cubes.
(left) House with shadows.

ACKNOWLEDGEMENTS

The research is part of a project sponsored by the National Science Foundation under a grant number DCR74-14694 entitled "Development of Computer Graphics Techniques and Applications" (Dr. Donald P. Greenberg, Principle Investigator). The authors wish to particularly thank Ted Crane and David Bessel for their work in the implementation of the color display system.

REFERENCES

1. Appel, A., "The Notion of Quantitative invisibility and the Machine Rendering of Solids", Proceedings ACM National Conference (1967), pp. 387-393.

2. Atherton, Peter R., "Polygon Shadow Generation", M.S. Thesis, Cornell University, Ithaca, N.Y. (1977), (forthcoming).

3. Bouknight, W.J., "A Procedure for Generation of Three Dimensional Half-toned Computer Graphics Representations", Comm. ACM, 13, 9 (Sept. 1970) pp. 527-536.

4. Galimberti, R., and Montanari, U., "An Algorithm for Hidden-Line Elimination", Comm. ACM, 12, 4, (April 1969), pp. 206-211.

5. Greenberg, Donald P., "An Interdisciplinary Laboratory for Graphics Research and Applications", Proceedings of the Fourth Annual Conference on Computer Graphics, Interactive Techniques and Image Processing - SIGGRAPH, 1977.

6. Myers, A.J., "An Efficient Visible Surface Program", CGRG, Ohio State U., (July 1975).

7. Newell, M.E., Newell, R.G. and Sancha, T.L., "A Solution to the Hidden Surface Problem", Proceedings ACM National Conference, (1972), pp. 443-450.

8. Roberts, L.G., "Machine Perception of Three-Dimensional Solids", MIT Lincoln Laboratory, TR 315, (May 1963).

9. Schumacher, R.A., Brand, B., Gilliand, M. and Sharp, W., "Study for Applying Computer Generated Images to Visual Simulation", AFHRL-TR-69-14, U.S. Air Force Human Resources Laboratory, (Sept. 1969).

10. Sutherland, I.E., and Hodgman, G.W., "Reentrant Polygon Clipping", Communications of the ACM, Vol. 17, No. 1, (Jan. 1974), pp. 32-42.

11. Sutherland, I.E., Sproull, R.F., and Schumacker, R.A., "A Characterization of Ten Hidden Surface Algorithms", ACM Computing Surveys, Vol. 6, No. 1, (Mar. 1974), pp. 1-55.

12. Warnock, J.E., "A Hidden Surface Algorithm for Computer Generated Halftone Pictures", Dept. Comp. Sci., U. of Utah, (1969).

13. Watkins, G.S., "A Real-Time Visible Surface Algorithm", Comp. Sci, Dept., U. of Utah, UTECH-CSC-70-101, (June 1975).

14. Weiler, Kevin J., "Hidden Surface Removal Using Polygon Area Sorting", M.S. Thesis, Cornell University, Ithaca, N.Y. (1977), (forthcoming).

A LINEAR TIME EXACT HIDDEN SURFACE ALGORITHM *

Wm. Randolph Franklin

Electrical and Systems Engineering Dept.
Rensselaer Polytechnic Institute
Troy, NY, 12181

ABSTRACT

This paper presents a new hidden surface algorithm. Its output is the set of the visible pieces of edges and faces, and is as accurate as the arithmetic precision of the computer. Thus calculating the hidden surfaces for a higher resolution device takes no more time. If the faces are independently and identically distributed, then the execution time is linear in the number of faces. In particular, the execution time does not increase with the depth complexity.

This algorithm overlays a grid on the screen whose fineness depends on the number and size of the faces. Edges and faces are sorted into grid cells. Only objects in the same cell can intersect or hide each other. Also, if a face completely covers a cell then nothing behind it in the cell is relevant.

Three programs have tested this algorithm. The first verified the variable grid concept on 50,000 intersecting edges. The second verified the linear time, fast speed, and irrelevance of depth complexity for hidden lines on 10,000 spheres. This also tested depth complexities up to 30, and showed that perspective scenes with the farther objects smaller are even faster to calculate. The third verified this for hidden surfaces on 3000 squares.

Keywords: hidden surface, hidden line, computational geometry, geometric intersections, variable grid, computer graphics, molecular models, space-filling, algorithms analysis

CR categories: 8.2, 3.74, 5.31, 3.13.

----

* This material is based upon work supported by the National Science Foundation under grant no. ENG-7908139.

LIST OF SYMBOLS

1. $F(N) = \theta(G(N))$ means that for all $0<a<b$, there exists N_0 such that $N>N_0 \Rightarrow$ $aG(N) \le F(N) \le bG(N)$.
2. $F(N)>\theta(G(N))$ and $G(N) <\theta(F(N))$ mean that for all $c > 0$, there exists N_0 such that $N > N_0 \Rightarrow F(N) >c\, G(N)$.
3. $F(N) \ge \theta(G(N))$, equivalently $G(N) \le \theta(F(N))$, means $F(N) = \theta(G(N))$ or $F(N) \ge \theta(\overline{G}(N))$.

   Informally, 1 means F grows asymptotically as fast as G, 2 means F grows faster, and 3 means F grows at least as fast.
4. Let $\lfloor x \rfloor$ = the largest integer $\le x$ (truncation).
5. Let B be the fineness of the variable grid, that is the number of cells along one side of the screen.
6. Let C be an unspecified constant.
7. Let D be the depth complexity of the scene.
8. Let E be an edge.
9. Let F be a face.
10. Let F_b be the blocking face of a cell.
11. Let G be a grid cell.
12. Let L be the length of a projected edge (assuming the screen is one-by-one).
13. Let N be the number of edges in the scene.
14. Let P be a point.
15. Let R be either a region of the screen corresponding to the visible part of a face, or the radius for a projected sphere.

INTRODUCTION

The hidden surface problem has been actively researched for 15 years. For an excellent summary as of 7 years ago, see Sutherland [13]. Lately,

"A Linear Time Exact Hidden Surface Algorithm" by W.R. Franklin from *Proceedings of SIGGRAPH '80,* 1980, pages 117-123. Copyright 1980, Association for Computing Machinery, Inc., reprinted by permission.

attention has turned to photographic quality output, Blinn [3,4], Crow [5], Newell [4], and Whitted [3]. The algorithm presented here falls in both object and image space in Sutherland's classification. Although it does many calculations on the display screen, in contrast to image space algorithms, its output is exact, and its time does not increase with depth complexity (the average number of projected faces on each point on the screen). Algorithms which compare all faces that cross a scan line take at least quadratic time in the depth complexity. In contrast to other object space algorithms, it takes linear time on a large class of input scenes.

Intuitively, the reason that the depth complexity, which is related to the size of the faces, does not matter, is as follows: Either the faces are large or they are small. If they are large then they overlap so much that most of them are totally hidden. After these are quickly detected and deleted, the resulting problem is much simpler. On the other hand, if the faces are small, then each face overlaps few, if any, other faces. This, too, can be detected efficiently. Therefore, the size of the faces does not slow the algorithm.

This algorithm is similar to that of Weiler and Atherton [14], except that it is faster, but does not yet texture the faces. Since the output of this algorithm has meaning, and is not just a set of pixel intensities, it could also accommodate shadows and textures. This algorithm is similar in spirit to the computational geometry ideas of Bentley [12].

On the surface, this algorithm is similar to Warnock's. However, it has the following differences:

1. Here the one level grid is a temporary scaffolding and the visible pieces are returned whole, while in Warnock's algorithm the visible pieces are returned cut up arbitrarily by the hierarchical grid.
2. This algorithm produces exact results while Warnock's algorithm stops subdividing at about half a pixel, and doubling its resolution doubles its time.

This algorithm takes worse than linear time on scenes where the faces' positions are correlated so as to make them all intersect each other with each of them partly visible. However here the complexity of the output is $>\theta(N)$, so the algorithm could not possibly be linear.

Knowlton [9] and Max [10] have a good hidden surface algorithm for shading with space filling molecular models.

An earlier version of this linear algorithm developed and implemented by the author in 1972-1976 is described in [6,7].

ASSUMPTIONS

The speed of this algorithm depends on several assumptions about how the nature of the scene changes as N increases.

a. The projected edges in any given scene are all the same length. This can be weakened to allow the ratio of the average edge length to the shortest length to be merely bounded above since then all edges could be cut into pieces as long as the shortest edge without changing N by more than a constant factor.

   It might seem that this assumption rules out perspectively projected scenes since the further edges are smaller. However, in practice these scenes are faster to calculate, not slower. This is because in this case a few big faces in front totally hide many small faces in the rear, and this algorithm can quickly eliminate totally hidden faces. On the other hand, if the closer edges were smaller, then this algorithm would slow down.

b. The faces' and edges' positions are independently and uniformly distributed. This is never exactly true since otherwise the probability of two faces meeting at an edge would be zero. However, these effects become relatively smaller as N grows. Even if the 3-D scene is highly correlated, as in figure 3, the projected scene is less correlated. Finally, correlation of distant objects is irrelevant since it doesn't affect their probability of intersecting, which remains zero.

c. The objects in big scenes are "similar" to those in small scenes in the sense that the same number of edges meet at a vertex, that faces do not get longer and thinner, and so on. This appears to hold for realistic scenes. A scene of N faces with length one and width 1/N would be very slow to calculate.

d. Border effects at the edge of the screen are ignored. They become progressively less important as the objects get smaller, unless the depth complexity is very large, say 100.

A NAIVE ALGORITHM

The new algorithm is a refinement on the following naive algorithm operating in time $T \geq \theta(N^2)$:

1. Intersect all the projected edges pair by pair, to cut each edge into segments. Each segment is completely visible or else completely hidden.
2. Compare each segment against all the faces to see if it is visible.
3. Draw the visible segments and use them to divide the screen into regions, each corresponding to a visible part of a face.
4. Compare each region against all the faces to see which it corresponds to and shade it accordingly.

Note that not only any algorithm that compares all the edges will be too slow (i.e., worse than linear), but any algorithm that finds all the edge segments is too slow since the number of segments is $\theta(N^2L^2 + N)$ which can be $> \theta(N)$. For example, let the scene be a cubical array of cubes. If there are K^3 cubes, each of side $1/K$, then $N=12K^3$ and $L=1/K$. so $L=\theta(N^{-1/3})$. Then there are $\theta(N^{4/3})$ line segments, and testing their visibility takes time $T=\theta(N^{7/3})$, which is worse than quadratic.

DATA STRUCTURES

This algorithm has the following logical data structures:

1. The array of faces.
2. The array of edges.
3. A B x B grid of square cells overlaid on the projected scene. Each cell has the following three elements which are initially empty:

3a. The number of the closest <u>blocking face</u>, F_b, if any, of this cell. F_b's projection completely covers the cell so that nothing behind can be seen.

3b. The set of faces whose projections intersect the cell, and which are in front of F_b.

3c. The set of edges whose projections intersect the cell, and which are in front of F_b.

4. A set of pairs of intersecting edges. This set contains all the visible, and some of the hidden, intersections.
5. The set of visible line segments.
6. The set of visible regions, R. Each R is a connected visible part of one face.

THE LINEAR ALGORITHM

1. Project and scale the scene to fit a 1 by 1 square on the plotter screen. These techniques are well known. They may be found in the textbooks by Newman and Sproull [11], and Rogers and Adams [12].
2. Let $B = \lfloor c \min(\sqrt{N}, L^{-1}) \rfloor$, for $0 < c < 1$. c, which is an unspecified constant, is used to fine-tune the algorithm. Fine-tuning is discussed later.
3. Overlay a B by B grid of cells onto the scene
4. Initialize the grid cell data structures.
5. Repeat for each projected face F:

   5a. Determine which cells, G, F falls partly or wholly in. This is not done by comparing each of the B^2 cells with F. Instead, the minimal box of cells enclosing F gives a good approximation. A more accurate determination can be made by considering F's edges. If extra cells are included then the algorithm will later run slower but will still give the correct output.

   5b. Repeat the following for each G that contains F:

   i. If G has a blocking face, F_b, determine whether, throughout G, F_b is always in front of F. False negatives are alright at this step. Thus a convenient way is to compare the distance of F from the viewpoint at the 4 corners of G with the distance of F_b at these points. Since the faces are convex and do not interpenetrate, if F is behind F_b at those 4 point, it is always behind F_b. (The converse is not always true.)

   If F is behind F_b, do not consider this G further with F and go back to (i) to process the next G.

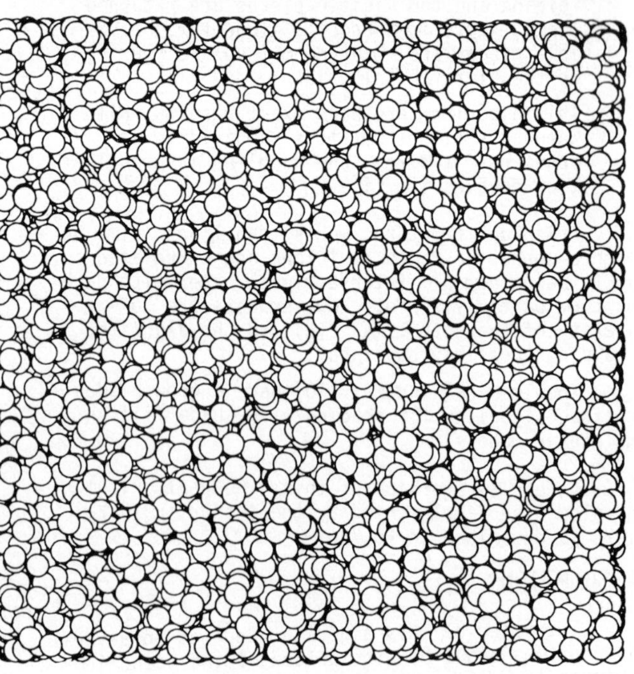

Figure 1: 10,000 spheres before and after removing the hidden lines

ii. Otherwise, determine whether F is itself a blocking face of G. This is true if and only if G's 4 corners are inside F. If F does cover G, then update F_b to be F.

iii. Otherwise add F to the set of faces in G.

5c. If F is not added to any G, then to save space delete it and its edges from the arrays since it is certainly invisible. If there are many big faces, most of them may get deleted at this point.

6. Repeat for each cell, G:

6a. Compare the blocking face, F_b, against all the faces on G's set. Delete from the set any that are behind F_b within G. The method of 5a(i) can be used. The reason that there may be faces to delete is that F_b may have been changed as the faces were processed. Thus a face, F, may have been added to G's list at a time when F was in front of the current F_b. Then later F_b was replaced with a closer face that was in front of F. F would be deleted in this step. Although we could clean out the list every time that we updated F_b, doing it all at once is faster. The initial check in 5a(i) was done to save space.

7. Repeat for each projected edge, E:

7a. Determine which cells, G, E passes through. Repeat for each G:

i. Test whether E is behind F_b. Do this by clipping E at the borders of G to E' and then testing whether the end-points of E' are both behind F_b.

ii. If not, then add E to the set of edges in G. Note that we add the complete E to the list, not its clipped version.

7b. If E is not added to any G, then delete it from the array of edges, since it is certainly invisible. However, note that a face may be partly visible even though none of its edges are.

8. Repeat for each cell, G:

8a. Repeat for each pair of edges, E_1 and E_2 in G's set of edges:

i. Test whether they intersect.

ii. If so, test whether the intersection is in G. (This catches duplications caused by the fact that the same pair of edges may pass through several cells).

iii. If so, then add E_1 to the list of edges intersecting E_2, and E_2 to the list of E_1.

However, if only the visible lines are wanted, and not the visible surfaces, do the following steps instead of (iii):

iv. Determine which one of E_1 and E_2 is in front of the other in 3-D at the point of intersection. Without loss of generality, let it be E_1.

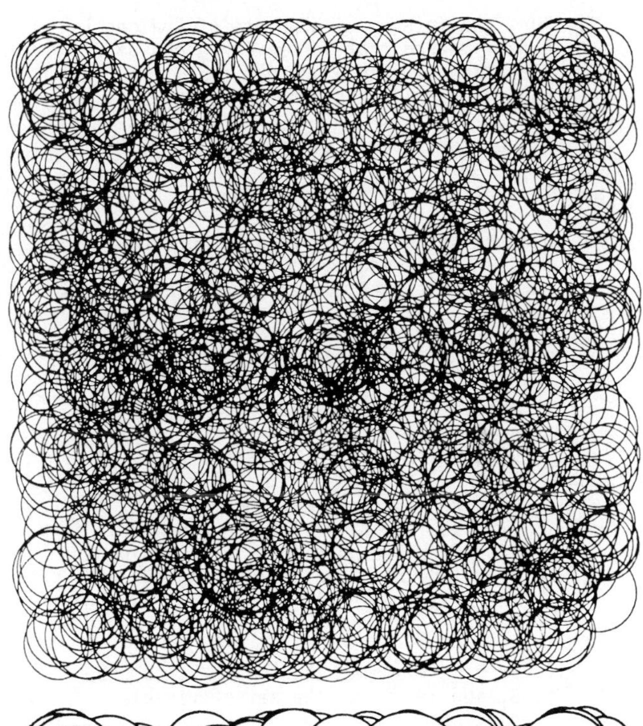

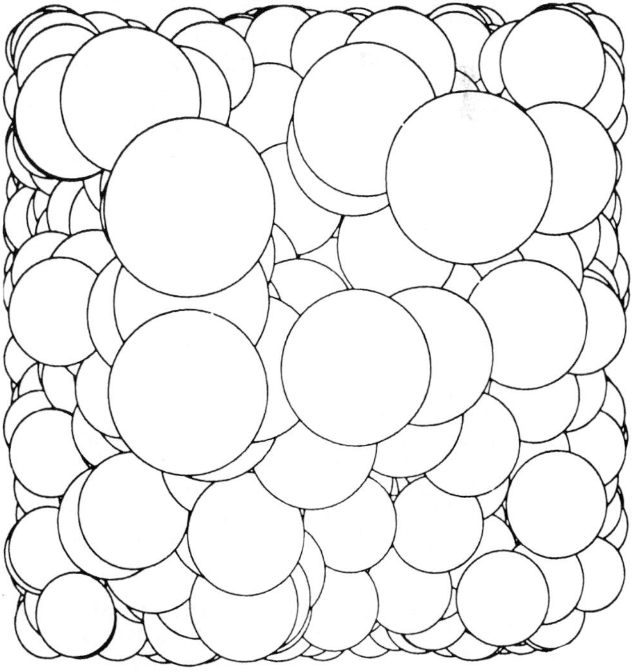

Figure 2: 1,000 spheres in perspective, before and after removing hidden lines

v. Add the intersection point to only E_2's list. This is because the visibility of E_1 is not changed by E_2's passing behind it. Nevertheless, we must still cut E_1 when we are shading if we want the visible regions to be properly defined.

9. Repeat for each edge, E:

9a. Sort the intersection points of E along E. A fast method that works regardless of E's slope and is stable against small floating-point errors in coordinates is this:

i. Let the intersections be (X_a, Y_a).

ii. Sort them by $ABS(X_a) + ABS(Y_a)$.

9b. Use the sorted points to split E into segments, S. An edge with no intersections forms one segment (unless it was previously deleted).

9c. Repeat for each segment, S:

i. Find its midpoint, P.

ii. Find which cell, G, contains P.

iii. Compare P against all the faces, F, in G to see if any hide P. F hides P if it satisfies 2 conditions: P is behind the 3-D plane of F (possibly extended) and the projected P is inside the projected F.

iv. If P is visible, then so is S, so draw S, and add it to the set of visible segments.

10. Determine the regions, R, of the planar graph formed by the visible segments, using standard algorithms.

11. Repeat for each region, R:

11a. Find a point, P, in it. The centroid will suffice except for some cases when R is concave.

11b. Find which cell, G, contains P.

11c. Compare P against the faces, F, in G. Find the closest of those faces whose projections contain P. The distance is measured by taking the length of a ray from the viewpoint towards P, possibly extended, until the 3-D plane of F. Note that in general the ordering of 2 faces in G will depend on where P is, so it is impossible to presort them by distance.

11d. R corresponds to a visible part of the closest face, F, so shade R accordingly. If P does not fall in any face, then R corresponds to background, and can be appropriately shaded. There may be more than one region per face.

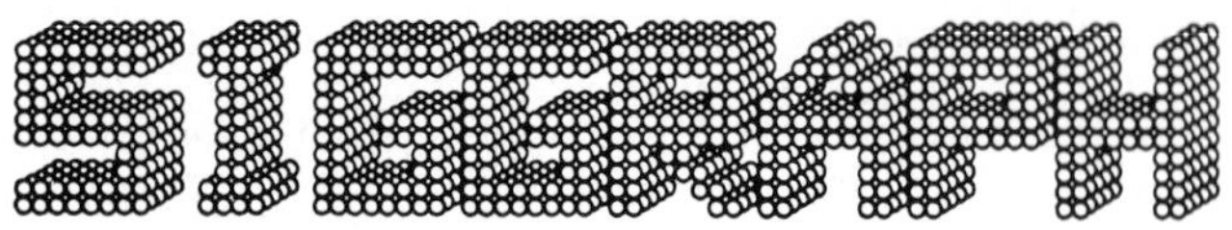

Figure 3: 1,470 spheres in a regular arrangement, with hidden lines removed

TIMING

There are 2 cases to be considered because of the definition of

$$B = \lfloor c \min(\sqrt{N}, L^{-1}) \rfloor .$$

$$\simeq c \min(\sqrt{N}, L^{-1})$$

since the floor function is asymptotically unimportant.

Case 1: $L \geq \theta(N^{-1/2})$

$$\text{so } B = \frac{c}{L} .$$

Since the cell size is a constant fraction of the face size as N increases, the probability that a given face will completely cover a cell that it partly covers is a constant, say p. If the faces are square with sides parallel to the grid, then

$$p = \left(\frac{c-1}{c+1}\right)^2 \quad , c \geq 1 .$$

Now as the number of faces in the cell increases to infinity, the expected number of the first blocking face is

$$q = \sum_{i=1}^{\infty} i\, p\, (1-p)^{i-1}$$

$$= \frac{1}{p}$$

$$= \left(\frac{c+1}{c-1}\right)^2$$

Thus, and this is crucial to the algorithm, although the expected number of faces per cell may grow to infinity, the expected number after faces hidden by the blocking face have been removed is bounded above by q.

Let r = the expected number of cells a face falls in.

Then $r = (c+1)^2$.

Let $s = \frac{\text{number of faces}}{N}$

Then the number of faces per cell before deletions is

$$\frac{rsN}{B^2}$$

of which q faces per cell are not deleted. Thus the fraction of faces left is

$$\frac{qB^2}{rsN} = \left(\frac{c}{c-1}\right)^2 \frac{1}{sL^2N} .$$

Since the edges are distributed in 3-D as the faces are, this is also the fraction of edge segments that will not be deleted for falling behind a blocking face.

Let u = average number of cells an edge falls in

$= c+1$.

Then the average number of edges per cell is

$$\frac{uN}{B^2}$$

Then the average number of edges per cell left after deletions is

$$\frac{qB^2}{rsN} \cdot \frac{uN}{B^2} = \frac{qu}{rs} = \frac{(c+1)}{(c-1)^2 s}$$

again a constant. Then intersecting the edges in the cell, pair by pair, takes constant time per cell. The total time is B^2.

Since each cell has a constant average number of edges in it, the number of intersections found is $\theta(B^2)$ so the number of segments the edges are cut into is $\theta(N + B^2)$. Testing a segment for visibility takes time proportional to the number of faces in the cell that that segment's center falls in, which is constant. Thus the total time for the hidden line part of the algorithm, obtained by summing times for the operations given above, and adding $\theta(N)$ for bookkeeping is

$$T = \theta(N + B^2)$$

$$= \theta(N)$$

Thus the hidden line algorithm is linear.

For the hidden surface algorithm, the number of visible segments is $\leq$ the number of segments = $\theta(N + B^2) = \theta(N)$. So the number of regions on the plotter screen is $\theta(N)$. Determining them takes an expected time of $\theta(N)$. Finding which face a region corresponds to takes time proportional to the number of faces in the cell being used for that region, which is constant. Thus, the total time to identify the regions is $\theta(N)$.

Case 2: $L < \theta(N^{-1/2})$

The analysis is similar to Case 1 and gives the same result. Therefore, the complete hidden surface algorithm takes time $T = \theta(N)$ in either case.

IMPLEMENTATION

Three different programs have been written to test various aspects of this algorithm. All the implementations were on a Prime 500 midicomputer with a 16 bit wordlength and 1 MB of memory. The Prime performs a single precision floating multiply in about 5 microseconds. The results were plotted either on an Imlac or an IBM 3277 graphics attachment.

The first was designed to test the concept of a variable grid. It calculated the intersections among random edges. It was tested with different numbers of edges, edge lengths and grid sizes. For example, with 10,000 edges of lengths about 0.01 (on a 1 by 1 square), and a 100 by 100 grid, it took only 77 seconds to find all 1814 intersections out of the 50 million possibilities. The number of (edge,cell) pairs was 19931. The optimal grid size was determined experimentally, and within a factor of 2 made little difference. The algorithm behaved as expected as N and L varied, except that the optimal grid size was hard to predict since it depends on the relative speeds of various parts of the program.

The second implementation, SPHERES, is described in detail in Franklin [8]. It uses the same concepts, but is a different algorithm designed to calculate hidden lines for scenes composed of spheres, as in a molecular model. SPHERES has been tested at depth complexities up to 30, and the time for fixed N even drops slightly as D increases at this point. For D = 10, SPHERES has been tested for N up to 10,000. This case took only 383 seconds to calculate. Figure 1 shows 10000 spheres packed 10 deep before and after hidden lines are removed. Figure 2 shows 1000 spheres with D = 10 in a perspective projection before and after. This case takes 1/3 less time than N = 1000, D = 10 with fixed R. Figure 3 shows the hidden lines removed from a regular array of 1970 spheres. Table 1 shows how T varies with N if D = 10. If N is fixed while D varies from .1 to 30 (by changing R), T is largest for D = 5, and declines slowly as D increases.

The third implementation removes hidden surfaces for random squares. Figure 4 shows 300 squares with the visible surfaces crosshatched at an angle proportional to their distance. This has been tested up to N = 3000 and table 2 shows that the time is still linear. This last case has D = 77.

This algorithm is now being extended to hierarchical or rotating scenes and is being incorporated into a general 3-D object manipulation package.

EXTENSIONS

It would be worthwhile to collect statistics on a scene before processing to determine the optimal B. If the scene is inhomogeneous, a hierarchical grid may be faster, although there exist sequences of scenes that still execute slowly.

ACKNOWLEDGEMENTS

Leong Shin Loong and Abel Shi Lo, while Mechanical Engineering students at RPI, helped with these implementations. Their assistance is gratefully appreciated.

REFERENCES

1. Bentley, J.L., Stanat, D.F., and Williams, E.H., Jr. The Complexity of finding fixed radius near neighbors. Info. Proc. Lett. 6, 6 (Dec. 1977), 209-212.

2. Bentley, J.L., Ottmann, T.A. Algorithms for reporting and counting geometric intersections. IEEE T. Comput. C-28, 9 (Sept. 1979), 643-647.

3. Blinn, J.F., Carpenter, L.C., Lane, J.M., and Whitted, T. Scan Line methods for displaying parametrically defined surfaces. Comm. ACM 23, 1 (Jan. 1980), 23-24.

4. Blinn, J.F., Newell, M.E. Texture and reflection in computer generated images. Comm. ACM 19, 10 (Oct. 1976), 542-547.

5. Crow, F.C. Shadow algorithms for computer graphics. Computer Graphics 11, 2 (Summer 1977), 242-248.

6. Franklin, W.R. VIEWPLOT summary, program logic manual, and user's manual. Harvard Lab for Computer Graphics, (July, Dec. 1976).

7. Franklin, W.R. Combinatorics of hidden surface algorithms. Harvard University Center for Research in Computing Technology, TR12-78, (June 1978).

8. Franklin, W.R. An Exact hidden sphere algorithm that operates in linear time. Computer Graphics and Image Processing, to appear.

9. Knowlton, K., and Cherry, L. ATOMS - a 3-D opaque molecular system. Computers and Chemistry 1, 3 (1977), 161-166.

10. Max, N.L. ATOMLLL - ATOMS with shading and highlights. Computer Graphics 13, 2 (Aug. 1979), 165-173.

11. Newman, W., and Sproull, R.F. Principles of Interactive Computer Graphics, 2nd edition. McGraw-Hill, 1979.

12. Rogers, D.F. and Adams, J.A. Mathematical Elements for Computer Graphics. McGraw-Hill, 1976.

13. Sutherland, I.E., Sproull, R.F., and Schumacker, R.A. A Characterization of ten hidden surface algorithms. Computing Surveys 6, 1 (Mar. 1974), 1-55.

14. Weiler, K., and Atherton, P. Hidden surface removal using polygon area sorting. Computer Graphics 11, 2 (Summer 1977), 214-222.

Table 1: Times for hidden spheres calculations for D = 10

N	R	B	T
30	0.326	7	4.1
100	0.178	13	5.6
300	0.03	23	10.3
1,000	0.0564	42	31.1
3,000	0.0326	72	97.5
10,000	0.0178	142	383.

Table 2: Times for hidden surface calculations for squares

N	L	B	D	T
1,000	0.16	12	25.6	527
3,000	0.16	12	76.8	1792

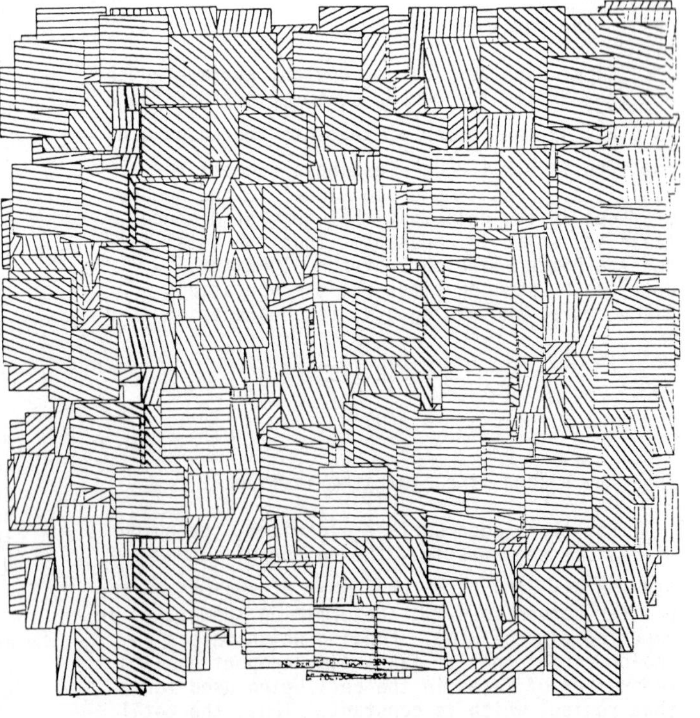

Figure 4: 300 squares with visible surfaces shaded

Chapter 7: Shading Algorithms

Introduction

The problem of shading is to model the interaction of illumination with surface reflection properties in order to calculate the appropriate color and intensity at a point in an image. This introductory chapter is somewhat longer than the others and more mathematical, as we attempt to provide a theoretical basis for such shading models, to supplement the reprinted paper of Cook and Torrance [Cook82] with material from Cook's master's thesis [Cook81], and to discuss techniques of indirect illumination. We start by assuming that the illumination is known as a function of incoming direction at all points on a surface.

Let (x,y,z) be a point on a surface and assume we wish to compute the intensity $I(x,y,z)$ of this point as seen by the "viewer." This intensity depends on the illumination coming from the environment towards the point (x,y,z) and on the reflecting properties of the surface. Whitted and Cook [Whit85] (included in this chapter) express this dependence as an integral

$$I(x,y,z) = \int_0^{2\pi}\int_0^{\pi/2} L(x,y,z,\phi,\theta)R(\phi,\theta)\sin\phi\, d\phi d\theta \quad (1)$$

where $L(x,y,z,\phi,\theta)$ is the illumination reaching (x,y,z) from the direction (ϕ,θ) in spherical coordinates with the surface normal as the axis, $R(\phi,\theta)$ is the reflectance toward the viewer from the surface for light coming from the direction (ϕ,θ), and $\sin\phi d\phi d\theta$ is an element of solid angle (also written as $d\omega$). The integrals are over the hemisphere above the surface.

The notation $R(\phi,\theta)$ is a simplification, since the reflectance usually depends on the angle of the viewpoint as well as the angle of the incoming illumination. However, a perfectly diffuse surface appears equally bright from all directions, so the notation is adequate in this case.

A Calculation of Lambert's Law

The reflectance $R(\phi,\theta)$ for diffuse surfaces obeys Lambert's law, and it is instructive to derive this law from energy considerations.

By definition, radiant flux is the light energy passing through a surface-per-unit time. Suppose we have a collimated beam coming from a small solid angle $d\omega_{in}$ about an incident direction (ϕ_{in},θ_{in}), with flux density S_{in} per unit area measured normal to the beam. In Figure 7.1, dA is a small area normal to the beam, intercepting the same flux as the area dB along the surface. Thus $dB = \frac{dA}{\cos\phi_{in}}$, so the incident flux density E_{in} per unit area on the surface is

$$E_{in} = S_{in}\cos\phi_{in} \quad (2)$$

By definition, the intensity of a beam of light is the radiant flux per unit solid angle per unit area measured normal to the beam. If the surface is perfectly diffuse, it will appear to have the intensity I_{ref} from all viewing directions. By geometric reasoning, similar to that in Figure 7.1, the flux per solid angle per unit surface area leaving in a direction $(\phi_{ref},\theta_{ref})$ must be $I_{ref}\cos\phi_{ref}$, where, in this case, I_{ref} is a constant, independent of viewing direction. Then the total flux E_{ref} leaving per unit surface area is

$$\begin{aligned} E_{ref} &= \int_0^{2\pi}\int_0^{\pi/2} I_{ref}\cos\phi_{ref}\sin\phi_{ref}\, d\phi_{ref}\, d\theta_{ref} \\ &= \int_0^{2\pi}\int_0^{\pi/2} \frac{1}{2}\sin(2\phi_{ref})\, d\phi_{ref}\, d\theta_{ref} \quad (3) \\ &= \int_0^{2\pi} \frac{1}{2}\, d\theta_{ref} \\ &= \pi I_{ref} \end{aligned}$$

If E_{ref} represents a constant fraction r of E_{in}, then $\pi I_{ref} = E_{ref} = rE_{in} = rS_{in}\cos\phi_{in}$, so

$$I_{ref} = \frac{r\cos\phi_{in} S_{in}}{\pi} \quad (4)$$

To use equation 1 for a collimated beam of light coming from the single direction (ϕ_{in},θ_{in}), we need to take the limit as the solid angle $d\omega_{in}$ of the incoming beam approaches zero, while its intensity approaches infinity, keeping their product, the flux density S_{in}, constant. To do this, we use the spherical-coordinate delta function $\delta(\phi,\theta;\phi_{in},\theta_{in})$, which is zero unless $\phi = \phi_{in}$ and $\theta = \theta_{in}$, but has the property that

$$\int_\phi\int_\theta \delta(\phi,\theta;\phi_{in},\theta_{in}) f(\phi,\theta)\sin\phi\, d\theta d\phi = f(\phi_{in},\theta_{in}) \quad (5)$$

for any function $f(\phi,\theta)$. Then we take $L(\phi,\theta) = S_{in}\delta(\phi,\theta;\phi_{in},\theta_{in})$. Substituting in equation 1 and using equation 3, we find $I_{ref} = R(\theta_{in},\phi_{in})S_{in}$. The energy computation gave $I_{ref} = (r\cos\phi_{in}/\pi)S_{in}$ so we can conclude that $R(\theta_{in},\phi_{in}) = r\cos\phi_{in}/\pi$, which is proportional to $\cos\phi_{in}$. This is Lambert's law, $R(\theta_{in},\phi_{in}) = k\cos\phi_{in}$, with $k = r/\pi$.

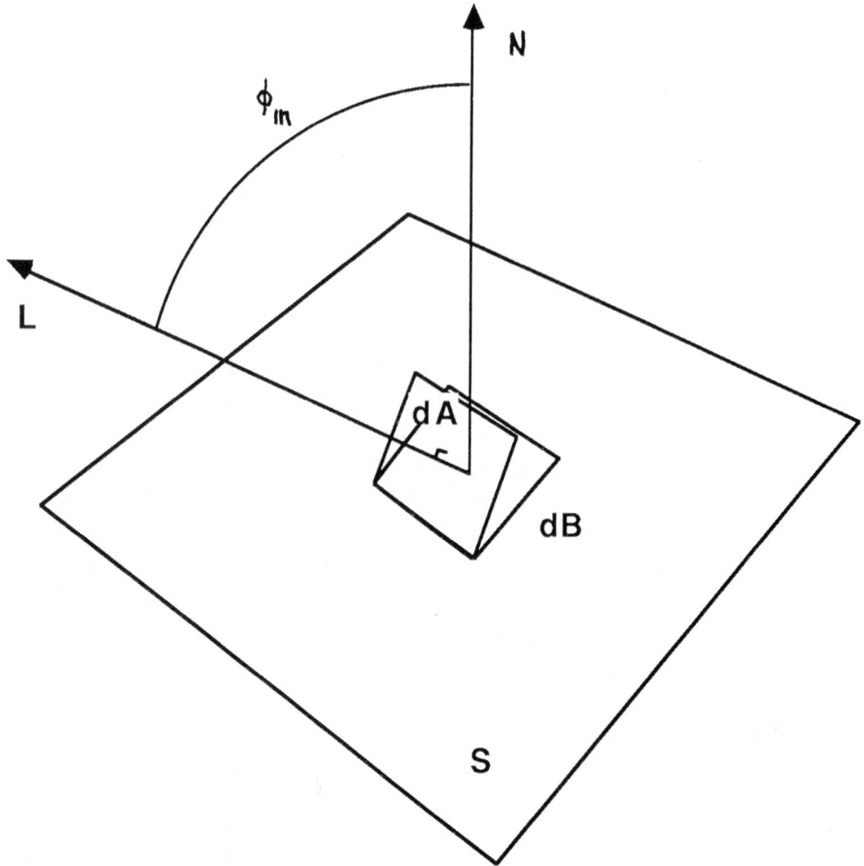

A surface S, with normal N, and light incident from a direction L with spherical coordinates (ϕ_{in}, θ_{in}). The surface dA is perpendicular to L, and dB is its shadow on S.

Figure 7.1: Flux per Solid Angle Leaving the Surface

Phong Shading

A general reflection function $R(\phi_{in},\theta_{in};\phi_{ref},\theta_{ref})$ depends on both the incident direction (ϕ_{in},θ_{in}) and the reflection direction $(\phi_{ref},\theta_{ref})$ and is, therefore, often called a bidirectional reflection function. It is sometimes convenient to represent R as the sum of two terms, a diffuse term that reflects according to Lambert's law, and a specular term that adds the shiny or glossy reflection concentrated near the mirror direction. Thus

$$R(\phi_{in},\theta_{in};\phi_{ref},\theta_{ref}) = k_d \cos \phi_{in} + R_{spec}(\phi_{in},\theta_{in};\phi_{ref},\theta_{ref}) \quad (6)$$

One early model for R_{spec} was proposed by Phong Bui-Toung [BuiT75]. Here we set $R_{spec} = k_s(\cos \beta)^n$, where k_s is a constant and β is the angle between the viewing direction $(\phi_{ref},\theta_{ref})$ and the perfect mirror reflection direction $(\phi_{mir},\theta_{mir}) = (\phi_{in},\theta_{in}+\pi)$. The exponent n controls the shininess of the surface; increasing n concentrates the highlight nearer to the position where $(\phi_{ref},\theta_{ref}) = (\phi_{mir},\theta_{mir})$. For a point light source at (ϕ_{in},θ_{in}), Phong calculated $\cos\beta$ from the direction of the normal $N(x,y,z)$ at a surface point (x,y,z). At an interior point of a polygon approximating a smooth surface, $N(x,y,z)$ was calculated by using bilinear interpolation between normals specified at the vertices. This interpolated vector was normalized to a unit vector and $\cos\beta$ was calculated as the dot product of this unit normal with the unit vector in the direction of $(\phi_{mir},\theta_{mir})$. The interpolation of the normals allows a specular highlight to appear in the middle of a polygon, even if $(\phi_{ref},\theta_{ref})$ is far from $(\phi_{mir},\theta_{mir})$ at the vertices.

A variant, which has also become known as Phong shading, is $R_{spec} = k_s(\cos\alpha)^m$, where α is the angle between the surface normal N and the vector H halfway between the direction of the light source (ϕ_{in},θ_{in}), and the viewing direction $(\phi_{ref},\theta_{ref})$. The vector H is the normal direction to a perfect mirror that would reflect the light source directly toward the viewer. If ϕ_{in} is not too large, α is approximately one half of β. This, and the properties of $\cos x$, for small x, means that m should be equal to $4n$ to get the same highlight appearance as Phong's original formulation. This variant is analyzed by Duff [Duff79], who shows how the necessary quantities can be calculated incrementally across a visible segment of a polygon along a scan line. If both the light source and the viewpoint are assumed to be at infinite distance, the calculation is greatly simplified because H is then independent of the point (x,y,z) being viewed.

These Phong models are usually used with point light sources, but most natural scenes also have ambient light coming from all directions. If we assume this ambient intensity L_A is equal in all directions and that there are N point light sources of brightness L_i in direction (ϕ_i,θ_i), for $i = 1 \ldots N$, then we can write

$$L(\theta_{in},\phi_{in}) = L_A + \sum_{i=1}^{n} L_i \delta(\phi_{in},\theta_{in};\phi_i,\theta_i) \tag{7}$$

Substituting in equation 1, we get

$$I_{ref} = L_A \int_\phi \int_\theta R(\phi,\theta) \sin\phi \;\; d\phi\, d\theta + \sum_{i=1}^{n} L_i R(\phi_i,\theta_i) \tag{8}$$

The integral after L_A is a constant k_A dependent only on the properties of the reflecting surface. If we separate R into specular and diffuse terms, as in equation 6, we get the popular formula

$$I_{ref} = k_a L_A + \sum_{i=1}^{n} k_d L_i \cos\phi_i + \sum_{i=1}^{n} L_i R_{spec}(\phi_i,\theta_i) \tag{9}$$

in which one of the two Phong expressions are commonly used for R_{spec}.

Miller and Hoffman [Mill84] have improved on this for environments at infinity of the sort considered by Blinn and Newell [Blin76], where $L(x,y,z,\phi,\theta)$ is assumed to depend only on ϕ and θ. If we substitute equation 6 into equation 1, we get

$$I_{ref} = \int_0^{2\pi}\int_0^{\pi/2} L(\phi_{in},\theta_{in}) k_d \cos\phi_{in} \sin\phi_{in}\, d\phi_{in}\, d\theta_{in} + \int_0^{2\pi}\int_0^{\pi/2} L(\phi_{in},\theta_{in})\, R_{spec}(\phi_{in},\theta_{in};\phi_{ref},\theta_{ref}) \sin\phi_{in}\, d\phi_{in}\, d\theta_{in} \tag{10}$$

The first integral depends only on the direction of the normal vector, which determines the hemisphere of integration and its (θ_{in},ϕ_{in}) coordinate system, so the result can be tabulated as a texture function of the normal vector. For the second integral, there are two alternatives. Miller and Hoffman used a perfectly shiny surface, so that

$$R(\phi_{in},\theta_{in};\phi_{ref},\theta_{ref}) = \delta(\phi_{in},\theta_{in};\phi_{perf},\theta_{perf}) \tag{11}$$

where $(\phi_{perf},\theta_{perf}) = (\phi_{ref},\theta_{ref} + \pi)$ is the perfect mirror reflection of the viewing direction $(\phi_{ref},\theta_{ref})$. This is the situation in Blinn and Newell [Blin76]. By equation 5 and the definition of the δ function in spherical coordinates, the second integral reduces to the tabulated illumination function $L(\phi,\theta)$ evaluated at $(\phi_{perf},\theta_{perf})$.

Alternatively, one can use Phong's original form of R_{spec}, which depends only on the angle β between (ϕ_{in},θ_{in}) and $(\phi_{perf},\theta_{perf})$. Then the second integral depends only on $(\phi_{perf},\theta_{perf})$ and can again be tabulated as a function of these angles.

In any of these table-based methods for glossy reflections, care must be taken with antialiasing: the table values which contribute to the reflections for a pixel on a highly curved region of the surface must be correctly averaged. Blinn and Newell's article [Blin76] deals with this problem for their specific context, while the paper by Heckbert [Heck86a] deals with it in the context of general texture mapping. Antialiasing and texturing are discussed in the next two chapters of this volume.

The variants of the Phong formula for the bidirectional-reflection function are not based on any physical or geometrical theory of reflection. Instead, they were designed to provide realistically shaped glossy highlights from point source illumination with a minimum of computation.

Cook-Torrance Shading

In 1967, Torrance and Sparrow [Torr67] presented a theory for reflections from roughened surfaces based on geometric optics. They modeled the roughness of the surface by a series of randomly oriented wedge-shaped grooves whose two sides had equal, but opposite, slopes. The slopes were also random and their distribution determined the roughness or shininess of the surface. Torrace and Sparrow calculated the distribution of the light reflected from all the slanted sides of the grooves, taking into account that one side of a groove might shadow the incident light aimed toward the opposite side of the groove or occlude the reflected beam on the way out. Diffraction was not considered, but the physical properties of the material were included by utilizing Fresnel's law in the calculations. This law defines the reflectivity of a perfect mirror in terms of the angle of incidence and two properties of the material, the index of refraction, and the extinction coefficient. The Torrance-Sparrow model successfully reproduced the experimentally observed fact that for large angles of incidence to a roughened surface, the angle for maximum reflection is slightly larger than the angle of incidence. This is called an "off-specular" peak. (Recall that in Phong's models, the maximum specular reflection occurs at the perfect mirror reflection direction.)

Blinn [Blin77] was the first to apply this reflection model to computer graphics. Cook and Torrance [Cook82] (included in this chapter) have improved Blinn's method to give more realistic colored reflections. Their basic equation is

$$R_{bd} = \frac{F}{\pi} \frac{D}{(N \cdot L)} \frac{G}{(N \cdot V)} \tag{12}$$

where N is the unit surface normal, L is the unit vector in the direction of the incident light, and V is a unit vector in the direction of the viewer. The angles ϕ_{in} and θ_{in} determine L, and ϕ_{ref} and θ_{ref} determine V, so R_{bd} is a bidirectional-reflection function.

However, it is used somewhat differently, because R_{bd} is defined as the ratio of the reflected intensity to the incident radiant flux per unit area of the surface

$$R_{bd} = \frac{I_{ref}}{E_{in}} \tag{13}$$

Suppose a beam of light of intensity I_{in}, from a solid angle $d\omega_{in}$ around an incident direction L meets a surface with normal N, as shown in Figure 7.1. By the definition of intensity as radiant flux per unit solid angle per unit area normal to the beam, we can multiply I_{in} by $d\omega_{in}$ to get the flux density, S_{in}, per unit area normal to the beam. In the geometry of Figure 7.1, $\cos\phi_{in} = N \cdot L$. Substituting in equation 2, which is based on this figure, we find that the incident flux E_{in} per unit surface area is

$$E_{in} = S_{in}\cos\phi_{in} = I_{in}\, d\omega_{in}\,(N \cdot L) \tag{14}$$

Then, by definition,

$$R_{bd} = \frac{I_{ref}}{E_{in}} = \frac{I_{ref}}{I_{in}\, d\omega_{in}\,(N \cdot L)} \tag{15}$$

so

$$I_{ref} = R_{bd} I_{in}\, d\omega_{in}\,(N \cdot L) \tag{16}$$

This reflected intensity I_{ref} is due only to the light incident on the surface from the small solid angle $d\omega$ about the incident direction (θ_{in}, ϕ_{in}). If we integrate such intensity contributions over the whole hemisphere above the surface, with varying incident intensity $I_{in}(\phi_{in},\theta_{in})$, we get the total reflected intensity I:

$$\begin{aligned} I &= \int R_{bd}(\phi_{in}, \theta_{in}; \phi_{ref}, \theta_{ref})\, I_{in}(\phi_{in}, \theta_{in})(N \cdot L)\, d\omega_{in} \\ &= \int_0^{2\pi}\left[\int_0^{\pi/2} I_{in}(\phi_{in},\theta_{in})\, R_{bd}(\phi_{in},\theta_{in};\phi_{ref},\theta_{ref}) \right. \\ &\qquad \left. \cos\phi_{in}\sin\phi_{in}\, d\phi_{in}\right] d\theta_{in} \end{aligned} \tag{17}$$

Compare this to equation 1, and note the extra factor of $\cos\phi_{in}$ which arises from the definition of R_{bd}.

In equation 12, the D expresses the probability density of finding small facets in the reflecting surface (with the appropriate perfect mirror normal H). It is a function of α, the angle between H and the surface normal N. Blinn [Blin77] and the Cook-Torrance paper [Cook82] give several different possibilities for $D(\alpha)$. The actual meaning of D is not explained completely in the paper by Cook and Torrance. Additional details appear in section 3.1 of Cook's master's thesis [Cook81], which we now summarize.

Suppose that all the facets have equal area f_a, that H is a potential facet-normal direction, and that $d\omega_H$ is an infinitesimal solid angle containing H. If $P(H)$ is the density of facets per unit surface area, per solid angle of facet normal, then $f_a\, P(H) d\omega_H\, dA$ is the total facet area with normals within $d\omega_H$ around H, lying on a surface area dA. If we multiply this facet area by the cosine of the angle between the facet normal H and the light direction L, we get the intercepted area dA_I, normal to the incoming light beam

$$dA_I = f_a\, P(H)\, d\omega_H\, dA(H \cdot L) \tag{18}$$

If I_{in} is the incident from a solid angle $d\omega_{in}$ about the incident direction L, then the flux dF_{in} on these facets is

$$\begin{aligned} dF_{in} &= I_{in}\, d\omega_{in}\, dA_I \\ &= I_{in}\, d\omega_{in} f_a\, P(H)\, d_H\, dA(H \cdot L) \end{aligned} \tag{19}$$

If 100 percent of this incident flux were reflected, then the reflected flux dF_{ref} is the same as dF_{in}. This flux is reflected into a solid angle $d\omega_{ref}$ about the viewing direction V and comes from a surface area dA. By a version of the geometry in Figure 7.1, reorganized for the reflected direction V, the area dA projects to an area $dA(V \cdot N)$ normal to the reflected beam. The intensity I_{ref} reflected from this collection of facets is the flux per unit solid angle per unit area normal to the reflected beam, so

$$\begin{aligned} I_{ref} &= \frac{dF_{ref}}{d\omega_{ref}\, dA(V \cdot N)} \\ &= \frac{I_{in}\, d\omega_{in} f_a\, P(H)\, d\omega_H\, d\,A(H \cdot L)}{d\omega_{ref}\, dA(V \cdot N)} \\ &= I_{in}\, d\omega_{in} f_a\, P(H)\, \frac{(H \cdot L)\, d\omega_H}{(V \cdot N)\, d\omega_{ref}} \end{aligned} \tag{20}$$

Now, from equation 14, $E_{in} = I_{in}\, d\omega_{in}(N \cdot L)$, so

$$R_{bd} = \frac{I_{ref}}{E_{in}} = \frac{f_a\, P(H)(H \cdot L)\, d\omega_H}{(N \cdot L)(V \cdot N)\, d\omega_{ref}} \tag{21}$$

We now consider the concentration factor $d\omega_H / d\omega_{ref}$. This factor is necessary because the intensity of a reflected beam is defined as flux per solid angle and must be integrated to get an actual flux. Thus the cone $d\omega_{ref}$ would be the solid angle of integration about the vector V subtended by the pupil of the eye, or the aperture of a camera, and $d\omega_H$ would measure the collection of facet normals, which could aim a reflected glint into this aperture. When the angle between L and H is close to 90 degrees, the angle of reflection V varies very slowly as H is rotated by dH_I around the axis L (see Figure 7.2), so reflections from a large range of facet normals are concentrated into a small solid angle near V.

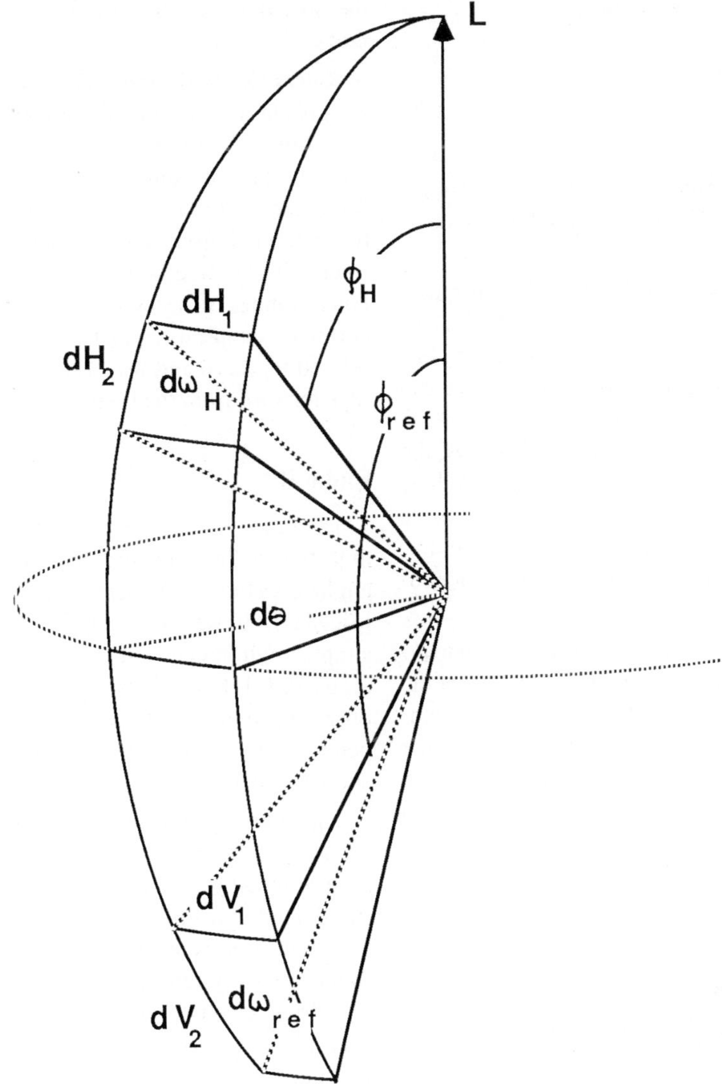

A solid angle $d\omega_H = dH_1 \cdot dH_2$ reflects light from a single direction L to a solid angle $d\omega_{ref} = dV_1 \cdot dV_2$ of reflected directions. If L is taken as the axis of spherical coordinates, then $dH_1 = d\theta \sin\phi_H$, $dV_1 = d\theta \sin\phi_{ref}$, $dV_2 = 2dH_2$, and $\phi_{ref} = 2\phi_H$.

Figure 7.2: Calculation of dw_H

By analyzing Figure 7.2 in spherical coordinates, with the north pole in the direction L, one can derive the concentration ratio $d\omega_H / d\omega_{ref} = 1/(4H \cdot L)$. (See [Rens50].)

Substituting this factor in equation 21, we get

$$R_{bd} = \frac{f_a P(H)(H \cdot L)}{(N \cdot L)(V \cdot N)} \frac{1}{4(H \cdot L)} = \frac{f_a P(H)}{4(N \cdot L)(V \cdot N)} \quad (22)$$

Now the facets actually do not reflect 100 percent of the incident energy. Even if they are perfectly shiny, Fresnel's law, derived from the physical behavior of electromagnetic waves, predicts that only a fraction of the energy incident on the facets is reflected. This fraction F depends on the material, the angle of incidence (embodied by $(N \cdot L)$, and the wavelength of the light.

In addition, facets may be hidden from the light source or the viewer by other facets which are in the way. The geometric attenuation factor G expresses the fraction of a beam aimed toward a facet with the correct H which is neither shadowed on the way in nor obscured on the way out. A careful derivation of this factor for surfaces roughened by grooves is presented in [Blin77]. A general method of determining G directly from a table of surface bump heights is given by Cabral et al. [Cabr87].

When the F and G factors are multiplied into equation 22, we get

$$R_{bd} = \frac{FGf_a P(H)}{4(N \cdot L)(N \cdot V)} \quad (23)$$

To turn this into equation 12, Cook defined

$$D = \frac{\pi f_a P(H)}{4} \qquad (24)$$

which puts the π in the denominator, as in the formula $k = 1/\pi$ derived in equation 24 for the Lambert's law coefficient k.

The chief improvement of the Cook-Torrance paper [Cook82] over Blinn's [Blin77] was in the color of the highlights. Blinn and previous authors, such as Phong, had assumed that the specular reflection was from light that did not penetrate into the material and, therefore, retained the color of the incident light. So, for white light, they used the material's color for the diffuse reflections and then added the highlights in white. This assumption is correct for plastics and some paints, where colored pigment particles are embedded in a colorless carrier, but it is not true for homogeneous materials such as metal.

In the formula given by equation 12 for the specular-reflection coefficient, only the Fresnel factor F depends on the material; the other factors just depend on the surface roughness and the viewing geometry. Fresnel's law involves the index of refraction, which can vary with the wavelength (i.e., color) of the incident light. Cook and Torrance give a method of estimating this variation, and therefore, of estimating the color of the highlights, to give very realistic appearing metal surfaces.

Extended Shading Techniques

Once the bidirectional-reflection function has been determined, the intensity must be computed by calculating the integrals in equations 1 or 17. As mentioned previously, this is much easier if $L(x,y,z,\phi,\theta)$ is independent of the position (x,y,z) of the surface point. In this case, the environment can be considered to be painted on a sphere at infinity, and the methods of Blinn and Newell [Blin76], Miller and Hoffman [Mill84] or Cabral et al. [Cabr87] can be used to calculate the intensity efficiently.

But in most actual environments, objects are close to each other, and light reflecting from one surface to another should influence the shading. The two methods, which have been developed to calculate this effect are ray tracing and radiosity.

Ray tracing is the subject of Chapter 5 of this book. As usually conceived, rays are traced backwards from the viewpoint into the environment, and secondary rays traced back from a surface can sample the environmental illumination. The original paper of Whitted [Whit80] (included in Chapter 5: Ray-Tracing Algorithms) traced only one "inverse reflection" ray in the perfect mirror direction, and thus could model only shiny surfaces. However, distributed ray tracing, developed by Cook et al. [Cook84a] (included in Chapter 5: Ray-Tracing Algorithms) can trace several secondary rays near this mirror direction and thus can sample the specular reflection of the environment in glossy surfaces.

Kajiya [Kaji86] extended this concept to include secondary rays in non-specular directions, which are used to simulate diffuse interreflections between surfaces. The above three groups of authors also consider secondary "inverse refraction" rays, and Kajiya's method can model the caustics refracted from a light source onto a diffuse surface. Even with the tree pruning suggested by Kajiya, a tremendous number of secondary diffuse rays must be traced to correctly sample rays that reach a light source by inverse refraction. Arvo and Kirk [Arvo86] have suggested tracing rays forward from the light source in such cases.

Radiosity

The other method for considering interreflections among objects is called radiosity and was originally developed by engineers studying radiative heat transfer (See [Spar78] or [Sieg81]). It was first applied to computer graphics for simple environments, such as an empty room, by Goral et al. [Gora84]. Extensions to the general case, where there are obscuring objects between surfaces, were published independently by Nishita and Nakamae [Nish85b] and by Cohen and Greenberg [Cohe85](included in this chapter).

The radiosity of a surface is the total light flux leaving it: the sum of the reflected light and any emitted light if the surface is self-luminous. The objects in the environment are subdivided into surface elements, on which the radiosity is assumed to be constant. The unknown radiosities are then found from a system of equations expressing the interactions of light in the environment.

In the case that all surfaces are diffusely reflecting, the fraction of the radiosity leaving one surface element which lands on another is independent of the direction from which incoming energy hits the first surface. This fraction, called the form factor, depends only on the geometrical relationship between the surfaces.

Form factors have traditionally been calculated by integration. In the absence of occlusion, the necessary area integrals over both surface elements can be reduced to line integrals (see [Spar78]).

Cohen and Greenberg chose to approximate the form factors by performing a Z-buffer hidden-surface computation from a viewpoint at the center of each surface element. A hemispherical field of view was required, but since flat projection planes are computationally simpler, half of a cube (a "hemicube") was used. The form factor between one element and another can then be found from the collection of pixels at which the second element is visible on the first element's hemicube.

Suppose the diffuse-reflection coefficients are known for all surface elements and suppose all form factors have been computed. Then the reflection integral, given by equation 1, for each element can be broken up into a sum over the other elements visible at its center, to give the radiosity at the element as a function of all the other radiosities. Each term in the sum is the product of a radiosity (for L), a diffuse-reflection coefficient (for R), and a form factor (for the solid angle of integration). If there are N elements, this gives N equations in the N unknown radiosities. These can be solved by Gauss-Seidel iteration. Each step in the iteration is equivalent to propagating the light from the self-luminous-source elements through one-and-one-half additional stages of surface reflection.

The radiosities found at the center of each element can be interpolated to shade other points on the surface. One advantage of this method is that the radiosity solution is independent of the viewpoint, and need not be repeated if the same scene is rendered from a different viewpoint.

The radiosity method has been further developed and generalized by Donald Greenberg and his students and colleagues in the Cornell University Program of Computer Graphics. One improvement, by Cohen et al. [Cohe86], subdivided the surfaces more finely at regions of high radiosity gradients such as the edges of shadows. The M elements resulting from this subdivision are grouped together into N patches of more uniform size, and a form factor is computed between each element and each patch. The element-to-patch form factors are summed to give patch-to-patch form factors. These are used as discussed previously to compute coarse patch radiosities by solving an $N \times N$ system of linear equations. The patch radiosities are then substituted into M equations, involving the MN element-to-patch form factors, to determine the element radiosities, which are used in the shading.

After this computation is complete, elements at which the resulting radiosity is found to change substantially can be further subdivided, without repeating the solution for the patch radiosities. In addition, the initial subdivision of patches into elements allows more accurate computation of the patch-to-patch form factors, since the summation accurately accounts for the variation across one patch in the visibility of the other.

A second extension, by Immel et al. [Imme86], included nondiffuse reflection. In this case, the reflected intensity, and thereby the radiosity, depends on the direction. Thus, the number of unknowns is the number N of surface elements times the number J of directions considered. These are related by NJ equations whose coefficients involve the bidirectional-reflection functions as well as the form factors. Solving this tremendous system of equations is extremely time consuming, but once this is done, the image from any viewpoint can be found in a shorter period of time.

A third extension, by Rushmeier and Torrance [Rush87], simulates light scattering and absorption by a "participating medium," such as dusty, smoky, or misty air, by including radiosities of volume elements of the medium. The Gauss-Seidel iteration for solving the resulting equations calculates the successive scattering of light in the medium as well as from the surfaces. Simpler single-scattering models for the medium were analyzed by Blinn [Blin82b], Max [Max86b] (included in Chapter 4: Scan-Line Algorithms) and Nishita et al. [Nish87].

Wallace et al. [Wall87] have improved on this performance by combining the best features of the ray tracing and radiosity methods. They use the radiosity method to compute the diffuse component of each surface intensity, independent of the viewpoint, and then use a view-dependent distributed-ray-tracing calculation for the specular component.

An earlier version of this article was included in *Unpublished Course Notes, State of the Art in Image Synthesis, SIGGRAPH '85 Course Notes # 11*, 1985, by Association for Computing Machinery, Inc.

A Comprehensive Shading Model [1]

Turner Whitted
Numerical Design Limited
Chapel Hill, North Carolina 27514

Rob Cook
PIXAR
San Rafael, California 94912

As part of the search for better display algorithms, we have tried to classify existing shading techniques within the most comprehensive model that we could devise. Shading is a function which depends on the illumination and reflection at visible points in a scene. Reflection depends in turn on the geometry and surface properties at the point of reflection. We define a general and comprehensive model of the image synthesis process in a "pixel equation" whose right hand side expresses a combination of the illumination and reflection components. We then describe various shading techniques as approximations to this expression to illustrate the limitations of typical shading models.

Computer Image Synthesis

Image synthesis has three functions: 1) geometric mapping, 2) shading, and 3) filtering and sampling. The geometric processing includes object space to screen space transformations and visibility calculations. The filtering and sampling functions are required to accommodate the computer's discrete representation of images that we would like to think of as continuous functions. This paper is

[1]The original version of this paper predates the introduction of radiosity methods to computer graphics[Goral84] and the very general "rendering equation" [Kajiya86]. The word "comprehensive" in the title should be interpreted with this in mind.

devoted to the remaining process, shading, which simulates the reflection of light from a visible surface point to the viewpoint in synthetic scenes.

Early shaded rendering methods were extensions of line drawing techniques. Shading amounted to little more than filling in the region between edges with an appropriate color. The realization that careful selection of the "appropriate color" could produce a realistic appearance lead to serious development of sophisticated shading methods.

As shaders have become more elaborate, the principles of the early rendering techniques have become less important to image synthesis as a whole since the execution time of most display algorithms is limited by shading time. It may be useful then to examine shading techniques by themselves and worry about the geometric mapping and filtering and sampling functions later. In this paper we examine the models of reflection and illumination that yield realistic appearance. The commonly used models turn out to be special cases of a comprehensive, but difficult to evaluate, "pixel equation."

Physical Models of Reflection

The most accurate simulations of reflection are based on physical models. Nevertheless, there is a certain amount of *ad-hoc* approximation in commonly used reflection functions. One successful approximation combines a diffuse and a specular component of reflected light in relative proportions that depend on surface properties. The models used for the diffuse and specular terms are quite different.

Perfectly diffusing surfaces reflect light in all directions equally. The amount of light reflected depends only on the surface's exposure to the light source. The amount of light falling on a unit area of the surface is greatest at normal incidence and least at grazing incidence, falling off as the cosine of the angle between the light source direction and the surface normal, *i.e.* for a single point light source

$$R_d = k_d \, I_L \, (\mathbf{N} \cdot \mathbf{L}) \tag{1}$$

Here **N** is the surface normal, **L** is the direction to the light source, and I_L is the intensity of the light source. The percentage of incident light reflected is the coefficient of diffuse reflection, k_d. Used alone, this reflection function produces surfaces with a chalky, matte finish.

An effective physical model of specular reflection for computer graphics is derived from the Torrance-Sparrow model [Blinn77] [Cook82]. This model assumes that a reflecting surface consists of microscopic mirrors whose orientation is distributed randomly about a mean surface normal. The specular reflection function has the form

$$R_s = \frac{k_s\, F\, G\, D}{(\mathbf{N}\cdot\mathbf{L})(\mathbf{N}\cdot\mathbf{E})} \tag{2}$$

where F is the Fresnel attenuation function, G accounts for shadowing between microfacets, and D is the distribution of orientations of microfacets for the surface. D then accounts for the surface roughness; G is a purely geometric term; and F is a function of the angle of incidence of illumination as well as the dielectric constant of the reflecting material. The two dot products in the denominator account for the area of the reflecting surface visible to a unit area at the light source and at the viewpoint respectively. Reflection is reduced to a function of four geometric terms and a term which is a function of both geometric elements and electrical properties. The constant k_s can be used either to relate the reflection to real physical quantities or merely to gain a degree of control over the shading process.

A Gaussian distribution works well for D, although more accurate ones have been proposed [Cook82]. As the variance of the distribution increases the specular highlight produced by the shading function becomes broader.

Illumination

While a reflection model defines the interaction of light with a surface in terms of the surface's physical properties, an illumination model defines the incident light itself. The illumination model is often geometric, but gross simplifications of the geometry are sufficient in many cases.

In most environments there is ambient light from a variety of sources bouncing around. Rather than model the individual light sources, we can make the simplifying assumption that ambient light comes equally from all directions. Then we can model the reflection of this ambient light as a constant term that has no dependence on viewer, light source, or surface normal directions.

Slightly more complex is a point source of light with no shape, no orientation, and, if located infinitely far from the point of reflection, only a partially specified position. In other words, the point source at infinity is specified only in terms of a direction, $\mathbf{L}$, and an intensity, I_L. Near light sources are specified by position rather than direction. Once the point of reflection is established the direction to the light source is simply

$$\mathbf{L}(x,y,z) = \mathbf{P}_L - \mathbf{P}_r.$$

where $\mathbf{P}_L$ is the light source position and $\mathbf{P}_r$ is the point of reflection.

Geometric illumination models can become progressively more complex to include lists of point light sources, and to ultimately include areas defined by geometric surfaces. Illumination models may also be expressed as functions of geometric terms. The simplest such function is a sky map stored in a look-up table. In this case, illumination falling on a surface is accessed by an index derived from the direction of the illumination. Alternatively, the illumination may be a function of the orientation of the light source (*e.g.* street lamps). Non-geometric aspects of illumination include spectrum, variations over time, etc.

One should note that although the illumination model can be used directly, without reflection, to model backgrounds and emitters, we are primarily interested in using it with a companion reflection model.

The Pixel Equation

The intensity of reflected light at a point on a visible surface can be expressed as the integral over the hemisphere above the reflecting surface of an illumination function, $L(t,x,y,z,\phi,\theta,\lambda)$, times a reflectance function, $R(t,x,y,z,\phi,\theta,\lambda)$. Here ϕ and θ are polar coordinates of illumination direction vectors, t is time, and λ is the wavelength of incident and reflected light, and (x,y,z) is the point of reflection.

We refer to the following as the "pixel equation" [Cook83]:

$$I_r(x,y,z) = \int_{t=-\infty}^{+\infty} \int_{\lambda=580}^{760} \int_{\phi=0}^{\pi/2} \int_{\theta=0}^{2\pi} L(t,x,y,z,\phi,\theta,\lambda) R(t,\phi,\theta,\lambda)\, d\theta\, d\phi\, d\lambda\, dt. \quad (3)$$

The pixel equation encompasses sampling in time and wavelength. It can be extended to include sampling in space, but that extension has little effect on the reflected intensity. Since the point of reflection is fixed each time this integral is evaluated, the (x,y,z) dependence of $L()$ and $R()$ is constant. For further simplicity we eliminate the time and wavelength, dependencies and write

$$I_r = \int_{\phi}\int_{\theta} L(\phi,\theta) R(\phi,\theta)\, d\phi\, d\theta. \quad (4)$$

The geometry of reflection is shown in figure 1.

One should note that objects can transmit as well as reflect light according to an equation in which the reflection function is replaced by a transmission function, $T(t,x,y,z,\phi,\theta,\lambda)$:

$$I_t(x,y,z) = \int_{t=-\infty}^{+\infty} \int_{\lambda=580}^{760} \int_{\phi=-\pi/2}^{0} \int_{\theta=0}^{2\pi} L(t,x,y,z,\phi,\theta,\lambda)T(t,x,y,z,\phi,\theta,\lambda)\, d\theta\, d\phi\, d\lambda\, dt. \quad (5)$$

Of course, the hemispherical domain of integration in (5) is on the under side of the surface.

The intensity expression can be evaluated as often as several times per pixel and must therefore be simple enough to permit rapid calculation. Reducing the expression by using an approximate $L()$ function, approximate $R()$ and $T()$ functions, or both generally eases the evaluation of the integral and significantly cuts the image generation time. As we shall see, simplifying approximations also limit the degree of realism that a shading model can achieve.

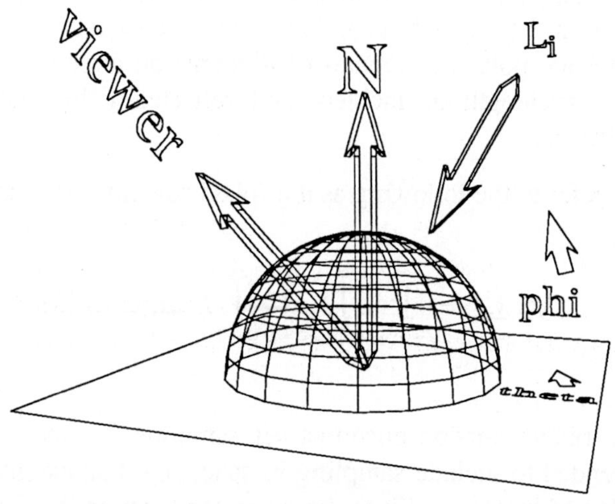

Figure 1. The geometry of reflection from a single point.

Conventional Shading Procedures and the Pixel Equation

Assume that all surfaces discussed here are polygonal or approximations composed of collections of polygons. Further assume that light sources are points which can be described in terms of position, color, and intensity.

Flat Shading with Point Light Sources

In the simplest case, each polygon is assigned a fixed intensity value. Then whenever that polygon is visible, the fixed shade is written into the appropriate pixel. The shade assigned to each polygon can assigned manually, according to some function that has special meaning to the viewer, or according to a shading model such as the ones described below.

For point light sources, the $L()$ function in (4) is a delta function times the intensity of the light source, $I_{L_i}\delta(\phi,\theta)$. If a delta function for each of N point light sources is substituted into the intensity expression the need to evaluate the integral disappears:

$$\int_{\phi}\int_{\theta}\sum_{i=1}^{N} I_{L_i}\delta(\phi_{L_i},\theta_{L_i})R(\phi,\theta)d\phi d\theta = \sum_{i=1}^{N} I_{L_i}R(\phi_{L_i},\theta_{L_i})$$

where ϕ_{L_i} and θ_{L_i} are polar coordinates of the direction from (x,y,z) to the ith light source. Intensity becomes solely a function of the reflection model and is much easier to compute.

With a perfectly diffusing surface, light is scattered equally in all directions and the viewer's position with respect to the surface and light source do not matter. If the light source is infinitely distant from the scene, then shade can be computed once for each polygon since the surface normal direction, and consequently the angle between the surface normal and the light source, are constant. With a combination of constant ambient light and point light sources the reflected intensity can be expressed as:

$$I = I_a + \sum_{i=1}^{N} k_d I_{L_i}(\mathbf{N}\cdot\mathbf{L}_i) \qquad (6)$$

where I is the intensity of the reflected light, I_a is a constant intensity due to reflected ambient light, and the diffuse reflection from each point source is simulated by equation (1).

Interpolated Shading and Highlights

Gouraud [Gouraud71] introduced the notion of interpolating intensities across the surface of polygons to simulate the smooth appearance of curved surfaces. The expression given in (6) works well with interpolated shading. However, reflection functions which include specular reflection terms yield artifacts in the final image whenever the specular term varies significantly within the span of a single polygon.

Phong [Phong75] devised the idea of interpolating the geometric elements in the intensity function instead of the intensity itself. In addition, Phong introduced an shading function that included a specular term,

$$I = I_a + \sum_{i=1}^{N} k_d I_{L_i} (\mathbf{N} \cdot \mathbf{L}_i) + k_s \sum_{i=1}^{N} I_{L_i} R_s \tag{7}$$

Phong's specular reflection function is a very much simplified version of the one in (2) with $R_s = FD$ where D is approximated by $D = (\mathbf{N} \cdot \mathbf{L})^n$ and n is a parameter related to surface smoothness.

Whether Phong's approximation, the full model of (2), or some other approximation is used, the evaluation of the shading function avoids integration as long as the lighting environment contains only an ambient term and point sources.

Extended Lighting Environment Models

The first attempts to provide a realistic simulation of the lighting environment were shadow algorithms [Bouknight70] [Atherton78] [Crow77]. Further enhancements were provided by models for transparency [Newell73] [Kay79a]. In the case of shadows these improvements amount to nothing more than modulation of the point light sources; they retain the limitations of point sources.

Area Sources

Other improvements in realism have come from more elaborate models of the lighting function, $L(\phi,\theta)$, than simple point sources. For glossy surfaces, reflections from one object to another are a desirable effect, but one that is very difficult to obtain. For planar, mirror-smooth surfaces, this effect can be achieved by treating the reflecting surface as a new image plane an computing a new viewing transformation for that view (for an example, see Catmull's 142 bottles and glasses [Catmull74]). This is a widely used but limited trick.

Blinn and Newell [Blinn76] created a two dimensional table of values of $L(phi,\theta)$ which has come to be known as *environment map* or *illumination map*. The shader computes a direction of maximum specular reflection and accesses the environment map with indices formed from the polar coordinates of that direction. It would appear that using a single direction of maximum reflection is equivalent to multiplying $R(\phi,\theta)$ by a delta function, but as pointed out in [Miller84] and [Greene86], it is possible to evaluate

$$\int_{\phi}\int_{\theta} L(\phi,\theta)D(\phi,\theta)d\phi d\theta$$

where D is the distribution function in (2) for each entry in the map. It is not possible to fold more of the reflection function into the table since the other terms depend on the direction from the point of reflection to the light source. Environment mapping's real limitation comes from the assumption that each element of the environment is infinitely distant from the point of reflection , i.e. L is only a function of ϕ and θ with no dependence on (x,y,z).

Ray Tracing

A less limited approach to accurately modeling the lighting environment using ray tracted approach to accurately modeling the lighting environment using ray tracing is described by Kay [Kay79b] and Whitted [Whitted80]. Ray tracing differs from previous methods in that shading and visibility are recursive with each point of reflection forming a new viewpoint.

In the simplest of environments (*i.e.* a single surface) all reflected and refracted light comes from explicit light sources. In real environments, light is reflected from one surface to another and transmitted from one surface through another. To simulate a real environment, a recursive intensity expression is used. Light reflected to the viewer from a visible point on a surface may reach the viewer from another point on another surface, and so on. To support this recursive intensity expression, a ray casting visibility calculation is applied recursively to build a tree of rays. Figure 2 shows the geometry of reflection and refraction of light for a ray traced pixel.

In addition to reflection and refraction, rays traced from a visible point to each point light source can be used to simulate shadows. If shadow rays encounter any surface closer than the light source, then the point of origin of the ray is in shadow with respect to that light source. In practice, the specular term can come from intensity incident along a reflected ray if the reflected ray intersects some object, or from a conventional expression, such as Phong's, if the reflected ray hits nothing. The refracted ray is omitted for opaque surfaces.

A very simple recursive shading expression that supports the features of ray tracing is:

$$I = \sum_{i=1}^{N} f_i(shadow)(k_d(\mathbf{N}\cdot\mathbf{L}_i) + k_s R_s) + I_{reflect}() + I_{refract}() \quad (8)$$

Each $f_i(shadow)$ function is just I_{L_i} modulated by a visibility test along a ray from the point of reflection to the light source L_i.

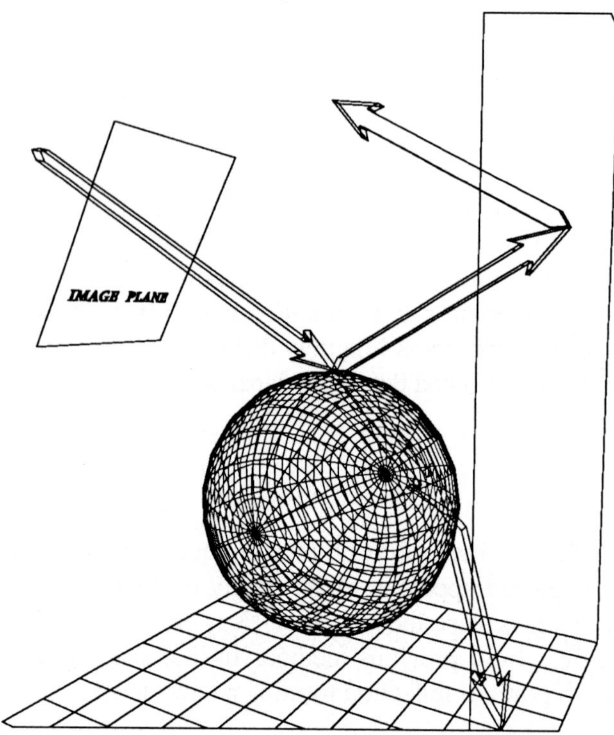

Figure 2. Light rays reflected and refracted for one pixel of a ray traced image.

The $I_{reflect}()$ and $I_{refract}()$ terms are the recursive parts of (8). Since visibility is determined only along an infinitesimally narrow path, using ray tracing in a lighting model is equivalent to replacing $R(\phi,\theta)$ with a delta function times the reflectance in the direction of maximum specular reflection.

The reflected intensity expression, $I_{reflect}$ becomes

$$I_r = \int_\phi \int_\theta R_s \delta(\phi_1,\theta_1) L(\phi,\theta)\, d\theta d\phi$$

$$= L(\phi_1,\theta_1)$$

There are numerous deficiencies of the simple ray tracing technique because most real surfaces are not perfect mirrors and most light sources are not points. In spite of the improvements applied to simple ray tracing, examination of the images produced reveal its drawbacks. This is most evident in the sharpness of shadows and reflection.

Hall and Greenberg [Hall83] extend the basic recursive shading function of (8) by incorporating a more complete approximation of (2) and by retaining the spectral dependence that is eliminated in (4). However the artifacts of evaluating R_s for only one direction remain.

Algorithms which permit the evaluation of R_s over a range of directions include *cone tracing* [Amanatides84] and *beam tracing* [Heckbert84].

Distributed Ray Tracing

Distributed ray tracing [Cook84], is a Monte Carlo evaluation of the right hand side of the pixel equation in which the functions under the integrals are treated as distribution functions. As seen in figure 3, rays are traced in random directions from the point of reflection. Actual implementations would not necessarily cast multiple rays at each point of reflection since oversampling of one kind or another is generally used for anti-aliasing.

In this "non-deterministic" shading function a sum of delta functions replaces the $L()$ function as in simple ray tracing, but the D term in (2) selects the most probable directions for $L()$. The approach not only permits the rendering of soft shadows and soft reflections, but it extends to the time domain to enable motion blurring. At the cost of tracing additional rays, it yields a close approximation to (4).

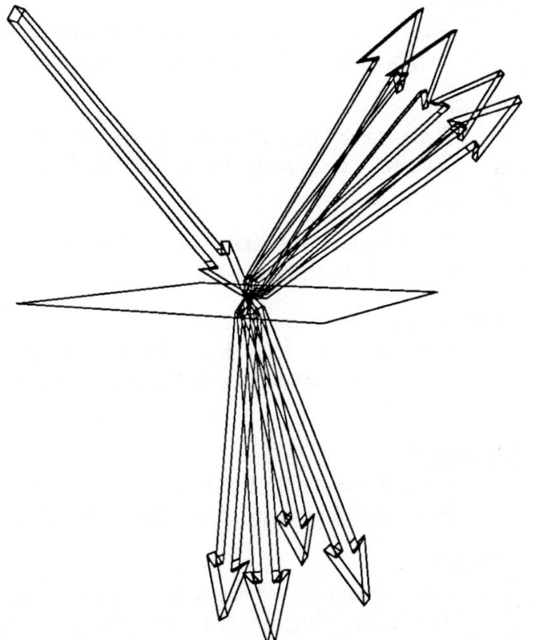

Figure 3. Rays distributed from the point of reflection.

Summary

To avoid the integration required in the most general expression of a shading function, conventional shading models approximate either the illumination term or the reflection term with a sum of delta functions. The approximations restrict the amount of realism that can be achieved with the respective model. If the number and distribution of delta functions is appropriately chosen, as in distributed ray tracing, then a close approximation to the general shading equation can be made.

References

[Amanatides84]
Amanatides, J., "Ray Tracing with Cones," *Computer Graphics*, Vol. 18, no. 3, (July 1984), pp. 129-135.

[Atherton78]
Atherton, P.R., K.J. Weiler, and D.P. Greenberg, "Polygon Shadow Generation," *Computer Graphics*, Vol. 12, no. 2, (Aug. 1978), pp. 275-281.

[Blinn76]
Blinn, James F., and Martin E. Newell, "Texture and Reflection in Computer Generated Images," *Comm. ACM*, **19**, 10 (Oct. 1976), pp. 542-547.

[Blinn77]
Blinn, James F., "Models of Light Reflection for Computer Synthesized Pictures," *Computer Graphics*, **11**, 2, July 1977.

[Bouknight70]
Bouknight, W.J., and K.C. Kelley, "An Algorithm for Producing Half-Tone Computer Graphics Presentations with Shadows and Movable Light Sources," *Proc. of SJCC, AFIPS*, v. 36, 1970.

[Catmull74]
Catmull, Edwin E. *A Subdivision Algorithm for Computer Display of Curved Surfaces*. Ph.D. Diss. University of Utah December 1974

[Cook82]
Cook, Robert L., and Kenneth E. Torrance, "A Reflectance Model for Computer Graphics," *ACM Trans. Graphics*, **1**, *1 (Jan. 1982), pp. 7-24.*

[Cook83]
Cook, Robert L., Donald P. Greenberg, and Turner Whitted, unpublished notes, 1983.

[Cook84]
Cook, Robert L., Thomas Porter, and Loren Carpenter, "Distributed Ray Tracing," *Computer Graphics*, **18**, 3, SIGGRAPH ACM, Jul. 1984, pp. 137-145.

[Crow77]
Crow, Franklin C., "Shadow Algorithms for Computer Graphics," *Computer Graphics*, **11**, 2, SIGGRAPH ACM, Jul. 1977, pp. 242-248.

[Goral84]
Goral, Cindy M., Kenneth E. Torrance, Donald P. Greenberg, and Bennett Battaile, "Modeling the Interaction of Light Between Diffuse Surfaces," *Computer Graphics* (Proceedings of Siggraph '84), July 1984, pp. 213-222.

[Gouraud71]
Gouraud, H., "Computer Display of Curved Surfaces," *IEEE Trans. Comp.*, **C-20**, 6, June 1971. Greene[86] Greene, Ned, "Applications of World Projections," *Proceedings of Graphics Interface '86*, (May 1986), pp. 108-114.

[Hall83]
Hall, Roy, and Donald P. Greenberg, "A TestBed for Realistic Image Synthesis," *IEEE CG&A*, **3**, 8, (Nov. 1983), pp. 10-20.

[Heckbert84]
Heckbert, P.S., and P. Hanrahan, "Beam Tracing Polygonal Objects," *Computer Graphics*, Vol. 18, no. 3, (July 1984), pp.119-127.

[Kajiya86]
Kajiya, James T., "The Rendering Equation," *Computer Graphics*, Vol. 20, no. 4, (August 1986), pp. 143-150.

[Kay79a]
Kay, D.S., Transparency, Refraction, and Ray Tracing for Computer Synthesized Images, Master's Thesis, Cornell University, Jan. 1979.

[Kay79a]
Kay, D.S., and D.P. Greenberg, "Transparency for Computer Synthesized Images," *Computer Graphics*, Vol. 13, no. 2, (August 1979) pp. 158-164.

[Miller84]
Miller, Gene S., and Robert Hoffman, "Illumination and Reflection Maps: Simulated Objects in Simulated and Real Environments," *Siggraph '84 Advanced Computer Graphics Animation Seminar*, (July 1984).

[Newell72]
Newell, M.E., R.G. Newell, and T.L. Sancha, "A New Approach to the Shaded Picture Problem," *Proc. ACM National Conf.*, 1972.

[Phong75]
Bui-Tuong Phong, "Illumination for Computer Generated Pictures," *Comm. ACM*, **18**, 3, (July 1975), pp. 311-317.

[Whitted80]
Whitted, Turner, "An Improved Illumination Model for Shaded Display," *Comm. ACM*, **23**, 6, June 1980.

A REFLECTANCE MODEL FOR COMPUTER GRAPHICS

Robert L. Cook
Program of Computer Graphics
Cornell University
Ithaca, New York 14853

Kenneth E. Torrance
Sibley School of Mechanical and Aerospace Engineering
Cornell University
Ithaca, New York 14853

Abstract

This paper presents a new reflectance model for rendering computer synthesized images. The model accounts for the relative brightness of different materials and light sources in the same scene. It describes the directional distribution of the reflected light and a color shift that occurs as the reflectance changes with incidence angle. The paper presents a method for obtaining the spectral energy distribution of the light reflected from an object made of a specific real material and discusses a procedure for accurately reproducing the color associated with the spectral energy distribution. The model is applied to the simulation of a metal and a plastic.

Key words: computer graphics, image synthesis, reflectance, shading

Computing Reviews category: 8.2

Introduction

The rendering of realistic images in computer graphics requires a model of how objects reflect light. The reflectance model must describe both the color and the spatial distribution of the reflected light. The model is independent of the other aspects of image synthesis, such as the surface geometry representation and the hidden surface algorithm.

Most real surfaces are neither ideal specular (mirror-like) reflectors nor ideal diffuse (Lambertian) reflectors. Phong [13,14] proposed a reflectance model for computer graphics that was a linear combination of specular and diffuse reflection. The specular component was spread out around the specular direction by using a cosine function raised to a power. Subsequently, Blinn [5,6] used similar ideas together with a specular reflection model from [22] which accounts for the off-specular peaks that occur when the incident light is at a grazing angle relative to the surface normal. Whitted [23] extended these models by adding a term for ideal specular reflection from perfectly smooth surfaces. All of these models are based on geometrical optics (ray theory).

The foregoing models treat reflection as consisting of three components: ambient, diffuse and specular. The ambient component represents light that is assumed to be uniformly incident from the environment and that is reflected equally in all directions by the surface. The diffuse and specular components are associated with light from specific light sources. The diffuse component represents light that is scattered equally in all directions. The specular component represents highlights, light that is concentrated around the mirror direction. The specular component was assumed to be the color of the light source and the Fresnel equation was used to obtain the angular variation of the intensity, but not the color, of the specular component. The ambient and diffuse components were assumed to be the color of the material. The resulting models produce images that look realistic for certain types of materials.

This paper presents a reflectance model for rough surfaces that is more general than previous models. It is based on geometrical optics and is applicable to a broad range of materials, surface conditions, and lighting situations. The basis of this model is a reflectance definition that relates the brightness of an object to the intensity and size of each light source that illuminates it. The model predicts the directional distribution and spectral composition of the reflected light. A procedure is described for calculating RGB values from the spectral energy distribution. The new reflectance model is then applied to the simulation of a metal and a plastic, with an explanation of why images rendered with previous models often look plastic and how this plastic appearance can be avoided.

The Reflectance Model

Given a light source, a surface, and an observer, a reflectance model describes the intensity and spectral composition of the reflected light reaching the observer. The intensity of the reflected light is determined by the intensity and size of the light source and by the reflecting ability and surface properties of the material. The spectral composition of the reflected light is determined by the spectral composition of the light source and the wavelength-selective reflection of the surface. In this section, the appropriate reflectance definitions are introduced and are combined into a general reflectance model. Figure 1 contains a summary of the symbols used in this model.

The geometry of reflection is shown in Figure 2. An observer is looking at a point P on a surface. V is the unit vector in the direction of the viewer, N is the unit normal to the surface, and L is the unit vector in the direction of a specific light source. H is a normalized vector in the direction of the angular bisector of V and L, and is defined by

$$H = \frac{V+L}{\mathrm{len}(V+L)} \quad .$$

It is the unit normal to a hypothetical surface that would specularly reflect light from the light source to the viewer. α is the angle between H and N, and θ is the angle between H and V, so that $\cos(\theta) = V \cdot H = L \cdot H$.

The energy of the incident light is expressed as energy per unit time and per unit area of the reflecting surface. The intensity of the incident light is similar, but is expressed per unit projected area and, in addition, per unit solid angle [19]. The energy in an incoming beam of light is

$$E_i = I_i (N \cdot L) d\omega_i \quad .$$

Except for mirrors or near-mirrors, the incoming beam is reflected over a wide range of angles. For this reason, the reflected intensity in any given direction depends on the incident energy, not just on the incident intensity. The ratio of the reflected intensity in a given direction to the incident energy from another direction (within a small solid angle) is called the <u>bidirectional reflectance</u>. This reflectance is fundamental for the study of reflection (for additional discussion, see [19]). For each light source, the bidirectional reflectance R is thus

$$R = \frac{I_r}{E_i} \quad .$$

The reflected intensity reaching the viewer from each light source is then

$$I_r = RE_i$$
$$= RI_i (N \cdot L) d\omega_i \quad .$$

The bidirectional reflectance may be split into two components, specular and diffuse. The specular component represents light that is reflected from the surface of the material. The diffuse component originates from internal scattering (in which the incident light penetrates beneath the surface of the material) or from multiple surface reflections (which occur if the surface is sufficiently rough). The specular and diffuse components can have different colors if the material is not homogeneous. The bidirectional reflectance is thus

$$R = sR_s + dR_d \ , \quad \text{where } s+d=1.$$

In addition to direct illumination by individual light sources, an object may be illuminated by background or ambient illumination. All light that is not direct illumination from a specific light source is lumped together into ambient illumination. The amount of light reflected toward the viewer from any particular direction of ambient illumination is small, but the effect is significant when integrated over the entire hemisphere of illuminating angles. Consequently, it is convenient to introduce an ambient (or

α	angle between N and H
θ	angle between L and H or V and H
D	facet slope distribution function
d	fraction of reflectance that is diffuse
$d\omega_i$	solid angle of a beam of incident light
E_i	energy of the incident light
F	reflectance of a perfectly smooth surface
f	unblocked fraction of the hemisphere
G	geometrical attenuation factor
H	unit angular bisector of V and L
I_i	average intensity of the incident light
I_{ia}	intensity of the incident ambient light
I_r	intensity of the reflected light
I_{ra}	intensity of the reflected ambient light
L	unit vector in the direction of a light
k	extinction coefficient
m	root mean square slope of facets
N	unit surface normal
n	index of refraction
R_a	ambient reflectance
R	total bidirectional reflectance
R_d	diffuse bidirectional reflectance
R_s	specular bidirectional reflectance
s	fraction of reflectance that is specular
V	unit vector in direction of the viewer
wm	relative weight of a facet slope

Figure 1. Summary of symbols.

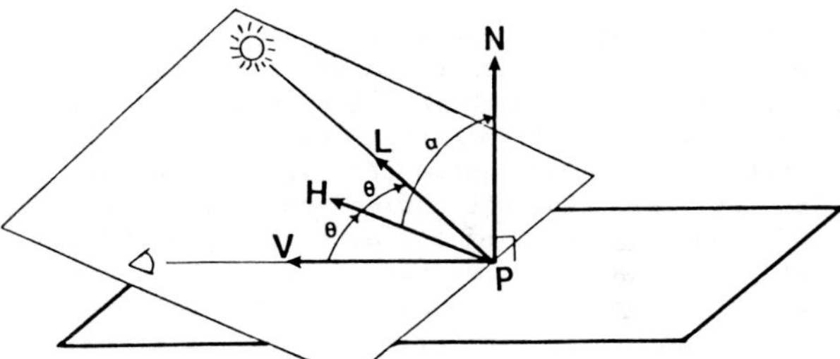

Figure 2. The geometry of reflection.

hemispherical-directional) reflectance, R_a. This reflectance is an integral of the bidirectional reflectance R and is thus a linear combination of R_s and R_d. For simplicity, we assume that R_a is independent of viewing direction. In addition we assume that the ambient illumination is uniformly incident. The reflected intensity due to ambient illumination is defined by

$$I_{ra} = R_a I_{ia} f \quad .$$

The term f is the fraction of the illuminating hemisphere that is not blocked by nearby objects (such as a corner) [24]. It is given by

$$f = \frac{1}{\pi} \int (N \cdot L) d\omega_i \quad ,$$

where the integration is done over the unblocked part of the illuminating hemisphere.

The total intensity of the light reaching the observer is the sum of the reflected intensities from all light sources plus the reflected intensity from any ambient illumination. Assuming that f=1, the basic reflectance model used in this paper becomes:

$$I_r = I_{ia} R_a + \sum_{\ell} I_{i\ell} (N \cdot L_\ell) d\omega_{i\ell} (sR_s + dR_d) \quad .$$

This formulation accounts for the effect of light sources with different intensities and different projected areas which may illuminate a scene. For example, an illuminating beam with the same intensity (I_i) and angle of illumination (N·L) as another beam, but with twice the solid angle ($d\omega_i$) of that beam, will make a surface appear twice as bright. An illuminating beam with twice the intensity of another beam, but with the same angle of illumination and solid angle, will also make a surface appear twice as bright.

This paper does not consider the reflection of light from other objects in the environment. This reflection can be calculated as in [23] or [6] if the surface is perfectly smooth, but even this pure specular reflection should be wavelength dependent.

The above reflectance model implicitly depends on several variables. For example, the intensities depend on wavelength, s and d depend on the material, and the reflectances depend on these variables plus the reflection geometry and the surface roughness. The next two sections consider the directional and wavelength dependence of the reflectance model.

Directional Distribution of the Reflected Light

The ambient and diffuse components reflect light equally in all directions. Thus, R_a and R_d do not depend on the location of the observer. On the other hand, the specular component reflects more light in some directions than in others, so that R_s does depend on the location of the observer.

The angular spread of the specular component can be described by assuming that the surface consists of microfacets, each of which reflects specularly [22]. Only facets whose normal is in the direction H contribute to the specular component of reflection from L to V. The specular component is

$$R_s = \frac{F}{\pi} \frac{D}{(N \cdot L)} \frac{G}{(N \cdot V)} \quad .$$

The Fresnel term F describes how light is reflected from each smooth microfacet. It is a function of incidence angle and wavelength and is discussed in the next section. G, the geometrical attenuation factor, accounts for the shadowing and masking of one facet by another and is discussed elsewhere in detail [5,6,22]. Briefly it is

$$G = \min \left\{ 1, \frac{2(N \cdot H)(N \cdot V)}{(V \cdot H)}, \frac{2(N \cdot H)(N \cdot L)}{(V \cdot H)} \right\} \quad .$$

The facet slope distribution function D represents the fraction of the facets that are oriented in the direction H. Various facet slope distribution functions have been considered by Blinn [5,6]. One of the formulations he described is the Gaussian model [22]:

$$D = ce^{-(\alpha/m)^2} \quad ,$$

where c is an arbitrary constant.

In addition to the ones mentioned by Blinn, other facet slope distribution models are possible. In particular, models for the scattering of radar and infrared radiation from surfaces are available, and are applicable to visible wavelengths. For example, Davies [8] described the spatial distribution of electromagnetic radiation reflected from a rough surface made of a perfect electrical conductor. Bennett and Porteus [3] extended these results to real metals, and Torrance and Sparrow [21] showed that they apply to nonmetals as well. Beckmann [2] provided a comprehensive theory that encompasses all of these materials and is applicable to a wide range of surface conditions ranging from smooth to very rough. For rough surfaces, the Beckmann distribution function is

$$D = \frac{1}{m^2 \cos^4 \alpha} e^{-\left[\frac{\tan^2 \alpha}{m^2}\right]} \quad .$$

This distribution function is similar in shape to the three functions mentioned by Blinn. The advantage of the Beckmann function is that it gives the absolute magnitude of the reflectance without introducing arbitrary constants; the disadvantage is that it requires more computation.

In all of the facet slope distribution functions, the spread of the specular component depends on the rms slope m. Small values of m signify gentle facet slopes and give a distribution that is highly directional around the specular direction, as shown in Figure 3a for the Beckmann distribution model and in Figure 3b for the Gaussian model. Large values of m imply steep facet slopes and give a distribution that is spread out, as shown in Figures 3c and 3d for the Beckmann and Gaussian models, respectively. Note the similarity between the two models.

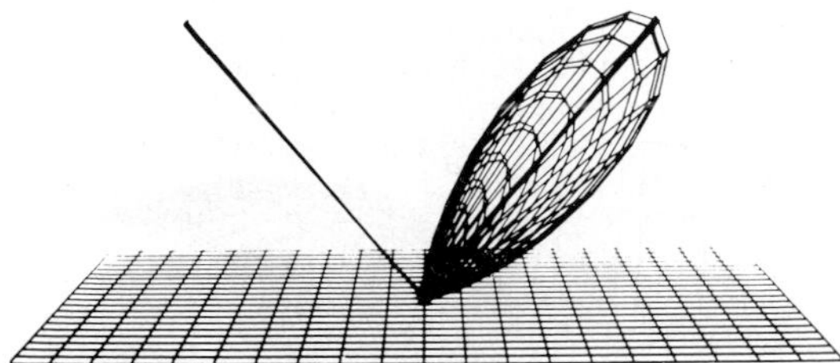

Figure 3a. Beckmann distribution for m=0.2.

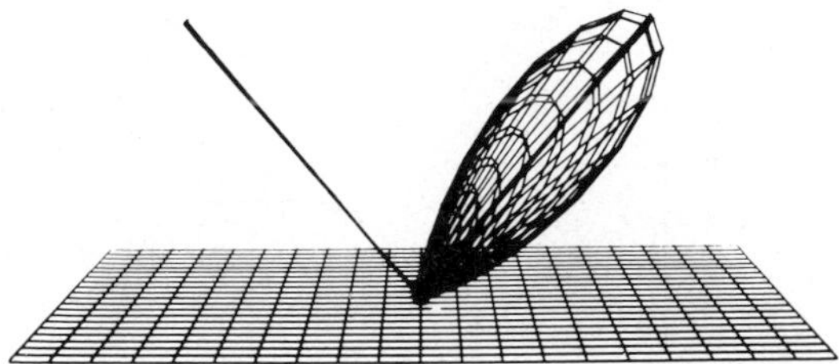

Figure 3b. Gaussian distribution for m=0.2.

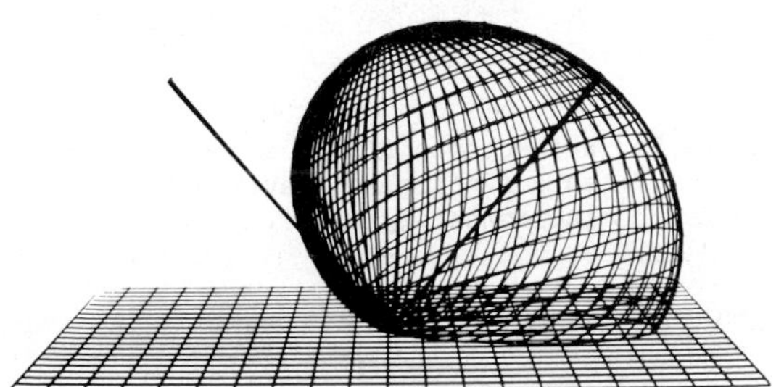

Figure 3c. Beckmann distribution for m=0.6.

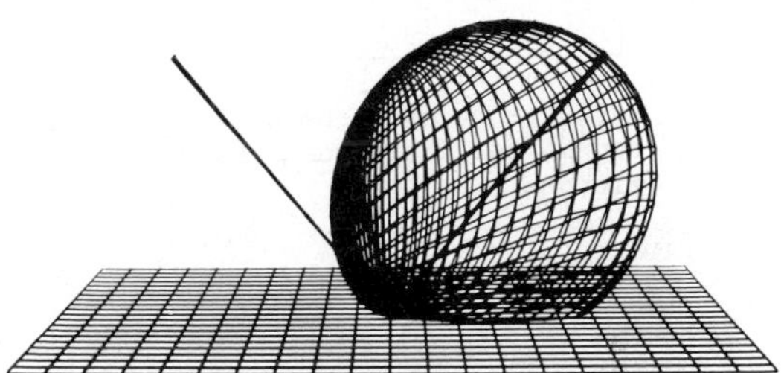

Figure 3d. Gaussian distribution for m=0.6.

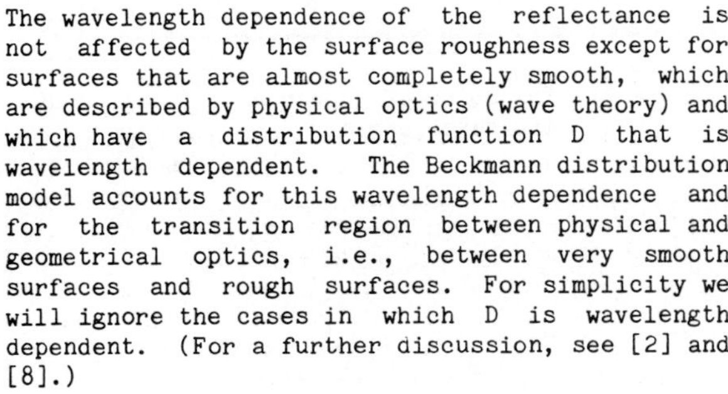

The wavelength dependence of the reflectance is not affected by the surface roughness except for surfaces that are almost completely smooth, which are described by physical optics (wave theory) and which have a distribution function D that is wavelength dependent. The Beckmann distribution model accounts for this wavelength dependence and for the transition region between physical and geometrical optics, i.e., between very smooth surfaces and rough surfaces. For simplicity we will ignore the cases in which D is wavelength dependent. (For a further discussion, see [2] and [8].)

Some surfaces have two or more scales of roughness, or slope m, and can be modeled by using two or more distribution functions [15]. In such cases, D is expressed as a weighted sum of the distribution functions, each with a different value of m:

$$D = \sum_j wm_j D(m_j) \quad ,$$

where m_j = rms slope of the jth distribution.
wm_j = weight of the jth distribution. The sum of these weights is 1.

Spectral Composition of the Reflected Light

The ambient, diffuse, and specular reflectances all depend on wavelength. R_a, R_d, and the F term of R_s may be obtained from the appropriate reflectance spectra for the material. A nonhomogeneous material may have different reflectance spectra for each of the three reflectances, though R_a is restricted to being a linear combination of R_s and R_d.

Reflectance spectra have been measured for thousands of materials and have been collected in [9,16-18]. The reflectance data are usually for illumination at normal incidence. These values are normally measured for polished surfaces and must be multiplied by $1/\pi$ to obtain the bidirectional reflectance for a rough surface [19]. Most materials were measured at only a few wavelengths in the visible range (typically around 10 to 15), so that values for intermediate wavelengths must be interpolated (a simple linear interpolation seems to be sufficient). The reflectance spectrum of a copper mirror for normal incidence is shown for visible wavelengths in Figure 4a. In choosing a reflectance spectrum, careful consideration must be given to the conditions under which which the measurements were made. For example, some metals develop an oxide layer with time which can drastically alter the color [1].

The spectral energy distribution of the reflected light is found by multiplying the spectral energy distribution of the incident light by the reflectance spectrum of the surface. An example of this is shown in Figure 4b. The spectral energy distributions of the sun and a number of CIE standard illuminants are available in [7]. The spectral energy distribution of CIE standard illuminant D6500, which approximates sunlight on a cloudy day, is the top curve shown in Figure 4b. The lower curve shows the corresponding spectral energy distribution of light reflected from a copper mirror illuminated by CIE standard illuminant D6500 at normal incidence. It is obtained by multiplying the top curve by the reflectance spectrum in Figure 4a.

In general, R_d and F will vary with the geometry of reflection. For convenience, we will subsequently take R_d to be the bidirectional

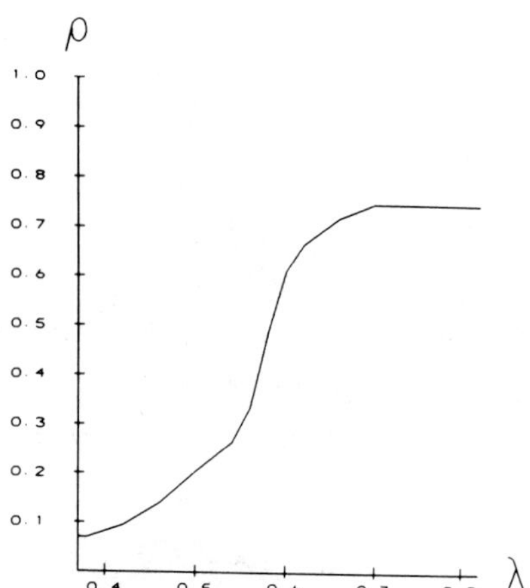

Figure 4a. Reflectance spectrum of a copper mirror for normal incidence. Wavelength is in microns.

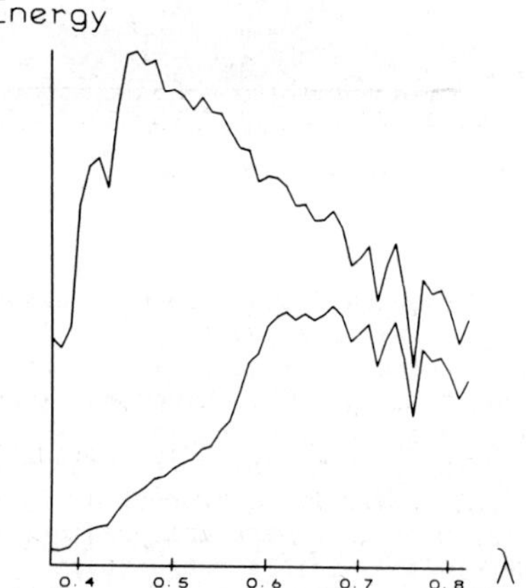

Figure 4b. Top curve: Spectral energy distribution of CIE standard illuminant D6500. Bottom curve: Spectral energy distribution of light reflected from a copper mirror illuminated by D6500.

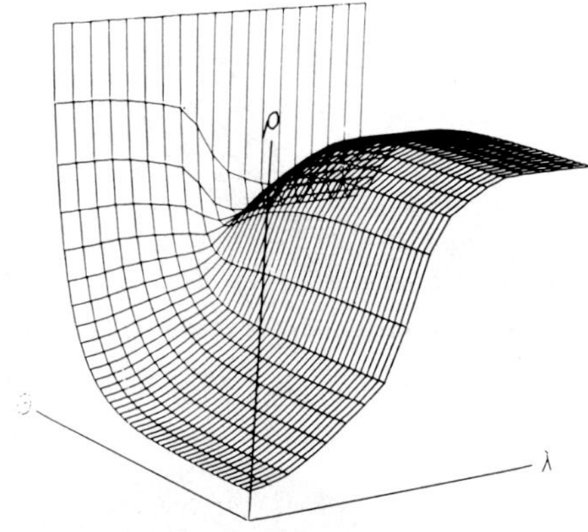

Figure 5a. Reflectance (ρ) of a copper mirror as a function of wavelength (λ) and incidence angle (θ).

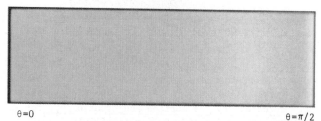

Figure 5b. The color of copper as a function of incidence angle.

Figure 5c. The color of copper as approximated by the method discussed in this paper.

reflectance for illumination in a direction normal to the reflecting surface. This is reasonable because the reflectance varies only slightly for incidence angles within about 70 degrees of the surface normal [20]. We will specifically allow for the directional dependence of F, however, as this leads to a color shift when the directions of incidence and reflection are near grazing.

The reflectance F may be obtained theoretically from the Fresnel equation [20]. This equation expresses the reflectance of a perfectly smooth, mirror-like surface in terms of the index of refraction (n) and the extinction coefficient (k) of the surface and the angle of illumination (θ). In general, both n and k vary with wavelength but their values are frequently not known. On the other hand, experimentally measured values of the reflectance at normal incidence are frequently known.

To obtain the spectral and angular variation of F, we have adopted a practical compromise. If n and k are known, we use the Fresnel equation. If not, but the normal reflectance is known, we fit the Fresnel equation to the measured normal reflectance for a polished surface. For nonmetals, for which k=0, this immediately gives us an estimate of the index of refraction n. For metals, for which k is generally not 0, we set k=0 and get an effective value for n from the normal reflectance. The angular dependence of F is then available from the Fresnel equation. The foregoing procedure yields the correct value of F for normal incidence and a good estimate of its angular dependence, which is only weakly dependent on the extinction coefficient k.

To illustrate this procedure, the Fresnel equation for unpolarized incident light and k=0 is

$$F = \frac{1}{2}\frac{(g-c)^2}{(g+c)^2}\left\{1+\frac{(c(g+c)-1)^2}{(c(g-c)+1)^2}\right\},$$

where

$c = \cos(\theta) = V \cdot H$

$g^2 = n^2 + c^2 - 1.$

(Note that a similar expression in [5] is missing the 1/2 factor.) At normal incidence, $\theta = 0$, so $c=1$, $g=n$ and

$$F_0 = \left\{\frac{n-1}{n+1}\right\}^2 .$$

Solving for n gives the equation

$$n = \frac{1+\sqrt{F_0}}{1-\sqrt{F_0}} .$$

Values of n determined in this way are then substituted into the original Fresnel equation to obtain the reflectance F at other angles of incidence. The procedure may repeated at other wavelengths to obtain the spectral and directional dependence of the reflectance.

The dependence of the reflectance on wavelength and the angle of incidence implies that the color of the reflected light changes with the incidence angle. Reflectance spectra for copper are shown in Figure 5a. As the incidence angle (θ) approaches $\pi/2$, the color of the reflected light approaches the color of the light source (since the reflectance F approaches unity). The colors corresponding to the reflection of white light (CIE standard illuminant D6500) from copper are shown as a function of θ in Figure 5b. It is evident that the color shift from the Fresnel equations only becomes important as θ approaches $\pi/2$ (i.e., as the angle between V and L approaches π).

Calculation of the color shift is computationally expensive. It can be simplified in one of two ways: by creating lookup tables or by using the following approximation. Values of F are first calculated for a value of n corresponding to the average normal reflectance. These values are then used to interpolate between the color of the material at $\theta=0$ and the color at $\theta=\pi/2$, which is the color of the light source because $F_{\pi/2}$ is 1.0 at every wavelength. For example, let the red component of the color at normal incidence be Red_0 and let the red component of the color of the incident light be $Red_{\pi/2}$. Then the red component of the color at other angles is

$$Red_\theta = Red_0 + (Red_{\pi/2} - Red_0)\,\frac{\max(0, F_\theta - F_0)}{F_{\pi/2} - F_0} .$$

The green and blue components are interpolated similarly. Figure 5c shows the effect of using the approximate procedure to estimate the color of copper as a function of incidence angle. The approximate procedure yields results that are similar to those from the complete (but more expensive) procedure (Figure 5b). The foregoing approximation must always be used if the spectral energy distribution of the reflected light is not known, in which case all of the RGB values are estimates.

Determining the RGB Values

For a computer synthesized scene to be realistic, the color sensation of an observer watching the synthesized scene on a color television monitor must be approximately equivalent to the color sensation of an observer watching a corresponding scene in the real world. To produce this equivalent color sensation, the laws of trichromatic color reproduction are used to convert the spectral energy distribution of the reflected light to the appropriate RGB values for the particular monitor being used.

Every color sensation can be uniquely described by its location in a three dimensional color space. One such color space is called the XYZ space. A point in this space is specified with three coordinates, the color's XYZ tristimulus values. Each spectral energy distribution is associated with a point in the XYZ color space and thus with tristimulus values. If two spectral energy distributions are associated with the same tristimulus values, they produce the same color sensation and are called metamers. The red, green, and blue phosphors of a monitor can be illuminated in proportions to produce a set of spectral energy distributions which define a region of XYZ space called the gamut of the monitor. The goal, then, is to find the proportions of phosphor illumination that produce a spectral energy distribution that is a metamer of the spectral energy distribution of the reflected light.

These proportions are determined by calculating the XYZ tristimulus values that are associated with the spectral energy distribution of the reflected light and then calculating the RGB values that produce a spectral energy distribution with these tristimulus values. To do this, the spectral energy distribution of the reflected light is multiplied by the XYZ matching functions (obtained from [7]) at every wavelength. The resulting spectra are then integrated to obtain the XYZ tristimulus values. These XYZ values are converted by a matrix multiplication to RGB linear luminance values for a particular set of phosphors and monitor white point. The linear luminances are then converted to RGB voltages, taking into account the nonlinearities of the monitor and the effects of viewing conditions. For a more complete description of this procedure, see [12].

The monitor has a maximum luminance at which it can reproduce a given chromaticity. Any XYZ values that represent luminances greater than this maximum are outside the gamut of the monitor. To avoid this problem, all XYZ values in the scene are scaled equally so that they all lie inside the monitor gamut and usually so that the color with the greatest luminance is reproduced on the monitor at the maximum luminance possible for its chromaticity. But even with scaling, some spectral energy distributions are associated with trimstimulus values that lie outside the gamut of the monitor. Because such a color cannot be reproduced on the monitor at any luminance, it must be approximated by a similar color that lies inside the monitor gamut. This color may be chosen in many different ways; in this case we have decided it is appropriate to maintain the same hue, desaturating the color as necessary. To do this, the tristimulus XYZ values are converted to a color space in which locations are specified by dominant wavelength and purity. The purity is then reduced while the dominant wavelength (and thus roughly the hue) is held constant until the color lies inside the monitor gamut. The resulting color is then converted back to XYZ space. (For a discussion of dominant wavelength and purity, see [11].)

Applications

This section discusses the application of the reflectance model to two particular classes of materials, metals and plastics. The main consideration is the homogeneity of the material. Substances that are composed of different materials, such that there is one material at the surface and another beneath the surface, are nonhomogeneous and may have specular and diffuse components that differ in color.

A typical plastic has a substrate that is transparent or white, with embedded pigment particles [10]. Thus, the light reflected directly from the surface is only slightly altered in color from the light source. Any color alterations are a result of the reflectance of the surface material. Light that penetrates into the material interacts with the pigments. Internal reflections thus give rise to a colored, uniformly distributed diffuse reflection.

A plastic may thus be simulated by using a colored diffuse component and a white specular component. This is just the model used by Phong and Blinn and is why so many computer graphics images that have a significant specular component look like plastic. Figure 6a shows a simulated copper-colored plastic vase. This figure was generated with the following parameters:

- 2 lights: I_i = CIE standard illuminant D6500
  - $d\omega_i$ = 0.0001 and 0.0002
- Specular: s = 0.1
  - F = the reflectance of a vinyl mirror
  - D = Beckmann function with m = 0.15
- Diffuse: d = 0.9
  - R_d = the bidirectional reflectance of copper for normal incidence
- Ambient: I_{ia} = 0.01 I_i
  - R_a = πR_d

Metals conduct electricity. An impinging electromagnetic wave can stimulate the motion of electrons near the surface, which in turn lead to re-emission (reflection) of a wave. There is little depth penetration, and the depth penetration decreases with increasing values of the extinction coefficient k. As a result, reflection from a metal occurs essentially at the surface [16]. Thus internal reflections are not present to contribute to a diffuse component, which can be important for a nonmetal. When the rms roughness slope m is small, multiple surface reflections may also be neglected and the entire diffuse component disappears. Figure 6b shows a simulated copper vase. This figure was generated with the following parameters:

- 2 lights: I_i = CIE standard illuminant D6500
  - $d\omega_i$ = 0.0001 and 0.0002
- Specular: s = 1.0
  - F = the reflectance of a copper

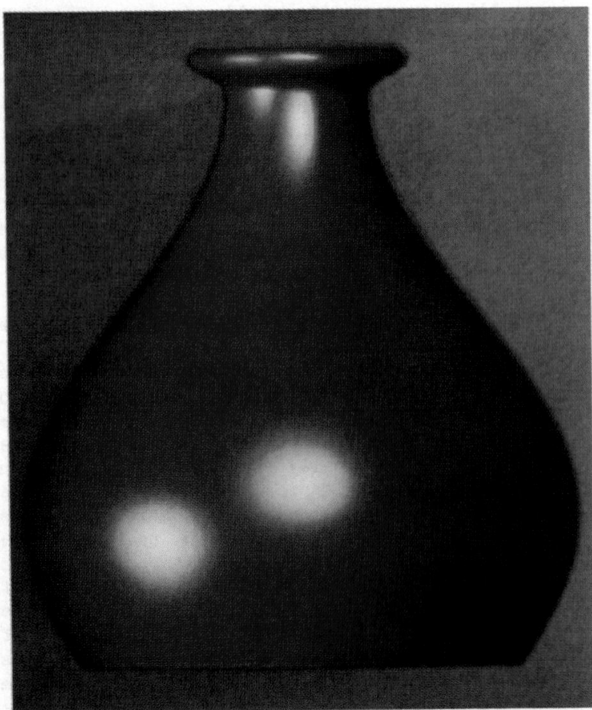

Figure 6a. A copper-colored plastic vase.

Figure 6b. A copper vase.

mirror
D = Beckmann function with
m_1 = 0.4
wm_1 = 0.4
m_2 = 0.2
wm_2 = 0.6
Diffuse: d = 0.0
R_d = the bidirectional reflectance of copper for normal incidence
Ambient: I_{ia} = 0.01 I_i
R_a = πR_d

Note that two values for the rms slope are employed to generate a realistic rough surface finish. The specular reflectance component has a copper color. The copper vase in Figure 6b does not display the plastic appearance of the vase in Figure 6a, showing that a correct treatment of the color of the specular component is needed to obtain a realistic nonplastic appearance.

Figure 7 shows vases made of a variety of materials. In every case, the specular and diffuse components have the same color (i.e., $R_d=F_0/\pi$). The lighting conditions for all of the vases are identical to the lighting conditions for Figures 6a and 6b. The six metals were generated with the same parameters used for Figure 6b, except for the reflectance spectra. The six nonmetals were generated with the the following parameters:

Material	s	d	m
Carbon	0.3	0.7	0.40
Rubber	0.4	0.6	0.30
Obsidian	0.8	0.2	0.15
Lunardust	0.0	1.0	not used
ArmyOlive	0.3	0.7	0.50
Ironox	0.2	0.8	0.35

Figure 8 shows a watch made with a variety of materials and surface conditions. It is illuminated by a single light source. The outer band of the watch is made of gold, and the inner band is made of stainless steel. The pattern on the links of the outer band was made by using a rougher surface for the interior than for the border. The LEDs are standard red 640 nanometer LEDs, and their color was approximated by using a color with the same dominant wavelength.

Conclusions

1. The specular component is usually the color of the material, not the color of the light source. The ambient, diffuse, and specular components may have different colors if the material is not homogeneous.
2. The concept of bidirectional reflectance is necessary to simulate different light sources and materials in the same scene.
3. The facet slope distribution models used by Blinn are easy to calculate and are very similar to others in the optics literature. More than one facet slope distribution function can be combined to represent a surface.
4. The Fresnel equation predicts a color shift of the specular component at grazing angles. Calculating this color shift is computationally expensive unless an approximate procedure or a lookup table is used.
5. The spectral energy distribution of light reflected from a specific material can be obtained by using the reflectance model together with the spectral energy distribution of the light source and the reflectance

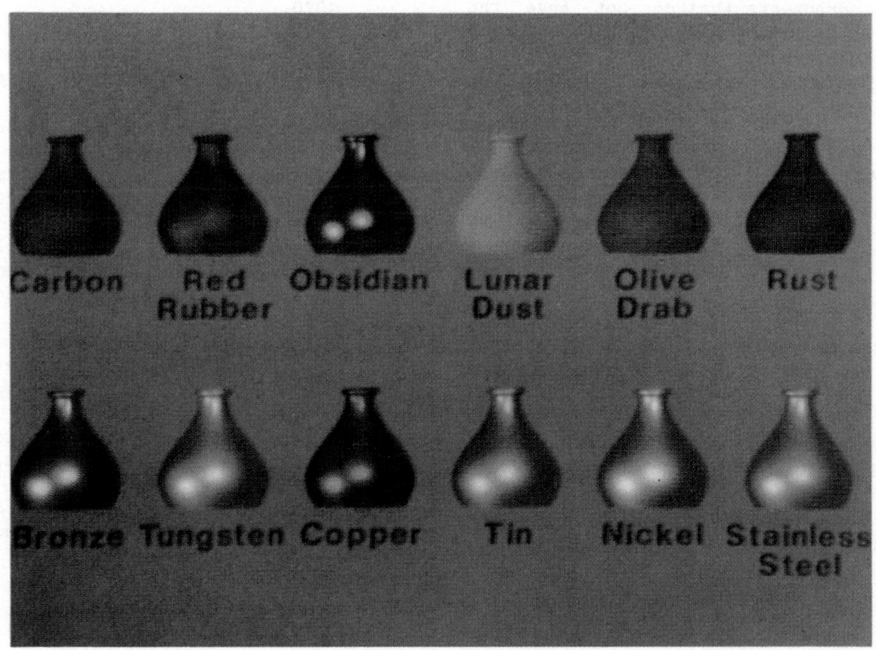

Figure 7. A variety of vases.

Figure 8. A watch.

spectrum of the material. The laws of trichromatic color reproduction can be used to convert this spectral energy distribution to the appropriate RGB values for the particular monitor being used.

6. Certain types of materials, notably some painted objects and plastics, have specular and diffuse components that do not have the same color. Metals have a specular component with a color determined by the light source and the reflectance of the metal. The diffuse component is often negligible for metals.

Acknowledgements

The work was performed at the Program of Computer Graphics of Cornell University, which is partially sponsored by the National Science Foundation (MCS-7811984).

The authors thank Gary Meyer for the invaluable contributions he made to this paper. His color software and photometric measurements of the monitors made it possible to accurately convert spectral energy distributions into RGB values. The authors also thank Dr. Donald Greenberg for his helpful discussions and valuable suggestions at every stage of the research. The watch was the result of a joint effort with Stuart Sechrest.

References

1. Barkman, E. F., "Specular and Diffuse Reflectance Measurements of Aluminum Surfaces," Appearance of Metallic Surfaces, American Society for Testing and Materials Special Technical Publication 478, pp.46-58, 1970.
2. Beckmann, Petr and Spizzichino, Andre, The Scattering of Electromagnetic Waves from Rough Surfaces, MacMillan, pp.1-33, 70-98, 1963.
3. Bennett, H. E. and Porteus, J. O., "Relation Between Surface Roughness and Specular Reflectance at Normal Incidence," Journal of the Optical Society of America, v.51 pp.123-129, 1961.
4. Blinn, James F. and Newell, Martin E., "Texture and Reflection in Computer Generated Images," Communications of the ACM, v.19 pp. 542-547, 1976.
5. Blinn, James F., "Models of Light Reflection for Computer Synthesized Pictures," SIGGRAPH 1977 Proceedings, Computer Graphics, v.11 #2 pp.192-198, 1977.
6. Blinn, James F., "Computer Display of Curved Surfaces," PhD dissertation, University of Utah, Salt Lake City, 1978.
7. CIE International Commission on Illumination, "Official Recommendations of the

International Commission on Illumination," Publication CIE No. 15, Colorimetry (E-1.3.1), Bureau Central de la CIE, Paris, 1970.

8. Davies, H., "The Reflection of Electromagnetic Waves from a Rough Surface," Proceedings of the Institution of Electrical Engineers, v.101 pp.209-214, 1954.
9. Gubareff, G. G., Janssen, J. E., and Torborg, R. H., Thermal Radiation Properties Survey: A Review of the Literature, Honeywell Research Center, Minneapolis, 1960.
10. Hunter, Richard S., The Measurement of Appearance, John Wiley & Sons, New York, pp.26-30, 1975.
11. Judd, Deane B., and Wyszecki, Guenter, Color in Business, Science, and Industry, John Wiley & Sons, New York, pp.170-172, 1975.
12. Meyer, Gary W., and Greenberg, Donald P., "Perceptual Color Spaces for Computer Graphics," SIGGRAPH 1980 Proceedings, Computer Graphics, v.14 #3 pp.254-261, 1980.
13. Phong, Bui Tuong, "Illumination for Computer-Generated Images," PhD dissertation, University of Utah, Salt Lake City, 1973.
14. Phong, Bui Tuong, "Illumination for Computer Generated Pictures," Communications of the ACM, v.18 pp.311-317, 1975.
15. Porteus, J. O., "Relation between the Height Distribution of a Rough Surface and the Reflectance at Normal Incidence," Journal of the Optical Society of America, v.53 pp.1394-1402, 1963.
16. Purdue University, Thermophysical Properties of Matter, vol. 7: Thermal Radiative Properties of Metals, 1970.
17. Purdue University, Thermophysical Properties of Matter, vol. 8: Thermal Radiative Properties of Nonmetallic Solids, 1970.
18. Purdue University, Thermophysical Properties of Matter, vol. 9: Thermal Radiative Properties of Coatings, 1970.
19. Siegel, Robert and Howell, John R., Thermal Radiation Heat Transfer, McGraw-Hill, New York, pp.64-73, 1980.
20. Sparrow, Ephraim M. and Cess, R. D., Radiation Heat Transfer, McGraw-Hill, New York, pp.64-68, 1978.
21. Torrance, Kenneth E. and Sparrow, Ephraim M., "Biangular Reflectance of an Electric Nonconductor as a Function of Wavelength and Surface Roughness," Journal of Heat Transfer, v.87 pp.283-292, 1965.
22. Torrance, Kenneth E. and Sparrow, Ephraim M., "Theory for Off-Specular Reflection From Roughened Surfaces," Journal of the Optical Society of America, v.57 pp.1105-1114, September 1967.
23. Whitted, Turner, "An Improved Illumination Model for Shaded Display," Communications of the ACM, v.23 pp. 343-349, 1980.
24. Whitted, Turner, private communication.

"The Hemi-Cube: A Radiosity Solution for Complex Environments" by M.F. Cohen and D.P. Greenberg from *Proceedings of SIGGRAPH '85*, 1985, pages 31-40. Copyright 1985, Association for Computing Machinery, Inc., reprinted by permission.

THE HEMI-CUBE
A RADIOSITY SOLUTION FOR COMPLEX ENVIRONMENTS

Michael F. Cohen and Donald P. Greenberg
Cornell University
Ithaca, N. Y. 14853

ABSTRACT

This paper presents a comprehensive method to calculate object to object diffuse reflections within complex environments containing hidden surfaces and shadows. In essence, each object in the environment is treated as a secondary light source. The method provides an accurate representation of the "diffuse" and "ambient" terms found in typical image synthesis algorithms. The phenomena of "color bleeding" from one surface to another, shading within shadow envelopes, and penumbras along shadow boundaries are accurately reproduced. Additional advantages result because computations are independent of viewer position. This allows the efficient rendering of multiple views of the same scene for dynamic sequences. Light sources can be modulated and object reflectivities can be changed, with minimal extra computation. The procedures extend the radiosity method beyond the bounds previously imposed.

CR Categories and Subject Descriptors: I.3.7 [Computer Graphics]: Three-Dimensional Graphics and Realism; I.3.3 [Computer Graphics]: Picture/Image Generation

General Terms: Algorithms

Additional Keywords and Phrases: Radiosity, diffuse reflections, hidden surface, form-factors, depth buffer.

INTRODUCTION

The representation of a realistic image of both actual and imagined scenes has been the goal of artists and scholars for centuries. The invention of the camera allowed the photographer to mechanically record the light passing through a lens and focused onto a piece of film, thus producing a realistic image. Today, within the field of computer graphics, one aspect of current research has been the attempt to produce realistic images of non-existent scenes. This is accomplished by simulating the distribution of light energy given a geometric and physical description of the environment. One major difficulty has been the correct simulation of the global illumination effects.

Light leaving an object surface originates from the surface by direct emission, as from a light source, or by the reflection or transmission of incident light. The incident light on a surface can arrive directly from a light source (along a direct line of sight) or indirectly by generally complex intermediate reflections and transmissions from other surfaces within the environment. Previously these secondary light "sources" have been ignored in computer graphics image generation algorithms. The summation of these sources have usually been approximated by an added constant term, referred to as the ambient component. [9] Some aspect of the global illumination has been achieved by the addition of a specular component found in ray tracing algorithms [13]. In essence, rays are traced only in the mirror reflection or transmission directions, point sampling the environment at the specific surface intersections. Ray tracing with

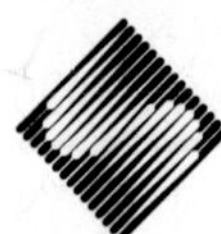

cones [1] or distributed ray tracing [2] extends this procedure by gathering light from more than one point per ray, but can not accurately model the global environmental lighting effects.

The majority of surfaces in a real environment are "diffuse" reflectors, i.e., an incident beam of light is reflected or scattered in all directions within the entire hemisphere above the reflecting surface. A special case of diffuse reflection is the so-called "ideal" diffuse or "Lambertian" reflection. In this case, the incident light is reflected from a surface with equal intensity in all directions. Ideal diffuse reflection is assumed in this paper. Specular reflections, from mirror-like surfaces, which account for a much smaller proportion of the reflected light energy, are not considered.

Thermal engineers have previously developed methods to determine the exchange of radiant energy between surfaces. [10] [11] Methods have been developed to determine the energy exchange within enclosures. The application of one such method, known as the radiosity method to computer graphics, was outlined in a paper by Goral. [5]

This paper extends the use of the radiosity method, to a broader class of problems. In particular, complex environments with occluded surfaces are allowed. In addition, very efficient procedures to render an image from the radiosity data are discussed and illustrated with examples.

RADIOSITY

The radiosity method describes an equilibrium energy balance within an enclosure. The essential features are summarized here for completeness. [5] It is assumed that all emission and reflection processes are ideal diffuse. Thus, after reflection from a surface, the past history or direction of a ray is lost.

The light leaving a surface (its radiosity) consists of self-emitted light and reflected or transmitted incident light. The amount of light arriving at a surface requires a complete specification of the geometric relationships among all reflecting and transmitting surfaces, as well as the light leaving every other surface. This relationship is given by:

$$\text{Radiosity}_i = \text{Emission}_i + \text{Reflectivity}_i \int_{env} \text{Radiosity}_j \, \text{Form-factor}_{ij} \tag{1}$$

Radiosity (B): The total rate of energy leaving a surface. Sum of emitted and reflected energy. (energy/unit time/unit area)

Emission (E): The rate of energy (light) emitted from a surface. (energy/unit time/unit area)

Reflectivity (P): The fraction of incident light which is reflected back into the environment. (unitless)

Form-factor (F): The fraction of the energy leaving one surface which lands on another surface. (unitless)

This equation states that the amount of energy (or light) leaving a particular surface is equal to the self-emitted light plus the reflected light. The reflected light is equal to the light leaving every other surface multiplied by both the fraction of that light which reaches the surface in question, and the reflectivity of the receiving surface. The sum of the reflected light from a given surface plus the light emitted directly from the surface is termed its radiosity. (Figure 1)

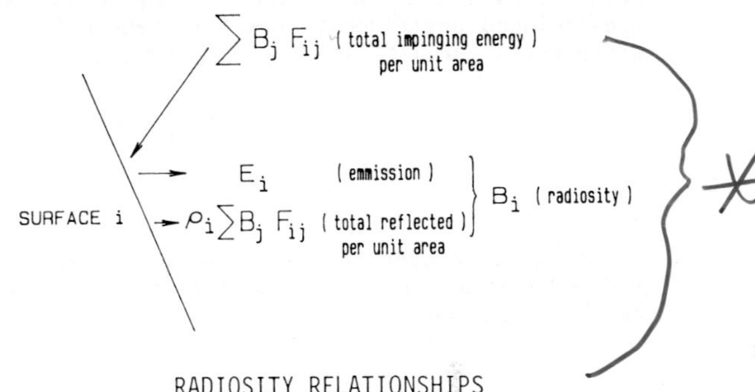

RADIOSITY RELATIONSHIPS

Figure 1

If the environment is subdivided into discrete surface elements or "patches", for which a constant radiosity is assumed, a set of simultaneous equations can be generated to describe the interaction of light energy within the environment. [5]

These equations take the form: (2)

$$\begin{bmatrix} 1-\rho_1F_{11} & -\rho_1F_{12} & \cdots & -\rho_1F_{1N} \\ -\rho_2F_{21} & 1-\rho_2F_{2N} & \cdots & -\rho_2F_{2N} \\ \cdot & \cdot & & \cdot \\ \cdot & \cdot & & \cdot \\ -\rho_NF_{N1} & -\rho_NF_{N2} & \cdots & 1-\rho_NF_{NN} \end{bmatrix} \begin{bmatrix} B_1 \\ B_2 \\ \cdot \\ \cdot \\ B_N \end{bmatrix} = \begin{bmatrix} E_1 \\ E_2 \\ \cdot \\ \cdot \\ E_N \end{bmatrix}$$

The color of an object is determined by its reflectivity (or emission in the case of a light source) at each wavelength of the visible spectrum. The reflectivity and emission terms in the above equations are, therefore, valid for a particular wavelength or band of wavelengths. It is necessary to form and solve the above matrix for each band of interest in order to determine the full radiosity of each patch. For the current discussion, it is sufficient to state that each point or patch is assumed to have a single constant radiosity B, even though this radiosity may be a set of three or more values to represent the radiosity at the different bands of interest. It is important to note that the form-factors are solely a function of geometry and are thus independent of any color considerations.

The FORM-FACTOR

The form-factor specifies the fraction of the energy leaving one surface which lands on another. By definition the sum of all the form-factors from a particular point or patch is equal to unity. Previous derivations do not account for occluding surfaces, and have therefore not reproduced shadows and penumbras.

The geometric terms in the form-factor derivation are illustrated in Figure 2. For non-occluded environments the form-factor for one differential area to another is given by:

$$F_{dAi\ dAj} = \frac{\cos\phi_i \cos\phi_j}{\pi r^2} \qquad (3)$$

By integrating over area j , the form-factor from a finite area (or patch) to a differential area can be expressed:

$$F_{dAi\ Aj} = \int_{A_j} \frac{\cos\phi_i \cos\phi_j}{\pi r^2}\, dAj \qquad (4)$$

The form-factor between finite surfaces (patches) is defined as the area average and is thus:

$$F_{Ai\ Aj} = \frac{1}{Ai} \int_{Ai}\int_{Aj} \frac{\cos\phi_i \cos\phi_j}{\pi r^2}\, dAj\, dAi \qquad (5)$$

This expression for the form-factor does not account for the possibility of occluding objects hiding all or part of one patch from another. There is, therefore, a missing term within the integrand if hidden surfaces are to be accounted for.

$$F_{Ai\ Aj} = \frac{1}{Ai} \int_{Ai}\int_{Aj} \frac{\cos\phi_i \cos\phi_j}{\pi r^2}\, \mathrm{HID}\, dAj\, dAi \qquad (6)$$

The function (HID) takes on a value of one or zero depending on whether differential area i can "see" differential area j. The HID function has the effect of producing the projection of area j visible from differential area i. It is the solution for this double area integral (6), which must be found to solve for radiosities in any non-convex environment.

In the past this double area integral has proven difficult to solve analytically for general applications. Form-factors between specific shapes and orientations, such as parallel rectanglar plates or circular disks, have been solved and tabulated [10]. An area integral, which is a double integral itself, can be transformed via Stoke's theorem into a single contour integral which can then be evaluated [5] [11]. For non-occluded environments the double area integral can be transformed into a double contour integral. A more general approach is needed to handle complex geometries.

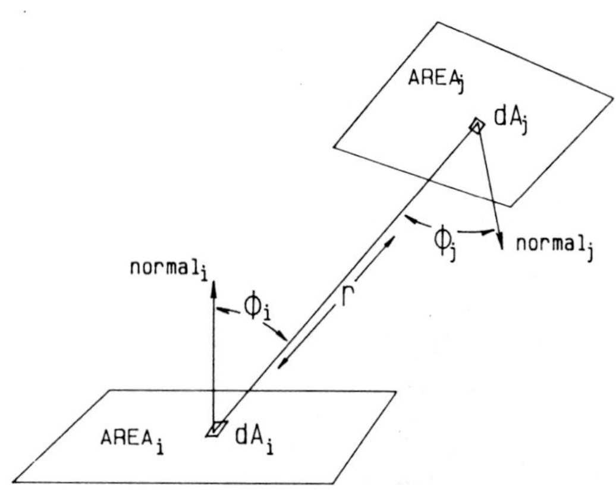

FORM-FACTOR GEOMETRY

Figure 2

Numerical techniques can provide a more efficient means to compute form-factors for general complex environments. Starting from a geometric analog to the analytic derivation, a numerical method is outlined to approximate the patch to patch form-factors which includes the hidden surface effects.

If the distance between the two patches is large compared to their size, and they are not partially occluded from one another, it can be seen that the integrand of the inner integral remains almost constant. In that case the effect of the outer integral is simply a multiplication by one and finding a solution to the inner integral will provide a good approximation for the form-factor. If the patches are close together relative to their size, or there is partial occlusion, the patches can be subdivided into smaller patches and the single integral equation approximation can still be used.

The form-factor from patch to patch is approximated with the differential area to finite area equation (4) by using the center point of patch i to represent the average position of patch i. Each patch has as its "view" of the environment, the hemisphere surrounding its normal.

A geometric analog for the form-factor integral was developed by Nusselt [10] and has been used to obtain form-factors by both photography and planimetry. (Figure 3). For a finite area, the form-factor is equivalent to the fraction of the circle (which is the base of the hemisphere) covered by projecting the area onto the hemisphere and then orthographically down onto the circle.

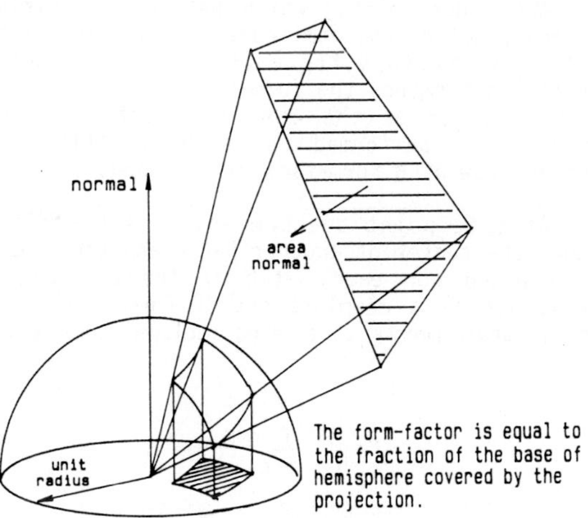

The projection onto the hemisphere accounts for the 1/r term as well as the cosine of the angle between the normal of the projecting patch and the r vector. The orthographic projection onto the circle has the effect of multiplying by the cosine of the angle between the "r" vector and the normal of the receiving patch. The PI in the denominator accounts for the area of a circle with unit radius.

NUSSELT ANALOG

Figure 3

This hemisphere can be broken into small delta solid angles, each representing a delta form-factor. The delta form-factor is equal to the fraction of the hemisphere subtended by the delta solid angle multiplied by the cosine of the angle from the normal. The form-factor to a patch is equal to the sum of the delta form-factors covered when projecting the patch onto the hemisphere. If all the patches in the environment are projected onto the hemisphere, removing the more distant areas in the case of an overlap, the final projection and summations would provide the form-factors to all patches from the patch represented at the center of the hemisphere. This procedure would then intrinsically include the effects of hidden surfaces.

In order to perform the summation of delta form-factors for each patch one would like a convenient means for discretizing the surface of the hemisphere. An evaluation can then be made as to which patch projects onto that discrete area. Difficulty in creating equal sized elements on a sphere as well as creating a set of linear coordinates to uniquely describe locations on its surface makes this approach impractical.

THE HEMI-CUBE

An efficient algorithm to compute form factors in general complex environments is described below.

From the definition of the form-factor it can be seen that any two patches in the environment, which when projected onto the hemisphere occupy the same area and location, will have the same form-factor value. This is also true for projections onto any other surrounding surface. (Figure 4)

Instead of projecting onto a sphere, an imaginary cube is constructed around the center of the receiving patch. (Figure 5) The environment is transformed to set the patch's center at the origin with the patch's normal coinciding with the positive Z axis. In this orientation the hemisphere described above is replaced by the upper half of the surface of the cube, the lower half being below the "horizon" of the patch. One full face, facing in the Z direction and four half-faces, facing in the +X -X +Y and -Y directions replace the hemisphere. These faces are divided into square "pixels" at a given resolution, generally between 50 x 50 and 100 x 100, and the environment is then projected onto the five planar surfaces. (Figure 6) Each full face of the cube covers exactly a 90 degree frustum as viewed from the center of the cube. This creates clipping planes of Z = X , Z = -X , Z = Y, and Z = -Y , allowing for simple comparisons to determine which side of a clipping plane any point lies. Every other patch in the environment is clipped to the frustum using a Sutherland-Hodgman type polygon clipper [8] streamlined to handle 90 degree frustums.

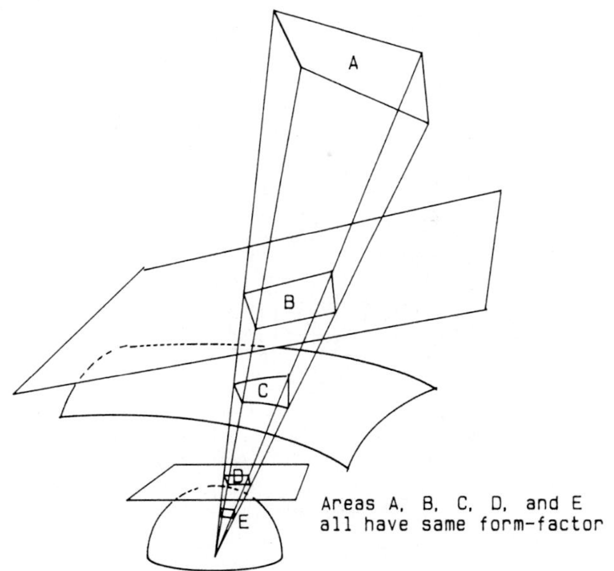

AREAS WITH IDENTICAL FORM-FACTOR

Figure 4

If two patches project onto the same pixel on the cube, a depth determination is made as to which patch is "seen" in that particular direction by comparing distances to each patch and selecting the nearer one. This depth buffer type hidden surface algorithm is well known in computer graphics. [3] However, rather than maintaining intensity information, an item buffer is maintained of which patch is seen at each pixel on the cube. [12]

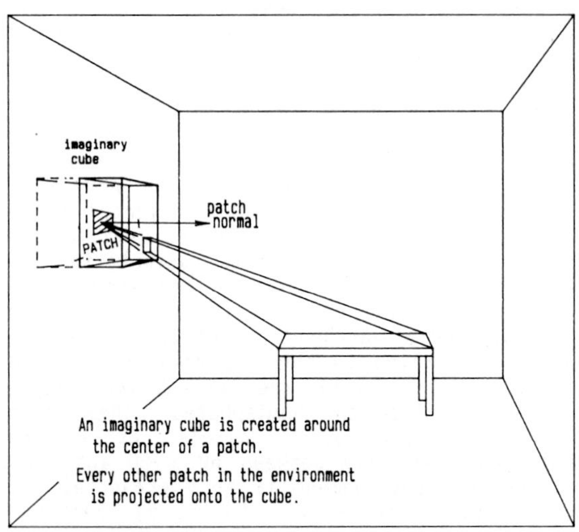

PROJECTION OF THE ENVIRONMENT ONTO THE HEMI-CUBE

Figure 5

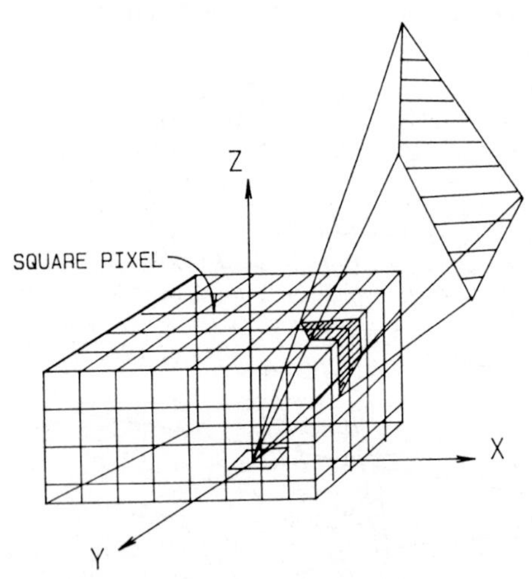

THE HEMI-CUBE

Figure 6

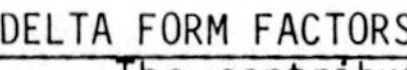

DELTA FORM FACTORS

The contribution of each pixel on the cube's surface to the form-factor value varies and is dependent on the pixel location and orientation. (Figure 7)

A specific delta form-factor value for each pixel on the cube is found from equation (3) for the differential area to differential area form-factor and stored in a lookup table. This table need only contain values for one eighth of the top face and one quarter of one side face due to symmetry.

After determining which patch(j) is visible at each pixel on the hemi-cube, a summation of the delta form-factors for each pixel occupied by patch(j) determines the form-factor from patch (i) at the center of the cube to patch(j). This summation is performed for each patch(j) and a complete row of N form-factors is found.

At this point the hemi-cube is positioned around the center of another patch and the process is repeated for each patch in the environment. The result is a complete set of form-factors for complex environments containing occluded surfaces.

$$F_{ij} = \sum_{q=1}^{R} \Delta F_q \qquad (7)$$

ΔF_q = Delta form-factor associated with pixel_q on hemi-cube

R = Number of hemi-cube pixels covered by projection of patch onto the hemi-cube

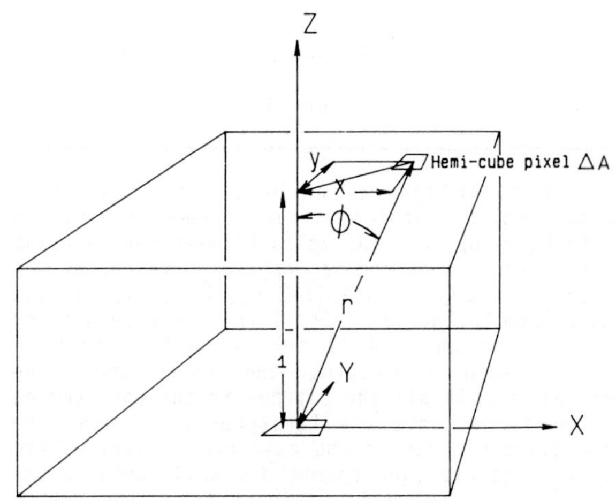

TOP OF HEMI-CUBE

$$r = \sqrt{x^2 + y^2 + 1}$$

$$\cos\phi_i = \cos\phi_j$$

$$\cos\phi = \frac{1}{\sqrt{x^2 + y^2 + 1}}$$

$$\Delta\text{Form-factor} = \frac{\cos\phi_i \cos\phi_j}{\pi r^2}\Delta A$$

$$= \frac{1}{\pi (x^2 + y^2 + 1)^2}\Delta A$$

DERIVATION OF DELTA FORM-FACTORS

Figure 7a

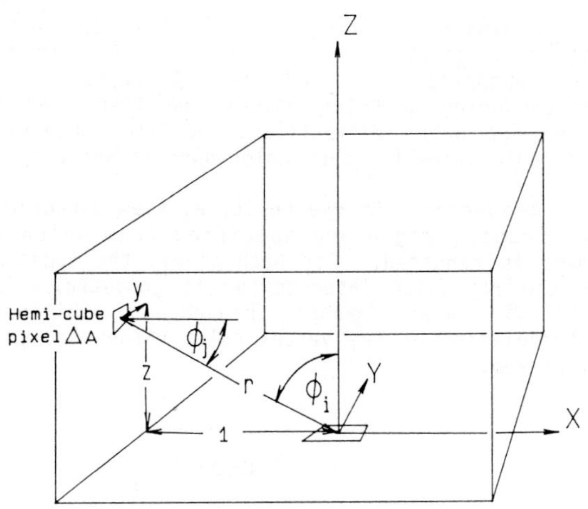

SIDE OF HEMI-CUBE

$$r = \sqrt{y^2 + z^2 + 1}$$

$$\cos \phi_i = \frac{z}{\sqrt{y^2 + z^2 + 1}}$$

$$\cos \phi_j = \frac{1}{\sqrt{y^2 + z^2 + 1}}$$

$$\Delta \text{Form-factor} = \frac{\cos \phi_i \cos \phi_j}{\pi \quad r^2} \Delta A$$

$$= \frac{z}{\pi \ (y^2 + z^2 + 1)^2} \Delta A$$

DERIVATION OF DELTA FORM-FACTORS

Figure 7b

THE ENERGY BALANCE SOLUTION

The solution for the series of simultaneous equations can be performed with any standard equation solver. However, a Gauss-Siedel iterative approach has a number of advantages. [6] The matrix is well suited to this technique due to the fact that it is diagonally dominant (the sum of the absolute values of each row is less than the main diagonal term). This is always true since, by definition, the sum of any row of form-factors is equal to unity. In the matrix to be solved, each form factor term is multiplied by its surface reflectivity, which is also less than unity. Thus the summation of the absolute values of all terms in any row exclusive of the main diagonal term is also less than one. The main diagonal term is equal to one minus its own form-factor. Since any polygonal (or convex) patch cannot see itself, its own form-factor is equal to zero. Therefore, the main diagonal term is always equal to one, the matrix is strictly diagonally dominant, and guaranteed to converge rapidly to a solution.

An initial guess for the radiosities, which must be supplied for the first iteration, is simply the emission of each patch (only the primary light sources have any initial radiosity). During each iteration each radiosity is solved for, using the previously found values of the other radiosities. Iterations continue until no radiosity value changes by more than a preselected small percentage. The iterative process converges very rapidly, generally in six to eight iterations, and a solution is found in a fraction of the time needed for standard elimination techniques.

Additional computational savings are made by compressing the null entries from the matrix. Zero valued form-factors will occur when one patch cannot "see" another due to occluding surfaces, if they belong to the same polygon, or face away from each other. Zeros will also occur in the matrix if reflectivities are equal to zero.

The matrix is formed and solved for the radiosities from the computed form-factors for each color band of interest. This is generally performed for three channels (red, green, blue) but could be done on a wavelength basis if desired.

RENDERING

To render an image the discretized radiosity information is used to create a continuous shading across a given surface (or polygon). A number of shading schemes have been devised in the past [5], however, most of these take place in image space and are axis dependent. An object space smoothing algorithm is desired in order to be able to render sequences of different views such that the same point in space would retain the same intensity values.

The adopted method uses a bilinear interpolation within each patch. This bilinear variation of radiosities insures first order continuity at patch edges. In order to perform the interpolation, radiosity values must be transferred from the patches themselves to each vertex of the patches. (Figure 8a)

For each polygon, the radiosities of patch vertices which are interior to the polygon containing the patch are computed as the average of radiosities of the surrounding patches. Exterior vertex radiosities are extrapolated values from the adjacent interior vertex radiosities through an average of the adjacent patch radiosities. Finally, the resulting vertex radiosities are used for the bilinear interpolation within each patch. (Figure 8b)

The radiosity solution is independent of view position and direction. To render an image on a raster display device, the eye position as well as the viewing direction and frustum angle must be specified. A transformation matrix sets the eye and view direction within the environment. A depth-buffer/item-buffer algorithm determines which patch is seen at each pixel of the screen.

Finding the intersection between a line from the eye through a pixel, and the plane of the patch which occupies the pixel provides a location within the patch. In order to perform the bilinear interpolation within the patch, this x,y,z position is converted to parametric (u,v) coordinates within the patch.

With this information bilinear interpolation of the three radiosity values are made and the pixel displayed.

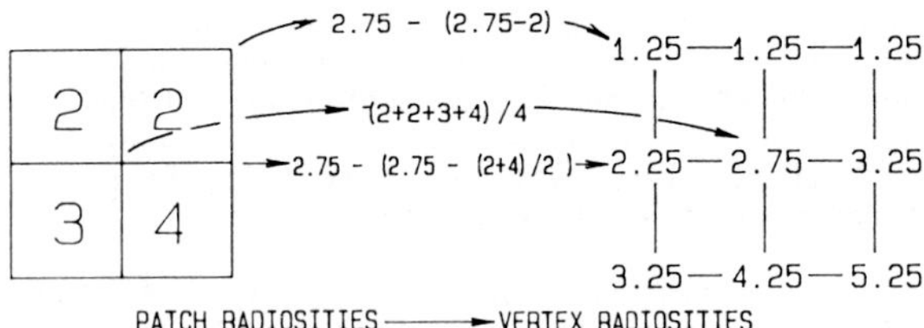

VERTEX RADIOSITIES

Figure 8a

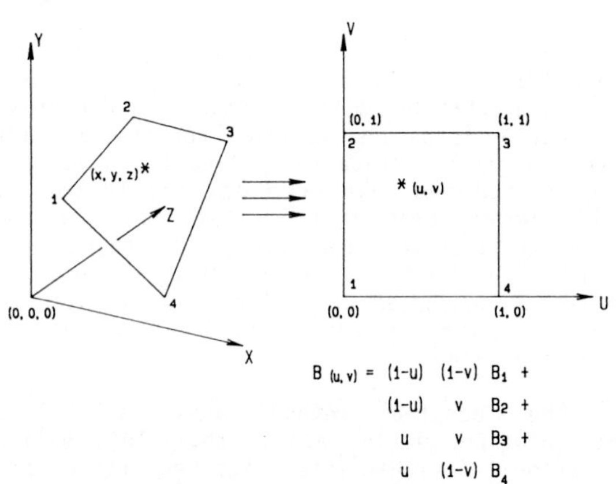

BILINEAR INTERPOLATION OF PIXEL RADIOSITY FROM VERTEX RADIOSITIES

Figure 8b

PROGRAM SUMMARY (Figure 9)

Input: The environment geometry is input from a file containing polygon descriptions and the associated vertex coordinates. Associated with each polygon are reflectivity and emission values for each color band and a parameter for subdividing the polygon into patches.

Form-factors: After the patches are defined, the hemi-cube is set around the center of each patch and a row of form-factors is determined from that patch to all others through their projections onto the cube. A file containing the matrix of form-factors is created.

Radiosity solution: For each color band a matrix is constructed using the form-factors and the appropriate set of reflectivities. The corresponding emission values are then used to solve for patch radiosities. A file containing the radiosities for each color band is written.

Rendering: An eye position, view direction, and frustum angle are specified from which an image is rendered. For each pixel, the location of the ray-patch intersection is computed. The color(s) are found through a bilinear interpolation of the vertex color values and then displayed.

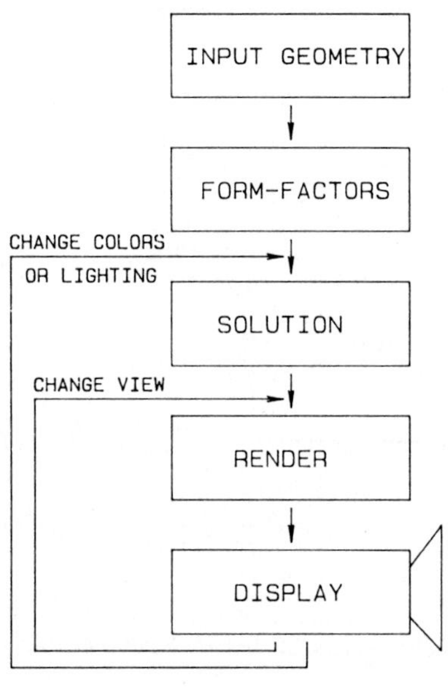

PROGRAM FLOW

Figure 9

SIMULATION VS REALITY

An experimental setup was devised to test the accuracy of computer simulations. A physical model of the simple environment simulated in figure 10 was constructed of wood and cardboard. The light and painted surfaces were made as diffuse as possible. Radiometric measurements were made at locations on the model and compared with the calculated values. A visual side-by-side comparison was made by a group of experimental subjects. Great lengths were taken to control the test conditions for both methods of comparisons. The results from both tests provide conclusive validation of the radiosity method. Details and illustrations of the experimental setup and the results are contained in an article by Meyer et. al. [7].

Figure 10

The environment simulated above, although simple in geometry displays a variety of shading characteristics. The patch radiosities are displayed on the top as constantly shaded and on the bottom after the bilinear interpolation for pixel radiosities.

Note:

(1) The distinct color bleeding onto the white and yellow boxes.

(2) The red shadow to the left of the yellow box. The majority of the light which reaches the shaded area arrives indirectly from the red wall, thus the red shadow.

(3) The variation of light intensity on the walls due to the diffuse light source.

No. of Patches: 2370

Form-factor computation: 337 Min.

Solution of matrices: 18 Min.

Rendering and display: 14 Min.

(A)

(B)

(C)

Figure 11

*All computation was performed on a VAX 11/780. The images were displayed on a Grinnell 512 x 480 frame buffer.

The images of figure 11 demonstrate the computational savings achieved when rendering multiple images of the same environment.

No. of patches: 1740	Image A	Image B	Image C
Form-factor comp.:	180 Min.	0 Min.	0 Min.
Matrix solution:	10 Min.	10 Min.	0 Min.
Rendering:	16 Min.	16 Min.	16 Min.
TOTAL:	208 Min.	26 Min.	16 Min.

By changing only the viewing parameters, only the rendering portion of the computation was repeated to produce Image C, thus the savings in total time.

CONCLUSION

The extension of the radiosity solution to environments with occluded surfaces allows the simulation of complex scenes. All surfaces are treated as light sources and thus the global illumination effects are correctly modeled. The influence of occluded surfaces is contained within the solution for the form-factors, and thus shadows and shadow boundaries are properly reproduced.

It should be emphasized that the object space intensity computations are performed independent of the view position and direction. Thus, each phase of the procedure is independent of the modules which follow it. The independence of the algorithm steps permits rendering of dynamic sequences with little additional computation. The rendering can be repeated from different viewpoints without recomputing form-factors or radiosities. If the geometry of the environment remains static, the information to render changes in the lighting conditions is already contained in the form-factors. Thus lights can be turned on/off and object colors can be changed simply by resolving the matrices. The iterative solution converges rapidly, typically in six to eight interations, regardless of the size of the matrix. The entire process need be repeated only with changes in geometry.

The extension of the radiosity method to occluded environments permits the rendering of complex scenes, and thus should have great relevance to computer generated imagery. The computational expense is minimal compared to ray-tracing algorithms especially when rendering dynamic sequences within a static geometry.

A number of issues must be addressed in order to make the radiosity method both general and efficient. Since the accuracy/fineness of the numerical integration of the form-factor depends partially upon the area projected onto the hemi-cube, problems can occur due to aliasing for small projections. In general, objects whose projection onto the hemi-cube is small have little effect. However, for very bright patches such as light sources, the effect of the inaccuracy can have a substantial deleterious effect.

Generalizations must be made to accomodate curved surfaces. Polygonal approximation that would allow use of the same algorithms may suffice for the form-factor computations. However, the exact surface description should be used during rendering.

Since the size of the radiosity computation grows with the square of the number of patches, methods of approximation must be developed to keep the computation manageable as the complexity of the environment increases. Small variations in intensity across a patch have little effect on the overall global illumination. Rather than continue the subdivision of the patches to discern small radiosity variations, more detailed intensity information within a patch can be derived from a coarse patch radiosity solution. In this way the number of patches, and thus the computation time, can be kept to a minimum while allowing complex environments to be rendered. Texture mapping falls into the same category, and can be handled by treating a textured patch's effect on the environment as one average intensity during the radiosity solution.

Provisions must be made to incorporate specular and transparent surfaces into the rendering process or, better yet, into the initial radiosity formulation.

The radiosity method offers a fundamentally new approach to image synthesis by beginning from basic principles of conservation of energy. The radiosity method has been shown to be able to render complex environments. Radiosity should play a major role in future realistic image synthesis systems.

ACKNOWLEDGEMENTS

This research was conducted at the Cornell University Program of Computer Graphics and was supported by the National Science Foundation grant DCR8203979. As with all of the research efforts at CUPCG, this paper is the result of a team effort. Thanks must go to Cindy Goral and Professor Kenneth Torrance for their groundwork introducing radiosity to the computer graphics community. Thanks to David Immel, Philip Brock, and Channing Verbeck for help in software development, to Jutta Joesch, Lisa Maynes, and James Ferwerda for editing the text. Also to Gary Meyer and Holly Rushmeier for conduting experiments to verify the radiosity algorithms, to Janet Brown in preparing the text, and to Emil Ghinger for photography. Thank you, reviewers, for your helpful comments.

REFERENCES

[1] Amanatides, John. Ray Tracing with Cones. ACM Computer Graphics (Proceedings 1985), pp. 129-135.

[2] Cook, Robert. Distributed Ray Tracing. ACM Computer Graphics (Proceedings 1984), pp. 137-145.

[3] Foley, J. D. and Van Dam, A. Fundamentals of Computer Graphics. Addison-Wesley Publishing Co., 1982.

[4] Goral, Cindy M., Torrance, Kenneth E., Greenberg, Donald P., Battaile, Bennett, Modeling the Interaction of Light Between Diffuse Surfaces, ACM Computer Graphics (Proceedings 1984), pp. 213-222.

[5] Gouraud, Henri, Computer Display of Curved Surfaces, Ph.D. Dissertation, University of Utah, 1971.

[6] Hornbeck, Robert W., Numerical Methods. Quantum Publishers, 1975, pp. 101-106.

[7] Meyer, Gary W., Rushmeier, Holly E., Cohen, Michael F., Greenberg, Donald P., Torrance, Kenneth E., Assessing the Realism of Computer Graphics Images, submitted for publication, 1985.

[8] Newman, William M. and Sproull, Robert F., Principles of Interactive Computer Graphics, McGraw Hill, 1979.

[9] Phong, Bui Tuong, Illumination for Computer Generated Images, Ph.D. Dissertation, University of Utah, 1973.

[10] Siegel, Robert and Howell, John R., Thermal Radiation Heat Transfer, Hemisphere Publishing Corp., 1978.

[11] Sparrow, E. M. and Cess R. D., Radiation Heat Transfer, Hemisphere Publishing Corp., 1978.

[12] Weghorst, Hank, Hooper, Gary, and Greenberg, Donald P., Improved Computational Methods for Ray Tracing, ACM Transactions on Graphics, Jan, 1984, pp. 52-69.

[13] Whitted, Turner, An Improved Illumination Model for Shaded Display, Communications of the ACM, June, 1980.

Chapter 8: Antialiasing

Introduction

The phenomenon of aliasing in the field of signal processing is well understood. Aliasing can occur when one is attempting to reconstruct a continuous signal from a set of discrete samples of the signal. Consider the one-dimensional signal, $i(t)$, in Figure 8.1. The signal is periodically sampled by multiplying it by $\Pi(t)$, an impulse train, or comb function, resulting in a set of samples, $s(k)$. Let $r(t)$ be a continuous signal reconstructed from the samples $s(k)$ with the constraint that $r(t)$ is the smoothest signal that passes through the points of $s(k)$. As can be seen, a high-frequency signal can be incorrectly reconstructed as a lower frequency signal, an *alias* for the signal.

The effect of aliasing in two dimensions, which is common in computer graphics, is shown in Figure 8.2. The low-frequency ripples, stairsteps, or jaggies are aliases caused by the high-frequency components of the polygon edges. The sharp corners of the stairsteps are not caused by aliasing but by a reconstruction error that introduces unwanted high-frequency components. The low-frequency components of the stairsteps are caused by aliasing. A good example of aliasing is given by Cook [Cook86] (which is included in this chapter).

In the early days of computer graphics, it was assumed that as the resolution of display devices increased the need for antialiasing would go away. The idea was that any errors introduced by aliasing would be so small that they could not be noticed. This has proven to be false. Aliasing tends to produce regular patterns that are easily spotted by the pattern-recognition mechanisms built into the human eye and brain. Even very high-resolution displays improve when the images are antialiased. When animation is generated with computer graphics, aliasing is even more difficult (see [Szab83]), and can cause

- classical temporal aliasing—like the backwards spinning wagon wheel in the movies
- strobing—causing a fast moving object to appear to jump in discrete steps
- scintillation—small particles that drift between samples blinking on and off
- the "crawling ants effect"—the spatial aliasing "jaggies" slowly changing between frames
- stretching and shrinking—a slowly moving small object (a few pixels in size) will seem to stretch and shrink in one pixel steps as it crawls across the screen
- beating—vertically moving objects beating with the interlace of broadcast TV

The sampling theorem (see [Oppe75]) states that the input signal can be reconstructed exactly from its samples only if it is bandlimited to some maximum frequency which is less than one-half the sampling rate. This frequency limit is called the Nyquist limit. Any frequency component of the signal that is higher than this limit will be reconstructed as a lower frequency alias. The spatial-sampling rate of a synthetic image is fixed by the final resolution of the image. To reduce the effects of aliasing in the final image, the obvious method is to filter the image to remove or reduce the high-frequency components before sampling.[1]

An image, $i(x,y)$, is linearly filtered by convolving it with a kernel or point spread function, $f(x,y)$. The filtering and sampling process that yields the samples, $s(i,j)$, can be described by the equation

$$\hat{s}(x,y) = (i(x,y) * f(x,y))\Pi(x,y)w(x,y) \qquad (1)$$

where, $w(x,y)$ represents a two-dimensional rectangular window function, which is the same size as the image, and $s(i,j) = \hat{s}(x,y)$ when $i = x$, $j = y$, and i and j are integers.

Performing these operations in this order is far too difficult to implement as it involves convolving two complicated continuous functions then throwing away most of this work by sampling the result. This formula can be reorganized into

$$s(i,j) = \int_{-\infty}^{+\infty}\int_{-\infty}^{+\infty} i(x+i,y+j)\,f(x,y)\,dx\,dy \qquad (2)$$

which is called *the antialiasing integral*. If we are generating a sequence of frames for an animation, aliasing can occur in the temporal dimension as well as in the spatial dimensions. The corresponding integral for spatial and temporal antialiasing is:

$$s(i,j,\tau) = \int_{-\infty}^{+\infty}\int_{-\infty}^{+\infty}\int_{-\infty}^{+\infty} i(x+i,y+j,t+\tau)\,f(x,y,t)\,dx\,dy\,dt$$

[1]Strictly speaking, raster images cannot meet the requirements of the sampling theorem, since we are assuming they have a finite extent and thus cannot be bandlimited. The effects of bandlimited/finite-extent assumptions and their relation to the real world are explored by [Slep72]. This formal contradiction does not present much of a problem in practice. Perfect antialiasing is never attempted.

EH0281-6/88/0000/0265$01.00 © 1988 IEEE

i(t)

II(t)

s(k)

r(t)

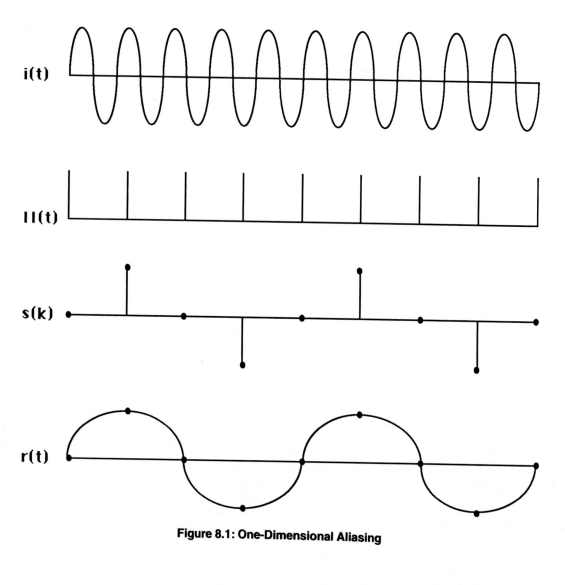

Figure 8.1: One-Dimensional Aliasing

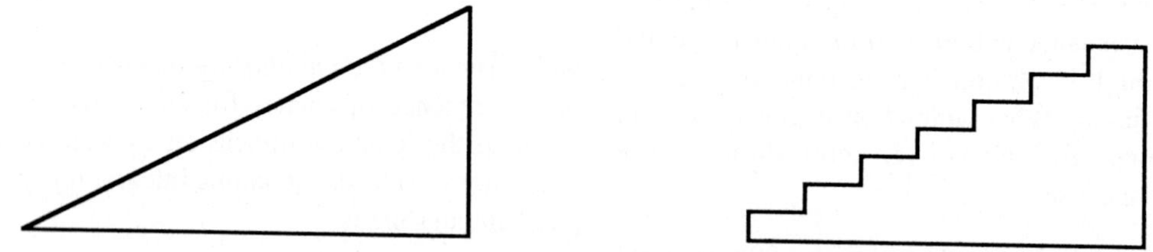

Figure 8.2: Two-Dimensional Aliasing

All antialiasing algorithms attempt to solve or approximate this integral at each pixel, $s(i,j)$. Algorithms vary in how this calculation is done and what point-spread function $f(x,y)$ is used.

What is the ideal filter for antialiasing? Clearly, the ideal filter should produce the best looking pictures. Unfortunately, the notion of "bestlooking" is badly defined since it involves how the human eye/brain system extracts information from an image, which has not been modeled in sufficient detail (see [Stoc72] for a good start). Many assume that an ideal low-pass filter (the sinc point-spread function, $(\sin\pi x)/\pi x)$ is optimum because it completely removes the high-frequency information without distorting the low-frequency information. There are several problems with this type of filter when it is applied to images. The point-spread function of the ideal low-pass filter decays very slowly ($O(1/x)$); thus small portions of the original image can affect large sections of the filtered image. Sharp transitions in the original image cause noticeable ringing in the filtered image (this is the Gibbs phenomenon). Even though images are constrained to have positive intensities, filtering can produce regions with negative intensities. A filter with a smooth, all positive, nearly finite[2] extent point-spread function, and smooth, nearly finite frequency response would seem to be superior for processing images for human viewing. The Gaussian, e^{-x^2}, is one such function that works well.

There are two types of antialiasing algorithms used in computer graphics. These are directly related to the two types of visible-surface algorithms in use, continuous and point sampling. The process of filtering and sampling the image plane is constrained by what type of information about the image plane is available. Continuous visible-surface algorithms provide known intensities over continuous areas. The antialiasing integral can be performed directly with this data (if its form is simple enough) to yield the filtered sample values. Point-sampling algorithms can only provide intensity information at single points. In this case, the antialiasing integral must be approximated by using only the values of the point samples.

Continuous antialiasing algorithms solve the antialiasing integral directly. Typically, these are limited to simple primitives and point-spread functions so this integral can be solved. The earliest algorithm with continuous antialiasing was that of Catmull [Catm78] (which is included in this chapter), which limited the primitives to polygons and used the "area sampling" filter point-spread function

$$f(x,y) = \begin{cases} 1 & \text{over a unit square centered on the current pixel} \\ 0 & \text{elsewhere.} \end{cases} \quad (3)$$

This filter function and choice of primitives makes it particularly easy to calculate the antialiasing integral, since it reduces to the area of the primitive times its intensity. Although this integral is easy to calculate, the high-frequency cutoff of this filter is fairly poor. While it is much better than no filtering at all, some aliasing artifacts remain.

Feibush et al. [Feib80] (included in this chapter) allowed filters with radially symmetric, small extent point spread functions. By exploiting the symmetry of the filter, a two-dimensional lookup-table was used to hold precomputed integrals of the filter point-spread function over various triangular domains. Since all the integration was precomputed, any type of complex radially symmetric filter could be used without any run-time performance penalty. This paper also included an approximate filtering method for textured polygons, but the most significant contribution was the table driven algorithm for calculating the antialiasing integral. The antialiasing performance of this algorithm was very good—virtually eliminating aliasing artifacts.

By approximating some of the geometric aspects of the two-dimensional lookup-table algorithm, Turkowski [Turk82] developed an algorithm by using a much smaller one-dimensional lookup table. Many aspects of the antialiasing calculations were performed by using cordic-arithmetic algorithms, which were fast and suitable for hardware implementation. Antialiasing performance for this algorithm is very good on the edges of polygons but is only approximate at vertices.

Abram et al. [Abra85] present an algorithm for continuous antialiasing that is structured somewhat differently than the Feibush algorithm. Efficiency is maintained by using precomputed lookup tables and bit-masks.

There are several techniques for approximating the antialiasing integral by using only point samples. These techniques generally rely on taking several point samples and on using them to approximate the continuous image in the area of interest.

One of the first techniques developed was *regular supersampling*. In this algorithm, an intermediate image is computed at a higher resolution than the final output. The output pixels are then formed by combining several of the pixels in the high-resolution intermediate image. Combining only those intermediate pixels, which overlap the output pixel by using an unweighted averaging, yield a discrete version of Catmull's area sampling. Combining intermediate pixels over a wider range, by using a weighted average, provides superior results. Crow compares several techniques in [Crow81].

Supersampling can be very expensive if a large number of samples are used to form each output pixel. *Adaptive supersampling* is an attempt to reduce the number of samples required in sections of the image that are relatively uniform. This was first described for ray tracing by Whitted [Whit80]. Samples are taken at the corners of square regions within a pixel. If the intensity values at the samples are sufficiently close to each other, the square region is assumed to have a uniform intensity. If the intensities differ sufficiently, then the area is divided into four smaller squares and the process is applied recursively to each. The resulting intensities of the smaller squares are averaged to approximate the actual intensity of the larger square. This saves a great deal of calculation in uniform parts of the image and concentrates the sampling in the areas where it is needed most.

Stratified sampling, introduced by Lee et al. [Lee85], is an enhanced adaptive supersampling technique where samples are placed and weighted based on the estimated local variance of the signal near the sample. The usefulness of this technique is limited by the need to estimate the local variance of the image.

Aliasing caused by regularly spaced sampling produces regularly spaced artifacts that are easily detected by the human eye. Perturbing the sampling locations slightly breaks up the regularity of the aliasing artifacts, which can be thought of as applying a small random phase shift to each sample. Although low-frequency signals are not affected much by this phase shift, high-frequency signals with wave-

[2]By "nearly finite," we mean that the total energy beyond some finite point is less than some threshold and can be considered to be negligible.

lengths close to or less than the amount of phase shift are broken up. This is called *jittered sampling* or *stochastic sampling* and is discussed extensively by Cook [Cook86] (included in this chapter) and Dippé and Wold [Dipp85b]. By using jittered sampling, high-frequency components alias as random noise rather than as coherent low frequencies. It is much easier for the human eye to ignore small amounts of random noise than to ignore a low-frequency regular pattern. Therefore, pictures improve if the samples are not uniform, even though the same energy is present in the artifacts. There is some disagreement as to what type of sampling pattern produces the best looking pictures. The two-dimensional Poisson-disk distribution and the jittered regular grid have both been used.

Frequently, different antialiasing methods are combined in actual implementations. Scan-line algorithms may do continuous antialiasing in the direction of the scan lines, but supersample (or do nothing) in the other dimension where less information is available. The A-buffer algorithm of Carpenter [Carp84] performs continuous antialiasing at each pixel for the simple cases, but drops back to supersampling when things get complex.

Several researchers have attacked the problems of temporal antialiasing, which is loosely called *motion blur*. Correct temporal antialiasing requires solving all visibility problems as a function of time, then filtering the results. Norton et al. [Nort82] perform spatial and temporal antialiasing of frequency domain texture functions. Korein and Badler [Kore83] use a simple continuous one-dimensional antialiasing algorithm in the temporal dimension while supersampling in the spatial dimensions. Potmesil and Chakravarty [Potm83] blur moving objects as a postprocess. Temporal antialiasing is elegantly integrated in the distributed-ray-tracing system of Cook et al. [Cook84a]. Catmull [Catm84] implements a motion-blur approximation by shrinking the polygons in the direction of motion before visible surfaces are calculated. Dippé [Dipp85a] presents an integrated spatial and temporal antialiasing method based on tetrahedral splines. The Feibush et al. [Feib80] two-dimensional lookup-table algorithm was extended to three dimensions for combined spatial and temporal antialiasing by using radially symmetric filters by Grant [Gran85]. Max [Max85] presents two techniques for temporal antialiasing in the 2½-dimensional compositing environment. The algorithms [Nort82, Potm83, Catm84, Max85] all blur images after calculating visibility at one sample point in time. The algorithms [Kore83, Cook84a, Dipp85a, Gran85] calculate visibility at different times and perform true temporal antialiasing.

In the distributed-ray-tracing system of Cook et al. [Cook84a], it was recognized that antialiasing in several dimensions could be performed efficiently by distributing the samples independently and randomly in each dimension. This was a major breakthrough over previous inefficient sampling strategies.

In addition to the papers in this section, some of the papers in other sections of this volume contain significant developments in antialiasing. These are: Whitted's ray-tracing paper [Whit80] with adaptive subdivision, the distributed ray tracing of Cook et al. [Cook84a], the antialiased compositing of Porter and Duff [Port84], the stochastic antialiasing Z-buffer algorithm of Cook et al. [Cook87], the A-buffer algorithm of Carpenter [Carp84], and Whitted and Weimer [Whit82] who utilized trapezoidal antialiased spans in a scan-line algorithm.

A HIDDEN-SURFACE ALGORITHM WITH ANTI-ALIASING

Edwin Catmull
Computer Graphics Lab
New York Institute of Technology
Old Westbury, New York 11568

ABSTRACT

In recent years we have gained understanding about aliasing in computer generated pictures and about methods for reducing the symptoms of aliasing. The chief symptoms are staircasing along edges and objects that pop on and off in time. The method for reducing these symptoms is to filter the image before sampling at the display resolution. One filter that is easy to understand and that works quite effectively is equivalent to integrating the visible intensities over the area that the pixel covers. There have been several implementations of this method - mostly unpublished - however most algorithms break down when the data for the pixel is complicated. Unfortunately, as the quality of displays and the complexity of pictures increase, the small errors that can occur in a single pixel become quite noticeable. A correct solution for this filter requires a hidden-surface algorithm at each pixel! If the data at the pixel is presented as a depth-ordered list of polygons then the average visible intensity can be found using a polygon clipper in a way similar to that employed by two known hidden-surface algorithms. All of the polygons in a pixel are clipped against some front unclipped edge into two lists of polygons. The algorithm is recursively entered with each new list and halts when the front polygon is clipped on all sides, thereby obscuring the polygons behind. The area weighted colors are then returned as the value to be added to the other pieces in the pixel.

Key words: aliasing, clipping, computer graphics, filtering, hidden-surface removal, sampling.

CR classification: 8.2

INTRODUCTION

Aliasing is now being recognized as an important factor in analysis of image synthesizing algorithms. Attention has turned to anti-aliasing partly because of the need to refine pictures but mostly because the complexity of scenes has increased and with it the need to have pictures free of aliasing symptoms.

A polygon hidden-surface algorithm is presented here with the focus of attention on anti-aliasing. One goal has been to produce a "correct" image for the anti-aliasing technique used. Speed, while important, has played a secondary role.

The techniques for hidden-surface elimination have improved in the last few years with the Sutherland et al [7] paper providing coherence to the development. Several new algorithms have come along [3,8,9], each adding new insight into the ways that we can take advantage of coherence for some class of objects to facilitate display.

Progress for anti-aliasing has been slower. In general pictures have not been extremely complicated and the more obvious effects of aliasing, like jagged edges, could be fixed up with ad hoc techniques. Methods for anti-aliasing have been presented in [1,2,4]. Frank Crow's dissertation was devoted to the topic and the results were published in [2].

ANTI-ALIASING

In general, the aliasing problem has been grossly underestimated in computer graphics. Its symptoms include:

1. jagged edges
2. small objects popping on and off the screen in successive frames
3. moire patterns in rendering periodic images
4. fine detail breaking up.

The problem occurs chiefly because image space is sampled at discrete points corresponding to the pixels.

There are several unpublished schemes for alleviating the problem for simple cases - in particular the symptom of jagged edges. They are unpublished because either they are incidental to some other algorithm or they are proprietary.

Frank Crow has written about anti-aliasing in [2]. From his study we can extract some key ideas:

1. The image space objects have sharpness and detail that cannot possibly be reproduced on a raster display. It is the attempt to sample that detail at discrete points in the image that causes the problem.

2. Point sampling of an unfiltered object is never correct at any resolution. It is frequently thought that the symptoms of aliasing will not be noticeable if the resolution is high enough. Unfortunately, this is not true.

3. The image should be filtered to eliminate detail that is too fine. After filtering the image can be sampled.

One simple filter is to integrate the visible intensities over the area of each pixel. In other words we take the average visible intensity over the square area represented by each pixel if the image is divided into a rectangular grid. This corresponds to convolving the continuous image with a two-dimensional Fourier (box) window. While there are better filters, this one is easy to understand and easier to implement analytically than other filters. The use of this filter will be called "area sampling."

The difference between point sampling and area sampling is qualitative while the difference between area sampling and better filters is quantitative. The sum of all intensities for a point sampled picture will vary as the object is translated, ie. for a fine picket fence the picture can be all white in one picture and all black in the next. The sum of all intensities for an area sampled picture will be constant under translation because area sampling integrates all the intensities. The difference between area sampling and better filters is quantitative since most reasonable filters would also integrate the intensities. The difference between filtered pictures is lowered as the resolution is increased since the sum of intensities in a local area will be the same or nearly so. We cannot say this when comparing point sampling with sampling of filtered images at high resolution. A line that is much thinner than a pixel will appear dotted using point sampling and jagged using area sampling. As the resolution is increased, point sampling will still produce dots but area sampling will produce a nice line.

In order to truly filter the image before sampling, an analytic continuous solution to both the hidden-surface problem and the filter convolution must be found. The magnitude of this problem grows dramatically with the order of the filter employed. There are several approaches or simplifications that one might take to implement filtering. This paper presents an approach that uses an analytic solution for area sampling.

The problem then is to correctly integrate the intensities of all visible objects at a single pixel. This seems to require some kind of hidden-surface algorithm at every pixel!

As an example where some algorithms might fail see figure 1.

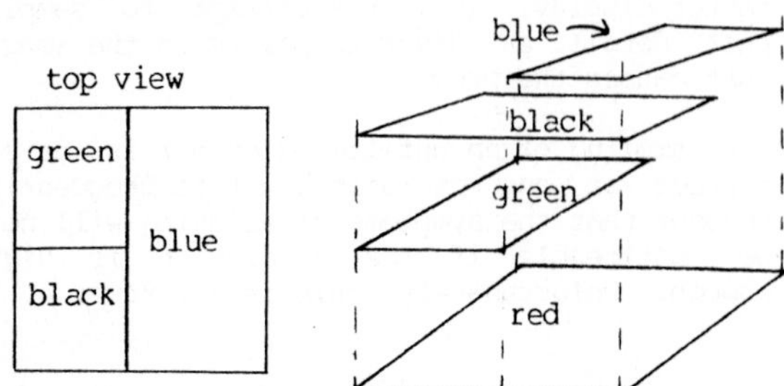

Figure 1

The correct integration would be 25% green, 25% black, 50% blue and no red. A simple minded algorithm that did not properly take into account what was hidden might distribute the intensities incorrectly and may even let some red show through. Unfortunately for computer graphics our eyes are quite capable of seeing errors like these even though they may be only one millionth of the area of the screen.

AN ALGORITHM WITH ANTI-ALIASING

In terms of the Sutherland et al criteria the algorithm presented here:

1. sorts all polygons in y.
2. sorts all active polygons for a scanline with an x-bucket sort.
3. sorts in z by searching a z-list for each entering edge.
4. does not use scanline-to-scanline coherence because an x-bucket is used.
5. Uses point-to-point coherence since order in the z-list does not change.

While this order of techniques probably has not been used before, it is not new in any spectacular way. However, care has been taken to ensure that everything necessary for anti-aliasing is available and to a much higher precision than the display.

The last step is to determine the intensity at the pixel given the z-list. An integrating algorithm is presented here that determines which pieces of polygons in the pixel are visible and then analytically calculates the average intensity.

Finding which pieces of polygons in the pixel are visible is not unlike the original hidden-surface problem except that we have two simplifications: 1) we are only interested in the sum of the intensities of each piece weighted by its area and 2) the higher level hidden-surface algorithm may have already determined the order of the polygons.

CLIPPING

Clipping is an important part of the algorithm. The clipping algorithm used was originally introduced in [6]. A variation is presented here for completeness.

When a polygon is clipped against a line it is divided into two polygons. See figure 2.

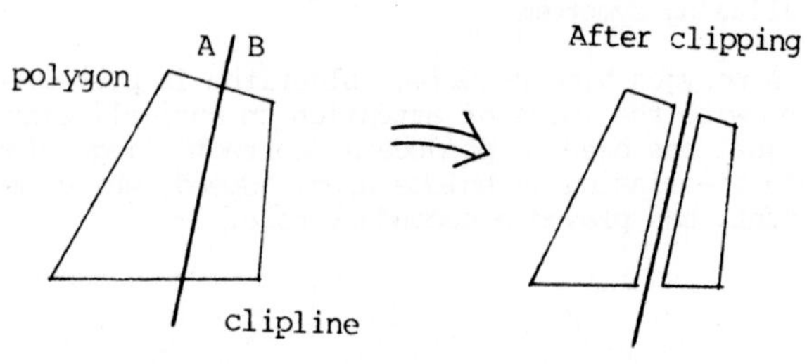

Figure 2

We can determine if a point is on side A or side B by inserting the coordinates of the point into the equation of the line:

$d = ax + by + c.$

If d is less than zero then the point is on side A, otherwise it is on side B. We are going to generate an A and a B polygon.

The Clipping Algorithm

I. A polygon is a list of points P1, P2,...Pn.

II. Call Pn the previous point. Determine which side it is on.

III. Loop through each point, called the current point.

A. If current point on A side then:

1. If previous point on A side then:

Copy current point to A polygon.

2. If previous point on B side then:

Calculate intersection of line with edge formed from current point and previous point.

Copy calculated point to A and B polygons.

Copy current point to A polygon.

B. If current point on B side then:

1. If previous point on B side then:

Copy current point to B polygon.

2. If previous point on A side then:

Calculate intersection of line with edge formed from current point and previous point.

Copy calculated point to A and B polygons.

Copy current point to B polygon.

C. Call the current point the previous point.

FINDING VISIBLE SURFACES

The image space polygons handled by this algorithm are of the following form:

1. There is a list of vertices on the left and the right.
2. The first vertex of each list is the highest in y.
3. Each succeeding vertex is lower in y than the preceding one.
4. The edge formed by the left vertices does not cross the edge of the right.

This form of polygon definition (see figure 3) is optimized for polygons with large numbers of edges. See figure 8 where the colored areas and the black line are both specified with polygons. The black lines are long thin polygons.

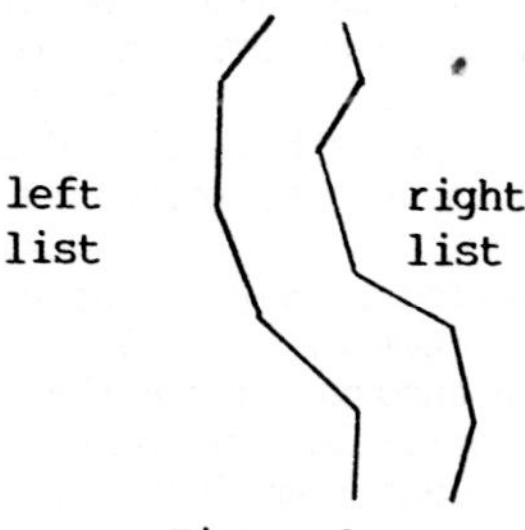

Figure 3

All other polygons in various stages of the algorithm are in the more conventional form of a list of vertices. It is assumed that an edge connects the first and last vertex. This form is necessary for the clipping algorithm presented above.

The purpose of the first level of the algorithm is to find all polygons that overlap a particular scanline and then to clip away everything that doesn't overlap it. Since the scanline has the width of one pixel we are left with a list of very narrow horizontal polygons.

The next step is to find which of those narrow polygons on the scanline overlap a particular pixel and then clip away those not over the pixel. If the closest polygon completely covers the pixel then its intensity value can be put into an array for the scanline, otherwise the list of polygons needs to be passed to the integrater.

Of course one objective is to do the above very quickly. To do so requires that we take advantage of coherence and sorting techniques to quickly reduce the number of items for consideration at each step.

The algorithm proceeds sequentially to each scanline beginning at the highest. At each scanline there is a list of active polygons that overlap that scanline. Note that a scanline is really a strip with width. At each scanline a horizontal strip is clipped off of each active polygon leaving only that part of the polygon which lies below the scanline. (See figure 4.)

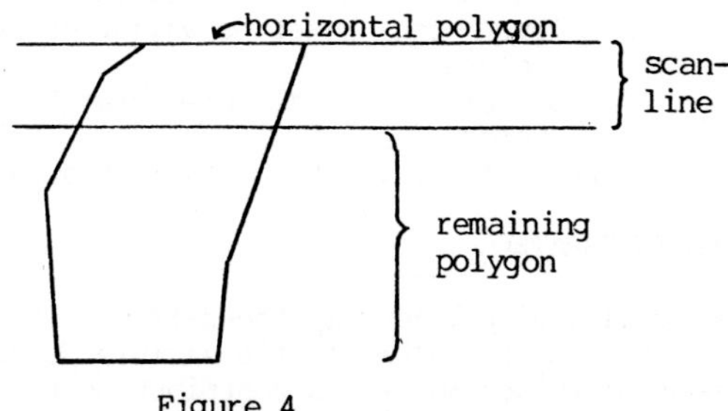

Figure 4

Similarly at each pixel, the horizontal strip is clipped at the right edge of the pixel to determine the polygons within the square pixel area.

For efficiency it is worth noting that the middle of most horizontal polygons completely covers the respective pixels. It would be wasteful to clip at each pixel in that case. We treat the middle as a solid run or segment and only need to count the pixels that it covers (see figure 5). The ends can be clipped off at the boundary of a solid segment and treated as indicated above.

The depth ordering is maintained with a sorted z-list. The first item in the list is the closest. When a new edge is encountered in the x-bucket it is entered into the z-list in order. If intersections are allowed, each item in the z-list must be checked against the incoming item over its full extent to check for possible intersection which would require splitting a polygon.

<u>The Hidden-surface Algorithm</u>

I. Sort all polygons on highest y value.
II. Initialize active polygon list to be empty.
III. Repeat for each scanline:
  A. Add polygons from y-list that enter on this scanline to active polygon list.
  B. Initialize the x-bucket to be empty and the scanline array to background.
  C. Loop through each polygon in active polygon list
    1. Clip off of each polygon the piece that lies on the current scanline. See figure 5.
    2. Replace polygon in list with polygon that has piece clipped off.
    3. If there are pixels under the piece that are completely covered, then for efficiency reasons we can break the piece into three pieces: the center solid piece and two polygons clipped off at the ends at the pixel boundaries. The two end polygons are called irregular pieces.
    4. The pieces are sorted into the x-bucket according to the leftmost pixel covered.
  D. Initialize the z-list to be empty.
  E. Repeat for each pixel across the scanline:
    1. Sort every entry at the current x position of the x-bucket into the z-list.
    2. Evaluate the z-list if not empty:
      a. If a solid piece, get its color
         else if an irregular piece is in front of a solid piece then find the area of the irregular piece over the pixel to weight the two colors
         else call the pixel integrater to get color
      b. Write the color into scanline array.

THE PIXEL INTEGRATER

Given a list of polygons in the z-list, it is necessary to find the area of each visible polygon piece in order to determine its contribution to the pixel intensity. The polygons in the z-list are in sorted z-order with the first polygon being the closest.

One of the key ideas of this algorithm is that the list of polygons can be divided into two lists with an edge of a polygon being used as the dividing line. A generalization of this idea based on using planes for dividing polygon lists is due to Ivan Sutherland [5] and in fact is part of a complete hidden-surface algorithm that he invented. This technique was used in another hidden-surface algorithm subsequently developed at Cornell[9].

Since the polygons are already in sorted order, we pick an edge of the first polygon to use as the dividing line. If this algorithm is recursively applied to both of the resulting lists of polygons then very shortly the front polygon of a list will cover all polygons behind it since everything else will have been clipped away. The area of the front polygon can then be found to weight the intensity. The sum of the weighted intensities from all the lists gives the final average intensity.

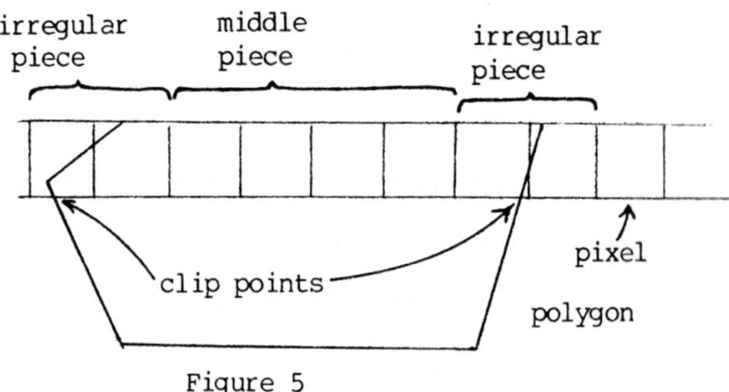

Figure 5

For this algorithm we make the following observations:

1. Since z order is implied in the list, there is no need for any z calculations. We may therefore think of the polygons as two-dimensional; they will be clipped against a line and not a vertical plane.

2. A pixel polygon for this algorithm is a list of vertices with implied connection of the first and last vertices.

3. A vertex consists of x, y, and clipflag, where clipflag is used to indicate whether or not the edge connecting that vertex and the next one has been clipped.

4. A pixel polygon that completely covers a pixel will be called a "solid polygon."

To prepare the z-list for the algorithm:

1. Each polygon will be transferred to a pixel polygon list in order until a solid polygon is reached. If there is no solid polygon, a dummy solid polygon is added with the background as its color.

2. All polygons are clipped to the pixel boundaries.

3. All edges that lie concurrent with the pixel boundaries are marked as clipped, ie. the last polygon should cover the pixel and all four edges are marked as clipped.

The Basic Algorithm for Integrating

1. Consider the first polygon in the list (which is also the closest).

2. Look for the first unclipped edge.
   If there is no unclipped edge or there is only one polygon in the list then return the color of the polygon weighted by its area.

3. Clip all polygons in the list against the edge and put them in two lists, one for each side of the edge.
   Set clipflag for each edge that lies along the clipping line as it is clipped.

4. Reenter this algorithm for each of the two lists.

5. Combine and return the two results.

IMPLEMENTATION

The hidden-surface algorithm and pixel integrater were implemented by the author at the Computer Graphics Lab at the New York Institute of Technology. The polygons to be rendered were flat colored with many edges to satisfy the needs of cartoon animation. These pictures are characterized by a large number of pixels that have more than two polygons. See figure 6. The hashed polygon C covers the boundary between polygons A and B. The pixel pointed at by P has four polygons in it, three of which are visible.

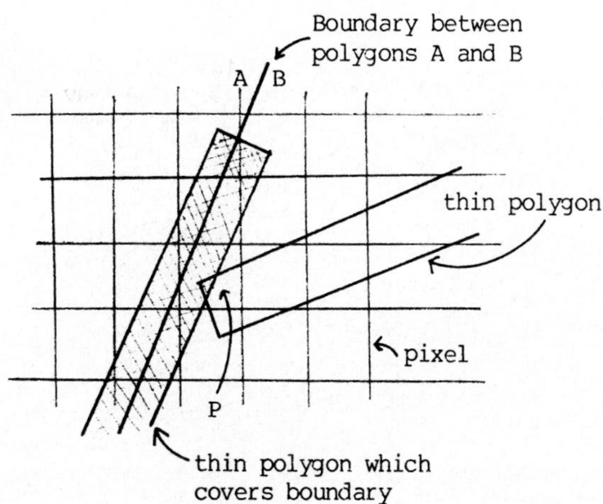

Figure 6

The ability to call the pixel integrater is under user control. The user can request jagged edges with the result that the program runs approximately three times faster for complicated pictures. Full anti-aliasing is only required for quality recording. Figure 7 shows a picture with aliasing.

We have been able to use and evaluate the algorithm. See figure 8,9, and 10 which were made at 512x512 resolution with 8 bits each for red, green and blue. Movies generated using this algorithm have not shown any aliasing symptoms for the class of images created. This has made the effort worthwhile.

ACKNOWLEDGMENT

The Computer Graphics Lab was conceived and sponsored by Dr. Alexander Schure, President of New York Institute of Technology. Lance Williams provided critical reading of the first draft.

REFERENCES

1. Catmull, Edwin, A subdivision algorithm for computer display of curved surfaces, Technical report UTEC-CSs-74-133 University of Utah, 1974

2. Crow, Frank, The aliasing problem in Computer-generated shaded images, CACM November 1977

3. Myers, Allan J., An efficient visible surface program, Ohio State University, Computer Graphics Research Group, report to NSF, July 1975

4. Shoup, R.G., Some quantization effects in digitally-generated pictures, Society for Information Display, 1973 proceedings.

5. Sutherland, I.E., Polygon sorting by subdivision: A solution to the hidden-surface problem, Unpublished manuscript, October 1973, Also public lecture at University of Utah 1973.

6. Sutherland, I.E., and Hodgman, G.W., Reentrant polygon clipping, CACM January 1974.

7. Sutherland, I.E., Sproull, R.F., and Schumacker, R.A., A characterization of ten hidden-surface algorithms, ACM Computing Surveys, March 1974.

8. Hamlin, Griffith Jr., and Gear, C.W., Raster-scan hidden surface algorithm techniques, Siggraph 1977 proceedings.

9. Weiler, K. and Atherton, P., Hidden surface removal using polygon area sorting, Siggraph 1977 proceedings.

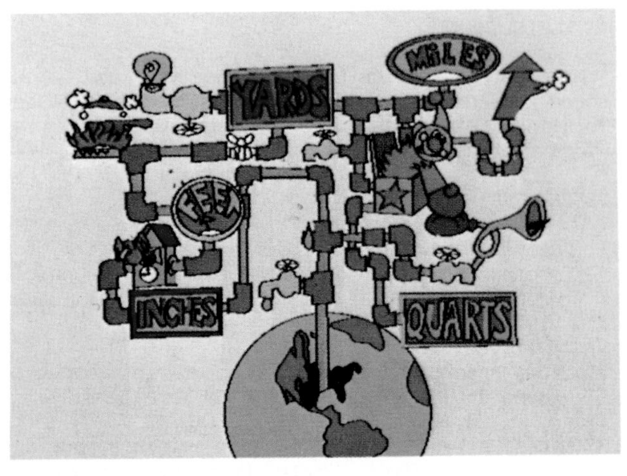

figure 7

figure 8

figure 9

figure 10

SYNTHETIC TEXTURING USING DIGITAL FILTERS

by

Eliot A. Feibush, Marc Levoy, Robert L. Cook
Program of Computer Graphics
Cornell University
Ithaca, New York 14853

ABSTRACT

Aliasing artifacts are eliminated from computer generated images of textured polygons by equivalently filtering both the texture and the edges of the polygons. Different filters can be easily compared because the weighting functions that define the shape of the filters are pre-computed and stored in lookup tables. A polygon subdivision algorithm removes the hidden surfaces so that the polygons are rendered sequentially to minimize accessing the texture definition files. An implementation of the texture rendering procedure is described.

COMPUTING REVIEWS CATEGORY: 8.2

KEYWORDS: Computer Graphics, Anti-Aliasing, Sampling, Digital Filtering, Texturing, Hidden Surface Removal

1. INTRODUCTION

Sampling converts a function into a sequence of discrete values so the function can be reproduced at a finite resolution. If the sampling rate is insufficient for the function, then the discrete values will contain aliasing artifacts. The most common aliasing artifacts in computer generated images are jagged edges and Moiré patterns. Animated sequences can also suffer from temporal aliasing artifacts such as strobing and false motion (e.g., wagon wheels that appear to spin backwards).

There are two solutions to the aliasing problem in computer graphics: increasing the sampling rate and filtering the original function. Increasing the sampling rate means computing and displaying the image at a higher resolution. Filtering the original function means blurring the image before sampling. The two approaches are not mutually exclusive. Catmull and Crow point out that if the only goal is to eliminate aliasing, then filtering the original function is better than increasing the sampling rate (4,5). Furthermore, it is often impossible to increase the sampling rate without more costly display technology.

Filtering was introduced to the computer graphics literature by Catmull in (3) and was studied comprehensively by Crow in (5). Since then, several researchers have made filtering an integral part of their synthetic imaging systems. These systems can be classified by the type of data they display:

1. Continuous functions (parametric data):
   1. Crow (5) (parabolas)
2. Objects (polygonal or patch data):
   1. Catmull (3) (patches)
   2. Crow (5) (polygons)
   3. Crow (6) (vectors)
   4. Catmull (4) (polygons)
   5. Whitted (9) (polygons)
3. Textures (pixel data):
   1. Catmull (3) (on patches)
   2. Blinn and Newell (2) (on patches)
   3. Crow (6) (characters)
   4. Blinn (1) (on patches)

Most of the above implementations that filter only edges use an unweighted filter (i.e., a filter with a weighting function that is constant throughout the convolution mask). This is far better than no filter at all, but not as good as a weighted filter. Unweighted filters have been used to avoid the computational expense of weighting functions. Researchers who have used weighted filters for the texture did not use the same filter for the edges of the surfaces.

The texture and the edges of each surface should be filtered separately and equivalently to produce correct renderings. The texture should be filtered first to remove excessively ,high frequencies that could cause aliasing in the form of Moiré patterns. Then the edges of surfaces should be filtered to eliminate the excessively high frequencies that could cause aliasing in the form of "jaggies." Of the implementations listed above that include texturing, only Catmull's (3) applies equivalent filters to both the texture and the edges. He uses unweighted filters to display environments of textured patches.

2. IMPLEMENTATION

This paper describes the implementation of two filtering processes used for displaying textured polygons. Both the texture filter and the edge filter are based on a polygon subdivision hidden surface algorithm, and both procedures use pre-computed lookup tables to define any desired filter shape.

2.1 DATA REPRESENTATION

Objects in this texture rendering system are defined by planar polygons. These polygons may be concave, may contain holes, and may be coplanar with other polygons in the environment to create detail faces within larger faces. Each polygon is assigned a texture which completely covers its surface. A texture is a two-dimensional array of texture definition points. The color of each point is represented by either one intensity value, producing a gray scale texture, or three intensity values, producing a full color texture.

The construction of the database, including the creation and assignment of textures to polygons, is handled by an interactive geometric modeling package which is described by Feibush (7). The textures can be generated by any of several methods, including optical scanning or synthetic airbrushing. In practice, several techniques are usually combined for each texture.

The word "pixel" (picture element) must be clearly defined. A pixel is often thought of as a rectangular block whose width is equal to the distance between centers of adjacent blocks. In this paper, however, a pixel is defined as an infinitesimal point having an intensity value.

2.2 COORDINATE SYSTEMS

Three coordinate systems are used:

1. Texture definition space.
2. Object definition space.
3. Image display space.

The first coordinate system is a two-dimensional space for defining textures. The textures are created and stored on the X - Y plane shown in Figure 1a. The second coordinate system is a three-dimensional space used for defining the polygons. When a texture is assigned to a polygon, a matrix is constructed that transforms the polygon from its location in object space to the X - Y plane in texture space, as shown in Figure 1b. The third coordinate system is a three-dimensional space used for displaying the object. A single matrix is used to transform the polygons from object space to image space and create the perspective distortion, as shown in Figure 1c.

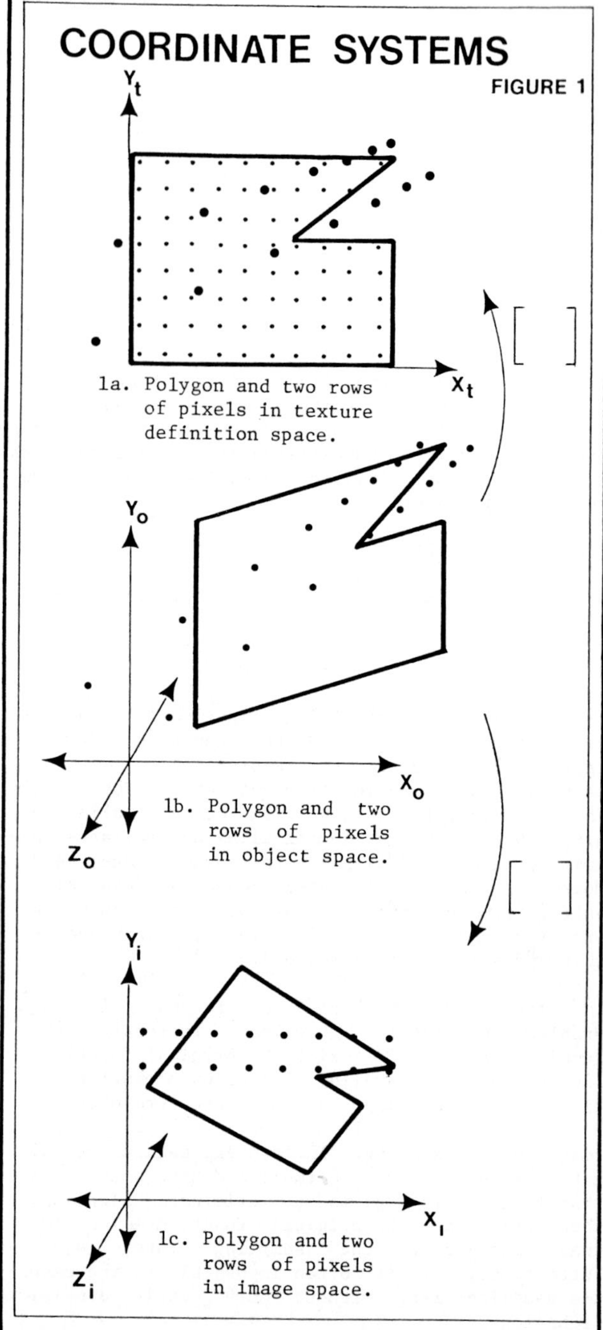

Also shown in the figure are two rows of display pixels which are drawn as points in accordance with the above definition of the term "pixel." These display pixels are initially defined in image space and can be transformed to object space (care must be taken in reversing the perspective distortion), and then to texture definition space, as shown in the figure.

2.3 HIDDEN SURFACE ALGORITHM

Most researchers use a scanline hidden surface algorithm to determine the contribution of each polygon in the object to the display pixels. In a scanline algorithm, all the polygons contributing to the color of a pixel are processed simultaneously. The color of each pixel can therefore be computed in a single pass. An alternative solution presented here is to use a polygon subdivision hidden surface algorithm to compute the visible portions of all the polygons before computing the color of the display pixels. The color of each pixel is built up piecemeal from the visible portions of each contributing polygon. The polygon hidden surface algorithm developed by Weiler (8) has been implemented.

Separating the hidden surface removal from the filtering process has a significant advantage over approaches that do both tasks simultaneously. Rendering a textured polygon involves accessing its texture definition file. A scanline algorithm requires simultaneous access to the texture files of all the polygons that are visible on each scanline. The storage problems this entails can not be taken lightly even in a virtual memory machine, particularly if the textures are high resolution color images. The polygon subdivision hidden surface algorithm produces a list of visible polygons defined at machine precision so that the polygons can be rendered sequentially. Hence only one texture file has to be accessible at a given time, and each texture file is processed completely before another one is needed.

2.4 TEXTURE FILTERING

Whenever a polygon is displayed in perspective and is not parallel to the picture plane, the amount of blurring required to avoid aliasing varies across the polygon and is different in the horizontal and vertical directions. The method described in this paper produces sufficient blurring at each display pixel by selecting specific texture definition points that correspond to the pixel and then filtering the points to determine the color of the pixel. A description of the procedure follows:

1. For a given view of the object, use the polygon subdivision hidden surface algorithm to make a list of the portions of the polygons that are visible in image space. The visible portions are called display polygons.

2. Working with one display polygon at a time, make a list of all the pixels that contribute to the display of the polygon. A convolution mask, whose shape is determined by the weighting function of the filter, is centered at each display pixel. Each pixel has a bounding rectangle, which is the smallest rectangle that completely bounds the pixel's convolution mask. The bounding rectangles may overlap depending on the size and shape of the convolution masks. List every display pixel whose bounding rectangle is completely or partially within the polygon, as shown in Figure 2a. Also save a list of the intersections of each bounding rectangle with the polygon.

3. For each display pixel, transform its bounding rectangle from image space to object space and then to texture definition space. The rectangle can be transformed to texture definition space because its vertices have three-dimensional coordinates coplanar with the display polygon. The rectangle in image space transforms to a quadrilateral in texture space, as shown in Figure 2b. The texture definition points within this quadrilateral contribute to the color of the display pixel. To simplify the selection of these points, a rectangle is constructed around the bounding quadrilateral. This rectangle includes some texture definition points that do not contribute to the color of the pixel, but these extra points will be eliminated from the filtering in step 6.

4. Transform the parent polygon of the current display polygon from object space to texture definition space. Clip the rectangle around the convolution mask quadrilateral against the parent polygon. The texture definition points within this area will be filtered, as in Figure 2c.

5. Transform each texture point that will be filtered to object space and then to image space, as shown in Figure 2d.

6. Eliminate the extra points selected in step 3 by clipping the transformed texture points against the bounding rectangle of the convolution mask in image space, as shown in Figure 2e.

7. Filter the selected texture points by computing the weighted average of their color values. Points near the center of the convolution mask are weighted more heavily than those near the edge. The cone shown in Figure 2f represents one possible weighting function. The weighting function is computed at a number of locations and the values are stored in a two-dimensional lookup table. The location of each transformed texture point within the convolution mask is used as an index to the lookup table. The color values of all the texture definition points are multiplied by their respective values in the lookup table and summed together in a weighted average. When the transformed texture points do not coincide precisely with the discrete locations at which the weighting function is calculated, the nearest value is used.

This completes the texture filtering. The edges of the polygons are filtered next to complete the rendering procedure.

TEXTURE FILTERING

FIGURE 2

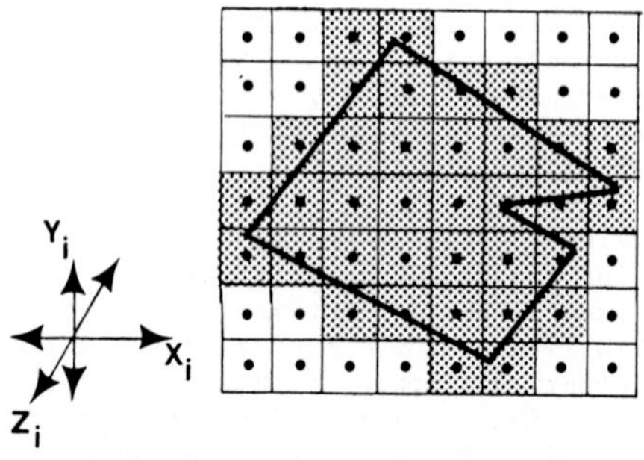

2a. Select the pixels that contribute to the display of the polygon. For clarity, the bounding rectangles shown do not overlap. Figures 2b-2f illustrate the texture calculation for each selected pixel.

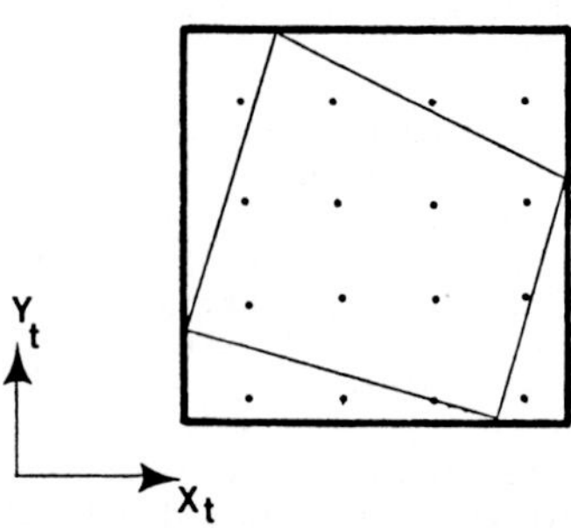

2b. Transform the bounding rectangle to texture space and select texture definition points.

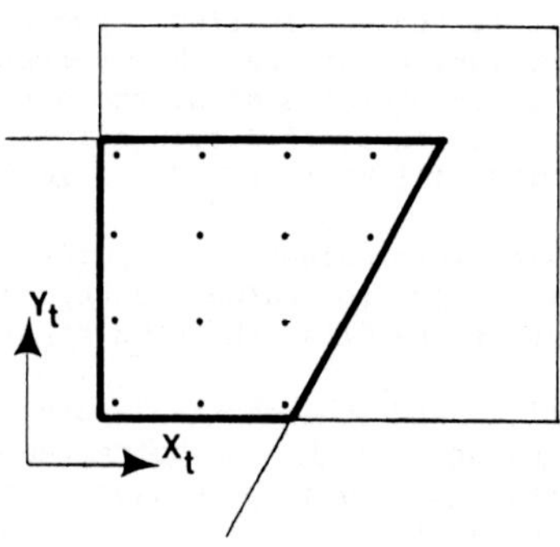

2c. Select the points inside the transformed parent polygon.

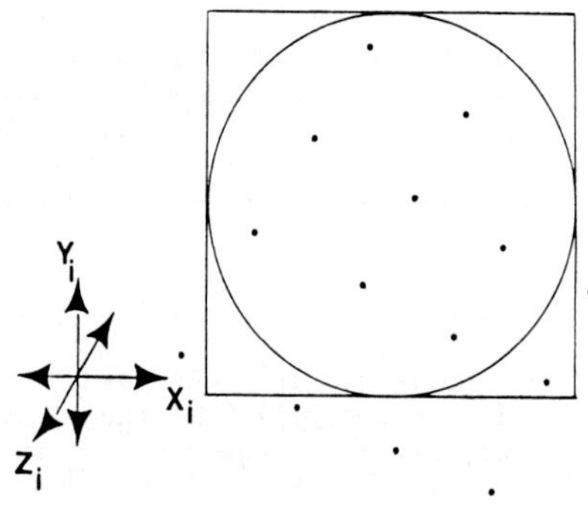

2d. Transform the points to image space.

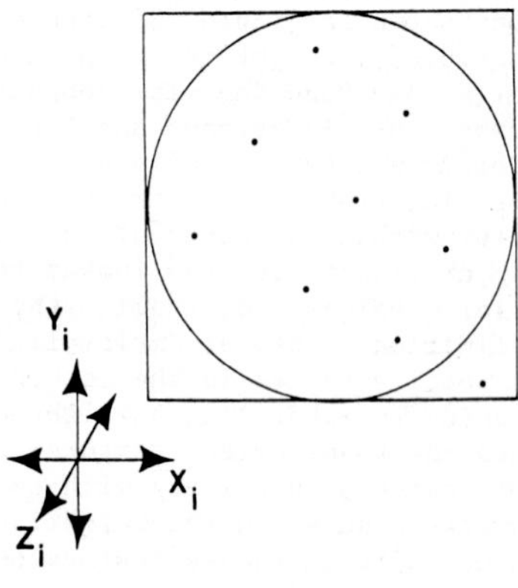

2e. Select the points inside the bounding rectangle.

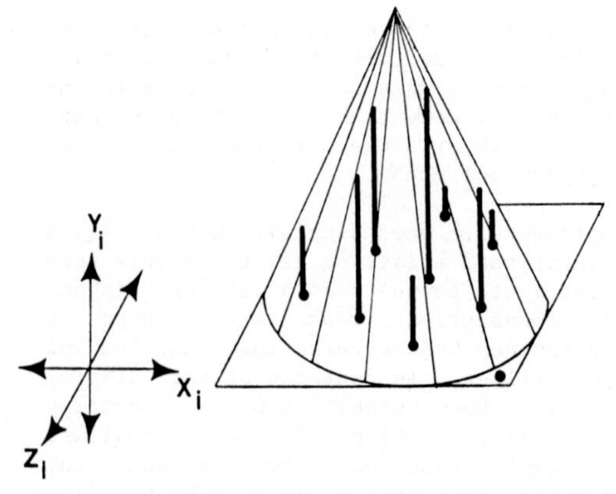

2f. Compute the weighted average of the selected points.

2.5 EDGE FILTERING

The intensity of a pixel whose convolution mask is completely within one display polygon is determined just by the texture filter. The intensity of a pixel near an edge of a polygon is only partly determined by the texture filter because its convolution mask covers more than one display polygon. The intensity of a pixel computed by the texture filter for one polygon is weighted by the percentage of the total intensity of the pixel that is contributed by that polygon. The total intensity of a display pixel is built up sequentially as each polygon is rendered by accumulating the partial intensities in a frame buffer.

The contribution of a polygon to a pixel is determined by filtering its edges with the same weighting function that was used for the texture filter. But unlike the texture, which is defined by discrete points, the edges of the polygon are defined by a continuous function. Edge filtering is therefore an analytic problem. The cone above the convolution mask shown in Figure 3a represents one possible weighting function for the filter. The value of the weighting function at any point in the convolution mask is the distance from the point to the surface above it. The contribution of a polygon to the pixel is the percentage of the volume of the entire cone that is above the polygon, as shown by the shaded volume in Figure 3a. The calculation of this volume is described below.

1. Clip the display polygon against the bounding rectangle of the convolution mask, as shown in Figure 3b. The points of intersection of each polygon edge with the bounding rectangle are already known from step 2 above. The clipped polygon may be concave and may contain holes.

2. For each vertex of the clipped polygon, construct a triangle with the following sides (as shown in Figure 3c):

    1. BASE is the line segment between the current vertex and the next vertex (going clockwise around the polygon).

    2. SIDE1 is the line segment between the current vertex and the pixel.

    3. SIDE2 is the line segment between the next vertex and the pixel.

3. Calculate the volume above the polygon from the volumes above all the triangles constructed in step 2, as shown in Figure 3c. The volume above a single triangle is added to the total if the cross product of SIDE1 and SIDE2 is negative; it is subtracted from the total if the cross product is positive.

4. The task of finding the volume above an arbitrary polygon has now been simplified to finding the volume above a series of triangles, each having one vertex at the pixel. The problem can be simplified further. For each triangle, the perpendicular from the pixel to BASE (or to its extension) forms two right triangles. The volume above the original triangle is the sum of the volumes above the two right triangles if the perpendicular lies within the triangle, as shown in Figure 3d; it is the difference of the volumes if the perpendicular lies outside of the triangle, as shown in Figure 3e.

5. The problem has now been simplified to finding the volume above a group of right triangles. The base and height of each triangle are used as indices to a lookup table that contains the volume above this triangle for the given weighting function. Care must be taken in computing the lookup table so that areas inside the bounding rectangle but outside the convolution mask have no volume above them. Only the shaded area of Figure 3f has volume above it.

Each filter shape needs only one lookup table, regardless of the filter's absolute size. The filter size can be changed by scaling the indices to the lookup table.

The organization of the lookup table assumes that the filter function is circularly symmetric. For a filter that is not circularly symmetric, one more parameter describing the location of the right triangles (such as a polar sweep angle) is required. A four parameter lookup table would give the volume above the original triangle without constructing the two right triangles. The X and Y positions of the two vertices of BASE of the original triangle would be used as the indices to the four parameter lookup table. This further simplifies the filtering computation but requires significantly more table storage.

3. EXAMPLES

A polygon textured with alternating red and white vertical stripes has been rendered by the system described in this paper. Due to the rotation and perspective transformations, the number of texture definition points that were filtered for each display pixel varied considerably. The images were computed at a resolution of 512 x 512 and displayed on a 24-bit color frame buffer.

The five images of the polygon demonstrate the effectiveness of different filters, as shown in Figures 4a-e. Figure 4a shows the polygon in texture definition space. In Figure 4b this polygon is displayed in image space with no filtering. In Figure 4c it is displayed using an unweighted filter with a square convolution mask whose sides are equal to the distance between adjacent display pixels. In Figure 4d the polygon is displayed using a filter with a Gaussian weighting function that has a standard deviation equal to the distance between adjacent display pixels. The convolution mask is a circle whose radius is equal to twice the standard deviation of

EDGE FILTERING

FIGURE 3

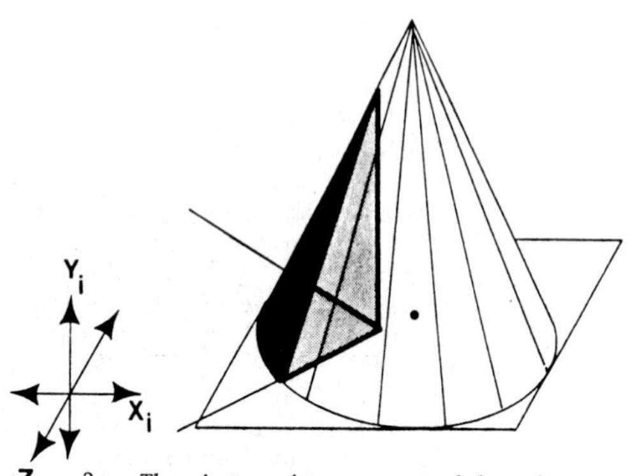

3a. The intensity computed by the texture filter is weighted by the ratio of the shaded volume to the total volume of the cone.

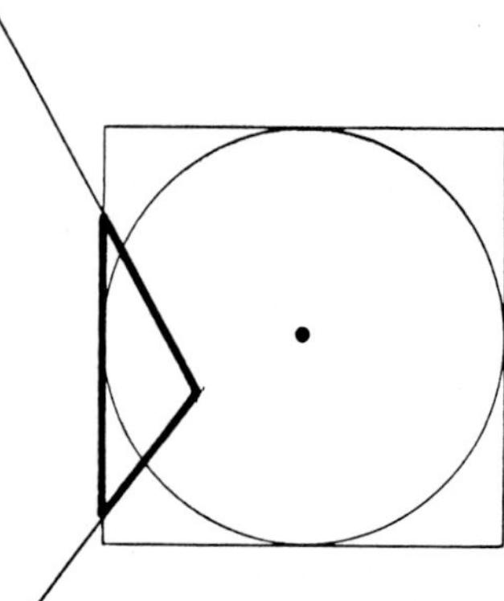

3b. Clip the polygon to the bounding rectangle of the pixel's convolution mask.

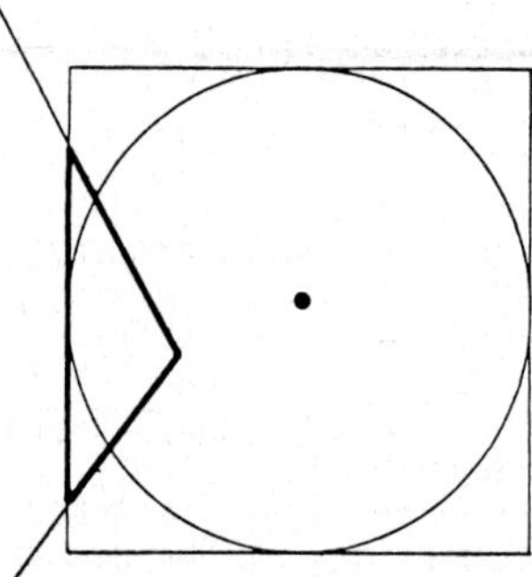

=

+

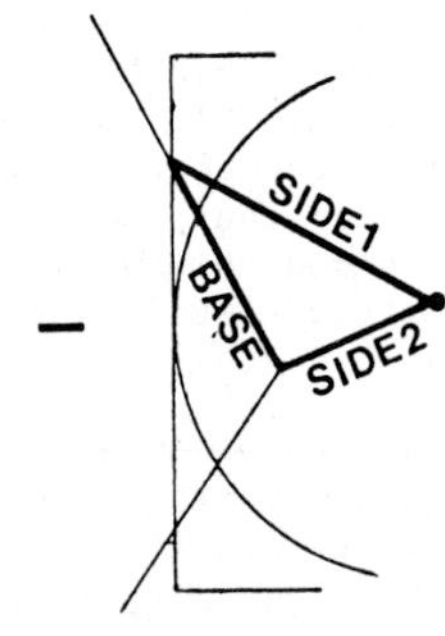

–

SIDE1
BASE
SIDE2

–

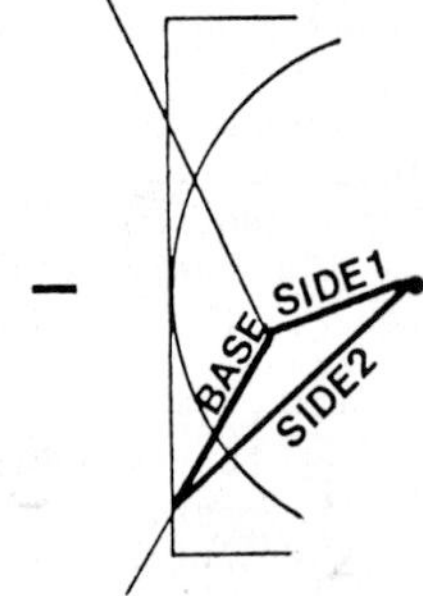

3c. For each vertex of the clipped polygon, construct the triangle formed by the vertex, the next vertex (going clockwise), and the pixel. From the volumes above these triangles, calculate the volume above the clipped polygon as shown in Figures 3d-f.

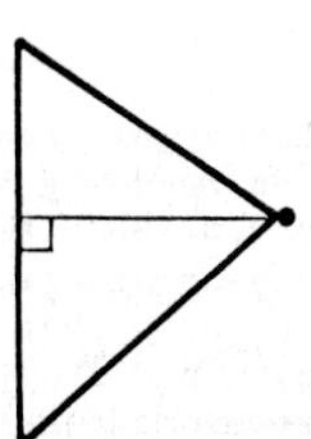

=

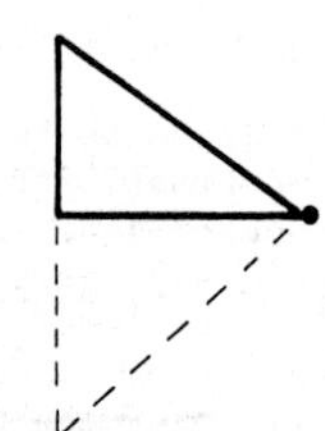

+

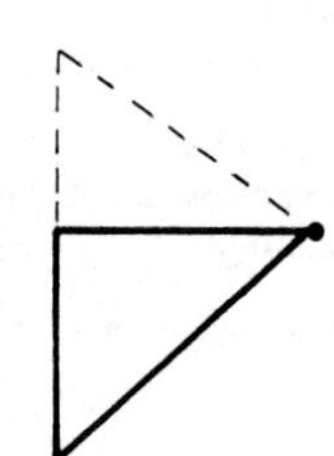

3d. For each triangle, construct the perpendicular from the pixel to BASE. If the perpendicular is inside the triangle, then the volume above the triangle is the sum of the volumes above the two right triangles formed by the perpendicular.

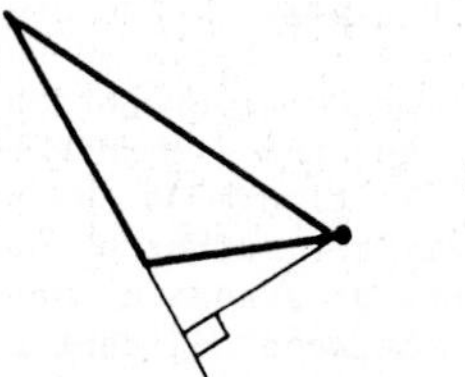

=

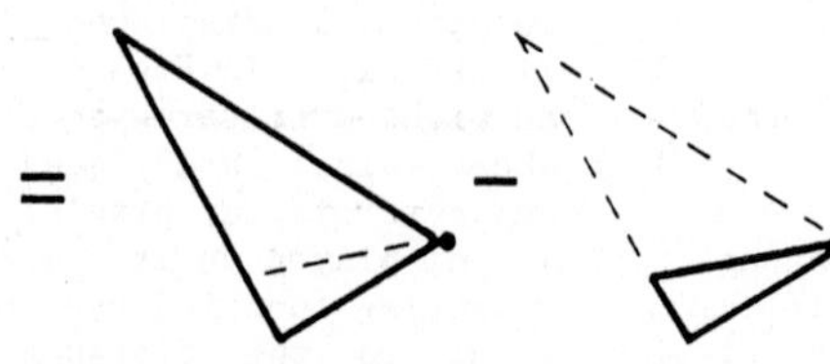

3e. If the perpendicular is outside the triangle, then the volume above the triangle is the difference of the volumes above the two right triangles formed by the perpendicular.

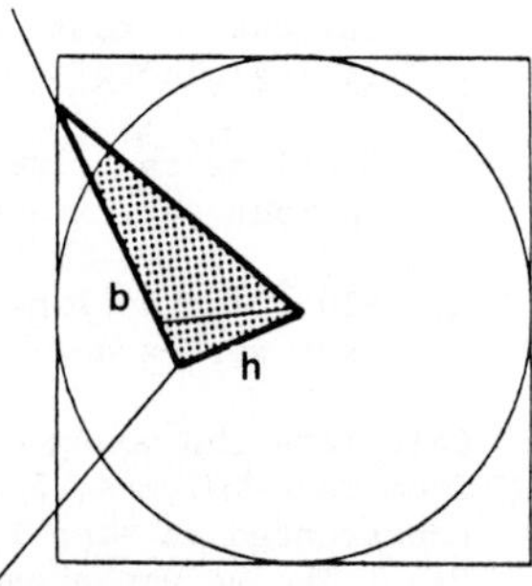

3f. Find the volume above each right triangle by using its height (h) and base (b) as indices to a lookup table. The value stored in the lookup table includes only the volume above the shaded portion of the triangle.

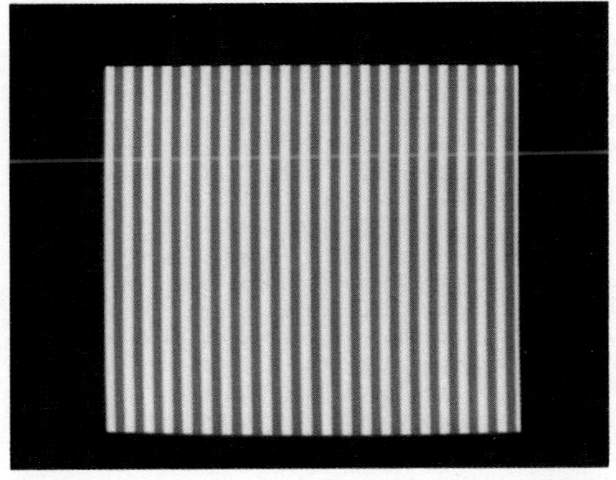

Figure 4a. Texture definition.

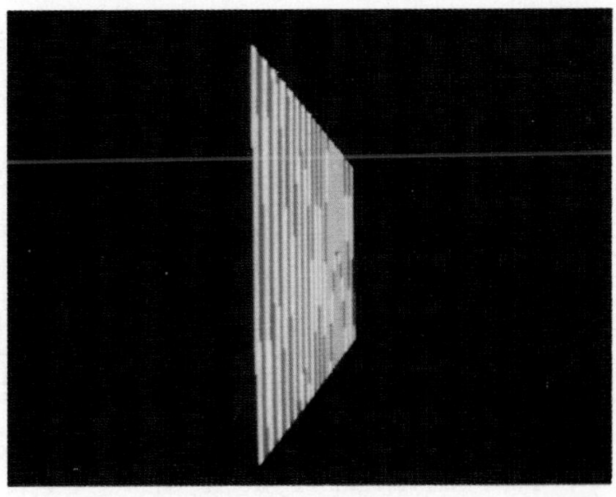

Figure 4b. No filter.

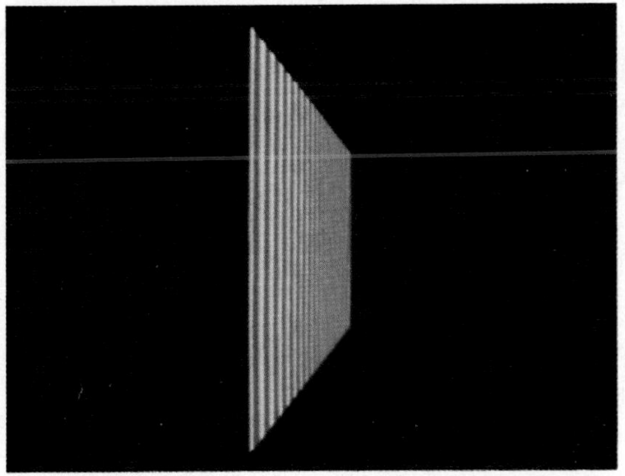

Figure 4c. Unweighted filter.

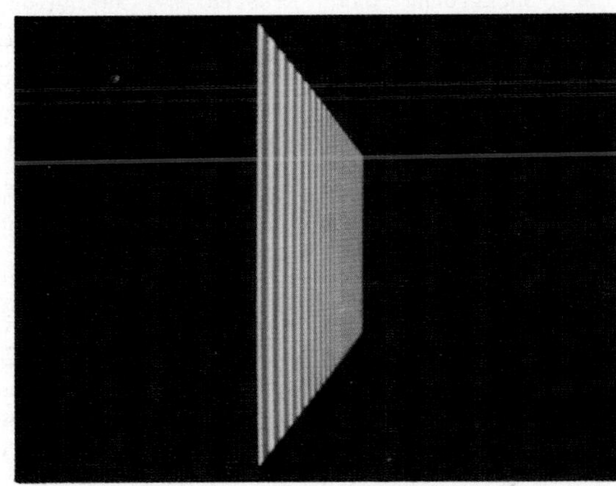

Figure 4d. Gaussian filter.

Figure 4e. Hardware magnification.

Figure 5. House.

the Gaussian.

Displaying the polygon with no filtering is completely unsatisfactory due to the jaggedness of not only the edges of the polygon but also the stripes in the texture. Using an unweighted filter is better and nearly satisfactory along the edges, but Moiré is still evident in the center of the polygon. The weighted filter, however, produces an excellent image. In the hardware magnification shown in Figure 4e, the polygon is inclined slightly more than in Figures 4b-d to enhance the visibility of the filtering. Notice that the filtering along the left edge of the polygon is equivalent to the filtering along the stripes of the texture.

The final image, Figure 5 shows the front facade of an imaginary house that has been rendered by the system described in this paper. It demonstrates an application of the system to a complex database composed of many polygons and textures. The textures were extracted from optically scanned photographs of real objects. The background was created by assigning an optically scanned photograph of a real site to the rearmost polygon in the environment.

4. LIMITATIONS

It is possible to obtain views where textures are magnified beyond their original resolution (i.e., zooming into a texture). During the texture filtering process, the area of the texture definition that corresponds to a display pixel will contain only a few texture definition points. To avoid reproducing these texture definition points as large square areas, the color values of the closest texture definition points are bilinearly interpolated.

Bilinear interpolation of the texture definition points is also necessary when the edges of two polygons are very close to each other, but do not actually touch. The hidden surface algorithm will detect the narrow slot between the polygons, so texture definition points of the polygon seen through the slot should be selected for filtering. If no texture definition points from the background polygon fall within the slot, then the nearby texture definition points are bilinearly interpolated.

More blurring is required to avoid aliasing if there are high frequency components in the texture definition. Aliasing that is not noticeable in a static image may become visible if the image is part of an animated sequence, so that additional blurring is needed.

5. CONCLUSIONS

Two filtering processes, one for the textures and one for the edges, are necessary for displaying textured polygons without introducing aliasing artifacts. A weighted filter, such as the Gaussian used in the examples, produces more realistic images than an unweighted filter or no filter at all.

A polygon subdivision hidden surface algorithm is superior to a scanline hidden surface algorithm for displaying textured polygons. By making a list of all the visible portions of the polygons before computing the color of the display pixels, the polygons can be filtered sequentially to minimize accessing each of the texture definition files.

Complex filters no longer have to be considered prohibitively expensive. If the filter's weighting function is stored in a lookup table instead of being computed at each pixel, an image can be computed in the same amount of time regardless of the complexity of the filter. The filter can be changed just by using a different lookup table.

ACKNOWLEDGEMENTS

This research has been performed at the Program of Computer Graphics at Cornell University and was funded in part by the National Science Foundation.

The authors thank Theodore Crane and Stuart Sechrest for implementing the polygon subdivision hidden surface algorithm.

REFERENCES

1. Blinn, James, "Computer Display of Curved Surfaces", Dissertation, University of Utah, 1978

2. Blinn, James, and Newell, Martin, "Texture and Reflection in Computer Generated Images", Communications of the ACM, Vol. 19, No. 10, Oct., 1976

3. Catmull, Edwin, "A Subdivision Algorithm for Computer Display of Curved Surfaces", Dissertation, University of Utah, 1974

4. Catmull, Edwin, "A Hidden-Surface Algorithm with Anti-Aliasing", Computer Graphics, Vol. 12, No. 3, Aug., 1978 (Siggraph '78)

5. Crow, Franklin, "The Aliasing Problem in Computer Synthesized Shaded Images", Dissertation, University of Utah, 1976

6. Crow, Franklin, "The Use of Grayscale for Improved Raster Display of Vectors and Characters", Computer Graphics, Vol. 12, No. 3, Aug., 1978 (Siggraph '78)

7. Feibush, Eliot, "Texture Rendering for Architectural Design", Computer Aided Design, Vol. 12, No. 2, Mar., 1980

8. Weiler, Kevin, "Hidden Surface Removal Using Polygon Area Sorting", Masters thesis, Cornell University, 1978

9. Whitted, Turner, "An Improved Illumination Model for Shaded Display", Preliminary papers to be published in Communications of the ACM, Aug., 1979

Stochastic Sampling in Computer Graphics

ROBERT L. COOK
Pixar

Ray tracing, ray casting, and other forms of point sampling are important techniques in computer graphics, but their usefulness has been undermined by aliasing artifacts. In this paper it is shown that these artifacts are not an inherent part of point sampling, but a consequence of using regularly spaced samples. If the samples occur at appropriate nonuniformly spaced locations, frequencies above the Nyquist limit do not alias, but instead appear as noise of the correct average intensity. This noise is much less objectionable to our visual system than aliasing. In ray tracing, the rays can be stochastically distributed to perform a Monte Carlo evaluation of integrals in the rendering equation. This is called *distributed ray tracing* and can be used to simulate motion blur, depth of field, penumbrae, gloss, and translucency.

Categories and Subject Descriptors: I.3.3 [**Computer Graphics**]: Picture/Image Generation; I.3.7 [**Computer Graphics**]: Three-Dimensional Graphics and Realism

General Terms: Algorithms

Additional Key Words and Phrases: Antialiasing, filtering, image synthesis, Monte Carlo integration, motion blur, raster graphics, ray tracing, sampling, stochastic sampling

1. INTRODUCTION

Because pixels are discrete, computer graphics is inherently a sampling process. The pixel size determines an upper limit to the frequencies that can be displayed. This limit, one cycle every two pixels, is called the *Nyquist limit.* An attempt to display frequencies greater than the Nyquist limit can produce aliasing artifacts, such as "jaggies" on the edges of objects [6], jagged highlights [26], strobing and other forms of temporal aliasing [19], and Moiré patterns in textures [6]. These artifacts are tolerated in some real-time applications in which speed is more vital than beauty, but they are unacceptable in realistic image synthesis.

Rendering algorithms can be classified as *analytic* or *discrete* according to how they approach the aliasing problem. Analytic algorithms can filter out the high frequencies that cause aliasing before sampling the pixel values. This filtering tends to be complicated and time consuming, but it can eliminate certain types of aliasing very effectively [3, 6, 8, 9, 15]. Discrete algorithms, such as ray tracing,

This research was done when Pixar was the computer division of Lucasfilm Ltd. An earlier version of this paper was prepared as an unpublished Lucasfilm Technical Memo #94, "Antialiased Point Sampling," 1983.
Author's address: Pixar, P.O. Box 13719, San Rafael, CA 94913-3719.

ACM Transactions on Graphics, Vol. 5, No. 1, January 1986, Pages 51–72.

only consider the image at regularly spaced sample points. Since they ignore everything not at these points, they appear by their nature to preclude filtering the image. Thus they are plagued by seemingly inherent aliasing artifacts. This is unfortunate, for these algorithms are much simpler, more elegant, and more amenable to hardware implementation than the analytic methods. They are also capable of many features that are difficult to do analytically, such as shadows, reflection, refraction [13, 24], constructive solid geometry [21], motion blur, and depth of field [5].

There are two existing discrete approaches to alleviating the aliasing problem: *supersampling* and *adaptive sampling*. Supersampling involves using more than one regularly spaced sample per pixel. It reduces aliasing by raising the Nyquist limit, but it does not eliminate aliasing. No matter how many samples are used, there are still frequencies that will alias. In adaptive sampling, additional rays are traced near edges [24]; the additional rays are traced midway between previously traced rays. Unlike supersampling, this approach can antialias edges reliably, but it may require a large number of rays, and it complicates an otherwise simple algorithm.

In this paper a new discrete approach to antialiasing called *stochastic sampling* is presented. Stochastic sampling is a Monte Carlo technique [11] in which the image is sampled at appropriate nonuniformly spaced locations rather than at regularly spaced locations. This approach is inherently different from either supersampling or adaptive sampling, though it can be combined with either of them. Stochastic sampling can eliminate all forms of aliasing, including unruly forms such as highlight aliasing.

With stochastic sampling, aliasing is replaced by noise of the correct average intensity. Frequencies above the Nyquist limit are still inadequately sampled, and they still appear as artifacts in the image. But a highly objectionable artifact (aliasing) is replaced with an artifact that our visual systems tolerate very well (noise).

In addition to providing a solution to the aliasing problem, stochastic sampling also provides new capabilities for discrete algorithms such as ray tracing. The physical equations simulated in the rendering process involve integrals over time, lens area, specular reflection angle, etc. Image-synthesis algorithms have usually avoided performing these integrals by resorting to crude approximations that assume instantaneous shutters, pinhole cameras, mirror or diffuse reflections, etc. But these integrals can be easily evaluated by stochastically sampling them, a process called Monte Carlo integration. In a ray-tracing algorithm, this involves stochastically distributing the rays in time, lens area, reflection angle, etc. This is called *probabilistic* or *distributed ray tracing* [5]. Distributed ray tracing allows the simulation of fuzzy phenomena, such as motion blur, depth of field, penumbrae, gloss, and translucency.

2. UNIFORM POINT SAMPLING

Before discussing stochastic sampling, we first review uniform sampling and the source of aliasing. In a point-sampled picture, frequencies greater than the Nyquist limit are inadequately sampled. If the samples are uniformly spaced, these frequencies can appear as aliases, that is, they can appear falsely as low frequencies [4, 17, 20].

To see how this happens, consider for the moment one-dimensional sampling; we refer to the dimension as time. Let a signal $f(t)$ be sampled at regular intervals of time, that is, at times nT for integer n, where T is the time period between samples, so that $1/T$ is the sampling frequency. The Nyquist limit is half the sampling frequency, or $0.5/T$. This sampling is equivalent to multiplication by the *shah* function $\text{III}(t/T)$, where

$$\text{III}(x) = \sum_{n=-\infty}^{\infty} \delta(x - n),$$

where δ is the Kronecker delta function. After sampling, information about the original signal $f(t)$ is preserved only at the sample points. The sampling theorem states that, if $f(t)$ contains no frequencies above the Nyquist limit, then sampling followed by an ideal reconstruction filter reproduces the original signal $f(t)$ exactly.

This situation is shown in Figure 1 for a sine wave. In Figure 1a, the frequency of the sine wave is below the Nyquist limit of the samples, and the sampled values accurately represent the function. But, in Figure 1b, the frequency of the sine wave is above the Nyquist limit of the samples. The sampled values do not accurately represent the sampled sine wave; instead they look as if they came from a low-frequency sine wave. The high-frequency sine wave appears incorrectly under the alias of this low-frequency sine wave.

Figure 2 shows this situation in the frequency domain. The Fourier transform of f is denoted by F; the Fourier transform of the shah function $\text{III}(t/T)$ is another shah function $(1/T)\text{III}(tT)$. Figure 2a shows the Fourier transform of the signal in Figure 1a, a single sine wave whose frequency is below the Nyquist limit. Sampling involves convolving the signal with the sampling grid of Figure 2b to produce the spectrum shown in Figure 2c. An ideal reconstruction filter, shown in Figure 2d, would extract the original signal, as in Figure 2e. In Figures 2f–2j, the same process is repeated for the signal in Figure 1b, a single sine wave whose frequency is above the Nyquist limit. In this case, the sampling process can fold the high-frequency sine wave into low frequencies, as shown in Figure 2h. These false frequencies, or aliases, cannot be separated from frequencies that are a part of the original signal. The part of the spectrum extracted by the reconstruction filter contains these aliases, as shown in Figure 2j.

Sampling theory thus predicts that, with a regular sampling grid, frequencies greater than the Nyquist limit can alias. The inability to reproduce those frequencies is inherent in the sampling process, but their appearance as aliases is a consequence of the regularity of the sampling grid. If the sample points are not regularly spaced, the energy in those frequencies can appear as noise, an artifact that is much less objectionable than aliasing. In the case of uniform sampling, aliasing is precisely defined; in the case of nonuniform sampling, we use the term aliasing to mean artifacts with distinct frequency components, as opposed to noise.

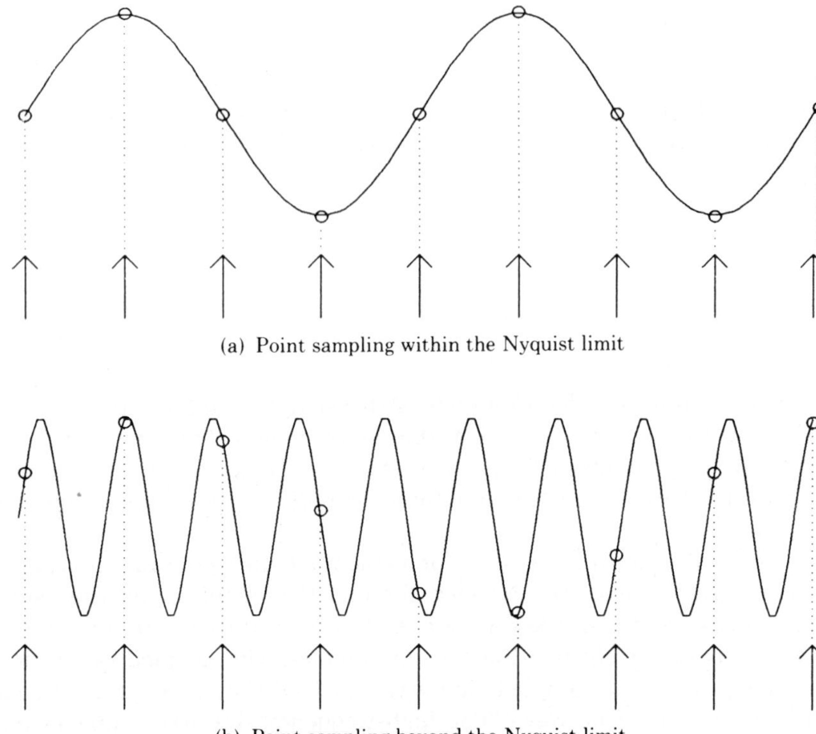

(a) Point sampling within the Nyquist limit
(b) Point sampling beyond the Nyquist limit

Fig. 1. Point sampling shown in the spatial domain. The arrows indicate the sample locations, and the circles indicate the sampled values. In (a), the sine wave frequency is within the Nyquist limit, so the sampled values accurately represent the signal. In (b), the sine wave frequency is above the Nyquist limit, and the sampled values incorrectly represent a low-frequency sine wave that is not present in the signal.

3. POISSON DISK SAMPLING

An excellent example of a nonuniform distribution of sample locations is found in the human eye. The eye has a limited number of photoreceptors, and, like any other sampling process, it has a Nyquist limit. Yet our eyes are not normally prone to aliasing [25]. In the fovea, the cells are tightly packed in a hexagonal pattern, and aliasing is avoided because the lens acts as a low-pass filter. Outside of the fovea, however, the cells are further apart and thus the sampling rate is lower, so we might expect to see aliasing artifacts. In this region, aliasing is avoided by a nonuniform distribution of the cells.

The distribution of cones in the eye has been studied by Yellott [27]. Figure 3a is a picture of the distribution of cones in an extrafoveal region of the eye of a rhesus monkey, which has a photoreceptor distribution similar to that in the human eye. Yellott took the optical Fourier transform of this distribution, with the result shown in Figure 3b. This distribution is called a *Poisson disk distribution,* and it is shown schematically in the frequency domain in Figure 4b. There is a spike at the origin (the dc component) and a sea of noise beyond the Nyquist

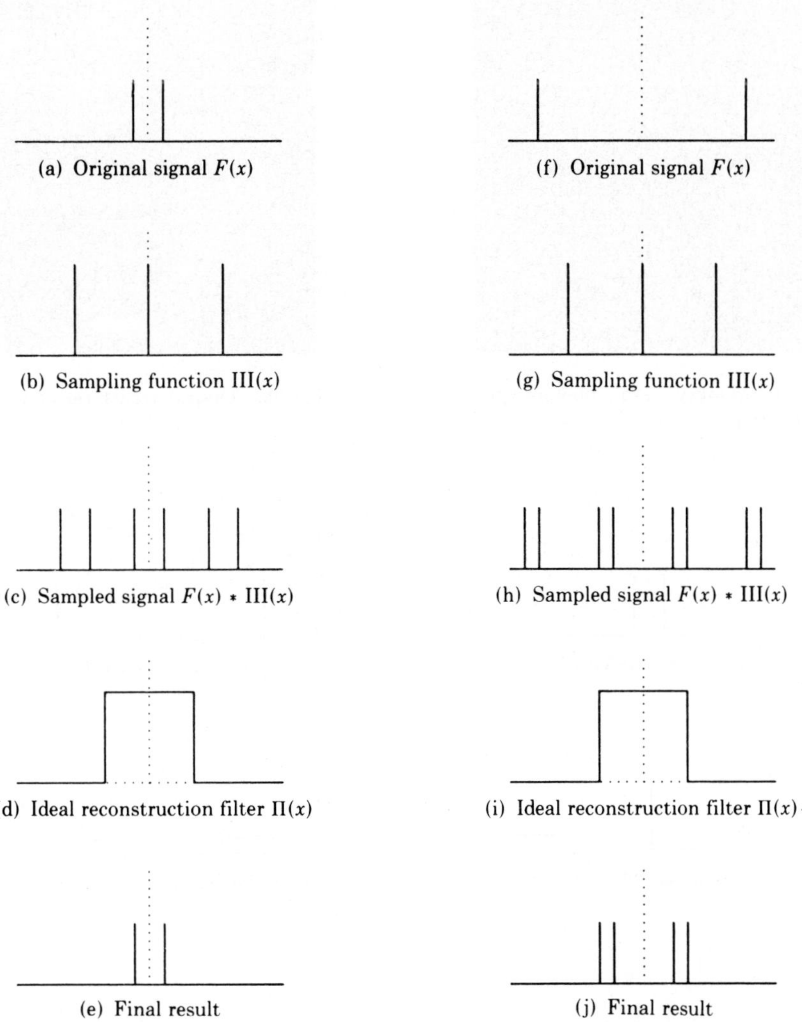

Fig. 2. Point sampling shown in the frequency domain. The original signal $F(x)$ is convolved with the sampling grid $III(x)$, and the result is multiplied by an ideal reconstruction filter $\Pi(x)$. The process is shown for a sine wave with a frequency below the Nyquist limit in (a)–(e) and above the Nyquist limit in (f)–(j).

limit. In effect, the samples are randomly placed with the restriction that no two samples are closer together than a certain distance.

Now let us analyze point sampling using a Poisson disk sampling distribution instead of a regular grid. Figure 4a shows a signal that is a single sine wave whose frequency is below the Nyquist limit. Convolution with the Poisson sampling grid of Figure 4b produces the spectrum in Figure 4c. The ideal reconstruction filter of Figure 4d would extract the original signal, Figure 4e. Figure 4f shows a sine wave whose frequency is above the Nyquist limit. Convolution with the Poisson sampling grid produces the spectrum in Figure 4h. An ideal reconstruc-

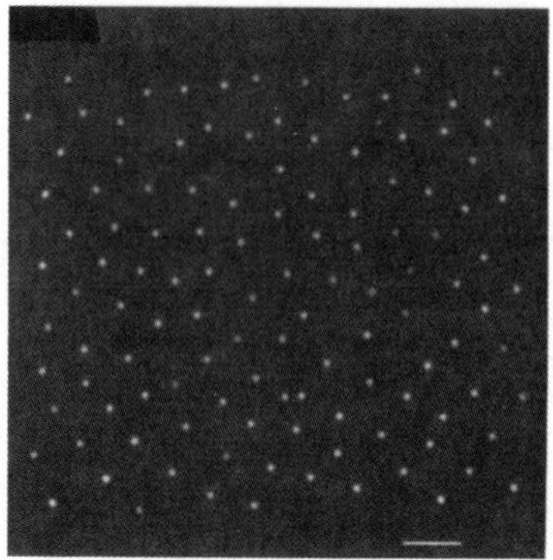

Fig. 3a. Monkey eye photoreceptor distribution.

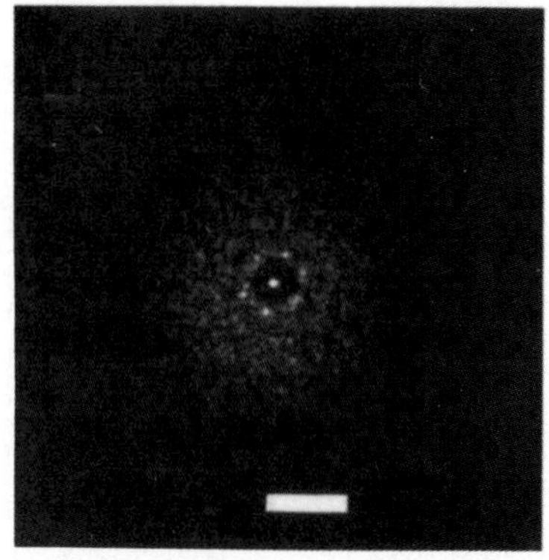

Fig. 3b. Optical transform of monkey eye.

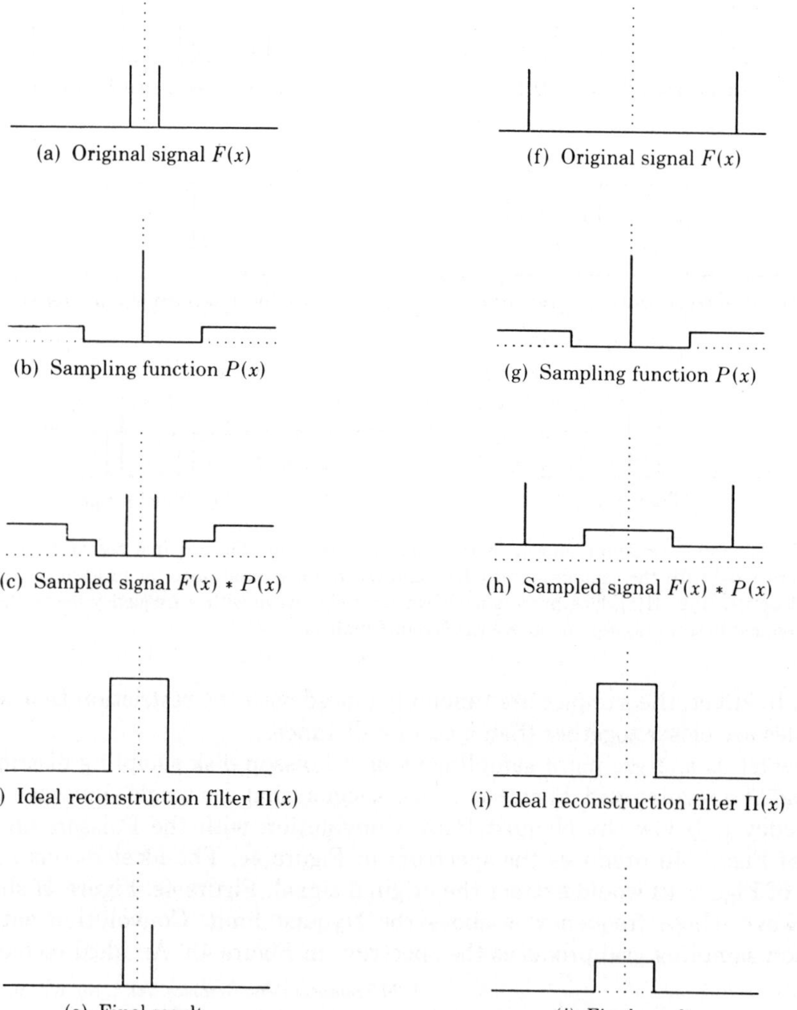

Fig. 4. Poisson disk sampling shown in the frequency domain.

tion filter would extract noise, as shown in Figure 4j. This noise replaces the aliasing of Figure 2j.

The minimum distance restriction decreases the magnitude of the noise. For example, film grain appears to have a random distribution [23], but without the minimum distance restriction of a Poisson disk distribution. With a purely random distribution, the samples tend to bunch up in some places and leave large gaps in other places. Film does not alias, but it is more prone to noise than the eye.

One possible implementation of Poisson disk sampling to image rendering is straightforward, though expensive. A lookup table is created by generating random sample locations and discarding any locations that are closer than a certain distance to any of the locations already chosen. Locations are generated until the sampling region is full. Filter values that describe how each sample affects the neighboring pixels are calculated, and these filter values must be normalized. The locations and filter values are stored in a table. This method would produce good pictures, but it would also require a large lookup table. An alternative method, jittering a regular grid, is discussed in the next section.

4. JITTERING A REGULAR GRID

4.1 Theory

Jittering, or adding noise to sample locations, is a form of stochastic sampling that can be used to approximate a Poisson disk distribution. There are many types of jitter; among these is additive random jitter, which can eliminate aliasing completely [22]. But the discussion in this paper is limited to one particular type of jitter: the jittering of a regular grid. This type of jitter produces good results and is particularly well suited to image-rendering algorithms.

The Fourier transform of a jittered grid (shown later in Figure 11b) is similar to the Fourier transform of a Poisson disk distribution (shown in Figure 4b). An analysis like that in Figures 2 and 4 shows that the results are not quite so good as those obtained with Poisson disk sampling. The images are somewhat noisier and some very small amount of aliasing can remain. We now look at this noise and aliasing quantitatively.

Jitter was analyzed in one dimension (time) by Balakrishnan [2], who calculated the effect of *time jitter*, in which the nth sample is jittered by an amount ζ_n so that it occurs at time $nT + \zeta_n$, where T is the sampling period (see Figure 5a). If the ζ_n are uncorrelated, Balakrishnan reports that jittering has the following effects:

—High frequencies are attenuated.

—The energy lost to the attenuation appears as uniform noise. The intensity of the noise equals the intensity of the attenuated part of the signal.

—The basic composition of the spectrum otherwise does not change.

Sampling by itself cannot be regarded as a filter, because sampling is not a linearly shift-invariant process. Balakrishnan showed, however, that the combination of jittered sampling plus an ideal reconstruction filter is a linearly shift-invariant process, even though the sampling by itself is not [2], so it is in this context that we can talk about frequency attenuation.

Fig. 5a. Time jitter. Regularly spaced sample times are shown as dashed lines, and the corresponding jittered times are shown as solid lines. Each sample time is jittered by an amount ζ so that the nth sample occurs at time $nT + \zeta_n$ instead of at time nT, where T is the sample period.

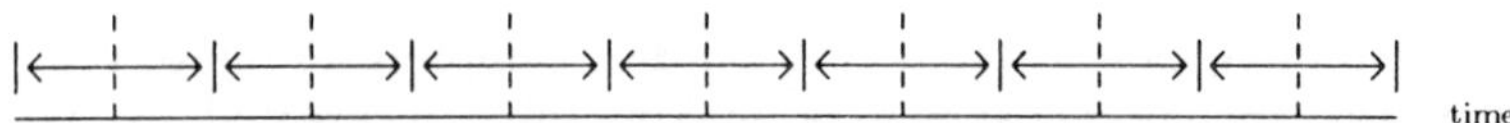

Fig. 5b. White noise jitter for $\gamma = 0.5$. Regularly spaced samples, shown as dashed lines, are jittered so that every time has an equal chance of being sampled.

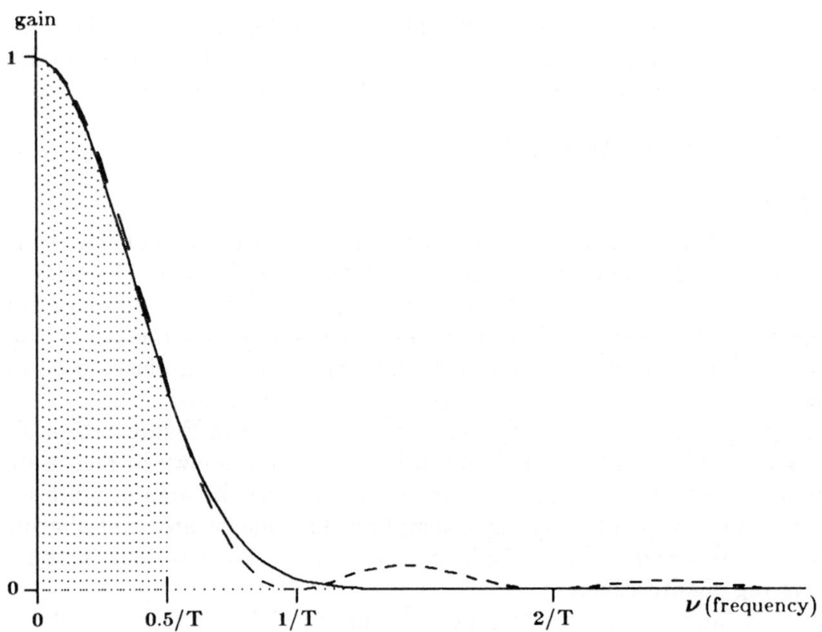

Fig. 6. Attenuation due to jitter. The broken line shows the filter for white noise jitter, the solid line for Gaussian jitter. The shaded area is inside the Nyquist limit.

Uncorrelated jitter is jitter in which any two jitter amounts ζ_n and ζ_m are uncorrelated. Balakrishnan analyzed two types of uncorrelated jitter: *Gaussian jitter* and *white noise jitter*. For Gaussian jitter, the values of ζ are chosen according to a Gaussian distribution with a variance of σ^2. The gain as a function of frequency ν is then

$$e^{-(2\pi\nu\sigma)^2}. \tag{1}$$

This function is plotted with a solid line in Figure 6 for $\sigma = T/6.5$. With white noise jitter, the values of ζ are uniformly distributed between $-\gamma T$ and γT (see

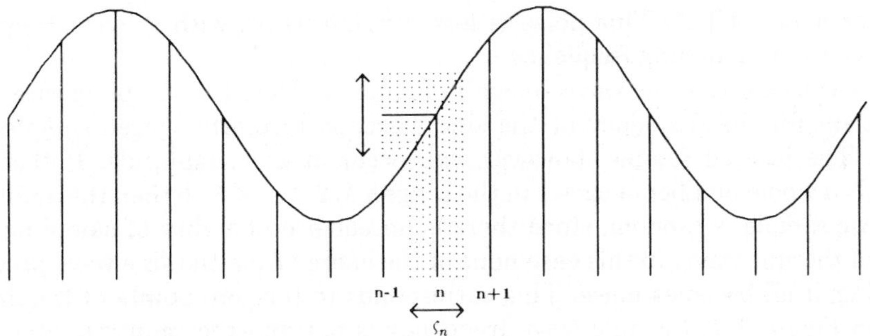

Fig. 7a. The effect of white noise jitter on a sine wave with a frequency below the Nyquist limit. Sample n occurs at a random location in the dotted region. The jitter indicated by the horizontal arrow results in a sampled value that can vary by the amount indicated by the vertical arrow.

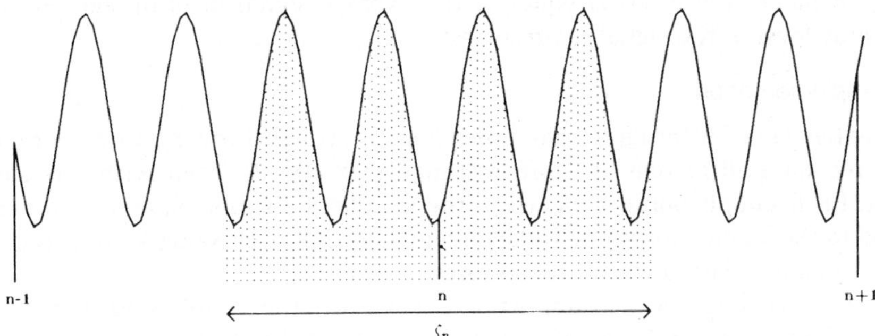

Fig. 7b. The effect of white noise jitter on a sine wave with a frequency above the Nyquist limit. The jitter indicated by the horizontal arrow results in a sampled value that is almost pure noise.

Figure 5b). The gain in this case is

$$\left[\frac{\sin(2\pi\gamma\nu T)}{2\pi\gamma\nu T}\right]^2, \tag{2}$$

as shown with a dashed line in Figure 6 for $\gamma = \frac{1}{2}$.

From this we can see that jittering a regular grid does not eliminate aliasing completely, but it does reduce it substantially. The Nyquist limit of $0.5/T$ is indicated in the figure by the shaded area. Notice that the width of the filter can be scaled by adjusting γ or σ. This gives control of the trade-off between decreased aliasing and increased noise.

For an intuitive explanation of these equations, consider the sine wave shown in Figure 7a, with samples at regularly spaced intervals λ as shown. These samples are inside the Nyquist limit and therefore sample the sine wave properly. Jittering the location of each sample n by some ζ_n in the range $-\lambda/2 < \zeta_n < \lambda/2$ is similar to adding some noise to the amplitude; note that the basic sine wave frequency is not lost. This noise is less for sine waves with a lower frequency relative to the sampling frequency.

Now consider the sine wave shown in Figure 7b. Here the sampling rate is not sufficient for the frequency of the sine wave, so regularly spaced samples can alias. The jittered sample, however, can occur at any amplitude. If there are exactly a whole number of cycles in the range $-\lambda/2 < \zeta_n < \lambda/2$, then the amplitude that we sample is random, since there is an equal probability of sampling each part of the sine wave. In this case none of the energy from the sine wave produces aliasing; it all becomes noise. This corresponds to the zero points of the dashed line in Figure 6. If the sine wave frequency is not an exact multiple of λ, then some parts of the wave will be more likely to be sampled than others. In this case there is some attenuated aliasing and some noise because there is some chance of hitting each part of the wave. This attenuation is greater for higher frequencies because with more cycles of the wave there is less preference for one part of the wave over another. Note also that the average signal level of the noise (the dc component or gray level) is equal to the average signal level of the sine wave. The gray level of the signal is preserved.

4.2 Implementation

The extension of jittering to two dimensions is straightforward. Consider a pixel as a regular grid of one or more rectangular *subpixels*, each with one sample point. Each sample point is placed in the middle of a subpixel, and then noise is added to the x and y locations independently so that each sample point occurs at some random location within its subpixel.

Once the visibility at the sample points is known, the sample values are filtered with a reconstruction filter and resampled on a regular grid of pixel locations to obtain the pixel values. How to do this reconstruction properly is an open problem. The easiest reconstruction filter to compute is a box filter. Each pixel value is obtained by simply averaging the sample values in that pixel. Weighted reconstruction filters with wider filter kernels give better variance reduction. In this case the filter values are a function of the position of each sample point relative to the surrounding pixels. The value of each pixel is the sum of the values of the nearby sample points multiplied by their respective filter values; this total is normalized by dividing by the total of the filter values.

If the random components of the sample locations are small compared with the width of the filter, the effect of the random components on the filter values can usually be ignored. The filter values can then be calculated in advance for the regularly spaced grid locations. These filter values can be prenormalized and stored in a lookup table. Changing filters is simply a matter of changing the lookup table.

5. DISTRIBUTED RAY TRACING

In the previous section, we applied stochastic sampling to the two-dimensional distribution of the sample points used for determining visibility in a z buffer or ray-casting algorithm. But the intensity of a pixel on the screen is an analytic function that may involve several nested integrals: integrals over time, over the pixel region, and over the lens area, as well as an integral of reflectance times illumination over the reflected hemisphere and an integral of transmittance times illumination over the transmitted hemisphere. These integrals can be tremendously complicated.

Image-rendering algorithms have made certain simplifying assumptions in order to avoid the evaluation of these integrals. But the evaluation of these integrals is essential for rendering a whole range of fuzzy phenomena, such as penumbrae, blurry reflections, translucency, depth of field, and motion blur. Thus image rendering has usually been limited to sharp shadows, sharp reflections, sharp refractions, pinhole cameras, and instantaneous shutters. Recent exceptions to this are the radiosity method [10] and cone tracing [1].

The rendering integrals can be evaluated with stochastic sampling. If we regard the variables of integration as additional dimensions, we can perform a Monte Carlo evaluation of the integrals by stochastically distributing the sample points (rays) in those additional dimensions. This is called probabilistic or distributed ray tracing.

—Distributing reflected rays according to the specular distribution function produces gloss (blurry reflection).
—Distributing transmitted rays produces translucency (blurry transparency).
—Distributing shadow rays through the solid angle of each light source produces penumbrae.
—Distributing ray origins over the camera lens area produces depth of field.
—Distributing rays in time produces motion blur.

Distributed ray tracing is discussed in detail in a previous paper [5], and others have extended the results found there [7, 12, 14] (also personal communications from D. Mitchell and from T. Whitted). This section summarizes the distributed ray-tracing algorithm from the viewpoint of stochastic sampling.

5.1 Nonspatial Jittering

One way to distribute the rays in the additional dimensions is with uncorrelated random values. For example, one could pick a random time for each ray or a random point on a light source for each shadow ray. This approach produces pictures that are exceedingly noisy, owing to the bunching up of samples (as illustrated later in Figure 11d). We can reduce the noise level by using a Poisson disk distribution, ensuring that the samples do not bunch up or leave large gaps that are unsampled. As before, we use jittering to approximate a Poisson disk distribution.

To jitter in a nonspatial dimension, we use randomly created prototype patterns in screen space to associate the sample points with a range of that dimension to sample, then jitter to pick the exact location within each range. In the case of sampling in time to produce motion blur, we divide the frame time into slices and randomly assign a slice of time to each sample point. The exact time within each slice is then determined by jittering.

For example, to assign times in a pixel with a 4-by-4 grid of sample points, one could use a random distribution of the numbers 1–16, such as the one shown in

7	11	3	14
4	15	13	9
16	1	8	12
6	10	5	2

Fig. 8. Example of a prototype time pattern.

Figure 8. The sample in the xth column and the yth row would have a prototype time

$$t_{xy} = \frac{P_{xy} - 0.5}{16},$$

where P_{xy} is the value shown in the xth column and the yth row of the prototype pattern in Figure 8. A random jitter of $\pm\frac{1}{32}$ is then added to this prototype time to obtain the actual time for a sample. For example, the sample in the upper left subpixel would have a time $\frac{6}{16} \leq t \leq \frac{7}{16}$.

Note that correlation between the spatial locations and the locations in other dimensions can cause aliasing. For example, if the samples on the left side of the pixel are consistently at an earlier time than those on the right side of the pixel, an object moving from right to left might be missed by every sample, whereas an object moving from left to right might be hit by every sample.

5.2 Weighted Distributions

Sometimes we need to weight the samples. For example, we may want to weight the reflected samples according to the specular reflection function, or we may want to use a weighted temporal filter. One approach would be to distribute the samples evenly and then later weight each ray according to the filter. A better approach is *importance sampling* [11], in which the sample points are distributed so that the chance of a location being sampled is proportional to the value of the filter at that location. This avoids the multiplications necessary for the weighting and also puts the samples where they will do the most good.

In order to use jitter to do importance sampling, we divide the filter into regions of equal area, as shown in Figure 9. Each region is sampled by one sample point, with the samples spaced further apart for smaller filter values and closer together for larger filter values. Each sample point is positioned at the center of its region and then jittered to a random location in the region. Note that the size of the jitter varies from sample to sample. If the filter shape is known ahead of time, a list of the centers and jitter magnitudes for each region can be precomputed and stored in a lookup table.

For example, for the reflection ray, we create a lookup table based on the specular reflection function. Given the angle between the surface normal and the incident ray, this lookup table gives a range of reflection angles plus a jitter magnitude for determining an exact reflection angle within that range. For any given reflection ray, the index into this table is determined using its ancestral

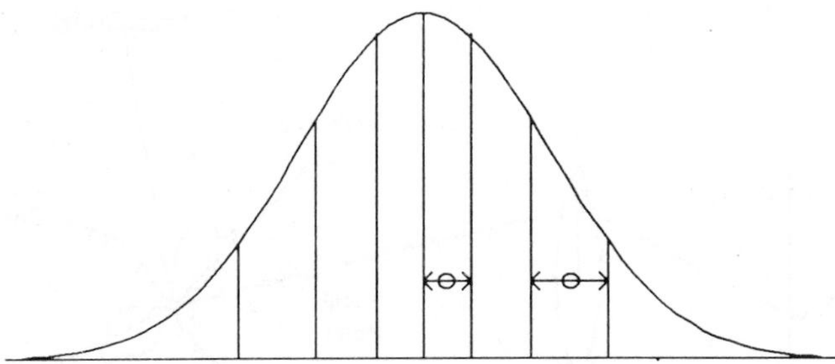

Fig. 9. Importance sampling. The samples are distributed so that they sample regions of equal area under the weighting function. The prototype sample location and jitter range is shown for two of the sampling regions.

primary ray in screen space to associate it with a randomly generated prototype pattern of table indices.

5.3 Summary of Distributed Ray Tracing

The distributed ray-tracing algorithm is illustrated in Figure 10. For each primary ray:

—Determine the spatial location of the ray by jittering.

—Determine the time for the ray from jittered prototype patterns.

—Move the camera and the objects to their location at that time.

—Determine the focal point by constructing a ray from the eye point (center of the lens) through the screen location of the ray. The focal point is located on this ray so that its distance from the eye point is equal to the focal distance.

—Determine the lens location for the ray by jittering a location selected from a prototype pattern of lens locations.

—The primary ray starts at the lens location and goes through the focal point. Determine the visible point for this ray using standard ray-casting or ray-tracing techniques.

—Trace a reflection ray. The direction of the reflection ray is determined by jittering a set of directions that are distributed according to the specular reflection function. This is done with a lookup table; the lookup table index is based on a screen space prototype pattern that assigns indices to primary rays and their descendants. The reflection direction is obtained from the lookup table and then jittered. The range of the jitter is also stored in the table.

—Trace a transparency ray if the visible object is transparent. The direction of the transparency ray is determined by jittering a set of directions that are distributed according to the specular transmission function.

—Trace the shadow rays. For each light source, determine the location on the light for the shadow ray, and trace a ray from the visible point to that location on the light. The chance of tracing the ray to a location on the light should be proportional to the intensity and projected area of that location as seen from the visible point on the surface.

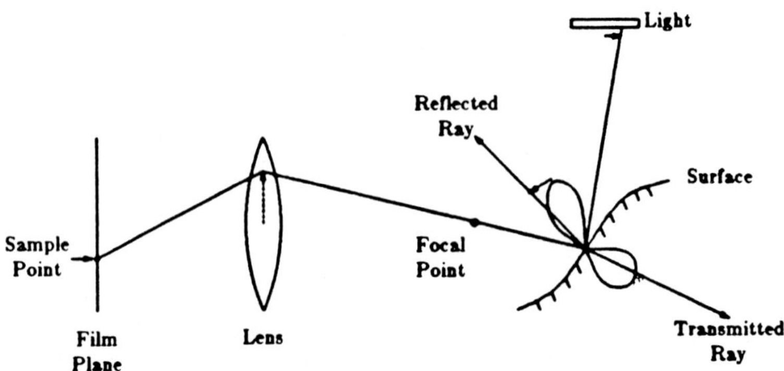

Fig. 10. Distributed ray tracing.

6. EXAMPLES

The jitter used in these examples is white noise jitter with $\gamma = 0.5$. An example of this distribution is shown in Figure 11a, and the Fourier transform of Figure 11a is shown in Figure 11b. Notice how Figure 11b resembles the Fourier transform of a Poisson disk distribution (shown in Figure 4b). By contrast, a pure Poisson distribution of samples with no minimum distance restriction is shown in Figure 11d, and the Fourier transform of Figure 11d is shown in Figure 11e. The C code in Figure 11c was used to generate Figure 11a, and the C code in Figure 11f was used to generate Figure 11d.

In Figures 12 and 13, a box filter was used for a reconstruction filter to accentuate the noise problems. In all of the other examples, the following Gaussian filter was used:

$$e^{-d^2} - e^{-w^2},$$

where d is the distance from the center of the sampling region to the center of the pixel, and $w = 1.5$ is the filter width distance, beyond which the filter was set to zero. The effect of jitter on the filter values was ignored.

Consider the comb of triangular slivers illustrated in Figure 12a. Each triangle is 1.01 pixels wide at the base and 50 pixels high. The triangles are placed in a horizontal row 1.01 pixels apart. If the comb is sampled with a regular grid, aliasing can result as depicted in Figure 12b. A comb containing 200 such triangular slivers is rendered in Figures 12c–f.

In Figure 12c the comb is rendered with a single sample at the center of each pixel. Figure 12d also has one sample per pixel, but the sample location is jittered by $\zeta = \pm\frac{1}{2}$ pixel in x and y. Figure 12c is grossly aliased: there are just a few large triangles spaced 100 pixels apart. This aliasing is replaced by noise in Figure 12d. Because there is only one sample per pixel, each pixel can only be white or black, but in any given region, the percentage of white pixels equals the percentage of that region that is covered by the triangles. Note that the white pixels are denser at the bottom, where the triangles are wider.

In Figure 12e the same comb is rendered with a regular 4-by-4 grid of samples. In Figure 12f the regular 4-by-4 grid is jittered by $\zeta = \pm\frac{1}{8}$ pixel in x and y. Again the regularly spaced samples alias; this time there are a few large overlapping triangles spaced $\frac{100}{4} = 25$ pixels apart. This aliasing is replaced by noise in the

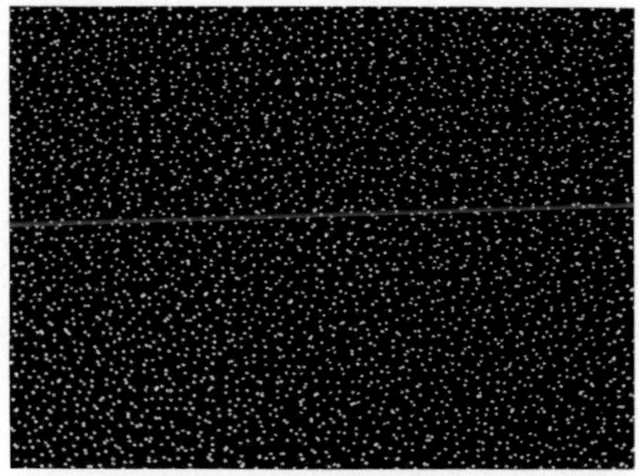

Fig. 11a. Distribution pattern of jittered samples.

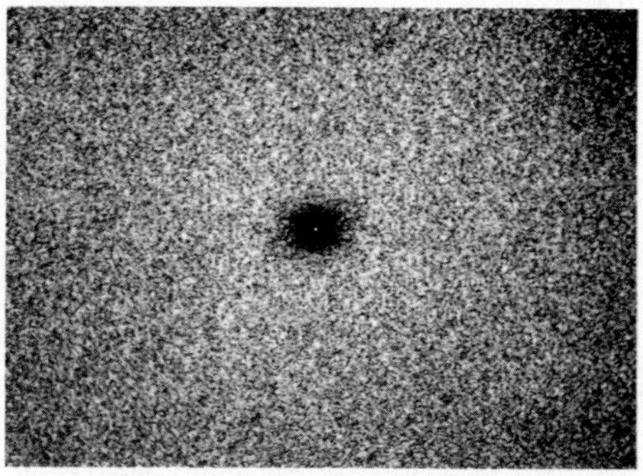

Fig. 11b. Fourier transform of the pattern in Figure 11a.

```
/* Draw a jittered sample pattern in a 512x512 frame buffer. There is one  */
 * sample in each sample region of 8x8 pixels, for a total of 4096 samples. */
DrawJitterPattern() {
      double Random();                    /* returns a random number in the range 0-1 */
      int x,y;                            /* (x,y) is the corner of the sample region */
      int jx,jy;                          /* (jx,jy) is the jitter */
      for (y=0; y<512; y+=8) {
            for (x=0; x<512; x+=8) {
                  jx = 8*Random();
                  jy = 8*Random();
                  SetPixelToWhite(x+jx,y+jy);
            }
      }
}
```

Fig. 11c. C program that generated the pattern in Fig. 11a.

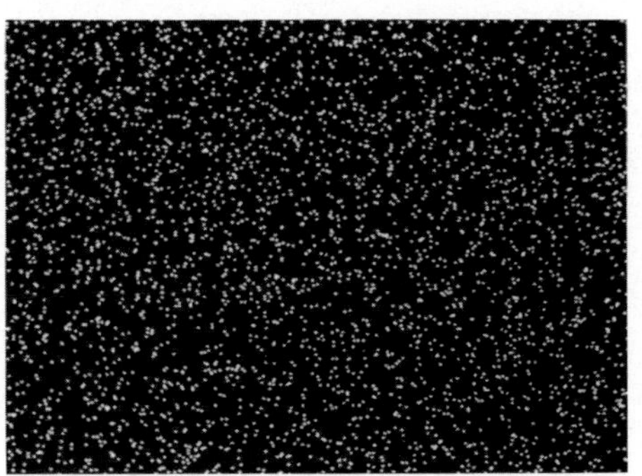

Fig. 11d. Distribution pattern of randomly placed samples.

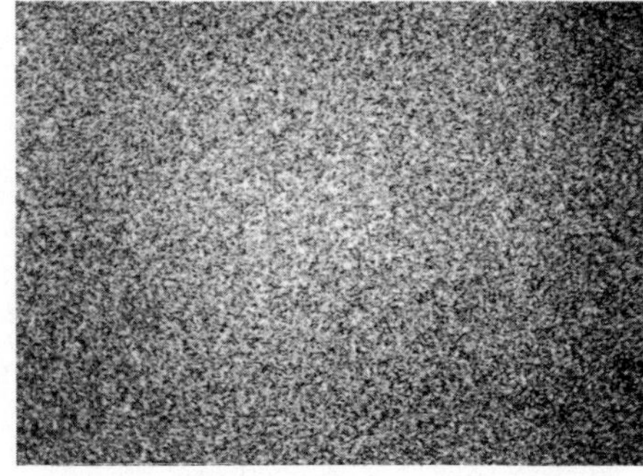

Fig. 11e. Fourier transform of the pattern in Fig. 11d.

```
/* Draw a random sample pattern with 4096 samples. */
DrawPoissonPattern() {
      double Random();                    /* returns a random number in the range 0-1 */
      int n, sx,sy;                       /* (sx,sy) is the sample location */
      for (n=0; n<4096; n++) {
            sx = 512*Random();
            sy = 512*Random();
            SetPixelToWhite(sx,sy);
      }
}
```

Fig. 11f. C program that generated the pattern in Fig. 11d.

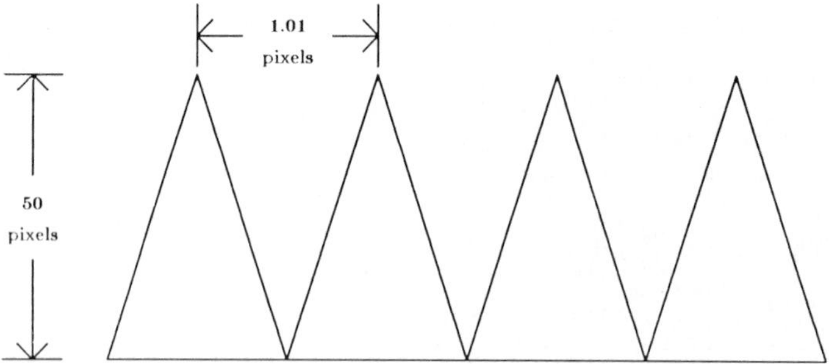

Fig. 12a. Schematic diagram of the comb of triangles example. The triangles are 50 pixels high and 1.01 pixels apart.

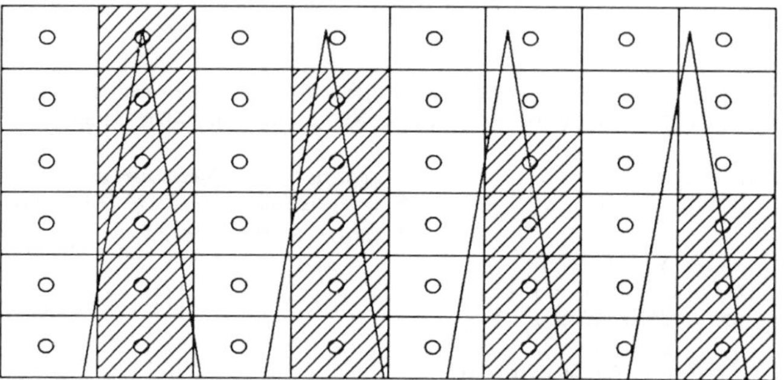

Fig. 12b. The comb of triangles aliases when rendered with a regular grid of sample points in the manner shown here. Samples are shown as circles, and pixels are shown as rectangles. Pixels with samples inside a triangle are shaded.

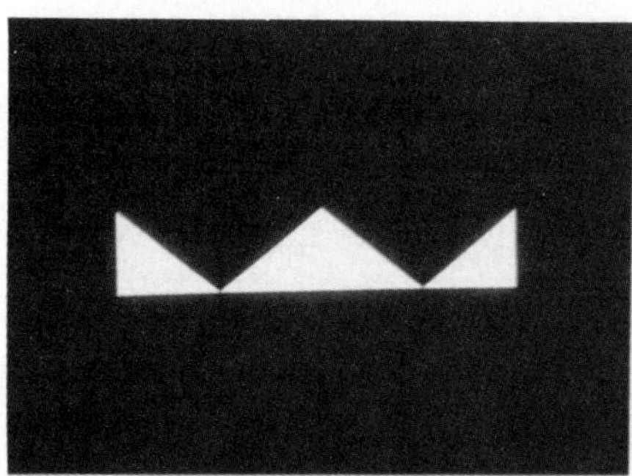

Fig. 12c. Comb rendered with a regular grid, one sample per pixel.

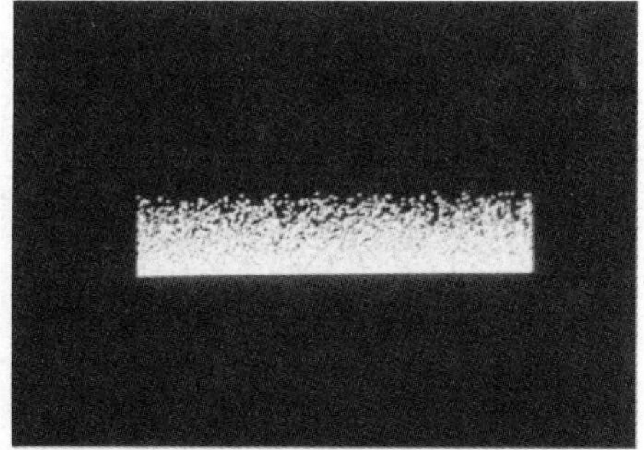

Fig. 12d. Comb rendered with a jittered grid, one sample per pixel.

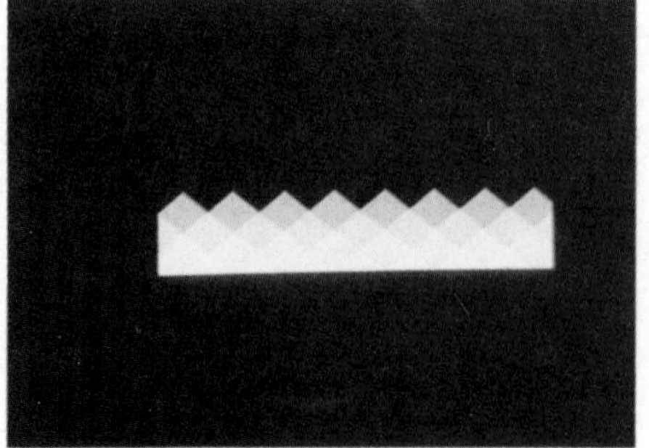

Fig. 12e. Comb rendered with a regular grid, 16 samples per pixel.

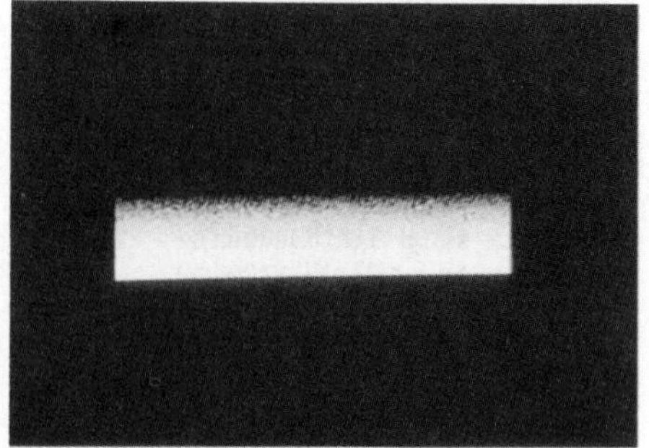

Fig. 12f. Comb rendered with a jittered grid, 16 samples per pixel.

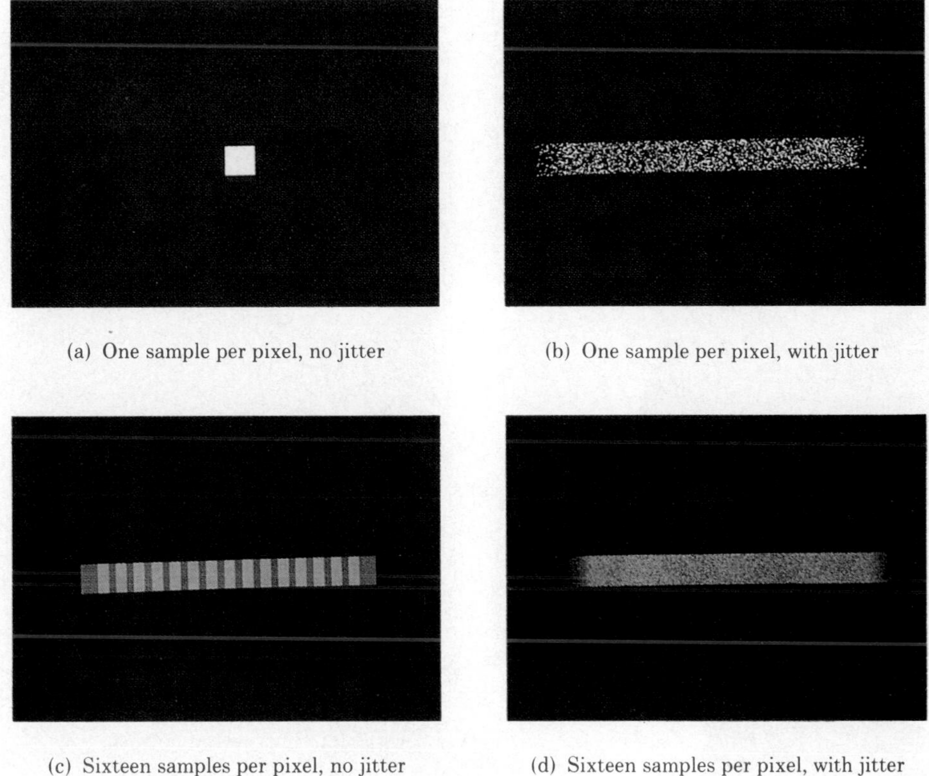

(a) One sample per pixel, no jitter

(b) One sample per pixel, with jitter

(c) Sixteen samples per pixel, no jitter

(d) Sixteen samples per pixel, with jitter

Fig. 13. Fast-moving polygon.

jittered version, Figure 12f. Notice, though, that the noise is greatly reduced compared with Figure 12d.

Figure 13 shows a small white square moving across the screen. Figure 13a was rendered with no jitter and one sample per pixel, so the image is still. Figure 13b was rendered with jitter and one sample per pixel; the image is now blurred but is extremely noisy because, with only one sample, each pixel can be only one of two colors—the color of the square or the color of the background. Notice, though, that in any given region the number of pixels that are white is proportional to the amount of time the square covered that region; thus the percentage of white pixels is constant in the middle and ramps off at the ends. Figure 13c was rendered with no jitter and 16 samples per pixel, and Figure 13d with jitter and 16 samples per pixel. Notice the reduction in the noise level with the additional samples.

Figure 14a is the ray-traced picture *1984*, with a closeup of the 4-ball shown in Figure 14b. The 4-ball remains stationary for most of the time the shutter is open and moves quickly to the upper right just before the shutter closes. The blur is quite extreme, and yet the image looks noisy instead of aliased. This picture was made with 16 samples per pixel.

Figures 15a and 15b are two frames from the short film *The Adventures of André & Wally B.* [18]. These extreme examples of motion blur were rendered

Fig. 14a. *1984*, by Thomas Porter.

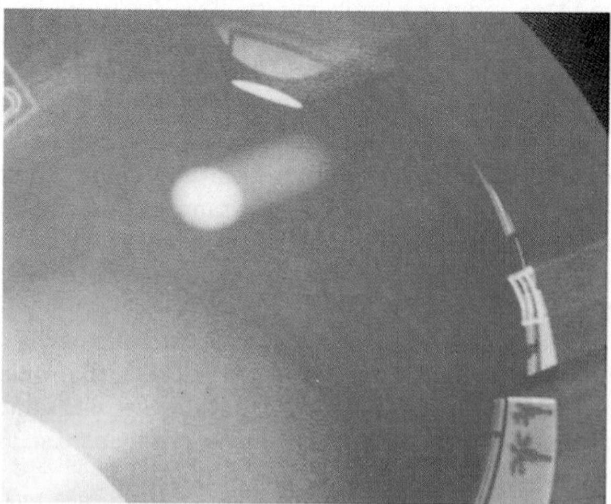

Fig. 14b. Close-up of *1984*.

Fig. 15a. Example of motion blur from *The Adventures of André & Wally B.*

Fig. 15b. Example of motion blur from *The Adventures of André & Wally B.*

with a scan-line algorithm that uses point sampling and a z buffer to determine visibility. In these frames a very simple adaptive method automatically used 16 samples per pixel for most pixels and 64 samples per pixel for pixels that contain objects that move more than 8 pixels in x or y within the frame time.

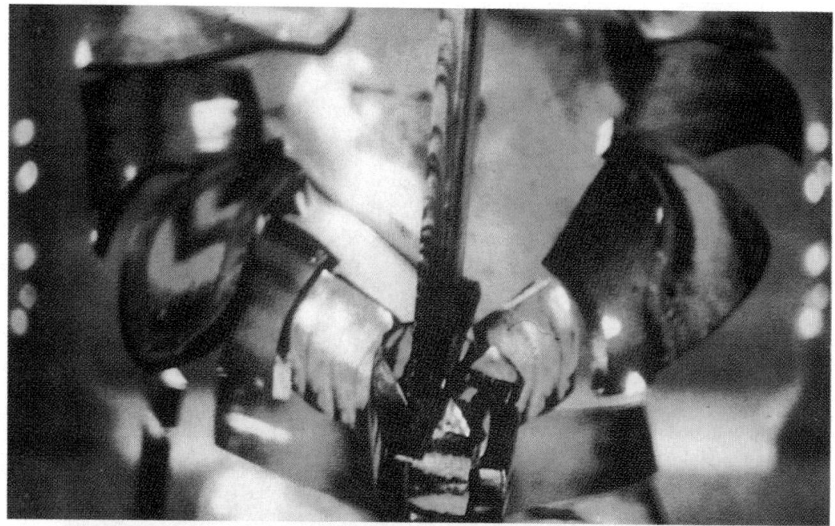

Fig. 16. Example of depth of field from *Young Sherlock Holmes* (Copyright 1985, Paramount Pictures Corp.).

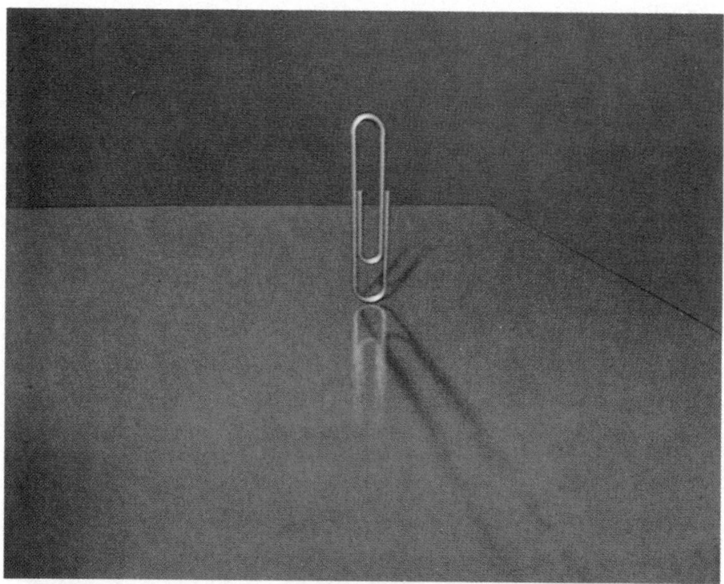

Fig. 17. Example of penumbrae and blurry reflection.

This cuts down considerably on the noise level and helps avoid needless computation. Others have since found ways to add more samples adaptively based on an estimate of the variance of the image in each pixel [12, 14].

Figure 16 shows a frame of a computer-synthesized stained-glass man from *Young Sherlock Holmes* [16]. The camera is focused on the sword, with the body out of focus. This was also rendered with a scan-line algorithm, but in this case, no adaptive method was used to change the number of samples per pixel; instead, there were always 16 samples per pixel. The sequence is also motion blurred.

The paper clip in Figure 17 shows penumbrae and blurry reflection, rendered with 16 samples per pixel. Other examples of distributed ray tracing have appeared in a previous paper [5]. In all cases, areas of extreme blur become noisy instead of aliasing.

7. DISCUSSION AND CONCLUSIONS

With correctly chosen nonuniform sample locations, high frequencies appear as noise instead of aliasing. The magnitude of this noise is determined by the sampling frequency. We have found that using 16 samples per pixel produces an acceptable noise level in most situations, with more needed only for high-frequency situations, such as frames that are extremely motion blurred or out of focus. Stochastic sampling should also work well when integrated with adaptive sampling. This has been the subject of some recent research [12, 14].

The human eye uses a Poisson disk distribution of photoreceptors. A simple and effective approximation to a Poisson disk distribution can be obtained by jittering a regular grid. When this technique is extended to distributed ray tracing, the locations in the nonspatial dimensions can be chosen by jittering randomly generated prototype patterns. Weighted functions can be evaluated using importance sampling.

Stochastic sampling involves some additional computation. Because the samples are not regularly spaced, forward differencing cannot be used to exploit pixel-to-pixel coherence. Compared with standard ray tracing, distributed ray tracing requires additional calculations to move objects to their correct location for each ray. Moving and out-of-focus objects also require a more sophisticated bounding calculation, and these objects must often be intersected with a larger number of rays.

Aliasing has been a major problem for ray-tracing and ray-casting algorithms, and this problem is solved by stochastic sampling. The shading calculations, which have traditionally been point sampled, are automatically antialiased with stochastic sampling, eliminating problems such as highlight aliasing. Another potential application is texture map sampling. Extended to distributed ray tracing, stochastic sampling also provides a solution to motion blur, depth of field, penumbrae, blurry reflections, and translucency.

ACKNOWLEDGMENTS

I would especially like to thank Tom Porter, who made the *1984* picture, suggested the extension of the two-dimensional technique to motion blur, and helped test many of the ideas. Alvy Ray Smith found the article on the distribution of cells in the eye. Andy Moorer and Jim Kajiya helped with the theory, and a number of discussions with Loren Carpenter were invaluable. The idea of dithering sample locations originally came from Rodney Stock, who provided inspiration and motivation for this work. Jack Yellott provided the pictures in Figure 3. Thanks also to the many people at Lucasfilm who made *The Adventures of André & Wally B.* and the stained-glass man sequence from *Young Sherlock Holmes*.

REFERENCES

1. AMANATIDES, J. Ray tracing with cones. *Comput. Graph. 18*, 3 (July 1984), 129–145.
2. BALAKRISHNAN, A. V. On the problem of time jitter in sampling. *IRE Trans. Inf. Theory* (Apr. 1962), 226–236.
3. BLINN, J. F. Computer display of curved surfaces. Ph.D. dissertation, Computer Science Dept., Univ. of Utah, Salt Lake City, 1978.
4. BRACEWELL, R. N. *The Fourier Transform and Its Applications.* McGraw-Hill, New York, 1978.
5. COOK, R. L., PORTER, T., AND CARPENTER, L. Distributed ray tracing. *Comput. Graph. 18*, 3 (July 1984), 137–145.
6. CROW, F. The use of greyscale for improved raster display of vectors and characters. *Comput. Graph. 12*, 3 (Aug. 1978), 1–5.
7. DIPPE, M. A. Z., AND WOLD, E. H. Antialiasing through stochastic sampling. *Comput. Graph. 19*, 3 (July 1985), 69–78.
8. FEIBUSH, E., LEVOY, M., AND COOK, R. L. Synthetic texturing using digital filtering. *Comput. Graph. 14*, 3 (July 1980), 294–301.
9. GARDNER, G. Y. Simulation of natural scenes using textured quadric surfaces. *Comput. Graph. 18*, 3 (July 1984), 11–20.
10. GORAL, C. M., TORRANCE, K. E., GREENBERG, D. P., AND BATTAILE, B. Modeling the interaction of light between diffuse surfaces. *Comput. Graph. 18*, 3 (July 1984), 213–222.
11. HALTON, J. H. A retrospective and prospective survey of the Monte Carlo method. *SIAM Rev. 12*, 1 (Jan. 1970), 1–63.
12. KAJIYA, J. T. The rendering equation. *Comput. Graph. 20*, 4 (Aug. 1986), 143–150.
13. KAY, D. S., AND GREENBERG, D. P. Transparency for computer synthesized images. *Comput. Graph. 13*, 2 (Aug. 1979), 158–164.
14. LEE, M. E., REDNER, R. A., AND USELTON, S. P. Statistically optimized sampling for distributed ray tracing. *Comput. Graph. 19*, 3 (July 1985), 61–67.
15. NORTON, A., ROCKWOOD, A. P., AND SKOLMOSKI, P. T. Clamping: A method of antialiasing textured surfaces by bandwidth limiting in object space. *Comput. Graph. 16*, 3 (July 1982), 1–8.
16. PARAMOUNT PICTURES CORP. *Young Sherlock Holmes.* Stained glass man sequence by D. Carson, E. Christiansen, D. Conway, R. Cook, D. DiFrancesco, J. Ellis, L. Ellis, C. Good, J. Lasseter, S. Leffler, D. Muren, T. Noggle, E. Ostby, W. Reeves, D. Salesin, and K. Smith. Pixar and Lucasfilm Ltd., 1985.
17. PEARSON, D. E. *Transmission and Display of Pictorial Information.* Pentech Press, London, 1975.
18. PIXAR. *The Adventures of André & Wally B.* By L. Carpenter, E. Catmull, R. Cook, T. Duff, C. Good, J. Lasseter, S. Leffler, E. Ostby, T. Porter, W. Reeves, D. Salesin, and A. Smith. July 1984.
19. POTMESIL, M., AND CHAKRAVARTY, I. Modeling motion blur in computer-generated images. *Comput. Graph. 17*, 3 (July 1983), 389–399.
20. PRATT, W. K. *Digital Image Processing.* Wiley, New York, 1978.
21. ROTH, S. D. Ray casting for modeling solids. *Comput. Graph. Image Process. 18* (1982), 109–144.
22. SHAPIRO, H. S., AND SILVERMAN, R. A. Alias-free sampling of random noise. *SIAM J. 8*, 2 (June 1960), 225–248.
23. SOCIETY OF PHOTOGRAPHIC SCIENTISTS AND ENGINEERS. *SPSE Handbook of Photographic Science and Engineering.* Wiley, New York, 1973.
24. WHITTED, T. An improved illumination model for shaded display. *Commun. ACM 23*, 6 (June 1980), 343–349.
25. WILLIAMS, D. R., AND COLLIER, R. Consequences of spatial sampling by a human photoreceptor mosaic. *Science 221* (July 22, 1983), 385–387.
26. WILLIAMS, L. Pyramidal parametrics. *Comput. Graph. 17*, 3 (July 1983), 1–11.
27. YELLOTT, J. I., JR. Spectral consequences of photoreceptor sampling in the rhesus retina. *Science 221* (July 22, 1983), 382–385.

Received March 1985; accepted June 1986

Chapter 9: Texturing Algorithms

Introduction

In computer graphics, the generated surface detail of a displayed object is called texture. Two aspects of texture that are usually considered are the addition of a prespecified pattern to a smooth surface and the addition of the appearance of roughness to the surface. Both of these aspects can be considered mapping functions and have been applied to a number of surface attributes including surface intensity, color, reflection properties, normal, transparency, illumination, and displacement (see [Heck86b], which is included in this chapter).

Since the basis of adding texture patterns to smooth surfaces is mapping, the texture problem reduces to the specification of a transformation from one coordinate system to another. A texture mapping is defined as a transformation from texture space to object space (see Figure 9.1). Depending on the visibility algorithm used, rendering objects with a texture can be accomplished in two ways:

- utilizing the direct mapping from the texture space to the object space, along with the image transformation that takes object space into image space
- utilizing the inverse mapping from image space to texture space.

These two methods have been characterized by Cook et al. [Cook87] as methods that generate the texture in a coherent-access fashion (direct map), or methods that generate the texture in a random-access fashion (inverse map). Object-space algorithms can usually use the direct mapping. Image-space algorithms usually use the inverse mapping (if it exists), or an approximation.

The first mention of texturing in the literature was by Catmull [Catm74]. In this algorithm, the surface patches are subdivided until they are pixel sized. A texture pattern may be mapped onto a surface by performing a corresponding subdivision to the texture pattern in texture space. Each subpixel sized patch may then be flat shaded with a weighted average of the intensities on the corresponding texture subpatch, which is also the method given in Cook et al. [Cook87] where the entities in the scene are subdivided into flat shaded micropolygons, which can be simply textured by performing a corresponding subdivision in texture space. Via the subdivision, the direct mapping can be utilized.

Unfortunately, for image-space algorithms, the inverse image of a pixel in image space must be calculated—and the inverse image of a square pixel in image space need not be square in texture space (see Figure 9.1). Much of the research in texturing is related to this problem, and the potential aliasing effects that can be caused by sampling the texture.

It is possible to approximately calculate the area covered by a pixel in image space and then transform this area to texture space. The intensity of the pixel in image space is determined by averaging the intensity of the pixels covered by the corresponding area in texture space. If the texture pattern is discretized, then the intensity of the subpatch is taken as a weighted average of the intensities for the texture pixels that cover the inverse image of the subpatch. Blinn and Newell [Blin76] used this method with a simple pyramidal filter. Feibush et al. [Feib80] (included in Chapter 8: Antialiasing) developed an approximate method based upon lookup tables to better calculate this average for arbitrary polygonal areas.

Even with considerable optimization, these methods can take a substantial amount of computer time, since the inverse transformation of every pixel must be calculated. To speed up the process, the texture can be prefiltered so that during rendering only a few samples will be accessed for each screen pixel. Williams [Will83] performed the first such prefiltering, by utilizing a pyramidal prefiltering scheme. The pyramid was generated by box filtering successive levels of the pyramid. Accesses to the pyramid can be shown to be at a constant cost. Crow [Crow84] defines a "summed-area table," which is preintegrated in the u and v directions and allows filtering of rectangular areas. Glassner [Glas86] has shown how to successively refine the rectangles into quadrilaterals, giving better general filtering of textures. Perlin [Perl85a] has developed a generalized method of prefiltering for the summed-area-table technique. An excellent review of these methods is given in Heckbert [Heck86b] (which is included in this chapter).

Catmull and Smith [Catm80] (included in this chapter) have taken a novel approach to this problem, by transforming the texture onto the screenspace image of the surface on which it is to be mapped. The transformations are algorithmically separated into two streams, each of which corresponds to a one-dimensional transformation of the pattern along horizontal- or vertical-scan lines, and thus can be performed quickly. The mapping of the texture onto the surface in image space is then trivial.

To add the appearance of roughness to a surface, Blinn [Blin78] (included in this chapter) developed a method similar to texturing that can be used to perturb the normal vector of a surface. This perturbation will affect the illumination calculation, by creating the appearance of a rough-textured or bumpy surface. Blinn used patterns defined on a simple grid, often represented by a two-dimensional look-

EH0281-6/88/0000/0305$01.00

up table and indexed by the parameters of the surface patch, to generate his mapping.

Multi-dimensional texturing has been developed concurrently by Perlin [Perl85b] and Peachey [Peac85]. In this scheme, a texture is defined in n-dimensional space. When, in the image rendering algorithm, a surface point is determined to be visible, a multi-dimensional function

$$I = I(x, y, z, u, v, \ldots) \quad (1)$$

is evaluated to determine the texture values. If the function depends only upon the surface point, then the object will appear to be "carved" from the texture. Other effects can be obtained with more complex functions.

Typically these functions are defined at a discrete set of points, and smooth spline interpolations are used to calculate function values for arguments not lying on this set. Perlin has also described a small texturing language, by detailing several of the functions of the language in his paper.

Whereas the majority of the texturing algorithms have been applied to surface color, intensity, and normal perturbation, the basic methods have also been applied to other scene characteristics. For example, Cook [Cook84b] and Cook et al. [Cook87] have used the technique to define surface displacement (before inserting their micropolygons into the rendering portion of the algorithm, the vertices of the polygon are displaced by values taken from displacement maps); Max [Max86a] has utilized Blinn's bump mapping technique to calculate accurate shadows on surfaces that have normal vector perturbation; Reeves and Blau [Reev85] has used illumination maps to create shadows; Wood textures have been created by Cook [Cook84b]; and Gardner [Gard84] has utilized transparency textures in his generation of clouds.

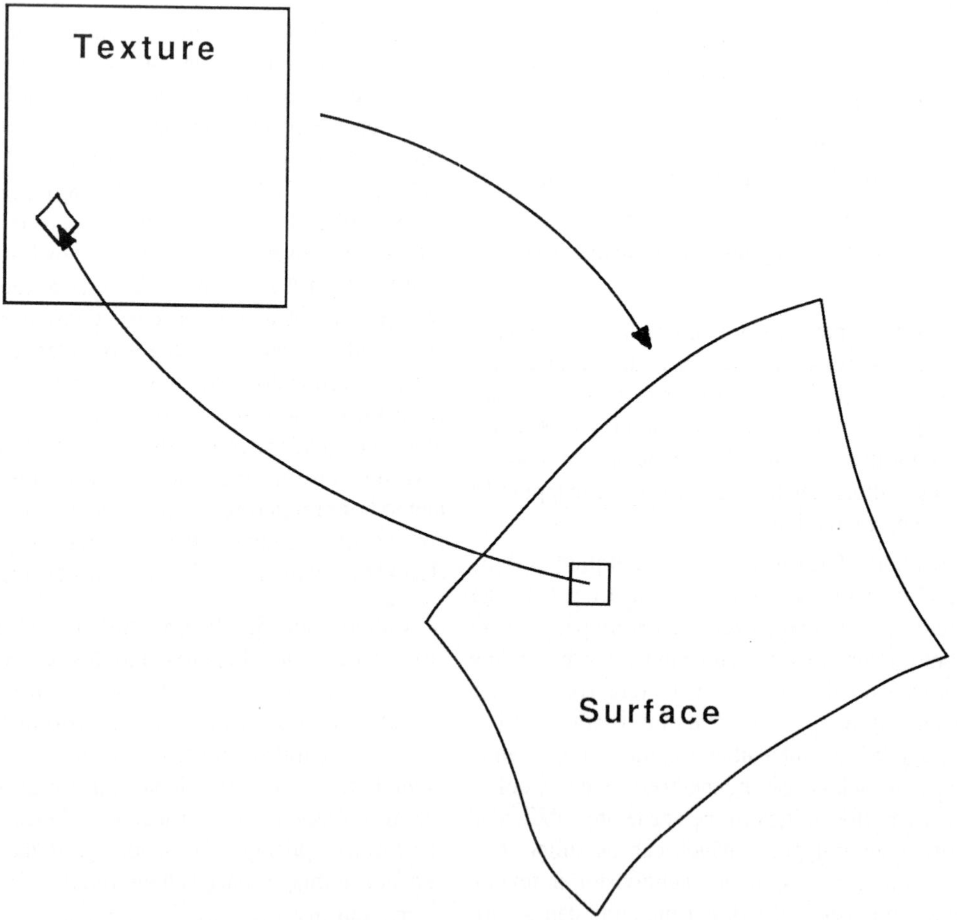

Figure 9.1: Texture Mapping

SIMULATION OF WRINKLED SURFACES

James F. Blinn
Caltech/JPL

Abstract

Computer generated shaded images have reached an impressive degree of realism with the current state of the art. They are not so realistic, however, that they would fool many people into believing they are real. One problem is that the surfaces tend to look artificial due to their extreme smoothness. What is needed is a means of sim{ulating the surface irregularities that are on real surfaces. In 1973 Ed Catmull introduced the idea of using the parameter values of parametrically defined surfaces to index into a texture definition function which scales the intensity of the reflected light. By tying the texture pattern to the parameter values, the texture is guaranteed to rotate and move with the object. This is good for showing patterns painted on the surface, but attempts to simulate rough surfaces in this way are unconvincing. This paper presents a method of using a texturing function to perform a small perturbation on the direction of the surface normal before using it in the intensity calculations. This process yields images with realistic looking surface wrinkles without the need to model each wrinkle as a separate surface element. Several samples of images made with this technique are included.

1. INTRODUCTION

Recent work in computer graphics has been devoted to the development of algorithms for making pictures of objects modelled by other than the conventional polygonal facet technique. In particular, several algorithms [4,5,7] have been devised for making images of parametric surface patches. Such surfaces are defined by the values of three bivariate functions:

$$X = X(u,v)$$
$$Y = Y(u,v)$$
$$Z = Z(u,v)$$

as the parameters vary between 0 and 1. Such algorithms basically consist of techniques for inverting the X and Y functions. That is, given the X and Y of a picture element, the corresponding u and v parameter values are found. This parameter pair is then used to find the Z coordinate of the surface to perform depth comparisons with other objects. The intensity of the resultant picture element is then found by a simulation of the light reflecting off the surface. Functions for performing this computation are described in [3].

The prime component in the calculation of the intensity of a picture element is the direction of the surface normal at that picture element. To calculate the surface normal we first examine the derivatives of the surface definition functions. If the coordinates of a point on the patch is represented by the vector P:

$$\vec{P} = (X,Y,Z)$$

The partial derivatives of these functions form two new vectors which we will call Pu and Pv.

$$\vec{Pu} = (Xu,Yu,Zu)$$

$$\vec{Pv} = (Xv,Yv,Zv)$$

These two vectors define a plane tangent to the surface at that point. Their cross product is thus a vector normal to the surface.

$$\vec{N} = \vec{Pu} \times \vec{Pv}$$

These vectors are illustrated in figure 1. Before using the normal in intensity calculations it must first be scaled to a length of 1.0 by dividing by its length.

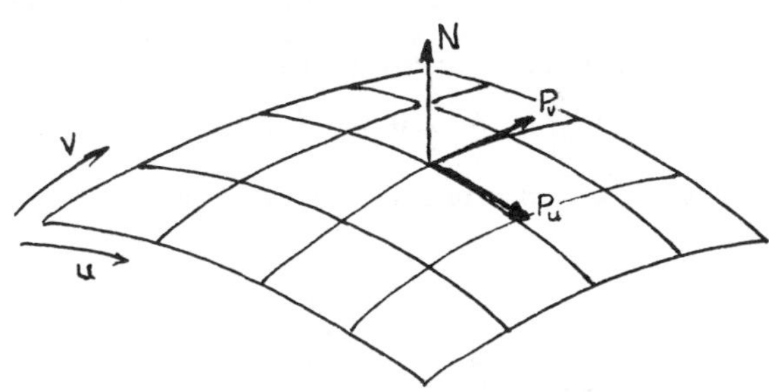

Figure 1 - Definition of Normal Vector

Images of smooth surfaces made directly from the patch description do not have the usual artifacts associated with polygonal facets, they do indeed look smooth. In fact they sometimes look too smooth. To make them look less artificial it is necessary to simulate some of the surface irregularities of real surfaces. Catmull [5] made some progress in this direction with process called texture mapping. Effectively the color of the surface was defined as a fourth bivariate function, C(u,v), and was used to scale the intensity of the generated picture at each point. This technique was good a generating pictures of objects with patterns painted on them. In order to simulate bumpy or wrinkly surfaces one might use, as the defining texture pattern, a digitized photograph of a bumpy or wrinkly

"Simulation of Wrinkled Surfaces" by J.F. Blinn from *Proceedings of SIGGRAPH '78*, 1978, pages 286-292.

surface. Attempts to do this were not very sucessful. The images usually looked like smooth surfaces with photographs of wrinkles glued on. The main reason for this is that the light source direction when making the texture photograph was rarely the same as that used when synthesizing the image. In fact, if the surface (and thus the mapped texture pattern) is curved, the angle of the light source vector with the surface is not even the same at different locations on the patch.

2. NORMAL VECTOR PERTURBATION

To best generate images of macroscopic surface wrinkles and irregularities we must actually model them as such. Modelling each surface wrinkle as a separate patch would probably be prohibitively expensive. We are saved from this fate by the realization that the effect of wrinkles on the perceived intensity is primarily due to their effect on the direction of the surface normal (and thus the light reflected) rather than their effect on the position of the surface. We can expect, therefore, to get a good effect from having a texturing function which performs a small perturbation on the direction of the surface normal before using it in the intensity formula. This is similar to the technique used by Batson et al. [1] to synthesize aerial picutres of mountain ranges from topographic data.

The normal vector perturbation is defined in terms of a function which gives the displacement of the irregular surface from the ideal smooth one. We will call this function F(u,v). On the wrinkled patch the position of a point is displaced in the direction of the surface normal by an amount equal to the value of F(u,v). The new position vector can then be written as:

$$\vec{P}' = \vec{P} + F\,\vec{N}/|N|$$

This is shown in cross section in figure 2.

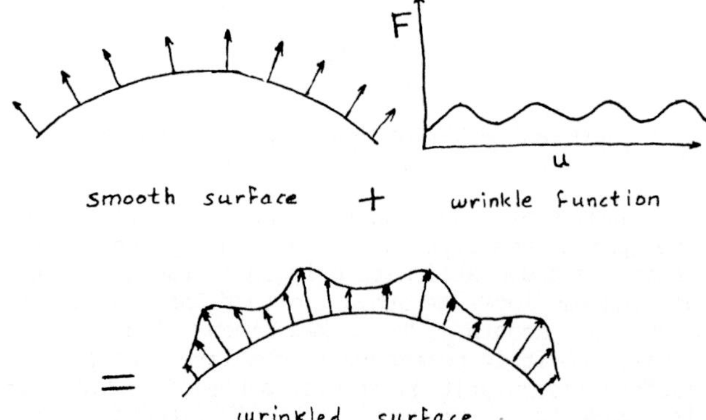

Figure 2 - Mapping Bump Function

The normal vector to this new surface is derived by taking the cross product of its partial derivatives.

$$\vec{N}' = \vec{P}u' \times \vec{P}v'$$

The partial derivatives involved are evaluated by the chain rule. So

$$\begin{aligned}\vec{P}u' &= d/du\,\vec{P}' = d/du(\vec{P} + F\,\vec{N}/|N|)\\ &= \vec{P}u + Fu\,\vec{N}/|N| + F\,(\vec{N}/|N|)u\end{aligned}$$

$$\begin{aligned}\vec{P}v' &= d/dv\,\vec{P}' = d/dv(\vec{P} + F\,\vec{N}/|N|)\\ &= \vec{P}v + Fv\,\vec{N}/|N| + F\,(\vec{N}/|N|)v\end{aligned}$$

The formulation of the normal to the wrinkled surface is now in terms of the original surface definition functions, their derivatives, and the bump function, F, and its derivatives. It is, however, rather complicated. We can simplify matters considerably by invoking the approximation that the value of F is negligably small. This is reasonable for the types of surface irregularities for which this process is intended where the height of the wrinkles in a surface is small compared to the extent of the surface. With this simplification we have

$$\vec{P}u' \approx \vec{P}u + Fu\,\vec{N}/|N|$$

$$\vec{P}v' \approx \vec{P}v + Fv\,\vec{N}/|N|$$

The new normal is then

$$\begin{aligned}\vec{N}' &= (\vec{P}u + Fu\,\vec{N}/|N|) \times (\vec{P}v + Fv\,\vec{N}/|N|)\\ &= (\vec{P}u \times \vec{P}v) + Fu\,(\vec{N} \times \vec{P}v)/|N|\\ &\quad + Fv\,(\vec{P}u \times \vec{N})/|N| + Fu\,Fv\,(\vec{N}\times\vec{N})/|N|^2\end{aligned}$$

The first term of this is, by definition, N. The last term is identically zero. The net expression for the perturbed normal vector is then

$$\vec{N}' = \vec{N} + \vec{D}$$

$$\text{where } \vec{D} = (\,Fu\,(\vec{N} \times \vec{P}v) - Fv\,(\vec{N} \times \vec{P}u)\,)\,/\,|N|$$

This can be interpreted geometrically by observing that (N x Pv) and (N x Pu) are two vectors in the tangent plane to the surface. An amount of each of them proportional to the u and v derivatives of F are added to the original, unperturbed normal vector. See figure 3

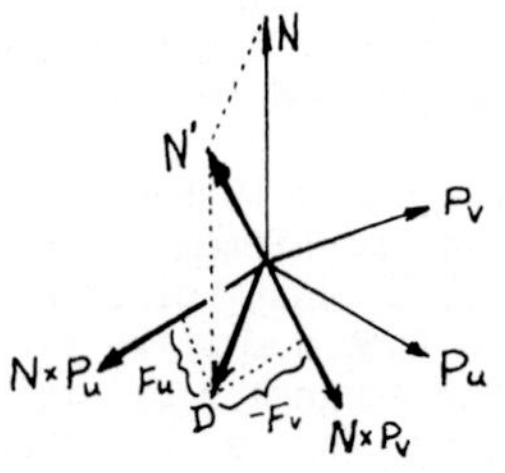

Figure 3 - Perturbed Normal Vector

Another geometric interpretation is that the vector N' comes from rotating the original vector N about some axis in the tangent plane to the surface. This axis vector can be found as the cross product of N and N'.

$$\vec{N} \times \vec{N}' = \vec{N} \times (\vec{N}+\vec{D}) = \vec{N} \times \vec{D}$$

$$= \frac{Fu\ (\vec{N} \times (\vec{N} \times \vec{Pv})) - Fv\ (\vec{N} \times (\vec{N} \times \vec{Pu}))}{|N|}$$

Invoking the vector identity Qx(RxS) = R(Q.S) - S(Q.R) and the fact that N.Pu = N.Pv = 0 this axis of rotation reduces to

$$\vec{N}\mathrm{x}\vec{N}' = |N|(Fv\ \vec{Pu} - Fu\ \vec{Pv}) \equiv |N|\ \vec{A}$$

This vector, A, is just the perpendicular to the gradient vector of F, (Fu,Fv) when expressed in the tangent plane coordinate system with basis vectors Pu and Pv. Thus the perturbed normal vector will be tipped "downhill" from the slope due to F. Note that, since NxD=|N| A and since N is perpendicular to D then

$$|NxD| = |N|\ |D|$$

so

$$|D| = |A|$$

Next, since the vectors N, D and N' form a right triangle, the effective angle of rotation is

$$\tan\vartheta = |D|/|N|$$

this is illustrated in figure 4.

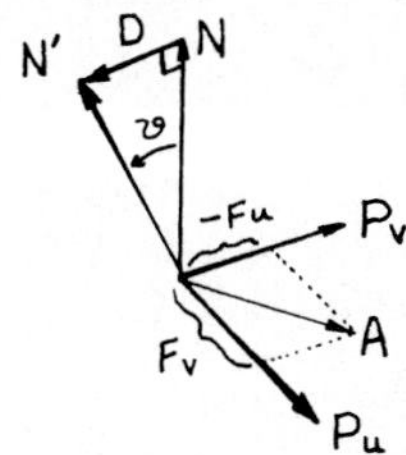

Figure 4 - Rotated Normal Vector

In summary, we can now calculate the perturbed normal vector, N', at any desired u and v parameter value. This vector must still be scaled to a length of 1 by dividing by its length. The result is then passed to the intensity calculation routines in place of the actual normal N.

3. TEXTURE FUNCTION DEFINITION

The formulation of the perturbed normal vector is in terms of the position functions X, Y, and Z and the bump displacement function F. To perform calculations we only need a means of evaluating the u and v derivatives of F(u,v) at any required parameter value. In this section we discuss some ways that such functions have been defined, means of evaluating them and show some resultant pictures.

The function F could, of course, be defined analytically as a bivariate polynomial or bivariate Fourier series. In order to generate a function with a sufficient amount of complexity to be interesting, however, an excessive number of coefficients are required. A much simpler way to define complex functions is by a table lookup. Since F has two parameters, this table takes the form of a doubly indexed array of values of F at various fractional parameter values. If the array is 64 by 64 elements and the parameters are between 0 and 1 a simple means of evaluating F (using Fortran style indexing) at u and v would be

```
FUNCTION FVAL(U,V)
     IU = IFIX(64*U)
     IV = IFIX(64*V)
     FVAL = FARRAY(IU+1,IV+1)
```

(We will duscuss the problem of overflow of the indices shortly). This will yield a function made of a checkerboard of constant valued squares 1/64 on a side. A smoother function can be obtained by interpolating values between table entries. The simplest interpolation technique is bilinear interpolation. Such an algorithm would look like

```
FUNCTION FVAL(U,V)
     IU=IFIX(64*U)
     DU=64*U - IU
     IV=IFIX(64*V)
     DV=64*V - IV
     F00 = FARRAY(IU+1,IV+1)
     F10 = FARRAY(IU+2,IV+1)
     F01 = FARRAY(IU+1,IV+2)
     F11 = FARRAY(IU+2,IV+2)
     FU0 = F00 + DU*(F10-F00)
     FU1 = F01 + DU*(F11-F01)
     FVAL= FU0 + DV*(FU1-FU0)
```

This yields a function which is continuous in value but discontinuous in derivative. Since the function F appears in the calculation only in terms of its derivative we should use a higher order interpolation scheme which is continuous in derivative. Otherwise the lines between function samples may show up as creases in the surface. Third order interpolation schemes (e.g. B-splines) are the standard solution to such a situation, but their generality is not really needed here. A cheaper, continuous interpolation scheme for derivatives consists of differencing the (bilinearly interpolated) function along the parametric directions. The increment between which differencing occurs is the distance between function sample values. The function generated by this interpolation scheme has continuity of derivative but not of value. The values of F are not used anyway. Thus

```
E = 1/64.
FU = (FVAL(U+E,V )-FVAL(U-E,V )) / (2*E)
FV = (FVAL(U ,V+E)-FVAL(U ,V-E)) / (2*E)
```

This is the form used in the pictures shown here. It is about as simple as can be obtained and has proven to be quite adequate.

In the above examples, the integer part of the scaled up parameter values were used directly as indices into the F array. In practive, one should protect against array overflow occurring when the parameter happens to be slightly less than 0 or greater than 1. In fact, for the bilinear interpolation case, all parameter values between 63/64 and 1 will attempt to interpolate to a table entry at index 65. The question of what is the function value at parameters outside the range of the table can be answered in a variety of ways. A simple method is to make the function periodic, with the table defining one period.

sample results that can be achieved with this technique. The first pattern, a hand drawn unit cell of bricks was mapped onto the sphere on the cover.

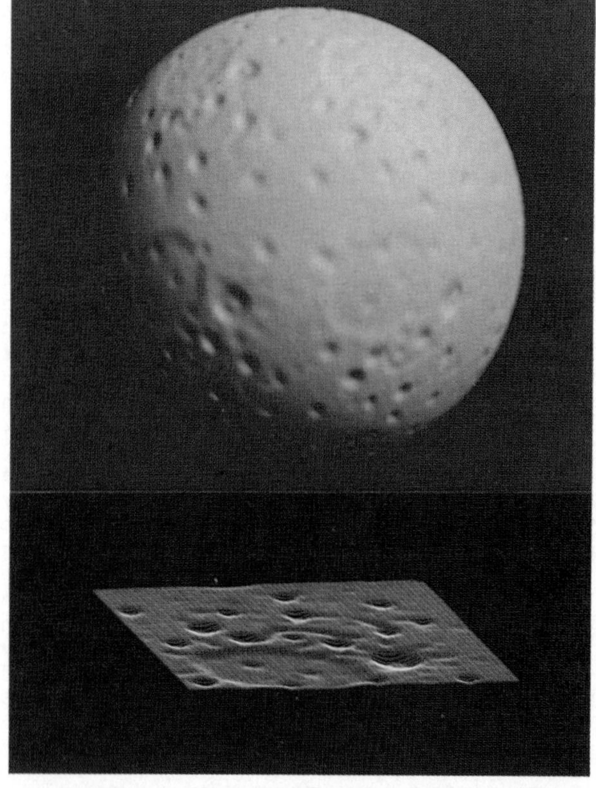

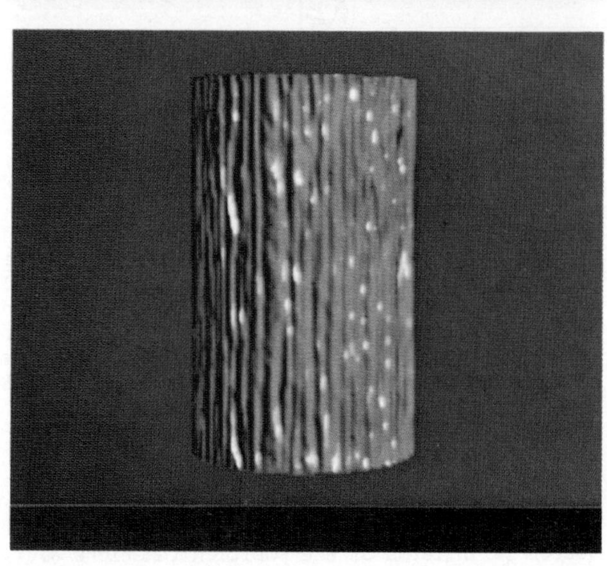

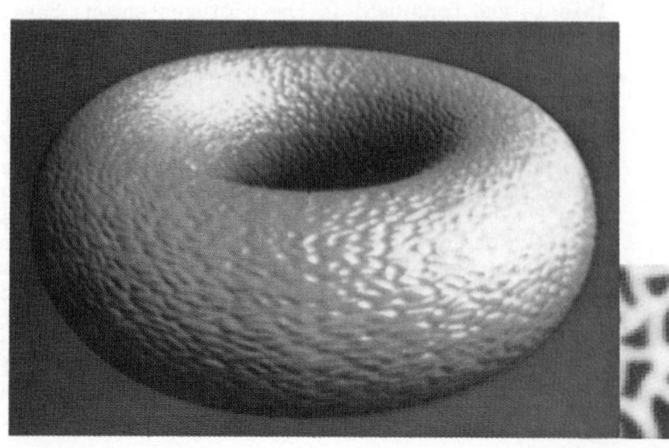

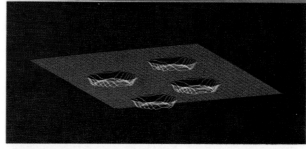

Figure 8 - Hand Drawn Bump Functions

This is easily accomplished by masking off all but the low 6 bits of the IU and IV values. This also makes it easy to have the table represent a unit cell pattern to be replicated many times per patch. The function values U and V are merely scaled up by the replication count before being passed to FVAL.

Now that we know what to do with the table entries we turn to the question of how to generate them in the first place. Some simple geometric patterns can be generated algorithmically. One such is a gridwork of high and low values. The table entries of the F function for such a grid are shown plotted as a 3D line drawing in figure 5. The result when mapped onto a flat patch with one corner bent back is also shown.

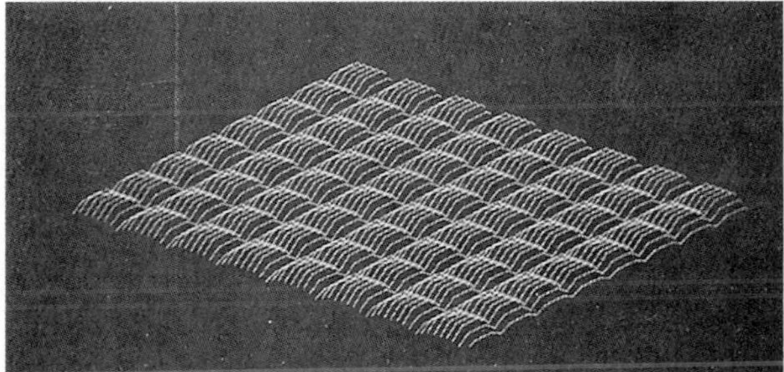

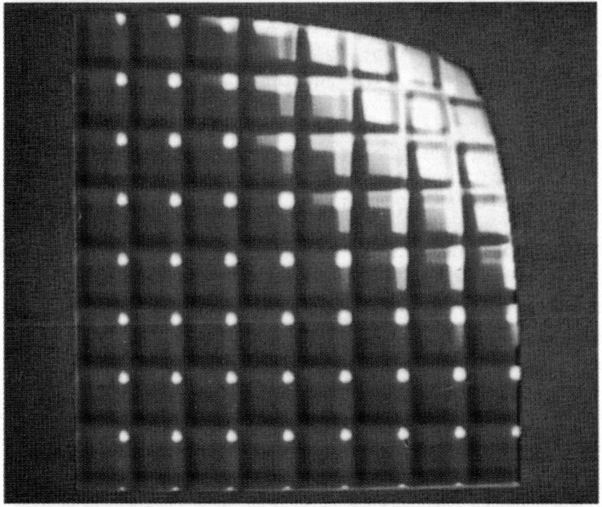

Figure 5 - Simple Grid Pattern

Embossed letters can be generated by using a bit-map character set as used to display text on a raster scan display. Such a texture array appears in figure 6. This pattern was used to make the title on the ribbon on the logo of the cover of these proceedings.

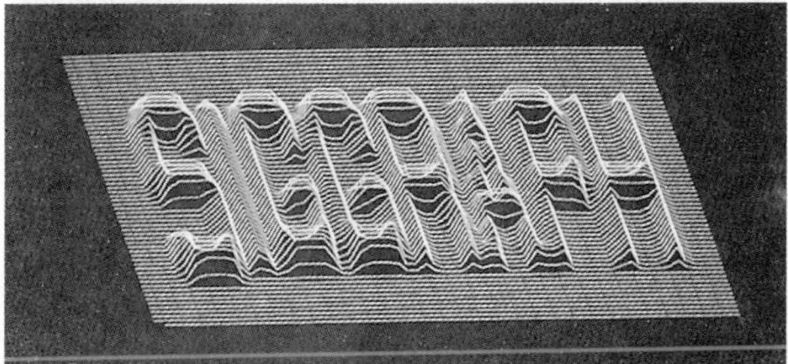

Figure 6 - Embossed Letter Pattern

Another method of generating bump functions derives from image synthesis algorithms which use Z-buffers or depth buffers to perform the hidden surface comparisons [5]. The actual Z values left in the depth buffer after running such an algorithm can be used to define the table entries for a bump function. In figure 7 an image of a sphere was generated using such an algorithm and the resultant Z-buffer replicated several times to generate the rivet-like pattern. This is the pattern mapped onto the cube on the cover logo. Similarly, a 3D character set was used with a Z-buffer algorithm to generate the pattern showing the date also in figure 7. This was used on the ribbon on the cover.

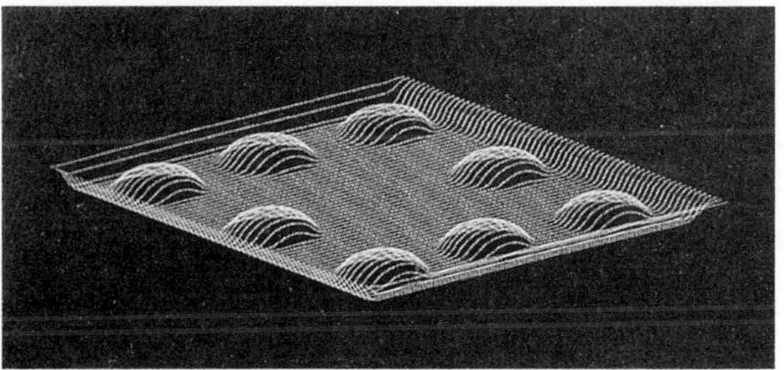

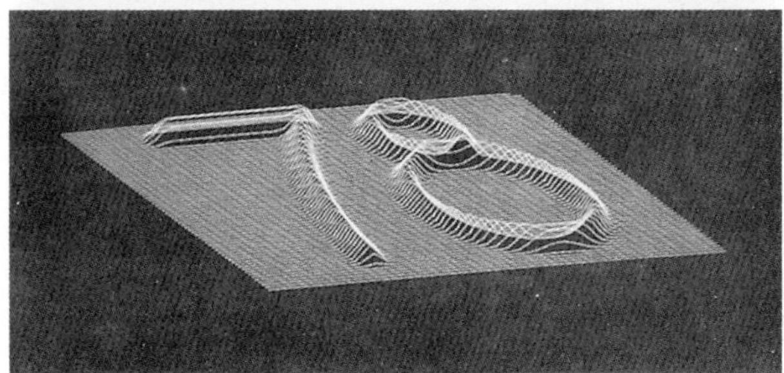

Figure 7 - Z-Buffer Patterns

The most general method of generating bump functions relies on video frame buffer technology and its standard tool, the painting program. Briefly, a frame buffer is a large digital memory with one word per picture element of an image. A video signal is continually synthesized from this memory so that the screen displays an image of what is in memory. A painting program utilizes a digitizing tablet to control the alteration of the values in the memory to achieve the effect of painting on the screen. By utilizing a region of the frame buffer as the defining table of the F function, a user can actually paint in the function values. The interpretation of the image will be such that black areas produce small values of F and white areas produce large values. Since only the derivatives of F are used in the normal vector perturbation, any area of constant intensity will look smooth on the final image. However, places where the image becomes darker will appear as dents and places where it becomes brighter will appear as bumps. (This correspondance will be reversed if the base patch is rotated to view the back side). The generation of interesting patterns which fit together end-to-end to form a continuous join between patches then becomes primarily an artistic effort on the part of the drawer. Figure 8 shows some

4. DEPENDANCE ON SCALE

One feature of the perturbation calculation is that the perturbation amount is not invariant with the scale at which the object is drawn. If the X, Y, and Z surface definiton functions are scaled up by 2 then the normal vector length, $|N|$, is scaled up by a factor of 4 while the perturbation amount, $|D|$, is only scaled by 2. This effect is due to the fact that the object is being scaled but the displacement function F is not. (Scale changes due to the object moving nearer or farther from the viewer in perspective space do not affect the size of the wrinkles, only scale shanges applied directly to the object.) The net effect of this is that if an object is scaled up, the wrinkles flatten out. This is illustrated in figure 9.

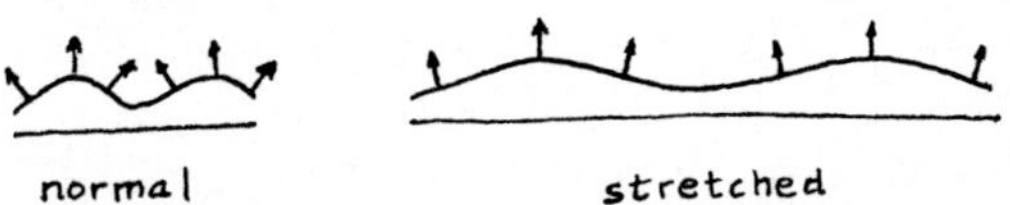

Figure 9 - Stretched Bump Texture

This effect might be desirable for some applications but undesirable for others. A scale invariant perturbation, D', must scale at the same rate as N. An obvious choice for this is

$$D' = a\, D\, |N|/|D|$$

so

$$|D'| = a\, |N|$$

where a is independant of scales in P. The value of a is then the tangent of the effective rotation angle.

$$\tan\vartheta' = |D'|/|N| = a$$

This can be defined in various ways. One simple choice is a generalization from the simple, flat unit square patch

$$X(u,v) = u$$
$$Y(u,v) = v$$
$$Z(u,v) = 0$$

For this patch the original normal vector perturbation gives

$$N = (0,0,1)$$
$$D = (-F_u, -F_v, 0)$$
$$\tan\vartheta = \mathrm{sqrt}(F_u^2 + F_v^2)$$

Here the value of a is purely a function of F. Use of the same function for arbitrary patches corresponds to a perturbation of

$$a = \mathrm{sqrt}(F_u^2 + F_v^2)$$
$$D' = a\, D\, |N|/|D|$$
$$N'' = N + D'$$

The texture defining function F is now no longer being used as an actual displacement added to the position of the surface. It just serves to provide (in the form if its derivatives) a means of defining the rotation axis and angle as functions of u and v.

5. ALIASING

In an earlier paper [2], the author described the effect of aliasing on images made with color texture mapping. The same problems can arise with this new form. That is, undesirable artifacts can enter the image in regions where the texture pattern maps into a small screen region. The solution applied to color textures was to average the texture pattern over the region corresponding to each picture element in the final image. The bump texture definition function, however, does not have a linear relationship to the intensity of the final image. If the bump texture is averaged the effect will be to smooth out the bumps rather than average the intensities. The correct solution to this problem would be to compute the intensities at some high sub-pixel resolution and average them. Simply filtering the bump function can, however, reduce the more offensive artifacts of aliasing. Figure 10 shows the result of such an operation.

Before

After

Figure 10 - Filtering Bump Texture

6. RESULTS

Surfaces appearing in images made with this technique look quite convincingly wrinkled. An especially nice effect is the interaction of the bumps with calculated highlights. We must realize, however, that the wrinkles are purely illusory. They only come from some playing with the parameters used in intensity calculations. They do not, for example, alter the smooth silhouette edges of the object. A useful test of any image generation algorithm is to see how well the objects look as they move in animation sequences. Some sample frames from such an animation sequence appear in figure 11. The illusion of wrinkles continues to be convincing and the smoothness of the silhouette edges is not overly bothersome.

Some simple timing measurements indicate that bump mapping takes about 4 times as long as Phong shading and about 2 times as long as color texture mapping. The pictures in this paper took from 3 to 7 minutes each to produce.

The author would like to thank Lance Williams and the New York Institute of Technology Computer Graphics Laboratory for providing some of the artwork and assistance in preparing the logo on the cover made with the techniques described in this paper.

REFERENCES

[1] Batson, R. M., Edwards, E. and Eliason, E. M. "Computer Generated Shaded Relief Images", Jour, Research U.S. Geol. Survey, Vol. 3, No. 4, July-Aug 1975, p. 401-408.

[2] Blinn, J. F., and Newell, M. E., "Texture and Reflection in Computer Generated Images", CACM 19, 10, Oct 1976, pp 542-547.

[3] Blinn, J. F., "Models of Light Reflection for Computer Synthesized Pictures", Proc. 4th Conference on Computer Graphics and Interactive Techniques, 1977.

[4] Blinn, J. F., "A Scan Line Algorithm for Displaying Parametrically Defined Surfaces", Proc. 5th Conference on Computer Graphics and Interactive Techniques, 1978.

[5] Catmull, E. E., "Computer Display of Curved Surfaces", Proc. IEEE Conf. on Computer Graphics, Pattern Recognition and Data Structures, Los Angeles (May 1975)11.

[6] Whitted, J. T., "A Scan Line Algorithm for Computer Display of Curved Surfaces", Proc. 5th Conference on Computer Graphics ond Interactive Techniques, 1978.

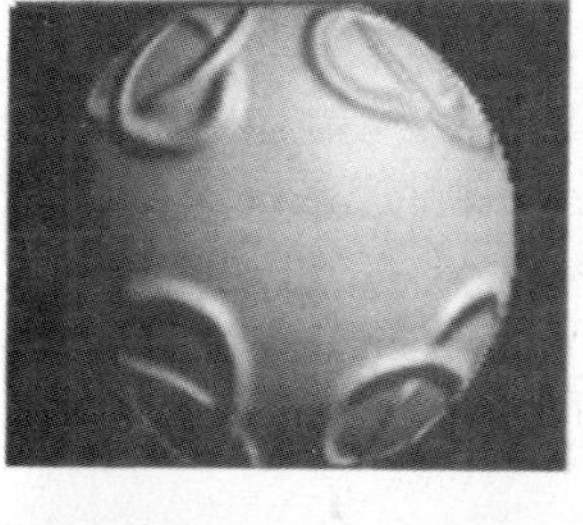
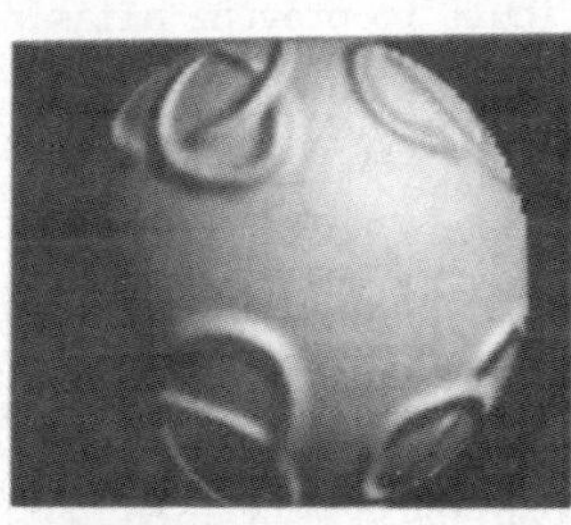
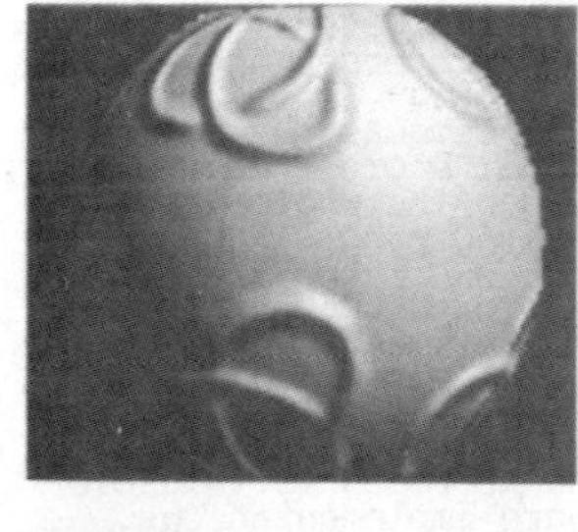
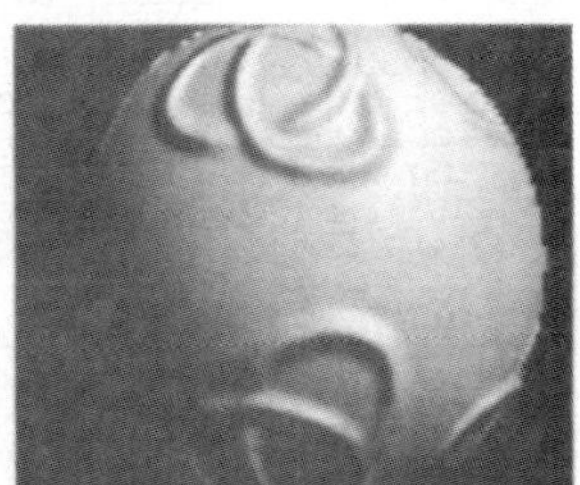

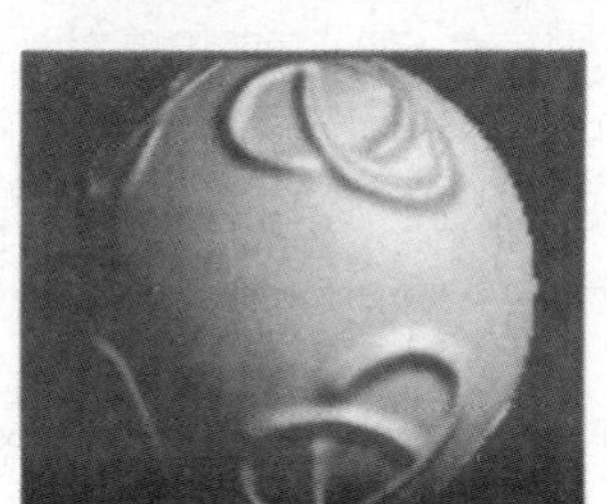
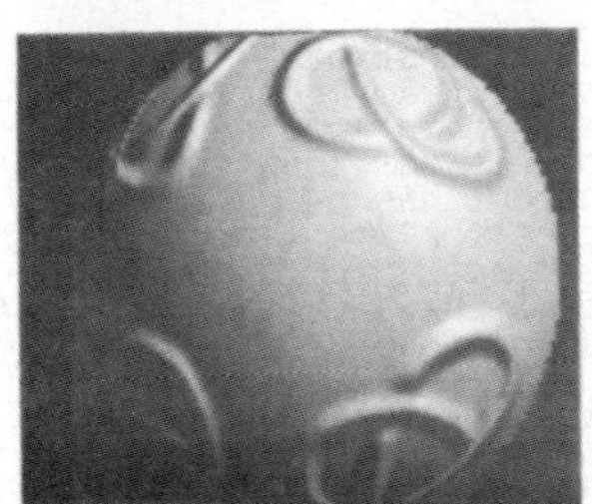
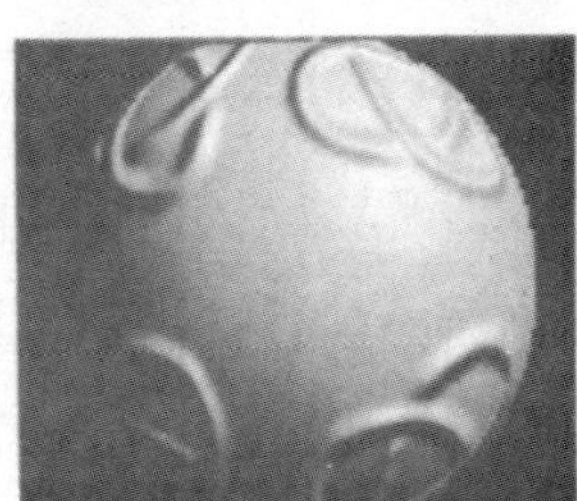

Figure 11 - Rotating Textured Sphere

"3-D Transformations of Images in Scanline Order" by E. Catmull and A.R. Smith from *Proceedings of SIGGRAPH '80*, 1980, pages 279-285. Copyright 1980, Association for Computing Machinery, Inc., reprinted by permission.

3-D TRANSFORMATIONS OF IMAGES IN SCANLINE ORDER

Ed Catmull and Alvy Ray Smith
Lucasfilm Ltd.
P.O.Box 7
San Anselmo, CA 94960

ABSTRACT - Currently texture mapping onto projections of 3-D surfaces is time consuming and subject to considerable aliasing errors. Usually the procedure is to perform some inverse mapping from the area of the pixel onto the surface texture. It is difficult to do this correctly. There is an alternate approach where the texture surface is transformed as a 2-D image until it conforms to a projection of a polygon placed arbitrarily in 3-space. The great advantage of this approach is that the 2-D transformation can be decomposed into two simple transforms, one in horizontal and the other in vertical scanline order. horizontal scanline order. Sophisticated light calculation is also time consuming and difficult to calculate correctly on projected polygons. Instead of calculating the lighting based on the position of the polygon, lights, and eye, the lights and eye can be transformed to a corresponding position for a unit square which we can consider to be a canonical polygon. After this canonical polygon is correctly textured and shaded it can be easily conformed to the projection of the 3-D surface.

KEY WORDS AND PHRASES: texture mapping, scanline algorithm, spatial transforms, 2-pass algorithm, stream processor, warping, bottleneck, foldover

CR CATEGORY: 8.2

INTRODUCTION

Texture mapping is an immensely powerful idea now being exploited in computer graphics. It was first developed by one of the authors [2] and extended by Blinn [1] who produced some startling pictures. In this paper we present a new approach to texture mapping that is potentially much faster than previous techniques and has fewer problems.

The two chief difficulties have been aliasing and the time it takes to do the transformation of a picture onto the projection of some patch. Usually the procedure is to perform some inverse mapping of a pixel onto a surface texture (Fig. 1). It is difficult to do this correctly because the inverse mapping does not happen in scanline order and also because we must integrate under the whole inverse image in order to prevent sampling errors.

We present in this paper an approach that does the mapping in scanline order both in scanning the texture map and in producing the projected image. Processing pixels in scanline order allows us to specify hardware that may work at video rates. We emphasize, however, that the approach is valuable for software as well as hardware implementations.

One of the key concepts we use is that of a "stream processor". Pixels enter the stream processor at video rate, are modified or merged in some way with another incoming stream of pixels and then sent to the output (Fig. 2). This concept has been implemented by several manufacturers for image processing. A generalization of the concept would be to allow the framebuffers to feed the streams in either horizontal or vertical scanline order.

We will show here that the class of transformations that can be applied to streams is much broader than previously believed. For example, an image in a frame buffer may be rotated by some arbitrary angle even though the data is sent through the processor in scanline order only. While this concept has been known for some time [3,4], we show here that the technique can be generalized to perspective projections. Further generalizations include quadric and bivariate curved surfaces. The ability to transform a whole raster image very quickly lets us consider doing shading calculations on a unit square where the calculations may be more amenable to stream processing and then transforming the results.

When we say "scanline order", we use a slightly broader meaning than normal. Usually this means that the order of the pixels is from left to right across a scanline and that the scanlines come in top to bottom order. We broaden the definition to include vertical scanline order. In addition, the scanlines may also occur in bottom to top or right to left order. This gives us trivially a 90 degree rotate and flopping a picture over in one pass through the picture.

EXAMPLE: SIMPLE ROTATION

For illustration, we present the simple case of rotation. We would like to rotate an entire image in the framebuffer. The rotation matrix is:

$$[x' \; y'] = \begin{bmatrix} c & -s \\ s & c \end{bmatrix} \begin{bmatrix} x \\ y \end{bmatrix}$$

where x and y refer to coordinates in the original picture and x', y' are the new coordinates (c=cos, s=sin).

We want to transform every pixel in the original picture. If we hold y constant and move along x then we are transforming the data in scanline order but the results are not coming out in scanline order. Not only is this inconvenient, it is also difficult to prevent aliasing errors.

There is an alternate method for transforming all of the pixels, and that is to evaluate only the x' in a first pass and then the y' in a second pass.

So again hold y constant, but just evaluate x':

$$[x' \; y] = [cx-sy \;\; y].$$

We now have a picture that has been skewed and scaled in the x direction, but every pixel has its original y value. See Fig.4, where Fig.4a is the original picture and Fig.4b is after the horizontal scanline computation.

Next we can transform the intermediate picture by holding x' constant and calculating y. Unfortunately, the equation y' = sx+cy can't be used because the x value for that vertical scanline is not the right one for the equation. So let us invert x' to get the correct x. We need x in terms of x'.

Recall x' = cx-sy, so

$$x = x'/c + sy/c.$$

Plug this into y' = sx + cy to get:

$$y' = (sx' + y)/c.$$

Now we transform the y value of the pixels in the intermediate picture in vertical scanline order to get the final picture, Fig.4c.

The first pass went in horizontal scanline order on input and output. The second was vertical in both. So in two passes the entire picture was rotated.

Before we generalize, two points should be noted.

(1) A 90 degree rotate would cause the intermediate picture to collapse to a line. It would be better to read the scanlines horizontally from the source buffer and write them vertically to effect that rotate. It follows that an 80 degree rotate should be performed by first rotating 90 degrees as noted then by -10 degrees using the 2-pass algorithm.

(2) The rate at which pixels are read from the input buffer is generally different than the rate at which they are sent to the output buffer. If we're not careful we could get sampling problems. However, since all of the pixels pass through the processor, it is not difficult to filter and integrate the incoming values to get an output value.

Next we generalize to:

$$[x'\ y'] = [X(x,y)\ \ Y(x,y)].$$

This generalization will include perspective. Whatever the transformation is, we shall show that we can do the x transforms first, followed by the y transforms, but in order to do the y transforms we must be able to find the inverse of x'. This may be very difficult to do and x' may even have multiple values. So we present first a more formal way of talking about the method before addressing some of the difficulties.

THE 2-PASS TECHNIQUE

We are interested in mapping the 2-D region bounded by a unit square into a 3-D surface which is projected back into 2-D for final viewing. Since the unit square (by which we mean the enclosed points also) may be represented by point samples in a digital framebuffer, and since a framebuffer is typically arranged in rows and columns, we are interested in row-ordered or column-ordered implementations of these mappings. The technique we now present is a means of decomposing a 2-D mapping into a succession of two 1-D mappings, or scanline-ordered mappings, where a scanline may be either horizontal (a row) or vertical (a column). The technique is quite general as we shall show subsequently.

This figure illustrates the 2-pass technique:

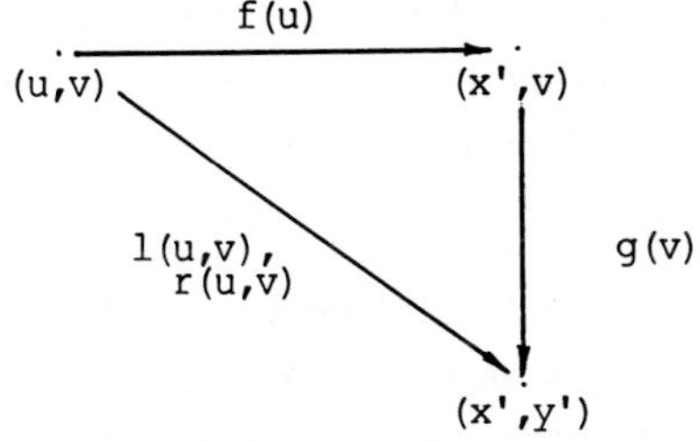

We want to map the set of points $\{(u,v):0\leq u<1, 0<v<1\}$ in the unit square into the set $\{(x',y')\}$ where the desired mapping is given as an arbitrary pair of functions

$$x'=l(u,v)$$
$$y'=r(u,v).$$

We wish to replace this pair of functions with the pair

$$x'=f(u)$$
$$y'=g(v)$$

where it is understood that f(u) is applied to all points in the unit square before g(v) is applied to any of them. We call the application of f the h-pass (for horizontal) and the application of g the v-pass (for vertical).

In general, there will be a different f(u) for each value of v, so f might be thought of as a function of (u,v). We prefer however to think of v as a parameter which selects a particular f(u) to be applied to all u on scanline v. To emphasize when v is being held constant like this, we will use the notation $\tilde{v}$. Thus $\tilde{v}$ is an index into a table of horizontal mappings. Similarly, there will in general be a different g(v) for each vertical scanline x' (where the prime indicates that the h-pass has already occurred). We will use the notation $\tilde{x}'$ to indicate a given vertical scanline just prior to the v-pass.

In this section, we will always have the v-pass follow the h-pass. This is just a convenience. The decomposition into the other order proceeds similarly, and we will have occasion to choose one order over the other in a later section.

An algorithm for the decomposition of l,r into f,g is the following:

(1) $f(u)=l(u,\tilde{v})$ is the function f for scanline $\tilde{v}$.

(2) Solve the equation $l(u,v)-\tilde{x}'=0$ for u to obtain $u=h(v)$ for scanline $\tilde{x}'$.

(3) $g(v)=r(h(v),v)$ is the function g for scanline $\tilde{x}'$.

We simply take f(u) as defined in (1) and show that g(v) in (3) is consistent with it. The h-pass takes the set of points $\{(u,v)\}$ into the set $\{(x',v)\}$. We desire a function which may be applied at this time to scanline $\tilde{x}'$. But being given $\tilde{x}'$ is equivalent to being given the equation

$$\tilde{x}'=l(u,v).$$

If this equation can be rearranged to have the form $u=h(v)$, then $r(h(v),v)$ is a function of v only and is the desired g.

Thus solving the equation $l(u,v)-\tilde{x}'=0$ for u is the key to the technique. We shall show some cases where this is simple, but in general it is not. An iterative solution such as provided by Newton-Raphson iteration could be used but is expensive. We shall treat these problems in the following sections.

It should be noted that we have placed no restrictions on functions l,r. So the 2-pass technique can be applied to a large class of picture transformations and distortions, only a few examples of which will be presented here. In particular, we henceforth restrict our attention to ratios of polynomials.

We shall illustrate the 2-pass technique by applying it, in detail, to the case of a rectangle undergoing affine transformations followed by a perspective transformation and projection into 2-space. Then, in less detail, we will treat bilinear and biquadratic patches under the same type of transformation. This should serve to indicate how the method can be extended to higher degree surfaces.

THE SIMPLE RECTANGLE

Consider the (trivial) parametric representation of a rectangle given by $x(u,v)=u$, $y(u,v)=v$, $z(u,v)=0$, $w(u,v)=1$. The class of transformations we apply are exactly those which can be represented by a 4x4 matrix multiplying a 3-space vector represented in homogeneous coordinates as indicated below:

$$[x\ y\ z\ w]\begin{bmatrix} a & e & i & m \\ b & f & j & n \\ c & g & k & o \\ d & h & l & p \end{bmatrix} = [x''\ y''\ z''\ w''].$$

Then projection into 2-space is accomplished by dividing through the homogeneous coordinate w":

$$[x'\ y'\ z'] = [x''/w''\ \ y''/w''\ \ z''/w''].$$

Replacing x, y, z, and w with their parametric forms and expanding the equations above gives

$$x' = (au+bv+d)/(mu+nv+p) = l(u,v)$$

$$y' = (eu+fv+h)/(mu+nv+p) = r(u,v).$$

We are interested in the 2-D projection only so we shall ignore z' from here on.

The functions l,r in this case represent an ordinary linear transformation of the unit square, followed by a perspective projection. Notice that they are both rational linear polynomials - i.e., a linear polynomial divided by a linear polynomial.

Applying the 2-pass algorithm to the functions l,r gives:

(1) The h-pass function for scanline $\tilde{v}$ is

$$f(u) = (Au+B)/(Cu+D)$$

where $A=a$, $B=b\tilde{v}+d$, $C=m$, $D=n\tilde{v}+p$.

(2) u=h(v) is obtained by solving

$$\tilde{x}' = (au+bv+d)/(mu+nv+p)$$

for u:

$$u = Ev+F$$

where $E=(b-n\tilde{x}')/(m\tilde{x}'-a)$ and $F=(d-p\tilde{x}')/(m\tilde{x}'-a)$.

(3) Thus

$$g(v) = (e(Ev+F)+fv+h)/(m(Ev+F)+nv+p) = (Gv+H)/(Iv+J)$$

is the v-pass function for scanline $\tilde{x}'$, where $G=f+eE$, $H=h+eF$, $I=n+mE$, $J=p+mF$.

Fig.5 shows the results of applying this f,g pair. Fig.5a is the original rectangular texture. Fig.5b is its appearance after the h-pass, and Fig.5c is the result of the v-pass.

Following are several points about this computation:

(1) The sampled image (Fig.5a) was reconstructed with a first-order filter (the so-called Bartlett window) then resampled with a zeroth-order filter (the Fourier window). This is only minimal use of sampling theory. A piece of hardware or software for production quality work would certainly employ more sophisticated filtering. Our figures look surprisingly nice despite use of the low-order filters mentioned above. (The edges are not antialiased, however.)

(2) Clipping is natural. The f function generates the final value of x'. If this value should fall outside the limits of the output buffer then it does so with no loss. The g function, which operates only on the scanlines output by f, will never need values clipped in the h-pass.

(3) The 2-pass technique does not avoid the ordinary problems of perspective projections. For example, the transformation can blow up if the denominator of either f or g goes to zero. This corresponds to the usual problem of wraparound through infinity and requires the normal solution of clipping before transformation.

(4) There is a problem introduced by the 2-pass technique not encountered before. This is what we call the "bottleneck problem". We shall discuss this in greater detail and offer a solution to it in the next section, then return to the examples.

BOTTLENECK

With the perspective transformation we have a problem analogous to that of the 90 degree rotate, that is, it is possible to have an intermediate picture collapse. In the case of rotation the solution was simple: rotate the texture 90 degrees and change the tranformation by that amount. The solution for the perspective case is the same, however it is more difficult to tell from the transformation matrix when a problem will occur.

We base our criteria on the area of the image in the intermediate picture. There are four possible ways to generate an intermediate picture:

1. transform x first
2. transform y first
3. rotate 90 degrees and transform x first
4. rotate 90 degrees and transform y first

In each case the area is easily found by integrating the area between x'(0,y) and x'(1,y) where

$$x' = (ax+by+c)/(dx+ey+f)$$

and y varies from 0 to 1. This gives

$$area = K*\ln(1+e/(d+f)) - k*\ln(1+e/f)$$

where $K=((ce-bf)+(ae-bd))/ee$, and $k=(cd-bf)/ee$. We use the method that gives the maximum intermediate area.

THE BILINEAR PATCH

The preceding class of transformations of the rectangle does not generate all quadrilaterals - e.g., nonplanar quadrilaterals. Since in general we cannot guarantee that all quadrilaterals are planar, we generalize to the bilinear patch.

The general bilinear patch (Fig.3a) has a parametric representation

$$x(u,v) = [u\ 1]\begin{bmatrix} a00 & a01 \\ a10 & a11 \end{bmatrix}\begin{bmatrix} v \\ 1 \end{bmatrix}$$

where $a00=(x3-x2)-(x1-x0)$, $a01=x1-x0$, $a10=x2-x0$, $a11=x0$. There are similar representations for y(u,v), z(u,v), and w(u,v), where bij, cij, and dij correspond respectively to the aij for x(u,v).

As in the preceding example we transform a bilinear patch with a 4x4 matrix multiply followed by a projection into 2-space. Hence we shall again ignore z' (but see discussion of foldover below). The transformation may be represented by the following matrix equation:

$$[x''\ y''\ z''\ w''] =$$

$$[x\ y\ z\ w]\begin{bmatrix} a & e & i & m \\ b & f & j & n \\ c & g & k & o \\ d & h & l & p \end{bmatrix} =$$

$$[uv\ u\ v\ 1]\begin{bmatrix} a00 & b00 & c00 & d00 \\ a01 & b01 & c01 & d01 \\ a10 & b10 & c10 & d10 \\ a11 & b11 & c11 & d11 \end{bmatrix}\begin{bmatrix} a & e & i & m \\ b & f & j & n \\ c & g & k & o \\ d & h & l & p \end{bmatrix} =$$

$$[uv\ u\ v\ 1]\begin{bmatrix} A & E & I & M \\ B & F & J & N \\ C & G & K & O \\ D & H & L & P \end{bmatrix}$$

After the homogeneous divide

$$x' = (Auv+Bu+Cv+D)/(Muv+Nu+Ov+P) = l(u,v)$$

$$y' = (Euv+Fu+Gv+H)/(Muv+Nu+Ov+P) = r(u,v).$$

The 2-pass algorithm gives:

(1) $f(u)=(A'u+B')/(C'u+D')$ for scanline $\tilde{v}$, where $A'=A\tilde{v}+B$, $B'=C\tilde{v}+D$, $C'=M\tilde{v}+N$, $D'=O\tilde{v}+P$.

(2) For vertical scanline $\tilde{x}'$, it can be shown that

$$g(v) = (A''vv+B''v+C'')/(D''vv+E''v+F'')$$

where $A''=EE'+GG'$, $B''=EF'+FE'+GH'+HG'$, $C''=FF'+HH'$, $D''=ME'+OG'$, $E''=MF'+NE'+OH'+PG'$, $F''=NF'+PH'$ with $E'=C-O\tilde{x}'$, $F'=D-P\tilde{x}'$, $G'=M\tilde{x}'-A$, $H'=N\tilde{x}'-B$.

Fig.6 shows a planar bilinear patch representing the texture in Fig.5a twisted about its center point. For this particular example, the h-pass is the identity function f(u)=u and hence is not shown. Fig.7 shows the h-pass and v-pass for a nonplanar patch transformation. Note the foldover. Fig.5a is the source texture again.

All of the considerations discussed for the simple rectangle apply here also. In addition we have new problems introduced due to the higher complexity of the surface. A bilinear patch may be nonplanar, so from some views it may be double valued. That is, a line from the viewpoint through the surface may intersect the surface twice. In terms of the scanline functions, g(v) can map scanline $\tilde{x}'$ back over We call this problem "foldover". It occurs at a silhouette edge of the projected surface. The solution is to compute z' for v=0 and for v=1. The endpoint of scanline $\tilde{x}'$ which maps into the z' farthest from the is transformed first, so that later points overwrite points that would be obscured anyway. For antialiasing purposes, the location of the foldover point must be remembered and an appropriate weight computed for combining the pixel there with a background.

THE BIQUADRATIC PATCH

The highest order patch we shall discuss here is the biquadratic patch (Fig.3b). It is particularly interesting because surface patches on quadric surfaces (e.g., ellipsoids) may be represented as biquadratic patches. The parametric equation of x for a biquadratic patch has form

$$x(u,v) = [uu\ u\ 1] \begin{bmatrix} a00 & a01 & a02 \\ a10 & a11 & a12 \\ a20 & a21 & a22 \end{bmatrix} \begin{bmatrix} vv \\ v \\ 1 \end{bmatrix}$$

and similarly for y(u,v), z(u,v), and w(u,v).

$$[x''\ y''\ z''\ w''] =$$

$$[uuvv\ uuv\ uu\ uvv\ uv\ u\ vv\ v\ 1] \begin{bmatrix} A0 & B0 & C0 & D0 \\ A1 & B1 & C1 & D1 \\ A2 & B2 & C2 & D2 \\ & \cdots & & \\ A8 & B8 & C8 & D8 \end{bmatrix}$$

It can be shown, in a manner analogous to that used for the bilinear patch, that f(u) is a ratio of quadratic polynomials and g(v) is a ratio of 4th-degree polynomials. Actually there are two v-pass functions - say gi(v), i=0 or 1 - one corresponding to each of two solutions of a quadratic equation encountered in the derivation. The fact that there are two v-pass functions requires an explanation. We now turn to this and other considerations which have been added because of the introduction of higher degree surfaces.

First, we present a technique for reducing gi(v) from a ratio of 4th-degree forms to a rational quadratic polynomial like f(u). Presumably we could implement the gi(v) as they stand. However, besides being computationally nasty, they are difficult to interpret and hence hide many pitfalls. For example, the foldover problem discussed in the bilinear case could occur three times in a scanline with attendant antialiasing problems. We prefer to introduce a method which, at the cost of more memory, greatly reduces the complexity of the gi(v). It can also be applied to the simple rectangle and bilinear patch. Its utility comes however in extending the methods of this paper to higher degree - e.g., to the transformation of bicubic patches in perspective - which we reserve for a future paper.

The notion is that during the h-pass we have already computed the u's which we need in the v-pass. It is the recomputation of these u's (step (2) in the 2-pass algorithm) which makes the v-pass more difficult than the h-pass. We propose a high-precision framebuffer (e.g., 16 bits per pixel) to hold the u's as they are computed during the h-pass. Thus, if uj maps into xj' under f(u), then at location xj' in one framebuffer we store the intensity computed from the neighborhood of uj in the source picture and in another framebuffer (the one with higher precision) the value uj itself. Then during the v-pass on scanline $\tilde{x}j'$, we merely lookup in the extra framebuffer the value of uj mapped by the h-pass into the current pixel, say $(\tilde{x}j', y)$, on the vertical scanline. It will be the uj at $(\tilde{x}j', y)$ in the extra framebuffer.

A difficulty which arises is that the h-pass function f(u) can cause a foldover on horizontal scanlines. This means that the intensity computed at location xj' is a function of one of two different uj's. Our solution is to have two auxiliary location framebuffers and one additional intensity framebuffer. During the h-pass a scanline is computed in an order where the deepest points are generated first, as discussed in the bilinear case. As each uj is determined, it is written into only one of the location framebuffers and the corresponding intensity is written into one of the intensity framebuffers only. This occurs until the uj corresponding to the point of foldover occurs. From this point on all uj's are stored in only the other location framebuffer and the corresponding intensities in the other intensity framebuffer. The final image is a combination of the two intensity framebuffers. In general, we believe this to be a difficult hidden surface problem and do not treat it further here.

The simplification produced by the addition of the three extra framebuffers reduces the gi(v) to

$$g(v) = (B0'vv+B1'v+B2')/(D0'vv+D1'v+D2')$$

where, for example, B0'=B0ujuj+B3uj+B6 with uj being obtained by table lookup. The problem of which gi(v) is to be used is replaced with the problem of computing in two framebuffers and solving the hidden surface problem implied.

Notice that g(v) may cause foldover in both intensity framebuffers, but in any one framebuffer there is only a single foldover per vertical scanline instead of the triple foldover implied by the original gi(v) and no auxiliary framebuffers.

We have claimed that the use of additional memory makes unnecessary the determination of the uj, the inverses of x' under f(u). To make this strictly true, we must make the following observations. A typical way to implement the function f(u) is to step along x' in equal increments (e.g., one pixel increments) and compute the inverse image u. The neighborhood of u is then used to compute the intensity at location x'. Of course, this defeats the whole purpose of avoiding inverses, assuming they can be computed at all. We propose "straightahead" mapping for implementing f(u) to avoid inverses altogether. The idea here is to step along u in equal increments, computing x'=f(u) after each increment. Let xj' be a value of x' for which we wish to know its inverse image Let ui be values of u at the equal increment points used as samples of u. Then when xi'=f(ui) is less than xj' and x(i+1)'=f(u(i+1)) is greater than xj', we either

(1) iterate on the interval [ui,u(i+1)] to obtain the desired inverse image uj, or

(2) approximate uj by uj=ui+a(u(i+1)-ui), where a=xj'-xi'.

The figures used to illustrate this paper were generated using the approximation (2) above. Filtering and sampling require integration of the intensity function of u. This integration requires computation at each ui, so the cost, if any, of straightahead implementation is a small addition to that already required.

SIMPLIFICATIONS

Much of the heavy machinery in the examples above becomes unnecessary in the following two special cases:

No perspective: It is easy to see that the division at each output pixel is unnecessary in this case - i.e., the scanline mappings are polynomials instead of ratios of polynomials.

Planar patch: If the patch is known to be 2-D then, regardless of the order of its bounding curves, there can be no foldover problem with the rigid-body transformations considered here. (Lines can completely reverse direction however (Fig.6).) Hence no extra framebuffers are needed. The problem simplifies substantially, becoming a 2-D "warp" of a rectangular texture.

For example, a planar biquadratic patch under affine projection only (no perspective) has scanline functions of form f(u)=auu+bu+c and g(v)=dvv+ev+f and can be accomplished in only one framebuffer.

SHADING

People who have implemented hidden surface programs with sophisticated lighting models have discovered that the time spent for the lighting calculation is much greater than the time spent solving the hidden surface problem. We propose here that it may be faster to perform the light calculations on a square canonical polygon and then to transform the results.

Typically, normals for a polygon are determined and then interpolated across segments. The normal at each pixel is dotted with vectors to the lights and eye in some function to find the shading.

While framebuffers have been used to store intensities and depth values, they can also be used to store normal values. The normal values can be kept in a buffer at arbitrary resolution. The stream processor can then interpolate or approximate those normals to get normals at a higher resolution, normalize them, dot them with other streams of normals, and use the dot products in intensity calculatons. The approach is:

1. Transform eye and lights relative to canonical polygon.

2. The canonical polygon normal framebuffer is filled with normals at some resolution (say 4 by 4).

3. Generate a high resolution array of normals using cubic splines (we used b-splines) first in the vertical direction, then the horizontal.

4. Normalize the normals.

5. The stream of normals is dotted with a stream of light vectors and/or eye vectors to implement the lighting function.

6. The results are transformed into position into the final frame buffer yielding the shaded polygon.

7. If we are also doing texture mapping, then the intensity of each pixel in the texture is used as the color in the lighting function and the results

The approximation of normals with cubic curves can be done in a stream processor by using difference equations. Each overlapping set of four values can be used to generate a difference equation with a matrix multiply. Then the difference equation is used to generate all of the values. Until normalization, x, y, and z may be treated alike and independently.

CONCLUSIONS

We have presented what we believe to be a powerful new way of looking at 3-D surface rendering in computer graphics. It is based on the old notion of transforming to a canonical form, where the difficult work may be performed with relative ease, then transforming back. The success of this notion in 3-D surface graphics depends on the ease of realization of the transformations to and from canonical form. We have shown that a stream processor and the 2-pass decomposition technique give a technologically feasible realization of the notion for modern computer graphics.

There is much work to be done to fully explore this approach. This paper begins the exploration of this territory and points out several of the difficulties peculiar to it.

ACKNOWLEDGEMENTS

Although we do not know the details of their work, we are aware that Larry Evans and Steve Gabriel have been pursuing an apparently similar line of research and wish to acknowledge them here. Mike Shantz and his colleagues at De Anza Systems Inc. have also done independent work on separable transformations. They have implemented second-order polynomial coordinate transformations in hardware.

The photographs for this paper were prepared by David DiFrancesco at the Jet Propulsion Lab (JPL). The source picture in all cases was generated by Turner Whitted of Bell Labs for SIGGRAPH '79 and is used with his permission and that of the CACM.

Computing facilities at JPL were generously provided by Jim Blinn and Bob Holzman. Facilities were also provided by Tom Ferrin and Bob Langridge of the University of California at San Francisco.

REFERENCES

[1] James F. Blinn, "Simulation of Wrinkled Surfaces", SIGGRAPH Proceedings, August 1978, 286-292.

[2] Edwin Catmull, "Computer Display of Curved Surfaces", Proc. IEEE Conference on Computer Graphics, Pattern Recognition, and Data Structures, Los Angeles, May 1975.

[3] Steven A. Coons, "Transformations and Matrices", Course Notes No. 6, University of Michigan, Nov. 26, 1969.

[4] A. Robin Forrest, "Coordinates, Transformations, and Visualization Techniques", University of Cambridge, Computer Laboratory CAD Document 45, June 1969.

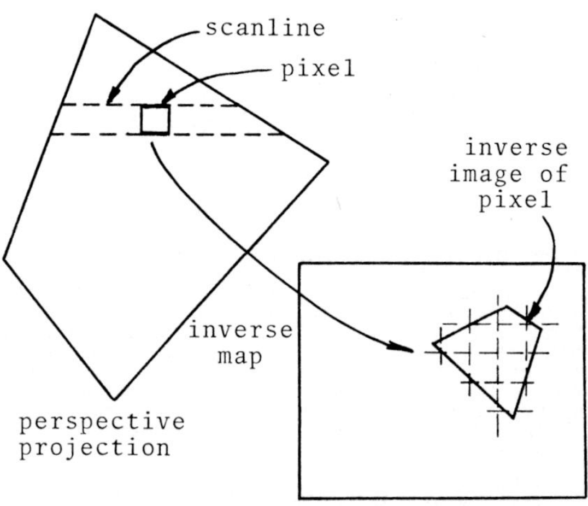

Fig.1. Texture mapping.

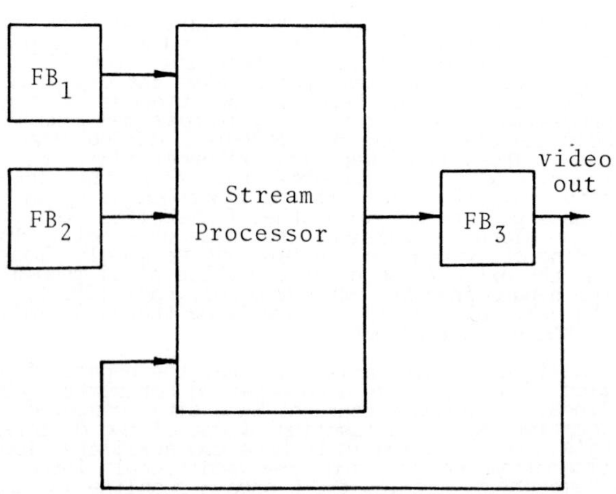

Fig.2. Stream processor.

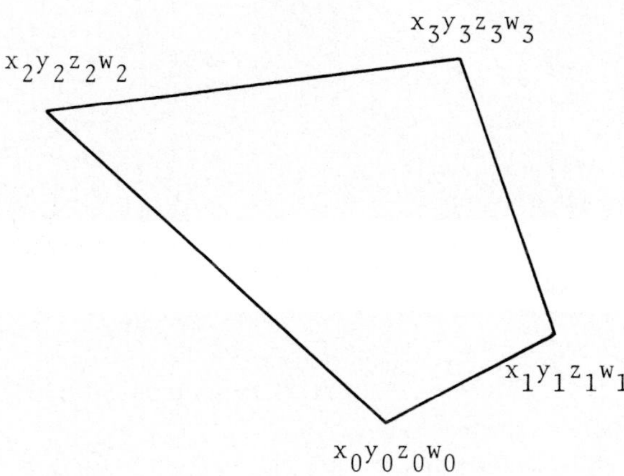

Fig.3a. Bilinear patch.

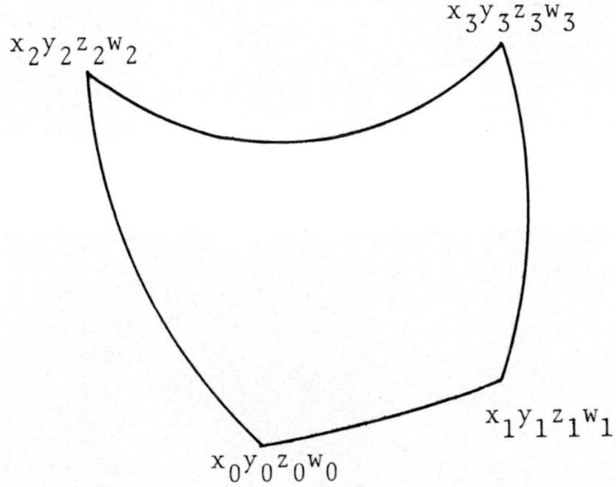

Fig.3b. Biquadratic patch.

Fig.4a. Source texture by Turner Whitted. (By permission of CACM).

Fig.4b. Simple rotate h-pass.

Fig.4c. Simple rotate v-pass.

Fig.5a. Source texture by Turner Whitted. (By permission of CACM).

Fig.5b. Simple rectangle in perspective, h-pass.

Fig.5c. Simple rectangle in perspective, v-pass.

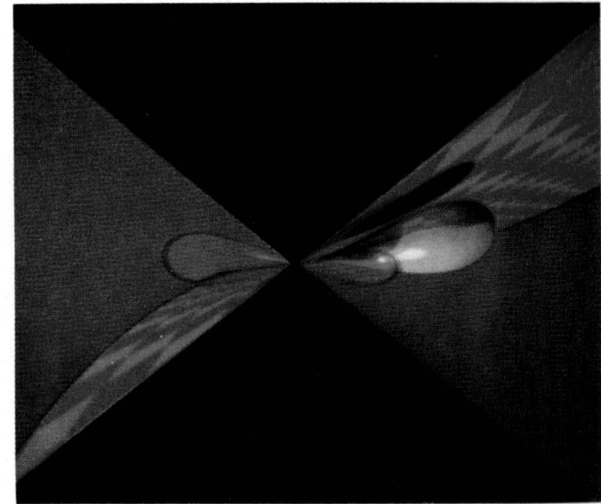

Fig.6. Planar bilinear patch twisted about midpoint.

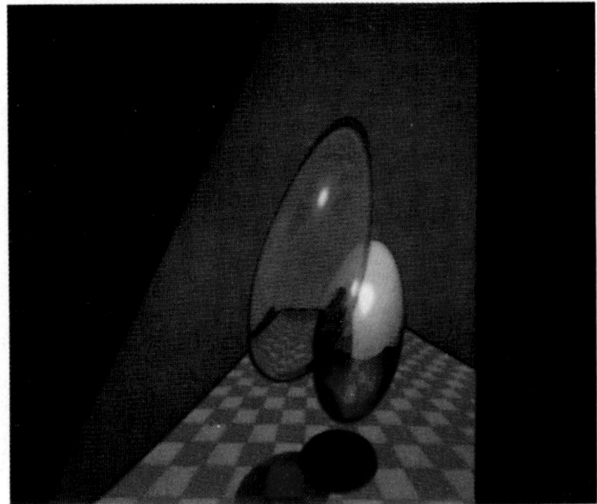

Fig.7a. Nonplanar bilinear patch h-pass.

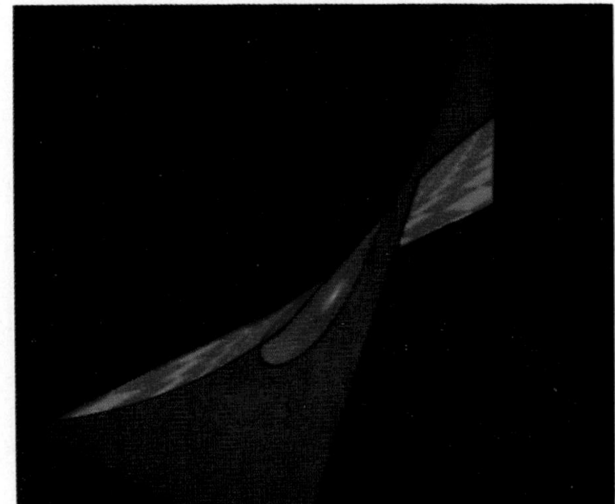

Fig.7b. Nonplanar bilinear patch v-pass.

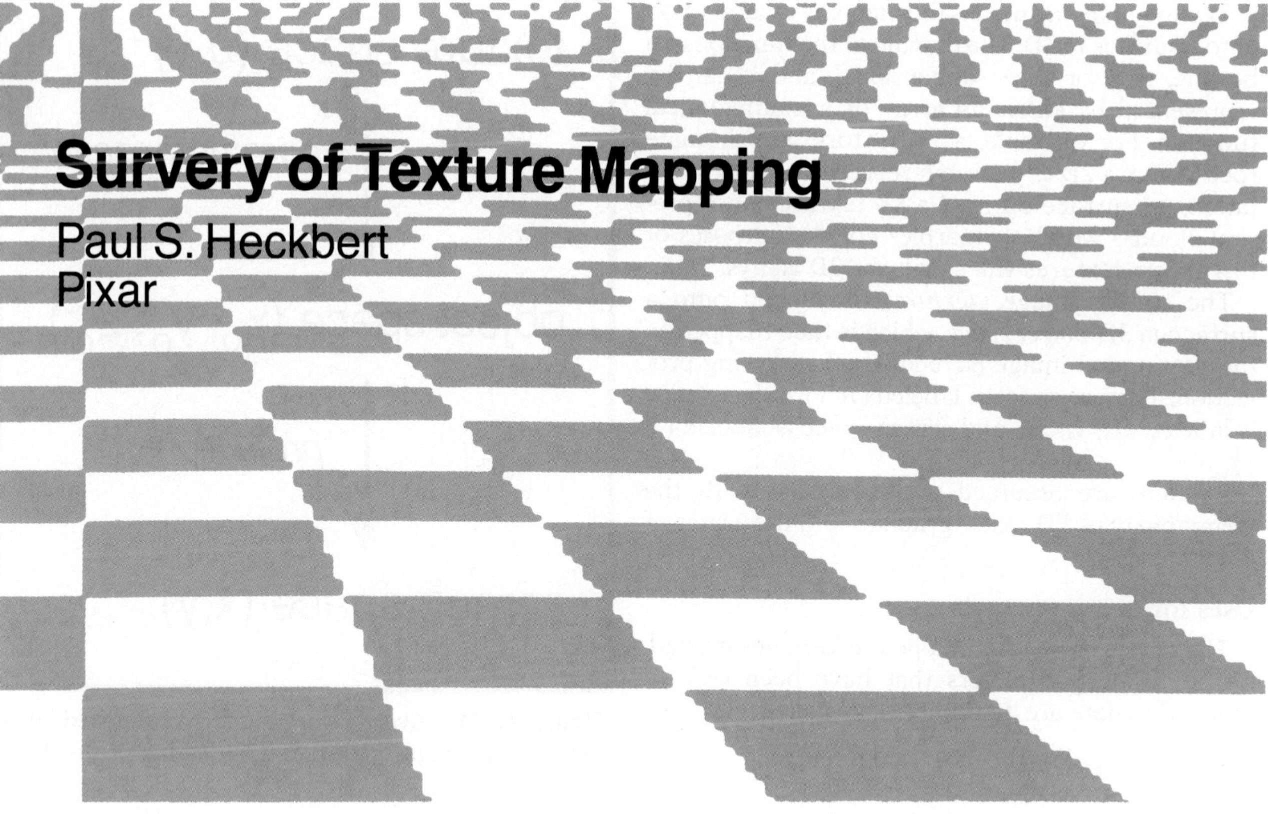

Survery of Texture Mapping

Paul S. Heckbert
Pixar

Reprinted from *IEEE Computer Graphics and Applications*, November 1986, pages 56-67.

Texture mapping is one of the most successful new techniques in high-quality image synthesis. It can enhance the visual richness of raster-scan images immensely while entailing only a relatively small increase in computation. The technique has been applied to a number of surface attributes: surface color, surface normal, specularity, transparency, illumination, and surface displacement—to name a few. Although the list is potentially endless, the techniques of texture mapping are essentially the same in all cases.

This article surveys the ,fundamentals of texture mapping, which can be split into two topics: the geometric mapping that warps a texture onto a surface, and the filtering necessary to avoid aliasing. An extensive bibliography is included.

One of the most frequent criticisms of early synthesized raster images was the extreme smoothness of surfaces: They showed no texture, bumps, scratches, dirt, or fingerprints. Realism demands complexity, or at least the appearance of complexity. Texture mapping is a relatively efficient way to create the appearance of complexity without the tedium of modeling and rendering every 3D detail of a surface.

An earlier version of this article appeared in *Proc. Graphics Interface 86*.

Overview of texture mapping

The study of texture mapping is valuable because its methods are applicable throughout computer graphics and image processing. Geometric mappings are relevant to the modeling of parametric surfaces in CAD and to general 2D image distortions for image restoration and artistic uses. The study of texture filtering leads to the development of space-variant filters, which are useful for image processing, artistic effects, depth-of-field simulation, and motion blur.

Definitions

A *texture* is defined rather loosely: It can be a texture in the usual sense (cloth, wood, gravel)—a detailed pattern repeated many times to tile the plane—or, more generally, it can be a multidimensional image mapped to a multidimensional space. The latter definition encompasses nontiling images such as billboards and paintings.

Texture mapping means the mapping of a function onto a surface in 3D. The domain of the function can be one, two, or three dimensional, and it can be represented by either an array or a mathematical function. For example, a 1D texture can simulate rock strata; a 2D texture can represent waves, vegetation,[1] or surface bumps;[2] a 3D texture can represent clouds,[3] wood,[4] or marble.[5] For the purposes of this article, textures will usually be 2D arrays.

The source image (*texture*) is mapped onto a surface in 3D *object space*, which is then mapped to the destination image (screen) by the viewing projection. Texture space is labeled (u, v), object space is labeled (x_o, y_o, z_o), and screen space is labeled (x, y).

Readers are assumed to be familiar with the terminology of 3D raster graphics and the issues of antialiasing.[6,7]

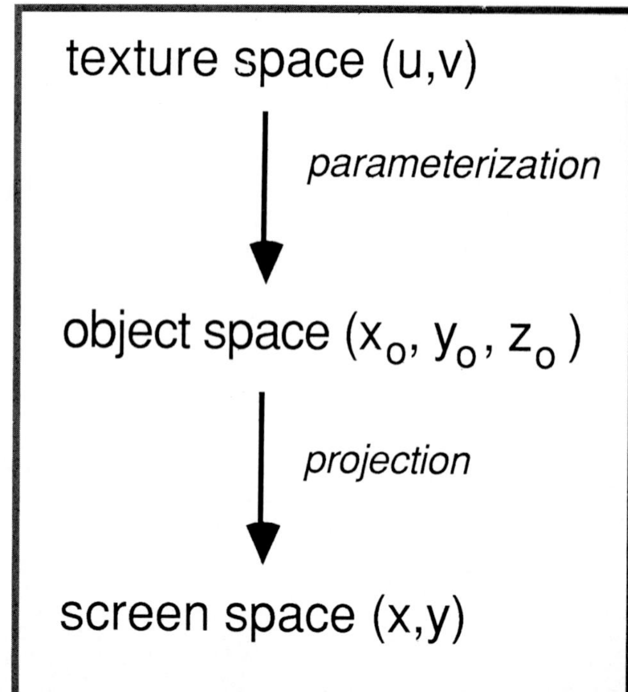

Figure 1. The overall mapping is composed of a surface parameterization and a viewing projection.

Uses for texture mapping

The possible uses for mapped texture are myriad. Some of the parameters that have been texture mapped to date are, in roughly chronological order,

- surface color (the most common use)[8]
- specular reflection[9]
- normal vector perturbation ("bump mapping")[10]
- specularity (the glossiness coefficient)[11]
- transparency[3]
- diffuse reflection[12]
- shadows, surface displacement, and mixing coefficients[13]
- local coordinate system ("frame mapping")[14]

The focus in this article is on the computational aspects of texturing—those tasks common to all types of texture mapping. I will not attempt a thorough survey of the optical and semantic implications of texturing, a careful review of which is available.[15] However, one type of texture mapping—illumination mapping—warrants particular attention.

Illumination mapping is the mapping of specular or diffuse reflection. It is also known as reflection mapping or environment mapping. Mapping illumination is rather different from mapping other parameters, since an illumination map is not associated with a particular object in the scene but with an imaginary infinite-radius sphere, cylinder, or cube surrounding the scene.[16] Whereas standard texture maps are indexed by the surface parameters u and v, a specular reflection map is indexed by the reflected ray direction,[9] and a diffuse reflection map is indexed by the surface normal direction.[12] The technique can be generalized for transparency as well, indexing by the refracted ray direction.[17] In the special case that all surfaces have the same reflectance and are viewed orthographically, the total reflected intensity is a function of surface orientation only, so the diffuse and specular maps can be merged into one.[18] Efficient filtering is especially important for illumination mapping, where high surface curvature often requires that broad areas of the sky be averaged.

Illumination mapping facilitates the simulation of complex lighting environments, since the time required to shade a point is independent of the number of light sources. There are other reasons for its recent popularity: It is one of the few demonstrated techniques for antialiasing highlights,[19] and it is an inexpensive approximation to ray tracing for mirror reflection and to radiosity methods[20] for diffuse reflection of objects in the environment.

Mapping

The mapping from texture space to screen space is split into two phases, as shown in Figure 1. First is the surface parameterization that maps texture space to object space, followed by the standard modeling and viewing transformations that map object space to screen space, typically with a perspective projection.[7] These two mappings are composed to find the overall 2D texture space to 2D screen space mapping, and the intermediate 3D space is often forgotten. This simplification suggests texture mapping's close ties with image warping and geometric distortion.

Scanning order

There are three general approaches to drawing a texture-mapped surface: a scan in screen space, a scan in texture space, and two-pass methods. The three algorithms are outlined below:

```
SCREEN SCANNING:
  for y
    for x
      compute u(x,y) and v(x,y)
      copy TEX[u,v] to SCR[x,y]

TEXTURE SCANNING:
  for v
    for u
      compute x(u,v) and y(u,v)
      copy TEX[u,v] to SCR[x,y]

TWO-PASS:
  for v
    for u
      compute x(u,v)
      copy TEX[u,v] to TEMP[x,v]
  for x
    for v
      compute y(x,v)
      copy TEMP[x,v] to SCR[x,y]
```

where TEX is the texture array, SCR is the screen array, and TEMP is a temporary array. Note that copying pixels involves filtering.

Screen order, sometimes called inverse mapping, is the most common method. For each pixel in screen space, the pre-image of the pixel in texture space is found and this area is filtered. This method is preferable when the screen must be written sequentially (for example, when output is going to a film recorder), the mapping is readily invertible, and the texture is random access.

Texture order may seem simpler than screen order, since inverting the mapping is unnecessary, but doing texture order correctly requires subtlety. Unfortunately, uniform sampling of texture space does not guarantee uniform sampling of screen space except for affine (linear) mappings. Thus, for nonaffine mappings texture subdivision must often be done adaptively; otherwise holes or overlaps will result in screen space. Scanning the texture is preferable when the texture-to-screen mapping is difficult to invert, or when the texture image must be read sequentially (for example, from tape) and will not fit in random access memory.

Two-pass methods decompose a 2D mapping into two 1D mappings, with the first pass applied to the rows of an image and the second pass applied to the columns.[21] These methods work particularly well for affine and perspective mappings, where the warps for each pass are linear or rational linear functions. Because the mapping and filter are 1D, they are amenable to stream-processing techniques such as pipelining. Two-pass methods are preferable when the source image cannot be accessed randomly but has rapid row and column access, and when a buffer for the intermediate image is available.

Parameterization

Mapping a 2D texture onto a surface in 3D requires a parameterization of the surface. This comes naturally for surfaces that are defined parametrically, such as bicubic patches, but less naturally for other surfaces such as polygons and quadrics, which are usually defined implicitly. The parameterization can be by surface coordinates u and v, as in standard texture mapping; by the direction of a normal vector or light ray, as in illumination mapping; or by spatial coordinates x_o, y_o, and z_o, for objects that should look as if they have been carved out of a solid material. Solid textures can be modeled using arbitrary 3D functions[5] or by sweeping a 2D function through space.[4,22]

Parameterizing planes and polygons

Let's focus our attention on the simplest surfaces for texture mapping: planar polygons. First we will look at the parameterization, and later at the composite mapping.

A triangle is easily parameterized by specifying the texture space coordinates (u, v) at each of its three vertices. This defines an affine mapping between texture space and 3D object space; each of x_o, y_o, and z_o has the form $Au + Bv + C$. For polygons with more than three sides, nonlinear functions are needed in general, and one must decide whether the flexibility is worth the expense. The alternative is to assume linear parameterizations and subdivide into triangles where necessary.

One nonlinear parameterization that is sometimes used is the bilinear patch:

$$[x_o \;\; y_o \;\; z_o] = [uv \;\; u \;\; v \;\; 1] \begin{bmatrix} A & E & I \\ B & F & J \\ C & G & K \\ D & H & L \end{bmatrix}$$

which maps rectangles to planar or nonplanar quadrilaterals.[23] This parameterization has the strange property of preserving lines and equal spacing along vertical and horizontal texture axes but not along diagonals. The use of this parameterization for planar quadrilaterals is not recommended, however, since inverting it requires the solution of quadratic equations.

A better parameterization for planar quadrilaterals is the "perspective mapping":[24]

$$[x_o w_o \;\; y_o w_o \;\; z_o w_o \;\; w_o] = [u \;\; v \;\; 1] \begin{bmatrix} A & D & G & J \\ B & E & H & K \\ C & F & I & L \end{bmatrix}$$

where w_o is the homogeneous coordinate that is divided through to calculate the true object-space coordinates.[7,25] Object coordinates x_o, y_o, and z_o are thus of the form $(Au + Bv + C)/(Ju + Kv + L)$. The perspective mapping preserves lines at all orientations but sacrifices equal spacing. Affine mappings are the subset of perspective matrices for which $J = K = 0$. Note that a perspective mapping might be used for the parameterization whether or not the viewing projection is perspective.

Projecting polygons

Commonly used projections are the orthographic and perspective projections.

Orthographic projection

Orthographic projections of linearly parameterized planar textures have an affine composite mapping. The inverse of this mapping, of course, is affine as well. This makes them particularly easy to scan in screen order; the cost is only two adds per pixel, disregarding filtering.[26] Affine mappings can also be performed by scanning the texture, thus producing the screen image in non-scan-line order. Most of these methods are quite ingenious.

Braccini and Marino show that by depositing the pixels of a texture scan line along the path of a Bresenham digital line, an image can be rotated or sheared.[27] To fill the holes that sometimes result between adjacent lines, they draw an extra pixel at each kink in the line. This results in some redundancy. They also use Bresenham's algorithm[7] in a totally different way: to resample an array. This is possible because distributing m source pixels to n screen pixels is analogous to drawing a line with slope n/m.

Weiman also uses Bresenham's algorithm for scaling but does not draw diagonally across the screen.[28] Instead he decomposes rotation into four scan-line operations: *x*scale, *y*scale, *x*shear, and *y*shear. He does box filtering by averaging several phases of the scaled image.

Affine mappings can be performed with multiple-pass methods in several ways. Catmull and Smith decompose such mappings into a composition of two shear-and-scale passes: one horizontal and the other vertical.[21] In a simpler variation discovered by Paeth, a rotational mapping is decomposed into three passes of shears: the first horizontal, the second vertical, and the third horizontal.[29] Filtering for this three-pass rotation is particularly simple because resampling the scan lines involves no scaling.

Perspective projection

A naive method for texture mapping in perspective is to linearly interpolate the texture coordinates u and v along the sides of the polygon and across each scan line, much as Gouraud or Phong shading[6] is done. However, linear interpolation will never give the proper effect of nonlinear foreshortening;[26] it is not rotationally invariant, and the error is obvious in animation. One solution is to subdivide each polygon into many small polygons. The correct solution, however, is to replace linear interpolation with the true formula, which requires a division at each pixel. In fact, Gouraud and Phong shading in perspective, which are usually implemented with linear interpolation, share the same problem, but the errors are so slight that they're rarely noticed.

Perspective mapping of a planar texture can be expressed using homogeneous matrix notation:[24]

$$[xw \;\; yw \;\; w] = [u \;\; v \;\; 1] \begin{bmatrix} A & D & G \\ B & E & H \\ C & F & I \end{bmatrix}$$

This mapping is analogous to the more familiar 3D perspective transformation using 4 × 4 homogeneous matrices. The inverse of this mapping (calculated using the adjoint matrix) is of the same form:

$$[uq \;\; vq \;\; q] = [x \;\; y \;\; 1] \begin{bmatrix} a & d & g \\ b & e & h \\ c & f & i \end{bmatrix} =$$

$$[x \;\; y \;\; 1] \begin{bmatrix} EI-FH & FG-DI & DH-EG \\ CH-BI & AI-CG & BG-AH \\ BF-CE & CD-AF & AE-BD \end{bmatrix}$$

The composition of two perspective mappings is also a perspective mapping. Consequently, a plane using a perspective parameterization that is viewed in perspective will have a compound mapping of the perspective form. For screen scanning we compute u and v from x and y as follows:

$$u = \frac{ax+by+c}{gx+hy+i}, \quad v = \frac{dx+ey+f}{gx+hy+i}$$

Perspective mapping simplifies to the affine form when $G = H = g = h = 0$, which occurs when the surface is parallel to the projection plane.

Aoki and Levine demonstrate texture mapping polygons in perspective using formulas equivalent to the above.[30] Smith proves that the division is necessary in general and shows how u and v can be calculated incrementally from x and y as a polygon is scanned.[26] As discussed earlier, Catmull and Smith decompose perspective mappings into two passes of shears and scales.[21] Gangnet, Perny, and Coueignoux explore an alternative decomposition that rotates screen and texture space so that the perspective occurs along one of the image axes.[31]

In "Texture Mapping Polygons in Perspective"[24] I promote the homogeneous matrix notation for perspective texture mapping and discuss techniques for scanning in screen space. Since the formulas for u and v above are quotients of linear expressions, they can be computed incrementally at a cost of three adds and two divides per screen pixel. I also discuss methods for computing the 3×3 matrices. Since they are homogeneous, all scalar multiples of these matrices are equivalent. If we arbitrarily choose $i = 1$, this leaves eight degrees of freedom. These eight values can be computed empirically by solving an 8×8 system of linear equations, which is defined by the texture and screen coordinates of four points in the plane.

Patches

Texture mapping is quite popular for surfaces modeled from patches, probably for two reasons: the parameterization comes for free, and the cost of texture mapping is small relative to the cost of patch rendering. Patches are usually rendered using a subdivision algorithm whereby screen and texture-space areas are subdivided in parallel.[8] As an alternative technique, Catmull and Smith demonstrate, theoretically at least, that it is possible to perform texture mapping on bilinear, biquadratic, and bicubic patches with two-pass algorithms.[21] Shantz, along with Fraser, Schowengerdt, and Briggs, explores a similar method for the purpose of geometric image distortions.[32,33] Two-pass algorithms require 1D space-variant texture filters.

Filtering

After the mapping is computed and the texture warped, the image must be resampled on the screen grid. This process is called filtering.

The cheapest texture filtering method is point sampling, wherein the pixel nearest the desired sample point is used. It works relatively well on unscaled images, but for stretched images the texture pixels are visible as large blocks, and for shrunken images aliasing can cause distracting moire patterns.

Aliasing

Aliasing can result when a signal has unreproducible high frequencies.[34,35] In texture mapping it is most noticeable on high-contrast, high-frequency textures. Rather than accept the aliasing that results from point sampling or avoid models that exhibit it, we prefer a high-quality, robust image-synthesis system that does the extra work required to eliminate it. In practice, total eradication of aliasing is often impractical, and we must settle for approximations that merely reduce it to unobjectionable levels.

Two approaches to the aliasing problem are (1) point sampling at higher resolution and (2) low-pass filtering before sampling.

The first method theoretically implies sampling at a resolution determined by the highest frequencies present in the image. Since a surface viewed obliquely can create arbitrarily high frequencies, this resolution can be extremely high. It is therefore desirable to limit dense supersampling to regions of high frequency and high contrast by adapting the sampling rate to the local intensity variance.[36] Whether adaptive or uniform point sampling is used, stochastic sampling can improve the appearance of images significantly by trading off aliasing for noise.[37]

The second method, low-pass filtering before sampling, is preferable because it addresses the causes of aliasing rather than its symptoms. To eliminate aliasing, our signals must be band-limited (contain no frequencies above the Nyquist limit). When a signal is warped and resampled, the following steps theoretically must be performed:[38]

1. Reconstruct continuous signal from input samples by convolution.
2. Warp the abscissa of the signal.
3. Low-pass-filter the signal using convolution.
4. Resample the signal at the output sample points.

These methods are well understood for linear warps, where the theory of linear systems lends support;[39] but for nonlinear warps such as perspective, the theory is lacking, and a number of approximate methods have sprung up.

Space-invariant filtering

For affine image warps, the filter is *space invariant;* the filter shape remains constant as it moves across the image. The four steps above can be simplified to

1. Low-pass-filter the input signal using convolution.
2. Warp the abscissa of the signal.
3. Resample the signal at the output sample points.

Space-invariant filtering is often done using an FFT, a multiply, and an inverse FFT.[39] The cost of this operation is independent of the filter size.

Space-variant filtering

Nonlinear mappings require *space-variant* filters, whose shape varies as they move across the image. Space-variant filters are more complex and less well understood than space-invariant filters.

In general, a square screen pixel that intersects a curved surface has a curvilinear quadrilateral pre-image in texture space. Most methods approximate the true mapping by the locally tangent perspective or linear mapping, so that the curvilinear pre-image is approximated by a quadrilateral or parallelogram. If pixels are regarded instead as circles, their pre-images are ellipses. This model is often simpler because an ellipse has five degrees of freedom (two for position, two for radii, and one for angle), while a quadrilateral has eight. Figure 2 shows the pre-images of several square screen pixels and illustrates how pixels near a horizon or silhouette require filtering of large, highly elongated areas. One of texture filtering's greatest challenges is finding efficient algorithms for filtering fairly general areas (such as arbitrarily oriented ellipses or quadrilaterals).

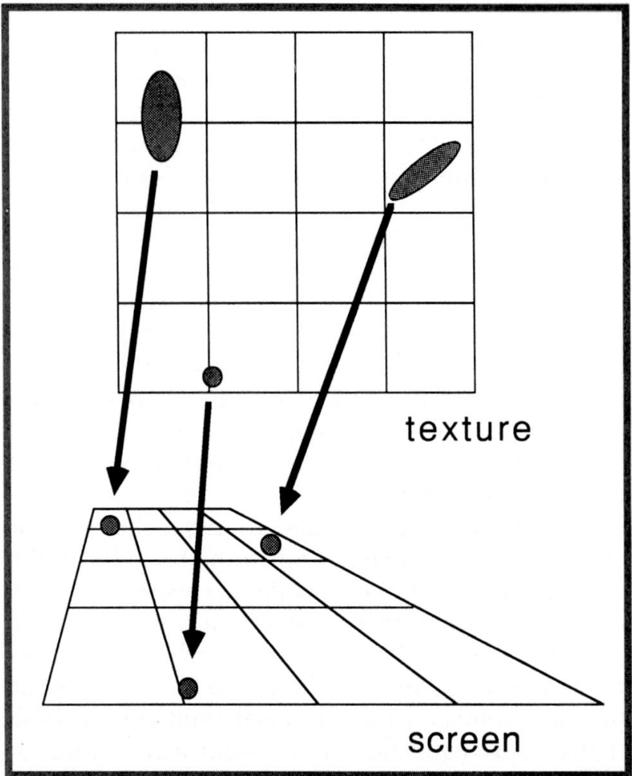

Figure 2. Corresponding areas in texture space and screen space. Circular pixels in screen space correspond to elliptical areas in texture space. Texture ellipses get very large near horizons and silhouettes.

The cross-sectional shape of the filter is also important. Theoretically we should use the ideal low-pass filter, $sinc(x) = \sin(\pi x)/\pi x$, but its infinite width makes it impractical for computation. In practice we must use a finite impulse response (FIR) filter.[39] Commonly used FIR filters are the box, the triangle, the cubic B-spline, and the truncated Gaussian (Figure 3).

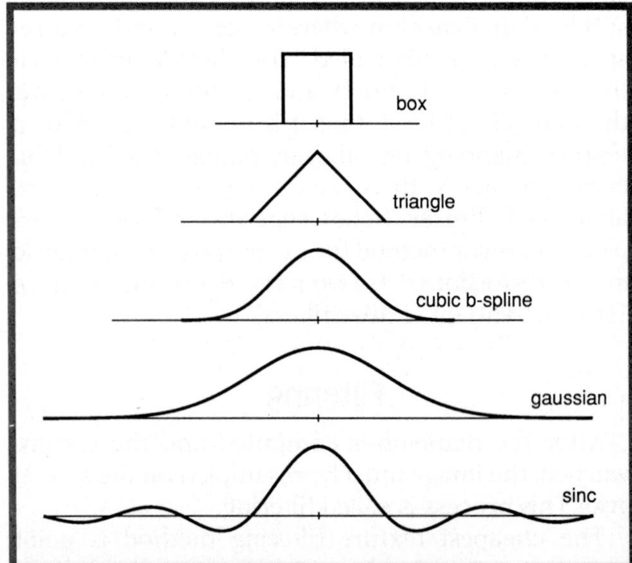

Figure 3. Cross sections of some common texture filters, ordered by quality. The top three are finite impulse response filters.

Most algorithms for texture filtering allow filtering requests to be made in arbitrary order. Such a random access capability is important for applications such as reflection mapping or ray tracing, which produce widely scattered requests.

Methods for random access space-variant filtering can be categorized as

- direct convolution
- prefiltering (pyramid or integrated array)
- Fourier series

Direct convolution

The most straightforward filtering technique is *direct convolution*, which directly computes a weighted average of texture samples. I will summarize several direct convolution methods.

Catmull, 1974

In his subdivision patch renderer, Catmull computes an unweighted average of the texture pixels corresponding to each screen pixel.[8] He gives few details, but his filter appears to be a quadrilateral with a box cross section.

Blinn and Newell, 1976

Blinn and Newell improve on this with a triangular filter that forms overlapping square pyramids two pixels wide in screen space.[9] At each pixel the pyramid is distorted to fit the approximating parallelogram in texture space, and a weighted average is computed.

Feibush, Levoy, and Cook, 1980

The filter used by Feibush, Levoy, and Cook is more elaborate.[40] The following steps are taken at each screen pixel:

1. Center the filter function (box, cylinder, cone, or Gaussian) on the pixel and find its bounding rectangle.
2. Transform the rectangle to texture space, where it is a quadrilateral. The sides of this quadrilateral are assumed to be straight. Find a bounding rectangle for this quadrilateral.
3. Map all pixels inside the texture space rectangle to screen space.
4. Form a weighted average of the mapped texture pixels using a two-dimensional lookup table indexed by each sample's location within the pixel.

Since the filter function is in a lookup table, it can be a Gaussian or other high-quality filter.

Gangnet, Perny, and Coueignoux, 1982

The texture filter proposed by Gangnet, Perny, and Coueignoux is quite similar to the method of Feibush et al., but they subdivide uniformly in screen space rather than in texture space.[31]

Pixels are assumed to be circular and overlapping. The pre-image of a screen circle is a texture ellipse whose major axis corresponds to the direction of greatest compression. A square intermediate supersampling grid oriented orthogonally to the screen is constructed. The supersampling rate is determined from the longest diagonal of the parallelogram approximating the texture ellipse. Each of the sample points on the intermediate grid is mapped to texture space, and bilinear interpolation is used to reconstruct the texture values at these sample points. The texture values are then weighted by a truncated *sinc* two pixels wide in screen space and summed.

The authors contrast Feibush's "back transforming" method with their own "direct transforming" method, claiming that the latter produces more accurate results because the sampling grid is in screen space rather than in texture space. Other differences are more significant. For example, Gangnet's method requires a bilinear interpolation for each sample point, while Feibush's does not. Also, Gangnet samples at an unnecessarily high frequency along the minor axis of the texture ellipse. For these two reasons, Feibush's algorithm is probably faster.

Greene and Heckbert, 1986

The elliptical weighted average (EWA) filter that I proposed[41] is similar to Gangnet's method in that it assumes overlapping circular pixels that map to arbitrarily oriented ellipses, and it is like Feibush's method because the filter function is stored in a lookup table. Instead of mapping texture pixels to screen space, however, the filter is mapped to texture space. The filter shape, a circularly symmetric function in screen space, is warped by an elliptic paraboloid function into an ellipse in texture space. The elliptic paraboloid is computed incrementally and used for both ellipse inclusion testing and filter table index. The cost per texture pixel is just a few arithmetic operations, in contrast to Feibush's and Gangnet's methods, which both require mapping each pixel from texture space to screen space, or vice versa.

Comparison of direct convolution methods

All five methods have a cost per screen pixel proportional to the number of texture pixels accessed, and this cost is highest for Feibush and Gangnet. Since the EWA filter is comparable in quality to these other two techniques at much lower cost, it appears to be the fastest algorithm for high-quality direct convolution.

Prefiltering

Even with optimization, the methods above are often extremely slow, since a pixel pre-image can be arbitrarily large along silhouettes or at the horizon of a textured plane. Horizon pixels can easily require the averaging of thousands of texture pixels. We would prefer a texture filter whose cost does not grow in proportion to texture area.

To speed up the process, the texture can be prefiltered so that during rendering only a few samples will be accessed for each screen pixel. The access cost of the filter will thus be constant, unlike direct convolution methods. Two data structures have been used for prefiltering: image pyramids and integrated arrays.

Pyramid data structures are commonly used in image processing and computer vision.[42,43] Their application to texture mapping was apparently first proposed in Catmull's PhD work.

Several texture filters that employ prefiltering are summarized below. Each method makes its own trade-off between speed and filter quality.

Pyramid

Dungan, Stenger, and Sutty prefilter their texture "tiles" to form a pyramid with power of 2 resolutions.[44] To filter an elliptical texture area, one of the pyramid levels is selected on the basis of the average diameter of the ellipse, and that level is point sampled. The memory cost for this type of texture pyramid is $1 + 1/4 + 1/16 + \ldots = 4/3$ times that required for an unfiltered texture. Others have used four-dimensional image pyramids which prefilter differentially in u and v to resolutions of the form $2^{\Delta u} \times 2^{\Delta v}$.

In a previously cited work I discussed Williams' trilinear interpolation scheme for pyramids (see below) and its efficient use in perspective texture mapping of polygons.[24] Choosing the pyramid level is equivalent to approximating a texture quadrilateral with a square, as shown in Figure 4a. The recommended formula for the diameter d of the square is the maximum of the side lengths of the quadrilateral. Aliasing results if the area filtered is too small, and blurring results if it's too big; one or the other is inevitable. (It is customary to err on the blurry, conservative side.)

Williams improves upon Dungan's point sampling by proposing a trilinear interpolation scheme for pyramidal images. Bilinear interpolation is performed on two levels of the pyramid, and linear interpolation is performed between them.[19] The output of this filter is thus a continuous function of position (u, v) and diameter d. His filter has a constant cost of eight pixel accesses and seven multiplies per screen pixel. Williams uses a box filter to construct the image pyramid, but Gaussian filters can also be used.[45] He also proposes a particular layout for color image pyramids called the "mip-map."

EWA on pyramid

Attempting to decouple the data structure from the access function, Greene suggests using the EWA filter on an image pyramid.[41] Unlike the other prefiltering techniques such as trilinear interpolation on a pyramid or the summed-area table, EWA allows arbitrarily oriented ellipses to be filtered, yielding higher quality.

Summed-area table

Crow proposes the summed-area table, an alternative to the pyramidal filtering of earlier methods. It allows orthogonally oriented rectangular areas to be filtered in constant time.[46] The original texture is preintegrated in the u and v directions and stored in a high-precision summed-area table. To filter a rectangular area, the table is sampled in four places (much as one evaluates a definite integral by sampling an indefinite integral). To do this without artifacts requires 16 accesses and 14 multiplies in general, but an optimization for large areas cuts the cost to four accesses and two multiplies. The high-precision table requires two to four times the memory cost of the original image.

The method was developed independently by Ferrari and Sklansky, who show how convolution with arbitrary rectilinear polygons can easily be performed using a summed-area table.[47,48]

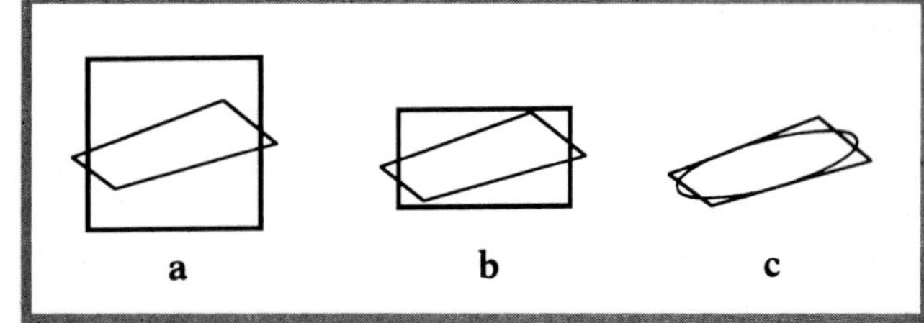

Figure 4. Approximating a quadrilateral texture area with (a) a square, (b) a rectangle, and (c) an ellipse. Too small an area causes aliasing; too large an area causes blurring.

The summed-area table is generally more costly than the texture pyramid in both memory and time, but it can perform better filtering than the pyramid, since it filters rectangular areas, not just squares, as shown in Figure 4b. Glassner has shown how the rectangle can be successively refined to approximate a quadrilateral.[49] As an optimization, he also suggests that this refinement be done only in areas of high local texture variance. To compute variance over a rectangle, he precomputes variances of 3×3 areas and forms a summed-area table of them. A more accurate method for computing rectangle variance would be to precompute summed-area tables of the texture values and their squares. Using these two tables, variance can be computed as $\sigma^2 = \Sigma x_i^2/n - (\Sigma x_i/n)^2$. Of course, accessing a variance table requires considerable overhead in time and memory.

Repeated integration filtering

This elegant generalization of the summed-area table was developed independently by Perlin and by Ferrari et al.[50-52] If an image is preintegrated in u and v n times, an orthogonally oriented elliptical area can be filtered by sampling the array at $(n + 1)^2$ points and weighting them appropriately. The effective filter is a box convolved with itself n times (an nth order B-spline) whose size can be selected at each screen pixel. If $n = 0$, the method degenerates to point sampling; if $n = 1$, it is equivalent to the summed-area table with its box filter; $n = 2$ uses a triangular filter, and $n = 3$ uses a parabolic filter. As n increases, the filter shape approaches a Gaussian, and the memory and time costs increase. The method can be generalized to arbitrary spline filters.[51] One difficulty with the method is that high-precision arithmetic (more than 32 bits) is required for $n \geq 2$.

Comparison of prefiltering methods

Table 1 summarizes the prefiltering methods I have discussed. The high-quality direct convolution

Table 1. Summary of prefiltering methods.

Method	Filter	Shape	DOF	Time	Memory
Point sampling	Impulse	Point	2	1, 0	1
Point-sampled pyramid[44]	Box	Square	3	1, 0	1.33
Trilinear interp. on pyramid[19,24]	Box	Square	3	8, 7	1.33
4D pyramid (scaling u, v)	Box	Rectangle	4	16, 15	4
EWA on pyramid[41]	Any	Ellipse	5	Unlimited?	1.33
Summed-area table[46–48]	Box	Rectangle	4	16, 14; or 4, 2	2-4
Repeated integration (order 2)[50–52]	Triangle	Rectangle	4	36, 31; or 9, 4	2-6
Direct convolution[31,40]	Any	Any	5+	Unlimited	1

methods of Feibush and Gangnet have been included at the bottom for comparison. In this table, "filter" means cross section, while "shape" is 2D filter shape. The number of degrees of freedom (DOF) of the 2D filter shape provides an approximate ranking of filter quality: the more degrees of freedom available, the greater the filter shape control. The numbers under "time" are texture pixel accesses and multiplies per screen pixel. "Memory" is the ratio of memory required relative to an unfiltered texture.

We see that the integrated-array techniques of Crow and Perlin have rather high memory costs relative to the pyramid methods, but they allow rectangular or orthogonally oriented elliptical areas to be filtered. Traditionally, pyramid techniques have lower memory cost but allow only squares to be filtered.

Since prefiltering usually entails a setup expense proportional to the square of the texture resolution, its cost is proportional to that of direct convolution—if the texture is only used once. But if the texture is used many times, as part of a periodic pattern, or if it appears on several objects or in several frames of animation, the setup cost can be amortized over each use.

Figure 5 illustrates several of these texture filters on a checkerboard in perspective, which is an excellent test of a texture filter, since it has a range of frequencies at high contrast. Note that parallel to the horizon, trilinear interpolation on a pyramid blurs excessively, but integrated arrays do not. Second-order repeated integration does just as well as EWA for vertically oriented texture ellipses (on the left of the images), but there is a striking difference between Gaussian EWA and the other prefiltering methods for ellipses at 45 degrees (on the right of the images).

Fourier series

An alternative to texture space filtering is to transform the texture to frequency space and low-pass-filter its spectrum. This is most convenient when the texture is represented by a Fourier series rather than a texture array. Norton, Rockwood, and Skolmoski explore this approach for flight simulator applications and propose a simple technique for clamping high-frequency terms.[1] Gardner employs 3D Fourier series as a transparency texture function with which he generates surprisingly convincing pictures of trees and clouds.[3]

Perlin's "image synthesizer" uses band-limited pseudorandom functions as texture primitives.[5] Creating textures in this way eases transitions from macroscopic to microscopic views of a surface. In the macroscopic range the surface characteristics are built into the scattering statistics of the illumination model; in the intermediate range they are modeled using bump mapping; and in the microscopic range the surface is explicit geometry.[2,14] Each term in the texture series can make the transition independently at a scale appropriate to its frequency range.

Filtering recommendations

The best filtering algorithm for a given task depends on the texture representation in use. When filtering a texture array, the minimal texture filter should be trilinear interpolation on a pyramid. This blurs excessively, but it eliminates most aliasing and costs little more than point sampling. Next in quality and cost are integrated arrays of order 1 (box filter) or order 2 (triangle filter). These allow elongated vertical or horizontal areas to be filtered much more accurately (resulting in less blurring at horizons and silhouettes), but blur is still excessive for elongated areas at an angle (such as an eccentric ellipse at 45 degrees). For near-perfect quality at a cost far below that of direct convolution, the EWA or similar filter on a pyramid is recommended. Its cost is not strictly bounded like that of most prefiltering methods but is proportional to ellipse eccentricity. The cost of direct convolution, meanwhile, is proportional to

Figure 5. Comparison of five texture filters.

(a) Point sampling.

(d) Second-order repeated integration.

(b) Trilinear interpolation on a pyramid.

(e) EWA filter with Gaussian cross section on a pyramid.

(c) First-order repeated integration (summed-area table).

ellipse area. Any of these methods could probably benefit from adaptive refinement according to local texture variance.[49]

In the case of arbitrary texture functions, which can be much harder to integrate than texture arrays, adaptive stochastic sampling methods are called for.[36]

Future research on texture filters will continue to improve their quality by providing greater filter shape control while retaining low time and memory costs. Researchers would like to find a constant-cost method for high-quality filtering of arbitrarily oriented areas.

System support for texture mapping

So far I have emphasized tasks common to all types of texture mapping. I will now summarize some of the special provisions a modeling and rendering system must make to support different varieties of texture mapping. I assume that the rendering program is scanning in screen space.

The primary requirements of standard texture mapping are texture space coordinates (u, v) for each screen pixel plus the partial derivatives of u and v with respect to screen x and y for good antialiasing. If the analytic formulas for these partials are not available, they can be approximated by differencing the u and v of neighboring pixels.

Bump mapping requires additional information at each pixel: two vectors tangent to the surface pointing in the u and v directions. For facet-shaded polygons, these tangents are constant across the polygon, but for Phong-shaded polygons they vary. To ensure artifact-free bump mapping on Phong-shaded polygons, these tangents must be continuous across polygon seams. One way to guarantee this is to compute tangents at all polygon vertices during model preparation and interpolate them across the polygon. The normal vector can be computed as the cross product of the tangents.

Proper antialiasing of illumination mapping requires some measure of surface curvature to calculate the solid angle of sky to filter. This is usually provided in the form of the partials of the normal vector with respect to screen space. When direct rendering support for illumination mapping is unavailable, however, tricks can be employed that give a visually acceptable approximation. Rather than calculate the exact ray direction at each pixel, one can compute the reflected or refracted ray direction at polygon vertices only and interpolate it, in the form of u and v texture indices, across the polygon using standard methods.

Although texture maps are usually much more compact than brute-force 3D modeling of surface details, they can be bulky, especially when they represent a high-resolution image as opposed to a low-resolution texture pattern replicated many times. Keeping several of these in random access memory is often a burden on the rendering program. This problem is especially acute for rendering algorithms that generate the image in scan-line order rather than in object order, since a given scan line could access hundreds of texture maps. Further work is needed on memory management for texture map access.

Summary

Texture mapping has become widely used because of its generality and efficiency. It has even made its way into everyday broadcast TV, thanks to new real-time video texture mapping hardware such as the Ampex ADO and Quantel Mirage. Rendering systems of the near future will allow any conceivable surface parameter to be texture mapped. Despite the recent explosion of diverse applications for texture mapping, a common set of fundamental concepts and algorithms is emerging. I have surveyed a number of these fundamentals: alternative techniques for parameterization, scanning, texture representation, direct convolution, and prefiltering. Further work is needed on quantifying texture filter quality and collecting theoretical and practical comparisons of various methods. ■

Acknowledgments

My introduction to textures came while mapping Aspen's facades for Walter Bender's Quick and Dirty Animation System at the Massachusetts Institute of Technology's Architecture Machine Group; we learned the hard way that point sampling and linear u, v aren't good enough. I did most of the research that evolved into this article while at the New York Institute of Technology's Computer Graphics Lab, where Pat Hanrahan and Mike Chou contributed many ideas, and Ned Greene, Jules Bloomenthal, and Lance Williams supplied the cheeseburger incentives. Thanks also to Rob Cook at Pixar for his encouragement, and to all the good folks at Pacific Data Images.

References

Recommended reading: Rogers' book[6] is an excellent introduction to image synthesis. For a good introduction to texture mapping, see Blinn and Newell's paper.[9] Smith[38] provides a helpful theoretical/intuitive introduction to digital image filtering, and Feibush et al.[40] describe texture filtering in detail. Two-pass methods are described by Catmull and Smith.[21] The best references on bump mapping and illumination mapping are by Blinn[10] and Miller and Hoffman,[12] respectively. Systems aspects of texture mapping are discussed by Cook[13] and Perlin.[5]

1. Alan Norton, Alyn P. Rockwood, and Philip T. Skolmoski, "Clamping: A Method of Antialiasing Textured Surfaces by Bandwidth Limiting in Object Space," *Computer Graphics* (Proc. SIGGRAPH 82), Vol. 16, No. 3, July 1982, pp.1-8.
2. Ken Perlin, "A Unified Texture/Reflectance Model," *SIGGRAPH 84: Advanced Image Synthesis Seminar Notes*, July 1984.
3. Geoffrey Y. Gardner, "Visual Simulation of Clouds," *Computer Graphics* (Proc. SIGGRAPH 85), Vol. 19, No. 3, July 1985, pp.297-303.
4. Darwyn R. Peachey, "Solid Texturing of Complex Surfaces," *Computer Graphics* (Proc. SIGGRAPH 85), Vol. 19, No. 3, July 1985, pp.279-286.
5. Ken Perlin, "An Image Synthesizer," *Computer Graphics* (Proc. SIGGRAPH 85), Vol. 19, No. 3, July 1985, pp.287-296.
6. David F. Rogers, *Procedural Elements for Computer Graphics*, McGraw-Hill, New York, 1985.
7. James D. Foley and Andries van Dam, *Fundamentals of Interactive Computer Graphics*, Addison-Wesley, Reading, Mass., 1982.
8. Ed Catmull, "A Subdivision Algorithm for Computer Display of Curved Surfaces," PhD thesis, Univ. of Utah, Dec. 1974.
9. James F. Blinn and Martin E. Newell, "Texture and Reflection in Computer Generated Images," *Comm. ACM*, Vol. 19, No. 10, Oct. 1976, pp.542-547.
10. James F. Blinn, "Simulation of Wrinkled Surfaces," *Computer Graphics* (Proc. SIGGRAPH 78), Vol. 12, No. 3, Aug. 1978, pp.286-292.
11. James F. Blinn, "Computer Display of Curved Surfaces," PhD thesis, Univ. of Utah, 1978.
12. Gene S. Miller and C. Robert Hoffman, "Illumination and Reflection Maps: Simulated Objects in Simulated and Real Environments," *SIGGRAPH 84: Advanced Computer Graphics Animation Seminar Notes*, July 1984.
13. Robert L. Cook, "Shade Trees," *Computer Graphics* (Proc. SIGGRAPH 84), Vol. 18, No. 3, July 1984, pp.223-231.
14. James T. Kajiya, "Anisotropic Reflection Models," *Computer Graphics* (Proc. SIGGRAPH 85), Vol. 19, No. 3, July 1985, pp.15-21.
15. Richard J. Carey and Donald P. Greenberg, "Textures for Realistic Image Synthesis," *Computers and Graphics*, Vol. 9, No. 2, 1985, pp.125-138.
16. Ned Greene, "Environment Mapping and Other Applications of World Projections," *IEEE CG&A*, Vol. 6, No. 11, Nov. 1986, pp.21-29. An earlier version appeared in *Proc. Graphics Interface 86*, May 1986, pp.108-114.
17. Douglas S. Kay and Donald P. Greenberg, "Transparency for Computer Synthesized Images," *Computer Graphics* (Proc. SIGGRAPH 79), Vol. 13, No. 3, Aug. 1979, pp.158-164.

18. Berthold K.P. Horn, "Hill Shading and the Reflectance Map," *Proc. IEEE,* Vol. 69, No. 1, Jan. 1981, pp.14-47.

19. Lance Williams, "Pyramidal Parametrics," *Computer Graphics* (Proc. SIGGRAPH 83), Vol. 17, No. 3, July 1983, pp.1-11.

20. Cindy M. Goral et al., "Modeling the Interaction of Light Between Diffuse Surfaces," *Computer Graphics* (Proc. SIGGRAPH 84), Vol. 18, No. 3, July 1984, pp.213-222.

21. Ed Catmull and Alvy Ray Smith, "3D Transformations of Images in Scanline Order," *Computer Graphics* (Proc. SIGGRAPH 80), Vol. 14, No. 3, July 1980, pp.279-285.

22. Eric A. Bier and Kenneth R. Sloan, Jr., "Two-Part Texture Mappings," *IEEE CG&A,* Vol. 6, No. 9, Sept. 1986, pp.40-53.

23. J.C. Hourcade and A. Nicolas, "Inverse Perspective Mapping in Scanline Order onto Non-Planar Quadrilaterals," *Eurographics 83,* pp.309-319.

24. Paul S. Heckbert, "Texture Mapping Polygons in Perspective," Tech. Memo No. 13, NYIT Computer Graphics Lab, Apr. 1983.

25. Lawrence G. Roberts, "Homogeneous Matrix Representation and Manipulation of N-Dimensional Constructs," MS-1045, Lincoln Lab, Lexington, Mass., July 1966.

26. Alvy Ray Smith, "Incremental Rendering of Textures in Perspective," *SIGGRAPH 80: Animation Graphics Seminar Notes,* July 1980.

27. Carlo Braccini and Giuseppe Marino, "Fast Geometrical Manipulations of Digital Images," *Computer Graphics and Image Processing,* Vol. 13, 1980, pp.127-141.

28. Carl F.R. Weiman, "Continuous Anti-Aliased Rotation and Zoom of Raster Images," *Computer Graphics* (Proc. SIGGRAPH 80), Vol. 14, No. 3, July 1980, pp.286-293.

29. Alan W. Paeth, "A Fast Algorithm for General Raster Rotation," *Graphics Interface 86,* May 1986, pp.77-81.

30. Masayoshi Aoki and Martin D. Levine, "Computer Generation of Realistic Pictures," *Computers and Graphics,* Vol. 3, 1978, pp.149-161.

31. Michel Gangnet, Didier Perny, and Philippe Coueignoux, "Perspective Mapping of Planar Textures," *Eurographics 82,* pp.57-71 (slightly superior to the version that appeared in *Computer Graphics,* Vol. 16, No. 1, May 1982).

32. Michael Shantz, "Two Pass Warp Algorithm for Hardware Implementation," *Proc. SPIE, Processing and Display of Three Dimensional Data,* Vol. 367, 1982, pp.160-164.

33. Donald Fraser, Robert A. Schowengerdt, and Ian Briggs, "Rectification of Multichannel Images in Mass Storage Using Image Transposition," *Computer Vision, Graphics, and Image Processing,* Vol. 29, No. 1, Jan. 1985, pp.23-36.

34. Franklin C. Crow, "The Aliasing Problem in Computer-Generated Shaded Images," *Comm. ACM,* Vol. 20, Nov. 1977, pp.799-805.

35. Turner Whitted, "The Causes of Aliasing in Computer Generated Images," *SIGGRAPH 81: Advanced Image Synthesis Seminar Notes,* Aug. 1981.

36. Mark E. Lee, Richard A. Redner, and Samuel P. Uselton, "Statistically Optimized Sampling for Distributed Ray Tracing," *Computer Graphics* (Proc. SIGGRAPH 85), Vol. 19, No. 3, July 1985, pp.61-67.

37. Robert L. Cook, "Antialiasing by Stochastic Sampling," *ACM Trans. Graphics,* 1986, to appear.

38. Alvy Ray Smith, "Digital Filtering Tutorial for Computer Graphics," parts 1 and 2, *SIGGRAPH 83: Introduction to Computer Animation Seminar Notes,* July 1983, pp.244-261, 262-272.

39. Alan V. Oppenheim and Ronald W. Schafer, *Digital Signal Processing,* Prentice-Hall, Englewood Cliffs, N.J., 1975.

40. Eliot A. Feibush, Marc Levoy, and Robert L. Cook, "Synthetic Texturing Using Digital Filters," *Computer Graphics* (Proc. SIGGRAPH 80), Vol. 14, No. 3, July 1980, pp.294-301.

41. Ned Greene and Paul S. Heckbert, "Creating Raster Omnimax Images from Multiple Perspective Views Using the Elliptical Weighted Average Filter," *IEEE CG&A,* Vol. 6, No. 6, June 1986, pp.21-27.

42. S.L. Tanimoto and Theo Pavlidis, "A Hierarchical Data Structure for Picture Processing," *Computer Graphics and Image Processing,* Vol. 4, No. 2, June 1975, pp.104-119.

43. A. Rosenfeld, *Multiresolution Image Processing and Analysis,* Springer-Verlag, Berlin, 1984.

44. William Dungan, Jr., Anthony Stenger, and George Sutty, "Texture Tile Considerations for Raster Graphics," *Computer Graphics* (Proc. SIGGRAPH 78), Vol. 12, No. 3, Aug. 1978, pp.130-134.

45. Peter J. Burt, "Fast Filter Transforms for Image Processing," *Computer Graphics and Image Processing,* Vol. 16, 1981, pp.20-51.

46. Franklin C. Crow, "Summed-Area Tables for Texture Mapping," *Computer Graphics* (Proc. SIGGRAPH 84), Vol. 18, No. 3, July 1984, pp.207-212.

47. Leonard A. Ferrari and Jack Sklansky, "A Fast Recursive Algorithm for Binary-Valued Two-Dimensional Filters," *Computer Vision, Graphics, and Image Processing,* Vol. 26, No. 3, June 1984, pp.292-302.

48. Leonard A. Ferrari and Jack Sklansky, "A Note on Duhamel Integrals and Running Average Filters," *Computer Vision, Graphics, and Image Processing,* Vol. 29, Mar. 1985, pp. 358-360.

49. Andrew S. Glassner, "Adaptive Precision in Texture Mapping," *Computer Graphics* (Proc. SIGGRAPH 86), Vol. 20, No. 4, Aug. 1986, pp.297-306.

50. Kenneth Perlin, "Course Notes," *SIGGRAPH 85: State of the Art in Image Synthesis Seminar Notes,* July 1985, pp.297-300.

51. Paul S. Heckbert, "Filtering by Repeated Integration," *Computer Graphics* (Proc. SIGGRAPH 86), Vol. 20, No. 4, Aug. 1986, pp.317-321.

52. Leonard A. Ferrari et al., "Efficient Two-Dimensional Filters Using B-Spline Approximations," *Computer Vision, Graphics, and Image Processing,* to appear.

Paul S. Heckbert is currently doing animation research and development at Pixar in San Rafael, California. From 1980 to 1985 he was software manager at the New York Institute of Technology's Computer Graphics Lab. His research interests include mathematical modeling, simulation of nature, image synthesis, and image processing.

Heckbert received a BS in applied mathematics from the Massachusetts Institute of Technology in 1980 while learning computer graphics at MIT's Architecture Machine Group. He is a member of ACM SIGGRAPH.

The author can be contacted at Pixar, PO Box 13719, San Rafael, CA 94913.

"An Image Synthesizer" by K. Perlin from *Proceedings of SIGGRAPH '85*, 1985, pages 287-296. Copyright 1985, Association for Computing Machinery, Inc., reprinted by permission.

An Image Synthesizer

Ken Perlin

Courant Institute of Mathematical Sciences
New York University

Abstract

We introduce the concept of a Pixel Stream Editor. This forms the basis for an interactive synthesizer for designing highly realistic Computer Generated Imagery. The designer works in an interactive Very High Level programming environment which provides a very fast concept/implement/view iteration cycle.

Naturalistic visual complexity is built up by composition of non-linear functions, as opposed to the more conventional texture mapping or growth model algorithms. Powerful primitives are included for creating controlled stochastic effects. We introduce the concept of "solid texture" to the field of CGI.

We have used this system to create very convincing representations of clouds, fire, water, stars, marble, wood, rock, soap films and crystal. The algorithms created with this paradigm are generally extremely fast, highly realistic, and asynchronously parallelizable at the pixel level.

CR CATEGORIES AND SUBJECT DESCRIPTORS: I.3.5 [Computer Graphics]: Three-Dimensional Graphics and Realism

ADDITIONAL KEYWORDS AND PHRASES: pixel stream editor, interactive, algorithm development, functional composition, space function, stochastic modelling, solid texture, fire, waves, turbulence

Introduction

This work arose out of some experiments into developing efficient naturalistic looking textures. Several years ago we developed a simple way of creating well behaved stochastic functions. We found that combinations of such functions yielded a remarkably rich set of visual textures. We soon found it cumbersome to continually rewrite, recompile, and rerun programs in order to try out different function combinations.

This motivated the development of a Pixel Stream Editing language (PSE). Cook [1] has proposed an expression parser for this purpose. We have taken the same idea somewhat farther by providing an entire high level programming language available at the pixel level. Unlike [1], The PSE contains general flow of control structures, allowing arbitrarily asynchronous operations at different pixels.

With the PSE we may interactively compose functions defined over modelling space. By starting with the right choice of primitive functions we can build up some rather convincing naturalistic detail with surprisingly simple and efficient algorithms.

We will first describe the PSE language and environment. Then we will introduce the concept of *solid texture*, together with our well behaved stochastic functions. Finally we will give some examples of how these concepts work together in actual practice.

A Pixel Stream Editing Language

Consider any list of variable names. We will call any list of corresponding values for these variables a "pixel". For example, one possible pixel for the variable list [red green blue] is [0.5 0.3 0.7]. We will call any list of names together with a two dimensional array of pixels an "image".

A Pixel Stream Editor (PSE) is simply a filter which converts input images to output images by running the same program at every pixel. We always read and write image pixels in some canonical order. At any one pixel, all that the program "knows" about each image are its variable names and their current values.

The PSE we have designed has a rather high level language. All of the familiar programming constructs are supported, including conditional and looping control structures, function procedure definitions, and a full compliment of arithmetic and logical operators and mathematical functions. Assignment and the equality operator are denoted by "=" and "==", respectively, as in the C programming language [2]. For any infix operator *op*, *a op= b* denotes *a = a op b*.

Variables may be scalars, or else vectors of scalars and/or vectors (recursively). Typing is implicit, determined by assignment. Program blocks are indicated by indenting. All operators will work on scalars or vectors. For example $a+b$ is a scalar sum if a and b are scalars, and a vector sum if a and b are vectors.

The following simple example will illustrate. Suppose the input image contains the variable list [surface point normal], where *surface* is a surface identifier, *point* is the location in space of the surface visible at this pixel, and *normal* is the surface normal direction at *point*. This image in particular would generally be the output of some visible surface finding algorithm.

Let the output image consist of [color]. If we interpret color as a [red green blue] vector, then the procedure :

```
if surface == 1
      color = [1 0 0] * max(0.1, dot(normal, [1 0 0]))
else
      color = [0 0 0.1]
```

will produce an image of a diffusely shaded red object lit from the positive x direction against a dark blue background. The function "*dot*()" is simply a built in function returning the dot product of two vectors.

Spotted Donut

Bumpy Donut

Stucco Donut

Disgusting Donut

Bozo's Donut

Wrinkled Donut

Note that in the above example, "[1 0 0]" is used in one place to denote the color red, and in another to denote a direction in space. Such looseness and ambiguity was a deliberate design decision in creating the language. In using the system we obtained some of the most striking visual effects only by stepping over (real or imagined) semantic distinctions.

We find that the PSE is most useful as a design tool when used as interactively as possible. For this reason we have placed it in an interactive design cycle :

1. Edit PSE program
2. Run it on a *low* resolution image
3. View the results on a color monitor

Design resolution is generally chosen to allow a design cycle time of under one minute.

Space Functions and Solid Texture

A number of researchers have proposed procedural texture, notably [3], [5], and [6]. As far as we know all prior work in this direction has been with functions which vary over a two dimensional domain.

Suppose we extend this to functions which vary over a three dimensional domain. We call any function whose domain is the entirety of (x,y,z) space a "space function".

Any space function may be thought of as representing a solid material. If we evaluate this function at the visible surface points of an object then we will obtain the surface texture that would have occured had we "sculpted" the object out of the material. We will call a texture so formed a "solid texture".

This approach has several advantages over texture mapping :

1. Shape and texture become independent. The texture does not need to be "fit" onto the surface. If we change the shape or carve a piece out of it, the appearance of the solid material will accurately change.

2. As with all procedural textures, the database is extremely small.

Although it is not immediately obvious, this paradigm is a superset of conventional texture mapping techniques. Any stored texture algorithm may be cast as a table lookup function composed with a projection function from three dimensions to two.

We will use solid texture repeatedly over the course of this paper to simulate a variety of materials.

Noise()

In order to get the most out of the PSE and the solid texture approach we have provided some primitive stochastic functions with which to bootstrap visual complexity. We now introduce the most fundamental of these.

Noise() is a scalar valued function which takes a three dimensional vector as its argument. It has the following properties :

Statistical invariance under rotation
(no matter how we rotate its domain,
it has the same statistical character)

A narrow bandpass limit in frequency
(its has no visible features larger or smaller
than within a certain narrow size range)

Statistical invariance under translation
(no matter how we translate its domain,
it has the same statistical character)

Noise() is a good texture modeling primitive since we may use it in a straightforward manner to create surfaces with desired stochastic characteristics at different visual scales, without losing control over the effects of rotation, scaling, and translation. This works well with the human vision system, which tends to analyze incoming images in terms of levels of differently sized detail [4].

The author has developed a number of surprisingly different implementations of the *Noise*() function. Some real tradeoffs are involved between time, storage space, algorithmic complexity, and adherence to the three defining statistical constraints.

Because of space limitations, we will describe only the simplest such technique. Although generally adequate, this procedure only approximately conforms to the bandwidth and rotational invariance constraints.

1. Consider the set of all points in space whose x, y, and z coordinates are all integer valued. We call this set the *integer lattice*.

   Associate with each point in the integer lattice a pseudo-random value and x, y, and z gradient values. More precisely, map each ordered sequence of three integers into an uncorrelated ordered sequence of four real numbers: $[a,b,c,d] = H([x,y,z])$, where $[a,b,c,d]$ define a linear equation with gradient $[a,b,c]$ and value d at $[x,y,z]$. $H()$ is best implemented as a hash function.

2. If $[x,y,z]$ is on the integer lattice, we define $Noise([x,y,z]) = d_{[x,y,z]}$.

   If $[x,y,z]$ is not on the integer lattice we compute a smooth (eg. cubic polynomial) interpolation between lattice equation coefficients, applied first in x (along lattice edges), then in y (within lattice z-faces), then in z. We then evaluate this interpolated linear equation at $[x,y,z]$.

We will now show some of the simpler uses of *Noise*(). We will assume that "*point*" and "*normal*" are vector valued input image variables.

By evaluating *Noise*() at visible surface points of simulated objects we may create a simple "random" surface texture (figure Spotted.Donut) :

```
color = white * Noise(point)
```

The above texture has a band-limited character to it; there is no detail outside of a certain range of size. This is equivalent to saying that the texture's frequency spectrum falls off away from some central peak frequency.

Through functional composition we may do many different things with the value returned by the *Noise*() function. For example, we might wish to map different ranges of values into different colors (figure Bozo's.Donut) :

```
color = Colorful(Noise(k * point))
```

In the above example we have scaled the texture by multiplying the domain of *Noise*() by a constant *k*. An nice feature of the functional composition approach is the ease with which such modifications may be made.

Another convenient primitive is the vector valued differential of the *Noise*() signal, defined by the instantaneous rate of change of *Noise*() along the x, y, and z directions, respectively. We will call this function *Dnoise*().

Water Crystal

Art Glass

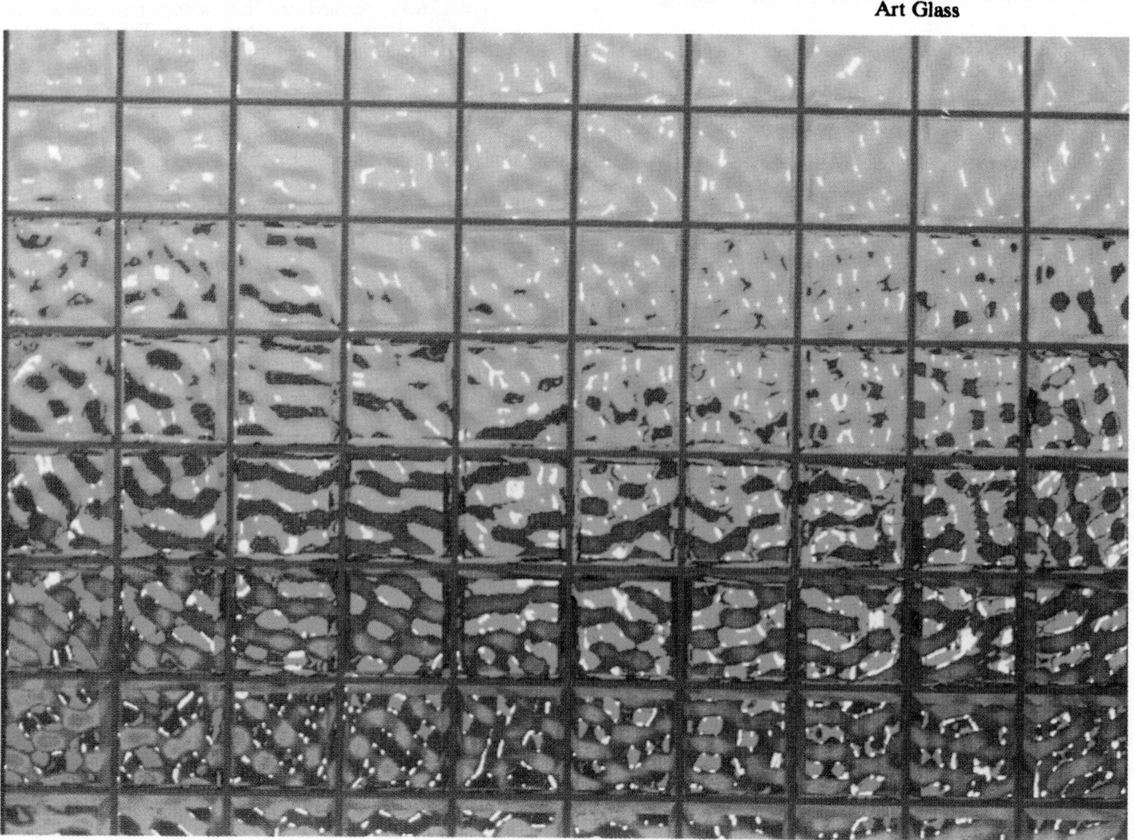

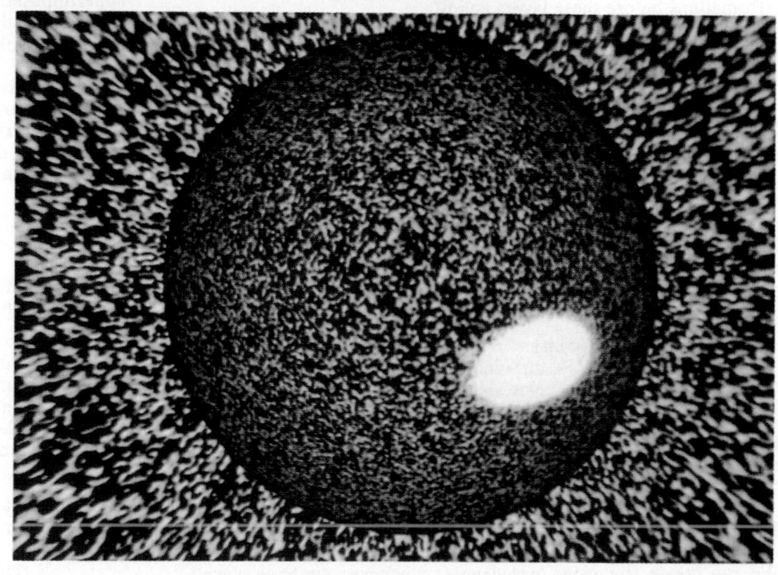

Dnoise() provides a simple way of specifying normal perturbation [7] (figure Bumpy.Donut) :

```
normal += Dnoise(point)
```

By using functions of *Noise*() to control the amount of *Dnoise*() perturbation, we may simulate various types of surface (figure Stucco.Donut), and use these in turn to design other types of surface (figure Disgusting.Donut).

As another example, a $1/f$ signal over space can be simulated by looping over octaves (powers of 2 in frequency) :

$$\sum_{i} \frac{Noise(point * 2^i)}{2^i}$$

In order to create $1/f$ texture we observe that the differential of a function with a $1/f$ frequency spectrum is a vector valued function with a flat frequency spectrum (ie. gradients of $1/f$ functions are similar at all scales). This means that we must create similar normal perturbation in all octaves (figure Wrinkled.Donut) :

```
f = 1
while f < pixel_freq
      normal += Dnoise(f * point)
      f *= 2
```

Note that the calculation stops at the pixel level. In this way unwanted higher frequencies are automatically clamped.

Unlike subdivision based [5] or Fourier space [14] fractal simulations, the above algorithm proceeds independently at all sample points. There is no need to create and modify special data structures in order to provide spacial coherence. This results in a considerable time savings. As with all of the algorithms we will present, the calculation at different pixels can be done in any order, in parallel, or even on different machines.

Marble - An Example of a Solid Texture

We can use *Noise*() to create function *turbulence*() which gives a reasonable visual appearance of turbulent flow (see Appendix). We may then use *turbulence*() to simulate the appearance of marble.

We observe that marble consists of heterogeneous layers. The "marble" look derives from turbulent forces which create deformations before these layers solidify.

The unperturbed layers alone can be modeled by a simple color-filtered sine wave :

```
function boring_marble(point)
      x = point[1]
      return marble_color(sin(x))
```

where *point*[1] denotes the first (ie. x) component of the *point* vector and *marble_color*() has been defined as a spline function mapping scalars to color vectors. To go from this to realistic marble we need only perturb the layers :

```
function marble(point)
      x = point[1] + turbulence(point)
      return marble_color(sin(x))
```

By invoking this procedure at visible surface points we can create quite realistic simulations of marble objects (figure Marble.Vase).

Fire

We can create fire using *turbulence*() whenever we have a well defined flow.

For example, suppose we wish to simulate a solar corona. We will assume that the following entities :

norm()	scalar length (ie. norm) of a vector
direction()	the (unit length) direction of a vector
frame	global time variable (ie. one frame click)

have already been defined.

A corona is hottest near the emitting sphere and cools down with radial distance from the sphere center. At any value of radius, and hence of temperature, a particular spectral emission is visible. Assume we have defined a function *color_of_emission*() which models emission color as a function of radius.

Modeled as a smooth flow, the corona would be implemented by :

```
smooth_corona(point - center)

function smooth_corona(v)
      radius = norm(v)
      return color_of_emission(radius)
```

By adding turbulence to the radial flow we can turn this into a realistic simulation of a corona (figure Corona) :

```
function corona(v)
      radius = norm(v)
      dr = turbulence(v)
      return color_of_corona(radius + dr)
```

To animate this we linearly couple the domain of turbulence to time :

```
function moving_corona(v)
      radius = norm(v)
      dr = turbulence(v - frame * direction(v))
      return color_of_corona(radius + dr)
```

Water

Suppose we wish to create the appearance of waves on a surface. To simplify things we will use normal perturbation [7] instead of actually modifying the surface position.

Max [8] approached this problem by using a collection of superimposed linear wave fronts. Linear fronts have a notable deficiency - they form a self-replicating pattern when viewed over any reasonably large area.

To avoid this we use spherical wave fronts eminating from point source centers [17]. More precisely, suppose at a given pixel a particular surface point is visible. For any wave source center, we will perturb the surface normal towards the center by a cycloidal function of the center's distance from the surface point :

```
normal += wave(point - center)

function wave(v)
      return direction(v) * cycloid(norm(v))
```

We can create multiple centers, let's say distributed randomly around the unit sphere, by using the direction of *Dnoise*() over any collection of widely spaced points. This works because (by definition) the value of *Dnoise*() is uncorrelated for *any* two points which are spaced widely enough apart :

```
function makewaves(n)
      for i in [1 .. n]
            center[i] = direction(Dnoise(i * [100 0 0] ))
      return center
```

To make a wave model with 20 sources we would enter :

```
if begin_frame
      center = makewaves(20)
for c in center
      normal += wave(point - c)
```

Note that the surface need not be planar. By making our wave signal defined over 3-space we have ensured shape independence. This means that we can run the above procedure on *any* shape. The illustration "Water Crystal" was made using 20 sources (figure Water.Crystal). A similar procedure was used to simulate an "Art Glass" partition (figure Art.Glass).

Waves of greater realism are created by distributing the wave-front spacial frequencies using a $1/f$ relationship of amplitude to frequency. If we assign a random frequency f to each center, the last line of the procedure then becomes :

```
normal += wave((point - c) * f) / f
```

Using this refinement (again with 20 sources) we can realistically simulate ocean surfaces (figure Ocean.Sunset).

Since each wave front moves outward linearly with time we may animate these images by adding a linear function of time to the argument passed to *cycloid*() :

```
function moving_wave(v, Dphase)
      return direction(v) * cycloid(norm(v) - frame * Dphase)
```

where *Dphase* is the rate of phase change. For greatest realism we make *Dphase* proportional to $f^{1/2}$ [9]. The wave images pictured are actually stills from such animations.

Other Examples - Clouds and Bubbles

The two bubble images were designed by Carl Ludwig using the PSE. The various elements were all created and assembled by functional composition in the PSE.

For example, in the topmost bubble image the background clouds were created by composing a color spline function with *turbulence*(). The reflection and refraction from the bubble surface were done by using simple vector valued functions to modify an incoming direction vector in accordance with the appropriate physical laws. These were composed with the cloud function and added together.

In the center image, a function corresponding to the shape of an illuminated window was composed with reflection and refraction functions.

The appearance of variable bubble thickness was simulated by multiplying *turbulence*() by each of a red, green, and blue frequency and using *sin*() of this to create constructive and destructive interference fringes. In the PSE this looks like :

```
color *= 1 + sin([rfreq gfreq bfreq] * turbulence(point))
```

Compositing

We can use the PSE simply as a digital image compositor, in which case it functions as a generalization of [10]. We can also use it to combine and modify images in more unusual ways.

Suppose for example that we wish to synthesize some flame on the PSE, knowing that later we will receive some other animation to be composited with our synthetic flame.

We may defer the aesthetic decision of how to color the flame until after looking at this footage. We do this by computing the flame in two passes. The first pass outputs only a scalar flame value. The second and simpler pass maps this scalar quantity to the appropriate color vector.

Note that this process involves no recalculation of the flame itelf. The second pass through the PSE is being used only as a general color splining filter, at a small fraction of the total computing cost.

In an actual commercial production this ability to split computation costs and defer post-production decisions adds enormously to throughput.

In more unusual cases we may use the scalar flame to modulate the frequency distribution or height of water waves, or the amount of rocklike character to give to a surface. In this context our approach is similar to that of [1] and [10], the difference being the extra flexibility we gain by the ability to specify arbitrary asynchronous pixel operations.

Considerations of Efficiency

The efficiency of an implementation is a rather elusive thing. This is because it consists of three fairly different considerations. Most familiar is time efficiency. There is also space efficiency, which often is inversely proportional to time efficiency (as in "should we use a procedure or a lookup table?").

The third consideration, often overlooked, is flexibility. Many of us are familiar with archaic and monolithic "dinosaur" programs that nobody dare modify lest they fall apart altogether. Such programs must be used "as is" or else scrapped and rewritten from scratch.

The approach we offer here does not always produce the most efficient algorithms. What it does offer is the opportunity to try out new approaches quickly and painlessly. For CGI in particular this is of the utmost importance. We generally want to see what the picture looks like before proceeding with optimization. Once implemented, PSE algorithms lend themselves readily to optimization by virtue of their simplicity and high degree of modularity.

In addition, a number of effects are ideally suited to a functional composition paradigm; generally when there is interplay between a simple regular structure and a complex stochastic structure. This is because we can use nonlinear functional composition to model the stochastic part of the structure. This will result in both good time efficiency and good space efficiency.

The flame model constitutes such a "best case" for our approach. The final motion picture quality animation ran in about 10 minutes a frame, written entirely in an unoptimized interpreted pseudo-code implementation of the design language on a Gould SEL 3287 Minicomputer. This appears to be much faster than the particle system approach of Reeves [11]. With optimization and true compilation a speedup of a factor of 5 is indicated. The marble vase, with twice as large an area of visible turbulence, took about 20 minutes to compute.

In all cases, the low resolution interactive design loop took between 15 seconds and 1 minute per iteration.

Now What?

We plan to make a number of improvements to the system. We are developing an optimized compiler for the design language which recognizes quantities that vary slowly over the image stream and computes quantities dependent these only as necessary. We are also adding a general facility for direct insertion of large data bases into the image prior to pixel streaming.

We are currently using the same paradigm of composition with stochastic functions for motion and shape modelling.

We have applied our approach to modelling stochastic motion not only for continuous turbulence models, but also for such things as falling leaves, swaying trees, flocks of birds, and muscular

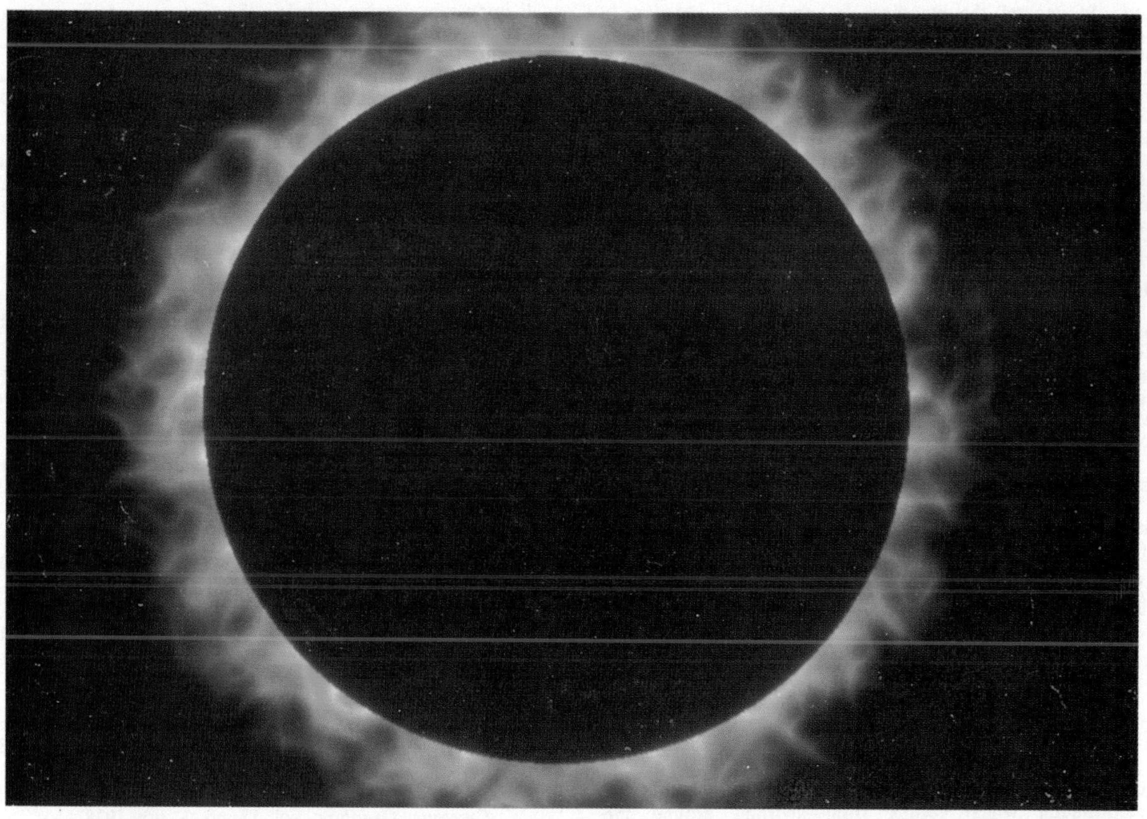

Corona

Ocean Sunset

rippling. In general the paradigm is appropriate whenever a regular, well defined macroscopic motion contains some stochastic component.

To create interesting stochastic shapes, we have generalized on the work of Blinn [15]. Given any space filling scalar valued function, we may consider the shape formed by any isosurface (surface of constant value) of the function. It turns out that a very rich class of shapes may be created in this manner (for example, we can actually build the three dimensional structure of the flame shown in figure Corona). We understand that Lance Williams of NYIT [16] is pursuing a similar line of research.

Conclusions

We have shown a new approach to the design of realistic CGI algorithms. We have introduced the concepts of the Pixel Stream Editor and of solid texture. We have demonstrated a number of effects which would have been considerably more difficult and expensive, and in some cases impossible, to generate by previously known techniques.

Appendix - Turbulence

A suitable procedure for the simulation of turbulence using the *Noise*() signal is :

```
function turbulence(p)
        t = 0
        scale = 1
        while (scale > pixelsize)
                t += abs(Noise(p / scale) * scale)
                scale /= 2
        return t
```

This is actually a simplified approximation to the magnitude of the deformation which results from swirling around the isosurfaces of the *Noise*() domain along the instantaneous vector field :

$$e^{-Noise(point)^2}\ (normal\ X\ Dnoise(point))$$

This formulation is part of a synthetic turbulence model developed by the author [12]. We use the simplified *turbulence*() procedure because it is fast and the pictures it produces look good enough.

Even so it is interesting to examine, with only minimal comment, the algorithmic structure of *turbulence*(). Note the expression

```
Noise(p / scale) * scale
```

inside the loop. This says that at each scale the amount of *Noise*() added is proportional to its size. Thus we obtain a self-similar, or $1/f$, pattern of perturbation. This will give a visual impression of brownian motion. Also, while the deformation is continuous everywhere, the *abs*() at each iteration assures that its gradient will have discontinuous boundaries at all scales. This will give a visual impression of discontinuous flow, which will be interpreted by the viewer as turbulent.

Acknowledgements

The management of MAGI very graciously allowed me the use of its facilities for this research. Frank Crow got me to publish. I'd also like to thank my Ph.D. advisor David Lowe, the faculty of the Courant Institute at NYU, and R/Greenberg Associates for their continuing support.

Gene Miller at MAGI designed "Bozo's Donut" and made a number of valuable suggestions for this paper.

Carl Ludwig made the bubbles and the lovely ocean sunset image. He also codeveloped the wave algorithm, made countless good suggestions for the system and for this paper, and performed the all important service of being the first *user* of the system other than the author.

Mike Ferraro originated the crucial concept of using functional composition to create texture [13]. Much of this paper has its roots in his powerful idea.

Lastly, this paper probably could not have been written were it not for all I have learned over the years about images, algorithms and true elegance of design from working with Josh Pines.

References

1. Cook, R., "Shade Trees," *Computer Graphics*, vol. 18, no. 3, July 1984.

2. Kernighan B., Ritchie D., *The C programming language*, Prentice Hall, Englewood Cliffs, 1978.

3. Gardner, G., "Simulation of natural scenes using textured quadric surfaces," *Computer Graphics*, vol. 18, no. 3, July 1984.

4. Marr, D., *Vision*, W. H. Freeman and Company, San Francisco, 1982.

5. Fournier, A., Fussel, D., and Carpenter, L., "Computer rendering of stochastic models," *Comm. ACM* 25, 6 (June 1982), 371-384.

6. Schacter, B., "Long-crested wave models," *Computer Graphics* and *Image Processing*, vol 12., 1980.

7. Blinn, J., "Simulation of wrinkled surfaces," *Computer Graphics*, vol. 12, no. 3, July 1978.

8. Max, N., "Vectorized procedure models for natural terrain: waves and islands in the sunset," *Computer Graphics*, vol. 15, no. 3, August 1981.

9. Sverdrup, Johnson & Fleming, *The Oceans*, Prentice Hall, Englewood Cliffs, 1942.

10. Porter, T., Duff, T., "Compositing digital images," *Computer Graphics*, vol. 18, no. 3, July 1984.

11. Reeves, W., "Particle systems, - A technique for modeling a class of fuzzy objects," *ACM Transactions on Graphics*, vol. 2, no. 2, April 1983.

12. Perlin, K., Author's unpublished Ph.D. dissertation - work in progress.

13. Mike Ferraro, personal communication.

14. Voss, R., *Fractal Lunar Mist*, Cover of SIGGRAPH '83 proceedings, July 1983.

15. Blinn, J., "A Generalization of Algebraic Surface Drawing." *ACM Transactions on Graphics*, vol. 1, pp 235., 1982.

16. Lance Williams, personal communication.

17. Suggested by Carl Ludwig, personal communication.

Chapter 10: Glossary of Terms

(Terms in *italics* in definition are also defined in the glossary. Definitions of terms are in the context of computer graphics. Many of the terms have a more general use outside of graphics which is not reflected in the definition.)

A-buffer: an extension of the *Z-buffer*, where the "A" stands for "antialiased, area-averaged, accumulating." The A-buffer augments the z-depth information contained in the Z-buffer to allow more accurate antialiasing.

adaptive sampling: a technique to reduce the expense of supersampling at a fixed resolution. Areas of little change receive fewer samples than areas of larger changes.

aliasing: an artifact caused by the inability of the frequency components of a signal above the *Nyquist limit* to be reconstructed from discrete samples. Those high-frequency components will instead be reconstructed as incorrect lower-frequency components not present in the original signal. These low-frequency components are "aliases" of the high-frequency components. The most common visual artifact of spatial aliasing in an image is the jagged stairstepping of slanted edges.

alpha channel: a method for providing the additional information needed for *compositing* separately rendered *antialiased* images in such a way that the final image is still antialiased. This channel augments the RGB channels that carry the color intensity information. The value of alpha varies between 0 and 1 and indicates the extent of coverage of a pixel by the separate image.

antialiasing: any technique to reduce the effects of *aliasing*

area coherence: one of a number of types of *coherence*. Algorithms that use area coherence take advantage of the fact that adjacent pixels in the x and y directions tend to be similar. Thus, in those portions of an image that exhibit area coherence, the rendering of one pixel allows for the rendering of nearby pixels with significantly less computation.

area subdivision algorithms: a class of continuous algorithms which operate by dividing the image plane into sections until each section has only one visible object.

area sampling: a method of computing the average intensity over the square area represented by each pixel to reduce *aliasing*. This is a particular type of *filtering* also known as a box filter. Also see *point sampling*.

atmospheric scattering: light scattering from particles (e.g., water, dust) in the atmosphere. This makes the atmosphere itself appear visible.

back face culling: a specific form of *culling* in which faces that lie on the back side of an object, relative to the *viewpoint*, and thus cannot be seen, are removed from the description of the scene prior to performing more complex computations.

b-rep: see *boundary representation*.

bicubic surface patch: a *parametric surface* patch in which the equations defining $X = X(u,v)$, $Y = Y(u,v)$, $Z = Z(u,v)$ are cubic in u and v.

bidirectional reflectance: the ratio of the reflected intensity in a given direction to the incident energy from another direction within a small solid angle.

blobbies: a class of algebraic surface defined by summing density distributions centered at different points.

boundary representation: one of two common forms for describing solid models. Also see *Constructive Solid Geometry (CSG)*. The surface of the solid is approximated by polygonal facets or tiles.

bounding volume: a simple volume, such as a box or sphere, which tightly encloses the object of interest. These are useful in *culling* operations based on the spatial extents of the objects.

BSP tree: (binary space partitioning tree) a tree data structure which divides space into two disjoint sections at each level. This data structure is used for spatial searching and sorting in several visible-surface algorithms.

bump maps: a *texture map* which contains perturbations of the normal vector of the surface.

coherence: the property that "near by" things should be similar and thus easier to calculate. Area, scan-line, frame-to-frame, and object coherence are types of coherence used in visible-surface determination.

compositing: the operation of combining several prerendered images into a single image.

Constructive Solid Geometry: a technique for constructing a solid model by combining primitive building blocks by using volumetric Boolean set operations. The other common technique is *boundary representation*.

cracks: defects that may occur in the rendering of curved primitives with some subdivision algorithms. The crack can occur when one patch is considered flat enough to render as a planar polygon while an adjoining patch is subdivided again before passing the flatness test.

CSG: see *Constructive Solid Geometry*.

depth of field: the distance over which images formed through a lens are in focus. In computer graphics, images are frequently rendered with infinite depth of field, so that objects at all distances from the viewer are in focus. More recently, some algorithms allow a realistic simulation of depth of field.

diffuse reflection: the component of reflection that represents light scattered equally in all directions.

direct illumination: the light that reaches objects directly from one or more of the light sources. Those parts of objects that do not receive direct illumination are in *shadow*.

distributed light source: a light source with physical extent (not a point light source). Shadows from such a light source will have *penumbras* (see *shadows*).

distributed ray tracing: a multidimensional sampling technique where a sample is chosen by independent random variables in each dimension. This greatly reduces the number of samples required for a given accuracy compared to sampling on a multidimensional fixed grid. This allowed such phenomena as *motion blur*, *depth of field*, *penumbras*, and *gloss* to be simulated efficiently.

environment maps: a type of *texture map* that contains an image of the background environment. This is useful for calculating an approximation to a true reflection in a complex environment.

extent: The region of space occupied by an object. (Also see *bounding volume*.)

filtering: reducing the fine detail from an image before sampling it. In other words, reducing the high-frequency components of the image that cause the *aliasing* problem. (Also see *area sampling, point sampling*.)

flatness test: used in some techniques for rendering primitives that are curved. These primitives are divided into smaller and smaller pieces until a piece can be considered "flat" for visible-surface determination. This test is used to determine if a primitive is "flat."

form factor: the fraction of the *radiosity* (light flux) leaving one diffusely reflecting surface that enters another. The form factors are thus independent of viewpoint and depend only on the positions of the objects.

fractals: a particular *stochastic model* developed by B. Mandelbrot and adapted to computer graphics. While the graphics use of the word differs from the original definition, no precise alternate word is in common use. The word "fractals" is derived from the term "fractional Brownian motion." Fractals are useful because they allow the generation of quite realistic images of natural phenomenon such as coastlines or terrain to arbitrary degrees of detail from a very compact database.

global illumination model: see *illumination model*.

gloss: reflections that are blurred rather than the simpler mirror reflections originally simulated in computer graphics.

hemicube: used in the *radiosity* technique in the calculation of *form factors*. This "half-cube" is an approximation to the hemispherical field of view from a viewpoint. The hemisphere is projected onto the flat projection planes of the hemicube.

hidden-line removal: the name most frequently used in the days of vector displays to describe the problem of removing those lines that should not be visible when the description of a three-dimensional object is converted to a two-dimensional screen image. (Also see *visible-surface algorithm*.)

hidden-surface removal: the process of visible-surface determination. (Also see *visible-surface algorithm*.)

illumination model: the process of determining how much light reaches the viewer from each point in the scene based on the light sources present, the viewer's position, and the surface properties and locations of the objects in the scene. An illumination or shading model is said to be local if it deals only with the light sources and surface orientation. The model is said to be global if it deals with the interaction of objects to simulate true reflection, shadows, and refraction.

image plane: the plane onto which the objects are projected for final viewing. The visible image is contained in a rectangular portion of the image plane.

image space: the three-dimensional space the image is displayed in. *Object space* is transformed into image space by applying the viewing transformation. (Also see *object space*.)

image synthesis: that part of computer graphics that addresses the production of realistic images. Image synthesis includes illumination, image formation, and shading.

indirect illumination: light that reaches an object by reflecting from or refracting through other objects.

jitter: one type of *stochastic sampling* in which a random perturbation is applied to regularly spaced points.

lighting model: see *illumination model.*

local illumination model: see *illumination model.*

motion blur: the blur seen on photographs of moving objects, which is the result of the camera lens being open for a finite period of time. This blur is an integration of visible intensities multiplied by a temporal weighting function. Accurate calculation of this integral yields correct temporal antialiasing. Blurring visible objects calculated at one point in time is an approximation subject to aliasing.

Nyquist limit: the upper limit of frequencies that can be represented at a fixed sampling rate. The Nyquist limit is equal to one half the sampling rate. Attempts to represent higher frequencies will result in *aliasing*.

object coherence: one of a number of types of *coherence*. Algorithms that exploit object coherence look at the relationships between parts of the same object.

object space: the three-dimensional space that objects are described in. (Also see *image space*.)

octree data structure: a structure that represents a three-dimensional scene by recursively subdividing it into octants.

parametric surfaces: surfaces defined by three bivariate functions, $X = X(u,v)$, $Y = Y(u,v)$, $Z = Z(u,v)$ in which u and v vary over some range.

particle systems: a method for modeling fuzzy objects such as fire and clouds by utilizing a cloud of tiny particles. The particles are usually generated and controlled by stochastic processes.

penumbra: see *shadow*.

pixel: an abbreviation for the term 'picture element.' The display surface is made up of some number of scan lines, each of which is broken up into a number of discrete pieces. These individual picture elements are the pixels.

point-light source: a mathematical light source consisting of light coming from a single point, which is used in most illumination models.

point sampling: the process of sampling the area covered by each *pixel* at a single mathematical point. This sampling typically misrepresents the intensity information that is available for the entire square which is the pixel. This is the cause of *aliasing*.

procedural model: a model described by an algorithmic formulation rather than the mathematical definition of a single primitive.

radiosity: the total light flux leaving a surface, including the self-emitted light and the reflected and transmitted incident light. See *radiosity method.*

radiosity method: a method for approximating the indirect illumination within an environment based on an equilibrium energy balance in an enclosure.

ray/surface-intersection calculation: the mathematical calculation of finding the intersection of a line (representing the ray) and a surface. This is the most time consuming step in the class of *ray-tracing* algorithms.

ray tracing: a family of algorithms for performing the visible-surface calculation that is based upon the technique of tracing individual sight rays through an environment.

reflection: the process of light bouncing off the surface of a material.

refraction: the bending of light rays as they pass through materials such as glass.

rendering: the process of converting the description of a scene into the color values of the individual pixels of a display surface.

scan conversion: the process of converting an image-space object into the screen-space pixels that are covered by the object.

scan lines: the horizontal lines of finite width into which the display device, and thus the *image plane*, is divided. Each scan line is subdivided into discrete pieces, which are called *pixels*.

scan-line algorithms: algorithms that determine which pixels are to be illuminated by processing a scene along consecutive scan lines. These algorithms exploit the scan-line *coherence* present in most images.

screen space: the space in which the x and y values correspond to pixel locations.

shader: the portion of the graphics system, responsible for the determination of the light intensity transmitted to the camera position, taking into consideration direct and indirect illumination and the position of the camera in the scene.

shadow: those parts of a scene that are visible from the viewer's position but not from the position of a light source. The shadow is made up of two components: the *umbra,* in which the light source is totally obscured, and the *penumbra,* in which the light source is partially obscured.

shadow polygons: polygons that bound the shadow volume created by a *point-light source* and a polygonal object.

shadow volume: the volume of space defined by the shadow of an object. (See *shadow polygons*.)

silhouette edge: the points on a surface where the normal vector to the surface is perpendicular to a vector in the direction of the camera. When producing a hidden-line view of the surface, these points would be represented as an edge.

specular reflection: light reflected directly from the outer surface of an object—typically modeled as a highlight on the object. (See also *diffuse reflection.*)

stochastic model: a model in which the object is represented by the sample path of a stochastic process of one or more variables rather than by deterministic primitives such as polygons or patches. One particular stochastic model is *fractals*.

stochastic sampling: sampling at nonuniformly spaced locations instead of on a regular grid. This causes the aliasing effects, generated by frequencies above the *Nyquist limit*, to be converted into noise which is more pleasing to the eye.

stochastic supersampling: more than one sample per pixel, with the samples chosen stochastically rather than on a regular grid. (See *stochastic sampling* and *supersampling.*)

supersampling: a technique to reduce the artifacts caused by *aliasing*. With this technique, more than one sample per pixel is taken on a regular grid.

texture maps: arrays containing intensity information which are mapped onto primitives during the final stages of rendering. (Also see *texturing, bump maps, and environment maps.*)

texturing: a technique developed to allow the addition of texture (surface features) to a primitive such as a polygon or a surface patch.

translucency: blurred transparency. Images seen through translucent objects are not as distinct or sharp as objects seen through transparent objects.

transparency: a property of materials that allows light to be transmitted through objects.

umbra: see *shadow*.

visible-surface algorithm: a method used to determine which objects, or portions of objects, should be visible when the description of a three-dimensional object is converted to a two-dimensional screen image. (See also *hidden-line removal* and *hidden-surface* removal.)

voxel: a three-dimensional analog of a *pixel*, in which the raster grid is conceptually extended to a grid of "volume elements."

Z-buffer: a data structure that allows retention of depth values for each of the pixels in the image memory. The term also refers to those algorithms that utilize such a structure.

Chapter 11: Annotated Bibliography

References

[Abra85] Abram, Greg, Lee Westover, and Turner Whitted, "Efficient Alias-Free Rendering Using Bit-Masks and Look-Up Tables," *Proceedings of SIGGRAPH '85* (San Francisco, Calif., July 22-26, 1985). In *Computer Graphics, 19,* 3 (July 1985), 53-59

This paper presents fast methods for antialiasing polygons. The filtering algorithm loops in reverse order compared to the Feibush et al. [Feib80] filtering algorithm. Polygons are broken into pixel fragments and the contribution of each fragment is looked up in a precomputed table.

[Aman84] Amanatides, John, "Ray Tracing with Cones," *Proceedings of SIGGRAPH '84* (Minneapolis, Minn., July 23-27, 1984). In *Computer Graphics, 18,* 3 (July 1984), 129-135

This paper extends the basic ray-tracing paradigm by utilizing "cones" in the place of rays. Antialiasing techniques can then be applied by averaging the contributions of the visible components within the beam of the cone. Extensions are made to include fuzzy shadows, dull reflections, and translucency. Applications of this technique have been limited by the available cone/object-intersection tests and representation of partial cones.

[Appe67] Appel, A., "The Notion of Quantitative Invisibility and the Machine Rendering of Solids," *Proceedings of the ACM National Conference*, ACM, Inc., New York, N.Y., Vol. 14, 1967, 387-393 (reprinted in [Free80])

This paper, a visible-line algorithm, introduces the *quantitative invisibility* of a point as the number of relevant faces that lie between the point and the viewpoint. The solution to the visible-line problem requires the computation of the quantitative visibility of every point on each relevant edge, and the paper gives a method of doing this incrementally as the edge crosses others in the image plane.

[Appe68] Appel, A., "Some Techniques for Shading Machine Renderings of Solids," *Proceedings of the AFIPS Spring Joint Computer Conference*, AFIPS Press, Reston, Va., Vol. 32, 1968, 37-49

This paper is typically referenced as the first to suggest the technique of ray tracing (i.e., tracing rays in reverse from the eyepoint). It is also credited with being the first to suggest the incorporation of shadows.

[Arno83] Arnon, Dennis S., "Topologically Reliable Display of Algebraic Curves," *Proceedings of SIGGRAPH '83* (Detroit, Mich., July 25-29, 1983). In *Computer Graphics, 17,* 3 (July 1983), 219-227

This paper describes methods for algebraic curve display, correctly portraying the topological structure of the curve. The algorithm is based upon the cylindrical algebraic decomposition algorithm of the field of computer algebra.

[Arvo86] Arvo, J. and D. Kirk, "Forward Ray Tracing," (Unpublished Course Notes, Tutorial on Ray Tracing, SIGGRAPH '86 course notes, Dallas, Tex., Aug. 18-22, 1986)

This paper addresses the global-illumination problem by introducing a limited forward-ray-tracing step from the light source. Rays are traced from the *light source* into the scene and illumination information is collected on the surfaces that make up the scene. This illumination information is then utilized in the common ray-tracing method.

[Arvo87] Arvo, James and David Kirk, "Fast Ray Tracing by Ray Classification," *Proceedings of SIGGRAPH '87* (Anaheim, Calif., July 27-31, 1987). In *Computer Graphics, 21,* 4 (July 1987), 55-64

This paper, which is included in Chapter 5 of this tutorial, describes an efficient method of speeding up the ray-tracing operation by subdividing a scene by both the spatial coordinates of the object space and the spherical coordinates of the potential rays leaving a spatial area. This five-dimensional system limits the number of ray/surface-intersection calculations performed by the ray-tracing system.

[Athe78] Atherton, Peter, Kevin Weiler, and Donald Greenberg, "Polygon Shadow Generation," *Proceedings of SIGGRAPH '78* (Atlanta, Ga., Aug. 23-25, 1978). In *Computer Graphics, 12,* 3 (Aug. 1978), 275-281

This paper is a continuation of the "cookie cutter" method by the authors [Weil77], in which shadow information is generated by first performing a visible-surface calculation from the light-source positions. The visible surfaces in this case are in shadow. By using a marking procedure, this information can be utilized in the regular visible-surface computation to decrease the illumination on those entities in shadow.

[Athe83] Atherton, Peter R., "A Scan-Line Hidden Surface Removal Procedure for Constructive Solid Geometry," *Proceedings of SIGGRAPH '83* (Detroit, Mich., July 25-29, 1983). In *Computer Graphics, 17,* 3 (July 1983), 73-82

This paper, which is included in Chapter 4 of this tutorial, discusses a scan-line algorithm that can be utilized in scenes containing primitives generated through constructive solid geometry. Depth lists, which can be utilized in the CSG visibility procedure, are calculated at each span endpoint. Differences in visibility at successive span endpoints are resolved by recursive subdivision of the span, with generation of additional depth lists at the generated subdivision points.

[Baha87] Bahar, Ezekiel and Swapan Chakrabarti, "Full-Wave Theory Applied to Computer-Aided Graphics for 3D Objects," *IEEE Computer Graphics and Applications, 7,* 7 (July 1987), 46-60

This paper develops a full-wave shading model for synthesis of metallic objects. The work is based on an analysis of electromagnetic scattering by rough surfaces.

[Barr81] Barr, Alan H., "Superquadrics and Angle-Preserving Transformations," *IEEE Computer Graphics and Applications, 1,* 1 (Jan. 1981), 11-23

This paper introduces a new family of modeling primitives, the superquadrics, and discusses rendering methods to display these primitives. The superquadric is of interest in the ray-tracing paradigm in that it has a closed-form expression for the ray/surface-intersection problem that can be solved explicitly.

[Barr84] Barr, Alan H., "Global and Local Deformations of Solid Primitives," *Proceedings of SIGGRAPH '84* (Minneapolis, Minn., July 23-27, 1984). In *Computer Graphics, 18*, 3 (July 1984), 21-30

This paper introduces hierarchical-modeling operations that simulate twisting, bending, and tapering of geometric objects. Results are given that show that the normal of the transformed surface can be calculated directly from the surface normal of the untransformed surface.

[Barr86] Barr, Alan H., "Ray Tracing Deformed Surfaces," *Proceedings of SIGGRAPH '86* (Dallas, Tex., Aug. 18-22, 1986). In *Computer Graphics, 20*, 4 (Aug. 1986), 287-296

This paper introduces methods for ray-tracing differentiable surfaces. Methods are given by which a set of simpler surfaces, in which the ray/surface-intersection calculation can be accomplished, can be substituted for the complex surface.

[Beat82] Beatty, John C. and Kellogg S. Booth, (Eds.) *Tutorial: Computer Graphics (Second Edition),* Computer Society Press, Washington, D.C., 1982

A revised version of the first collection of papers, in the field of computer graphics. This collection contains many fundamental papers.

[Berg86] Bergeron, Philippe, "A General Version of Crow's Shadow Volumes," *IEEE Computer Graphics and Applications, 6,* 9 (Sept. 1986), 17-28

This paper discusses a generalization of Crow's shadow-volume method [Crow77a]. Its primary use is illustrated in scenes from the computer-generated film *Tony de Peltrie*.

[Berl85] Berlin, E.P., "Efficiency Considerations in Image Synthesis," (Unpublished Course Notes, Tutorial on State of the Art in Image Synthesis, SIGGRAPH '85 course notes #11, San Francisco, Calif., July 22-26, 1985)

This paper discusses the inclusion of shadows and reflection into a painter's algorithm. The method utilizes the BSP-tree algorithm of Fuchs et al. [Fuch80], by integrating the shadow and reflection calculations with tree traversal methods. These results are similar to those of Garcia [Garc86].

[Blin76] Blinn, James F. and Martin E. Newell, "Texture and Reflection in Computer Generated Images," *Communications of the ACM, 19,* 10 (Oct. 1976), 542-547 (reprinted in [Beat82])

This paper builds on the original results of Catmull [Catm74] in describing methods by which patterns can be mapped onto surfaces. Weighted averages of the pattern are calculated to reduce aliasing artifacts in the generated images.

[Blin77] Blinn, James F., "Models of Light Reflection for Computer Synthesized Pictures," *Proceedings of SIGGRAPH '77* (San Jose, Calif., July 20-22, 1977). In *Computer Graphics, 11*, 2 (Summer 1977), 192-198 (reprinted in [Free80])

This paper applies the reflection model of Torrance and Sparrow [Torr67] to computer graphics.

[Blin78] Blinn, James F., "Simulation of Wrinkled Surfaces," *Proceedings of SIGGRAPH '78* (Atlanta, Ga., Aug. 23-25, 1978). In *Computer Graphics, 12*, 3 (Aug. 1978), 286-292

This paper, which is included in Chapter 9, introduces the concept of generating "bump-mapped surfaces" to the field of computer graphics. The essential step in the algorithm is applying a perturbation to the calculated normal vector of a surface, which generates simulated bumps through the shading process.

[Blin79] Blinn, James F., "Computer Display of Curved Surfaces," Ph.D. Dissertation, University of Utah, Salt Lake City, Utah, 1978

The essential part of this thesis is a much expanded version of the "edge tracking algorithm" given in Lane et al. [Lane80a].

[Blin82a] Blinn, James F., "A Generalization of Algebraic Surface Drawing," *ACM Transactions on Graphics, 1,* 3 (July 1982), 235-256

This paper introduces the modeling primitive commonly called "blobby" surfaces, which are contour surfaces to a density function of position, defined by summing spherical-symmetric density distributions around a collection of point centers. It also discusses rendering methods by which scenes composed of these primitives can be generated. Ray tracing is used, with efficient sorting of the density spheres, and numerical techniques for the ray/surface-intersection calculations.

[Blin82b] Blinn, James F., "Light Reflection Functions for Simulation of Clouds and Dusty Surfaces," *Proceedings of SIGGRAPH '82* (Boston, Mass., July 26-30, 1982). In *Computer Graphics, 16,* 3 (July 1982), 21-29

This paper discusses a probabilistic simulation of light passing through, and being reflected by clouds of small particles. The author applies these techniques to the simulation of clouds and rings in his planetary-simulation films.

[Bloo83] Bloomenthal, Jules, "Edge Inference with Application to Antialiasing," *Proceedings of SIGGRAPH '83* (Detroit, Mich., July 25-29, 1983). In *Computer Graphics, 17,* 3 (July 1983), 157-162

This paper gives a method which, from the set of vertical and horizontal segments that form the aliased-staircase image, can approximate the original edge with a precision beyond that of a raster element. The approximations can then be used to reshade the pixels they intersect, which results in antialiasing of the edges.

[Bouk70a] Bouknight, W. Jack, "A Procedure for Generation of Three-Dimensional Half-Toned Computer Graphics Presentations," *Communications of the ACM, 13,* 9 (Sept. 1970), 527-536 (reprinted in [Free80])

This paper is considered one of the first scan-line algorithms. It includes discussions of the *y*-sorted lists and *x*-sorted lists, and with Watkins [Watk70] was one of the first to utilize coherence in the algorithm.

[Bouk70b] Bouknight, W.J. and K.C. Kelley, "An Algorithm for Producing Half-Tone Computer Graphics Presentations with Shadows and Movable Light Sources," *Proceedings of the AFIPS Spring Joint Computer Conference*, AFIPS Press, Reston, Va., Vol. 36, 1970, 1-10.

This paper is considered one of the first shadow papers. Whereas the visibility algorithm is based upon a scan-line paradigm, the shadow calculation is essentially a ray trace. The scene is projected onto a sphere centered at the light-source and bounding-box tests are used on the projected polygons to eliminate most tests.

[Bouv85] Bouville, Christian, "Bounding Ellipsoids for Ray-Fractal Intersection," *Proceedings of SIGGRAPH '85* (San Francisco, Calif., July 22-26, 1985). In *Computer Graphics, 19,* 3 (July 1985), 45-52

This paper gives a method by which bounding volumes can be easily generated for the efficient ray tracing of fractal surfaces. The method is simple, in that it utilizes only coordinate transformations in the description of an ellipsoid that bounds a fractal component. The paper improves on the "cheesecake" bounding volumes of Kajiya [Kaji83], and also provides probabilistic bounds when the vertex-displacement distribution has infinite range.

[Bres65] Breshenham, J.E., "Algorithm for the Control of a Digital Plotter," *IBM Systems Journal, IV,* 1, (1965), 25-30 (reprinted in [Free80])

This paper describes a method for the drawing of "straight lines" on a digital-plotter device. Its use has been extended to the generation of lines and circles (see [Bres77]) on raster devices, and the tracing of rays through three-dimensional space [Fuji86].

[Bres77] Breshenham, J.E., "An Incremental Algorithm for Digital Display of Circular Arcs," *Communications of the ACM, 20,* No. 2 (Feb. 1977), 100-106.

This paper presents an algorithm for generating a sequence of pixels that are along a circular arc.

[BuiT75] Bui-Tuong, Phong, "Illumination for Computer Generated Pictures," *Communications of the ACM, 18,*6 (June 1975), 311-317 (also *Technical Report UTEC-CSC-73-129*, Department of Computer Science, University of Utah, Salt Lake City, Utah), (reprinted in [Beat82])

This paper extends the results of Gouraud [Gour71] by proposing a method by which specular highlights of surfaces can be generated, and by describing a method for producing smooth-appearing surfaces by linearly interpolating the normal vector over polygons, and then by renormalizing to a unit vector at each pixel.

[Cabr87] Cabral, Brian, Nelson Max, and Rebecca Springmeyer, "Bidirectional Reflection Functions from Surface Bump Maps," *Proceedings of SIGGRAPH '87* (Anaheim, Calif., July 27-31, 1987). In *Computer Graphics, 21*, 4 (July 1987), 273-281

In this paper, the bump-mapping technique of Blinn [Blin78] is used to calculate the geometrical-attenuation factor in the calculation of the bidirectional-reflection coefficient (see [Cook82]). It also gives an efficient way to use these bidirectional coefficients in finding the effects of environmental illumination for surface shading.

[Care85] Carey, R.J. and D.P. Greenberg, "Textures for Realistic Image Synthesis," *Computers and Graphics 9*, 2, 1985, 125-138

This paper presents methods for simulating a variety of different textures. Two general types of textures, geometric and spectral, are simulated.

[Carp84] Carpenter, Loren, "The A-Buffer, An Antialiased Hidden Surface Method," *Proceedings of SIGGRAPH '84* (Minneapolis, Minn., July 23-27, 1984). In *Computer Graphics, 18*, 3 (July 1984), 103-108

This paper, which is included in Chapter 2 of this tutorial, extends the concept of a Z-buffer by the addition of a list of visible objects at each pixel. A 32-bit coverage mask is used for complex cases. Complex entity comparisons, for entities that intersect the same pixel, are implemented through Boolean operations. This technique effectively increases the resolution of the Z-buffer algorithm several times.

[Catm74] Catmull, E.E., "A Subdivision Algorithm for Computer Display of Curved Surfaces," Ph.D. Dissertation, University of Utah, Salt Lake City, Utah, Dec. 1974

This paper is one of the most important early works in the field of image synthesis. Within this work, the author introduced the concepts of Z-buffer, surface subdivision for rendering purposes, and texturing of computer-generated surfaces. This paper has been used as a foundation for much of the research in the area of image synthesis.

[Catm75] Catmull, E.E., "Computer Display of Curved Surfaces," *Proceedings of the IEEE Conference on Computer Graphics, Pattern Recognition and Data Structures*, May 1975, 11 (reprinted in [Free80])

This paper is an abbreviated version of the author's thesis work [Catm74] and is often referenced in its place.

[Catm78] Catmull, Edwin, "A Hidden-Surface Algorithm with Anti-Aliasing," *Proceedings of SIGGRAPH '78* (Atlanta, Ga., Aug. 23-25, 1978). In *Computer Graphics, 12*, 3 (Aug. 1978), 6-11 (reprinted in [Beat82])

This paper, which is included in Chapter 9 of this tutorial, proposes the first continuous polygon antialiasing method by essentially utilizing a visible-surface calculation at each pixel. All polygons within the pixel are clipped to all polygon boundaries, by creating a large set of polygon fragments. These fragments can then be culled by utilizing visibility criteria, and a correct shade for the pixel can be calculated by weighting the intensities of the polygon fragments by the area they cover in the pixel.

[Catm80] Catmull, Ed and Alvy Ray Smith, "3-D Transformation of Images in Scanline Order," *Proceedings of SIGGRAPH '80* (Seattle, Wash., July 14-18, 1980). In *Computer Graphics, 14*, 3 (July 1980), 279-285

This paper, which is included in Chapter 8 of this tutorial, proposes a method by which texture patterns can be transformed into the image space of the surface on which they are to be mapped. The transformations are algorithmically separated into two streams, each of which corresponds to a one-dimensional transformation of the pattern along scan lines.

[Catm84] Catmull, Edwin, "An Analytic Visible Surface Algorithm for Independent Pixel Processing," *Proceedings of SIGGRAPH '84* (Minneapolis, Minn., July 23-27, 1984). In *Computer Graphics, 18*, 3 (July 1984), 109-115

This paper proposes a parallel algorithm of independent pixel processing for image synthesis. The algorithm treats each pixel, and the entities that cover each pixel, as an independent entity. A special "head-tail" sort is utilized to generate a list of visible elements for each pixel, and the filtering method of Feibush et al. [Feib80] is used to generate the final antialiased images.

[Clar79] Clark, James H., "A Fast Scan-Line Algorithm for Rendering Parametric Surfaces," *Proceedings of SIGGRAPH '79* (Chicago, Ill., Aug. 8-10, 1979). In *Computer Graphics, 13*, 2 (Aug. 1979), 174

This paper, which is included in Chapter 4 of this tutorial, expands on the work of Catmull [Catm74] and Lane et al. [Lane80a] in addressing the problem of "cracks" in subdivided surfaces. The author uses screen-space curvature as the primary consideration in the flatness test, and a subdivision criterion based only upon the patch edges that avoids the cracks inherent in the straightforward subdivision method. A central-differencing scheme is utilized for efficiency. The paper appears in the SIGGRAPH *Proceedings* in abstract form only.

[Clea86] Cleary, J. G., B. M. Wyvill, G. M. Birtwistle, and R. Vatti, "Multiprocessor Ray Tracing," *Computer Graphics Forum 5*, 1 (March 1986), 3-12

This paper compares the two- and three-dimensional regular subdivision methods of decomposing object space between processors in a network for ray tracing. Ray packets are passed between processors. Processor and communications bottlenecks are considered.

[Cohe85] Cohen, Michael F. and Donald P. Greenberg, "The Hemi-Cube: A Radiosity Solution for Complex Environments," *Proceedings of SIGGRAPH '85* (San Francisco, Calif., July 22-26, 1985). In *Computer Graphics, 19*, 3 (July 1985), 31-40

This paper, which is included in Chapter 7 of this tutorial, is an extension of the initial radiosity method proposed by Goral et al. [Gora84]. This method provides a better approximation of the radiosity form factors by performing a Z-buffer visible-surface computation at the center of each surface element. Collection of the "visible" elements at each surface element can then be used to calculate the form factor.

[Cohe86] Cohen, Michael F., Donald P. Greenburg, David S. Immel, and Phillip J. Brock, "An Efficient Radiosity Approach for Realistic Image Synthesis," *IEEE Computer Graphics and Applications 6*, 3, (March 1986), 26-35

This paper improves on the basic radiosity results of Goral et al. [Gora84], and the hemicube results of Cohen and Greenberg [Cohe85] by calculating points in the scene where intensity gradients are high, and by calculating a finer discrete mesh on the surface about these points.

[Cook81] Cook, R., *A Reflection Model for Realistic Image Synthesis*, Master's Thesis, Cornell University, Ithaca, N.Y., 1981

This paper introduces the reflection model later published by Cook and Torrance [Cook82]. The author also proposes methods by which soft shadows and fuzzy reflections can be generated.

[Cook82] Cook, Robert L. and Kenneth E. Torrance, "A Reflectance Model for Computer Graphics," *ACM Transactions on Graphics, 1*, 1 (Jan. 1982), 7-24

This paper, which is included in Chapter 7 of this tutorial, extends the illumination models presented by Phong Bui-Toung [BuiT75] and Blinn [Blin77] to give realistic colored reflections. The model is applied to the simulation of the illumination characteristics for a variety of metallic surfaces that cannot be modeled with earlier methods.

[Cook84a] Cook, Robert L., Thomas Porter, and Loren Carpenter, "Distributed Ray Tracing," *Proceedings of SIGGRAPH '84* (Minneapolis, Minn., July 23-27, 1984). In *Computer Graphics, 18*, 3 (July 1984), 137-145

This paper, which is included in Chapter 5 of this tutorial, extends the original ray-tracing methods of Whitted [Whit80], who first distributed rays throughout a pixel to assist in the antialiasing process. This paper proposes methods by which rays can be distributed independently in multi-dimensional space, creating methods by which motion blur, fuzzy shadows, and depth-of-field effects can be simulated efficiently.

[Cook84b] Cook, Robert L., "Shade Trees," *Proceedings of SIGGRAPH '84* (Minneapolis, Minn., July 23-27, 1984). In *Computer Graphics, 18*, 3 (July 1984), 223-231

This paper proposes a method by which texturing methods and shading models can be combined. The author proposes a tree structure, which can be implemented dynamically, in which the user can specify most components of the illumination model.

[Cook86] Cook, Robert L., "Stochastic Sampling in Computer Graphics," *ACM Transactions on Graphics, 5*, 1 (Jan. 1986), 51-72

This paper, which is included in Chapter 8, addresses the method of utilizing nonregularly spaced samples in the point-sampling image-generation algorithms. By using this method, frequencies above the Nyquist limit can be made to appear as noise on the image, which is much less objectionable to the human visual system than aliasing.

[Cook87] Cook, Robert L., Loren Carpenter, and Edwin Catmull, "The REYES Image Rendering Architecture," *Proceedings of SIGGRAPH '87* (Anaheim, Calif., July 27-31, 1987). In *Computer Graphics, 21*, 4 (July 1987), 95-102

This paper, which is included in Chapter 2 of this tutorial, is a direct extension of the work of Catmull [Catm74] in which Z-buffer and subdivision methods are utilized in the rendering process. Catmull's results are improved upon by the introduction of stochastic-sampling methods [Cook86] in the Z-buffer, and the introduction of flat-shaded "micro-polygons" as a primitive, which allows the quick calculation of texturing.

[Croc84] Crocker, Gary A., "Invisibility Coherence for Faster Scan-Line Hidden Surface Algorithms," *Proceedings of SIGGRAPH '84* (Minneapolis, Minn., July 23-27, 1984). In *Computer Graphics, 18*, 3 (July 1984), 96-102

This paper expands on the basic scan-line paradigm by introducing a method in which global invisibility of objects is taken into consideration in calculation of the active and depth lists. Objects, which are invisible for long stretches throughout a scan line, are updated infrequently, resulting in a significant cost savings in the algorithm.

[Crow77a] Crow, Franklin C., "Shadow Algorithms for Computer Graphics," *Proceedings of SIGGRAPH '77* (San Jose, Calif., July 20-22, 1977). In *Computer Graphics, 11*, 2 (Summer 1977), 242-248 (reprinted in [Beat82])

This paper introduces the concept of shadow volumes to computer graphics, in which specific surfaces, representing the boundaries of the volumes in shadow, are added to a scene. When depth lists are formed in the rendering algorithm, a simple counting argument can be used to determine if the polygon at the front of the depth list is in shadow.

[Crow77b] Crow, Franklin C., "The Aliasing Problem in Computer-Generated Shaded Images," *Communications of the ACM, 20,* 11 (Nov. 1977), 799-805

This paper introduces the concept of antialiasing to computer graphics. Prefiltering methods are discussed, and compared to common postfiltering found in image-processing applications.

[Crow81] Crow, Franklin C., "A Comparison of Antialiasing Techniques," *IEEE Computer Graphics and Applications, 1,* 1 (Jan. 1981), 40-48

This paper presents a comparison of prefiltering (continuous) and postfiltering (point-sampling) antialiasing methods with a set of computer-generated images.

[Crow82] Crow, F. C., "A More Flexible Image Generation Environment," *Proceedings of SIGGRAPH '82* (Boston, Mass., July 26-30, 1982). In *Computer Graphics, 16*, 3 (July 1982), 9-18

This paper presents a rendering technique by which large components of an image are rendered separately, and are combined into the final image. The complete system that is used to create the scenes is described.

[Crow84] Crow, Franklin C., "Summed-Area Tables for Texture Mapping," *Proceedings of SIGGRAPH '84* (Minneapolis, Minn., July 23-27, 1984). In *Computer Graphics, 18*, 3 (July 1984), 207-212

This paper expands on the pyramidal prefiltering methods of Williams [Will83], creating a preintegrated-texture table that allows the quick filtering of rectangular areas.

[Dipp84] Dippé, Mark and John Swensen, "An Adaptive Subdivision Algorithm and Parallel Architecture for Realistic Image Synthesis," *Proceedings of SIGGRAPH '84* (Minneapolis, Minn., July 23-27, 1984). In *Computer Graphics, 18*, 3 (July 1984), 149-158

This paper proposes a general method for utilizing object-space decomposition methods for parallel ray tracing.

[Dipp85a] Dippé, Mark A. Z., *Antialiasing in Computer Graphics*, PhD. Dissertation, University of Calif., Berkeley, Calif., April 1985.

This work contains two main sections. The first is a tetrahedral-spline representation of an image varying in time with functional prefiltering for spatial and temporal antialiasing. The second section is on stochastic sampling.

[Dipp85b] Dippé, Mark A. Z. and Erling Henry Wold, "Antialiasing through Stochastic Sampling," *Proceedings of SIGGRAPH '85* (San Francisco, Calif., July 22-26, 1985). In *Computer Graphics, 19*, 3 (July 1985), 69-78

This paper, similar to Cook [Cook86], addresses the method of utilizing nonregularly spaced samples in the point-sampling image-generation algorithms.

[Duff79] Duff, Tom, "Smoothly Shaded Renderings of Polyhedral Objects on Raster Displays," *Proceedings of SIGGRAPH '79* (Chicago, Ill., Aug. 8-10, 1979). In *Computer Graphics, 13*, 2 (Aug. 1979), 270-275

This paper analyzes the effects (especially Mach banding) of Phong [BuiT75] and Gouraud [Gour71] shading and proposes an extended model in which Phong shading can be quickly calculated.

[Duff85] Duff, Tom, "Compositing 3-D Rendered Images," *Proceedings of SIGGRAPH '85* (San Francisco, Calif., July 22-26, 1985). In *Computer Graphics, 19*, 3 (July 1985), 41-44

This paper, which is included in Chapter 2 of this tutorial, extends the image-composition methods of Porter and Duff [Port84] to include depth information. For each pixel, a z-depth value is added to the RGBα formulation of Porter and Duff. This allows composition by depth in a three-dimensional fashion rather than the 2½-dimensional methods.

[Feib80] Feibush, Eliot A., Marc Levoy, and Robert L. Cook, "Synthetic Texturing Using Digital Filters," *Proceedings of SIGGRAPH '80* (Seattle, Wash., July 14-18, 1980). In *Computer Graphics, 14*, 3 (July 1980), 294-301

This paper, which is included in Chapter 8 of this tutorial, specifies a two-dimensional lookup-table method for filtering with radially symmetric, small extent point-spread functions. A method to approximate filter textures is also presented.

[Fium83] Fiume, Eugene, Alain Fournier, and Larry Rudolph, "A Parallel Scan Conversion Algorithm with Anti-Aliasing for a General-Purpose Ultracomputer," *Proceedings of SIGGRAPH '83* (Detroit, Mich., July 25-29, 1983). In *Computer Graphics, 17*, 3 (July 1983), 141-150

This paper utilizes an extended design of an ultracomputer to propose a parallel scan-line/Z-buffer algorithm.

[Fole82] Foley, J.D. and A. van Dam, *Fundamentals of Interactive Computer Graphics*, Addison-Wesley, Reading, Mass., 1982

This is a basic computer-graphics text that includes some aspects of image synthesis.

[Four82] Fournier, Alain, Don Fussell, and Loren C. Carpenter, "Computer Rendering of Stochastic Models," *Communications of the ACM, 25*, 6 (June 1982), 371-384

This paper, which is included in Chapter 4 of this tutorial, discusses database-enhancement techniques based upon fractal geometry. Rendering of the models is discussed.

[Four85] Fournier, Alain and Thomas Milligan, "Frame Buffer Algorithms for Stochastic Models," *IEEE Computer Graphics and Applications, 5*, 10 (Oct. 1985), 40-46

This paper expands on the rendering methods for fractal objects [Four82] by discussing a system in which the database enhancement takes place at the display level.

[Four86] Fournier, Alain and William T. Reeves, "A Simple Model of Ocean Waves," *Proceedings of SIGGRAPH '86* (Dallas, Tex., Aug. 18-22, 1986). In *Computer Graphics, 20*, 4 (Aug. 1986), 75-84

This paper discusses a mathematical model for the generation of waves and their refraction while traveling across an ocean bottom of varying depth. It is similar to that of Peachey [Peac86].

[Fran80] Franklin, William Randolph, "A Linear Time Exact Hidden Surface Algorithm," *Proceedings of SIGGRAPH '80* (Seattle, Wash., July 14-18, 1980). In *Computer Graphics, 14*, 3 (July 1980), 117-123

This paper, which is included in Chapter 6 of this tutorial, specifies an algorithm which, if input polygons are randomly distributed in space, will result in computation time which is linear in the number of input edges.

[Fran81] Franklin, William Randolph and Alan H. Barr, "Faster Calculation of Superquadric Shapes," *IEEE Computer Graphics and Applications, 1*, 3 (July 1981), 41-47

This paper expands on the results of Barr [Barr81], by proposing fast methods for rendering scenes composed of superquadric primitives.

[Free80] Freeman, Herbert, (Ed.), *Tutorial and Selected Readings in Interactive Computer Graphics*, Computer Society Press, Wash., D.C., 1980

A reprint collection from many areas of computer graphics. First presented at COMPCON S'80, San Francisco, Calif. This collection contains many fundamental papers.

[Frie85] Frieder, Gideon, Dan Gordon, and R. Anthony Reynolds, "Back-to-Front Display of Voxel-Based Objects," *IEEE Computer Graphics and Applications, 5*, 1 (Jan. 1985), 52-60

This paper discusses variations of the painter's algorithm for displaying objects composed of a grid of small cubes. Special-case sorting simplifications with this type of object lead to fast algorithms.

[Fuch80] Fuchs, Henry, Zvi M. Kedem, and Bruce F. Naylor, "On Visible Surface Generation by *A Priori* Tree Structures," *Proceedings of SIGGRAPH '80* (Seattle, Wash., July 14-18, 1980). In *Computer Graphics, 14*, 3 (July 1980), 124-133

This paper, which is included in Chapter 3 of this tutorial, discusses a method by which set of polygons can be ordered by depth, in preparation for rendering by a painting algorithm. The method utilizes a tree sort, with clipping to resolve depth conflicts.

[Fuch81] Fuchs, H. and J. Poulton, "Pixel-Planes: A VLSI-oriented Design for a Raster Graphics Engine," *VLSI Design, 3*, 3, 1981, 20-28

This paper discusses the development of "Pixel-Planes," a parallel-display architecture for computer graphics. This system utilizes one special-purpose processor for each pixel by using the Z-buffer algorithm, allowing extremely fast generation of images.

[Fuch83] Fuchs, Henry, Gregory D. Abram, and Eric D. Grant, "Near Real-Time Shaded Display of Rigid Objects," *Proceedings of SIGGRAPH '83* (Detroit, Mich., July 25-29, 1983). In *Computer Graphics, 17*, 3 (July 1983), 65-72

This paper expands on the results presented by Fuchs et al. [Fuch80] by introducing enhancements that allow the implementation of the algorithm on a high-speed graphics processor.

[Fuch85] Fuchs, Henry, Jack Goldfeather, Jeff P. Hultquist, Susan Spach, John D. Austin, Frederick P. Brooks, Jr., John G. Eyles, and John Poulton, "Fast Spheres, Shadows, Textures, Transparencies, and Image Enhancements in Pixel-Planes," *Proceedings of SIGGRAPH '85* (San Francisco, Calif., July 22-26, 1985). In *Computer Graphics, 19*, 3 (July 1985), 111-120

This paper expands on the results of Fuchs and Poulton [Fuch81] in implementing spheres, shadows, textures, and transparencies into the architecture of the Pixel-Planes graphics processor.

[Fuji83] Fujimoto, Akira and Kansei Iwata, "Jag-Free Image on Raster Displays," *IEEE Computer Graphics and Applications, 3*, 9, (Dec. 1983), 26-34.

This paper describes an antialiasing algorithm whose effects are achieved without inference, by post-processing a Z-buffer using information about the projections of the model's polygon edges.

[Fuji86] Fujimoto, Akira, Takayuki Tanaka, and Kansei Iwata, "ARTS: Accelerated Ray-Tracing System," *IEEE Computer Graphics and Applications, 6*, 4 (April 1986), 16-26

This paper, which is included in Chapter 5 of this tutorial, describes an integer based method of tracing rays through a three-dimensional array of cubes. This allows a general speedup in the ray-tracing process by enclosing object space within a three-dimensional array of cubes. Each cube holds a list of the objects in the scene that intersect it. Rays can be traced through the cube array, and ray/surface-intersection tests need only be made against those objects that intersect the cubes in the path of the ray.

[Garc86] Garcia, A., "Efficient Rendering of Synthetic Images," Ph.D. Thesis, Department of Electrical Engineering and Computer Science, Massachusetts Institute of Technology, Cambridge, Mass., 1986

This paper integrates direct image formation and reflection into a painter's algorithm using a BSP tree. Shadows are also calculated by polygon clipping by using the BSP tree.

[Gard84] Gardner, Geoffrey Y., "Simulation of Natural Scenes Using Textured Quadric Surfaces," *Proceedings of SIGGRAPH '84* (Minneapolis, Minn., July 23-27, 1984). In *Computer Graphics, 18*, 3 (July 1984), 11-20

This paper discusses modeling and rendering methods for textured quadric surfaces. These surfaces are utilized in the generation of clouds, trees, and earth for scenes containing natural terrain.

[Gard85] Gardner, Geoffrey Y., "Visual Simulation of Clouds," *Proceedings of SIGGRAPH '85* (San Francisco, Calif., July 22-26, 1985). In *Computer Graphics, 19*, 3 (July 1985), 297-303

This paper expands on the previous work of the author [Gard84] by specifying fast modeling and rendering methods for realistic clouds.

[Glas84] Glassner, Andrew S., "Space Subdivision for Fast Ray Tracing," *IEEE Computer Graphics and Applications, 4*, 10 (Oct. 1984), 15-22

This paper, which is included in Chapter 5 of this tutorial, is similar to the work of Fujimoto et al. [Fuji86] in that object space is broken into an array of cells. Each cell is used as a bucket, and holds a list of the objects in the scene that intersect the cell. The ray/surface-intersection calculation need only be made for the objects in the cells that are in the path of the ray. This paper proposes an octree method for subdividing the object space.

[Glas86] Glassner, Andrew, "Adaptive Precision in Texture Mapping," *Proceedings of SIGGRAPH '86* (Dallas, Tex., Aug. 18-22, 1986). In *Computer Graphics, 20*, 4 (Aug. 1986), 297-306

This paper discusses a method of utilizing a preintegrated-texture table, to filter areas approximated as the sum of quadrilaterals.

[Gold86] Goldfeather, Jack, Jeff P. M. Hultquist, and Henry Fuchs, "Fast Constructive Solid Geometry Display in the Pixel-Powers Graphics System," *Proceedings of SIGGRAPH '86* (Dallas, Tex., Aug. 18-22, 1986). In *Computer Graphics, 20*, 4 (Aug. 1986), 107-116

This paper discusses an extension of the Pixel-Planes architecture described by Fuchs and Poulton [Fuch81], which allows the display of CSG primitives.

[Gold71] Goldstein, R.A. and R. Nagel, "3-D Visual Simulation," *Simulation, 16*, 1, (Jan. 1971), 25-31

This paper describes the MAGI-Synthavision solid-modeling system. It contains one of the earliest known uses of ray tracing.

[Gora84] Goral, Cindy M., Kenneth E. Torrance, and Donald P. Greenberg, "Modeling the Interaction of Light between Diffuse Surfaces," *Proceedings of SIGGRAPH '84* (Minneapolis, Minn., July 23-27, 1984). In *Computer Graphics, 18*, 3 (July 1984), 213-222

This paper gives the original presentation of the radiosity method for determination of the global illumination in a scene. This method is an application of methods developed for radiative heat-transfer problems to the field of computer graphics. The objects in an environment are subdivided into surface elements, on which the radiosity is assumed constant. The unknown radiosities are then found from a system of equations, expressing the interactions of light in the environment. Once the radiosities are calculated, the scene can be rendered from any camera position.

[Gour71] Gouraud, H., "Computer Display of Curved Surfaces," *IEEE Transactions on Computers, C-20*, 6, (June 1971), 623-629 (reprinted in [Free80])

This paper presents the first attempts at smooth-surface shading. The method depends on a simple linear interpolation of intensity values, based on intensities calculated for the vertices of polygons.

[Gran85] Grant, Charles W., "Integrated Analytic Spatial and Temporal Anti-Aliasing for Polyhedra in 4-Space," *Proceedings of SIGGRAPH '85* (San Francisco, Calif., July 22-26, 1985). In *Computer Graphics, 19*, 3 (July 1985), 79-84

This paper extends the results of Feibush et al. [Feib80] from a two-dimensional lookup-table algorithm to a three-dimensional lookup-table algorithm for combined spatial and temporal antialiasing.

[Gran86] Grant, Charles W., "Shadow Mask Sweep Algorithm," *Technical Report UCRL-95948*, Lawrence Livermore National Laboratory, Livermore, Calif., 1986.

This paper extends the painter's algorithm to include the generation of shadows. The algorithm can be applied to render combinations of primitives, which include particle systems and nonuniform-density translucent volumes.

[Gran87] Grant, Charles W., "A Preliminary Taxonomy of Visible Surface Algorithms," *Workshop on Rendering Algorithms and Systems*, CHI + GI 87, Toronto, Ontario, April 1987. (Also *Technical Report UCRL-95810*, Lawrence Livermore National Laboratory, Livermore, Calif., 1987)

This paper presents an update of the visible-surface algorithm taxonomy of Sutherland et al. [Suth74].

[Gree86] Greenberg, D.P., M.F. Cohen, and K.E. Torrance, "Radiosity: A Method for Computing Global Illumination," *The Visual Computer 2*, 1986, 291-297

This paper gives a summary of the radiosity methods presented by Goral et al. [Gora84] and Cohen and Greenberg [Cohe85].

[Hain86] Haines, Eric A. and Donald P. Greenberg, "The Light Buffer: A Shadow-Testing Accelerator," *IEEE Computer Graphics and Applications, 6*, 9 (Sept. 1986), 6-16

This paper presents a method to reduce the shadow-testing computations in ray tracing. The method generates a partition of space for each light source. The partitions are used during shadow testing to quickly determine a small subset of objects that may have to be tested for intersections.

[Hall83] Hall, Roy A. and Donald P. Greenberg, "A Testbed for Realistic Image Synthesis," *IEEE Computer Graphics and Applications, 3*, 8 (Nov. 1983), 10-20

This paper describes the design of a system developed as a testing base for image synthesis. The paper also discusses enhancements to the illumination model of Whitted [Whit80], which includes the contribution of transmitted light from light sources.

[Hall86] Hall, R., "A Characterization of Illumination Models and Shading Techniques," *The Visual Computer 2*, 1986, 268-277

This paper presents an overall model for illumination models in image synthesis.

[Haml77] Hamlin, Jr., Griffith and C. William Gear, "Raster-Scan Hidden Surface Algorithm Techniques," *Proceedings of SIGGRAPH '77* (San Jose, Calif., July 20-22, 1977). In *Computer Graphics, 11*, 2 (Summer 1977), 206-213 (reprinted in [Free80])

This paper presents two techniques for reducing the number of depth calculations in scan-line visible-surface algorithms. The second of these is the scan-plane algorithm in which a continuously moving scan plane stops only at positions where the visibility could change, instead of at equally spaced scan lines.

[Hanr83] Hanrahan, Patrick, "Ray Tracing Algebraic Surfaces," *Proceedings of SIGGRAPH '83* (Detroit, Mich., July 25-29, 1983). In *Computer Graphics, 17*, 3 (July 1983), 83-90

This paper analyzes the ray/surface-intersection calculation for surfaces that can be described by polynomial equations of the spatial coordinates. In general, the ray/surface-intersection calculation can be shown to be equivalent to finding the roots of a polynomial, which can be directly solved if the degree of the polynomial equations is low. The implementation takes advantage of automated computer-algebra manipulations.

[Harr87] Harrington, S., *Computer Graphics: A Programming Approach,* Second Edition, McGraw-Hill Publishers, New York, N.Y., 1987.

A computer-graphics textbook.

[Haru84] Haruyama, Shinichiro and Brian A. Barsky, "Using Stochastic Modeling for Texture Generation," *IEEE Computer Graphics and Applications, 4,* 3 (March 1984), 7-19

This paper discusses algorithmic methods by which the fractal generation techniques of Fournier et al. [Four82] can be utilized by texturing functions.

[Hear86] Hearn, Donald and M. Pauline Baker, *Computer Graphics,* Prentice-Hall Publishers, Englewood Cliffs, N.J., 1986.

A computer-graphics textbook.

[Heck82] Heckbert, Paul S., "Color Image Quantization for Frame Buffer Display," *Proceedings of SIGGRAPH '82* (Boston, Mass., July 26-30, 1982). In *Computer Graphics, 16,* 3 (July 1982), 297-307

This paper discusses algorithms for quantization of color images. Several quantization algorithms are presented and their results are compared.

[Heck84] Heckbert, Paul S. and Pat Hanrahan, "Beam Tracing Polygonal Objects," *Proceedings of SIGGRAPH '84* (Minneapolis, Minn., July 23-27, 1984). In *Computer Graphics, 18,* 3 (July 1984), 119-127

This paper utilizes the "cookie cutter" clipper of Weiler and Atherton [Weil77] to clip beams of light as they intersect polygonal objects, thereby allowing the generation of a ray-tracing algorithm that avoids the usual point-sampling problems.

[Heck86a] Heckbert, Paul S., "Survey of Texture Mapping," *IEEE Computer Graphics and Applications, 6,* 11 (Nov. 1986), 56-67

This paper, which is included in Chapter 9 of this tutorial, surveys the field of texture mapping, by describing the relevant methodologies that have been developed to render surfaces with texture.

[Heck86b] Heckbert, Paul S., "Filtering by Repeated Integration," *Proceedings of SIGGRAPH '86* (Dallas, Tex., Aug. 18-22, 1986). In *Computer Graphics, 20,* 4 (Aug. 1986), 315-321

This paper extends the "summed-area" results of Crow [Crow84] and Perlin [Perl85a], by giving a generalized theory that develops a space-variant filtering method that can be used with any piecewise-polynomial kernel.

[Horn81] Hornung, Christoph, "An Approach to a Calculation Minimized Hidden Line Algorithm," in Encarnacao, J.L., (ed.), *Eurographics '81*, North-Holland Publishing Company, Amsterdam, The Netherlands, 1981, 31-42

This paper presents results that reduce the visible-surface computation time for networks of polygons. In these cases, the middle edges, shared by two polygons cannot change the visibility of the other polygon edges. This algorithm considers only the non-middle edges and determines the visible regions of the whole surface network. These regions are then subdivided by the middle edges into the visible regions of the individual polygons.

[Imme86] Immel, David S., Michael F. Cohen, and Donald P. Greenberg, "A Radiosity Method for Non-Diffuse Environments," *Proceedings of SIGGRAPH '86* (Dallas, Tex., Aug. 18-22, 1986). In *Computer Graphics, 20,* 4 (Aug. 1986), 133-142

This paper describes an extension to the radiosity method of Cohen and Greenberg [Cohe85] by including non-diffuse reflection.

[Joy86] Joy, Kenneth I. and Murthy N. Bhetanabhotla, "Ray Tracing Parametric Surface Patches Utilizing Numerical Techniques and Ray Coherence," *Proceedings of SIGGRAPH '86* (Dallas, Tex., Aug. 18-22, 1986). In *Computer Graphics, 20,* 4 (Aug. 1986), 279-285

This paper, which is included in Chapter 5 of this tutorial, gives a method by which the ray/surface-intersection calculation can be approximated for scenes consisting of bicubic patches. Numerical techniques are utilized in the basic calculation, with results from numerical calculations in adjoining pixels forming the initial approximations for new calculations.

[Kaji82] Kajiya, James T., "Ray Tracing Parametric Patches," *Proceedings of SIGGRAPH '82* (Boston, Mass., July 26-30, 1982). In *Computer Graphics, 16,* 3 (July 1982), 245-254

This paper discusses a method by which the the ray/surface-intersection calculation can be approximated for scenes consisting of bicubic patches. The method utilizes algebraic geometric techniques to obtain a numerical procedure for finding the intersection.

[Kaji83] Kajiya, James T., "New Techniques for Ray Tracing Procedurally Defined Objects," *Proceedings of SIGGRAPH '83* (Detroit, Mich., July 25-29, 1983). In *Computer Graphics, 17,* 3 (July 1983), 91-102

This paper, which is included in Chapter 5 of this tutorial, presents methods for which the ray/surface-intersection calculation can be accomplished for a variety of surface types. Fractal surfaces, volumes of revolution and geometric prisms are discussed. A bounding-box method to limit the number of ray/surface-intersection tests is also given.

[Kaji84] Kajiya, James T. and Brian P. Von Herzen, "Ray Tracing Volume Densities," *Proceedings of SIGGRAPH '84* (Minneapolis, Minn., July 23-27, 1984). In *Computer Graphics, 18*, 3 (July 1984), 165-174

This paper presents methods by which ray tracing may be utilized to render scenes consisting of volumes of arbitrary density. Single- and multiple-scattering models are discussed.

[Kaji85] Kajiya, James T., "Anisotropic Reflection Models," *Proceedings of SIGGRAPH '85* (San Francisco, Calif., July 22-26, 1985). In *Computer Graphics, 19*, 3 (July 1985), 15-21

This paper presents a shading model that describes the reflection and refraction of light from surfaces that exhibit anisotropy.

[Kaji86] Kajiya, James T., "The Rendering Equation," *Proceedings of SIGGRAPH '86* (Dallas, Tex., Aug. 18-22, 1986). In *Computer Graphics, 20*, 4 (Aug. 1986), 143-150

This paper presents a unified shading model in which the illumination models of Whitted [Whit80] and the radiosity methods [Gora84, Cohe85, Gree86, Imme86] are a subset. It provides a theoretical derivation of the distributed ray-tracing method of Cook et al. [Cook84a]. It suggests a pruning scheme for the ray tree, which increases the efficiency enough to allow ray tracing for diffuse reflections, and thus model caustics projected by transparent surfaces onto diffuse surfaces.

[Kapl85] Kaplan, M.R., "Space Tracing: A Constant Time Ray Tracer," 1985 SIGGRAPH Tutorial on State of the Art in Image Synthesis, San Francisco, Calif., July 1985

This paper, similar to that of Glassner [Glas84], utilizes object-space subdivision techniques to reduce the number of ray/surface-intersection tests in the ray-tracing operation. The algorithm utilizes a binary-tree subdivision of object space.

[Kay79] Kay, Douglas Scott and Donald Greenberg, "Transparency for Computer Synthesized Images," *Proceedings of SIGGRAPH '79* (Chicago, Ill., Aug. 8-10, 1979). In *Computer Graphics, 13*, 2 (Aug. 1979), 158-164

This paper describes an approximate method for simulating refraction in computer-generated images. The basic technique utilizes transforming the background image when overlaying a transparent object over an existing computer-generated image.

[Kay86] Kay, Timothy L. and James T. Kajiya, "Ray Tracing Complex Scenes," *Proceedings of SIGGRAPH '86* (Dallas, Tex., Aug. 18-22, 1986). In *Computer Graphics, 20*, 4 (Aug. 1986), 269-278

This paper discusses a bounding-box method by which the number of ray/surface-intersection tests in the ray-tracing operation can be limited. The method is based upon the prespecification of the planes used to form the bounding-box hierarchies. This system, utilized with the basic bounding-box algorithm given by Kajiya [Kaji83], results in a very efficient algorithm.

[Know77] Knowlton, K. and L. Cherry, "ATOMS, a Three-D Opaque Molecule System," *Computers and Chemistry, 1*, 3, (1977), 161-166.

This paper describes an area-based rendering system for chemical models consisting of spheres and cylinders. The rendering model treats areas that are bounded by pieces of circles and straight lines.

[Kore83] Korein, Jonathan and Norman I. Badler, "Temporal Anti-Aliasing in Computer Generated Animation," *Proceedings of SIGGRAPH '83* (Detroit, Mich., July 25-29, 1983). In *Computer Graphics, 17*, 3 (July 1983), 377-388.

This paper presents some of the first research in techniques for temporal antialiasing in computer graphics. Two algorithms are used: one that is continuous in the temporal dimension and discrete in the spatial dimension, and one that supersamples in the temporal dimension.

[Lane79] Lane, J.M. and L. Carpenter, "A Generalized Scan Line Algorithm for the Computer Display of Parametrically Defined Surfaces," *Computer Graphics and Image Processing, 11*, 1979, 290-297

This paper describes a method of subdivision of parametrically defined surfaces to minimize the "crack" problems inherent in such systems. The authors develop a measure by which it can be determined the number of times a patch must be subdivided in order to get smooth silhouettes and shading.

[Lane80a] Lane, Jeffery M., Loren C. Carpenter, Turner Whitted, and James F. Blinn, "Scan Line Methods for Displaying Parametrically Defined Surfaces," *Communications of the ACM, 23*, 1 (Jan. 1980), 23-34 (reprinted in [Beat82])

This paper, which is included in Chapter 4 of this tutorial, describes three algorithms for the display of parametric surfaces. The algorithms are based upon subdivision of the patch, insertion of internal edges into the patch, and edge tracking.

[Lane80b] Lane, J.M. and R.F. Riesenfeld, "A Theoretical Development of Computer Generation and Display of Piecewise Polynomial Surfaces," *IEEE Transactions on Pattern Analysis and Machine Intelligence, PAMI-2*, 1, Jan. 1980, 35-46

This paper develops a mathematical formulation of the subdivision process for Bézier patches and uniform B-spline patches.

[Lee85] Lee, Mark E., Richard A. Redner, and Samuel P. Uselton, "Statistically Optimized Sampling for Distributed Ray Tracing," *Proceedings of SIGGRAPH '85* (San Francisco, Calif., July 22-26, 1985). In *Computer Graphics, 19*, 3 (July 1985), 61-67

This paper discusses a stratified-sampling method of point-sampled antialiasing, where the variance of the intensities at samples throughout a pixel are estimated, and the number of samples increased, according to the quality of the desired result.

[Levo77] Levoy, Marc, "A Color Animation System Based on the Multiplane Technique," *Proceedings of SIGGRAPH '77* (San Jose, Calif., July 20-22, 1977). In *Computer Graphics, 11*, 2 (Summer 1977), 65-71

This paper describes a system that is based upon key-frame animation. Individual images are combined by using a multiplane cel-animation technique in two dimensions to produce depth and motion illusions.

[Max81] Max, Nelson L., "Vectorized Procedural Models for Natural Terrain: Waves and Islands in the Sunset," *Proceedings of SIGGRAPH '81* (Dallas, Tex., Aug. 3-7, 1981). In *Computer Graphics, 15*, 3 (Aug. 1981), 317-324

This paper discusses rendering methods based on ray tracing for height fields. The algorithms are described within the framework of the computer-generated film *Carla's Island*. Methods are described that enable this algorithm to be adapted to a vectorized supercomputer.

[Max85] Max, Nelson L. and Douglas M. Lerner, "A Two-and-a-Half-D Motion-Blur Algorithm," *Proceedings of SIGGRAPH '85* (San Francisco, Calif., July 22-26, 1985). In *Computer Graphics, 19*, 3 (July 1985), 85-93

This paper presents an algorithm for raster and vector motion blur that produces masks suitable for 2½-dimensional composition. Efficient one-dimensional blurring schemes are utilized to make the algorithm fast.

[Max86a] Max, Nelson L., "Shadows for Bump-Mapped Surfaces," in Kunii, T.L., (ed.), *Advanced Computer Graphics*, Springer Verlag, Tokyo, Japan, 1986, 145-156

This paper describes an enhancement to Blinn's bump-mapped surfaces [Blin77], which can be utilized to approximate shadows on the surfaces.

[Max86b] Max, Nelson L., "Atmospheric Illumination and Shadows," *Proceedings of SIGGRAPH '86* (Dallas, Tex., Aug. 18-22, 1986). In *Computer Graphics, 20*, 4 (Aug. 1986), 117-124

This paper, which is included in Chapter 4 of this tutorial, utilizes a novel adaptation of the scan-line algorithm to incorporate shadows into scenes. Scan lines are radiated from the light source, allowing shadows to be accumulated on the scan lines. Resampling of the image is necessary to produce the final rendered image. The algorithm can also be applied to atmospheric scattering of light.

[McKe87] McKenna, Michael, "Worst-Case Optimal Hidden-Surface Removal," *ACM Transactions on Graphics, 6*, 1 (Jan. 1987), 19-28

This paper gives an $O(n^2)$ visible-surface algorithm that can be shown to be optimal, for a worst-case picture with a maximal number of visible-edge intersections.

[Mehl84] Mehlhorn, Kurt, *Multi-Dimensional Searching and Computational Geometry*, Springer-Verlag, Berlin, West Germany, 1984.

This book is the third in a series on data structures and algorithms. There are two sections. The multidimensional data-structures section contains much information useful for graphics, especially multidimensional searches. The computational-geometry section covers many problems, including those with algorithms in the "sweep paradigm."

[Meye83] Meyer, G.W., "Colorimetry and Computer Graphics," *Technical Report 83-1*, Program of Computer Graphics, Cornell University, Ithaca, N.Y., April 1983

This paper presents a tutorial on color in computer graphics. Various color models are introduced and compared.

[Mill84] Miller, G. and R. Hoffman, "Illumination and Reflection Maps: Simulated Objects in Simulated Environments," (Unpublished Course Notes, Tutorial on Advanced Image Synthesis, SIGGRAPH '84 course notes, Minneapolis, Minn., July 23-27, 1984)

This paper presents an improvement to the illumination model of Phong [BuiT75], utilizing environments at infinity proposed by Blinn and Newell [Blin76]. Results are obtained that reduce much of the illumination calculation to calculation of a texture function of the normal vector of the surface.

[Mill86] Miller, Gavin S.P., "The Definition and Rendering of Terrain Maps," *Proceedings of SIGGRAPH '86* (Dallas, Tex., Aug. 18-22, 1986). In *Computer Graphics, 20*, 4 (Aug. 1986), 39-48

This paper presents an improvement to the fractal terrain generation scheme of Fournier [Four82] that eliminates artifacts that persist from the triangular tiling of the original fractal database. A method based upon quadratic splines is presented that eliminates these artifacts. A hybrid method of rendering scenes composed of these primitives is also discussed.

[Mora81] Moravec, Hans P., "3D Graphics and the Wave Theory," *Proceedings of SIGGRAPH '81* (Dallas, Tex., Aug. 3-7, 1981). In *Computer Graphics, 15*, 3 (Aug. 1981), 289-296

This paper discusses an alternative to the geometric-optics model usually preferred in computer graphics by introducing rendering with the wave model of light. The results were not encouraging.

[Mull86] Müller, H., "Image Generation by Space Sweep," *Computer Graphics Forum 5*, 1986, 189-196

This paper proposes an efficient method of ray tracing by utilizing a plane-sweep algorithm, and a two-dimensional bounding-box scheme to limit the number of ray/surface-intersection tests. This is currently one of the few algorithms to attempt to classify the rays in the scene, rather than the objects of the scene.

[Nayl86] Naylor, B.F. and W.C. Thibault, "Application of BSP Trees to Ray-Tracing and CSG Evaluation," *Technical Report GIT-ICS 86/03*, School of Information and Computer Science, Georgia Institute of Technology, Atlanta, Ga., 1986

This paper discusses a space-subdivision technique to limit the number of ray/surface-intersection tests in the ray-tracing operation. Scenes, consisting of polygonal elements, are subdivided according to the planes of the polygons and classified in a BSP Tree. Rays are tested against all objects in the closer subtree of a node, before being tested against the node itself and the further subtree.

[Newe72] Newell, M.E., R.G. Newell, and T.L. Sancha, "A New Approach to the Shaded Picture Problem," *Proceedings of the ACM National Conference*, 1972, 443 (reprinted in [Free80])

This paper gives one of the original presentations of the painter's algorithm in computer graphics. The algorithm is coupled with a special depth sort to reduce conflicts for overlapping objects and can be used to produce partial transparency effects.

[Newm79] Newman, W.M. and R.F. Sproull, *Principles of Interactive Computer Graphics, Second Edition*, McGraw-Hill Publishers, New York, N.Y., 1979.

The second edition of the first basic computer-graphics textbook.

[Nish83] Nishita, T. and E. Nakamae, "Half-Tone Representation of 3-D Objects Illuminated by Area Sources or Polyhedron Sources," *Proceedings of COMPSAC 1983*, Chicago, Ill., 1983, 237-242

This paper discusses the generation of accurate shadows for objects illuminated from polyhedral sources. Accurate umbras and penumbras are generated, by calculating the exact contribution of the light sources at discrete points on a polygon and utilizing linear interpolation to approximate the contribution at other points.

[Nish85a] Nishita, Tomoyuki, Isao Okamura, and Eihachiro Nakamae, "Shading Models for Point and Linear Sources," *ACM Transactions on Graphics, 4*, 2 (April 1985), 124-146

This paper utilizes the authors previous work [Nish83] and constructs models for shading from point and linear sources.

[Nish85b] Nishita, Tomoyuki and Eihachiro Nakamae, "Continuous Tone Representation of Three-Dimensional Objects Taking Account of Shadows and Interreflection," *Proceedings of SIGGRAPH '85* (San Francisco, Calif., July 22-26, 1985). In *Computer Graphics, 19*, 3 (July 1985), 23-30

This paper presents results similar to the radiosity results of Goral et al. [Gora84] and Cohen and Greenberg [Cohe85]. Shadows are calculated explicitly utilizing shadow volumes to better calculate the form factors for the radiosity solution.

[Nish86]Nishita, Tomoyuki and Eihachiro Nakamae, "Continuous Tone Representation of Three-Dimensional Objects Illuminated by Sky Light," *Proceedings of SIGGRAPH '86* (Dallas, Tex., Aug. 18-22, 1986). In *Computer Graphics, 20*, 4 (Aug. 1986), 125-132

This paper presents improved illumination models for natural lighting that considers both direct sunlight and scattered light caused by clouds. A model of the sky consisting of a large hemisphere is proposed that acts as a source of diffuse light with a non-uniform intensity.

[Nish87] Nishita, Tomoyuki, Yasuhiro Miyawaki, and Eihachiro Nakamae, "A Shading Model for Atmospheric Scattering Considering Luminous Intensity Distribution of Light Sources," *Proceedings of SIGGRAPH '87* (Anaheim, Calif., July 27-31, 1987). In *Computer Graphics, 21*, 4 (July 1987), 303-310

This paper presents a shading model for scattering and absorption of light caused by particles in the atmosphere. The algorithm takes into account the luminous intensity distribution of light, shadows due to obstacles, and the density of the particles.

[Nort82] Norton, Alan, Alyn P. Rockwood, and Philip T. Skolmoski, "Clamping: A Method of Antialiased Textured Surfaces by Bandwidth Limiting in Object Space," *Proceedings of SIGGRAPH '82* (Boston, Mass., July

26-30, 1982). In *Computer Graphics, 16*, 3 (July 1982), 1-8

This paper presents an antialiasing method that filters the input signal according to the rate at which it is to be reproduced. The higher-frequency terms, which are usually truncated, are selectively dampened by the algorithm according to a power series approximation of a box filter.

[Nurm85] Nurmi, O., "A Fast Line-Sweep Algorithm for Hidden Line Elimination," *BIT, 25*, 3, 1985, 466-472

This paper gives a method by which the scan-plane-sweep algorithm can be implemented, by using time and space proportional to $(n + k)\log n$, where n is the number of edges in the input data and k is the number of edge intersections in the picture plane. This is similar to the algorithm of McKenna [McKe87].

[Okin84] Okino, Norio, Yukinori Kakazu, and Masamichi Morimoto, "Extended Depth-Buffer Algorithms for Hidden-SurfaceVisualization," *IEEE Computer Graphics and Applications, 4*, 5 (May 1984), 79-88

This paper presents a Z-buffer algorithm that is utilized in a CSG-type rendering system. The algorithm keeps additional depth values per pixel to assist in the evaluation of the visible element.

[Oppe75] Oppenheim, A.V. and R.W. Shafer, *Digital Signal Processing*, Prentice-Hall, Englewood Cliffs, N.J., 1975

This is a standard textbook on digital-signal processing.

[Park80] Parke, Frederic I., "Simulation and Expected Performance Analysis of Multiple Processor Z-Buffer Systems," *Proceedings of SIGGRAPH '80* (Seattle, Wash., July 14-18, 1980). In *Computer Graphics, 14*, 3 (July 1980), 48-56

This paper analyzes the performance of rendering algorithms utilizing a parallel Z-buffer approach.

[Peac85] Peachey, Darwyn R., "Solid Texturing of Complex Surfaces," *Proceedings of SIGGRAPH '85* (San Francisco, Calif., July 22-26, 1985). In *Computer Graphics, 19*, 3 (July 1985), 279-286

This paper describes three-dimensional texturing of surfaces. The algorithm is similar to that of Perlin [Perl85b], and creates images that appear to be "carved" from a three-dimensional textured block.

[Peac86] Peachey, Darwyn R., "Modeling Waves and Surf," *Proceedings of SIGGRAPH '86* (Dallas, Tex., Aug. 18-22, 1986). In *Computer Graphics, 20*, 4 (Aug. 1986), 65-74

This paper presents a mathematical model of ocean waves that includes refraction by the underwater terrain. The work is similar to that of Fournier and Reeves [Four86].

[Perl85a] Perlin, K., (Untitled), (Unpublished Course Notes, Tutorial on State of the Art in Image Synthesis, SIGGRAPH '85 course notes #11, San Francisco, Calif., July 22-26, 1985)

This paper presents a generalization of the preintegrated-texture table (see also [Crow84] or [Heck86b]).

[Perl85b] Perlin, Ken, "An Image Synthesizer," *Proceedings of SIGGRAPH '85* (San Francisco, Calif., July 22-26, 1985). In *Computer Graphics, 19*, 3 (July 1985), 287-296

This paper, which is included in Chapter 9 of this tutorial, describes a method of multi-dimensional texturing. Whereas the basics of the algorithm is similar to that of Peachey [Peac86], this paper goes into some detail concerning implementation of such a system. The author proposes a small interpretive language that can be used to generate textures.

[Port78] Porter, Thomas K., "Spherical Shading," *Proceedings of SIGGRAPH '83* (Detroit, Mich., July 25-29, 1983). In *Computer Graphics, 17*, 3 (July 1983), 282-285.

This paper presents an algorithm for rendering images of atoms (spheres) by using Bresenham's incremental circle generating algorithm [Bres77]. It uses a single scan-line version of the Z-buffer algorithm. Porter attributes this idea to A. J. Meyers. Antialiasing of the spheres is also performed.

[Port84] Porter, Thomas and Tom Duff, "Compositing Digital Images," *Proceedings of SIGGRAPH '84* (Minneapolis, Minn., July 23-27, 1984). In *Computer Graphics, 18*, 3 (July 1984), 253-259

This paper, which is included in Chapter 3 of this tutorial, proposes the addition of a transparency channel (the α-channel) to the usual RGB color model. Matting operations are defined that illustrate its use in a 2½-dimensional visible-surface composition scheme.

[Potm81] Potmesil, Michael and Indranil Chakravarty, "A Lens and Aperture Camera Model for Synthetic Image Generation," *Proceedings of SIGGRAPH '81* (Dallas, Tex., Aug. 3-7, 1981). In *Computer Graphics, 15*, 3 (Aug. 1981), 297-305

This paper presents an extension of the basic ray-tracing scheme of Whitted [Whit80] from the pinhole camera model to a camera model whose lens has a non-zero area.

[Potm83] Potmesil, Michael and Indranil Chakravarty, "Modeling Motion Blur in Computer Generated Images," *Proceedings of SIGGRAPH '83* (Detroit, Mich., July 25-29, 1983). In *Computer Graphics, 17*, 3 (July 1983), 389-399.

This paper presents a technique for blurring parts of images as a post process based on the velocity of the objects at each pixel. This is not true temporal antialiasing.

[Prep85] Preparata, Franco P. and Michael Ian Shamos, *Computational Geometry: An Introduction*, Springer Verlag, New York, N.Y., 1985

This book is based on Shamos's doctoral dissertation, which created the field of computational geometry. Many types of geometric algorithms (searching, convex hull, intersections, proximity, etc.) are explored and many complexity results are presented.

[Reev83] Reeves, William T., "Particle Systems—A Techniques for Modelling a Class of Fuzzy Objects," *Proceedings of SIGGRAPH '83* (Detroit, Mich., July 25-29, 1983). In *Computer Graphics, 17*, 3 (July 1983), 359-376

This paper describes a modeling and rendering system that generates scenes consisting of small particles. The algorithm's use is illustrated with scenes made of light particles.

[Reev85] Reeves, William T. and Ricki Blau, "Approximate and Probabilistic Algorithms for Shading and Rendering Structured Particle Systems," *Proceedings of SIGGRAPH '85* (San Francisco, Calif., July 22-26, 1985). In *Computer Graphics, 19*, 3 (July 1985), 313-322

This paper, which is included in Chapter 3 of this tutorial, presents stochastic algorithms for generation of particles and approximate algorithms for shading and visible-surface determination by using the painter's algorithm.

[Reev87] Reeves, William T., David H. Salesin, and Robert L. Cook, "Rendering Antialiased Shadows with Depth Maps," *Proceedings of SIGGRAPH '87* (Anaheim, Calif., July 27-31, 1987). In *Computer Graphics, 21*, 4 (July 1987), 283-291

This paper extends the results of Williams [Will78] in the generation of shadows via the Z-buffer algorithm. The author's methods reduce the quantization and aliasing effects inherent in Williams' algorithm.

[Rens50] Rense, W.A., "Polarization Studies of Light Diffusely Reflected from Ground and Etched Glass Surfaces," *Journal of the Optical Society of America 40*, 1950, 55-59

This paper presents an illumination model derived from studies of glass surfaces. It is included here because it states the formula for the solid-angle compression factor used in Chapter 7 of this tutorial in deriving the bidirectional-reflection functions of Cook and Torrance [Cook82].

[Roge85] Rogers, D.F., *Procedural Elements for Computer Graphics*, McGraw Hill, New York, N.Y. 1985

A basic computer-graphics textbook.

[Ross86] Rossignac, Jaroslaw R. and Aristides A. G. Requicha, "Depth-Buffering Display Techniques for Constructive Solid Geometry," *IEEE Computer Graphics and Applications, 6*, 9 (Sept. 1986), 29-39

This paper applies the Z-buffer algorithm to scenes consisting of CSG primitives. A large set of points, generally one to a raster element, is generated on each surface making up the leaves of the CSG tree, and are tested for visibility both through the CSG tree and the Z-buffer.

[Roth82] Roth, S.D., "Ray Casting for Modeling Solids," *Computer Graphics and Image Processing, 18*, 2, Feb. 1982, 109-144

This paper describes several methods of rendering scenes containing modeled primitives with ray tracing. Focus is on methods pertaining to models arising through the CSG paradigm, and on using transformation matrices to position, rotate, or scale a small collection of primitive objects.

[Rubi80] Rubin, Steven M. and Turner Whitted, "A 3-Dimensional Representation for Fast Rendering of Complex Scenes," *Proceedings of SIGGRAPH '80* (Seattle, Wash., July 14-18, 1980). In *Computer Graphics, 14*, 3 (July 1980), 110-116

This paper describes the first bounding-box method by which scenes can be represented hierarchically, and rendered by the ray-tracing algorithm. The algorithm utilizes parallelpipeds for bounding boxes with an orientation that minimizes their size.

[Rush87] Rushmeier, Holly E. and Kenneth E. Torrance, "The Zonal Method for Calculating Light Intensities in the Presence of a Participating Medium," *Proceedings of SIGGRAPH '87* (Anaheim, Calif., July 27-31, 1987). In *Computer Graphics, 21*, 4 (July 1987), 293-302

This paper extends the radiosity methods of Goral et al. [Gora84] to simulate the light scattering and absorption by a "participating medium" such as dusty, smoky, or misty air. This is accomplished by including radiosities of volume elements of the medium.

[Schu69] Schumacker, R.A., B. Brand, M. Gilliland, and W. Sharp, "Study for Applying Computer-Generated Images to Visual Simulation," *Technical Report, AFHRL-TR-69-14,* U.S. Air Force Human Resources Lab., Sept. 1969, NTIS AD 700 375

This paper describes one of the original implementations of the painter's algorithm. It solves the order problem by considering a face-priority and cluster-priority algorithm, by generating a priority graph. Circuits in the graph, which would cause discrepancies in the image, are resolved manually.

[Schw82] Schweitzer, Dino and Elizabeth S. Cobb, "Scan-Line Rendering of Parametric Surfaces," *Proceedings of SIGGRAPH '82* (Boston, Mass., July 26-30, 1982). In *Computer Graphics, 16*, 3 (July 1982), 265-271

This paper presents a scan-line algorithm that renders bicubic patches directly from the parametric description without producing a polygonal tiling of the surface. The algorithm is similar to that of Whitted (in [Lane80a]), with shades being generated across a scan line by calculating a cubic approximation to the normal surface and performing a cubic interpolation of the edge normals in the scan line.

[Sech81] Sechrest, Stuart and Donald P. Greenberg, "A Visible Polygon Reconstruction Algorithm," *Proceedings of SIGGRAPH '81* (Dallas, Tex., Aug. 3-7, 1981). In *Computer Graphics, 15*, 3 (Aug. 1981), 17-27

This paper presents a polygons-in, polygons-out algorithm based on a scan-plane methodology. The algorithm is based on the method of Hamlin and Gear [Haml77] but utilizes the scan information to explicitly reconstruct the visible polygons as output. This work is similar to that of Séquin and Wensley [Sequ85].

[Sede84] Sederberg, Thomas W. and David C. Anderson, "Ray Tracing of Steiner Patches," *Proceedings of SIGGRAPH '84* (Minneapolis, Minn., July 23-27, 1984). In *Computer Graphics, 18*, 3 (July 1984), 159-164

This paper specifies a method of calculating the ray/surface intersection for triangular-surface patches for which points on the patch are defined parametrically by quadratic polynomials.

[Sequ85] Séquin, Carlo H. and Paul R. Wensley, "Visible Feature Return at Object Resolution," *IEEE Computer Graphics and Applications, 5*, 5 (May 1985), 37-50

This paper presents a polygons-in, polygons-out algorithm based on a scan-plane methodology. The algorithm is based on the method of Hamlin and Gear [Haml77]. Reconstruction utilizes the scan information to explicitly rebuild the visible polygons as output. This work is similar to that of Sechrest and Greenberg [Sech81].

[Sieg81] Siegel, Robert and John R. Howell, *Thermal Radiation Heat Transfer*, Hemisphere Publishing Corp., Washington, D.C., 1981.

This textbook is a standard source on radiative heat transfer. These techniques are utilized in the radiosity methods of image synthesis (see [Gora84] and [Gree86]).

[Shin87] Shinya, Mikio, Tokiichiro Takahashi, and Seiichiro Naito, "Principles and Applications of Pencil Tracing," *Proceedings of SIGGRAPH '87* (Anaheim, Calif., July 27-31, 1987). In *Computer Graphics, 21*, 4 (July 1987), 45-54

This paper describes methods by which, in the ray-tracing methodology, groups of rays may be traced as a packet (pencil), utilizing only one ray/surface-intersection test for the pencil of rays.

[Slep72] Slepian, D., "On Bandwidth," *Proceedings of the IEEE, 64*, 1972, 292-300.

This paper explores the relationship between measurements in the laboratory and mathematical models as related to bandwidth of signals. The concept of finite-extent bandlimited signals, to some tolerance, is developed. A version of the 2WT theorem is proved within this framework.

[Smit84] Smith, Alvy Ray, "Plants, Fractals and Formal Languages," *Proceedings of SIGGRAPH '84* (Minneapolis, Minn., July 23-27, 1984). In *Computer Graphics, 18*, 3 (July 1984), 1-10

This paper develops a general framework, based on formal language theory, for the database-enhancement techniques based on fractal geometry [Four82]. The author applies this model to the generation of plants.

[Spar78] Sparrow, E.M., *Radiation Heat Transfer*, McGraw-Hill, New York, N.Y., 1978

A basic physical and engineering textbook, containing radiation algorithms that have been applied to illumination and shading in computer graphics.

[Ster79] Stern, Garland, "SoftCel—An Application of Raster Scan Graphics to Conventional Cel Animation," *Proceedings of SIGGRAPH '79* (Chicago, Ill., Aug. 8-10, 1979). In *Computer Graphics, 13*, 2 (Aug. 1979), 284-288

This paper describes a system that uses the frame buffer to allow the copying, painting, and photographic operations that accompany conventional-animation practices. A simplified 2½-d rendering system is described that utilizes some transparency between images.

[Stoc72] Stockham, Thomas G., "Image Processing in the Context of a Visual Model," *Proceedings of the IEEE*, No. 6, July 1972, 829-842.

This paper applies a model of the early vision system based on homomorphic filtering to the problem of controlling subjective distortion in processed images. The model of the early vision system explains several effects including Mach bands and the eye's great dynamic range.

[Suth74] Sutherland, I.E., R.F. Sproull, and R.A. Schumacker, "A Characterization of Ten Hidden-Surface Algorithms," *Computing Surveys, 6*, 1, 1974, 1-55 (reprinted in [Beat82])

This paper, one of the most fundamental papers in computer graphics, describes a detailed study of 10 early visible-surface algorithms. This paper was the first to attempt to understand the similarities and differences of the current visible-surface algorithms, and thus to better understand their operation.

[Swee86] Sweeney, Michael A. J. and Richard H. Bartels, "Ray Tracing Free-Form B-Spline Surfaces," *IEEE Computer Graphics and Applications, 6*, 2 (Feb. 1986), 41-49

This paper presents an algorithm that can be used to calculate the ray/surface intersection for a B-spline surface. The B-spline surface subdivision technique is utilized to generate a close tiling of the surface with control points. These control points are used as initial approximations for Newton's method, which is used to generate the final intersection point.

[Szab83] Szabo, Nicholas S., "Digital Image Anomalies: Static and Dynamic," in *Computer Image Generation*, Bruce J. Schachter, Ed., John Wiley & Sons, New York, N.Y., 1983, 125-135.

This paper discusses the many different types of artifacts that can occur in synthetic images and animation.

[Thib87] Thibault, William C. and Bruce F. Naylor, "Set Operations on Polyhedra Using Binary Space Partitioning Trees," *Proceedings of SIGGRAPH '87* (Anaheim, Calif., July 27-31, 1987). In *Computer Graphics, 21*, 4 (July 1987), 153-162

This paper describes a Binary-State-Partitioning (BSP) tree method similar to that described by Fuchs et al. [Fuch80], for performing set operations on polyhedra. The operations are efficient and were used in the implementation of a near-real-time system.

[Torr67] Torrance, K.E. and E.M. Sparrow, "Theory for Off-Specular Reflection from Roughened Surfaces," *J. Opt. Soc. Am., 57*, 9 (Sept. 1967), 1105-1114

This is a fundamental paper in describing illumination models later used for computer graphics. The authors study surfaces made up of microfacets, and provide an estimate of the bidirectional reflection function for such surfaces. The paper was used as a base for the work of Blinn [Blin77] and Cook and Torrance [Cook82].

[Toth85] Toth, Daniel L., "On Ray Tracing Parametric Surfaces," *Proceedings of SIGGRAPH '85* (San Francisco, Calif., July 22-26, 1985). In *Computer Graphics, 19*, 3 (July 1985), 171-179

This paper utilizes the methods of interval mathematics, and the interval equivalent of Newton iteration, to accurately calculate the intersection of a ray and a Bézier patch.

[Turk82] Turkowski, Kenneth, "Anti-Aliasing through the Use of Coordinate Transformations," *ACM Transactions on Graphics, 1*, 3 (July 1982), 215-234

This paper describes an antialiasing algorithm that provides a simplification of the work of Feibush et al. [Feib80]. By approximating some of the geometric aspects of their two-dimensional lookup-table algorithm, an algorithm using a much smaller one-dimensional lookup table was produced. Many of the aspects of the antialiasing calculations were performed using cordic-arithmetic algorithms.

[vanW84] van Wijk, Jarke J., "Ray Tracing Objects Defined by Sweeping Planar Cubic Splines," *ACM Transactions on Graphics, 3*, 3 (July 1984), 223-237

This paper describes an algorithm that simplifies the calculations of the intersection of a ray and a surface defined using sweep methods. Translational, rotational, and conic sweeping of planar cubic splines is described and algorithms are developed for the ray/surface-intersection calculation in each case.

[vanW85] van Wijk, J.J., "Ray Tracing Objects Defined by Sweeping a Sphere," *Computers and Graphics 9*, 3, 1985, 283-290

This paper describes an algorithm that can be used to calculate the intersection of a ray and a surface defined by sweeping a sphere along an axis specified by a cubic spline.

[Verb84] Verbeck, Channing P. and Donald P. Greenberg, "A Comprehensive Light-Source Description for Computer Graphics," *IEEE Computer Graphics and Applications, 4*, 7, (July 1984), 66-75.

This paper describes a method to define light-source characteristics, including both the geometry and luminous-intensity distribution of a light source.

[Voss83] Voss, R., "Fourier Synthesis of Gaussian Fractals: *1/f* Noises, Landscapes, and Flakes," (Unpublished

Course Notes, Tutorial on State of the Art in Image Synthesis, SIGGRAPH '83 course notes #10, Detroit, Mich., July 25-29, 1983)

This paper discusses the Fourier synthesis method for generating fractal data, and briefly mentions the two-pass "slab method" for calculating scattered illumination through clouds.

[Wall81] Wallace, Bruce A., "Merging and Transformation of Raster Images for Cartoon Animation," *Proceedings of SIGGRAPH '81* (Dallas, Tex., Aug. 3-7, 1981). In *Computer Graphics, 15*, 3 (Aug. 1981), 253-263

This paper presents a 2½-dimensional visible-surface algorithm for merging of raster images for cartoon animation.

[Wall87] Wallace, John R., Michael F. Cohen, and Donald P. Greenberg, "A Two-Pass Solution to the Rendering Equation: A Synthesis of Ray Tracing and Radiosity Methods," *Proceedings of SIGGRAPH '87* (Anaheim, Calif., July 27-31, 1987). In *Computer Graphics, 21*, 4 (July 1987), 311-324

This paper brings together the radiosity-illumination model and the ray-tracing paradigm into one rendering system. View-independent and view-dependent components of the illumination model are separated in the rendering process, the view-independent calculations are accomplished through the radiosity model and the view dependent are calculations accomplished through ray tracing.

[Warn69] Warnock, J. E., "A Hidden Line Algorithm for Halftone Picture Representation," *Technical Report TR 4-15*, Computer Science Department, University of Utah, Salt Lake City, Utah, 1969

This paper presents an early algorithm using area coherence based on recursive subdivision of the image area into quarters. At each stage, the polygons overlapping the current area are compared to see if there is a "blocking" polygon that surrounds the area and is in front of all other polygons, or if only a single polygon overlaps the area. In these simple cases, the single visible polygon can be rendered directly into the area. Otherwise, the area is divided into quarters and each quarter is treated recursively.

[Warn83] Warn, David R., "Lighting Controls for Synthetic Images," *Proceedings of SIGGRAPH '83* (Detroit, Mich., July 25-29, 1983). In *Computer Graphics, 17*, 3 (July 1983), 13-21

This paper expands the use of illumination models typically used with point-light sources, to include light direction, light concentration, and methods for restricting the path of a light. Methods that use the color of the light source are also analyzed.

[Watk70] Watkins, G., *A Real Time Hidden Surface Algorithm*, Ph.D. Thesis, Computer Science Department, University of Utah, Salt Lake City, Utah, 1970. Also published as *Technical Report UTEC-CSC-70-101*, June 1970, NTIS AD 762 004

This paper, one of the original scan-line algorithms, was motivated by real-time considerations. Thus in most cases, the nature of this algorithm is more aggressive than its predecessors. It utilizes an efficient span-generation scheme, as well as a logarithmic search in the z-depth list.

[Wegh84] Weghorst, Hank, Gary Hooper, and Donald P. Greenberg, "Improved Computational Methods for Ray Tracing," *ACM Transactions on Graphics, 3,* 1 (Jan. 1984), 52-69

This paper discusses hierarchical bounding-box techniques that limit the number of ray/surface-intersection tests that must take place in the ray-tracing algorithm, and the speed tradeoffs in using spherical or rectangular bounds.

[Weil77] Weiler, Kevin and Peter Atherton, "Hidden Surface Removal Using Polygon Area Sorting," *Proceedings of SIGGRAPH '77* (San Jose, Calif., July 20-22, 1977). In *Computer Graphics, 11*, 2 (Summer 1977), 214-222

This paper, which is included in Chapter 6 of this tutorial, describes a polygons-in, polygon-out visible-surface method based upon a "cookie-cutter" clipper. The clipper described by the authors will perform three-dimensional clipping of one non-convex polygon against another. The result is that polygons in the front of the scene can be used as clippers for polygons behind them, with only the visible portions of the rear polygon being kept. After all polygons have been checked, the result is a set of visible polygons making up the scene.

[Whit80] Whitted, Turner, "An Improved Illumination Model for Shaded Display," *Communications of the ACM, 23*,6 (June 1980), 343-349

This paper, which is included in Chapter 5 of this tutorial, presents a full-illumination model for the ray-tracing paradigm, and is thought to be the most important paper in the area. The model includes contributions from both global reflected and transmitted light. Point-sampling problems are discussed, and antialiasing procedures are addressed.

[Whit82] Whitted, Turner and David M. Weimer, "A Software Testbed for the Development of 3D Raster Graphics Systems," *ACM Transactions on Graphics, 1,* 1 (Jan. 1982), 43-58

This paper, which is included in Chapter 4 of this tutorial, describes the implementation of a scan-line based rendering system that attempts to uncouple many of the rendering steps to provide a testbed framework for the development of raster algorithms. The authors explicitly calculate and store individual spans, with their illumination information as a set of "span buffers." These span buffers can then be piped to different processes in the display pipeline to produce various image effects.

[Whit85] Whitted, T. and R. Cook, "A Comprehensive Shading Model," (Unpublished Course Notes, Tutorial on State of the Art in Image Synthesis, SIGGRAPH '85 course notes #11, San Francisco, Calif., July 22-26, 1985, 4 pages)

An updated and expanded version of this paper, which is included in Chapter 7 of this tutorial, presents a general shading model. The paper expresses the total illumination as an integral of the illumination coming from the environment toward a point on the surface and on the reflecting properties of the surface. Methods are described by which this model can be simplified to generate other known illumination models.

[Will78] Williams, Lance, "Casting Curved Shadows on Curved Surfaces," *Proceedings of SIGGRAPH '78* (Atlanta, Ga., Aug. 23-25, 1978). In *Computer Graphics, 12*, 3 (Aug. 1978), 270-274

This paper, which is included in Chapter 2 of this tutorial, presents methods by which shadows can be generated in a Z-buffer algorithm. Two passes through the Z-buffer algorithm are made, one from the light source (creating the non-shadowed surfaces) and one from the camera position (utilizing the information from the first pass).

[Will83] Williams, Lance, "Pyramidal Parametrics," *Proceedings of SIGGRAPH '83* (Detroit, Mich., July 25-29, 1983). In *Computer Graphics, 17*, 3 (July 1983), 1-11

This paper presents a pyramidal-prefiltering scheme for fast texturing. The method gives an approximate technique for antialiasing of textures.

[Wyli67] Wylie, C., G.W. Romney, D.C. Evans, and A.C. Erdahl, "Halftone Perspective Drawings by Computer," *Proceedings of the Fall Joint Computer Conference*, 1967, Thompson Books, Washington, D.C., 49-58

This paper presents an early scan-line algorithm. The algorithm is thought to be the first to use the *y*-sorted list, *x*-sorted list, and z-depth search common to most scan-line algorithms today.

[Wyvi86] Wyvill, Geoff, Tosiyasu L. Kunii, and Yasuto Shirai, "Space Division for Ray Tracing in CSG," *IEEE Computer Graphics and Applications, 6*, 4 (April 1986), 28-34

This paper describes a rendering system based upon ray tracing that is utilized for scenes containing CSG primitives. An octree-based method is specified that allows the ray tracer to avoid calculating intersections of every ray with every primitive. The octree is generated from the CSG model, and closely conforms to the model.

Keyword Index

This section contains a keyword index to the annotated bibliography. References marked with a dagger (†) indicate papers included in the tutorial chapters.

IEEE Computer Society

Offices of the IEEE Computer Society

Headquarters Office
1730 Massachusetts Avenue, NW
Washington, DC 20036-1903
Phone: (202) 371-0101
Fax: (202) 728-9614

Publications Office
P.O. Box 3014
10662 Los Vaqueros Circle
Los Alamitos, CA 90720-1264
Membership and General Information: (714) 821-8380
Publication Orders: (800) 272-6657
Fax: (714) 821-4010

European Office
13, avenue de l'Aquilon
B-1200 Brussels, BELGIUM
Phone: 32-2-770-21-98
Fax: 32-3-770-8505

Asian Office
Ooshima Building
2-19-1 Minami-Aoyama, Minato-ku
Tokyo 107, JAPAN
Phone: 81-3-408-3118

IEEE Computer Society Press Publications

Monographs: A monograph is an authored book consisting of 100% original material.

Tutorials: A tutorial is a collection of original materials prepared by the editors and reprints of the best articles published in a subject area. They must contain at least five percent original material (15 to 20 percent original material is recommended).

Reprint Books: A reprint book is a collection of reprints divided into sections with a preface, table of contents, and section introductions that discuss the reprints and why they were selected. It contains less than five percent original material.

Technology Series: Each technology series is a collection of anthologies of reprints, each with a narrow focus on a subset of a particular discipline, such as networks, architecture, software, robotics, etc.

Submission of proposals: For guidelines on preparing CS Press Books, write Editor-in-Chief, IEEE Computer Society, P.O. Box 3014, 10662 Los Vaqueros Circle, Los Alamitos, CA 90720-1264 (or telephone 714-821-8380).

Purpose

The IEEE Computer Society advances the theory and practice of computer science and engineering, promotes the exchange of technical information among 100,000 members worldwide, and provides a wide range of services to members and nonmembers.

Membership

Members receive the acclaimed monthly magazine IEEE Computer, discounts, and opportunities to serve (all activities are led by volunteer members). Membership is open to all IEEE members, affiliate society members, and others seriously interested in the computer field.

Publications and Activities

IEEE Computer. An authoritative, easy-to-read magazine containing tutorials and in-depth articles on topics across the computer field, plus news, conferences, calendars, interviews, and new products.

Periodicals. The society publishes six magazines and four research transactions. Refer to membership application or request information as noted above.

Conference Proceedings, Tutorial Texts, Standards Documents. The IEEE Computer Society Press publishes more than 100 titles every year.

Standards Working Groups. Over 100 of these groups produce IEEE standards used throughout the industrial world.

Technical Committees. Over 30 TCs publish newsletters, provide interaction with peers in specialty areas, and directly influence standards, conferences, and education.

Conferences/Education. The society holds about 100 conferences each year and sponsors many educational activities, including computing science accreditation.

Chapters. Regular and student chapters worldwide provide the opportunity to interact with colleagues, hear technical experts, and serve the local professional community.

Other IEEE Computer Society Press Titles

Monographs

Analyzing Computer Architectures
Written by J.C. Huck and M.J. Flynn
(ISBN 0-8186-8857-2); 206 pages

Desktop Publishing for the Writer: Designing, Writing, and Developing
Written by Richard Ziegfeld and John Tarp
(ISBN 0-8186-8840-8); 380 pages

Digital Image Warping
Written by George Wolberg
(ISBN 0-8186-8944-7); 340 pages

Integrating Design and Test—CAE Tools for ATE Programming
Written by K.P. Parker
(ISBN 0-8186-8788-6); 160 pages

JSP and JSD—The Jackson Approach to Software Development (Second Edition)
Written by J.R. Cameron
(ISBN 0-8186-8858-0); 560 pages

National Computer Policies
Written by Ben G. Matley and Thomas A. McDannold
(ISBN 0-8186-8784-3); 192 pages

Physical Level Interfaces and Protocols
Written by Uyless Black
(ISBN 0-8186-8824-2); 240 pages

Protecting Your Proprietary Rights in Computer and Hi-Tech Industries
Written by Tobey B. Marzook, Esq.
(ISBN 0-8186-8754-1); 224 pages

Tutorials

Ada Programming Language
Edited by S.H. Saib and R.E. Fritz
(ISBN 0-8186-0456-5); 548 pages

Advanced Computer Architecture
Edited by D.P. Agrawal
(ISBN 0-8186-0667-3); 400 pages

Advanced Microprocessors and Hi-Level Language Computer Architectures
Edited by V. Mulutinovic
(ISBN 0-8186-0623-1); 608 pages

Advances in Distributed System Reliability
Edited by Suresh Rai an Dharma P. Agrawal
(ISBN 0-8186-8907-2); 352 pages

Computer Architecture
Edited by D.D. Gajski, V.M. Multinovic, H. Siegel, and B.P. Furht
(ISBN 0-8186-0704-1); 602 pages

Computer Arithmetic I
Edited by Earl E. Swartzlander, Jr.
(ISBN 0-8186-8931-5); 398 pages

Computer Arithmetic II
Edited by Earl E. Swartzlander, Jr.
(ISBN 0-8186-8945-5); 412 pages

Computer Communications: Architectures, Protocols and Standards (Second Edition)
Edited by William Stallings
(ISBN 0-8186-0790-4); 448 pages

Computer Graphics (Second Edition)
Edited by J.C. Beatty and K.S. Booth
(ISBN 0-8186-0425-5); 576 pages

Computer Graphics Hardware: Image Generation and Display
Edited by H.K. Reghbati and A.Y.C. Lee
(ISBN 0-8186-0753-X); 384 pages

Computer Graphics: Image Synthesis
Edited by Kenneth Joy, Max Nelson, Charles Grant, and Lansing Hatfield
(ISBN 0-8186-8854-8); 380.4 pages

Computer and Network Security
Edited by M.D. Abrams and H.J. Podell
(ISBN 0-8186-0756-4); 448 pages

Computer Networks (Fourth Edition)
Edited by M.D. Abrams and I.W. Cotton
(ISBN 0-8186-0568-5); 512 pages

Computer Text Recognition and Error Correction
Edited by S.N. Srihari
(ISBN 0-8186-0579-0); 364 pages

Computers for Artificial Intelligence Applications
Edited by B. Wah and G.J. Li
(ISBN 0-8186-0706-8); 656 pages

Database Management
Edited by J.A. Larson
(ISBN 0-8186-0714-9); 448 pages

Digital Image Processing and Analysis: Vol 1—Digital Image Processing
Edited by R. Chellappa and A.A. Sawchuk
(ISBN 0-8186-0665-7); 736 pages

Digital Image Processing and Analysis: Vol 2—Digital Image Analysis
Edited by H.A. Freeman and K.J. Thurber
(ISBN 0-8186-0605-3); 384 pages

Local Network Technology (Third Edition)
Edited by William Stallings
(ISBN 0-8186-0825-0); 512 pages

Microprogramming and Firmware Engineering
Edited by V. Milutinovic
(ISBN 0-8186-0839-0); 416 pages

Modeling and Control of Automated Manufacturing Systems
Edited by A. A. Desrochers
(ISBN 0-8186-8916-1); 384 pages

Modern Design and Analysis of Discrete-Event Computer Simulation
Edited by E.J. Dudewicz and Z. Karian
(ISBN 0-8186-0597-9); 486 pages

Nearest Neighbor Pattern Classification Techniques
Edited by Belur V. Dasarathy
(ISBN 0-8186-8930-); 500 pages

New Paradigms for Software Development
Edited by William Agresti
(ISBN 0-8186-0707-6); 304 pages

Object-Oriented Computing, Vol. 1: Concepts
Edited by Gerald E. Petersen
(ISBN 0-8186-0821-8); 214 pages

Object-Oriented Computing, Vol. 2: Implementations
Edited by Gerald E. Petersen
(ISBN 0-8186-0822-6); 324 pages

Office Automation Systems (Second Edition)
Edited by H.A. Freeman and K.J. Thurber
(ISBN 0-8186-0711-4); 324 pages

For Further Information:

IEEE Computer Society, 10662 Los Vaqueros Circle, P.O. Box 3014, Los Alamitos, CA 90720

IEEE Computer Society, 13, avenue de l'Aquilon, 2 B-1200 Brussels, BELGIUM

IEEE Computer Society, Ooshima Building, 2-19-1 Minami-Aoyama, Minato-ku, Tokyo 107, JAPAN

Parallel Architectures for Database Systems
Edited by A.R. Hurson, L.L. Miller, and S.H. Pakzad
(ISBN 0-8186-8838-6); 478 pages

Programming Productivity: Issues for '80s (Second Edition)
Edited by C. Jones
(ISBN 0-8186-0681-9); 472 pages

Recent Advances in Distributed Database Management
Edited by C. Mohan
(ISBN 0-8186-0571-5); 500 pages

Reduced Instruction Set Computers (RISC) (Second Edition)
Edited by William Stallings
(ISBN 0-8186-8943-9); 448 pages

Reliable Distributed System Software
Edited by J.A. Stankovic
(ISBN 0-8186-0570-7); 400 pages

Robotics (Second Edition)
Edited by C.S.G. Lee, R.C. Gonzalez, and K.S. Fu
(ISBN 0-8186-0570-7); 630 pages

Software Design Techniques (Fourth Edition)
Edited by P. Freeman and A.I. Wasserman
(ISBN 0-8186-0514-6); 736 pages

Software Engineering Project Management
Edited by R. Thayer
(ISBN 0-8186-0751-3); 512 pages

Software Maintenance and Computers
Edited by D.H. Longstreet
(ISBN 0-8186-8898-X); 304 pages

Software Management (Third Edition)
Edited by D.J. Reifer
(ISBN 0-8186-0678-9); 526 pages

Software-Oriented Computer Architecture
Edited by E. Fernandez and T.J. Lang
(ISBN 0-8186-0708-4); 376 pages

Software Quality Assurance: A Practical Approach
Edited by T.S. Chow
(ISBN 0-8186-0569-3); 506 pages

Software Restructuring
Edited by R.S. Arnold
(ISBN 0-8186-0680-0); 376 pages

Software Reusability
Edited by Peter Freeman
(ISBN 0-8186-0750-5); 304 pages

Software Reuse—Emerging Technology
Edited by Will Tracz
(ISBN 0-8186-0846-3); 400 pages

Software Risk Management
Edited by B.W. Boehm
(ISBN 0-8186-8906-4); 508 pages

Standards, Guidelines and Examples: System and Software Requirements Engineering
Edited by Merlin Dorfman and Richard H. Thayer
(ISBN 0-8186-8922-6); 626 pages

System and Software Requirements Engineering
Edited by Richard H. Thayer and Merlin Dorfman
(ISBN 0-8186-8921-8); 740 pages

Test Access Port and Boundary-Scan Architecture
Edited by C. M. Maunder and R. E. Tulloss
(ISBN 0-8186-9070-4); 400 pages

Test Generation for VLSI Chips
Edited by V.D. Agrawal and S.C. Seth
(ISBN 0-8186-8786-X); 416 pages

Visual Programming Environments: Paradigms and Systems
Edited by Ephraim Glinert
(ISBN 0-8186-8973-0); 680 pages

Visual Programming Environments: Applications and Issues
Edited by Ephraim Glinert
(ISBN 0-8186-8974-9); 704 pages

Visualization in Scientific Computing
Edited by G.M. Nielson, B. Shriver, and L. Rosenblum
(ISBN 0-8186-1979-1); 304 pages

VLSI Support Technologies: Computer-Aided Design
Edited by Rex Rice
(ISBN 0-8186-0386-1); 464 pages

VLSI Testing and Validation Techniques
Edited by H. Reghbati
(ISBN 0-8186-0668-1); 616 pages

Volume Visualization
Edited by Arie Kaufman
(ISBN 0-8186-9020-8); 494 pages

Reprint Collections

Dataflow and Reduction Architectures
Edited by S.S. Thakkar
(ISBN 0-8186-0759-9); 460 pages

Expert Systems: A Software Methodology for Modern Applications
Edited by Peter Raeth
(ISBN 0-8186-8904-8); 476 pages

Logic Design for Testability
Edited by C.C. Timoc
(ISBN 0-8186-0573-1); 324 pages

Milestones in Software Evolution
Edited by Paul W. Oman and Ted G. Lewis
(ISBN 0-8186-9033-X); 332 pages

Software (Third Edition)
Edited by M.V. Zelkowitz
(ISBN 0-8186-0789-0); 440 pages

Validation and Verification of Knowledge-Based Systems
Edited by Uma G. Gupta
(ISBN 0-8186-8995-1); 400 pages

VLSI Technologies and Computer Graphics
Edited by H. Fuchs
(ISBN 0-8186-0491-3); 490 pages

Artificial Neural Networks Technology Series

Artificial Neural Networks—Concept Learning
Edited by Joachim Diederich
(ISBN 0-8186-2015-3); 160 pages

Artificial Neural Networks—Electronic Implementation
Edited by Nelson Morgan
(ISBN 0-8186-2029-3); 144 pages

Artificial Neural Networks—Theoretical Concepts
Edited by V. Vemuri
(ISBN 0-8186-0855-2); 160 pages

Software Technology Series

Computer-Aided Software Engineering (CASE)
Edited by E.J. Chikofsky
(ISBN 0-8186-1917-1); 110 pages

Communications Technology Series

Multicast Communication in Distributed Systems
Edited by Mustaque Ahamad
(ISBN 0-8186-1970-8); 110 pages

Robotic Technology Series

Multirobot Systems
Edited by Rajiv Mehrotra and Murali R. Varanasi
(ISBN 0-8186-1977-5); 122 pages